CENTENARY REVIEW OF THE ASIATIC SOCIETY OF BENGAL

CENTENARY REVIEW OF THE ASIATIC SOCIETY OF BENGAL

RAJENDRALALA MITRA

Published by

FacsiMile Publisher
12 Pragati Market
Ashok Vihar, Ph-2
Delhi - 110052, India
Phone: 011-47034999
Email: www.facsimilepublishers.com
info@facsimilepublishers.com

Distribution Network
gyanbooks.com
India, USA, Canada, UK, Australia

ISBN: 978-93-6878-423-4 (HB)
First Published, 1885

2nd Impression 2026

Printed at: Gyan Press, Delhi.

CENTENARY REVIEW OF THE ASIATIC SOCIETY OF BENGAL
Author: RAJENDRALALA MITRA

CENTENARY REVIEW

OF THE

ASIATIC SOCIETY OF BENGAL

From 1784 to 1883.

Published by the Society.

CALCUTTA:
PRINTED BY THACKER, SPINK AND CO.

1885.

CONTENTS.

Part I.—History of the Society.
By Dr. Rajendralala Mitra.

Part II.—Archæology, History, Literature, &c.
By Dr. A. F. R. Hoernle.

Part III.—Natural Science, &c.
By Baboo P. N. Bose.

Proceedings of the Special Centenary Meeting of the Society.

CENTENARY REVIEW

OF THE

ASIATIC SOCIETY OF BENGAL

From 1784 to 1883.

PART I.

HISTORY OF THE SOCIETY.

BY

RAJENDRALALA MITRA, LL.D., C.I.E.

Published by the Society.

CONTENTS.

	PAGE.
Asiatic Researches	47
Beadroll	74
Bibliotheca Indica	61
Books, European	22
Busts	30
Coins	29
Committees, Special	15
Council	15
Funds	71
House	20
Inscription	28
Introduction	1
Journal	51
Library	22
———, Summary of the ...	27
Meetings	17
Members, Associate	11
———, Corresponding ...	11
———, Foundation ...	3
———, Honorary	10
———, Ordinary	7
———, Table of	83

	PAGE.
Museum	31
Name	3
Object	4
Oriental MSS.	24
Patrons	11
Pictures	30
Presidents	12
———, List of	84
Proceedings	53
Publications	47
———, List of	95
———, Miscellaneous ...	70
———, Oriental ...	55
Rules	5
Sanskrit MSS., Conservation of	66
Secretary	14
Secretaries, List of	84
Society, Foundation of the ...	2
Summary	80
Treasurer	14
Vice-President	13
Vice-Presidents, List of ...	84

Centenary Review

OF THE

ASIATIC SOCIETY OF BENGAL.

From 1784 to 1883.

Part I.

HISTORY OF THE SOCIETY.

Introduction — Foundation of the Society — Foundation Members — Name — Object — Rules — Ordinary Members — Honorary Members — Associate Members — Corresponding Members — Patrons — President — Vice-President — Secretary — Treasurer — Council — Special Committees — Meetings — House — Library — European books — Oriental Manuscripts — Summary of the Library — Inscriptions — Coins — Pictures and Busts — Museum — Publications — Asiatic Researches — Journal — Proceedings — Oriental Publications — Miscellaneous Publications — Conservation of Sanskrit Manuscripts — Funds — Bead-roll — Summary.

A HUNDRED years have elapsed—a century of arduous and unremitting labour, and the time has now arrived for a review of the progress made and of the services rendered to the cause of literature and science by the Asiatic Society of Bengal since its foundation. Such a review will be as useful in showing what has been accomplished, as in suggesting what has to be done in the vast field which remains yet unexplored. It will be to the Society what periodical stock-taking is to mercantile firms. It will also prove a source of profound satisfaction to those who now represent the Society for the eminent success with which they and their predecessors have worked for the advancement of knowledge.

For convenience of treatment, this Review will be divided into three parts—1*st*, giving a succinct history of the Society; 2*nd*, a *resumé* of the papers published on science generally; 3*rd*, a *précis* of all researches into archæology, history, literature, &c.

Foundation of the Society.

The idea of forming the Society was conceived by Sir William Jones, who came out to Calcutta in October 1783 as a Puisne Judge of the late Supreme Court at Fort William in Bengal. A distinguished scholar and linguist, who had already acquired considerable familiarity with some of the classics of India, and enthusiastically devoted to oriental researches, he soon noticed the want of an organized association in Calcutta as a drawback to progress. He felt, to quote his own language, "that, in the fluctuating, imperfect, and limited erudition of life, such enquiries and improvements could only be made by the united efforts of many, who are not easily brought, without some pressing inducement or strong impulse, to converge in a common point." Accordingly, while he engaged himself in the study of the Sanskrit language, which he had till then not acquired, he invited the co-operation of the leading men of the time in Calcutta for the formation of an institution where united action could be taken to promote the study of oriental literature and science, and where, by the co-operation of the many, the talents and abstract studies of the few would prove most effectual, and derive the stimulus which emulation, publicity, and a common interest never fail to excite. His exertions were warmly seconded by his friends, and a meeting was held on Thursday, the 15th of January, 1784, to come to some definite resolution. Thirty gentlemen attended this meeting, and they represented the *élite* of the European community in Calcutta at the time. The chair was taken by Sir Robert Chambers, and the proceedings were opened by Sir William Jones, who delivered a learned and very suggestive "Discourse on the Institution of a Society for enquiring into the History, civil and natural, the Antiquities, Arts, Sciences, and Literature of Asia." The address was enthusiastically received, and a resolution was come to establishing the Society under the name of the 'ASIATICK SOCIETY.'

Foundation Members.

The gentlemen who took part at this meeting and became the founders[1] of the Society were then, or subsequently became, the leading officers of the East India Company in this country, and included among them all the principal contributors to the pages of the Society's Transactions.

Name.

The name adopted for the Society at the inaugural meeting was borne on the records till the close of the fourth decade of this century. In 1829, soon after the establishment of the Asiatic Society of Great Britain and Ireland in London, and the affiliation of the Literary Society of Bombay with that institution, a letter was received from the latter offering to the Calcutta Society the privilege of being affiliated, and in this letter it was for the first time

---

[1] These were: Sir Robert Chambers, Kt., Chief Justice, Supreme Court; Mr. Justice Hyde, Puisne Judge, Supreme Court; Sir William Jones, Kt., Puisne Judge. Supreme Court; General John Carnac; Lieutenant-Colonel Henry Watson; David Anderson, Esq.; Henry Vansittart, Esq.; Charles Croftes, Esq.; William Chambers, Esq.; Richard Johnson, Esq.; John Shore, Esq. (afterwards a Baronet, and then Lord Teignmouth); Francis Gladwin, Esq.; Charles Chapman, Esq.; Nathaniel Middleton, Esq.; Major William Davy; Charles Wilkins, Esq. (afterwards knighted); Jonathan Duncan, Esq.; John Bristow, Esq.; Thomas Graham, Esq.; Francis Fowke, Esq.; Thomas Law, Esq.; Captain Jonathan Scott; Francis Balfour, Esq.; J. David Paterson, Esq.; Ralph Broome, Esq.; Burrish Crisp, Esq.; Lieutenant James Anderson; Lieutenant Charles Hamilton; T. Reuben Burrow, Esq.; and George Hillarow Barlow, Esq. (afterwards made a Baronet).

designated as the "Asiatic Society of Bengal;" but the Society did not accept the change.[1] As the parent of all the Asiatic Societies extant, it fitly retained its original name of THE Asiatic Society. In March 1832, when Mr. James Prinsep sought the sanction of the Society to use its name for the Journal he was then about to start, the resolution adopted used the words 'Asiatic Society' only (Journal, Vol. I, p. i); but the editor deemed it convenient for his purposes to add a local designation, and the Society took no notice of it. In 1843, when this Journal became the property of the Society, the new name had already become familiar, and it was formally introduced in the Code of Bye-laws published in 1851.

Object of the Society.

In the terms of the original resolution, the object of the Society was "enquiry into the history and antiquities, arts, sciences, and literature of Asia." Dilating on this definition, Sir William Jones remarked: "You will investigate whatever is rare in the stupendous fabric of nature; will correct the geography of Asia by new observations and discoveries; will trace the annals and even traditions of those nations who, from time to time, have peopled or desolated it; and will bring to light their various forms of Government, with their institutions, civil and religious; you will examine their improvements and methods in arithmetic and geometry—in trigonometry, mensuration, mechanics, optics, astronomy and general physics; their systems of morality, grammar, rhetoric and dialectic; their skill in chirurgery and medicine, and their advancement, whatever it may be, in anatomy and chemistry. To this you will add researches into their agriculture, manufacture, and trade;

---

[1] Proceedings, January 1830.

and, whilst you enquire into their music, architecture, painting, and poetry, will not neglect those inferior arts, by which comforts, and even elegances of social life, are supplied or improved." To give emphasis to these details, Sir William Jones added: "If now it be asked, what are the intended objects of our enquiries within these spacious limits, we answer, MAN and NATURE; whatever is performed by the one, or produced by the other." These words have since been paraphrased into—"The bounds of its investigations will be the geographical limits of Asia, and within these limits its enquiries will be extended to whatever is performed by man, or produced by nature," and this sentence now serves as the motto of the Society. How far this resolution has been faithfully and diligently carried out will be shown in the following pages.

Rules.

In his inaugural address Sir William Jones expressed a strong feeling of disapprobation against an elaborate code of rules. He said: "It may be advisable at first, in order to prevent any difference of sentiment on particular points not immediately before us, to establish but one rule,—namely, to have no rules at all." He, however, qualified this by adding, "This only I mean, that, in the infancy of any society, there ought to be no confinement, no trouble, no expense, no unnecessary formality. Let us, if you please, for the present, have weekly evening meetings in this hall for the purpose of hearing original papers read on such subjects as fall within our enquiries. Let all curious and learned men be invited to send their tracts to our Secretary, for which they ought immediately to receive our thanks; and if, towards the end of each year, we should be supplied with a sufficiency of valuable materials to fill a volume, let us present our ASIATIC Miscellany to the literary world, who have derived so much pleasure and information from the agreeable work of Kaempfer than which we can scarcely propose a better model, that they will accept with eagerness any fresh entertainment of the same kind. You will not perhaps be disposed to admit mere translations of considerable length, except of such unpublished essays or treatises as may be transmitted to us by native authors; but whether you will enrol as members any number of learned Natives you will hereafter decide, with many other questions as they happen to arise; and you will think, I presume, that all questions should be decided by ballot by a majority of two-thirds, and that nine members should be requisite to constitute a board for such decisions. * * * One thing only as essential to your dignity I recommend with earnestness—on no account to admit a new member who has not expressed a voluntary desire to become so; and in that case, you will not require, I suppose, any other qualification than a love of knowledge and a zeal for the promotion of it."[1] No formal resolution was adopted in regard to these suggestions, but they were unanimously accepted as the rules of the Society, and uniformly acted upon for several years. In August 1796, the necessity having been felt for devising "the best means of rendering the Institution permanent, and for determining whether a house should be provided for the future meetings of the Society,"[2] some new rules were framed, and the suggestions of the founder were reduced into the form of rules. Other rules were framed from time to time to meet special occasions, but nothing like a regular code was adopted until the beginning of the second half of this century. On the retirement of

---

[1] Jones's Works, Vol. I, p. 6. [2] Researches, Vol. VI, p. 590.

Mr. Henry Torrens, the affairs of the Society were found to be in great disorder, and considerable differences of opinion existed on many important matters. A complete code of rules, providing for all contingencies, was, therefore, deemed urgently necessary, and a committee was appointed to prepare the same. After much deliberation and examination of the rules of European societies, the Committee submitted a new Code of Bye-laws, which was formally adopted on January 5, 1851.[1] One important clause in the Code required that every candidate for admission as an ordinary member shall address a letter stating that "he is anxious to promote the progress of science and literature, and is desirous of becoming a member of the Society." This was done as much in accordance with the opinion of the founder, who had strongly urged in his inaugural address, "not to admit a new member who had not expressed a voluntary desire to become so," as with a view to prevent unseemly repudiation of membership which had occurred in some cases. In practice, however, this rule was found to be unworkable, and had soon to be rescinded. Other clauses were also found troublesome, and a general revision was called for in 1859. On the establishment of the Indian Museum, the altered circumstances of the Society requiring extensive changes in the rules, a new Code was adopted in 1869.[2] This had again to be recast in 1876,[3] and the last is the one now in force, with a few amendments since adopted.

Ordinary Members.

The founder's inaugural address did not suggest any rule for the selection of members, but at the second meeting of the Society (January 22, 1784) members were proposed, who were

---

[1] Proceedings. [2] *Ibid.*, January 1869, p. 10. [3] *Ibid.*, November 1876, p. 204.

*

balloted for and elected at the next meeting. At the third meeting such propositions were seconded, and ordered for ballot at the following meeting; and this plan has ever since been uniformly followed.

At first it was not expected that the Natives of this country would join the Society, and Sir William Jones said, "whether you will enrol as members any number of learned Natives you will hereáfter decide;" and the question was not mooted for many years afterwards. On January 7, 1829, Dr. H. H. Wilson proposed some native names, and they were elected; similar propositions were subsequently made from time to time, and duly adopted. In the Code of Rules now in force, it is laid down, that "persons of all nations shall be eligible as members of the Society."

As the Society met at the Grand Jury Rooms of the Supreme Court, and no expense of any kind had to be incurred, the Members were not called upon to make any pecuniary contribution to the Society. In 1796, when the idea of providing a suitable house was first mooted, funds had to be raised by subscription, and it was ruled that Ordinary Members should pay a quarterly contribution of one gold mohur each for the support of the Society, old Members being required to make up for their previous membership by a payment of two gold mohurs each, in lieu of the entrance-fee which all new Members were called upon to contribute. The rule regarding the quarterly subscriptions was altered in 1859, when the amount was reduced to Rs. 12 a quarter for resident members, and Rs. 6 for non-residents. Looking to the numerical weakness of European society in India, and to the arduous character of the various occupations in which its members are engaged, it would be unreasonable to expect that many men would be found to devote their time to literary and scientific pursuits. Such pursuits require leisure and ease of circumstances, early literary training, and an affluent retired life. Europeans coming to India have to fight the battle of existence, or to discharge onerous official duties, and when they have earned a competence and run through their allotted course of official career, they return to Europe to enjoy a life of ease. Natives, on the other hand, have, generally speaking, a defective education in early life, and cannot engage in researches, the fruits of which have to be recorded in a foreign language. The Asiatic Society has thus always laboured under a double disadvantage. But as Milton truly remarks,—"no man who hath tasted learning but will confess the many ways of profiting by those who, not contented with stale receipts, are able to manage and set forth new positions to the world," and the highly educated gentlemen, who came out in the civil, the medical, and the military services of the East India Company, fully bore out the truth of the observation. Notwithstanding the heavy duties they had to discharge in their respective spheres, many of them contributed largely to the efficiency, the stability, and the advancement of the Society by their literary labours and scientific researches. It is worthy of note, and not a little singular, that the members of the Civil Service took a much more prominent position in this respect than those of the more learned professions. As was to be expected, merchants, tradesmen, and other non-official Europeans took but a slender share in the work of the Society. The steady growth of the Society is best shewn in the statement given in Appendix A. It shows that, commencing with a total of 30 names, the number of members rose, at the close of 1788, to 89, and in 1876, when the subscription of resident members was brought down to Rs. 9 per quarter, to 285. It should be added, however, that the various lists from which the statement has been compiled are misleading, as they do not discriminate under one uniform rule the efficient from non-efficient and absent members.

There is no record, in the first volume of the Proceedings, of any resolution having been adopted, laying down a principle for the election of Honorary Members. The first person elected as an Honorary Member was M. Carpentier de Cossigny. He was proposed by an Ordinary Member, seconded by another, and balloted for and elected in due course. Other elections followed from time to time, but without any definite rule. Exception was, however, taken to this course in 1828 ; and, in January 1829, it was resolved "that Honorary Members be in future proposed only by the Committee of Papers, members of the Society not in the Committee communicating their recommendation of an individual as an Honorary Member to the Committee, either directly or through the Secretary. The Committee not to be expected to assign any reasons, should they not see cause to make the nomination." When the resolutions and rules of the Society were codified in 1851, the qualifications for an Honorary Member were laid down to be "eminence for his knowledge of, or encouragement given to, science or literature, or for services rendered to the Society, to be testified by a written statement and supported by the votes of a majority of three-fourths of the members present at a meeting," limiting the elections at the same time to thirty in all. In 1876, the rule was further modified by omitting all reference to services to the Society. The roll of the Society shows that, on the whole, the selections have been judiciously made : it includes the names of all the European *savans* who distinguished themselves

Honorary Members.

most by their oriental scholarship, and a great number of eminent scientific men of the last hundred years, as also two renowned Indian scholars,—Sir Rádhákánta, Baháдur, and Professor Bápudeva Sástrí.

Associate Members.

Another class of members was established on May 6, 1835, to secure the co-operation of competent persons in India, who would not offer themselves as candidates for ordinary membership. This was called Associate Member, to whom was assigned all the privileges of Ordinary Members except that of voting at the meetings of the Society. Under the rules now in force, this class is reserved for "persons well-known for their literary or scientific attainments, but who are not likely to become Ordinary Members." Their number is limited to 15.

Corresponding Members.

A fourth class of members was established in 1851 to recognize the services of correspondents in foreign countries, but it was not much appreciated, and therefore abolished in 1869.

Patrons.

At the second meeting of the Society, Sir William Jones submitted draft of a letter to Warren Hastings, Esq., Governor-General and President, and Edward Wheeler, John Macpherson, and John Stables, Esqs., Members of the Council of Fort William in Bengal, requesting them to become patrons of the Society. The draft was approved, and the assent of the Governor-General and Council having been obtained, they were, at a subsequent meeting, duly elected. This election became a precedent, which was regularly followed until the time of Lord William Bentinck : on his election as patron, the Members of his Council were left out. Since then the practice has been to elect only the Governor-General as patron.

Along with the letter above referred to, a second was addressed to Mr. Warren Hastings, requesting him to accept the office of President of the Society. The offer, however, was declined. While expressing his appreciation of the honor done him by the offer, Mr. Hastings said :—"From an early conviction of the utility of the institution, it was my anxious wish that I might be, by whatever means, instrumental in promoting the success of it; but not in the mode which you have proposed, which, I fear, would rather prove, if of any effect, an incumbrance on it. I have not the leisure requisite to discharge the functions of such a station, nor, if I did possess it, would it be consistent with the pride, which every man may be allowed to avow in the pursuit or support of the objects of his personal credit, to accept the first station in a department in which the superior talents of my immediate followers in it would shine with a lustre, from which mine must suffer much in the comparison, and to stand in so conspicuous a point of view the only ineffective member of a body, which is yet in its infancy, and composed of members with whose abilities I am, and have long been, in the habits of intimate communication, and know them to be all eminently qualified to fill their respective parts in it.

President.

"On these grounds I request your permission to decline the offer which you have done me the honor to make to me, and to yield my pretensions to the gentleman whose genius planned the institution, and is most capable of conducting it to the attainment of the great and splendid purposes of its formation.

"I at the same time earnestly solicit your acceptance of my services in any way in which they can be, and I hope that they may be, rendered useful to your researches."

In accordance with the suggestion contained in the above extract, Sir William Jones was elected President of the Society on February 5, 1784. He held the office till his demise on April 27, 1794. He was succeeded by Sir John Shore, who then held the office of Governor-General. In subsequent years, two other Governors-General, the Marquis of Hastings and Lord Hardinge, held the same office. It was found, however, that the reasons assigned by Mr. Warren Hastings were correct, and that the duties of so exalted an office as that of Governor-General of India did not admit of that close application on the part of the President to the duties of the Society, which was so desirable. The elections, therefore, have been confined to distinguished persons whose knowledge and zeal and opportunities were best calculated to promote the interests of the Society. The names of all the Presidents are shown in the Statement hereto annexed (Appendix B).

Vice-President.

In anticipation of the acceptance of the office of President by Mr. Warren Hastings, Sir William Jones was elected Vice-President at the second meeting of the Society. But on his election soon after to the Presidentship, the office became vacant, and none was appointed in his place. On his death, however, when the office of President was held by Sir John Shore, the then Governor-General of India, some inconvenience was felt owing to his inability to attend every meeting of the Society, and in 1796 a resolution was adopted to appoint two Vice-Presidents. The number was afterwards raised to 3, and subsequently to 4; but by the rules now in force it is limited to 3. The Statement given in Appendix B shows the names of all the Vice-Presidents.

Immediately after the establishment of the Society, Mr.

Secretary.

George Hillarow Barlow undertook the duties of Secretary; but, two months after, Mr. John Herbert Harington was appointed Secretary by formal resolution, and for fifty years afterwards, one Secretary, aided at times by a Deputy Secretary, sufficed for the despatch of the Society's ordinary business, the financial affairs being conducted by a Treasurer. On the retirement of Mr. James Prinsep, two Secretaries were deemed necessary, besides the Treasurer, and a third was added some time afterwards. Under the rules now in force, the number of Secretaries is not fixed, but four are generally appointed : one General Secretary, one Natural Science Secretary, one Philological Secretary, and one Treasurer.

Treasurer.

In 1796, when subscriptions first began to be collected, Mr. Trail, of the firm of Palmer and Co., Merchants, was appointed Treasurer, and his firm undertook to transact all banking business for the Society. In 1803, a native clerk was engaged to keep accounts, but all financial business continued to be conducted by Messrs. Palmer and Co. After a time, the duty of collecting subscriptions was made over to the clerk. On the failure of Palmer and Co. in 1828, the custody of the finances was made over to Messrs. Macintosh and Co., and, after their failure in 1833, to the Bank of Bengal. The clerk above referred to was the late Bábu Rámacomal Sen. He served the society for nearly forty years, latterly holding the office of what was called 'Native Secretary,' but really that of Treasurer. In 1840, Mr. Bolst, an uncovenanted assistant in the Bengal Secretariat, was appointed Treasurer, and he kept the records in the Bengal Office, or in his private dwelling. On his dismissal from the Bengal Office, the account-books of the Society could not be recovered.

In 1846, one of the Secretaries became the Treasurer, and that arrangement has continued since.

Council. Soon after its establishment, the Society appointed a Committee of Papers, consisting of the President, the Secretary, and four other members, to conduct its affairs. In November 1796, this Committee was strengthened by the addition of two Vice-Presidents, and four other members, and in 1849, another addition was made, bringing up the total to fifteen, including the office-bearers. Under the rules now in force, the minimun is fixed at fifteen, and the maximum at twenty.

In 1846, several active Committees having been organized, it was deemed expedient, with a view to prevent misunderstanding and confusion, to change the name of the Committee of Papers and to designate it the Council, as the governing body of the Society.

Special Committees. Although the Society was established with a view to hold weekly meetings for exchange of notes among members and reading of papers on subjects of interest, the necessity soon arose for appointing special Committees for the consideration of questions of importance. Such Committees were, however, generally temporary, and their functions ceased with the determination of the questions referred to them. On the completion of the Society's house, when the means and accommodation for steady, continuous, and combined action were easy of access, Dr. Hare, in June 1808, moved, seconded by Dr. Leyden, "that a Committee be appointed for the purpose of physical investigations, the collection of facts, specimens, and correspondence with individuals whose situations in this country may be favorable for such discussions and investigations." This the mover subsequently modified, and recommended two Committees, one for "Natural History, Philosophy, Medicine, Improvements of the Arts, and whatever is comprehended in the general term of Physics;" and another "for Literature, Philology, History, Antiquities, and whatever is comprehended under the general term of Literature." This recommendation was, after some consideration, formally adopted on September 7, 1808, and the following elections were made:—

Physical Committee.	*Literary Committee.*
J. Farquhar, Esq.	J. H. Harington, Esq.
Dr. J. Leyden.	Dr. J. Leyden.
Lieutenant A. Lockett.	Lieutenant A. Lockett.
George Davidson, Esq.	H. B. Bayley, Esq.
Rev. W. Carey.	H. P. Forbes, Esq.
W. Hunter, Esq.	Rev. W. Carey.
	W. Hunter, Esq.

It was at the same time resolved that other members of the Society should be invited to join the Committees and to frame rules for the conduct of their investigations. The Committees met several times, and prepared lists of desiderata and carried on some correspondence; but, after a time, they fell into disuetude, and no record is now extant of their proceedings. In 1818, the Physical Committee was revived, and it was in active work for several years; but its proceedings are not now forthcoming. At the annual meeting of the Society, on December 13, 1821, Dr. Wilson, then Secretary, proposed that "special Committees should be appointed to report upon the papers received by the Society and for other purposes, as also a House Committee, the President, one Vice-President, and the Secretary, being *ex officio* members of all the Committees." But its consideration was deferred, and never after taken up. In 1828, a Committee was appointed "to promote geological researches, working under the rules then in force for the Physical Committee, with such modifications as may be deemed expedient." Dr. Calder was appointed its Secretary. At the same time the Transactions of the Society were divided into two parts, one to be devoted to Physical, and the other to Literary, subjects. The Physical Committee was in active work for some time, and spent large sums of money in boring operations in Fort William and other researches. A Statistical and a Finance Committee were appointed soon after. No rules, however, were laid down for the annual election of the Committees, and thy fell again into abeyance. In 1847, the then Committee of Papers, adverting to the constitution of their body, which, though intended to represent the different objects of the Society, had at one time been almost exclusively composed of gentlemen who deemed Oriental Literature the paramount object of the Society, and at another period of those under whom researches in Oriental Philology were nearly abandoned in favor of Zoology and kindred sciences, recommended the appointment of Sections, or Standing Committees, for (1) Oriental Literature, (2) Zoology and Natural History, (3) Geology and Mineralogy, (4) Meteorology and Physics, (5) Geography and Indian Statistics, (6) Finances. The elections for these Committees took place at the annual meeting, and were followed up by fresh elections every year until the Byelaws of 1851 placed the appointment of Committees at the disposal of the Council. An Historical Committee and a Coin Committee have since been added.

Meetings.

As already incidentally noticed, the original object of the Society was to hold weekly meetings in imitation of the hebdomadal gatherings of the Royal Society two centuries ago, but this could not be regularly carried out for any length of time. In England, the professors of colleges, ministers of religion, and educated men of independent means and retired from business, have a great deal of leisure time, and a habitual liking for literary and scientific researches, for which they are regularly trained by their system of education. In Calcutta, on the other hand, at the close of the last century, these classes were entirely wanting. As stated in the Introduction to the first volume of the Researches, "a mere man of letters, retired from the world and allotting his whole time to philosophical or literary pursuits, is a character unknown among Europeans resident in India, where every individual is a man of business in the civil or military state, and constantly occupied either in the affairs of Government, in the administration of justice, in some department of revenue or commerce, or in one of the liberal professions; very few hours, therefore, in the day or night, can be reserved for any study that has no immediate connection with business, even by those who are most habituated to mental application, and it is impossible to preserve health in Bengal without regular exercise and reasonable relaxation of mind." And under the circumstances, notwithstanding the earnestness and devotion of the founders and a large body of very able men who placed themselves under the standard of the Society, papers could not be produced in such rapid succession as to keep up the interest of the weekly meetings. After the first few months, frequent interruptions followed, and during the close of the rains in the beginning of autumn, meetings had to be suspended for weeks. After the death of the founder, a resolution had to be adopted to hold monthly, instead of weekly, meetings.[1] In six months' time, even monthly meetings were found to

---

[1] Proceedings for December 5, 1799.

be too frequent, and a meeting once every three months was held sufficient.[1] The interval fixed by the last resolution, however, was found to be too long, and calculated to diminish the interest of the public in the Society, and after a short trial, the plan of monthly meetings was reverted to with occasional recess during the months of September and October. In 1818, some energetic members thought formal monthly meetings not sufficient for unrestrained friendly communications and conversation on literary and scientific subjects ; it was thereupon resolved (April 2, 1828) :—

I. That the apartments should be kept open for private meetings at 7-30 P.M. on the second and fourth Wednesdays of every month.

II. That the meetings shall be open to every member that chooses to attend and to every visitor whom he may wish to introduce.

III. That none of the official business of the Society shall be transacted at these meetings, and none of the officers of the Society shall attend, except in a private capacity.

IV. That the general attention of the Society at these meetings shall be confined to the promotion of those studies and enquiries which were originally contemplated in the institution of the Asiatic Society.

There is no record to show how these private meetings were attended, and when they were abandoned.

The day of the meeting was originally Thursday. When monthly meetings were resolved upon, the first Wednesday of every month was thought the most convenient, and it remains unchanged to this day. At the close of the last century, the time for dinner among Englishmen was early, and 7 P.M. was found a fit time for meetings, as

---

[1] Proceedings for July 2, 1800.

affording a means of recreation to men of literary habits after their meals; but changes in the social rules of the European community early in this century rendered 8, and subsequently 9, P.M. as the most convenient hour for the meetings of the Society. Under the rules now in force a recess is observed during the months of September and October.

The business at the annual meeting in the time of Sir William Jones was limited to the reading of the annual address. After his death such addresses were not forthcoming, and no annual meeting was held; the office-bearers were elected, since 1796, at the ordinary December meeting. In 1828 it was resolved, that the anniversary of the Society should be celebrated by an annual dinner, but it was not acted up to in subsequent years. In 1833, Mr. James Prinsep introduced, for the first time, the practice of submitting a brief annual report in January; Mr. Torrens discontinued it in 1841, but his successors revived the practice in 1847, and the rules of the Society now render it imperative. The Code of 1869 provided for an annual address from the Chair, and some very interesting addresses were delivered by Sir Joseph Fayrer, Sir John Phear, Mr. Oldham and Mr. Medlicott; but the practice of delivering such addresses has of late been dropped.

House.

During the presidency of Sir William Jones, no necessity was felt for a house for the Society. The Grand Jury Room of the late Supreme Court was always accessible for the meetings of the Society, and there being no office, no effects, and no establishment, no separate accommodation was wanted. On the demise of the founder, the case became different. The Court-house was not always so readily available; books, papers, records, and specimens of various kinds had accumulated, and they required a store-room, and a natural desire to secure permanency for these suggested the necessity of a local habitation. It was accordingly resolved[1] that an application should be made to Government for the grant of a free site for a house, and the members should pay a quarterly contribution of one gold mohur each and an entrance-fee of two gold mohurs, which, accumulating for a few years, would yield a sufficient sum to cover the expense of building a house. There is no record to show what reply was given by Government to this application. A second application was madé, on July 4, 1804, for a spot of land at the corner of Park Street, which had before been in the possession of a Riding School, but had subsequently reverted to Government, and the Government granted it with the exception of a small portion on the western side, which was "required by the Magistrate of Calcutta for the establishment of a Police Thannah and a Fire Engine." On the remodelling of the Calcutta Police in 1849, the Police-station at this spot was abolished, and, on the application of the Society, the spot was also given to it, free of all rent, for so long as the Society would be in existence. By a subsequent release, dated March 3, 1876, the Government has given the land free of all conditions. The pottah for the land is dated April 7, 1852, and covers an area of a little over three bigahs and a half.

In 1805, when the order of Government granting the land was received, the Society had accumulated a sufficient sum to be in a position to undertake the building of a house. Captain Lock, of the Bengal Engineers, designed a plan, which, after some modifications, was made over to one Jean Jacques Pichon, a Frenchman, settled as a builder in Calcutta, to erect the building. The contract with

[1] Proceedings for December 1, 1796.

the builder bears date February 1, 1806, and the cost settled was Rs. 24,000. It appears from subsequent Proceedings (April 6, 1808), that the contract amount had to be raised to Rs. 30,000. Extensive additions and alterations have since been made at a heavy cost. The Society took possession of the house at the beginning of 1808.

Although built at the cost, and for the exclusive use, of the Society, the house has been always accessible to the public for literary and scientific lectures. In 1822, the use of the meeting-room was permitted to the Serampore Missionaries for a course of lectures on phrenology, and the Medical and Physical Society of Calcutta held their meetings and had their office and library in the house for upwards of thirty years.

Library : European books.

One of the objects for which the house was built was to provide accommodation for a Library and a Museum. From soon after the foundation of the Society, books, papers, manuscripts, drawings, copperplates and other articles were, from time to time, presented to the Society, and they had to be kept, owing to want of a better place for their preservation, in the private dwelling-house of the Secretary for the time being; and as the exigencies of European official life in this country led to frequent changes, the risk of loss was serious. The new house at once removed this difficulty. The books that had been received up to the time formed the nucleus of a Library, and funds were sanctioned every year, and also on special occasions, for the purchase of new books. Mr. H. T. Colebrooke was also appointed as agent in London to select and purchase books for the Society (October 1, 1817). Exchanges of publications were also made with leading European Societies, and of duplicates in the Library with private individuals, and members retiring from the country sometimes presented selections from their private collections. A small but very valuable collection of works on art was given by Mr. Home, who was for several years a leading member of the Society, and a much larger one of historical and other works relating to India was got from Government on the abolition of the old College of Fort William as an educational institution, duplicates and works of general interest being given to the Calcutta Public Library. A very valuable collection of manuscripts, being diverse occasional papers and essays, and ten volumes of drawings of antiquarian and archæological subjects, belonging to Colonel Mackenzie, for a long time Surveyor-General of India, were received in December 1822. A set of abstract translations of the Puráṇas, prepared by native scholars under the superintendence of Dr. Wilson, and several translations from Persian works, have also come to the possession of the Society. A collection of some illustrated works on Botany was received from Dr. N. Wallich in June 1817, but it was subsequently sent to the Hon'ble East India Company's Botanical Gardens, at Sibpur, near Calcutta.

To facilitate the use of the Library by members a set of rules was framed in January 1820. A catalogue of the whole of the Society's library was published in 1833. It shows a total of about a thousand volumes. After the accession of the College of Fort William collection, a second catalogue of the European books was prepared by the late Dr. E. Roer, and that shows a total of 4,315 volumes. A third catalogue was prepared in 1856 by the writer of this Review, and that brought up the total to upwards of 7,000 volumes. Accessions to the Library have since been very numerous and valuable, comprising, besides sets, more or less complete, of the Transactions of all the leading European and American learned bodies, nearly all standard works of reference in science and oriental literature. The total, it is estimated, will exceed 20,000 volumes. Much inconvenience is felt by members from want of a good catalogue of this extensive and valuable collection—perhaps the richest in India. This, however, it is expected, will soon be supplied. There is now in the press an alphabetical catalogue carefully prepared under the superintendence of H. B. Medlicott, Esq., F.R.S., and it is expected to be completed before the close of the current year.

Library: Oriental Department.

The early history of the Oriental Library is very much the same as that of the European one. The Society depended mainly on casual gifts from members, and they were not numerous. The first accession of any importance was a gift from the Seringapatam Prize Committee (February 3, 1808). It included a selection from the Library taken in *loot* from the palace of Tipu Sultan. There were among them many old and rare works, including a great number of beautifully illuminated manuscripts of the Quran, and of that part of it called *Pansurah.* An exceedingly well written old text of the *Gulistán,* said to be the first copy from the original manuscript of the author, and a codex of the *Pádsháanámáh* bearing an autograph of the Emperor Shah Jehan, were among them. Presentations were also received, on diverse occasions, from the late College of Fort William and the General Committee of Public Instruction, of books published under their superintendence and from other sources. The total, however, did not, in 1835, exceed a thousand volumes. On the abolition of the College of Fort William, the whole of its Sanskrit, Arabian, Persian, and Urdu works, mostly in manuscript, collected at great expense and trouble under the superintendence of Gladwin, Carey, Gilchrist, and other distinguished oriental scholars, were placed under the custody of the Society, with a promise that they would, on the sanction of the Hon'ble Court of Directors being obtained, be given to the Society, subject only to two conditions, namely,—safe and careful preservation, and unrestricted accessibility to the public at all reasonable hours. Pending the receipt of the sanction, the Government defrayed the cost of the establishment, amounting to Rs. 78 per mensem. The sanction was obtained in 1846, when the monthly grant was stopped, and the books and manuscripts became the property of the Society, subject only to the two conditions aforesaid.

When the manuscripts came to the possession of the Society, it was all but certain that they would ultimately be its property, and in anticipation of the sanction of the Court of Directors, Mr. Prinsep, then Secretary, caused catalogues to be prepared and printed not only of the new accessions but of all the manuscripts owned by the Society. The Persian catalogue bears date 1837, and contains a total of 2,742 names, out of which 1,013 are Arabic, 1,418 Persian, and 311 Urdu,—a few of these being printed books. The Sanskrit catalogue was issued in 1838, and it includes, besides Sanskrit, a few Mágadhi, Bengali, Hindi, Carnáti, Tailinga and Mahratti names. The total is, in round numbers, 1,800. Annexed to this catalogue are lists of Sanskrit works then owned by the Sanskrit Colleges of Calcutta and Benares. These lists were very useful at the time, as shewing the extent of Sanskrit literature then known to exist. The catalogues were prepared by Maulvies and Pandits in the Indian style, and are not very convenient for reference now. They abound, too, in mistakes, and have become obsolete from the circumstance of the Library having been greatly extended since 1838. The accessions in the Persian Department have not been very numerous, in all 167, but several valuable codices have been obtained. The losses in this department have, however, been greater than the accession. The Sanskrit Library has been nearly doubled ; while the losses, though serious, do not exceed 250 codices. The want of a revised catalogue has, therefore, been much felt, and an attempt was sometime ago made to compile a *catalogue raisonné* of the Sanskrit works. It was then expected that the then Librarian of the Society would be able, with the assistance of a Pandit, to get the needful done. But on his retirement from the Society soon after, the work fell into abeyance. The writer of this Review, thereupon, undertook to finish what was then in the press, and brought out, in 1877, a royal octavo volume of 228 pages, containing descriptive accounts of all the manuscripts on Sanskrit grammar that were available in the Library. It comprised also a tabular statement of all the works of that class which had been met with in India. Other occupations did not, however, permit the editor to carry on the undertaking, and taking into consideration the immense time and labour necessary for such an elaborate work, it had to be finally abandoned. Dr. Hoernle has now in the press a nominal catalogue, which, it is believed, will be completed in a short time.

Besides these there are now in the custody of the Society 2,507 Sanskrit manuscripts, mostly new to the collection aforenamed, belonging to the Government of India, and some of great age and value. The ultimate destination of these has not yet been determined upon, but it is expected that they will be so kept by Government as to be always available to Indian and Anglo-Indian scholars.

In addition to the above, the Society possesses a rare collection of Tibetan xylographs, including one complete, and another somewhat defective, set of the Khahgyur and the Stangyur texts of the Buddhist Scriptures. For the complete set the Society is indebted to Mr. B. H. Hodgson, by whose liberality and earnest efforts, its Library and Museum have been so vastly enriched. The second copy was brought down by M. Csoma de Körös. Of these voluminous collections there exists no other copy in India, and only two in Europe, both sent by Mr. Hodgson. To that gentleman the Society also owes its thanks for a very large and exceedingly valuable collection of Sanskrit Buddhist manuscripts, of which an analytical catalogue, prepared by the writer of this Review, has lately been published by the Society.

The Society has also, in its Library, upwards of 350 Chinese xylographs, of which there is, in manuscript, a descriptive catalogue prepared by Mr. Alabaster, the author of a Life of Buddha, published under the name of "The Wheel of the Law." There are, likewise, palm-leaf manuscripts of Burmese, Siamese, Javanese, and Cingalese works, to the extent of about 125 bundles, of which, however, there is no inventory of any kind.

Summary of the Library.

It has not been possible to count, for the purposes of this Review, all the books and manuscripts contained in the Library, but partly from certain recent accounts and partly from memoranda prepared four years ago, it appears that the Society now owns, or has in custody, of—

English Books and Manuscripts	...	...	19,842	Vols.
Arabic ditto	...	...	1,161	„
Persian ditto	...	...	1,506	„
Urdu ditto	...	...	300	„
Sanskrit ditto	...	...	3,378	„
Ditto Manuscripts (Govt. property)			2,507	„
Tibetan Xylographs	...	...	256	„
Chinese ditto	...	...	350	„
Burmese, Siamese, &c., ditto, manuscripts on palm leaves	...	...	125	„
		Total	29,425	

For a colonial Library such a collection of nearly 30,000 volumes, of which upwards of 8,000 are in manuscript, is, it is believed, unrivalled, and the members may well congratulate themselves on their work, bearing in mind that the bulk of it has been got up by private enterprise without any pecuniary help from Government. The work done is highly creditable. Had the Society done nothing else in the course of its career of a hundred years, this collection would suffice to secure to it the thanks of future generations.

Inscriptions.

Inscriptions and coins are closely related to books; they differ only in the material in which they are preserved, but are fully as valuable as written history, and at times much more so, being far more authentic. Their decipherment has engaged the attention of the Society from a very early date, and some of the most brilliant discoveries in Indian history have been thereby effected. Records of this description are not plentiful; many exist on scarps of rocks and on ancient buildings or sculpture; others occur on stones not easily removable, while records on copperplates are title-deeds which their owners do not part with, and coins are intrinsically so valuable that they are not readily to be had. The members of the Society have, however, been assiduous in their endeavours to obtain them either in original or in facsimile, and a great number has been collected.

Of inscriptions the Society had at one time upwards of a hundred. On the removal, however, of the Society's collection of antiquities from its premises to the Indian Museum, it was deemed expedient to make over all inscribed stones to the Museum, leaving behind in the Library only the records—mostly land grants—on copperplates.

Coins.

Coins in gold and silver, when they cease to be current, are soon melted down, and in India, where the practice of wearing ornaments of precious metals is so universally prevalent, the cause of their destruction is constantly at work, while copper coins are not much cared for, and their material is subject to rapid deterioration by the influence of the climate. It is not remarkable, therefore, that the Society was never very rich in this description of relics. Many were exhibited at the meetings, and many more described in the Transactions of the Society, but few were given to it. Nevertheless, from time to time, a few coins were presented to it by various benefactors ; and after the death of Colonel Mackenzie, duplicates of such coins as existed in any number in his very large collection, were received through the liberality of the Government of Bengal. These made up the Society's collection of coins in 1832, when they were noticed by Professor H. H. Wilson in the Asiatic Researches.

"Subsequently a great many coins were received at different times; and an imperfect inventory of the collection was published by Dr. Roer in the Proceedings of 1843.

"The cabinet, as described by Roer, consisted at that time of 297 Roman coins, from Augustus down to the destruction of the Occidental Empire, mostly copper, and only a very few rare ones; of Greek coins there were 16; and of Bactrian, Indo-Scythian, Sassanian and Gupta coins only 116. There were at the time, however, two or three bags full of copper coins, which had not been described. A little later in the same year, it received a considerable addition of Norwegian coins.

"In the following year, 1844, it suffered a great loss, all the more intrinsically valuable specimens being stolen. A description of the Cabinet in this despoiled state, to which, however, a few more coins had been added in the meanwhile, was given by Mr. Freeling in the Proceedings for 1857. In order to retrieve the loss, the Society determined to purchase the well-known and magnificent collection of Colonel Stacy, which had been offered to it for sale at the reduced sum of Rs. 4,000, in November 1856. A subscription was opened by the Council among the members, the Society itself contributing Rs. 1,200 towards the purchase; and early in 1859, this valuable collection was successfully secured. A priced catalogue of it had already been published by Mr. E. Thomas in the Journal of the preceding year, 1858.

"Since then many additions have been made from year to year, some by presentations, but mostly by purchase. A catalogue of the Cabinet in its present state is in course of preparation. It is particularly rich in Delhi Patháns and Bengal Patháns, also in the later Bactrians, Indo-Scythians, Guptas, and the various sorts of ancient Hindu and Buddhist coins. It might be more complete in the Delhi Moghals; but it is most defective in the provincial Muhammadan coinages of Malwá, Guzarát, Jaunpur, &c., also in some of the more ancient classes, as the Sauráshtrian and Sassanian coins. A small collection of Roman coins in gold was obtained from General Cubbon some years ago. They are of peculiar interest as coming from a trove discovered in the Madras Presidency. Among the copper, lead, and inferior coins generally there are a very large number of duplicates. On the other hand, there are also in the Society's collection a few coins which are unique, and a not inconsiderable number which are more or less rare."

Pictures and Busts.

The Society has, moreover, a small but very valuable collection of oilpaintings and some busts, the latter memorials of the many great men, whose labours contributed so largely to establish and sustain the renown of the Society. Many of the paintings are also memorials, which the members secured of their distinguished collaborateurs; the others are of a miscellaneous character, and most of them belonged at one time to the studio of Mr. Home. That gentleman was an artist, and at the beginning of this century lived for several years in Calcutta, and took an active interest in the affairs of the Society. Subsequently he went up to Lucknow and made a fortune in the service of Gháziuddín Hyder, the then King of Oudh. During his tour in Europe he collected many rare pictures, and on his death his two sons, who were then in active service as officers in the Bengal army, deposited them with the Society on the condition that should they not be able to remove the collection within a reasonable time, it shall become the property of the Society, and remain as a memorial of their father. The sons died about forty years ago, and the pictures accordingly now belong to the Society. Among them there are originals by Rubens, Guido Rene, Domenichino, Reynolds, Canaletti, and Westmoreland. The Society has received from other sources originals by Chinery, Poe, and Daniel.[1] Looking to the satisfactory state of preservation of the old pictures, it is easy to infer that the idea about the Indian climate being prejudicial to pictures is untenable.

Museum.

In the inaugural address of the founder no reference was made to a Museum : but curiosities were sent in from time to time by mofussil members, and in 1796 the idea was started of having a suitable house for their reception and preservation. Nothing practical, however, could be done at the

[1] For a list of the Pictures and Busts, see the Society's printed Catalogue of Curiosities.

time, and it was not until some time after the completion of the house that measures were taken to carry out the object. On February 2, 1814, Dr. N. Wallich wrote a letter to the Society strongly advocating the formation of a Museum, and offering at the same time not only duplicates from his own rich collection to form a nucleus for it, but his own services to look after it, and in bringing the letter before the Society, the Committee of Papers submitted the following notes, which, though long, are worth quoting to show clearly what it was that the Society undertook:

"A collection of the substances which are the objects of science and of those reliques which illustrate ancient times and manners, has always been one of the first steps taken by Societies instituted for the dissemination of specific or universal knowledge. Such a collection was one of the first objects also of the Asiatic Society, and any person engaged in the study of the history and language of this country, or in the investigation of its natural productions, must have had frequent cause for regretting that such a purpose should have been hitherto so very incompletely carried into effect. No public repository yet exists to which the naturalist or scholar can refer, and the only sources of information, beyond verbal and often inaccurate description, have been found in the accidental accumulations of individuals, always of difficult access, indiscriminate selection, temporary duration, and little utility.

"The Asiatic Society is now called upon to adopt active measures for remedying this deficiency, and collecting, from the abundant matter which India offers, a Museum that shall be serviceable to history and science. In the former of these departments the Society is already in possession of several valuable articles, and there can be no doubt that enquiry and exertion, and the assurance of their being properly bestowed, would soon add considerably to the number. There are, however, many things of extremely easy attainment, that would afford much useful illustration, and the student of the original languages and compositions would be frequently extricated from perplexity and doubt by having it in his power to refer to specimens of various Eastern implements and instruments in daily and domestic use amongst the natives of these regions.

"It is, however, in the departments of science that a Museum in this country would be found most specially serviceable, and the facility of its accumulation is proportionable to the extent of its utility. In Natural History, Botany, Anatomy, Chemistry, Mineralogy and other branches, a collection would accumulate rapidly if once commenced; and from the first moment of its accumulation would furnish additional matter to the stock of knowledge. Many objects with which we are exceedingly familiar in this country are new or imperfectly known to general science, and a vast variety of articles may be derived from sources hourly acceptable, each of which would contribute some interesting supply to the extensive results of western enquiry.

"The importance of the measure is, however, so obvious, that it must be unnecessary to urge it further, and it only remains to consider the means by which it can be effected. The Society possesses accommodation fit for the purpose, and the expense of adapting these to the reception of contributions could not be any amount. The present establishment might perhaps be sufficient to take charge of it, at least for sometime, and at any rate no great addition could be requisite. The principal difficulty lies in the selection of a person willing and able to devote some time and trouble to procuring and arranging the materials of which such a Museum should consist, and the removal of this difficulty is the chief inducement at present for the Society to take the subject into serious consideration.

"Dr. Wallich offers, if the Society should determine to place the collection under his superintendence, to contribute to it the results of his own enquiries, to appropriate to it such further contributions as come within his reach, and to devote all the attention in his power to the arrangement and conservation of the whole."

After a careful consideration of the details submitted by the Committee of Papers, the Society came to the following resolutions :—

"Resolved accordingly that the Asiatic Society determine upon forming a Museum for the reception of all articles that may tend to illustrate oriental manners and history, or to elucidate the peculiarities of art or nature in the East.

"That this intention be made known to the public, and that contributions be solicited of the undermentioned nature :—

"Inscriptions on stone or brass.

"Ancient monuments, Muhummadan or Hindu.
"Figures of the Hindu deities.
"Ancient coins.
"Ancient manuscripts.
"Instruments of war peculiar to the East.
"Instruments of music.
"The vessels used in religious ceremonies.
"Implements of native art and manufacture, &c., &c.
"Animals peculiar to India, dried or preserved.
"Skeletons or particular bones of animals peculiar to India.
"Birds peculiar to India, stuffed or preserved.
"Dried plants, fruits, &c.
"Mineral or vegetable preparation peculiar to Eastern pharmacy.
"Ores of Metals.
"Native alloys of metals.
"Minerals of every description, &c., &c.

"That the names of persons contributing to the Museum or Library of the Society be hereafter published at the end of each volume of the Asiatic Researches.

"That the Hall on the groundfloor be fitted up for the reception of the articles that may be procured.

"That the plan and expense of so doing be regulated by the Committee of Papers and Secretary and the person under whose superintendence the Museum may be placed.

"That the expense which may be incurred in preparing materials that may be furnished in a state unfit for preservation be defrayed by the Society within a certain and fixed extent.

"That the thanks of the Society be given to Dr. Wallich for the tender of his services.

"That the services of Dr. Wallich be accepted, and that he be in consequence appointed Superintendent of the Oriental Museum of the Asiatic Society."

The Museum thus formed thrived rapidly. Contributions were received under all the heads noticed, and grants were made freely for their preservation. All coins, copper-plates, sculptures, inscriptions on stone, implements and miscellaneous articles received were placed in charge of the Librarian, while geological and zoological specimens were classified, arranged, and preserved under the superintendence of Dr. Wallich, who was appointed their curator, all donations being duly announced in the pages of the Society's Transactions.

The archæotectonic and miscellaneous collection was greatly enriched by contributions from Colonel Stuart, Dr. Tytler, General Mackenzie, Mr. B. H. Hodgson, Captain Dillon, Bábu Rámacomal Sen and others. A partial inventory of it was prepared by Dr. Roer in 1843, and a complete catalogue was compiled by the writer of this Review in 1847, and published in 1849.

The Natural History Museum remained in charge of Dr. Wallich for several years. On his resignation the Society found it necessary to employ one Mr. Gibbon as Superintendent on Rs. 50 per mensem.[1] The Museum, however, did not, and could not, under the circumstances, get on satisfactorily. What was wanted was a competent knowledge of Zoology and Geology, and that could not be secured for the remuneration offered. The Society had, therefore, to revert to gratuitous aid from amateurs in the ranks of the medical service of the East India Company. The new impulse given to the work of the Society by the appointment of the Physical Committee in 1828, led to the employment of a paid Superintendent on Rs. 150 per mensem, and one Mr. Hichins was selected for the post (June 17, 1828). His successor, three years after, was appointed on Rs. 200 per month.

The budget of 1836 showed that there were no means available for the payment of a Curator's salary. As it was, however, not desirable to dispense with the services of so

---

[1] Proceedings, August 1817.

experienced and useful an officer, a resolution was adopted to pay the amount from the vested fund. This was received with great disfavor by some of the leading members of the Society, and a formal dissent was placed by them on record. In the face of this, the plan of payment could not be continued in the following year. The Committee was thus driven to the alternative either of dispensing with the services of a Curator, or of reducing expenses in other departments. Neither, however, was deemed expedient; the latter course would seriously affect the progress of the Society, and the former was by no means desirable. "Viewing the maintenance of the Museum as a national object, and calculated to be of immense importance to science if placed upon a footing of efficiency, with a professional naturalist at the head, directing researches and systematizing information obtained from various sources, both public and private, in all the branches of Physical Science, but more particularly in regard to the Natural History of British India and Asia at large," it was felt that such a course would be highly reprehensible. It was accordingly resolved that "a full and urgent representation" should be submitted "to Government on the subject, and to solicit such support as is accorded in most other countries to similar institutions of national and scientific utility;" and "pending the result of the reference the Curator be retained."[1] The memorial submitted on the subject was written by Sir Edward Ryan, and its prayer was based on the high ground of public utility. After detailing the services rendered to the cause of literature and science by the Society, Sir Edward remarked: "It is not from a declining Society that an appeal is made,

---

[1] Journal, Vol. VI, pp. 399f.

to save it from impending ruin or to enable it to support its expenses on the same scale of efficiency as heretofore. On the contrary, the Society never had a more flourishing list of contributing members, nor was it ever more actively engaged on the multiplied objects of its attention. Indeed, it would be difficult to mention any department in which its duties have not materially increased within the last few years."[1] He then went on to say :—

"The Asiatic Society, or it may be allowable to say the Metropolis of British India, has had the germs of a national Museum as it were planted in its bosom. As at *Paris* a new era was opened in the history of its great museum, the Jardin des Plantes, through the discoveries of extinct and wondrous animal forms exhumed from the rocks on which the town was built, and which required all the adjuncts of comparative anatomy for their investigation even by the master hand of the great CUVIER; so in *Calcutta* through the munificence of a few individuals and development of fossil deposits in various parts of India hitherto unsuspected, we have become possessed of the basis of a grand collection, and we have been driven to seek recent specimens to elucidate them. Our desire has been warmly seconded by all who have enjoyed the opportunity of contributing; from *China*, from *New South Wales*, from the *Cape*, and from every quarter of the Honorable Company's possessions, specimens of natural history, of mineralogy and geology, have flowed in faster than they could be accommodated, and the too little attention they have received has alone prevented similar presentations from being much more numerous; for it is but reasonable to suppose that, of the stores continually despatched to England or the Continent, the Society would have received a larger share had it done proper honor to what it has received.

"In May 1835, the Society resolved to try the experiment of appointing salaried officers[2] to the charge of its Museum. For two years economy in other departments has enabled it to maintain this

---

[1] Journal, Vol. VI, p. 493. [2] Incorrect.

system, and the good effects of the measure are visible to all who visit the rooms. Yet, not being able to purchase more than a small portion of the time of a competent naturalist, the benefit has been comparatively limited, and now at the very commencement of the experiment, the state of the Society's funds will compel it to withhold further support from its incipient museum, unless some fresh source of income be provided.

"These then are the motives that have persuaded the Society of the propriety of an appeal to the Ruling Power:—not to contribute to the ordinary wants and engagements of the institution, but to convert that institution into a public and national concern by entrusting it with the foundation and superintendence of what has yet to be formed, for the instruction of our native fellow subjects, as much as for the furtherance of science,—a public depository of the products of nature in India and the surrounding countries properly preserved, properly arranged, and properly applied.

"To effect such an object it is indispensable that the services of a professional naturalist of high attainments should be engaged, and that he should have at his command the means of working effectually, and of devoting his whole time to the employment."[1]

The prayer of the memorial was limited to a grant of Rs. 200 per mensem. The Government admitted that the expense of establishing such a museum could not be met by voluntary subscriptions, nor could it "be maintained in the creditable and useful condition necessary for the attainment of the object desired, unless aided liberally by the Government, in like manner as similar institutions in Europe are supported from the public treasury;" but they were not prepared to accede to the request without a reference to the Court of Directors. They said:

"There are many circumstances which induce the Governor-General in Council to consider that the proposition submitted on this occasion is peculiarly one to be decided by the Home

[1] Journal, Vol. VI, pp. 494-5.

authorities, rather than by the Local Government. In the first place, the Honorable Court of Directors are themselves at considerable expense in keeping up a museum and library at the India House, and though his Lordship in Council concurs with you in thinking that such institutions in Europe, however perfect, do not supersede the necessity of providing similar in India likewise,—with reference especially to the spirit of literary inquiry and scientific research which it is desired to excite and encourage amongst the native youths of India; still the fact that the Honorable Court have a separate institution of their own, points to the propriety of making them the judges of its sufficiency or the contrary for Indian purposes. Moreover, were the Government of India to sanction a specific annual grant for a museum and library in Calcutta under the management of your Society, such a grant would reasonably be made a precedent for similar applications from learned Societies at other Presidencies, and his Lordship in Council is not prepared to decide without a reference to England upon the relative claims of such Societies with reference to the circumstances of the institutions themselves and of the Presidencies and places where they may be established." (June 1837.)

On the receipt of this, a second petition was submitted, from which the following is an extract :—

"The Society feel that they have every reason to be highly flattered with the condescension and consideration extended to their address by the members of Government; and although a reference to the Honorable the Court of Directors has been deemed indispensable before finally determining on the adoption of the Society's proposition for the formation of a national museum at the cost of the state, still they entertain the most sanguine assurance of a favorable issue under the encouragement and recommendation with which His Lordship in Council has been pleased to promise that the reference home shall be accompanied.

"On the strength of this confident expectation a very full meeting of the Society, held on the 5th instant, came to the resolution that it would be unadvisable at such a juncture to break up the establishment, and abandon the incipient Museum upon which they had for two years devoted so considerable a portion of their income, and thus perhaps have to recommence their collection a year hence, should the Honorable Court acquiesce in the proposed measure.

"It was consequently resolved that a second respectful application should be submitted to the Right Honorable the Governor-General in Council in immediate connection with their former address to inquire:—

"Whether, in order to maintain the Society's Museum in its present state of efficiency, pending the reference on the subject of its extension and conversion into a public institution, the Government would be disposed to sanction a monthly grant of 200 rupees, the actual sum which is now obliged to be withdrawn from this object on account of other calls on the Society's funds."[1]

This prayer was at once granted, and Dr. Pearson was appointed Curator. He was succeeded by Dr. McLelland. The reply of the Court of Directors came in their Despatch No. 17, of September 18, 1839. The Court fully recognized the claims of the Society, and, adverting to the Society's immediate permanent want of a qualified person to preserve its collections, remarked, that they "would not object to the Government allowing the Society a monthly sum of 200 or 250 rupees a month as salary to a Curator, with a further sum of 50 rupees a month for the cost of preparing specimens and maintaining the collection in order." They went further, and said: "We shall not object to your granting to the Society funds for special purchases, as occasions arise, as far as may be compatible with a due regard to public economy. On all such occasions, you will forward to our Museum a selection from the articles which may have been so procured."[2] The only condition attached to this was, that "the articles to be purchased should not be of a perishable nature."

[1] Proceedings. July 1837.

[2] *Ibid.*, November 1839.

The question now arose as to whether a competent Curator should be brought out from Europe, or one appointed in India. Opinion was very much divided, particularly as the officer then in charge of the Museum, Dr. McLelland, was thoroughly well-qualified for the office. That gentleman, however, did not agree to the terms proposed of two hours' daily attendance at the Museum, and a monthly report of progress. It was resolved, therefore, to write to Dr. Wilson, then the London Agent of the Society, to select a fit person. The person selected was Mr. Edward Blyth, who took charge of his office in September, 1841.

It was generally expected that the Curator sent out from England would be able to take scientific charge of the whole of the Museum; but this could not be done. Thoroughly competent as Mr. Blyth was as a naturalist, he had not studied geology to such an extent as to be fit to be a scientific curator of that department. In his letter to the Secretary, dated September 22, 1841, he himself said: "It is in the Mineral department, unfortunately, that I am at present less qualified, by previous study, to devote my immediate and first labors advantageously for the Society; but with the opportunities for study which are now before me, and with the liberal encouragement and support I may reckon upon receiving, I do not fear but that I shall soon render myself competent to discharge that portion of my duty which relates to the efficient management of the Museum of Economic Geology; this being a subject in which I feel the liveliest interest, and with the high importance of which I am deeply and thoroughly impressed."[1] This difficulty was, however, soon overcome. The satisfactory working of the coal mines at Rániganj, and the reports

---

[1] Journal, Vol. XL, pp. 756.

of Dr. Helfer and other scientific officers had invited the attention of Government to the mineral resources of the country, and a resolution was adopted in 1835 to establish a Museum of Economic Geology, in order to make typical specimens readily accessible for reference to the public. An officer was deputed to England to obtain such specimens. Captain Trimenheere came out with them in May 1841, and for want of suitable accommodation elsewhere the Government deposited them in the rooms of the Society. Provision was also made by Government for the custody of these by a competent curator on a salary of Rs. 250 a month, with an allowance of Rs. 64 for contingent charges. The money was placed at the disposal, and under the control, of the Society, which appointed Mr. Piddington as Curator, and placed under his charge the collections of the Museum of Economic Geology as also its own Geological and Palæontological specimens. Fossil bones belong as strictly to Zoology as recent ones, but, for the sake of convenience, and on account of the peculiar qualifications of the two Curators, the unscientific course adopted was unavoidable. This arrangement lasted till 1856, and the two departments thrived most satisfactorily under the management of the officers appointed. The usefulness of the Zoological collections was greatly enhanced by the publication of valuable catalogues of the Mammals and Birds by Mr. Blyth, of the Reptiles and Fresh-water Shells by Mr. W. Theobald, and of the Fossils by Dr. Hugh Falconer and Mr. H. Walker. Full monthly reports were submitted by both the Curators, and they were very favourably received by the scientific public.

The Geological Museum was never a cause of heavy expense to the Society, and at first the relief afforded by the Government grant enabled the Society to carry on the Zoological branch with but a small contribution from its general resources. But the collections increased rapidly under the energetic management of Mr. Blyth and the hearty co-operation of the mofussil members interested in Natural History, and the demands of the Museum soon outgrew the resources of the Society.

On the formation of a general Museum in connection with the then recently established department of Geological Survey of India, the Government desired the transfer there of the Museum of Economic Geology.[1] It proposed at the same time that the Society should deposit there its own collection of fossils and other geological specimens. The last proposal gave rise to much discussion. On the one hand it was obvious, that the collection would be better preserved, better laid out, and better taken care of by the very able officers under whom it would be placed than in the Society's premises. But on the other it was felt, that the dissociation of a part of the Museum, and that the least expensive but highly valuable, would prove injurious to the interests of the Society, if not to endanger its very existence, and at the same time postpone to an indefinite period the great object which the Society had cherished since 1837 of seeing a national museum worthy of the metropolis of British India established here. The offer of the Government was, therefore, declined.[2]

The removal of the Museum of Economic Geology enabled the Society to devote more space for the accommodation of its zoological collection, but it had already become an unmanageable burden which no private association could sustain. It required more room and more establish-

[1] Proceedings, July 11, 1856.

[2] *Ibid.*, November 5, 1856.

ment to preserve it than what the Society could provide. Taking these circumstances into mature consideration a resolution was adopted to the effect, that "the Council enter into a communication with the Government on the subject of the foundation at Calcutta of an Imperial Museum, to which the whole of the Society's collections, except the library, may be transferred, provided the locality, the general arrangement, and management be declared, on reference to the Society at large, to be perfectly satisfactory to its members."[1] The Mutiny of the native troops in the N. W. Provinces, however, soon after followed, and the matter was consequently left in abeyance. In October 1858, the question was revived, and a representation was submitted to Government, giving in detail the views of the Society on the subject of the proposed museum; but it failed in its object. The Government, while recognizing it as "its duty to establish in the metropolis an imperial museum for the collection and exposition of specimens of natural history in all its branches, and of other objects of interest—physical, economical and historical"—declined to entertain the project on financial grounds. At the same time it renewed its offer regarding the geological and palæontological collections. The Society, thereupon, submitted a memorial to the Secretary of State, and, while awaiting a reply to this, applied for an extra grant from the Government of Rs. 200 per mensem, which, though at the time declined,[2] was, on a renewal of the application two years after, sanctioned.

Adverting to previous correspondence, the Government, in May 1862, announced that, "in the opinion of the Governor-General in Council, the time had arrived when the

---

[1] Proceedings, May 6, 1857.

[2] *Ibid.*, April and June 1859.

foundation of a public museum in Calcutta, which had been generally accepted as a duty of the Government, may be taken into consideration with regard to its practical realization," and then gave a sketch of the terms on which the Society's collections may be transferred to it.[1] Negociations now followed, which were protracted till the middle of 1865, when the following conditions were finally settled, *viz.*:—

1. That, in consideration of the Society's making over its zoological, geological, and archæological collections to a public museum to be established and maintained by Government, and made over to a Board of Trustees, the Society shall be provided with suitable accommodation in the house which was to be built by Government for the museum, and to have exclusive possession, occupation, and control of the portion so alloted to it.

2. That the Society shall have the right of nominating from its own body one-third of the members of the said Board.

3. That it shall retain exclusive possession of its own house.

4. That it shall make over to the new museum all archæological and natural history specimens that it may, in future, receive from its members.

A law to this effect was passed in 1866 (Act XVII), and the collections were formally made over to an officer of the Board of Trustees appointed under it. An arrangement was also made to allow the collections to remain in the Society's premises until the proposed building could be completed.

The time occupied in building the new house was pro-

---

[1] Journal for 1862, p. 320.

tracted, and the inconvenience felt by the Society from want of room for the accommodation of its daily expanding Library was great; and a special house-allowance was granted by Government at the rate of Rs. 400 per mensem from December 1, 1874.

A misunderstanding arose about this time as to the number of rooms the Society should be permitted to occupy in the new house. The officers in charge of the Museum and the Board of Trustees were of opinion that the whole of the accommodation available in the house then in course of erection would be ultimately required for the purposes of their charge, while the members of the Society were reluctant to enter into a house where accommodation was insufficient, and freedom of action cramped. It was felt, too, that the Society's position as an independent body would be injured by its office being huddled in the corner of a house occupied by two such large Government establishments as the Geological Survey and the Natural History Museum, and forming as it were a mere annexe to them. The Government, thereupon, referred the matter for settlement to a Committee consisting of Sir Ashley Eden and Dr. Oldham, and, at their recommendation, paid the Society the sum of Rs. 1,50,000 as compensation for its claim to accommodation in the Museum building.[1] This arrangement has proved highly beneficial both to the Society and to the Museum.

The exertions made for the establishment of the national museum, and the endowment of it with the richest collection of specimens available in India, are acts for which the Society deserves high credit. To quote the language of an elegant writer in the 'Calcutta Review:'

---

[1] Proceedings, July 1876.

"Had it done nothing else to promote science during the last ten years, it would have entitled itself to the gratitude of posterity for the vigor with which it has prosecuted to success a project fraught with so much public usefulness."

Publications of the Society: Asiatic Researches.

Although Sir William Jones contemplated the publication of a volume of 'Asiatick Miscellany' every year, no attempt was made to get out such a periodical during the first three years of the Society's career. Most of the papers received during the first year were short and unimportant, and it was not until the middle of the year 1787 that the Society was in a position to go to press with the first volume of its Transactions. The Society, however, had no funds of its own at the time, and there was no publisher in Calcutta who could undertake the work at his own responsibility. Ultimately one Mr. Manuel Cantopher, of the Hon'ble East India Company's Printing Office, undertook the job as a private speculation, on the understanding that every Member of the Society would take the book at Rs. 20 a copy. The name then approved for the periodical was "Asiatick Researches," instead of what the founder had originally suggested. The first volume appeared in 1788, and the second followed in 1790. The third, the fourth, and the fifth volumes appeared successively in 1793, 1795, and 1797, under the same conditions, the price being reduced to Rs. 16 per copy. The work created quite a sensation in the literary world, and the demand for it was so great, that a pirated edition was brought out in England in 1798. This also sold so rapidly that, within the next five or six years, two other editions were brought out in octavo. The demand for the work was also urgent on the Continent, and a French translation was brought out in

Paris under the title of "Recherches Asiatiques."[1] In introducing it to the public, the translator, M. A. Labaume, remarked: "cette collection a inspiré en Angleterre un intérét, qu'il est a-peu-prés impossible de se procurer aujourdhui un exemplaire de l'edition originale de Calcutta, et qu'il en été fait à Londres trois editions, qui sont presque entierement épuisées: cependant elles sont fort incorrectes et remplies de fautes importantes." The translation was a faithful one, and it was enriched by a series of valuable notes on the philological and historical papers by M. Langlès, and on the scientific papers by MM. Cuvier, Delambre, Lamarck and Olievier. The estimation in which the work was then held was thus indicated by the editor: "la plus riche collection de faits qui existe sur l' Inde, ce pays qui attire les premiers regards de ceux qui veulent études l'histoire des hommes."

The plan of quarterly contributions from Members had placed the Society in some funds in 1798, when the sixth volume was about to be sent to press; and, looking to the rapid and profitable sale which the first five volumes had met with, the idea was taken up of bringing out the next volume on account of the Society. The proposal was that the same printer should continue to print the work, but at the cost of the Society, which was to reimburse its outlay by charging the Members at Rs. 12 a copy. Volumes VI — XII were published under this arrange-

---

[1] The full title of the translation runs thus: "Recherches Asiatiques, ou Mémoires de la Société établie au Bengale pour faire des recherches sur l'histoire et les antiquités, les arts, les sciences, et la literature de l' Asie; traduits de l' Anglois, par M. A. Labaume. Revus et Augmentés de notes pour la partie Orientale, Philologique et Historique, par M. Langlès, et pour la partie des Sciences exactes et naturelles, par MM. Cuvier, Delambre, Lamarck, et Olievier. Paris, 1805, 4to. 2 vols.

ment.[1] This arrangement did not, however, prove advantageous. The cost of printing became heavy, and the sale-proceeds did not fully recoup the outlay. In 1819, it was therefore proposed that the copyright should be sold to a London publisher, and the work brought out at shorter intervals than heretofore. The project, however, fell through. Following the example of European Societies, it was besides resolved that the Researches should be given to members gratis. This increased the responsibility of the Society, and caused greater delay in the publication of its Transactions. In 1829, when the Physical Class was in active work, a resolution was adopted to divide the Researches into two parts, one to be devoted wholly to scientific papers, and the other to literary contributions. This plan was carried out in Vols. XVII, XVIII, XIX, and XX, but as the two parts were intended to be bound together, no appreciable advantage was gained by it. On the contrary, the scientific parts did not sell so readily as the literary ones, and many copies of the stock were accordingly made defective. In 1837, Mr. James Prinsep brought out a very carefully prepared analytical index of the first eighteen volumes of the Researches. This was a valuable acquisition, as it made the rich treasures of the Society's Transactions readily accessible to students. It did not suffice, however, to revive public interest in the valuable but tardily-issued publication ; and soon after the completion of the second part of the twentieth volume of the Researches in 1839, the work was finally abandoned.

The causes which contributed to the stoppage of this

[1] The dates in which Vols. VI to XX were issued, were :—Vol. VI, in 1799 ; Vol. VII, in 1801 ; Vol. VIII, in 1805 ; Vol. IX, in 1807 ; Vol. X, in 1808 ; Vol. XI, in 1810 ; Vol. XII, in 1816 ; Vol. XIII, in 1820 ; Vol. XIV, in 1822 ; Vol. XV, in 1825 ; Vol. XVI, in 1828 ; Vol. XVII, in 1832 ; Vol. XVIII, in 1833 ; Vol. XIX, in 1836 ; and Vol. XX, in 1839.

once popular and highly esteemed periodical were manifold. The first and foremost was tardy publication. From the foundation of the Society in 1784 to the close of 1839, within a period of fifty-five years, the Society published only twenty volumes, or one volume at an average in every two years and nine months. In many instances the interval was greater. In the early days of the Society this was not much felt, but latterly it became a source of frequent complaint. On January 8, 1820, Dr. Gordon moved that "the great delay in completing and publishing the volumes of the Society's Transactions being a source of general complaint and discouraging to the authors of papers for the Researches, some remedy should be adopted for publishing the volumes in parts," and it was resolved that "the Committee of Papers cause the several copies printed by the Society to be distributed to the members applying for the same, in such parts as, and at such periods and as often as, may, by the Committee, be found most convenient; 12 copies of each paper or of the part containing it to be sent to the authors." This did not, however, suffice to remove the cause of complaint. Another frequent complaint was the form of the 'Researches.' A heavy quarto volume necessarily suggested elaborate and finished essays, and in the selection of papers for it, short notes, describing new discoveries or new ideas, however interesting, were frequently rejected. They were read at meetings, and then pigeonholed for decay. The Transactions in their quarto form could not be adapted for them. An outlet for these was, therefore, very much needed. For a time these found a place in the 'Quarterly Oriental Journal,' which Dr. Wilson started in 1821, while short notes on scientific subjects were published in the 'Transactions of the Medical and Physical Society.' Both those publications, however, were dropped in 1827. A substitute for these was provided in 1829 by Captain J. D. Herbert, Deputy Surveyor-General, in a monthly publication which he started under the name of 'Gleanings in Science.' His primary idea was to confine it to extracts and abstracts from European scientific publications, but original contributions poured in so rapidly that he had to abstain from extracts. The Society benefited by this publication so far that a *précis* of its monthly proceedings, which had heretofore been preserved in manuscript, was regularly published. Captain Herbert, however, was appointed Astronomer to His Majesty the King of Oudh in 1830, and Mr. James Prinsep, who had been associated with him in the undertaking, instead of dropping the work, proposed to change its name and call it 'The Journal of the Asiatic Society.' The sanction was given in March 1832. The 'Journal,' however, as it appeared in that month, bore the name of the 'Journal of the Asiatic Society of Bengal.' Its character, too, was entirely changed. Instead of being a scientific periodical, it became essentially literary. It came out also with the additional advantage of free postage, the Government having, in consideration of the Editor publishing Dr. Buchanan-Hamilton's 'Statistics of Bengal' as an appendix to it, conceded that privilege. For the first two years, moreover, it was given to the members free of charge. The frequency and regularity with which this Journal appeared recommended it strongly to the notice of authors, and many papers which would have been otherwise reserved for the pages of the 'Researches' found their way into the 'Journal.'

Journal.

The Journal, thus established and conducted, superceded the Researches. The privilege of franking allowed it was withdrawn after two years.[1] But it had already established its name and fame as a standard periodical of European reputation, and the Asiatic Society made up for the loss by purchasing the necessary number of copies for presentation to its members. The Court of Directors also extended to it their patronage by subscribing for 40 copies.[2] It was devoted to the publication almost exclusively of papers received by the Society, and it thus became its organ, though not officially so recognized. Although many scientific papers were published in it, its literary character was generally maintained, for at the time there were two rivals—the 'India Journal of Science' of Dr. Corbyn, and the 'Calcutta Journal of Natural History' of Dr. McLelland, which diverted many scientific papers from its pages. On the other hand, the Government, at the request of the Society, allowed it access to all official records likely to be of general interest, and no want was ever felt of fit materials for publication.

Financially, nevertheless, it involved a small, but steadily recurring, loss to the editor. It injured also the Researches, by withdrawing valuable papers and by stinting the resources of the Society, which, after paying for the Journal for its members, had little means left to defray the cost of printing the Researches. The two volumes and the Index printed since the commencement of the Journal had to be paid for out of vested funds. On the retirement of Mr. Prinsep in 1838, his successor, Mr. Henry Torrens, took up the work and carried it on at his own risk. Matters, however, came to a crisis at the close of 1842, when Mr. Torrens resigned the secretaryship as well as the editorship of the Journal, and no one could be

---

[1] Proceedings, June 1834.

[2] *Ibid.*, February 1838.

found to take his place. The only course then left to the Society was to recognize the Journal as its official organ, and finally to abandon the Researches.

The changes above adverted to did not in the least affect the character of the Journal. For ten years it had been recognized by the public, though not by the Society itself, as the organ of the Society, and it so continued to be, though it became a source of greater responsibility to the Society, inasmuch as the loss which had hitherto been borne by the editor and proprietor had now to be met by it; and with a view to the exercise of due discretion in the selection of papers, the Committee of Papers had to be invested with the duty of editing. Since 1837 its bulk had become so heavy that the annual volume had to be divided into two parts, and it was so kept up till 1845. In the following year grave financial difficulties rendered it necessary to reduce its size to the bulk of one part only. From the next year the two parts were again regularly published till 1850. The Society's resources were, however, taking into consideration its other responsibilities, never equal to so large a publication, and the size of the Journal was, accordingly, again reduced to one part, or six fasciculi, a year.

Proceedings.

Financially this arrangement was appropriate enough, but it gave rise to a new inconvenience. The précis of the Society's proceedings, which had been hitherto published regularly every month, could not be oftener issued than once in every two or three months, and it became a frequent matter of complaint. The obvious course in the case was to separate the Proceedings from the body of the Journal, and this was done in 1865. The value of the new series was also enhanced by inserting into it short notes, which were not deemed fit for introduction into the Journal, but which were, nevertheless, of sufficient interest to be worthy of publication. Another change was also at the time suggested. The complaints which necessitated the division of the Researches into two parts in 1829 were now brought to bear upon the Journal; and a similar division had to be adopted. Care was at the same time taken to keep these Parts so distinct by separate pagination and separate indexes as to form two separate serials, so that the scientific scholar may have the scientific matter without the admixture of what to him appeared as literary lumber, and the orientalist may not have to pay for scientific matter, in which he did not feel himself interested. This arrangement necessitated the employment of three Secretaries, one to look after the general business of the Society and edit the Proceedings, one to edit the scientific part of the Journal, and a third to take charge of the literary portion.

The most frequent contributors to the Journal have been Mr. J. Prinsep, Mr. B. H. Hodgson, Col. P. T. Cautley, Mr. E. Blyth, Mr. H. Piddington, Dr. H. Falconer, Dr. G. G. Spilsbury, Dr. J. Campbell, M. Csoma de Körös, Capt. J. D. Cunningham, General A. Cunningham, Col. R. Everest, Major M. Kittoe, Capt. Hutton, Capt. J. W. Sherwill, Col. J. Abbott, Capt. J. Newbold, Mr. H. F. Blanford, Mr. W. T. Blanford, Dr. R. Mitra, Mr. Wood-Mason, and Mr. H. Blochmann.

A list of all the contributors with the titles of their contributions will be found in Appendix D.

Counting each part as a volume, the Society has published, either directly or indirectly, and including the index, eighty-four volumes of the Journal, and nineteen volumes of the Proceedings.

These 103 volumes represent, roughly speaking, a total of 50,000 pages of closely printed matter, replete with innumerable essays, papers, monographs, and notes of great interest. Their bulk, however, has made their use a matter of great trouble. To obviate this the writer of this Review prepared, and published in 1856, an index to the last two volumes of the Asiatic Researches and the first 23 volumes of the Journal; but it was compiled, as stated in its preface, "to render the varied and valuable matter contained in the Transactions of the Society easy of reference to the compiler, and pretended to be nothing more than a resumé of the several-volume indexes to the Journal and Researches, giving, under the usual alphabetical arrangement, nothing more than the subjects, the names of authors, and the local connection of the articles as they appear in their titles." A carefully-arranged analytical index to the entire set is what is now much needed, and it is to be hoped that the beginning of the second century of the Society's career will be signalized by such a compilation.

The subject, nature, and value of the papers published in these volumes have been noticed at some length in the subsequent parts of this Review. Suffice it now to observe that they have contributed greatly to enhance the reputation of the Society.

Oriental Publications.

Though himself actively engaged in the translation of oriental works into the English language, Sir William Jones seems to have entertained no idea of the Asiatic Society immediately taking up the task of printing oriental texts, or of translating them; and it was not until several years afterwards that the subject was mooted. The first proposition came from the Brethren of the Baptist Mission at Serampore, who offered to undertake, under certain conditions, the publication of a series of Sanskrit works with translations,[1]

[1] Proceedings, May 15, 1806.

and the Society, on the recommendation of the Committee of Papers, agreed to give the Missionaries the aid required, the patronage being limited at the time to a single work to be selected by a Committee appointed for the purpose.[1] The work approved was the Rámáyana, and the Society agreed to pay a monthly contribution of Rs. 150, on the distinct understanding that the work would be completed in three years. On October 7, 1807, a second book was selected—the text of the Sánkhya,—and a resolution was come to to extend the monthly grant to a period of eighteen months after the expiration of the first three years. The plan, however, fell through, and the contribution was stopped after the publication of the first three volumes of the Rámáyana. While these negociations were proceeding, Sir James Mackintosh, then President of the 'Literary Society of Bombay,' submitted a scheme for the regular publication of Sanskrit texts; and on July 2, 1806, the Asiatic Society resolved to "publish, from time to time, as their funds will admit of it, in volumes distinct from the Asiatic Researches, translations of short works in the Sanskrit and other Asiatic languages, or extracts and descriptive accounts of books of greater length in those languages, which may be offered to the Society and appear deserving of publication," and "that, as this publication may be expected gradually to extend to all Asiatic books of which copies may be deposited in the Library of the Society, and even to all works extant in the learned languages of Asia, the series of volumes be entitled 'Bibliotheca Asiatica,' or a descriptive catalogue of Asiatic books, with extracts and translations." No action seems to have been taken in accordance with these resolutions, beyond a few casual grants in aid of oriental publications by private individuals.

[1] Proceedings, July 3, 1805.

On the arrival of M. Csoma de Körös at Almorah, after his long sojourn in Tibet, occasion arose for the Society to obtain from Government a grant for the publication of that distinguished scholar's Tibetan Grammar and Dictionary (1830). The Society at the same time sanctioned an allowance of Rs. 50 per mensem to that gentleman, who was then in very straitened circumstances. This allowance was continued to the day of his death in May 1843. Soon after, the Society undertook to print an Annamatican Dictionary, prepared by the Bishop of Isauropolis. Subsequently, grants were obtained for the publication of a Burmese and a Siamese Dictionary, as also for Mr. Macnaghten's edition of the *Sháhanámeh* and Mr. Brownlow's edition of the Macan manuscript of the *Alif Lailá*, the printing of which the Society undertook to superintend.

It was not, however, until 1835, that any systematic attempt was made for the publication of oriental works. The battle which had long raged between the Anglicists and the Orientalists, in regard to the language best adapted for the education of the people of this country, came to a close with the overthrow of the latter, and the Government adopted a resolution to put a stop to all oriental works which were then in the press on its account, directing the printed sheets 'to be sold' as 'waste paper.' The Society now intervened, and, after protracted discussions at two sittings, came to a resolution to undertake the completion of the abandoned works, and to arrange for the carrying on of similar works in future.[1] The last part of the resolution was referred to a Special Committee, consisting of Dr. Mill, Mr. Hay Macnaghten, Mr. Turton, Mr. William Grant, Mr. J. R. Colvin, and Mr. J. Prinsep, with a view

[1] Proceedings, April and June, 1835.

"to prepare a memorial from the Society to the Court of Directors and the Board of Control, stating that Government here have withdrawn the funds hitherto appropriated to the revival of oriental literature in this country,—and respectfully impressing upon the authorities at home the importance of having some public funds appropriated to this purpose, and requesting them to adopt such means as they think fit for providing a sufficient sum for this important subject."[1] A strong representation was got up, and forwarded under the signature of Sir Edward Ryan, then President of the Society, to the Court of Directors,[2] and an application submitted to Government for the gift of the printed sheets of the abandoned works.

The works abandoned were :—(1) The *Mahábhárata*, of which 1,400 pages had been printed, and 2,000 remained unfinished ; (2) the *Rájatarangini*, of which about 200, out of 620, pages had been printed ; (3) the *Naishadha*, of which 200, out of 600, had been printed ; (4) the *Sausruta*, of which about one half had been printed ; (5) the *Saríravidyá*, a Sanskrit translation of Hooper's *Vade Mecum*, of which a few pages only had been printed ; (6) the *Fatáwe Alamgiri*, in six volumes royal quarto, of which only two had been printed ; (7) the *Ináya*, in four volumes quarto, of which the last two had been printed ; (8) the *Kházánat ul Ilm*, a quarto volume of 620 pages, of which about one-fifth remained to be printed ; (9) the *Jawáme ul Ilm ul Riázi*, an Arabic translation of Hutton's 'Mathematics,' a quarto volume of 120 pages ; (10) the *Anis ul Musharrahín*, an Arabic translation of Hooper's *Vade Mecum* by Dr. Tytler ; and (11) a Treatise on Algebra in Arabic. The cost of finishing these works was estimated

---

[1] Journal, Vol. IV, 355. [2] *Ibid.*, Vol. IV, 472.

at Rs. 20,000, and in a Prospectus issued at the time, the patronage of the friends of oriental literature and of the public of India was solicited in aid and support of the important undertaking. The co-operation of European literary associations was also invited. The call was cordially responded to. The President of the Société Asiatique de Paris wrote a sympathizing letter, offering the co-operation of the Society he represented,[1] and the native public most warmly took up the cause. The Pandits and the Maulvies who had been employed by Government to edit the works volunteered their services free of charge, and one gentleman, Naváb Tauhar Jang, of Chitpur, undertook to defray the entire cost of printing the *Share ul Islám.*

The works, with two exceptions, were completed in four years. The exceptions were the *Saríravidyá* and the Treatise on Algebra. The former was, after protracted discussions, abandoned, because it was thought that it would be useless without a profusion of woodcut illustrations, which could not be procured in India at that time; and the latter, because there seemed to be no demand for it.

The petition of the Society to the Court of Directors was at first coldly received ; but through the exertions of Professor H. H. Wilson, then the London Agent of the Society, and of the President and other influential members of the Royal Asiatic Society, a grant of Rs. 500 per mensem was ultimately sanctioned. The correspondence on the subject appears in the Proceedings of June 1838. The following extract from the Court's Despatch will show the terms on which the grant was made. Writing to the Government of India, the Court said:—" Although the works formerly published may not always have been

[1] Proceedings, November 1836.

selected in the most judicious manner, we are still of opinion that the publication of works—and works on instruction in the Eastern languages—should not be abandoned; we therefore authorize you to devote a sum, not exceeding five hundred rupees a month, to the preparation and publication of such works, either through the medium of the Asiatic Society, or any equally appropriate channel, and we shall expect an annual return of the works published and ten copies of each book for distribution in this country."

The means thus placed at the disposal of the Society would have enabled Mr. James Prinsep to have done an immense deal of good, but his arduous and unremitting labours of several years in India had undermined his health, and he was obliged, immediately after the receipt of the Despatch, to retire from India for a change. It was hoped that the bracing air of his native land and abstinence from work would soon bring on a restoration; but he sank under his illness early in 1840. The estimate he had formed of the probable cost of completing the works was insufficient, and, at the time of his retirement, there was a heavy debt, for the payment of which his successors, Dr. O'Shaughnessy and Mr. Sutherland thought fit to confine their oriental works to the completion of the *Mahábhárata*. Mr. Henry Torrens was elected Secretary in May 1840. He was a distinguished scholar, an elegant writer, and a linguist, but he had neither the energy nor the aptitude to control financial details, and was withal unmindful of the restraints of rules, and under his management the grant was frittered away on works which did not come under the terms of the Court's Despatch. The annual account called for by the Court was not rendered during the whole time of his management to the close of 1846. The only new work published during his secretaryship was an edition of the *Tárikh-i-Nádiri* in Persian. A contribution of Rs. 500 was also paid to cover the cost of printing a selection of small poems in Sanskrit, under the name *Kávya-sangraha.* When the accounts were cast in the last named year, it was found that no less than Rs. 25,000 had been devoted to purposes unconnected with oriental literature.

Bibliotheca Indica.

The immediate question before the Council of 1847 was, how to utilize the grant, and a Committee was appointed to devise means to carry out the Court's wishes regarding the publication of the Vedas. The plan approved by the Society was, as suggested in a judicious minute by Mr. Laidley (dated December 1847) to start a monthly serial under the name of 'Bibliotheca Indica' and the editorship of a competent scholar, aided by a staff of Pandits. The work was taken in hand at the beginning of 1848. Dr. Roer was appointed the chief editor on a salary of Rs. 100 per mensem, and his principal duty was to supply English translations of the works taken in hand. The first work selected was the Sanhitá of the Rig Veda, but before four fasciculi of it could be published, news arrived that the Court of Directors had made arrangements with Dr. Max Müller for the publication of that work, together with an English translation by Dr. H. H. Wilson, and the Society's project had, therefore, to be abandoned. Dr. Roer then took up the Upanishads and some other works.

At the close of 1850, the Council appointed a Sub-Committee to report on the publication, and at their suggestion the post of chief editor was abolished, and rules were framed for the remuneration of editors according to the nature of the work done. The Committee further suggested, "that, whilst it is of the highest importance for translations to be made here in India with all Hindu assistance, it is not expedient to limit the publication of volumes in the 'Bibliotheca Indica' to works which the editors may be prepared at once to translate. It is evident that such a restriction would operate unfavorably, as in many cases, years must be spent before a perfectly satisfactory translation could be finished. At the same time the Committee recommend that no work should be printed without so much critical apparatus as is necessary for giving an account of the manuscripts made use of, their authority and age, &c., and a resumé of the contents of the volume."[1] These suggestions were unanimously approved, and they gave a new impulse to the publication. Distinguished scholars, such as Dr. Sprenger, Dr. Ballantyne, Pandit Isvarachandra Vidyáságara, tendered their services, and several very valuable works were taken in hand. The publications were carried on with great spirit and energy, soon outstripping the limit imposed by the amount of the grant, and in five years it became necessary to put a stop to the issue of the 'Bibliotheca' in order to pay off arrears.

About this time a letter was received from Professor Wilson, finding fault with some of the Arabic works then in course of publication, on the ground of their being unconnected with India, and therefore of little interest to local scholars, and not contemplated by the terms of the grant.[2] This was followed by a Despatch from the Court of Directors, in which the same arguments were repeated in an official form. Adverting to the excess of expenditure over income, the Court remarked:—

"This augmented activity and enhanced expense arise especially from the great impulse given to publications in Mahommedan litera-

[1] Journal, Vol. XIX, 629. [2] Proceedings, May 1856.

ture and the Arabic language. Of the 38 Nos. of the 'Bibliotheca Indica' issued in 1854, twenty-seven are Arabic, only ten are Sanskrit, and one English; the cost of the former is Rs. 6,752, of the ten latter less than half, *viz.*, Rs. 3,036. This is a disproportion which is inconsistent with the comparative claims of the two departments of literature, whether the ratios of the population or the value of the individual works be considered, for on referring to the Mahommedan works, we observe that they have no relation whatever to India, nor to any popular form even of the literature of the Indian Mahommedans; but they embrace to a very large extent abstruse Mahommedan theology and Sufyism, in works which none but a few of the most learned Moulvies can read, and which still fewer understand, works utterly worthless for the illustration of the past or present condition of India, and of little utility to European scholars. When we authorized the appropriation of a special grant to the encouragement of Indian literature, we had in view especially the literature of the Hindus, although, we did not purpose to exclude Mahommedan literature of local origin or interest, such as the historical works epitomized by Sir Henry Elliott; but we certainly did not contemplate a voluminous and costly publication of the theology and tradition and spiritual mysticism of the Mussulmans, which is the literature of Arabia and not at all that of India.

"We therefore direct that the encouragement of such works be hereafter withheld. The publications that have been commenced may be completed, but upon their completion we expect that the Asiatic Society, in applying part of the funds placed at its disposal to Arabic or Persian works, will have due regard to the light which they are calculated to throw, not upon the literature or theology of Arabia, but upon the literature and history of India."[1]

The principles here laid down have, since the date, been fully recognized and generally acted upon by the Society, though the varying ascendancy of Sanskrit and Semitic

[1] Proceedings, August 1856.

scholars in the Council of the Society have at times caused a slight preponderance on the one side or the other.

The practice now is to divide the grant into two parts, one of which is devoted to Sanskrit, and the other to works in Arabic, Persian and other languages. This apportionment was first brought to the notice of Government in 1868 by Mr. Whitley Stokes, then Legal Member of the Supreme Council, who, while accepting the propriety of it, remarked, that, in view of the vast extent and paramount importance of Sanskrit literature, and the little that has yet been done towards its preservation, the amount devoted to it was very small, and recommended it to be doubled. The Government approved of his suggestion, and the Society now receives an additional allowance of Rs. 250 per mensem exclusively for Sanskrit works.

The total number of Oriental works published by the Society up to date amounts to 140. Of these, one hundred and eleven have been published, or are in course of publication, in the 'Bibliotheca Indica.' The works may be noticed under two heads : 1st, Semitic ; 2nd, Sanskritic. The Semitic series includes, besides some standard law books in Arabic, all the standard works in Persian, on the general history of India, together with a critical edition and an English translation of the Ain-i-Akbari, the well-known Gazetteer of Akbar's extensive empire. An imperfect version of this work was published early in this century by Mr. Francis Gladwin, but it did not include the most important part of the work—its numerous tabular statements. The translation, moreover, had been long since out of print. The late Mr. Blochmann, therefore, undertook a new and faithful translation, and brought out the first volume in 1873, together with the whole of the text. For rigorous exactitude of rendering, for faithful representation of the spirit of the original, and for the richness, variety and profusion of its illustrative and explanatory notes, the book is a model of its kind. No Persian work has as yet had the benefit of so able and so faithful an interpreter. It is deeply to be regretted that the lamented death of its learned and enthusiastic Secretary has deprived the Society not only of his invaluable services, but also of the opportunity of completing the work in the same style.

The Sanskrit series includes the leading works of almost all the departments of Bráhmanic literature. The Vedas are represented by twenty-five different works ; the Purá-nas, by three ; the philosophical schools, by the text-books of all the six leading systems and several commentaries ; the Yotishah, by three, two with translations. The law-books, the rituals of the Vedas, grammar, rhetoric, and other branches have also been represented by important works. Notices of these in some detail will appear in a subsequent part of this Review. It is doubtful if any Society in Europe has, within fifty years, done for any classic literature as much as the Asiatic Society of Bengal has done for Sanskrit literature since 1847. This work alone has given to it the highest claim to the consideration and respect of the people of this country and of oriental scholars in all parts of the world.

Up to date, the Bibliotheca series has come up to a total of 747 fasciculi ; of these 280 are Semitic, including English translations of four works in 28 fasciculi. The names of the translations are: 1, Ain-i-Akbari; 2 Tabakát-i-Násiri ; 3 History of the Khalifs; 4 Shamshieh, or the Logic of the Arabians. The Sanskrit series takes up 467 fasciculi, including translations of twenty different works in 50 fasciculi. The works in the Semitic series have been edited by Dr. Aloys Sprenger, Captain Nassau

Lees, Hekekyan Bey, Mr. Henry Blochmann, Major Raverty, Captain Jarrett, and the Maulvies of the Calcutta Madrissa. The credit of the Sanskrit series is due to several scholars, of whom—

Dr. E. Roer	edited	33	fasc.
„ Fitz-Edward Hall	„	18	„
„ Ballantyne	„	5	„
„ E. B. Cowell	„	17	„
Professor Jayanáráyana Tarkapanchánan ...	„	19	„
„ Bharatachandra Siromani ...	„	16	„
„ Mahesachandra Nyáyaratna ...	„	19	„
Pandit Satyavrata Sámasrami	„	44	„
Dr. Rájendralála Mitra	„	83	„
„ Hoernle	„	12	„

Appendix C supplies a detailed list of all the works published.

As a preliminary to the publication of Sanskrit works, it was, at the beginning of this century, deemed expedient to collect information regarding the nature, extent, and character of Sanskrit manuscripts extant in this country. Dr. Farquhar accordingly proposed, on October 5, 1803, that "the Society immediately adopt some effectual steps to procure a catalogue of all the most useful Indian works now in existence, with an abstract of their contents." No action, however, could be taken on it, owing to want of organization for carrying out so vast an undertaking, until July 1, 1807, when a petition was submitted to Government, praying an annual grant of five to six thousand rupees to carry out the object. Mr. Colebrooke, then President of the Society, urged the following arguments in support of this prayer:—

Conservation of Sanskrit Manuscripts.

"The utility of such a catalogue is obvious. It would assist the researches of learned men, directing them to the books most likely to afford the information which they may require; it would promote the studies of oriental scholars, guiding them to the selection of books most deserving of their notice; and, on many points, it would furnish to the literary world as much information as is needed in particular branches of Indian knowledge.

"A catalogue, prepared according to the views of the Asiatic Society, would not only indicate the subject and scope of every valuable book, but would contain extracts of the most curious or important passages in it, besides notices of various topics connected with the work itself, with the history of its author, or that of the sovereign in whose reign he lived, and with the manners and opinions prevalent at the period when he wrote.

"It can scarcely be hoped that a work of so great extent should be undertaken and executed solely at the charge of individuals. The labor will be cheerfully borne by members of the Society, so far as their part of the task reaches, but much preparatory labor must be performed by learned natives, for whom remuneration will be requisite. Private Libraries will, no doubt, be open; but, however extensive some of those libraries may be, and among others, my own collection of Sanskrit manuscripts, it will be still necessary that considerable expense should be incurred in providing books, which may not there be found. It is desirable, for other reasons also, that reliance should not be exclusively placed on the precarious aid of private collections. A library of oriental manuscripts, accessible to the public under proper regulations, would be otherwise greatly beneficial. Asiatic knowledge would be there preserved. The learned, whether Natives or Europeans, would easily supply themselves with transcripts of scarce books, and whenever occasion arose for consulting numerous authorities, the irksome task of reference would be alleviated.

"On every consideration, the Asiatic Society is desirous of forming a collection, as well as of obtaining detailed catalogue, of manuscripts. But the funds of the Society are too limited for the undertaking: and, without aid, either the design must be relinquished, or, if it be prosecuted, a progress answerable to the public expectations cannot be looked for. On the other hand, if the

Asiatic Society had at its disposal a moderate addition to those funds, in an annual sum of five to six thousand rupees, the execution of the scheme might be immediately commenced; and its accomplishment might be expected at a period not very remote."

The Government received the proposition very favorably, and strongly recommended it to the notice of the Court of Directors ; but the Board of Control declined to make the grant, and the project dropped. Mr. Prinsep, in 1837, revived the idea ; and, in the Sanskrit catalogue of the Society's Library, included, by way of a first instalment, the names of all the works contained in the libraries of the Calcutta and the Benares Sanskrit Colleges. This, however, did not meet the requirements of the case, and, in 1867, Pandit Rádhákissen, of Lahore, urged the adoption of a comprehensive scheme that should bring to light the treasures of Sanskrit lore buried in private libraries in India. The Government of Lord Lawrence took it up warmly, and, acting upon the recommendation of Mr. Whitley Stokes, ordered that each of the several subordinate Governments should organize a scheme not only for the preparation of inventories, on a uniform plan, of all manuscripts that may be met with in private collections, but also for the purchasing or the preparation of transcripts of all valuable or rare manuscripts, promising at the same time special grants for the purchase of rare collections, whenever opportunities would offer for so doing. The Government, at the same time, named Dr. Buhler of Bombay, Dr. Kielhorn of Púná, Mr. Burnell of Madras, and the writer of this Review, as persons who, in its opinion, were fit to be entrusted with the management of the undertaking. The amount sanctioned for Bengal was Rs. 3,000 per annum, and the Asiatic Society was asked to superintend its disbursement.

The form recommended by Government was a tabular one, which did not admit of the contents of the manuscripts being given at length. The writer of this Review, when requested to undertake the work, pointed out this defect,[1] and, taking into consideration the fact that a work of this kind could be done only once for all, suggested certain modifications, especially with reference to abstracts of contents. His suggestions were approved both by the Society and the Government, but unfortunately his minute was not circulated to other Governments, and the opportunity for securing uniformity was lost.

The inventories prepared for the Society have been named "Notices of Sanskrit Manuscripts," and eighteen fasciculi of these have been published during the last twelve years. The descriptions given are full, and the contents of most of the works have been given in such a way as to obviate the necessity of a future more detailed analysis. In this respect it contrasts very favorably with the lists published in Madras, Bombay, and the N. W. Provinces. The model selected was the admirable catalogue of the Bodleian collection prepared by Dr. Aufrecht. A catalogue has also been prepared by the writer of the library of His Highness the Mahárájá Bikáner. It extends to 745 pages, and supplies more or less detailed notices of 1,794 manuscripts.

Although Sanskrit manuscripts are not marketable articles, and the sanctity attached to them by the people of this country render them extremely difficult of access, nevertheless, purchases have been made to the extent of 2,507 codices. These are now preserved in the library of the Asiatic Society.

---

[1] Proceedings, May 1869.

It has been incidentally noticed (*ante*, p. 57), that the Society obtained from Government contributions in support of the publication of certain oriental works ; nor were its efforts in this respect limited to works of that description. Scientific works taken in hand in India always found ready support from the Society, both by subscriptions from its own funds as well as by intercession with the Government for special grants. In certain cases the Society, likewise, undertook the task of superintending the printing of literary and scientific works for others. As instances, it may not be amiss here to cite the names of Colonel Dalton's magnificent work on the Ethnology of Bengal, Colonel Mainwaring's Lepcha Grammar and Dictionary, Mr. Beal's Biographical Dictionary, and Mr. Grierson's Grammar of the Northern Behar dialect. Circumstances also arose from time to time to print works independently of the Journal of the Society. The most important and recent work of this class is Messrs. Moore and Hewettson's description of Mr. Atkinson's collection of Indian Lepidoptera, a profusely illustrated quarto volume, which was most welcome to students of Entomology. In 1837, the Society came into possession of the original journals, correspondence, and researches of Messrs. Moorcroft and Trebeck's travels beyond the Himalayas, and immediately placed them in the hands of Messrs. Allen & Co., the charge of editing being entrusted to Dr. Wilson, then its London agent. The whole edition of the work, however, sold off in a short time, and the Society incurred no expense on account of it. Mr. Hodgson's Essay on 'the Coch, Bodo and Dhimal Tribes,' Mr. Laidley's Travels of Fahían, and some other minor works were also published solely, or mainly, at the expense of the Society. A list of these will be found in Appendix C.

Miscellaneous Works.

Funds.

It has been already stated that, during the first twelve years of its career, the Society possessed no income of any kind. Such small contingent expenses as were incurred in carrying on its affairs were defrayed by the President, or by the Secretary, or by both. When the rules regarding quarterly subscriptions were adopted in 1796, the great object was to accumulate a sufficient sum for the building of a house, and for sometime afterwards very little was spent for other purposes. It was not until the establishment of its museum and library that the ordinary expenses of the Society became heavy, and the periodical cost of the Researches, which subsequently began to be distributed gratis, swallowed up nearly the whole of its income. Moreover, whatever little savings it had, were lost by the failure of Messrs. Palmer and Co., who were the Society's agents till 1828. Difficulties, therefore, arose in 1829, when frequent grants had to be sanctioned for the researches of the Physical Class and for costly illustrations for the Transactions. The cost of the Museum was also steadily on the increase. A very timely relief was about this time received by a donation from the King of Oudh of Rs. 20,000, supplemented by another of Rs. 5,000 from his Prime Minister. This enabled the Society to pay off its debts, and still leave a considerable sum in the hands of its bankers. Unfortunately, however, the failure, in 1833, of Messrs. Mackintosh and Co., who had charge of the money, deprived it entirely of its cash balance. In 1834, one Mr. Bruce, who had been long a member of the Society, left a bequest of £2,000, and the amount was invested in Government Securities, from the interest of which it was expected that the cost of the Researches would be easily and regularly defrayed, and that publication would be independent of the ordinary resources of the Society; but the monthly contributions for the Journal and heavy expenses on account of the oriental publications began soon to trench upon this vested fund. In 1836, its amount had been reduced to Rs. 17,500, and a resolution was adopted to pay out of it Rs. 200 a month for a Curator.[1] This called forth a vigorous protest,[2] and as it may be of use for reference in future, it may be well to copy it here:—

"It appears to us that in a Society constituted as the Asiatic Society of Bengal is, the existence of a fund vested in Government Securities is absolutely necessary for the permanence of the foundation.

"We consider that such funds are intended to be reserved for cases of extreme emergency, and that the interest only of *such funds* should be carried to the current expenses of the Society.

"We also consider that any infringement of a law upon which the Society's existence may be said to depend, is injurious not only to the Society itself as a body, but to the interests of the members individually; and may be drawn in as a precedent for further encroachments, leading to the ultimate dissolution of the Society.

"For these reasons, we dissent from the resolution passed at the meeting of the Society of the 4th May, 1836, continuing the services of a Curator at two hundred rupees per mensem, the account current shewing a deficiency of Rs. 571-0-1, and the payment of the Curator's salary being proposed to be made out of the vested funds of MR. BRUCE. Further, in adverting to the Secretary's remark, 'that M. BOUCHEZ, the assistant and working Curator, would be competent to set up all new specimens and preserve the present collection,' we see no necessity, under the

---

[1] Proceedings, May 1836.

[2] *Ibid.*, January 1837.

present difficulties of the Society, of retaining the higher appointment."

Northern Doab, 14*th Dec.* 1836;	P. F. Cautley, *Capt., Arty.* H. Falconer, M.D. W. M. Durand, *Lieut., Engrs.* W. E. Baker, *Lieut., Engrs.*
and, Calcutta, 26*th Jan.* 1837.	Alexander Colvin, *Lieut.-Col., Engrs.* John Colvin."

This led to the stoppage of the Curator's allowance on the following year. But the mischief had already been done, and the lax management of the finances for some years afterwards, and the unnecessarily large establishment entertained, greatly embarrassed the position of the Society, and accumulated a debt, which in 1846 entirely swamped the vested fund. Retrenchments also became urgently necessary. Instead of a European Assistant Secretary on Rs. 200, a Librarian on Rs. 100, an Assistant Librarian on Rs. 40, a Maulvie and a Pandit on Rs. 30 each, and an Accountant on Rs. 60, total Rs. 460, a single native officer as Assistant Secretary and Librarian on Rs. 100 a month was found ample for the requirements of the Society, and the financial affairs of the Society were managed with perfect smoothness for some time after this change. With greatly extended business, it was not possible, however, to establish a vested fund. From 1847 to 1876, the Society lived on its annual income, but saved nothing. In 1858 a resolution was adopted to the effect, that the composition fees received from Life Members should be vested in Government Securities, and only the interest thereof should be devoted to current expenditure. Compositions, however, were few, and the vested fund therefore remained insignificant. The compensation received from Government in 1875 in lieu of the claim the Society had for accommodation in the Indian Museum building, enabled the Society to vest a large sum in Government Securities, and a portion of it is now held as a Permanent Reserve Fund under Rule 67, which runs thus : "Of the Funds of the Society now invested in Government Securities, Rs. 1,20,000 shall be considered as a *Permanent Reserve Fund* for the benefit of the Society, and it shall not be competent to the Council, or to any of the Society's officers, or to any Committee of the Society, to sell or otherwise alienate the said fund or any portion of it without first recommending the sale or alienation in question to the Society, and taking the votes of the general body of Members as provided in Rules 64 and 65, and, further, such sale or alienation shall only be lawful if carried by a majority of not less than three-fourths of the members who have voted. And should any portion of the Permanent Fund be sold or alienated by authority of the members of the Society, the remainder shall be preserved under this rule in the same manner as if the sum were intact." It is to be hoped that this rule will be scrupulously and most faithfully observed, and no occasion will arise in future for dissentients to record a protest similar to the one quoted above.

Beadroll.

In a brief history like the present it is not possible to give personal notices of all those whose labors have created and sustained the reputation of the Society. Were it otherwise, still sufficient information cannot now be collected regarding the earlier contributors. To make a selection would be an unpleasant and invidious task. Brief notices of most of the authors of papers have, besides, been given in subsequent parts of this Review. It is, nevertheless, desirable to refer here to a few of the most renowned scholars with whom the fame of the Society is intimately associated.

Their names stand on the beadroll of the Society, and as such are deserving of its highest respect.

1. The first and foremost name in this beadroll is that of Sir William Jones, born September 1746, died April 27, 1794. To him the Society owes its foundation and the distinction it attained in the earlier days of its career. No less than 29 papers were contributed by him in the first four volumes of the Asiatic Researches, and his translation of Manu has been a standard text-book of reference for lawyers for a hundred years. He, likewise, translated into English the *Sakuntalá* of Kálidása, and the *Gitagobinda* of Jayadeva. He was a scholar of world-wide renown, and his memory is dearly cherished by all oriental scholars.

2. Sir John Shore, Bart., afterwards Lord Teignmouth, succeeded Sir William Jones on May 26, 1794, and retired to England on May 2, 1797. He contributed only six papers to the Researches, but it was mainly through his exertions that the Society prospered in its infancy. His name is intimately associated with the foundation of the Society, but he is best remembered by the people of this country as the virtual author of the Permanent Settlement of the land-revenue in Bengal.

3. The name of Henry Thomas Colebrooke, born 1765, died March 18, 1837, comes next. He came to India as a writer in the service of the East India Company, and for a long time held the office of a Judge in the Sadar Dewáni Adálat. He was President of the Asiatic Society for ten years, from April 1806 to February 1, 1815, and contributed nineteen papers to the Transactions of the Society. On his retirement from India, he helped the Society as its London agent until the time of his demise. A great mathematician, zealous astronomer, and profound Sanskrit scholar,

he wrote nothing that did not at once command the highest attention from the public, and, notwithstanding the great advance that has been made in oriental researches of late years, his papers are still looked upon as models of their kind. He was the founder of the Royal Asiatic Society of Great Britain and Ireland, and contributed several valuable papers to its Transactions.

4. Sir Charles Wilkins, Kt., LL.D., born 1750, died 1833, came out to India as a writer in the East India Company's Civil Service, and devoted himself to the study of the Sanskrit language. He was the first Englishman who acquired a thorough mastery of it, and in 1779 published a grammar of that language. He, likewise, translated the *Bhagavadgítá*, which was published in 1785 under the auspices of Mr. Warren Hastings. He was the first also to bring his profound learning to bear upon Sanskrit palæography, and to decipher several inscriptions, which were unintelligible to the Pandits of his time. He was a scholar of unexampled perseverance, and his unremitting labors in the climate of Bengal forced him to retire from the Service at the close of the last century. In England he published a translation of the *Hitopadesa* and several extracts from the *Mahábhárata*. On the arrival in England of a large collection of oriental manuscripts, soon after the capture of Seringapatam, the Court of Directors appointed him the custodian of those treasures. He was thus the first Librarian of the India House Library. On the establishment of the College at Hailebury, in 1805, he was appointed a visitor of that Institution in the Oriental Department, and at about that time the University of Oxford conferred on him the honorary degree of Doctor in Civil Law. At a later period King George IV bestowed on him, in recognition of his high literary merits, the honor of

Knighthood, accompanying that act of favor with the badge of the Guelphic Order.

5. Samuel Davis, Esq., F. R. S., came out to India as an officer of Engineers in the Bengal Presidency, and accompanied the Embassy to Tibet in 1783, but was soon after admitted to the Civil Service of the East India Company. He joined the Society two months after its foundation, and contributed three papers to its Transactions. He was a mathematician and astronomer, and to him is due the credit of having first identified, by actual observations in the company of Pandits at Benares, the asterisms and many of the stars noticed in Sanskrit works. While employed as District Judge and Governor-General's Agent at Benares, he was deeply engaged in astronomical researches in an observatory which he had erected on the top of his house. Vizier Ali, the deposed Naváb of Oudh, revolted at this time, and attacked him with a large following of rowdies at the top of the staircase to his observatory. He defended himself for a long time with a pike, which now forms the crest of his family coat-of-arms. He became Chairman of the Court of Directors, and in that capacity wrote the celebrated Fifth Report on the Permanent Settlement. He was subsequently elected a fellow of the Royal Society of London.

6. Colonel Francis Wilford. He was an enthusiastic supporter of the Society. He wrote ten elaborate essays on historical subjects, which created quite a sensation in his time. Unfortunately, however, the Pandits on whom he relied for his quotations from Sanskrit works betrayed him, and his speculations, therefore, were subsequently found to be not very valuable.

7. Reuben Burrow, Esq., writer in the service of the East India Company. He was a distinguished mathema-

tician and astronomer, and contributed eleven papers in connexion with the mathematics and astronomy of the Hindus.

8. John Bentley, Esq., a writer in the Civil Service, distinguished himself by his researches into Hindu astronomy, for which he deservedly acquired high distinction in Europe.

9. Dr. H. H. Wilson, born 1784, died May 1860. He arrived at Calcutta in 1808, in the Medical Service of the East India Company, became Deputy Secretary to the Society on April 2, 1811, and in two months was elected full Secretary, which office he held till 1833, with two short breaks in 1815 and 1819. He first attracted public notice by an elegant translation of the *Meghadúta*, which was published in 1813. It was followed in rapid succession by other works, among which his 'Theatre of the Hindus' and the Sanskrit-English Dictionary deserve special mention. He contributed also largely to the periodical literature of the day, and to the Asiatic and the Medical and Physical Societies. In 1816, he was appointed Assay Master of the Calcutta Mint, which office he held to the last day of his sojourn in Calcutta. As visitor of the Sanskrit College of Calcutta, he superintended the publication of a large number of Sanskrit books, and, with the assistance of a native staff, had the bulk of the eighteen Puránas translated into English, from cut of which he selected the *Vishnu Purána* for publication. The Chair of Boden Professor of Sanskrit at Oxford was created in 1832, and he assumed it in the summer of the following year. His literary labors in England were incessant, and within a week before his death he completed his translation of the fourth volume of the Rig Veda and a critical review of Max Müller's Vedic Literature. His name stands conspicuous on the roll of those whose genius and labors have

contributed to enlighten the literary world on the early history and civilization of the Hindu race. His connexion with the Society extended over a quarter of a century, and during that period the stability and credit of the Society was thoroughly established.

10. James Prinsep, Esq., born August 20, 1799, died April 22, 1840. 'He was distinguished almost from his infancy for habits of minute attention to whatever fairly attracted his mind, and his ingenuity and skill in design pointed to the profession of an architect as especially appropriate.' But while studying under Pugin, his eyes suffered seriously, and he had to drop his study. This affection lasting long, all opportunity for entering into any learned profession was lost. On his recovery, he entered as an apprentice to Mr. Bingley, Assay Master of the Royal Mint, London, and in due course, receiving a certificate of proficiency, was sent out as assistant to the Assay Master of the Calcutta Mint, in 1819. After a few months' service he went up with Dr. Wilson, then Assay Master of Calcutta, to Benares, the Mint office where required special remodelling. Dr. Wilson returned after the completion of his mission, and Mr. Prinsep was left there as Assay Master for several years. In 1833, he succeeded Dr. Wilson at the Calcutta Mint. During his stay at Benares, he published a large illustrated work on the temples of that holy city. He, likewise, contributed to the pages of the 'Gleanings in Science,' of which he was for a time the editor. The Asiatic Society testified its respects for his services by voting a bust, which now graces its meeting-room; and the public of Calcutta, in recognition of his services, erected near Fort William a magnificent Ghat to his memory. His services to the Asiatic Society, from 1832 to 1838, have been frequently referred to in the preceding

pages, as also in the subsequent parts of this Review. Suffice it to say that his administration was the most brilliant and successful in the annals of the Society.

11. Rev. W. H. Mill, D.D., elected 1833, retired in 1842. He came out in the Ecclesiastical Service of the East India Company, and for a long time held the office of Principal of Bishop's College, Sibpur. His contributions to the Journal were not very numerous, but high encomium is due to his patience, perseverance, and learning in deciphering the inscriptions on the Allahabad column in one of the oldest Indian characters. He was a profound Sanskrit scholar, and universally held in high esteem. To mark their sense of veneration for him, the members of the Society have set up a bust to his honor.

12. Brian Houghton Hodgson, Esq., Bengal Civil Service, born 1799, living. He came out to India in 1819, and spent the greater part of his time in the Himalayas, holding for several years the office of Resident at the Court of Khatmandu, Nepal. He utilized to the utmost the very favourable opportunities he had of carrying on his literary and scientific pursuits in a till then untrodden field, and the service he has done to the cause of science is immense. His contributions to the Society amount to a total of 112 papers, besides large donations in exceedingly valuable manuscripts and specimens of Natural History. On his retirement from the Civil Service in 1843, the Society voted him a bust, and his name is intimately associated with the progress of the Society. Those of his collaborateurs who are still living cherish for him the kindest affection and respect.

Summary.

The details given above, meagre as they are, show that the Asiatic Society has, during its career of a hundred years, fully carried out the objects of its existence. To bring the record of its services to a focus :

1. It has provided for the use of scholars a commodious house, valued at Rs. 1,50,000.

2. It has got up a library, containing thirty thousand volumes, of which upwards of eight thousand are manuscripts.

3. It has a collection of ancient coins and medals, valued at ten thousand rupees.

4. It has a a small but valuable collection of pictures and memorial busts.

5. It got up an Archæological and Ethnological Museum of considerable extent, a Geological Museum rich in meteorites and Indian fossils, and a Zoological Museum, all but complete as regards the Avi-fauna of India.

6. It has published a total of 354 volumes, including 21 volumes of the Asiatic Researches and Index, 84 volumes of the Journal and Index, 19 volumes of Proceedings, 167 volumes of Oriental works of different kinds, 31 volumes of miscellaneous works relating to India, 14 volumes of catalogues of various kinds, and 18 volumes of 'Notices of Sanskrit Manuscripts.'

These are deeds which, for extent, variety, and usefulness, may well claim the consideration of the public. They compare very favorably with the works of other and older Societies in other parts of the earth. To the student of science in India they have proved of incalculable service. And it is in view of these the Society this day celebrates its Centenary Jubilee.

Appendix A.

Statement showing the number of Members on the rolls of the Society from time to time.

At the close of—	Members	At the close of—	Members
1788	89	1853	146
1790	101	1854	145
1792	110	1855	162
1795	123	1856	167
1797	151	1857	147
1799	174	1858	133
1802	197	1859	180
1805	200	1860	242
1807	204	1861	281
1808	215	1862	311
1810	216	1863	355
1815	263	1864	380
1820	252	1865	376
1825	243	1866	387
1828	285	1867	416
1832	267	1868	427
1833	258	1869	442
1834	274	1870	414
1835	306	1871	446
1838	126	1872	438
1839	125	1873	358
1843	126	1874	344
1844	125	1875	345
1845	119	1876	347
1846	136	1877	345
1847	219	1878	327
1848	218	1879	329
1849	207	1880	356
1850	142	1881	350
1851	130	1882	337
1852	139	1883	323

Appendix B.

List of Presidents, Vice-Presidents, and Secretaries of the Asiatic Society.

1784–89.

President—
Sir William Jones.

Secretaries—
George Hillarow Barlow.
John Herbert Harington.

1790.

President—
As in 1789.

Secretary—
John Herbert Harington.

At end of 1792, and in 1793.

President—
Sir William Jones.

Secretary—
Edmund Morris.

1794 and 1795.

President—
Sir John Shore.

Secretary—
Edmund Morris.

1796.

President—
As in 1794.

Secretary—
Captain Symes.

1797.

President—
As in 1795.

Vice-Presidents—
John Fleming.
John Herbert Harington.

Secretary—
Codrington Edmund Carrington.
Henry Trail, *Treasurer.*
W. C. Blacquiere (for a few months in 1798).

1799.

President—
Sir J. Anstruther, Bart.

Vice-Presidents—
John Fleming.
J. H. Harington.

Secretary—
W. Hunter.
Henry Trail, *Treasurer.*

1802.

President—
As in 1799.

Vice-Presidents—
As in 1799.

Secretary—
R. Home.
H. Trail, *Treasurer.*

1805.

President—
As in 1799.

Vice-Presidents—
J. H. Harington.
H. T. Colebrooke.

Secretary—
W. Hunter.
H. Trail and Palmer & Co., *Treasrs.*

1807.

President—
H. T. Colebrooke.

Vice-Presidents—
J. H. Harington.
Dr. J. Fleming.

Secretary—
W. Hunter.
H. Trail and Palmer & Co., *Treasrs.*

1810.

President—
As in 1807.

Vice-Presidents—
As in 1807.

Secretary—
Dr. W. Hunter.
Dr. J. Leyden, *Depy. Secy.*
Palmer & Co., *Treasurers.*

1815.

President—
Earl of Moira.

Vice-Presidents—
J. H. Harington.
Sir John Royds.
Right Rev. T. F. Middleton.

Secretary—
Dr. H. H. Wilson.
Major J. Weston.
W. L. Gibbons, *Depy. Secy.*
Palmer & Co., *Treasurers.*

1820.

President—
Marquis of Hastings.

Vice-Presidents—
Right Rev. T. F. Middleton.
Sir E. Hyde East, Kt.
Major-Genl. T. Hardwicke.
W. B. Bayley.

Secretary—
H. H. Wilson (absent).
Capt. A. Lockett (offg.)
Palmer & Co., *Treasurers.*

1822.

President—
As in 1820.

Vice-Presidents—
As in 1820.

Secretary—
H. H. Wilson.
Palmer & Co., *Treasurers.*

1825.

President—
Hon. J. H. Harington.

Vice-Presidents—
W. B. Bayley.
Rt. Rev. Reginald Heber.

Secretaries—
H. H. Wilson.
Dr. C. Abel, *Phys. Com. Secy.*

1828.

President—
Sir C. E. Grey.

Vice-Presidents—
Hon. W. B. Bayley.
Hon. Sir J. Franks.
Hon. Sir E. Ryan.
Hon. Sir C. Metcalfe.

Secretaries—

H. H. Wilson.

Palmer & Co., *Treasurers.*

Capt. F. Jenkins, } *Phy. Com. Secy.*
D. Ross, }

1832.

President—

Hon. Sir E. Ryan.

Vice-Presidents—

Hon. Sir J. Franks.

Hon. Sir C. Metcalfe.

J. Calder.

Secretaries—

H. H. Wilson.

J. Prinsep, *Phy. Com. Secy.*

Mackintosh & Co., *Treasurers.*

1833.

President—

As in 1832.

Vice-Presidents—

Hon. Sir J. Franks.

Hon. Sir C. Metcalfe.

Rev. W. H. Mill.

Secretaries—

J. Prinsep.

Babu Ramcomul Sen, *Nat. Secy.*

J. Prinsep, *Phy. Com. Secy.*

Bank of Bengal, *Treasurers.*

1834.

President—

As in 1832.

Vice-Presidents—

Hon. Sir J. Franks.

Hon. Sir C. Metcalfe.

Rev. W. H. Mill.

W. McNaghten.

Secretaries—

As in 1833

1835.

President—

As in 1832.

Vice-Presidents—

Rt. Rev. Lord Bishop.

Rev. Dr. Mill.

Sir J. P. Grant.

W. H. McNaghten.

Secretaries—

As in 1834.

1836.

President—

As in 1832.

Vice-Presidents—

Rev. Dr. Mill.

W. H. McNaghten.

Sir J. P. Grant.

Sir B. Malkin.

Secretaries—

As in 1834.

1837.

President—

As in 1832.

Vice-Presidents—

Rev. Dr. Mill.

W. H. McNaghten.

Sir J. P. Grant.

Sir B. Malkin.

H. T. Prinsep.

Secretaries.

As in 1834.

1838.

President—

As in 1832.

Vice-Presidents—

Rt. Rev. Lord Bishop.

Sir J. P. Grant.

H. T. Prinsep.

Col. D. MacLeod.

Secretaries —

J. Prinsep.
Rev. Mr. Malan.
Dr. W. B. O'Shaughnessy. } From Oct. 1838
Babu Ramcomul Sen.

1839.

President—

As in 1832.

Vice-Presidents—

As in 1838.

Secretaries—

Dr. W. B. O'Shaughnessy.
J. C. C. Sutherland.

1840.

President—

As in 1832.

Vice-Presidents—

Hon. Sir J. P. Grant.
Col. D. McLeod.
Hon. H. T. Prinsep.
Hon. Sir H. Seton.

Secretary—

H. W. Torrens.

1841.

President—

As in 1832.

Vice-Presidents—

Hon. Sir J. P. Grant.
Hon. Sir H. Seton.
Hon. H. T. Prinsep.
Hon. W. W. Bird.

Secretary—

H. W. Torrens.

1842.

President—

Hon. H. T. Prinsep.

Vice-Presidents—

Hon. Sir J. P. Grant.
Hon. W. W. Bird.
Hon. Sir H. W. Seton.
Rt. Rev. Lord Bishop.

Secretary—

As in 1841.

1843.

Presidents—

Hon. H. T. Prinsep.
Rt. Hon. W. W. Bird (from 30th March).

Vice-Presidents—

Rt. Rev. Lord Bishop.
Sir J. P. Grant.
Sir H. W. Seton.
H. W. Torrens.

Secretaries—

H. W. Torrens.
H. Piddington, *Sub-Secy.*

1844.

Presidents—

W. W. Bird.
Hon. Sir Henry Hardinge (from October).

Vice-Presidents—

As in 1843.

Secretaries—

As in 1843.

1845.

President—

As at close of 1844.

Vice-Presidents—

Rt. Bev. Lord Bishop.
Sir J. P. Grant.
Sir H. Seton.
H. W. Torrens.
Lt.-Col. W. N. Forbes.

Secretaries—

As in 1844.

1846.

President—

As in 1844.

Vice-Presidents—

As in 1845.

Secretaries—

H. W. Torrens.

Mr. T. resigned, and Dr. W. B. O'Shaughnessy appointed in Aug.

Mr. J. W. Laidlay appointed Co-Secretary in Nov.; Dr. Roer as Co-Secy., Oriental Dept.

1847.

President—

As in 1844.

Vice-Presidents—

Rt. Rev. Lord Bishop.
Hon. Sir J. P. Grant.
Hon. Sir H. Seton.
Lt.-Col. Forbes.

Secretaries—

J. W. Laidlay, *Genl., Nat. Hist. & Min.*
Dr. W. B. O'Shaughnessy, *Genl., Meteor. & Phys.*
Dr. E. Roer, *Ortl. Dept.*
S. G. T. Heatley, *Geoly. & Ind. Stat.*

1848.

President—

Hon. Sir J. W. Colvile, Kt.

Vice-Presidents—

Rt. Rev. Lord Bishop.
Hon. Sir J. P. Grant.
H. M. Elliot.
J. W. Laidlay.

Secretaries—

Dr. W. B. O'Shaughnessy.
J. W. Laidlay.
Dr. E. Roer, *Ortl. Dept.*

1849.

President—

As in 1848.

Vice-Presidents—

Rt. Rev. Lord Bishop.
Lt.-Col. W. N. Forbes.
J. W. Laidlay.
Dr. W. B. O'Shaughnessy.

Secretaries—

Dr. W. B. O'Shaughnessy, *Genl.*
J. W. Laidlay, *Nat. Hist.*
Dr. E. Roer, *Ortl. Dept.*

Dr. Walker and Dr. McClelland officiated for some months as Secretaries owing to the illness of Dr. O'Shaughnessy and absence of Mr. Laidlay.

1850.

President—

As in 1848.

Vice-Presidents—

Rt. Rev. Dan. Wilson, Bishop of Calcutta.
J. W. Laidlay.
Dr. W. B. O'Shaughnessy.
Welby Jackson.

Secretaries—

Dr. W. B. O'Shaughnessy, *Genl.*
J. W. Laidlay, *Nat. Hist.*
Dr. E. Roer, *Ortl. Dept.*

Capt. Hayes, elected Secy. in place of Dr. O'Shaughnessy (retired) in May 1850 (from February).

1851.

President—

As in 1848.

Vice-Presidents—

Rt. Rev. Lord Bishop.
W. Jackson.
J. W. Laidlay.
Dr. W. B. O'Shaughnessy.

Secretaries—

Capt. F. C. C. Hayes.

Dr. A. Sprenger, elected in place of Capt. Hayes (retired) in May.

In consequence of changes made in the organization of the Council, another election was held in June with the following results:—

President—

As in 1848.

Vice-Presidents—

Sir H. M. Elliot.

Dr. W. B. O'Shaughnessy.

Welby Jackson.

Secretary—

Dr. A. Sprenger.

1852.

President—

As in 1848.

Vice-Presidents—

Sir H. M. Elliot.

Dr. W. B. O'Shaughnessy.

Welby Jackson.

Secretaries—

Dr. A. Sprenger.

A. Grote, elected Jt. Secy. in April.

H. V. Bayley.

1853.

President—

As in 1848.

Vice-Presidents—

W. B. Jackson.

J. R. Colvin.

Ramgopal Ghose.

Secretaries—

A. Grote, *Genl.*

Dr. A. Sprenger, *Phil. Dept.*

1854.

President—

As in 1848.

Vice-Presidents—

Hon. Col. J. Low.

Sir H. M. Elliot.

Ramgopal Ghose.

Secretaries—

As in 1853.

1855.

President—

As in 1848.

Vice-Presidents—

Major-Genl. Hon. J. Low.

Lt.-Col. W. E. Baker.

Ramgopal Ghose.

Secretaries—

A. Grote.

H. V. Bayley.

W. S. Atkinson.

Mr. Grote resigned in July. H. V. Bayley and others officiated for him, and in December Mr. W. S. Atkinson was appointed.

1856.

President—

As in 1848.

Vice-Presidents—

Ramgopal Ghose.

Dr. G. G. Spilsbury.

A. Grote.

Secretary—

W. S. Atkinson.

1857.

President—

As in 1848.

Vice-Presidents—

As in 1856.

Secretaries—

W. S. Atkinson.

R. Mitra.

1858.

President—

As in 1848.

Vice-Presidents—

Ramgopal Ghose.

A. Grote.

Lt.-Col. R. Strachey.

Secretaries—

W. S. Atkinson.

E. B. Cowell.

1859 and 1860.

President—

A. Grote.

Vice-Presidents—

Col. R. Strachey.

Dr. T. Thomson.

Babu Ramaprasad Roy.

Secretaries—

As in 1858.

1861.

President—

As in 1859.

Vice-Presidents—

Dr. T. Thompson.

Major H. L. Thuillier.

Babu Rajendralala Mitra.

Secretaries—

As in 1858.

1862.

President—

As in 1359.

Vice-Presidents—

Lt.-Col. H. L. Thuillier.

Babu Rajendralala Mitra.

T. Oldham.

Secretaries—

As in 1858.

1863.

President—

Lt.-Col. H. L. Thuillier.

Do., resigned in April.

E. C. Bayley elected President in September.

Vice-Presidents—

A Grote.

Lt.-Col. R. Strachey.

Babu Rajendralala Mitra.

E. C. Bayley, in place of Col. Strachey in March.

Secretaries—

W. S. Atkinson (resigned in Aug.)

E. B. Cowell (resigned in July.)

H. F. Blanford elected Secy. in August.

1864.

President—

E. C. Bayley.

Vice-Presidents—

Capt. W. N. Lees.

Dr. T. Anderson.

Babu Rajendralala Mitra.

Secretaries—

H. F. Blanford.

W. L. Heeley.

1865.

President—

A. Grote.

Vice-Presidents—

Capt. W. N. Lees.

W. S. Atkinson.

Babu Rajendralala Mitra.

In July, Babu Jadava Krishna Singh, in place of R. Mitra, resigned.

Secretaries—

H. F. Blanford.

W. L. Heeley.

In July, on resignation of the two Secretaries, R. Mitra and Dr. J. Anderson came in.

Lt.-Col. J. E. Gastrell, *Treasurer.*

1866.

President—

E. C. Bayley.

Vice-Presidents—

Dr. G. B. Partridge.

Jadava Krishna Singh.

W. L. Heeley.

Secretaries—

H. F. Blanford, *Genl. Secy.*

R. Mitra, *Phil. Secy.*

Dr. J. Anderson, *Nat. Hist. Secy.*

Lt.-Col. J. E. Gastrell, *Treasurer.*

1867.

President—

Dr. J. Fayrer.

Vice-Presidents—

Dr. S. B. Partridge.

Hon. G. Campbell.

A. Grote.

Secretaries—

H. F. Blanford, *Genl. Secy.*

R. Mitra, *Phil. Secy.*

Dr. J. Anderson, *Nat. His. Secy.*

Lt.-Col. J. E. Gastrell, *Treasurer.*

In December, Dr. Colles was elected Nat. His. Secy. in place of Dr. Anderson, resigned.

1868.

President—

Dr. T. Oldham.

Vice-Presidents—

Hon. J. B. Phear.

A Grote.

Kumar Harendra Krishna Bahadur.

In July, Mr. Grote left for England, and Dr. J. Fayrer was elected V. P. in his stead.

Secretaries—

H. F. Blanford, *Gen. Secy.*

R. Mitra, *Phil. Secy.*

Dr. J. A. P. Colles, *Nat. His. Secy.*

Col. J. E. Gastrell, *Treasurer.*

In May, Mr. Blanford resigned, and W. H. Blochmann was appointed in July. In May, Dr. F. Stoliczka was elected Nat. Hist. Secy. in place of Dr. Colles, resigned.

1869.

President—

Dr. T. Oldham.

Vice-Presidents—

Dr. J. Fayrer, C.S.I.

Hon. J. B. Phear.

Kumar Harendra Krishna Bahadur.

Secretaries—

H. Blochmann, *Phil. Secy.*

Dr. F. Stoliczka, *Nat. His. Secy.*

Col. J. E. Gastrell, *Treasurer.*

In Sept., Col. Hyde was elected treasurer in place of Col. Gastrell, resigned. General duties of Secy. carried on by both Nat. His. and Phil. Secretaries.

1870.

President—

Hon. J. B. Phear.

Vice-Presidents—

Dr. T. Oldham.

Dr. J. Fayrer.

R. Mitra.

Secretaries—

H. Blochmann, *Phil. Secy.*

Dr. F. Stoliczka, *Nat. His. Secy.*

Lt.-Col. H. Hyde, *Treasurer.*

General duties of Secy. carried on by Phil. and Nat. His. Secretaries.

1871.

President—

As in 1870.

Vice-Presidents—

Dr. T. Oldham.

R. Mitra.

Lord Napier of Magdala.

Secretaries—

H. Blochmann, *Phil. Secy.*

Dr. F. Stoliczka, *Nat. His. Secy.*

Lt.-Col. H. Hyde, *Treasurer.*

General duties of Secy. carried on by Phil. and Nat. His. Secretaries.

In Aug., Col. J. F. Tennant succeeded Col. Hyde, resigned.

1872.

President—

Dr. T. Oldham.

Vice-Presidents—

Hon. J. B. Phear.

R. Mitra.

Hon. E. C. Bayley.

Secretaries—

H. Blochmann, *Phil. Secy.*

Dr. F. Stoliczka, *Nat. His. Secy.*

Col. J. F. Tennant, *Treasurer.*

Gen. Sec.'s duties carried on by Nat. Hist. & Phil. Secretaries till June, when Capt. Waterhouse was appointed Gen. Secretary.

Col. Gastrell resumed charge of Treasurership in February.

1873.

President—

Dr. T. Oldham.

In April, Col. H. Hyde was elected President in place of Dr. Oldham, resigned.

Vice-Presidents—

As in 1872.

Secretaries—

Capt. J. Waterhouse, *Genl. Secy.*

Dr. F. Stoliczka, *Nat. His. Secy.*

H. Blochmann, *Phil. Secy.*

Col. J. E. Gastrell, *Treasurer.*

In May, Mr. J. Wood-Mason appointed Nat. His. Secy. in place of Dr. F. Stoliczka.

1874.

President—

Col. H. Hyde.

Vice-Presidents—

As in 1872.

Secretaries—

Capt. J. Waterhouse, *Genl. Secy.*

H. Blochmann, *Phil. Secy.*

J. Wood-Mason, *Nat. His. Secy.*

Col. J. E. Gastrell, *Treasurer.*

1875.

President—

Hon. E. C. Bayley.

In April, Dr. T. Oldham elected President, Hon. E. C. Bayley resigned.

Vice-Presidents—

R. Mitra.

Col. H. Hyde.

Dr. T. Oldham.

Secretaries—

Capt. J. Waterhouse, *Genl. Secy.*
H. Blochmann, *Phil. Secy.*
J. Wood-Mason, *Nat. His Secy.*
Col. J. E. Gastrell, *Treasurer.*

Dr. Lewis officiated as Natural History Secretary for a short time.

1876.

President—

Dr. T. Oldham.

Vice-Presidents—

R. Mitra.
Hon. E. C. Bayley.
Col. H. L. Thuillier.

Secretaries—

Capt. J. Waterhouse, *Genl. Secy.*
H. Blochmann, *Phy. Secy.*
J. Wood-Mason, *Nat. His. Secy.*
Col. J. E. Gastrell, *Treasurer.*

Dr. Lewis officiated for a short time.

On Col. Gastrell's resignation, Mr. H. B. Medlicott succeeded him in June.

1877.

President—

Hon. Sir E. C. Bayley.

Vice-Presidents—

Dr. R. Mitra.
Col. H. L. Thuillier.
W. T. Blanford.

Secretaries—

Capt. J. Waterhouse, *Genl. Secy.*
H. Blochmann, *Phil. Secy.*
J. Wood-Mason, *Phy. Secy.*
H. B. Medlicott, *Treasurer.*

Mr. J. Wood-Mason resigned in July, Mr. W. T. Blanford and Capt. Waterhouse edited Part II of Journal.

1878.

President—

W. T. Blanford.

Vice-Presidents—

Dr. R. Mitra.
H. B. Medlicott.
T. S. Isaac.

Secretaries—

Capt. Waterhouse, *Genl. Secy.*
H. Blochmann, *Phil. Secy.*
R. Lydekher, *Nat. His. Secy.*
E. Gay, *Treasurer.*

In July, Mr. Blochmann died, and Mr. C. H. Tawney officiated. Dr. A. F. R. Hoernle was appointed in November. In August, Mr. Gay resigned, and Mr. H. Beverley was appointed Treasurer.

Mr. Lydekher resigned in March, and Capt. Waterhouse and Mr. W. T. Blanford again edited Part II of Journal.

1879.

President—

W. T. Blanford.

In Dec., Mr. H. B. Medlicott succeeded Mr. Blanford.

Vice-Presidents—

Dr. R. Mitra.
H. B. Medlicott.
T. S. Isaac.

In Decr., Messrs. C. H. Tawney and J. Westland succeeded Mr. H. B. Medlicott and Mr. T. S. Isaac.

Secretaries—

Capt. J. Waterhouse, *Genl. Secy.*
Dr. A. F. R. Hoernle, *Phil. Secy.*
H. Beverley, *Treasurer.*

Capt. J. Waterhouse edited Part II of Journal till October, when Mr. J. Wood-Mason was appointed Nat. Hist. Secy.

In Decr., Capt. Waterhouse resigned, and Mr. J. Crawford took his place.

1880.

President—

H. B. Medlicott.

Vice-Presidents—

Dr. R. Mitra.

J. Westland.

C. H. Tawney.

Secretaries—

J. Crawford, *Genl. Secy.*

Dr. A. F. R. Hoernle, *Phil. Secy.*

J. Wood-Mason, *Nat. His. Secy.*

H. Beverley, *Treasurer.*

In April, Mr. A. Pedler succeeded Mr. Crawford, resigned.

In April, Mr. J. C. Douglas succeeded Mr. H. Beverley, resigned.

1881.

President—

Hon. Sir Ashley Eden.

Vice-Presidents—

Dr. R. Mitra.

C. H. Tawney.

Hon. H. J. Reynolds.

Secretaries—

A. Pedler, *Genl. Secy.*

Dr. A. F. R. Hoernle, *Phil. Secy.*

J. Wood-Mason, *Nat. His. Secy.*

V. Ball, *Treasurer.*

In March, Mr. V. Ball succeeded Mr. J. C. Douglas, resigned.

In Sept., Mr. J. Eliot was appointed Treasurer in place of Mr. Ball, resigned.

In April, Mr. Pedler resigned, and Dr. H. W. M'Cann succeeded him.

1882.

President—

Hon. Sir A. Eden.

In May, Hon. H. J. Reynolds succeeded Sir A. Eden, resigned.

Vice-Presidents—

Dr. R. Mitra.

Hon. J. Gibbs.

Hon. H. J. Reynolds.

In May, Mr. H. F. Blanford succeeded Mr. H. J. Reynolds.

Secretaries—

Dr. H. W. M'Cann, *Genl. Secy.*

Dr. A. F. R. Hoernle, *Phil. Secy.*

J. Wood-Mason, *Nat. His. Secy.*

J. Eliot, *Treasurer.*

In Sept., Mr. Wood-Mason resigned, and Dr. J. Scully appointed in his place.

1883.

President—

Hon. H. J. Reynolds.

Vice-Presidents—

Dr. R. Mitra.

Hon. J. Gibbs.

H. F. Blanford.

Secretaries—

Dr. H. W. M'Cann, *Genl. Secy.*

Dr. A. F. R. Hoernle, *Phil. Secy.*

Dr. J. Scully, *Nat. His. Secy.*

J. Eliot, *Treasurer.*

Dr. J. Scully resigned in March, and Babu P. N. Bose was appointed in June.

Mr. J. Eliot resigned, and Mr. F. W. Peterson succeeded him in August.

Appendix C.

List of Books published, directly or indirectly, by the Asiatic Society of Bengal.

No. of vols.

TRANSACTIONS.

Asiatic Researches, Vols. I—XX, 1788—1839 (Vols. XVII—XX being in two parts). 4to. 20

Index to Vols. I—XVIII of the Asiatic Researches. 4to. 1

Journal, Vols. I—LII, 1832-83 (31 volumes being in two parts). 8vo. .. 83

Index to Vols. XIX—XX of the Asiatic Researches and Vols. I—XXIII of the Journal. 8vo. 1

Proceedings, published separately from the year 1865 to 1883. 8vo. ... 19

CATALOGUES.

Catalogue of the Books and Maps in the Library. Edition of 1833. Edited by Dr. Burlini. 8vo. 1

Ditto ditto. Edited by Dr. Roer. 1843. 8vo. 1

Ditto ditto. Edited by Dr. R. Mitra. 1856. 8vo. 1

Catalogue of the Sanskrit Books and Manuscripts of the Asiatic Society. 8vo. 1838 1

A Descriptive Catalogue of Sanskrit Manuscripts in the Library of the Asiatic Society of Bengal. Part I. Grammar. Edited by Dr. R. Mitra. Rl. 8vo. 1

Catalogue of Persian, Arabic, and Urdu Manuscripts and Books. 8vo. ... 1

Ditto of Nepalese Sanskrit Manuscripts, or the Buddhist Sanskrit Literature of Nepal. By Dr. R. Mitra. Rl. 8vo. 1882 1

Ditto of the Fossil Remains of Vertebrata from the Sewalik Hills, the Nerbudda, Perim Island, &c., in the Museum of the Asiatic Society of Bengal. By H. Falconer. 8vo. 1859 1

Ditto of the Recent Shells in the Museum of the Asiatic Society. By W. Theobald. 8vo. 1860 1

Ditto of the Reptiles in the Asiatic Society's Museum. By W. Theobald. (Extra No., J. A. S. B., 1875) 1

Ditto of Curiosities in the Museum of the Asiatic Society. By Dr. R. Mitra. 8vo. 1849 1

Ditto of the Birds in the Museum of the Asiatic Society. By Ed. Blyth. 8vo. 1849 1

Ditto of the Mammalia in the Museum of the Asiatic Society. By Ed. Blyth. 8vo. 1863 1

Ditto of Mammals and Birds of Burmah. By Ed. Blyth. (Extra No., J. A. S. B., 1875) 1

MISCELLANEOUS PUBLICATIONS.

	No. of vols.
General Cunningham's Archæological Survey Report for 1863-64. (Extra No., J. A. S. B., 1864)	1
Sketch of the Turki Language as spoken in Eastern Turkestan. Part II—Vocabulary. By R. B. Shaw. (Extra No., J. A. S. B., 1878) ...	1
A Grammar and Vocabulary of the Northern Balochi Language. By M. L. Dames. (Extra No., J. A. S. B., 1880)	1
Introduction to the Maithili Language of North Bihar. By G. A. Grierson. Part—I Grammar. (Extra No., J. A. S. B., 1880.) Part II—Chriestomathy and Vocabulary. (Extra No., J. A. S. B., 1882) ...	2
Vedántasára. Translated by Dr. E. Roer. 8vo.	1
Moore and Hewetson's Descriptions of New Indian Lepidoptera. Parts I and II. 4to.	2
Lassen's Bactrian Coins. Translated by Dr. E. Roer. 8vo. ...	1
On the Aborigines of India. Essay First, on the Coch, Bodo and Dhimal Tribes. By B. H. Hodgson. 8vo.	1

ORIENTAL PUBLICATIONS.

SANSKRIT.

Sausruta, a System of Medicine taught by Dhanvantari, and compiled by his pupil, Susruta. 8vo.	2
Naishadha Charita, an Epic Poem by Sri Harsha. Part I. Edited by Premachánd Tarkavágísa. 8vo. 1835	1
Harivansa, or the History of the Yádava Race. A Poem. 4to. ...	1
Rájatarangini, or History of Kashmir. 4to.	1
Mahábhárata, or a History of the Kurus and the Pándus. By Vyása. Vols. I—IV. 4to.	4
Ditto Index. 4to.	1

ARABIC.

Fatáwe 'Alamgírí, on Muhammadan Law. 4to.	6
Istiláhát-i-Súfiyá, or Technical Terms of the Súfis. Edited by Dr. A. Sprenger. 8vo.	1
Jawámi 'ul 'ilm ir Riází, on Surveying. 4to.	1
Khazánat ul 'ilm. 4to.	1
Sharáyat-ul Islám, Canonical Law of the Muhammadans. 4to. ...	1
Anís-ul Musharrahín, on Anatomy. Translation of Hooper's *Vade mecum.* 4to.	1
Inayah, a Commentary on the Hidáya, a work on Muhammadan Law. 4to.	4

PERSIAN.

Tárikh i Nádiri	1

ORIENTAL PUBLICATIONS.—(*Continued.*)

No. of vols.

BIBLIOTHECA INDICA SERIES.*

Sanskrit Works, complete.

The first two Lectures of the Sanhitá of the Rig Veda. Fasc. I—IV. Nos. 1—4. Edited by Dr. E. Roer 1

Naishadha Charita by Sri Harsha, with a Commentary. Part II, Edited by Dr. E. Roer, Fasc. I—XII. Nos. 39, 40, 42, 45, 46, 52, 67, 72, 87, 90, 120, 124. 2

Chaitanya-chandrodaya Nátaka, a Drama on the doctrine of Faith. By Kavikarnapura. Edited by Dr. R. Mitra. Fasc. I—III. Nos. 47, 48, 80 1

Vásavadattá, a Romance by Subandhu, with its Commentary, Darpana. Edited by Prof. F. E. Hall. Fasc. I—III. Nos. 116, 130, 148 ... 1

The Márkandeya Purána. Edited by Rev. K. M. Banerjea. Fasc. I—VII. Nos. 114, 127, 140, 163, 169, 177, 183 1

Vedánta Sútras, or Aphorisms of the Vedánta, by Bádaráyana, with the Commentary of Sankara Áchárya and the Gloss of Govindánanda. Edited by Pandita Rámanáráyana Vidyáratna. Fasc. I—XIII. Nos. 64, 89, 172, 174, 178, 184, 186, 194, 195, 198, 201 1

The Brihad Áranyaka Upanishad, with the Commentary of Sankara Áchárya and the Gloss of Ánanda Giri. Edited by Dr. E. Roer. Fasc. I—XI. Nos. 5—13, 16, 18 2

The Chhándogya Upanishad, with the Commentary of Sankara Áchárya and the Gloss of Ánanda Giri. Edited by Dr. E. Roer. Fasc. I—VI. Nos. 14, 15, 17, 20, 23, 25 1

The Taittiríya, the Aitareya, and the Svetásvatara Upanishads, with the Commentary of Sankara Áchárya and the Gloss of Ánanda Giri. Edited by Dr. E. Roer. Fasc. I—III. Nos. 22, 33, 34 1

The Ísá, Kéna, Katha, Prasna, Munda, and Mándukeya Upanishads, with the Commentary of Sankara Áchárya and the Gloss of Ánanda Giri. Edited by Dr. E. Roer. Fasc. I—VI. Nos. 24, 26, 28, 29, 30, 31 ... 1

Division of the Categories of the Nyáya Philosophy, with a Commentary by Visvanátha Panchánana. Edited and translated by Dr. E. Roer. Fasc. I—II. Nos. 32, 35 1

The Sáhitya Darpana, or Mirror of Composition. By Vísvanátha Kivirája. Edited by Dr. E. Roer. Fasc. I—V. Nos. 36, 37, 53, 54, 55 ... 1

The Lalita Vistara, or Memoirs of the Early Life of Sákya Sinha. Edited by Dr. R. Mitra. Fasc. I—VI. Nos. 51, 73, 143, 144, 145, 237 ... 1

Sarvadarsana Sangraha, or an Epitome of the Different Systems of Indian Philosophy. By Mádhavácharya. Edited by Pandita Ísvarachandra Vidyáságara. Fasc. I—II. Nos. 63, 142 1

* All are 8vo. except those otherwise marked.

No. of vols.

The Súrya-Siddhánta, an Ancient System of Hindu Astronomy, with Ranganátha's Exposition, the Gúdhártha-Prakásaka. Edited by Prof. F. E. Hall, with the assistance of Pandit Bápú Deva Sástrin. Fasc. I—IV. Nos. 79, 105, 115, 146 1

The Sánkhya-pravachana-bháshya, a Commentary on the Aphorisms of the Hindu Atheistic Philosophy. By Vijnána Bhikshu. Edited by Prof. F. E. Hall. Fasc. I—III. Nos. 94, 97, 141 1

Purána Sangraha, Part I, Text and Translation of the Márkandeya Purána (discontinued) 1

The Vaíseshika Darsana, with the Commentaries of Sánkara Mísra and of Jayanáráyana Tarkapanchánana. Edited by Pandita Jayanáráyana Tarkapanchánana. Fasc. I—V. Nos. 4—6, 8, 10 1

The Aphorisms of Sándilya, with the Commentary of Svapnesvara. Edited by Dr. J. R. Ballantyne. Fasc. I. No. 11 1

The Dasarúpa, or Hindu Canons of Dramaturgy, by Dhananjaya, with the Expositions of Dhanika, the Avaloka. Edited by Prof. F. E. Hall. Fasc. I—III. Nos. 12, 24, 82 1

The Nárada Pancharátra. Edited by Rev. K. M. Banerjea. Fasc. I—IV. Nos. 17, 25, 34, 75 1

The Kaushítaki-Brahmana-Upanishad, with the Commentary of Sankaránanda. Edited, with an English Translation, by Prof. E. B. Cowell. Fasc. I—III. Nos. 19-20 (3rd fasc. has no number) 1

The Kávyádarsa of Srí Dandin, with a Commentary. Edited by Pandita Premachandra Tarkavágísa. Fasc. I—V. Nos. 30, 33, 38, 39, 41 ... 1

The Maitri, or Maitráyana Upanishad, with the Commentary of Rámatírtha. Edited, with an English Translation, by Prof. E. B. Cowell. Fasc. I—III. Nos. 35, 40 (3rd fasc. has no number) 1

The Sankara-vijaya, or the Life and Polemics of Sankara Ácharya by Ánanda Giri. Edited by Prof. Jayanáráyana Tarkapanchánana. Fasc. I—III. Nos. 46, 137, 138... 1

The Brihat Sanhitá of Varáha-Mihira. Edited by Dr. H. Kern. Fasc. I—VII. Nos. 51, 54, 59, 63, 68, 72, 73 1

The Sráuta Sútra of Asvaláyana, with the Commentary of Gárgya Náráyana. Edited by Rámanáráyana Vidyáratna. Fasc. I—XI. Nos. 55, 61, 66, 69, 71, 80, 84, 86, 90, 93, 299 2

The Nyáya Darsana, with the Commentary of Vátsyáyana. Edited by Pandita Jayanáráyana Tarkapanchánana. Fasc. I—III. Nos. 56, 67, 70 1

The Taittiríya Áranyaka of the Black Yajur Veda, with the Commentary of Sáyana Ácharya. Edited by Dr. R. Mitra. Fasc. I—XI. Nos. 60, 74, 88, 97, 130, 144, 159, 169, 203, 226, 263 1

No. of vols.

Sánkhya-Sára; a Treatise of Sánkhya Philosophy. By Vijnána Bhikshu. Edited by Prof. F. E. Hall. Fasc. I. No. 83. 1

The Grihya Sútra of Asvaláyana, with the Commentary of Gáryga Náráyana. Edited by Rámanáráyana Vidyáratna and Anandachandra Vedántavágísa. Fasc. I—IV. Nos. 102, 132, 143, 164 ... 1

The Tándya Mahábráhmana, with the Commentary of Sáyana Ácharya. Edited by Ánandachandra Vedántavágísa. Fasc. I—XIX. Nos. 170, 175, 177, 179, 182, 188, 190, 191, 199, 206, 207, 212, 217, 219, 221, 225, 254, 256, 268 2

The Srauta Sútra of Látyáyana, with the Commentary of Agnisvámí. Edited by Ánandachandra Vedántavágísa. Fasc. I—IX. Nos. 181, 184, 185, 187, 196, 198, 202, 213, 260 1

The Gopála Tápaní of the Atharva Veda, with the Commentary of Visvesvara. Edited by Harachandra Vidyábhushana and Visvanátha Sástrí. Fasc. I. No. 183 1

Agni Púrana, a Collection of Hindu Mythology and Traditions. Edited by Dr. R. Mitra. Fasc. I—XIV. Nos. 189, 197, 201, 291, 306, 312, 313, 316, 357, 373, 390, 399, 404, 421 3

The Gopatha Bráhmana of the Atharva Veda. Edited by Dr. R. Mitra and Harachandra Vidyábhushana. Fasc. I—II. Nos. 215, 252 ... 1

The Nrisinha Tápaní of the Atharva Veda, with the Commentary of Sankara Ácharya. Edited by Prof. Rámamaya Tarkaratna. Fasc. I—III. Nos. 216, 223, 238 1

The Sáma Veda Sanhitá, with the Commentary of Sáyana Ácharya. Edited by Satyavrata Sámasramí. Vol. I. Nos. 1—10; Vol. II, Nos. 1—6; Vol. III, Nos. 1—7; Vol. IV, Nos. 1—6; Vol. V, Nos. 1—8. (37 Fasc.) Nos. 218, 224, 235, 244, 251, 270, 280, 285, 286, 293, 301, 321—324, 334, 339, 340, 342, 347, 348, 351, 355, 356, 361, 365, 366, 369, 371, 376, 382, 385, 389, 398, 402, 413, 414 5

The Gobhilíya Grihya Sútra, with a Commentary. Edited by Chandrakánta Tarkálankára. Fasc. I—XII. Nos. 229, 241, 246, 277, 300, 346, 383, 415, 416, 423, 425, 448 1

Chhandah Sútra of Pingala Ácharya, with the Commentary of Haláyudha. Edited by Pandita Visvanátha Sástrí. Fasc. I—III. Nos. 230, 258, 307 1

The Taittiríya Prátisákhya, with the Commentary entitled the Tribháshyaratna. Edited by Dr. R. Mitra. Fasc. I—III. Nos. 234, 253, 259 1

The Atharvana Upanishads, with the Commentary of Náráyana. Edited by Prof. Rámamaya Tarkaratna. Fasc. I—V. Nos. 249, 265, 276, 282, 305. (Publication discontinued) 1

No. of vols.

The A'itareya Aranyaka, with the Commentary of Sáyana Áchárya. Edited by Dr. R. Mitra. Fasc. I—V. Nos. 325, 329, 335, 337, 345 ... 1

Bhámatí, a Gloss on Sankara Ácharya's Commentary on the Brahma Sútras, by Váchaspati Misra. Edited by Pandita Bála Sástrí. Fasc. I—VIII. Nos. 328, 336, 343, 364. 384, 405, 427, 433 1

The Institutes of Vishnu, together with Extracts from the Sanskrit Commentary of Nanda Pandita, called Vaijayantí. Edited, with Critical Notes, an Anukramaniká, and Indexes of Words and Mantras, by Prof. J. Jolly. Fasc. I—II. Nos. 458, 463 1

The Yoga Aphorisms of Patanjali, with the Commentary of Bhoja Rájá and an English Translation. Edited and Translated by Dr. R. Mitra. Fasc. I—V. Nos. 462, 478, 482, 491, 492 1

Sanskrit Works, in progress.

The Elements of Polity by Kamandaki, with a Commentary. Edited by Dr. R. Mitra and Jaganmohan Tarkálankára. Fasc. I—IV. Nos. 19, 179, 206; and new series 338 1

The Taittiríya Bráhmana of the Black Yajur Veda, with the Commentary of Sáyana Áchárya. Edited by Dr. R. Mitra. Fasc. I—XXIV. Nos. 125, 126, 147, 150—155, 175, 176, 188—192, 196, 197, 204, 210, 216, 220, 222, 223 3

The Sanhitá of the Black Yajur Veda, with the Commentary of Mádhava A'chárya. Edited by Dr. E. Roer, Prof. E. B. Cowell, and Mahesachandra Nyáyaratna. Fasc. I—XXXII. Nos. (O.S.) 92, 117, 119, 122, 131, 133, 134, 137, 149, 157, 160, 161, 166, 171, 180, 185, 193, 202, 203, 218, 219, 221, 224, 228, 231, 233, 236, 239, 241; and (N.S.) 466 5

The Aphorisms of the Mímámsá by Jaimini, with the Commentary of Savara-Svámin. Edited by Pandit Mahesachandra Nyáyaratna. Fasc. I—XVI. Nos. (N.S.) 44, 85, 95, 101, 115, 142, 154, 174, 208, 209, 240, 315, 368, 388, 436, 470 2

Chaturvarga-chintámani by Hemádri. Edited by Panditás Bharatachandra Siromani, Yajnesvar Bhattácharya, and Kámákhyánátha Tarkaratna. Vol. I, Nos. 1—11; Vol. II, part i, Nos. 1—13; part ii, Nos. 1—12; Vol. III, Nos. 1—6 (42 Fasc.) Nos. (N. S.) 228, 237, 242, 245, 257, 262, 267, 274, 278, 281, 290, 326, 327, 331, 341, 344, 354, 360, 367, 372, 377, 381, 386, 391, 400, 401, 406, 506, 407, 410, 417—419, 422, 426, 429, 464, 475, 481, 486, 493, 495 4

Prithirája Rasau of Chand Bardai. Edited in the original old Hindí by John Beames and Dr. A. F. Rudolf Hoernle. Part I, Fasc. 1; Part II, Fasc. 1—4, (5 Fasc.), Nos. (N.S.) 269, 304, 408, 430, 489 ... 1

Kâtantra, with the Commentary of Durgasimha. Edited, with Notes and Indexes, by Prof. Julius Eggeling. Fasc. I—VI. Nos. (N.S.) 297, 298, 308, 309, 396, 397 1

No. of vols.

The Váyu Púrána, a System of Hindu Mythology and Tradition. Edited by Dr. R. Mitra. Vol. I, Fasc. 1—6; Vol. II, Fasc. 1—4; (10 Fasc.) Nos. (N.S.) 400, 424, 428, 434, 437, 445, 457, 476, 488, 499 2

The Nirukta, with Commentaries. Edited by Pandit Satyavrata Sámasrami. Fasc. I—VII. Nos. (N.S.) 449, 454, 460, 471, 477, 480, 494 2

The Srauta Sútra of Ápastamba, belonging to the Taittiríya Sanhitá, with the Commentary of Rudradatta. Edited by Dr. Richard Garbe. Fasc. I—VII. Nos. (N.S.) 461, 469, 474, 479, 483 3

Parásara Smriti. Edited by Pandit Chandrakánta Tarkálankára. Fasc. I. No. (N.S.) 487 1

Sthavirávalícharta, or Parisishtaparvan, being an Appendix of the Trishashti-sataka-purusha-charita. By Hemachandra. Edited by Dr. Hermann Jacobi. Fasc. I. No. (N.S.) 497 1

Arabic Works, complete.

Arabic Bibliography. Edited by Dr. A. Sprenger. Fasc. I. No. (O.S.) 21 1

Soyúty's Itqán, on the Exegetic Sciences of the Qorán. Edited by Mowlavies Sadeedood-deen Khán, Basheerood-deen, and Dr. A. Sprenger. Fasc. I—X. Nos. (O.S.) 44, 49, 57, 68, 70, 74, 77, 81, 99, 104 1

Fotooh-al-Sham: being an account of the Moslem Conquest in Syria. By Aboo Ismá'aíl, Mohammad bin 'Abd Alla, Al-Azdi, Al-Baçri. Edited by Ensign W. N. Lees. Fasc. I—IV. Nos. (O.S.) 56, 62, 84, 85 ... 1

Tusy's List of Shy'ah Books and 'Alam Alhodá's Notes on Shy'ah Biography. Edited by Dr. A. Sprenger, Mawlavy 'Abd Al-Haqq and Mawlavy Gholam Qadir. Fasc. I—IV. Nos. (O.S.) 60, 71, 91, 107 (Publication discontinued) 1

A Dictionary of the Technical Terms used in the Sciences of the Musalmans. Edited by Mawlavies Mohammad Wajih, Abd Al-Haqq, and Gholam Kadir, under the superintendence of Dr. Aloys Sprenger and Capt. W. Nassau Lees. Fasc. I—XX. Nos. (O.S.) 58, 65, 82, 88, 95, 100, 108, 109, 118, 129, 132, 156, 158, 159, 162, 165, 167, 170, 173, 183. 4to. 2

Shamshiyá, First Appendix to the Dictionary of the Technical Terms used in the Sciences of the Mussalmans, containing the Logic of the Arabians in the original Arabic. With an English translation. Edited and translated by Dr. A. Sprenger. Fasc. I. No. (O.S.) 88. 4to. .. 1

The Conquest of Syria, commonly ascribed to Aboo 'Abd Allah Mohammad B. 'Oma, Al-Waqidí. Edited by W. Nassau Lees. Fasc. I—IX. Nos. (O.S.) 59, 66, 96, 98, 102, 103, 164, 167, 187 2

History of Mohammad's Campaigns, by Aboo 'Abd Ollah Mohammad 'Bin Omar Alwâkidy. Edited by Alfred von Kremer. Fasc. I—V. Nos. 110, 112, 113, 121, 139 1

No. of vols.

The Nokhbat Al-Fikr and Nozhat Al-Nazr. By Shahat Al-Din Ahmad Ibn Hajar Al-'Asqaluni. Edited by Capt. W. Nassau Lees and Mawlavies Abd-Al-Haqq and Gholam Qadir. Fasc. I. No. (N.S.) 37 1

Arabic Works, in progress.

Içabah: a Biographical Dictionary of Persons who knew Mohammad, by Ibn Hajar. Edited by Mawlavies Mohammad Wajyh, 'Abd-al-Haqq, and Gholam Qádir, Dr. A. Sprenger, Capt. W. N. Lees and Mawlavi Abd ul-Hai. Vol. I, Nos. 1—12; Vol. II, Nos. 1—7; Vol. III, Nos. 1—5; Vol. IV, Nos. 1—10, with supplement (in all 35 Fasc.). Nos. (O.S.) 61, 69, 75, 83, 86, 93, 101, 106, 111, 123, 128, 136, 138, 205, 207, 208, 209, 211, 214, 215, 225, 226, 227, 232, 234, 235, 238, 240, 242, 248 3

Persian Works, complete.

Khirad-námah-i Iskandary, also called the Sikandar-námah-i Bahry. By Nitzámy. Edited by Dr. A. Sprenger, Aghá Mohammed Shoosteri and Mawlaví Aghá Ahmad 'Ali. Fasc. I—II. Nos. (O.S.) 43; (N.S.) 171. (Publication discontinued) 1

Táríkh-i Feroz-Sháhí of Ziaa al-Din Barni, commonly called Ziaa-i Barni. Edited by Saiyid Ahmad Khán, under the superintendence of Capt. W. Nassau Lees and Mawlavi Kabir-al-din. Fasc. I—VII. Nos. (N. S.) 2, 3, 7, 9, 14, 15, 23 1

Táríkh-i Baiháki, containing the Life of Massúd, son of Sultán Mahmúd of Ghaznín, being the 7th, 8th, and 9th parts of the 6th and 10th volumes of the Táríkh-i al-i Saboktageen. By Abu'l Fazl Al-Baihaqi. Edited by the late W. H. Morley, and printed under the supervision of Capt. W. Nassau Lees. Fasc. I—IX. Nos. (N.S.) 16, 18, 21, 22, 26, 27, 29, 31, 36 1

Tabaqát-i Násiri of Aboo 'Omar Minháj Al-dín 'Othmán, Ibn Siráj al-din al-Jawzjani. Edited by Capt. W. Nassau Lees and Mawlavis Khadim Hosain and 'Abd Al-Hai. Fasc. I—V. Nos. (N.S.) 42, 43, 45, 47, 50 1

Muntakhat al-Tawáríkh of Abd al-Qádir Bin-i-Malúk Sháh al-Badáoní. Edited by Capt. W. N. Lees and Maulaví Ahmad 'Alí. Fasc. I—XV. Nos. (N.S.) 57, 58, 62, 64, 65, 131, 135, 136, 139, 140, 145, 146, 152, 153, 161 3

Iqbálnámah-i Jahángírí of Motamad Khán. Edited by Mawlavis Abd al-Haii and Ahmad Ali, under the superintendence of Major W. N. Lees. Fasc. I—III. Nos. (N.S.) 77, 79 1

Álamgirnámah. By Muhammad Kázim Ibn-i- Muhammad Amin Munshi. Edited by Mawlavis Khádim Husain and Abd al-Hai, under the superintendence of Major W. N. Lees. Fasc. I—XIII. Nos. (N.S.) 87, 89, 91, 92, 94, 98, 99, 103, 104, 106, 109, 134, 288 ... 1

No. of vols.

Wís o Rámín: a Romance of Ancient Persia. Translated from the Pahlawi and rendered into verse by Fakhr Al-din, As'ad al-Astarábádi, Al-Fakhri, Al Gurgáni. Edited by Capt. W. N. Lees and Munshi Ahmed Ali. Fasc. I—V. Nos. (N.S.) 48, 49, 52, 53, 76 ... 1

The Bádsháhnámah. By 'Abd Al-Hamid Láhawrí. Edited by Mawlavis Kabír al-Din Ahmad and Abd al-Ráhim, under the superintendence of Major W. N. Lees. Fasc. I—XIX. Nos. (N.S.) 96, 100, 105, 107, 108, 110, 111, 114, 116, 118, 121, 125—129, 133 ... 2

Index of Names of Persons and Geographical Names occurring in the above. By Maulvi Abdur Rahim. Fasc. I. No. (N.S.) 261 ... 1

The Áín-i-Akbarí. By Abul Fazl-i-'Allámí. Edited by Prof. H. Blochmann. Fasc. I—XXII. Nos. (N.S.) 112, 113, 119, 120, 122, 141, 157, 162, 168, 176, 193, 211, 236, 248, 264, 275, 314, 349, 350, 370, 378, 387. 4to. 2

The Muntakhbát Al-Lubáb of Kháfi Khan. Edited by Maulavi Kabír al-Dín Ahmad. Fasc. I—XIX. Nos. (N.S) 147, 148, 150, 151, 155, 156, 160, 165—167, 172, 173, 178, 180, 186, 192, 204, 205, 292 ... 2

The Maásir i 'Álamgírí of Muhammad Sáqí Musta'id Khán. Edited by Maulaví Ághá Ahmad 'Alí. Fasc. 1—VI. Nos. (N.S.) 195, 210, 220, 232, 233, 289 1

The Farhang i Rashídí. A Persian Dictionary. By Sayyid 'Abdurrashíd of Tattah. Edited by Maulaví Zulfagár Alí. Fasc. I—XIV. Nos. (N.S.) 200, 222, 231, 239, 243, 250, 255, 266, 271, 279, 302, 303, 317, 318. 4to. 2

The Haft Ásmán, or History of the Masnawí of the Persians. By the late Maulaví Ághá Ahmad 'Alí. Printed with a Biographical Notice of the Author by Prof. H. Blochmann. Fasc. I. No. (N.S.) 294 ... 1

Persian Work, in progress.

The Akbarnámah. By Abul Fazl i Mubárak i 'Allámí. Edited by Maulaví 'Abd-ur-Rahím. Vol. I, Nos. 1—8; Vol. II, Nos. 1-6 (double Nos.); Vol. III, Nos. 1—4 (20 Fasc.), Nos. 283, 284, 319, 320, 352, 353, 362, 363, 374, 375, 379, 380, 411, 412, 431, 432, 467, 468, 484, 485. 4to. 3

Translations into English, complete.

The Taittaríya, Aitaréya, Svetásvatara, Kena, Isá, Katha, Prasna, Mundaka and Mándukya Upanishads. Translated by Dr. E. Roer. Fasc. I—II. Nos. (O.S.) 41 50 1

The Brihad Áranyaka Upanishad, and the Commentary of Sankara Ácharya on its first chapter. Translated by Dr. E. Roer. Fasc. I—III. Nos. (O.S.) 27, 38, 135 1

No. of vols.

The Chhándogya Upanishad of the Sáma Veda, with Extracts from the Commentary of Sankara Ácharya. Translated by Dr. R. Mitra. Fasc. I—II. Nos. (O.S.) 78, 181 1

The Sáhitya-Darpana, or Mirror of Composition: a Treatise on Literary Criticism by Viswanátha Kavirája. Translated by Pramadádása Mitra. Fasc. I—IV. Nos. (O.S.) 212, 213, 217; (N.S.) 330 1

Súrya Siddhánta. Translated by Pandit Bápú Deva Sástrí. Fasc. I. No. (N.S.) 1 1

Siddhánta Siromani. Translated by the late Lancelot Wilkinson. Revised by Pandit Bápú Deva Sástrí. Fasc. I—II. Nos. (N.S.) 13, 28 ... 1

The Sánkhya Aphorisms of Kapila, with Extracts from Vijnána Bhiksu's Commentary. Translated by Dr. J. R. Ballantyne. Fasc. I—II. Nos. (N.S.) 32, 81 1

Káchcháyano's Páli Grammar. Translated and arranged on European models; with Chrestomathy and Vocabulary. By Dr. Francis Mason. Fasc. I—II. Nos. (N.S.) 123, 124 1

The Áín-i-Akbarí. By Abul Fazl 'Allámí. Translated by Prof. H. Blochmann. Fasc. I—VII. Nos. (N.S.) 149, 158, 163, 194, 227, 247, 287. 1

The Brahma Sútras, with the Commentary of Sankaráchárya. Translated by Rev. K. M. Banerjea. Fasc. I. No. (N.S.) 214. (Publication discontinued) 1

The Aphorisms of Sándilya, with the Commentary of Svapnesvara, or the Hindu Doctrine of Faith. Translated by Prof. E. B. Cowell. Fasc. I. No. (N.S.) 409 1

History of the Caliphs. By Jalálu'ddín A's Suyúti. Translated by Major H. S. Jarrett. Fasc. I—VI. Nos. (N.S.) 440, 441, 443, 446, 451, 453 1

Translations of the following works have also been made, and have been published with the texts. They will be found entered in the Lists of Sanskrit and Arabic works, completed:

Division of the Categories of the Nyáya Philosophy.

The Maitri or Maitráyaníya Upanishad.

The Kaushítaki-Bráhmana-Upanishad.

The Yoga Aphorisms of Patanjali.

First Appendix to the Dictionary of the technical terms used in the Sciences of the Mussalmans.

Translations into English, in progress.

Tabkát-i-Násiri: A General History of the Muhammadan Dynasties of Asia, including Hindustan, from A. H. 194 (810 A.D.) to A. H. 658 (1260 A.D.), Vol. I and the Irruption of the Infidel Mughal into Islám. By the Mauláná, Minháj-ud-din, Abu-'Umar-i-'Usmán. Translated by Major H. G. Räverty. Fasc. I—XIV. Nos. (N.S.) 272, 273, 295, 296, 310, 311, 332, 333, 358, 359, 392—395 2

No. of vols.

The Kathá Sarit Ságara, or Ocean of the Streams of Story. Translated by C. H. Tawney. Vol. I. Nos. 1—8; Vol. II. Nos. 1—2; (10 Fasc.), Nos. (N.S.) 436, 438, 439, 442, 444, 450, 456, 459, 465, 472 ... 2

The Prithirája Rásau of Chand Bardái. Translated by Dr. A. F. Rudolf Hoernle. Part II. Fasc. I. No. (N.S.) 452 1

The Lalita-Vistara, or Memoirs of the Early Life of Sákya Sinha. Translated by Dr. R. Mitra. Fasc. I—II. Nos. (N.S.) 455, 473 ... 1

The Sausruta-Sanhitá: the Hindu System of Medicine according to Susruta. Translated by Dr. Udoy Chánd Dutt. Fasc. I. No. (N.S.) 490 1

Miscellaneous.

The Prithirája Rásau of Chand Baradai. Edited in the original old Hindí by John Beames and Dr. A. F. Rudolf Hoernle. Part I. Fasc. I; Part II. Fasc. I—V. (5 Fasc.), Nos. (N.S.) 269, 304, 408, 480, 489. 1

The Prákrita-Lakshanam, or Chanda's Grammar of the Ancient (Arsha) Pákrit. Edited by Dr. A. F. Rudolf Hoernle. Fasc. I. No. (N.S.) 447. 1

PUBLISHED WITH THE AID, OR UNDER THE SUPERVISION, OF THE SOCIETY.

The Rámáyana of Válmikí. Edited and translated by Drs. W. Carey and J. Marshman. 4to. 3

Tibetan Grammar. By Alexander Csoma de Körös. 4to. ... 1

Tibetan Dictionary. By ditto 1

The Alif Leilatun-o-Leilá, or the Arabian Nights in the original Arabic. Edited by J. Brownlow. 4to. 4

The Shábnámah, in Persian. Edited by W. H. Macnaghten. Fol. ... 2

Dictionarium Anamittico-Latinum. By A. J. L. Tabara 1

Kávya Sangraha. A Selection of small poems in Sanskrit. Edited by Dr. A. Hœberlin 1

Notices of Sanskrit Manuscripts. Compiled by Dr. R. Mitra. 8vo. Fasc. I—XVII. 18

Beale's Oriental Biographical Dictionary. Edited by H. G. Keene. 4to. 1

Travels in the Himalayan Provinces. By Moorcroft and Trebeck. 8vo... 2

Grammar of the Burmese Language. By Captain Latter. 4to. ... 1

Travels of Fahian. By J. W. Laidlay. 8vo. 1

Ethnology of Bengal. By Colonel Dalton. 4to... 1

Catalogue of Sanskrit Manuscripts in the Library of H. H. the Mahárání of Bikáner. By Dr. R. Mitra. 8vo. 1

A Grammar of the Lepcha Language. By Major Mainwaring. 4to. ... 1

Appendix D.

Index to the Papers and Contributions to the Asiatick Researches and the Journal and Proceedings of the Asiatic Society of Bengal.

☞ N.B.—The Papers are indexed under the Authors' Names. Anonymous Contributions are indexed under the Leading Word in the Title.

Abbey, W.—On Ethnology of Mergui. [*Proc.* 1866, 243.

Abbott, Colonel James.—Public Papers relating to the Nurma or Chanderi Cotton, in reference to queries by Mr. Piddington, Journal Asiatic Society, Vol. X, p. 716. [*Jl.* xi, 1188.

An Account of a Remarkable Aerolite, which fell at the village of Manicgaon, near Eidulabad, in Khandeesh. [*Jl.* xiii, 880.

On Kunker Formations, with specimens. [*Jl.* xiv, 442.

Account of certain Agate Splinters found in the clay stratum bordering the River Narbudda. [*Jl.* xiv, 756.

Remarks upon the Occurrence of Granite in the bed of the Narbudda. [*Jl.* xiv, 821.

Account of the Process employed for obtaining Gold from the Sand of the River Beyass; with a short Account of the Gold Mines of Siberia. [*Jl.* xvi, 266.

Process of Working the Damascus Blade of Goojrat. [*Jl.* xvi, 417.

On a Sculpture from the Site of the Indo-Greek City of Bucephalia. [*Jl.* xvi, 664.

Additional Observations on the Damask Blade of Goojrat. [*Jl.* xvi, 666.

Abbott, Colonel James (*contd.*)—Extracts from a letter, descriptive of Geological and Mineralogical Observations in the Huzaree district, dated Camp Puhli, in Huzaree, 19th June, 1847. [*Jl.* xvi, 1135.

Inundation of the Indus, taken from the lips of an eye-witness (Ushruff Khan), A. D. 1842. [*Jl.* xvii, pt. i, 230.

On the Manufacture of the Matchlock of Koteli [*Jl.* xvii, pt. i, 277.

Some Account of the Battlefield of Alexander and Porus. [*Jl.* xvii, pt. ii, 619.

Remains of Greek Sculpture in Potowar. [*Jl.* xviii, 131.

Addendum on the Battlefield of Alexander and Porus [*Jl.* xviii, 176.

List of the Rajahs of Sialkote. [*Jl.* xviii, 177.

On the Sites of Nikaia and Boukephalon. [*Jl.* xxi, 214.

Note on the Ruins at Maunkyala. [*Jl.* xxii, 570.

On the Ballads and Legends of the Punjab. [*Jl.* xxiii, 50.

On the Ballads and Legends of the Punjab. Rifacimento of the Legendof Russaloo. [*Jl.* xxiii, 123.

On the Mirage of India [*Jl.* xxiii, 163.

Gradus ad Aornos. [*Jl.* xxiii, 309.

Aornos. [*Jl.* xxxii, 409.

Memorandum on the Elephant Statues in the Delhi Palace. [*Jl.* xxxiii, 375.

Abdullatif, Maulvi.—On the Panthays. [*Proc.* 1868, 142.

Abdun Nubee, Hajee.—Notes taken on a Tour through parts of Baloochisthan, in 1838 and 1839. Arranged and translated by Major Robert Leech [*Jl.* xiii, 667, 786.

Abel, Dr. Clarke.—Some Account of an Orang Outang of remarkable height found on the Island of Sumatra, together with a description of certain remains of this Animal presented to the Asiatic Society by Capt. Cornfoot, and at present contained in its Museum. [*As. Res.* xv, 489.

Aborigines of the Eastern Ghâts. [*Jl.* xxv, 39.

Adam, Dr. J.—Account of Barren Island in the Bay of Bengal. [*Jl.* i, 128.

Memoranda on the Geology of Bundelcund and Jubbulpore. [*Jl.* xi, 392.

Aerolite, on an, presented to the Society. [*Jl.* viii, 822.

Agha Abbas.—Journal of a Tour through parts of the Punjab and Afghanistan, in the year 1837. Arranged and translated by Major R. Leech, by whom the tour was planned and instructions furnished. [*Jl.* xii, 564.

Aitchison, Dr. J. E. Tierney.—On the Vegetation of the Jhelum District of the Punjab. [*Jl.* xxxiii, 290.

Lagomys rufescens, sent by. [*Proc.* 1880, 173.

Alabaster, C.—Memorandum on Education in China drawn up from information afforded by the ex-Imperial Commissioner Yeh. [*Jl.* xxviii, 48.

Aleem-ulla, Mulla.—Account (Part II) of parts of the Cabul and Peshawar Territories, and of Samah, Sudoom, Bunher, Swah, Deer and Bajour, visited by Mulla Aleem-ulla of Peshawar, in the latter part of the year 1837. Arranged and translated by Major R. Leech, C.B., late Political Agent, Candahar, under whose instructions the tour was made. [*Jl.* xiv, 660.

Alexander, James.—On the Tenures and Fiscal Relations of the Owners and Occupants of the soil in Bengal, Behar, and Orissa. [*Jl.* xiv, 527.

Ali Ibrahim Khan.—On the Trial by Ordeal among the Hindus. [*As. Res.* i, 389.

Allahabad, Population of the City and District of. [*Jl.* iii, 244.

Allan, Lieut.-Col. A. S.—Notes on Father Tieffentaller. [*Proc.* 1872, 59.

Amery.—On Origin of Races. [*Proc.* 1867, 111.

Anderson, Andrew.—On a new species of Kite, and Notes on the genus *Milvus* generally. With a Note by W. E. Brooks. [*Proc.* 1873, 242.

Anderson, Capt.—On Andamanese. [*Proc.* 1867, 157.

Anderson, Dr. J.—On Ethnological Exhibition. [*Proc.* 1866, 83.

On a new species of *Pycnonotus.* [*Proc.* 1869, 265.

On a new species of *Scincus.* [*Proc.* 1871, 115.

On two Saurian genera Eurylepis and Plocederma. [*Proc.* 1871, 180.

A List of the Reptilian Accessions to the Indian Museum, Calcutta, from 1865 to 1870, with a description of some new species. [*Jl.* xl, pt. ii, 12.

Remarks on Rude Stone Monuments in Chutiá Nágpúr. [*Proc.* 1873, 132.

Exhibition of a living Bamboo Rat, with remarks and description. [*Proc.* 1877, 148.

On the Floral Simulation of *Gongylus gongylodes,* Linn. [*Proc.* 1877, 193.

Description of some new and little known Asiatic Shrews in the Indian Museum, Calcutta. [*Jl.* xlvi, pt. ii, 261.

On the Indian Species of the genus Erinaceus. [*Jl.* xlvii, pt. ii, 195.

On *Arvicola indica,* Gray, and its relations to the sub-genus *Nesokia,* with a description of the species of *Nesokia.* [*Jl.* xlvii, pt. ii, 214.

See **Blyth, E.**

Anderson, Dr. Thomas.—Notes on the Indian Species of Lycium. [*Jl.* xxvi, 52.

Notes on the Flora of Lucknow with Catalogues of the cultivated and indigenous Plants. [*Jl.* xxviii, 89.

On the Flora of Behar and the mountain Parasnath, with a list of the species collected by Messrs. Hooker, Edgeworth, Thomson and Anderson. [*Jl.* xxxii, 189.

Anderson, Major William.—An attempt to identify some of the places mentioned in the Itinerary of Hiuan Thsang. [*Jl.* xvi, 1183.

Notes on the Geography of Western Afghanistan. [*Jl.* xviii, 553.

Sketch of the Recorded Revenues of the states beyond the Sutluj about 1750 to 1800. [*Jl.* xviii, 822.

Anderson, Major William (*contd.*) —Translation of Ibn Huokul's Account of Scinde. [*Jl.* xxi, 49.
Ibn Huokul's Account of Seestan. translated. [*Jl.* xxi, 365.
Ibn Huokul's Account of Khorasan. [*Jl.* xxii, 152.

Arabic into Persian, on the Introduction of. [*As. Res.* ii, 205.

Armstrong, Dr. J.—A Description of some new species of Hydroid Zoophytes from the Indian Coasts and Seas. [*Jl* xlviii, pt. ii, 98.

Arracan Bell, Restoration and Translation of the Inscription on the large, now at Nadrohighat, Zillah Alligarh. [*Jl.* vii, 287.

Asiatic Languages, comparison of [*Jl.* vii, 707.

Assam, Earthquakes in: *See* **Earthquakes.**

Assam, Report of the Society of Arts on Specimens of Rice, Wool, &c., from Nepal and. [*Jl.* v, 365.

At'har Ali Khan.—On the Baya, or Indian Gross-Beak. [*As. Res.* ii, 109.
On the Cure of the Elephantiasis. [*As. Res.* ii, 149.

Atkinson, E. T. — Memorandum, accompanying a set of Photographs of the Ruins of Garhwa, near Sheorájpúr, in the Allahabad District. [*Proc.* 1874, 123.

Attar Singh.—History of the Village of Aṛuṛa, Ludhiáná. [*Proc.* 1871, 247.

Avdall, Johannes.—Memoir of the Life and Writings of St. Nierses Clajensis, surnamed the Graceful, Pontiff of Armenia. [*Jl.* v, 129.
Note on some of the Indo-Scythic Coins found by Mr. C. Masson at Beghrám, in the Kohistán of Kabul. [*Jl.* v, 266.
Memoir of a Hindu Colony in Ancient Armenia. [*Jl.* v, 331.
Note on the Origin of the Armenian Era, and the Reformation of the Haican Kalendar. [*Jl.* v, 384.
Singular Narrative of the Armenian King Arsaces and his contemporary Sapor, King of Persia; extracted from the Armenian Chronicles. [*Jl.* vi, 81.
A short Memoir of Mechithar Ghosh, the Armenian Legislator. [*Jl.* ix, 967.
On the Laws and Law-books of the Armenians. [*Jl.* x, 235.
On the Invention of the Armenian Alphabet. [*Jl.* xiv, 522.

Avdall, Johannes (*contd.*)—Authors of Armenian Grammars, from the earliest stages of Armenian literature up to the present day. [*Jl.* xxxvii, pt. i, 134.
A Covenant of 'Alí, granting certain privileges to the Armenians. [*Proc.* 1869, 249.
A Covenant of 'Alí, fourth Caliph of Baghdád. [*Jl.* xxxix, pt. i, 60.

Ayrton, W. E. — Observations on method of detecting bad insulators. [*Proc.* 1871, 76.
Some Remarks on the connection between Inertia and Time. [*Proc.* 1871, 160.
On a Galvanometer suitable for the Quantitative Measurement of Electromotive Force. [*Proc.* 1871, 217.
On a Quantitative Method of testing a "Telegraph Earth." [*Jl.* xl, pt. ii, 177.
On the Syphon Recorder. [*Proc.* 1872, 51.

Baddeley, Dr. P. F. H.—On the Dust-storms of India. [*Jl.* xix, 390.
On Dust Whirlwinds and Cyclones. [*Jl.* xxi, 140, 264, 333.

Baigas of Balaghat, Notes on the. [*Proc.* 1872, 172.

Baker, Capt. H. C.—Experiments on the Strength and Elasticity of Indian Woods. [*As. Res.* xviii, pt. ii, 215.

Baker, Major W. E.—Description of the Fossil Elephant's Tooth from Somrotee, near Nahun. [*Jl.* iii, 638.
On the Fossil Elk of the Himálaya. [*Jl.* iv, 506.
Selected Specimens of the Sub-Himalayan Fossils in the Dádúpur Collection. [*Jl.* iv, 565.
Note on the Fossil Camel of the Sub-Himálayas. [*Jl.* iv, 694.
Report on a line of Levels taken by order of the Right Honorable the Governor General, between the Jumna and Sutlej Rivers. [*Jl.* ix, 688.
Note on a Fossil Antelope, from the Dadoopoor Museum [*Jl.* xii, 769.
Memorandum on the prospect of remuneration in working the Iron Mines of the Raneegunge district. With a Report by Professor Oldham. [*Jl.* xxii, 484.

Baker, Major W. E.; and **Durand, H. M.**—Table of Sub-Himálayan Fossil Genera in the Dádúpur Collection. [*Jl.* v, 291.

Baker, Major W. E.; and Durand, H. M. (*contd.*) — Sub - Himálayan Fossil Remains of the Dádúpur Collection. [*Jl.* v, 486, 661. 739.
Fossil Remains of the smaller Carnivora from the Sub-Himálayas. [*Jl.* v, 576.

Baker, Rev.—On the Poetry of Madagascar. [*Jl.* i, 86.

Balfour, Edward.—On the Migratory Tribes of Natives in Central India. [*Jl.* xiii, 1.

Balfour, Dr. Francis.—A Treatise on the Barometer. [*As. Res.* iv. 195.
Observations respecting the remarkable Effects of Sol-Lunar Influence in the Fevers of India; with the Scheme of an Astronomical Ephemeris for the purposes of Medicine and Meteorology. [*As. Res.* viii, 1.
Extracts from the Tehzeebul Mantik, or "Essence of Logic," proposed as a small supplement to Arabic and Persian Grammar; and with a view to elucidate certain points connected with Oriental Literature. [*As. Res.* viii, 89.

Ball, Valentine.—On Stone Implements. [*Proc.* 1865, 127.
On Chipped Implements of Bengal. [*Proc.* 1867, 143.
On Synostosis of human skull. [*Proc.* 1867, 147.
List of Localities in India where ancient Stone Implements have been discovered. [*Proc.* 1867, 147.
On the Jungle Products used as articles of food by the Inhabitants of the districts of Manbhoom and Hazaribagh. [*Jl.* xxxvi, pt. ii, 73.
Remarks on Elephants. [*Proc.* 1868, 129.
On Stone Implements. [*Proc.* 1868, 177.
On the ancient Copper Miners of Singhbhúm. [*Proc.* 1869, 170.
Notes on the Flora of Manbhúm. [*Jl.* xxxviii, pt. ii, 112.
Remarks on Celts found in Singhbhúm. [*Proc.* 1870, 268.
Brief Notes on the Geology and on the Fauna in the neighbourhood of Nancowry Harbour, Nicobar Islands. [*Jl.* xxxix, pt. ii, 25.
Notes on the Geology of the vicinity of Port Blair, Andaman Islands. [*Jl.* xxxix, pt. ii, 231.
Notes on Birds observed in the neighbourhood of Port Blair, Andaman Islands, during the month of August, 1869. [*Jl.* xxxix, pt. ii, 239.

Ball, Valentine. (*contd.*)—Remarks on Birds captured in the Red and Arabian Seas. [*Proc.* 1871, 249.
Names of Birds, &c., in four of the aboriginal languages of Western Bengal. [*Jl.* xl, pt. i, 103.
Notes on a Collection of Birds made in the Andaman Islands by Assistant Surgeon G. E. Dobson, M.B., during the months of April and May. [*Jl.* xli, pt. ii, 273.
On the occurrence of *Tupai Ellioti*, Waterhouse. in the Sátpúra Hills, Central Provinces. [*Proc.* 1874, 95.
On an Ancient Perforated Stone found in the Sátpúra Hills. [*Proc.* 1874, 96.
On some Stone Implements of the Barmese type, found in Pargana Dálbhúm, District of Singhbhúm. [*Proc.* 1875. 118.
Remarks on two Specimens of Indian Boomerangs. [*Proc.* 1875, 136.
Exhibition of a Series. of Khond Weapons. &c.. from the Tributary States of Orissa. [*Proc.* 1876, 114.
On an Ancient Kitchen-Midden at Chaudwar, near Cuttack. [*Proc.* 1876, 120.
On Stone Implements found in the Tributary States of Orissa. [*Proc.* 1876, 122.
Remarks on the Abstract and Discussion of Dr. O. Feistmantel's Paper, entitled "Giant-Kettles (pot-holes) caused by water-action in Streams in the Rajmahal hills and the Barákur district." [*Proc.* 1877. 140.
Notes on certain Mammals occurring in the basin of Máhanadi. [*Proc.* 1877, 168.
Exhibition of two Stone Implements from Parisnáth Hill. [*Proc.* 1878. 125.
On a forgotten Record of the occurrence of the Lion in the district of Palamow and its connection with some other facts regarding the Geographical Distribution of Animals in India. [*Proc.* 1881, 3.
On Nature and Use of Fire Sticks. [*Proc.* 1881, 72.
Remarks on Relics from Buddha Gaya. [*Proc.* 1881, 89.
Remarks on Paper on Inhabitants of the Nicobars. [*Proc.* 1881, 110.
Exhibition of an ancient Stone Implement made of magnetic iron ore. [*Proc.* 1881. 120.
On the Origin of the so-called Kharakpur Meteorite. [*Proc.* 1881, 140.

Ball, Valentine (*contd.*) — On the Identification of certain Diamond Mines in India, which were known to and worked by the Ancients, especially those which were visited by Tavernier. With a Note on the history of the Koh-i-nur. [*Jl.* l, pt. ii, 31.

Additional Note on the Identification of the ancient Diamond Mines visited by Tavernier. [*Jl.* l, pt. ii, 219.

Ballantyne. Dr. J. R.—Sanskrit Inscription from Behar, with a Translation by Dr. Ballantyne and Remarks by Capt. M. Kittoe. [*Jl.* xvii, pt. i, 492.

Sanskrit Inscription from Behar. Translated, with Remarks, by Capt. M. Kittoe. [*Jl.* xviii. 492.

See **Kittoe, Capt. M.**; and **Roer, Dr. E.**

Bandyopadhyaya, Brajanatha.—Hamír Rásá, or a History of Hamír, Prince of Ranthambor. Translated from the Hindi. [*Jl.* xlviii, pt. i, 186.

Banerji, Revd. Krishna Mohana.—The "Mahimnastava," or a Hymn to Shiva; with an English translation. [*Jl.* viii, 355.

On Translation of Technical Terms. [*Proc.* 1866. 155, 173.

On Paper on Human Sacrifices in ancient India. [*Proc.* 1876, 53.

Banerji, Rangalal.—Identification of certain Tribes mentioned in the Puranas with those noticed in Col. Dalton's Ethnology of Bengal. [*Proc.* 1874, 7.

Note on a Copper-plate Grant found in the Record Office of the Cuttack Collectorate. [*Jl.* xlvi, pt. i, 149.

Banurji, Chandrasekhara. — Notes on the Antiquities of the Nálti, the Assia, and the Mahabinayaka Hills of Cuttack. [*Jl.* xxxix, pt. i, 158.

An Account of the Antiquities of Jájpúr in Orísá. [*Jt.* xl, pt. i, 151.

The Kaimur Range. [*Jl.* xlvi, pt. i, 16.

Barbe, Revd. M.—Some Account of the Hill Tribes in the interior of the district of Chittagong, in a letter to the Secretary of the Asiatic Society. [*Jl.* xiv, 380.

Barbe, Revd. P.—Notice of the Nicobar Islands. [*Jl.* xv, 344.

Barrow, H.—Horary Observations of the Barometer, Thermometer, and Wet-bulb Thermometer, made at Calcutta on the 21st and 22nd of December, 1858. [*Jl.* v, 51.

Barrow, H. (*contd.*)—Horary Observations of the Barometer, Thermometer and Wet-bulb Thermometer, made at Calcutta on the 21st and 22nd of March, 1836. [*Jl.* v, 243.

Basevi, Capt. J. P.—On the Pendulum operations about to be undertaken by the Great Trigonometrical Survey of India; with a sketch of the theory of their application to the determination of the earth's figure, and an account of some of principal observations hitherto made. [*Jl.* xxxiv, pt. ii, 251.

Bastian, Dr. A.—On some Siamese Inscriptions. [*Jl.* xxxiv, pt. i, 27.

Translation of an Inscription copied in the temple of Nakhon Vat, or the City of Monasteries. near the capital of ancient Kambodia. [*Jl.* xxxvi, pt. i, 76.

Basu, Durgarama.—Transcript and translation of a copper-plate grant of Govinda Chandra of Kanauj [*Proc.* 1876, 130.

Batsch, Revd. F.—Language of Dravidian Aborigines. Notes on the Oraon Language. [*Jl.* xxxv, pt. ii, Extra No., 251.

Batten, J. H.—Note on a Visit to the Nítí Pass of the grand Himálayan Chain. [*Jl.* vii. 310.

A few Notes on the subject of the Kumaon and Rohilcund Turaee. [*Jl.* xiii, 887.

See **Herbert, Capt.**; and **Manson, Capt.**

Bayley, Hon. E. C.—Note on some Sculptures found in Peshawar. [*Jl.* xxi, 606.

Note on two Inscriptions at Khunniara, in the Kangra district. [*Jl.* xxiii, 57.

Note on the Translation of a Bactrian Inscription from Wardak. [*Jl.* xxx, 347.

Remarks on Bactro-Buddhist Relics from Ráwal Pindi. [*Jl.* xxxi, 184.

On Arian Alphabets. [*Proc.* 1867, 43.

Note on a Coin from Major Strutt. [*Proc.* 1869, 201.

Memorandum on, and tentative reading of, the Súe Vihár Inscription from near Bháwalpúr. [*Jl.* xxxix, pt. i, 65.

Letter regarding a new Gold Mohur. [*Proc.* 1871, 83.

Letter on an Irish Celt. [*Proc.* 1872, 35.

Note on two Coins from Kausambhi. [*Jl.* xlii, pt. i, 109.

Further Note on Coins from Kausambhi. [*Jl.* xlii, pt. i, 191.

Bayley, Hon. E. C. (*contd.*)—Note on two Muhammadan Coins. [*Jl.* xlii, pt. i, 311.
Remarks on a Coin of Ghiyás-ud-dín A'zam Sháh. [*Proc.* 1874, 157.
Note on a Hoard of 543 Sassanian Coins in the possession of Col. H. Hyde, R. E. [*Jl.* xliii, pt. i, 99.
Remarks on Inscription of the time of Skanda Gupta. [*Proc.* 1875, 45.
Remarks on Human Sacrifices in ancient India. [*Proc.* 1876, 55.
Exhibition of Silver Cilician, Sassanian, and Parthian Coins, and of four Gold Coins belonging to Mr. J. R. Reid. [*Proc.* 1876, 219.
Exhibition of Partho-Persian Coins. [*Proc.* 1877, 2.
On a forged Pali Inscription. [*Proc.* 1877, 267.

Bayley, W. B.—Statistical View of the Population of Burdwan, &c. [*As. Res.* xii, 547.

Bayne, R. R.—Notes on the Remains of portions of Old Fort William discovered during the erection of the East Indian Railway Company's Offices. [*Jl.* lii, pt. i, 105.
Note on Further Discoveries made on the site of Old Fort William. [*Proc.* 1883, 42.

Beale, J. W.—Influence of the Moon on the Weather. [*Jl.* xxi, 501.

Beale, T. W.—Letter on a Persian MS., entitled '*Imárát-ul-Akbar.* [*Proc.* 1875, 117.

Beames, J.—On "Om" and "Amen." [*Proc.* 1866, 192.
Outlines of a Plea for the Arabic Element in Official Hindustani. [*Jl.* xxxv, pt. i, 1.
On the Arabic Element in Official Hindustani, No. 2. [*Jl.* xxxvi, pt. i, 145.
On Chand's Poems. [*Proc.* 1868, 242.
The Nineteenth Book of the Gestes of Prithiráj by Chand Bardái, translated into English. [*Proc.* 1869, 235.
The Nineteenth Book of the Gestes of Prithiráj by Chand Bardai, entitled "The Marriage with Padmavati," literally translated from the old Hindi. [*Jl.* xxxviii, pt. i, 145.
Reply to Mr. Growse. [*Jl.* xxxviii, pt. i, 171.
Letter regarding an Inscription. [*Proc.* 1870, 4.
On the Relation of Urya to other modern Aryan languages. [*Proc.* 1870, 192.

Beames, J. (*contd.*)—The Ruins at Kopari, Balasore district. [*Jl.* xl, pt. i, 247.
The Rhapsodies of Gambhir Rai, the bard of Núrpúr (A. D. 1650). [*Proc.* 1872, 156.
More Buddhist Remains in Orissa. [*Jl.* xli, pt. i, 7.
Translations of selected portions of Book I of Chand Bardai's Epic. [*Jl.* xli, pt. i, 42.
List of the Books contained in Chand's poem, the Prithirája Ráso. [*Jl.* xli, pt. i, 204.
Letter on his edition of Chand. [*Proc.* 1873, 122.
Studies in the Grammar of Chand Bardái. [*Jl.* xlii, pt. i, 165.
The Alti Hills in Cuttack. [*Jl.* xliv, pt. i, 19.
The Rhapsodies of Gambhír Rái, the bard of Núrpur, A. D. 1650. [*Jl.* xliv, pt. i, 192.
Reply to Dr. Mitra's remarks on paper on history of Orissa. [*Proc.* 1883, 42.
Old Dutch Hatchments in Chinsurah Church. [*Proc.* 1883, 145.
Notes on the History of Orissa under the Mahomedan, Maratha, and English rule. [*Jl.* lii, pt. i, 231.

Beavan, Capt. R. C.—On Antiquities of Manbhoom. [*Proc.* 1865, 66.
Contributions towards a history of *Panolia Eldi*: McLelland. [*Jl.* xxxvi, pt. ii, 175.

Becher, Major J. R.—Letter containing inquiries into a rumour respecting the stoppage of the River Indus in the year 1858. [*Jl.* xxviii, 219.

Bedford, J. R.—On the Meteorology of Rampore Bauleah. [*Jl.* xxi, 593.
Contributions to the Statistics of Bengal,—Income, Expenditure and Food. [*Jl.* xxii, 387.

Benson, W. H.—Account of a new genus of Land Snails, allied to the genus *Cyclostoma* of Lamarck; with a description of a species found on the outlying rocks of the Rajmahal range of hills. [*Jl.* i, 11.
Account of *Oxygyrus*: a new genus of Pelagian Shells allied to the genus *Atlanta* of Lesueur, with a Note on some other Pelagian Shells lately taken on board the ship *Malcolm.* [*Jl.* iv, 173.
Description of two Species of *Carinaria*, lately discovered in the Indian Ocean. [*Jl.* iv, 215.
Corrected Character of the genus *Cuvieria* of Rang and Notice of a second species inhabiting the tropical Indian Ocean. [*Jl.* iv, 698.

Benson, W. H. (*contd.*)—Descriptive Catalogue of Terrestrial and Fluviatile *Testacea*, chiefly from the North-East Frontier of Bengal. [*Jl.* v, 350.

Descriptive Catalogue of a Collection of Land and Fresh-water Shells, chiefly contained in the Museum of the Asiatic Society. [*Jl.* v, 741.

Description of the Shell and Animal of *Nematura*, a new genus of Mollusca, inhabiting situations subject to alternations of fresh and brackish water. [*Jl.* v, 781.

Notice on *Balantium*, a genus of the Pteropodous Mollusca; with the characters of a new species inhabiting the Southern Indian Ocean. [*Jl.* vi, 150.

Note on the genera *Oxygyrus* and *Bellerophon*. [*Jl.* vi, 316.

Note on the Affinities of *Galathea* of Lamarck (*Potamophila* of Sowerby), a genus of Fluviatile Testacea. [*Jl.* vii, 420.

Notes on the Rev. F. Mason's paper "On the Shells of the Tenasserim Provinces." [*Jl.* xviii, 164.

Chusan Shells. Described by W. H. Benson. Collected by Dr. T. Cantor. [*Jl.* xxiv, 119.

See **Hutton, Lieut. T.**

Bentley, John. — Remarks on the principal Æras and Dates of the ancient Hindus. [*As. Res.* v, 315.

On the Antiquity of the Súrya Siddhánta, and the formation of the Astronomical Cycles therein contained. [*As. Res.* vi, 537.

On the Hindu Systems of Astronomy, and their connection with History in ancient and modern times. [*As. Res.* viii, 193.

Benza, Dr. P. M. –Geological Sketch of the Nilgherries (Nil-giri). [*Jl.* iv, 413.

Beosi River, Iron Suspension Bridge over the, near Ságar, Central India. [*Jl.* ii, 538.

Berry, Dr. Andrew.—An Account of the Male Plant, which furnishes the Medicine generally called Columbo or Columba Root. [*As. Res.* x, 385.

Beveridge, H.—On a Copper-plate Inscription found at Bákirganj. [*Proc.* 1873, 171.

Were the Sundarbans inhabited in ancient times? [*Jl.* xlv, pt. i, 71.

The Antiquities of Bagurá (Bogra). [*Jl.* xlvii, pt. i, 89.

Beverley, H.—Knotted Ropes used by the Santáls in taking the census of 1872. [*Proc.* 1872, 192.

Beverley, H. (*contd.*)—Remarks on the Recent Census of the Town of Calcutta. [*Proc.* 1876, 111.

Remarks on old Maps of Calcutta, &c. [*Proc.* 1881, 90.

Bhattacharji, Rishi Kesh.—On the Identity of Upello with Upaplava. [*Jl.* l, pt. i, 130.

Biddulph, Major J.—Remarks on a Head of *ovis poli*. [*Proc.* 1879, 280.

Bidie, Dr. G.—The Pagoda or Varáha Coins of Southern India. [*Jl.* lii, pt. i, 33.

Bigge, Lieut. H. — Despatch from Lieut. H. Bigge, Assistant Agent, detached to the Naga Hills, to Capt. Jenkins, Agent, Governor Genera , N. E. Frontier. [*Jl.* x, 129.

Bijaya Mandir, Udayapur, &c., Inscription from the. [*Jl.* xvii, pt. i, 68.

Bird, James.—On the Historical Geography of Hindustan, and the Origin of the Social State among the Hindus. [*Jl.* ix, 848.

Bird, Dr. James.—Opening of the Topes at the Caves of Kanari, near Bombay, and the Relics found in them. [*Jl.* x, 94.

Birds, Catalogue of Indian. [*Jl.* i, 261, 313.

Black, F. C.—*See* **Smith, V. A.**

Blake, Captn.—Information regarding Illanoon Pirates. [*Jl.* vii, 978.

Bland, Dr. William.—Notes on Delhi Point, Pulo-Tinghie, &c., and on some Pelagic Fossil Remains found in the rocks of Pulo-Lédah. [*Jl.* v, 575.

Note on the Genus *Pterocyclos* of Mr. Benson and *Spiraculum* of Mr. Pearson. [*Jl.* v, 783.

Note on the Malay Woodpecker. [*Jl.* vi, 952.

Blanford, Henry F.—On Dr. Gerard's Collection of Fossils from the Spiti Valley, in the Asiatic Society's Museum. [*Jl.* xxxii, 124.

Note on a Tank section at Sealdah, Calcutta. [*Jl.* xxxiii, 154.

Note on the Hailstorm of Thursday the 24th March. [*Jl.* xxxiii, 530.

On Scientific Technology. [*Proc.* 1866, 168.

On Celts. [*Proc.* 1868, 59.

On certain protracted Irregularities of Atmospheric Pressure in Bengal in relation to the Monsoon Rainfall of 1868 and 1869. [*Jl.* xxxix, pt. ii, 123.

On the Normal Rainfall of Bengal. [*Jl.* xxxix, pt. ii, 243

On Barometric and other Meteorological Curves. [*Proc.* 1871, 60.

Blanford, Henry F. (*contd.*)—On some undescribed Species of *Camptoceras* and other Land-shells. [*Jl.* xl, pt. ii, 39.

Note on the Error of the Calcutta Standard Barometer, compared with those of Kew and Greenwich. [*Jl.* xl. pt. ii, 446.

Remarks on Rude Stone Monuments in Chutiá Nágpúr. [*Proc.* 1873, 130.

On the Climate of Bengal. [*Proc.* 1873, 178.

On some recent Evidence of the Variation of the Sun's Heat. [*Jl.* xliii, pt. ii, 21.

Exhibition of two series of Synoptical Weather Charts of India, with remarks thereon. [*Proc.* 1876, 218.

On certain protracted Irregularities of Atmospheric Pressure in the Indian Monsoon-region, and their relation to variations of the local Rainfall. [*Jl.* xlv, pt. ii, 27.

An Account of Experiments made in 1875 and 1876 in various parts of India, for the purpose of comparing the observed Temperature of the Dew-point with that computed from the Psychrometer by different methods of reduction. [*Jl.* xlv, pt. ii, 53.

Remarks on Himálayan Glaciation. [*Proc.* 1877, 3.

Note on the Variation of the Barometric Tides in connexion with Diurnal Land- and Sea-Breezes. [*Jl.* xlvi. pt. ii. 45.

Catalogue of the recorded Cyclones in the Bay of Bengal up to the end of 1876. [*Jl.* xlvi. pt. ii, 328.

Exhibition of Autographic Records of Nor'-Wester Storms and of Weather Charts. [*Proc.* 1878. 104.

Exhibition of an enlarged Photograph by M. Janssen of part of the Solar Disc. [*Proc.* 1879, 138.

On the Diurnal Variation of Rainfall Frequency at Calcutta. [*Jl.* xlviii, pt. ii, 41.

Exhibition of a Balfour Stewart's Actinometer. [*Proc.* 1880, 6.

Note to accompany some Drawings of large Hailstones. by Col. H. H. Godwin-Austen and Mr. S. E. Peal. [*Proc.* 1880, 103.

On the High Atmospheric Pressure of 1876-78 in Asia and Australia in relation to the Sun-spot Cycle. [*Jl.* xlix, pt. ii, 70.

On Photographs of the Van Rysselberghe Meteorograph. [*Proc.* 1881, 65.

Blanford, Henry F. (*contd.*)—On the Relations of Cloud and Rainfall to Temperature in India. and on the opposite Variations of Density in the higher and lower Atmospheric Strata. [*Jl.* l, pt. ii, 69.

Description of a Raingage with evapometer, for remote and secluded stations. [*Jl.* l, pt. ii, 8.

Some further results of Sun-thermometer observations with reference to atmospheric absorption and the supposed variation of solar heat. [*Jl.* li. pt. ii, 72.

Remarks on Hailstorm at Shamnagar. [*Proc.* 1883, 58.

Remarks on Paper on Air-temperature and Humidity at different elevations. [*Proc.* 1883, 87.

Remarks on Paper on Measurement of Solar Radiation. [*Proc.* 1883, 89.

See **Blanford, William T.; Harding, Chas.; Stoliczka, Dr. F.**

Blanford, William T.—On the Rocks of the Damúda group, and their associates in Eastern and Central India, as illustrated by the re-examination of the Ránigauj field. [*Jl.* xxix, 352.

Contributions to Indian Malacology, No. III. Description of new operculated Land-shells from Pegu. Arakan and the Khasi hills. (*See also* **Blanford, W. T.; and H. F.**) [*Jl.* xxxi, 135.

Account of a Visit to Puppá doung, an extinct volcano in Upper Burma. [*Jl.* xxxi. 215.

Contributions to Indian Malacology, No. IV. Descriptions of new Land-shells from Ava and other parts of Burma. [*Jl.* xxxii, 319.

Contributions to Indian Malacology, No. V. Descriptions of new Land-shells from Arakan. Pegu, and Ava; with Notes on the distribution of described species. [*Jl.* xxxiv, pt. ii, 66.

On worked Agates of stone-age. [*Proc.* 1866, 230.

Contributions to Indian Malacology, No. VI. Descriptions of new Land-shells from the Nilgiri and Anamullay Hills and other places in the Peninsula of India. [*Jl.* xxxv, pt. ii, 31.

Contributions to Indian Malacology, No. VII. List of species of Unio and Anodonta described as occurring in India, Ceylon and Burma. [*Jl.* xxxv, pt. ii, 134.

On Stone Implements. [*Proc.* 1867, 136.

Blanford, William T. (*contd.*)—

On the Superior Antiquity of Indian Stone-weapons. [*Proc.* 1867, 144.

Contributions to Indian Malacology, No. VIII. List of Estuary Shells collected in the delta of the Irrawady in Pegu, with descriptions of the new species. [*Jl.* xxxvi, pt. ii, 51.

Zoological Notes. [*Jl.* xxxvi, pt. ii, 189.

Letter from Aden. [*Proc.* 1868, 65.

Letter from Zulla, Abyssinia. [*Proc.* 1868, 83.

Letter from Senaffè. [*Proc.* 1868, 167.

Notes on a Journey in Northern Abyssinia. [*Proc.* 1868, 276.

Contributions to Indian Malacology. No. IX. Descriptions of new Diplommatinæ from Darjiling and the Khasi Hills. [*Jl.* xxxvii, pt. ii, 77.

Contributions to Indian Malacology, No. X. Descriptions of new species of Cyclophoridæ, of Ennea and Streptaxis, from the hills of Southern and South-Western India. [*Jl.* xxxviii, pt. ii, 125.

Ornithological Notes, chiefly on some Birds of Central, Western and Southern India. [*Jl.* xxxviii, pt. ii, 164.

Contributions to Indian Malacology, No. XI. Descriptions of new species of Paludomus, Cremnoconchus, Cyclostoma and of Helicidæ from various parts of India. [*Jl.* xxxix, pt. ii, 9.

Notes of some Reptilia and Amphibia from Central India. [*Jl.* xxxix, pt. ii, 335.

Note on Hemidactylus marmoratus, H. Kelaarti and Ablabes Humberti. [*Proc.* 1871, 173.

On chipped quartzite Implements found on the Godavery. [*Proc.* 1871, 179.

Note on Colonel McMaster's List of Birds from Nagpore, &c. [*Jl.* xl, pt. ii, 216.

List of Birds collected or observed in the Wardha Valley and its vicinity near Chanda. [*Jl.* xl, pt. ii, 268.

Account of a Visit to the Eastern and Northern Frontiers of Independent Sikkim; with Notes on the Zoology of the Alpine and Sub-Alpine regions. Part I. [*Jl.* xl, pt. ii, 367.

Blanford, William T. (*contd.*)—

Account of a Visit to the Eastern and Northern Frontiers of Independent Sikkim; with Notes on the Zoology of the Alpine and Sub-Alpine regions. Part II. [*Jl.* xli, pt. ii, 30.

On Birds from Sikkim. [*Jl.* xli, pt. ii, 152.

Monograph of Himalayan, Assamese, Barmese and Cingalese Clausiliæ. [*Jl.* xli, pt. ii, 199.

Note on the Genus Gymnops, W. Blanf. (Lacertidæ). [*Jl.* xlii, pt. ii, 144

On the Scientific Names of the Sind "Ibex," the Markhor, and the Indian Antelope. [*Jl.* xliii, pt. ii, 12.

Note on the Molluscan Genera *Cœlostele*, Benson and *Francesia* Paladilhe, and on some Species of Landshells from Aden. [*Jl.* xliii, pt. ii, 41.

Remarks on Flint Cores and Flakes from Sakhar and Rohri in Sind. [*Proc.* 1875, 134.

Exhibition of Skins of Thibetan *Mammalia.* [*Proc.* 1875, 197.

List of Mammalia collected by the late Dr. Stoliczka, when attached to the embassy under Sir D. Forsyth in Kashmir, Ladak, Eastern Turkestan and Wakhán; with Descriptions of new Species. [*Jl.* xliv, pt. ii, 105.

On the Species of Marmot inhabiting the Himalaya, Tibet and the adjoining regions. [*Jl.* xliv, pt. ii, 114.

List of Reptilia and Amphibia collected by the late Dr. Stoliczka in Kashmir, Ladák, Eastern Turkestán and Wakhán; with Descriptions of new Species. [*Jl.* xliv, pt. ii, 191.

Note on (i) *Elachistodon Westermanni*, (ii) *Platyceps semifasciatus*, and (iii) *Ablepharus pusillus* and *Blepharosteres agilis*. [*Jl.* xliv. pt. ii, 207.

Note on a large Hare inhabiting high elevations in Western Thibet. [*Jl.* xliv, pt. ii, 214.

On Iron Arrow-heads from Sind. [*Proc.* 1876, 116.

Exhibition of Drawings by Capt. E. Mockler, Pol. Agent, Guádar, representing Ancient Dwellings and Tombs near Guádar in Baluchistan, with Description. [*Proc.* 1876, 172

On some Lizards from Sind, with Descriptions of new Species of *Ptyodactylus*, *Stenodactylus* and *Trapelus*. [*Jl.* xlv, pt. ii, 18.

Description of *Felis Shawiana*, a new Lyncine Cat from Eastern Turkestan. [*Jl.* xlv, pt. ii, 49.

Blanford, William T. (*contd.*)—
On the Physical Geography of the Great Indian Desert with especial reference to the former Existence of the Sea in the Indus Valley; and on the Origin and Mode of Formation of the Sandhills. [*Jl.* xlv, pt. ii, 86.
Description of *Golunda Ellioti* from Sind. [*Jl.* xlv, pt. ii, 165.
Notes on some recent Researches by Prof. Jeitteles, of Vienna on the Origin of the Domestic Dog. [*Proc.* 1877, 114.
On an apparently undescribed Weasel from Yarkand. [*Proc.* 1877, 148.
Exhibition of a Collection of Pottery, &c., received from Major E. Mockler, Pol. Agent at Guádar, Balúchistán. [*Proc.* 1877, 157.
On an apparently undescribed Weasel from Yarkand. [*Jl.* xlvi, pt. ii, 259.
On the Metád Rat (*Golunda Meltada*, Gray) with a Note on *Golunda Ellioti.* [*Jl.* xlvi, pt. ii, 288.
Description of *Spiraculum Mastersi.* [*Jl.* xlvi, pt. ii, 313.
Note on two Species of Asiatic Bears, the "Mamh" of Baluchistan and *Ursus pruinosus*, Blyth, of Tibet, and on an apparently undescribed Fox from Baluchistán. [*Jl.* xlvi, pt. ii, 315.
On an apparently new Hare, and some other Mammalia from Gilgit. [*Jl.* xlvi, pt. ii, 323.
Exhibition of a Geological Map of Sind, with an Account of the Geology of the Province. [*Proc.* 1878, 3.
Descriptions of two apparently new Mammals from Tenasserim. [*Proc.* 1878, 71.
Exhibition of Skins of adult wild Swans from Sind and the Punjáb. [*Proc.* 1878, 138.
Remarks on *Arvicola indica*, Gray, and its relation to the Sub-genus *Nesokia*, Gray. [*Proc.* 1878, 195.
Description of *Ruticilla schisticeps*, Hodgs. [*Jl.* xlvii, pt. ii, 1.
Notes on some Reptilia from the Himalayas and Burma. [*Jl.* xlvii, pt. ii, 125.
On some Mammals from Tenasserim. [*Jl.* xlvii, pt. ii, 150.
Description of a supposed new Hedgehog from Muscat in Arabia. [*Jl.* xlvii, pt. ii, 212.
Note on the Mamh or Balúchistán Bear (*Ursus Gedrosianus*). [*Proc.* 1879, 4.

Blanford, William T. (*contd.*)—
Exhibition of a Specimen of Hippuritic Limestone from Afghanistan. [*Proc.* 1879, 202.
A second note on Mammalia collected by Major Biddulph in Gilgit. [*Jl.* xlviii, pt. ii, 95.
Notes on a Collection of Reptiles and Frogs from the neighbourhood of Ellore and Dumagudem. [*Jl.* xlviii, pt. ii, 110.
Note on a Collection of Reptiles made by Major O. B. St. John, R. E., at Ajmere in Rájputáná. [*Jl.* xlviii, pt. ii, 119.
Notes on Reptilia. [*Jl.* xlviii, pt. ii, 127.
On a Species of *Trochalopterum* from Travancore. [*Jl.* xlix, pt. ii, 142.
Contributions to Indian Malacology, No. XII. Descriptions of new Land- and Fresh-water Shells from Southern and Western India, Burmah, the Andaman Islands, &c. [*Jl.* xlix, pt. ii, 181.
Description of an *Arvicola* from the Punjáb Himalayas. [*Jl.* xlix, pt. ii, 244.
On the Voles (*Arvicola*) of the Himalayas, Tibet and Afghanistan. [*Jl.* l, pt. ii, 88.
On *Myospalax fuscicapillus*, Blyth. [*Jl.* l, pt. ii, 118.
Notes on an apparently undescribed *Varanus* from Tenasserim and on other Reptilia and Amphibia. [*Jl.* l, pt. ii, 239.
A numerical Estimate of the Species of Animals, chiefly Land and Freshwater, hitherto recorded from British India and its Dependencies. [*Jl.* l, pt. ii, 263.

Blanford, W. T.; and H. F.—Contributions to Indian Malacology, No. I. [*Jl.* xxix, 117.
Contributions to Indian Malacology, No. II. [*Jl.* xxx, 347*d*.

Blaquiere, W. C. — The Rhudhirádhayáya, or Sanguinary Chapter, translated from the Cálicá Puran. [*As. Res.* v, 371.

Blochmann, Henry.—On Palæography of India. [*Proc.* 1865, 171.
On Scientific Technology. [*Proc.* 1866, 163.
On "Om" and "Amen." [*Proc.* 1866, 195.
On new Arabic type. [*Proc.* 1867, 29.
Notes on Sirájuddaulah and the town of Murshidabád, taken from a Persian Manuscript of the Táríkh-i-Mançúrí. [*Jl.* xxxvi, pt. i, 85.

Blochmann, Henry (*contd.*) — On Persian Poets, styled Sultan. [*Proc.* 1868, 220.
Notes on a MS. of the Sirájallughát. [*Proc.* 1868, 262.
Remarks on the Sundarban. [*Proc.* 1868, 266.
Contributions to Persian Lexicography. [*Jl.* xxxvii. pt. i, 1.
Note on the Fall of a Meteorite at Jullunder, in April, A. D. 1621. [*Proc.* 1869, 167.
Observation on the Persian MS. of *Jámí's Khiradnâmah-i-Sikandarí.* [*Proc.* 1869, 190.
Contributions to the Chronology of the reigns of Timúr and his descendants up to Sháhjahán, No. 1. [*Proc.* 1869, 207.
Observations on Metrical Inscriptions found on Indian and Persian Coins. [*Proc.* 1869, 255.
Note on a Málwah Goldmuhur. [*Proc.* 1869, 266.
Badáoní and his Works. [*Jl.* xxxviii. pt. i, 105.
Observations on a Sanad, &c. [*Proc.* 1870, 6.
Notes on Places of Historical Interest in the district of Huglí, I. Madárau, and Panduah. [*Proc.* 1870. 109.
Note on a Persian MS. entitled Mirát-ul-Quds, a life of Christ; compiled, at the request of the Emperor Akbar, by Jerome Xavier. [*Proc.* 1870, 138.
On Coins sent by Mr Ferrar from Pertabgar. [*Proc.* 1870, 151.
Remarks on the *Balwantnámah.* [*Proc.* 1870, 218.
Remarks on the Arabic Inscription of the Bonhara Mosque. [*Proc.* 1870, 297.
On History of the Rájahs of Kharakpur. [*Proc.* 1870, 305.
Notes on the Arabic and Persian Inscriptions in the Húglí district. [*Jl.* xxxix, pt. i, 280.
Facsimiles of several Autographs of Jahángír, Sháhjahán and Prince Dárá Shikoh; together with Notes on the Literary Character and the Capture and Death of Dárá Shikoh. [*Jl.* xxxix, pt. i, 271.
Notes on Arabic and Persian Inscriptions. [*Proc.* 1871, 126.
Observations on a Persian MS. on the Lives of the twelve Apostles, by Jerome Xavier. [*Proc.* 1871, 138.
Remarks regarding the Birthplace of Todar Mall. [*Proc.* 1871, 178.
Note on three Arabic Inscriptions by early Bengal Kings. [*Proc.* 1871, 245.

Blochmann, Henry (*contd.*)— Notes from Muhammadan Historians on Chutiá Nágpúr, Pachet, and Palámau. [*Jl.* xl, pt. i, 111.
Notes on several Arabic and Persian Inscriptions. [*Jl.* xl, pt. i, 251.
Remarks on Mr. Ferrar's letter regarding Todar Mall. [*Proc.* 1872, 36.
Remarks on Inscriptions received from Mr. Wilson. [*Proc.* 1872. 47.
Remarks on Bengal and Dak'hin Silver Coins. [*Proc.* 1872, 118.
Inscription on a Tomb and Mosque at Sambhalherá. [*Proc.* 1872, 165.
Inscriptions from Kol. [*Proc.* 1872, 166.
Inscriptions from Miyán Mír. &c. [*Proc.* 1872, 168.
Inscription on Jahánárá Banú Begum's Tomb, Delhi. [*Proc.* 1872. 169.
Inscription on the Chase of one of the trophy guns formerly belonging to the Bengal Artillery. [*Proc.* 1872, 169.
Remarks on Readings of rare Bengal Coins [*Proc.* 1872, 202.
Koch Bihár, Koch Hájo, and Asám, in the 16th and 17th centuries, according to the Akbarnámah, the Padisháhnámah, and the Fathiyah i 'Ibriyah. [*Jl.* xli, pt. i, 49.
Notes on Arabic and Persian Inscriptions, No. II. [*Jl.* xli, pt. i, 102.
On a new King of Bengal ('Aláuddín Fírúz Sháh). and Notes on the Husaini Kings of Bengal and their Conquest of Chátgáon (Chittagong). [*Jl.* xli, pt. i, 331.
Remarks on Major Stubb's Inscriptions from Lakhnau. [*Proc.* 1873, 11.
Remarks on Mr Growse's Inscriptions from Mathura. [*Proc.* 1873, 12.
General Cunningham's Bengal Inscriptions (Muhammadan Period). [*Proc.* 1873, 17.
Remarks on Bengal Coins and Inscriptions. [*Proc.* 1873, 89.
On Mr. Delmerick's Arabic and Persian Inscriptions from Sonpat and Pánípat. [*Proc.* 1873, 94.
Babu Gunga Parshád's Inscriptions from the Murádábád district, with translations. [*Proc.* 1873, 98.
On Inscriptions received from Jaunpúr, Pánipat and Muzaffarnagar. [*Proc.* 1873, 138.
On two Coins received from the Rev. Mr. Carleton, Rúpar. [*Proc.* 1873, 155.
Readings of General Cunningham's Inscriptions from Raprí, Mahobá and Dihlí; and Mr. T. W. Beale's Inscriptions from Biánah, Ajmír and Agráh. [*Proc.* 1873, 156.

Blochmann, Henry (*contd.*)—
Readings of Col. Guthrie's cast of a Bengal Coin of Firuz Sháh the Second. [*Proc.* 1873, 171.
On Arabic and Persian Inscriptions received from General Cunningham. [*Proc.* 1873, 197.
Contributions to the Geography and History of Bengal (Muhammadan Period).—Pt. I., Geographical. Pt. II., Historical, based on Inscriptions received from General A. Cunningham, Dr. J. Wise, E. V. Westmacott. Esq., W. L. Heeley, Esq., Walter M. Bourke. Esq., &c., and on unpublished Coins; with Notes by E. V. Westmacott, Esq., and Dr. J. Wise. [*Jl.* xlii, pt. i, 209.
Remarks on some Inscriptions received from General Cunningham and Mr. Delmerick. [*Proc.* 1874. 69.
Remarks on a rare Coin of Mahmúd ibn Muhammad Sháh ibn Tughluq Sháh, received from Mr. Delmerick. [*Proc.* 1874, 92.
Remarks on some Inscriptions received from General Cunningham and Messrs. Atkinson and James. [*Proc.* 1874, 100.
Translations and Notes to Readings of Inscriptions received from Mr. T. W. Beale, Agrah. [*Proc.* 1874, 160.
Remarks on three Coins exhibited by Col. H. Hyde. [*Proc.* 1874. 207.
Exhibition of a Persian MS. with Sháhjahán's autograph. [*Proc.* 1874, 208.
Translations and Notes on Inscriptions from Agrah. Sikandrah and Narnaul. [*Proc.* 1874, 209.
Contributions to the Geography and History of Bengal (Muhammadan Period), No. II. [*Jl.* xliii, pt. i, 280.
Readings and Translations of Inscriptions from Jaunpur and Tilbegampur. [*Proc.* 1875, 14.
Exhibition of Bengal Coins belonging to Col. Hyde. [*Proc.* 1875, 112.
Readings of Muhammadan Inscriptions received from Capt. H. C. Marsh and Mr. T. W. Beale, Agrah. [*Proc.* 1875, 113.
Readings and Translations of Inscriptions received from Mr. J. G. Delmerick. [*Proc.* 1875, 212.
Contributions to the History and Geography of Bengal (Muhammadan Period), No. III. [*Jl.* xliv, pt. i, 275.
Readings and Translations of Arabic and Persian Inscriptions from Dihlí, Rohtás and Sahasrám, received from Messrs. Delmerick, Beglar and Major-General A. Cunningham, C.S.I. [*Proc.* 1876, 4.

Blochmann, Henry (*contd.*)—
Exhibition of Coins from Káshghar presented by Dr. Scully; of a unique Gold Coin of Náçir-uddín Mahmúd Sháh; and of a Gold Coin of Muhammad-bin-Tughluq. [*Proc.* 1876, 90.
Exhibition of Muhammadan Inscriptions from Dihlí, Hiçár Fírúzah and Murshídábád. [*Proc.* 1876, 91.
Remarks on a Silver Coin of Sháhjahan II. [*Proc.* 1876, 138.
Readings and Translations of Arabic and Persian Inscriptions received from Messrs. J. G. Delmerick and J. R. Reid. [*Proc.* 1877, 92.
Readings and Translations of some Arabic and Persian Inscriptions from Háñsí, received from Mr. J. G. Delmerick, Dihlí. [*Proc.* 1877, 117.
Exhibition of an Impression taken by General Cunningham from a Rupee struck by Muhammad 'Adil Shah. [*Proc* 1877, 156.
Exhibition of, and Remarks on, some Persian Inscriptions received from Mr. H. James Rainey, Jessore. [*Proc.* 1877, 256.
An unpublished Ghazal by Háfiz. [*Jl.* xlvi, pt. i, 237.
Exhibition of a unique Gold Coin of Julál-uddín Fírúz Sháh (II) of Dihlí. [*Proc.* 1878, 64.
Exhibition of a Persian MS., with a Note. [*Proc.* 1878, 88.
Exhibition of Silver Coins from Burmah. [*Proc.* 1878, 102.

Bloomfield, A.—Letter on pieces of copper and silver from Gungeria. [*Proc.* 1870. 113.

Blundell, E. A.—An Account of some of the Petty States lying north of the Tenasserim Provinces drawn up from the Journals and Reports of Dr. D. Richardson. [*Jl.* v. 601.
An Account of some of the Petty States lying north of the Tenasserim Provinces. [*Jl.* v, 688.

Blunt, Captain James T.—A Description of the Cuttub Minar. [*As. Res.* iv, 313.
Narrative of a Route from Chunarghur to Yertnagoodum, in the Ellore Circar. [*As. Res.* vii, 57.

Blyth, Edward.—A general Review of the Species of True Stag, or Elaphoid form of Cervus, comprising those more immediately related to the Red Deer of Europe. [*Jl.* x, 736.
Description of another new species of Pika (Lagomys) from the Himalaya. [*Jl.* x, 816.

Blyth, Edward (*contd.*)—A Monograph of the species of Wild Sheep. [*Jl.* x, 858.

Descriptions of three Indian Species of Bat, of the genus Taphozous. [*Jl.* x, 971.

Notes on various Indian and Malayan Birds, with Descriptions of some presumed new species. [*Jl.* xi, 160.

Notice of the predatory and sanguivorous habits of the Bats of the genus Megaderma; with some Remarks on the blood-sucking propensities of other Vespertilionidæ. [*Jl.* xi, 255.

A Monograph of the species of Lynx. [*Jl.* xi, 740.

Descriptive Notice of the Bat described as Taphozous longimanus, by Gen. Hardwicke. [*Jl.* xi, 784.

A Monograph of the Indian and Malayan Species of Cuculidæ, or Birds of the Cuckoo family. [*Jl.* xi, 897.

A Monograph of the Indian and Malayan species of Cuculidæ, or Birds of the Cuckoo family (concluded). [*Jl.* xi, 1095.

Supplement to the Monograph of the Indian and Malayan Species of Cuculidæ, or Birds of the Cuckoo family, published in Vol. XI. pp. 898, 1095, *et seq.* [*Jl.* xii, 240.

Notices of various Mammalia, with Description of many New Species. [*Jl.* xiii, 463.

"On the Leiotrichane Birds of the Subhemalayas," by B. H. Hodgson: with some additions and annotations,—a Synopsis of the Indian Pari,—and of the Indian Fringillidæ. [*Jl.* xiii, 933.

Notices and Descriptions of various new or little-known Species of Birds. [*Jl.* xiv, 173.

Description of Caprolagus, a new genus of Leporine Mammalia. [*Jl.* xiv, 247.

Notices and Descriptions of various new or little-known Species of Birds. [*Jl.* xiv, 546.

Drafts for a Fauna Indica. Comprising the Animals of the Himalaya Mountains, those of the Valley of the Indus, of the Provinces of Assam, Sylhet, Tipperah, Arracan, and of Ceylon; with Occasional Notices of Species from the Neighbouring Countries. [*Jl.* xiv, 845.

Notices and Descriptions of various new or little-known Species of Birds. [*Jl.* xv, 1.

Blyth, Edward (*contd.*) — Notices and Descriptions of various new or little-known Species of Birds. [*Jl.* xv, 280.

Notes on the Fauna of the Nicobar Islands. [*Jl.* xv, 367.

Notices and Descriptions of various new or little-known Species of Birds. [*Jl.* xvi, 117.

Some further Notice of the Species of Wild Sheep. [*Jl.* xvi, 350.

Notices and Descriptions of various new or little-known Species of Birds. [*Jl.* xvi, 428.

Reply to the Minute by Capt. Munro, regarding the MS. of the "Burnes Drawings." [*Jl.* xvi, 1168.

A Supplemental Note to the Catalogue of the Birds in the Asiatic Society's Museum. [*Jl.* xviii, 800.

Description of a New Species of Mole (Talpa leucura, Blyth.) [*Jl.* xix, 215.

Remarks on the Modes of Variation of nearly affined Species or Races of Birds, chiefly inhabitants of India. [*Jl.* xix, 221.

Conspectus of the Ornithology of India, Burma and the Malayan Peninsula, inclusive of Sindh, Asám, Ceylon and the Nicobar Islands. [*Jl.* xix, 229.

Conspectus of the Ornithology of India. [*Jl.* xix, 319.

Conspectus of the Ornithology of India, Burma and the Malayan Peninsula, inclusive of Sindh, Asám, Ceylon and the Nicobar Islands. [*Jl.* xix, 501.

Report on the Mammalia and more remarkable species of Birds inhabiting Ceylon. [*Jl.* xx, 153.

Notice of a Collection of Mammalia, Birds and Reptiles procured at or near the station of Chérra Punji in the Khásia hills, north of Sylhet. [*Jl.* xx, 517.

Remarks on the different species of Orang-utan. [*Jl.* xxii, 369.

Notices and Descriptions of various Reptiles, new or little-known. [*Jl.* xxii, 639.

Notices and Descriptions of various Reptiles, new or little-known. [*Jl.* xxiii, 287.

A Monograph of the Indian Species of Phylloscopus and its immediate affines [*Jl.* xxiii, 479.

A Memoir on the Indian Species of Shrews. [*Jl.* xxiv, 24.

Report on a Zoological Collection from the Somáli country. [*Jl.* xxiv, 291

Blyth, Edward (*contd.*) — Further Remarks on the different Species of Orang-utan. [*Jl.* xxiv, 518.
Description of a new Indian Pigeon, akin to the 'Stock Dove' of Europe; with Notices of other Columbinæ. [*Jl.* xxvi, 217.
•On the different Animals known as Wild Asses. [*Jl.* xxviii, 229.
On the Great Rorqual of the Indian Ocean, with Notices of other Cetals, and of the Syrenia or marine Pachyderms. [*Jl.* xxviii, 481.
Note on the Sciuri inhabiting Ceylon and those of the Tenasserim Provinces. [*Jl.* xviii, 600.
The Cartilaginous Fishes of Lower Bengal. [*Jl.* xxix, 35.
Report on some Fishes received chiefly from the Sitang River and its Tributary Streams, Tenasserim Provinces. [*Jl.* xxix, 138.
On the Flat-horned Taurine Cattle of S. E. Asia; with a Note on the Races of Rein Deer, and a Note on Domestic Animals in general. [*Jl.* xxix, 282.
Note on the Races of Rein Deer. [*Jl.* xxix, 37.
A Memoir on the living Asiatic specie of Rhinoceros. [*Jl.* xxxi, 151.
A Further Note on Elephants and Rhinoceroses. [*Jl.* xxxi, 196.
A Further Note on Wild Asses and alleged Wild Horses. [*Jl.* xxxi, 363.
A Memoir on the Rats and Mice of India. [*Jl.* xxxii, 327.
Catalogue of the Mammals of Burma. Edited, with Notes and Additions, by Dr. J. Anderson. [*Jl.* xliv, pt. ii, Extra No, 1.
Catalogue of the Birds of Burma. Edited, with Notes and Additions, by Arthur Viscount Walden. [*Jl.* xliv, pt. ii, Extra No., 34.
See **Hodgson, B. H.**; **Hutton, Capt. T.**

Boag, W.—On the Poison of Serpents. [*As. Res.* vi, 103.

Boats, Comparative Section and Tonnage of English and Indian, for River Navigation. [*Jl.* iii, 136.

Boileau, Major J. T.—Description of a Sundial in the Court of the Moti Musjid, in the Fort of Agra. [*Jl.* ii, 251.
Remarks on the Construction of Newman's Improved Portable Barometer, and on the mode of renewing the Gauge Point when lost. [*Jl.* x, 957.

Boileau, Major J. T. (*contd.*) — Observations of Meteors on the night between the 12th and 13th November 1841, made at the Magnetic Observatory at Simla. [*Jl.* x, 964.
Tables for determining the Elastic Force of Aqueous Vapour in the Atmosphere and the Temperature of the Dew-Point, by Observations of a Dry and Wet-bulb Thermometer: computed agreeably to Dr. Apjohn's Hygrometric Formula. [*Jl.* xiii, 135.
See **Ivory,**—

Boria, Cavelly.—Account of the Jains, collected from a Priest of this Sect; at Mudgeri. [*As. Res.* ix, 244.

Boring Experiment, Report of the Committee appointed on the 27th March, 1833, to consider on the expediency of recommending to the Government the continuance of the. [*Jl.* ii, 369.

Bose, Kishen Kant.—Some Account of the Country of Bhútan. [*As. Res.* xv, 128.

Bose, P. N.—Note on some Earthen Pots found in the alluvium at Mahesvara (Mahesar). [*Jl.* li, pt. i, 226.
Note on Máhishmatí or Mahesvara (Mahesar) on the Narmadá, and the Identification of Hiouen Thsang's 'Muhesvarapura.' [*Proc.* 1883, 127.

Bose, Rashbihari.—Extracts from my Diary regarding the Bonhara Temple near Omerpore, Behar and other Antiquities of the place. [*Jl.* xxxix, pt. i, 232.
Letter on Kharakpúr. [*Proc.* 1871, 98.
Extracts from my Diary regarding a Visit to Kharakpúr, in the district of Munger (Moughyr), and several places in the Banka Subdivision, Bhágalpúr. [*Jl.* xl, pt. i, 22.
Legends and Ballads connected with persons deified or held in great veneration in Bhágalpúr and the neighbouring districts (being extracts from diaries). [*Jl.* xl, pt. i, 183.

Boulderson, H. S. — Astronomical Observations at Barelly. [*Jl.* ii, 318.
Meteorological Register at Barelly in 1831. [*Jl.* ii, 641.
Abstract Statement of 412 Villages in Zilla Bareilly. Settlement under Regulation VII. 1822. [*Jl.* iii, 475.

Boulderson, S. M.—Abstract of a Meteorological Register kept at 'Caineville,' Mussooree (Masúrí). [*Jl.* iv, 230.

Bowring, L.—Descriptive Notice of the District of Jhilum. [*Jl.* xix, 43.

Bowring, L. (*contd.*)—On Mysore Inscriptions. [*Proc.* 1865, 112.
On Mysore Aerolites. [*Proc.* 1865, 195
Kashmírí Vocabulary and Grammatical Forms.
[*Jl.* xxxv, pt. ii, Extra No., 225.
Letter on Cromlechs in Coorg.
[*Proc* 1869, 59.

Boyes, Capt. W. J. E—Extract from Note Book regarding the genus Paussus. [*Jl.* xii, 421.

Brandis, Dr. D.—Exhibition of Specimens of Indian Timbers.
[*Proc.* 1878, 86.

Branfill, Lieut.-Col. B. R.—Physiographical Notes, &c., on Tanjore (Tanjá-úr). [*Jl.* xlvii, pt. ii, 179.
Description of the Great Siva Temple of Gangai Kondapuram and of some other places in the Trichinopoli district [*Jl.* xlix, pt. i, 1.
Rude Megalithic Monuments in North Arcot. [*Jl.* xlix, pt. i, 8.

Brett, F. H.—Concerning certain interesting Phenomena manifested in individuals born blind, and in those having little or no recollection of that sense, on their being restored to sight at various periods of life.
[*Jl.* vi, 47.

Broadley, A. M.—The Buddhistic Remains of Bihár. [*Jl.* xli, pt. i, 209.

Brodie, Capt.—Narrative of a Tour over that part of the Naga Hills lying between the Diko and Dyang river. [*Jl.* xiv, 828.

Brooke, Capt. J. C.—Note on the Zinc Mines of Jáwar. [*Jl.* xix, 212.
The Mines of Khetree in Rajpootana
[*Jl.* xxxiii, 519.

Brooks, W. E.—Description of a new Species of Abrornis. [*Proc.* 1871, 248
The Swans of India [*Proc.* 1872, 63.
The Imperial Eagles of India.
[*Proc.* 1872, 64.
On a New Indian Sylvia.
[*Proc.* 1872, 66.
On a New Species of Reguloides.
[*Proc.* 1872, 148.
Notes on the Ornithology of Cashmir.
[*Jl.* xli, pt. ii, 73.
On two undescribed Cashmir Birds.
[*Jl.* xli, pt. ii, 327.
Notes on *Aquila nævioides, A. fulvescens* and *A. vindhiana.*
[*Proc.* 1873, 173.
On an undescribed species of Lophophanes. [*Jl.* xlii, pt. ii, 57.
On Aquila bifasciata and Aquila orientalis. [*Jl.* xlii, pt. ii, 145.
Notes on the Certhiinæ of India.
[*Jl.* xlii, pt. ii, 255.

Brooks, W. E. (*contd.*)—Some Ornithological Notes and Corrections.
[*Jl.* xliii, pt. ii, 239.
On an apparently unnamed species of *Phænicopterus.* [*Proc.* 1875, 17.
Postscript to Description of *Phænicopterus Andersoni.* [*Proc.* 1875, 48.
See **Anderson, Dr. J.**

Broome, Lieut. A.; and Cunningham, Lieut. A.—Abstract Journal of the Routes of Lieutenants A. Broome and A. Cunningham, to the sources of the Punjab rivers.
[*Jl.* x, 1.

Brough, R. S.—On the proper relative Sectional Areas for Copper and Iron Lightning Rods. [*Jl.* xlvii, pt. ii, 191.
On a Case of Lightning, with an evolution of the Potential and Quantity of the Discharge in Absolute Measure [*Proc.* 1877, 56.
On the Diameter of the Wire to be employed in winding an Electromagnet in order to produce the maximum Magnetic effect.
[*Proc.* 1877, 134.
A Theoretical Deduction of the best Resistance of a Telegraph Receiving Instrument. [*Proc.* 1877, 184.
Exhibition of Professor Graham Bell's Telephone. [*Proc.* 1877, 252.
A few Magnetic Elements for Northern India. [*Proc.* 1878, 69.

Brown, A.—Ceremonies observed at the Coronation of a Hindu Raja.
[*As. Res.* xiii, 311.

Brown, Revd. N.—Alphabets of the Tai language. [*Jl.* vi, 17.
Comparison of Indo-Chinese Languages
[*Jl.* vi, 1023.
Memorandum of various Phænomena in 1843. [*Jl.* xii, 909.

Brown, Capt. Wm.—Account of an Ancient Temple at Hissar, and of the Ship Model at that place. [*Jl.* vii, 429.

Browne, Capt. H. A.—The Pegu Pagoda. [*Jl.* xxxvi, pt. i, 109.

Brownlow, C.—Note on the Occasional Existence of Fresh Water on the surface of the Ocean. [*Jl.* v, 236.
Description of a Bachelors' Hall among the Mikir Tribes, Assam.
[*Proc.* 1874, 17.

Bruce, C. A.—Report on the Manufacture of Tea, and on the Extent and Produce of the Tea Plantations in Assam. [*Jl.* viii, 497.

Bruce, J. G.—A Letter to the Secretary on the Nurma Cotton of Bundelcund. [*Jl.* x, 822.

Buchanan, Dr. Francis.—Description of the Tree called by the Burmas, Launzan. [*As. Res.* v, 123.
A Comparative Vocabulary of some of the Languages spoken in the Burma Empire. [*As. Res.* v, 219.
On the Religion and Literature of the Burmas. [*As. Res.* vi, 163.
History of Cooch Behár, being an extract of a passage from Dr. Buchanan's Account of Rungpur (Rungapura). [*Jl.* vii, 1.

Buddh Gya in Behár, translation of an Inscription in the Pali character and Burmese language on a stone at. [*Jl.* iii, 214.

Buhler, George.—A Translation of the Chapter on Ordeals, from the Vyavahâra Mayúkha [*Jl.* xxxv, pt. i, 14
A Notice of the S'aunaka Smriti. [*Jl.* xxxv, pt. i, 149.
Account of a Recent Tour through Western Rajputana in search of Sanskrit MSS. [*Proc.* 1874, 93.

Buist, Dr. George.—On the General Vibration, or Descent and Upheaval, which seems, at a recent Geological Period, to have occurred all over the Northern Hemisphere. [*Jl.* xix, 302.
On the Encrustation of Steam Boilers and Pipes in India. [*Jl.* xix, 419.
Floods in India for 1849. [*Jl.* xx, 186.
On the Adaptation of the Aneroid for the purposes of Surveying in India. [*Jl.* xx, 320.
On the Oriental Character of certain Northern Antiquities. [*Jl.* xxi, 127.

Burgess, James.—On Hypsometrical Measurements by means of the Barometer and the Boiling-point Thermometer. [*Jl.* xxvii, 337.

Burke, Dr.—Report on the Value of Life among the Officers and Men in H. Majesty's Troops in India. [*Jl.* viii, 48.

Burn, A.—On the Cotton called "Nurma," in Guzerat. [*Jl.* xi, 290.

Burnell, A. C.—Extract from a pamphlet on making Copies of Indian Inscriptions. [*Proc.* 1874, 125
On the Invasion of Bengal by the Chola King Kulottunga. [*Proc.* 1876, 107.

Burnes, Capt. Alexander. — Some Account of the Salt Mines of the Punjab. [*Jl.* i, 145,
Account of the Jain Temples on Mount Abú in Guzerat. [*Jl.* ii, 161.
Description of Bokhára. [*Jl.* ii, 224.

Burnes, Capt. Alexander (*contd.*)—
On the reputed Descendants of Alexander the Great, in the valley of the Oxus. [*Jl.* ii, 305.
On the "Topes" and Grecian Remains in Punjab. [*Jl.* ii, 308.
Description of the Salt Works at Panchpadder, Mewár. [*Jl.* ii, 365.
On the Colossal Idols of Bamián. [*Jl.* ii, 561.
On the Reg-Ruwan, or moving sand: a singular phenomenon of sound near Cabul. [*Jl.* vii, 324.
On the Siah-pósh Kaffirs, with specimens of their language and costume. [*Jl.* vii, 325.
Report on ten specimens of Coal from Capt. Burnes. [*Jl.* vii, 848.

Burnes, Capt. Alexander; and Gerard, Dr.—A Sketch of the Route and Progress of Lieut. A. Burnes and Dr. Gerard. [*Jl.* i. 139.
Continuation of the Route of Lieut. A. Burnes and Dr. Gerard, from Péshawar to Bokhara. [*Jl.* ii, 1.
Continuation of Dr. Gerard's Route with Lieut. Burnes, from Bokhara to Meshid. [*Jl.* ii, 143.

Burney, Lt.-Col. H.—Translation of an Inscription in the Burmese Language, discovered at Buddha Gaya, in 1833. [*As. Res.* xx, pt. i, 161.
Some Account of the Lacquered or Japanned Ware of Ava. [*Jl.* i, 169.
Memoir of Giuseppe d'Amato. [*Jl.* i, 349.
Notice of Pugan, the Ancient Capital of the Burmese Empire. [*Jl.* iv, 400.
Discovery of Buddhist Images with Deva-Nágarí Inscriptions at Tagoung, the Ancient Capital of the Burmese Empire. [*Jl.* v, 157.
Some Account of the Wars between Burmah and China, together with the Journals and Routes of three different Embassies sent to Pekin by the King of Ava; taken from Burmese documents. [*Jl.* vi, 121.
Some Account of the Wars between Burmah and China, together with the Journals and Routes of three different Embassies sent to Pekin by the King of Ava; taken from Burmese documents. [*Jl.* vi, 405, 542.

Burr, Captain C.B.—Extract from a journal, during the late Campaign in Egypt. [*As. Res.* viii, 35.

Burrow, Reuben.—Hints relative to Friction in Mechanics. [*As. Res.* i, 171.

Burrow, Reuben (*contd.*) — A Method of Calculating the Moon's Parallaxes, in Latitude and Longitude [*As. Res.* i, 320.

Remarks on the Artificial Horizons, &c. [*As. Res.* i, 327.

Demonstration of a Theorem concerning the Intersections of Curves. [*As. Res.* i, 330.

Corrections of the Lunar Method of finding the Longitude. [*As. Res.* i, 433.

A Synopsis of the different cases that may happen in deducing the Longitude of one place from another by means of Arnold's Chronometers, and of finding the rates when the differences of Longitude is given. [*As. Res.* ii, 473.

Memorandums concerning an old Building in the Hadjipur district, near the Gunduck river. [*As. Res.* ii, 477.

Observations of some Eclipses of Jupiter's Satellites. [*As. Res.* ii, 483.

A Proof that the Hindus had the Binomial Theorem. [*As. Res.* ii, 487.

A specimen of a Method of reducing Practical Tables and Calculations into more general and compendious forms. [*As. Res.* iii, 141.

Table of Latitudes and Longitudes of some principal places in India, determined from astronomical observations. [*As. Res.* iv, 325.

Burt, Adam.—On the Dissection of the Pangolin. [*As. Res.* ii, 353.

Burt, Capt. T. S.—Description of an Instrument for trisecting Angles. [*Jl.* i, 499.

Description of the Mode of extracting Salt from the damp Sand-beds of the River Jumna, as practised by the inhabitants of Bundelkhand. [*Jl.* iii, 33.

A Description, with Drawings, of the Ancient Stone Pillar at Allahabad called Bhim Sen's Gadá or Club, with accompanying copies of four inscriptions engraven in different characters upon its surface. [*Jl.* iii, 105.

Notice of an Inscription on a Slab discovered in February, 1838. [*Jl.* viii, 159.

Inscription found near Bhabra, three marches from Jeypore on the road to Delhi. [*Jl.* ix, 616.

Inscription taken from a Baolee at Bussuntgurh, at the foot of the southern range of hills running parallel to Mount Aboo. [*Jl.* x, 664.

Burt, Capt. T. S. (*contd.*) — Observations on a second Inscription taken in fac-simile from the neighbourhood of Mount Aboo. [*Jl.* x, 821.

Burt, Capt. T. S.; and Cunningham, Capt. A.—Lithographs and Translations of Inscriptions taken in ectype by Captain T. S. Burt: and of one from Ghosi taken by Captain A. Cunningham. [*Jl.* vii, 629.

Burt's Trisection Instrument, Defence of Lieutenant. [*Jl.* ii, 486.

Busteed, Dr. H. E.—On the Method of Assaying Silver adopted in the Assay Offices of H. M.'s Indian Mints. [*Jl.* xxxix. pt. ii, 377.

Butler Dr. D. — On the Preparation of Opium for the China market: written in March 1835, and then communicated to the Benares and Behár Agencies. [*Jl.* v, 165.

Butler, J. — Earthquakes in Assam. [*Jl.* xviii, 172.

Butler, Capt. John.—A Rough Comparative Vocabulary of Tribes in the Nágá Hills District. [*Jl.* xlii, pt. i, Appendix, I.

A Rough Comparative Vocabulary of two more of the Dialects spoken in the "Nágá Hills." [*Jl.* xliv, pt. i, 216.

Rough Notes on the Angámi Nágás and their Language. [*Jl.* xliv, pt. i, 307.

Bysack, Gaur Das.—On the Gopalpore Aerolite. [*Proc.* 1865, 94.

The Antiquities of Bagerhat. [*Jl.* xxxvi. pt. i, 118.

Note on Khánjá Khán Garh in the district of Bardwán, Jahánábád Subdivision, Bengal. [*Jl.* xlvi, pt. i, 165.

Calcutta, Bishop of — On Cave Temples. [*Proc.* 1865, 163.

On Temple in Kashmir. [*Proc.* 1865, 165.

Calcutta, Population and Mortality in. [*Jl.* vii, 888.

Calder, James. — General Observations on the Geology of India. [*As. Res* xviii, pt. i, 1.

Camel Draught, Documents relative to the application of, to Carriages. [*Jl* viii. 591.

Campbell, Dr. A.—On the Notice of Alum or Salájit of Nipal. [*Jl.* ii, 482.

Account of the Earthquake at Kathmandú. [*Jl.* ii, 564.

Further particulars of the Earthquake in Nipal. [*Jl.* ii, 636.

On the Népâlese Method of Refining Gold. [*Jl.* iii, 622.

Campbell, Dr. A. (*contd.*) — Notice of the Nipalese Spirit Still. [*Jl.* iv, 282.

Notes on the State of the Arts of Cotton Spinning. Weaving. Printing, and Dyeing in Nepál. [*Jl.* v, 219.

Notes taken at the post mortem examination of a Musk Deer. [*Jl.* vi, 118.

Abstract of a Meteorological Register kept at the Cathmandu Residency for 1837. [*Jl.* vi, 610.

Abstract of Meteorological Register kept at the Cathmandu Residency for July and August, 1837. [*Jl.* vi. 889.

Notes on the Musical Instruments and Agricultural and other Instruments of the Nipalese. [*Jl.* vi. 953.

Note on the Mechis, together with a small Vocabulary of the Language. [*Jl.* viii, 623.

Note on the Lepchas of Sikkim, with a Vocabulary of their Language. [*Jl.* ix, 379.

Note on the Limboos and other Hill Tribes hitherto undescribed. [*Jl.* ix, 495.

On the Literature and Origin of certain Hill Tribes in Sikkim. [*Jl.* xi, 4.

Report of the Death of Mr. Csoma de Körös, made to G. A. Bushby, Esq. Officiating Secretary, Political Department. [*Jl.* xi, 303

Memorandum on the "Bora Chung" of Bootan. [*Jl.* xi, 963.

Itinerary from Phari in Thibet to Lassa. with appended Routes from Darjeeling to Phari. [*Jl.* xvii, pt. i, 257.

Routes from Darjeeling to Thibet. [*Jl.* xvii, pt. ii, 488.

On the Elevation of Peaks in the Himalaya, &c. [*Jl.* xvii. pt. ii, 576.

Journal of a Trip to Sikim, in December 1848, with Sketch Map. [*Jl.* xviii, 482.

Answers to Mr. Piddington's Query about Winds, Storms, &c. in Thibet. [*Jl.* xix, 457.

A Journey through Sikim to the frontiers of Thibet. [*Jl.* xxi. 407.

A Journey through Sikim to the frontiers of Thibet. [*Jl.* xxi, 477.

A Journey through Sikim to the frontiers of Thibet. [*Jl.* xxi, 563.

Note on the Limboo Alphabet of the Sikim Himalaya. [*Jl.* xxiv, 202.

Notes on Eastern Thibet (with Sketch Map of Route to Lassa). [*Jl.* xxiv, 215.

A Register of the Temperature of the Surface of the Ocean from the Hooghly to the Thames. [*Jl.* xxvii, 170.

Campbell, Dr. A. (*contd.*) — *See* **Hodgson, B. H.; Lloyd, Lt.-Col.**

Campbell, C.—Memorandum on the life-sized Statues lately exhumed inside the Palace of Delhi. [*Jl.* xxxiii, 159.

Notes on the History and Topography of the Ancient Cities of Delhi. [*Jl.* xxxv, pt. i, 199.

Campbell, Hon'ble G. — On Indian Ethnology. [*Proc.* 1865, 142.

On Languages of Cashmir. [*Proc.* 1866, 46, 62.

On Ethnological Exhibition. [*Proc.* 1866, 71, 87, 188.

On Translation of Technical Terms. [*Proc.* 1866, 141, 177.

The Ethnology of India. [*Jl.* xxxv, pt. ii, Extra No., 1.

List of Words and Phrases to be noted and used as test-words for the discovery of the radical affinities of languages, and for easy comparison. Comparative Table of Aboriginal Words. Comparative Table of Northern and Arian Words. [*Jl.* xxxv, pt. ii, Extra No., 201.

On Mon Languages. [*Proc.* 1867, 51.

Campbell, Capt. J.—Report on the Soda Soils of the Barramahal. [*Jl.* x, 159.

Report on the Kaolin Earth of Mysore. [*Jl.* x, 163.

Report upon the Manufacture of Steel in Southern India. [*Jl.* xi, 217.

Report upon the Improvement of the Silk manufactured in Mysore and the Salem districts. [*Jl.* xi, 218.

Report upon the Construction of Philosophical Instruments in India. [*Jl.* xi, 293.

Manual of Chemistry. [*Jl.* xi, 297.

Campbell, J. F.—On Himalayan Glaciation. [*Jl.* xlvi, pt. ii, 1.

Campbell, Capt. J. H. — *See* **Piddington, H.**

Campbell, Capt. W. M. — Notes on the Transit of Venus of 1874. [*Proc.* 1874, 241.

Canal, Selections from Correspondence respecting the proposed formation of a, for Irrigation, to be supplied from the river Jumna, near the village of Kuttha Putthur, in the Deyra Doon. [*Jl.* xi, 761.

Cantor, Dr. Theodore. — Sketch of an undescribed Hooded Serpent with Fangs and Maxillar Teeth. [*As. Res.* xix, pt. i, 87.

Notice of a Skull (fragment) of a gigantic Fossil Batrachian. [*Jl.* vi, 538.

Cantor, Dr. Theodore (*contd.*) — Catalogue of Mammalia inhabiting the Malayan Peninsula and Islands, collected or observed. [*Jl.* xv, 171, 241.

On Teredo Navalis and a natural defence against its ravages, by Mr. Lehmann: from the Transactions of the Scandinavian Naturalists of Copenhagen, 1840; translated and communicated, [*Jl.* xvi, 487

Catalogue of Reptiles inhabiting the Malayan Peninsula and Islands, collected or observed. [*Jl.* xvi, 607, 897, 1026.

Catalogue of Malayan Fishes. [*Jl.* xviii, 987.

See **Benson, W. H.**

Carey, V. J.—On Stone Spindle Whorls. [*Proc.* 1866, 135.

Carey, Rev. Dr. William.—Remarks on the State of Agriculture in the District of Dinájpur. [*As. Res.* x, 1.

An Account of the Funeral Ceremonies of a Burman Priest. [*As. Res.* xii, 186.

Carlleyle, A. C. L.—Descriptions of two new species belonging to the genera *Varanus* and *Feranioides*, respectively. [*Jl.* xxxviii, pt. ii, 192.

Coins of the S'unga or Mitra Dynasty, found near Rámanagar or Ahichhatra, the ancient Capital of North Panchála, in Rohilkhand:—the property of H. Rivett-Carnac, Esq. [*Jl.* xlix, pt. i, 21.

Carloss, Lieut.—Account of a Journey to Beylah, and Memoir on the Province of Lus. [*Jl.* viii, 184.

Carnac, H. Rivett-.—*See* **Rivett-Carnac, H.**

Carnegy, Patrick.—Queries regarding the Races of India. [*Proc.* 1868, 86.

The Bhars of Audh and Banáras. [*Jl.* xlv, pt. i, 297.

Carte, W. E.—Notice of Amulets in use by the Trans-Himalayan Boodhists. [*Jl.* ix, 904.

Carter, H. J.—Report on Geological Specimens from the Persian Gulf, collected by Lieut. C. G. Constable, I. N. [*Jl.* xxviii, 41; xxix, 359.

Casi Raja, Pundit.—An Account of the Battle of Paniput, and of the events leading to it. [*As. Res.* iii, 91.

Caul, Goverdhan.—On the Literature of the Hindus. [*As. Res.* i, 340.

Cautley, Capt. P. T.—Notice of the occurrence of Coal and Lignite in the Himalaya. [*As. Res.* xvi, 387.

Note on the Fossil Crocodile of the Seválik Hills. [*As. Res.* xix, pt. i, 25.

Cautley, Capt. P. T. (*contd.*) — The Fossil Ghariál of the Siválik Hills. [*As. Res.* xix, pt. i, 32.

On Gypsum of the Himalaya. [*Jl.* i, 289.

Discovery of an ancient town near Behut, in the Doab. [*Jl.* iii, 43.

Further Account of the remains of an ancient town discovered at Behat, near Seharanpur. [*Jl.* iii, 221.

Note on the Gold Washing of the Gúmtí River. [*Jl.* iv, 279.

Note on the Teeth of the Mastodon à dents étroites of the Siwálik Hills. [*Jl.* v, 294.

Note on Mastodons of the Sewaliks. [*Jl.* v, 768.

Note on a Fossil Ruminant genus allied to Giraffidæ in the Siwalik Hills. [*Jl.* vii, 658.

On the Use of Wells, &c., in Foundations; as practised by the natives of the Northern Doab. [*Jl.* viii, 327.

On the Fossil Remains of Camelidæ of the Sewaliks. [*Jl.* ix, 620.

Cautley, Capt. P. T.; and Falconer, Dr. Hugh.—Note on the Ursus Sivalensis, a new fossil species from the Siválik Hills. [*As. Res.* xix, pt. i, 193.

Synopsis of Fossil Genera and Species from the upper deposits of the tertiary strata of the Siválik Hills, in the collection of the authors. [*Jl.* iv, 706.

See **Falconer, Dr. Hugh.**

Cayley, Dr. H.—Remarks on Himálayan Glaciation. [*Proc.* 1877, 4.

Celestial Objects, Catalogue of the most remarkable, visible in the horizon of Calcutta, arranged in order of Right Ascension. [*Jl.* ii, 252.

Cervus Duvaucelii of Cuvier, or C. Elaphoides and Bahraiya of Hodgson, Note on the. [*Jl.* v, 240.

Cesspools in Calcutta, on the utility of. [*Jl.* i, 100.

Chakravarti, Pandit Haradhandra.—*See* **Ghosha, Pratapa Chandra.**

Chambers, Sir Robert.—A Discourse delivered at a Meeting of the Asiatick Society on the 18th of January, 1798. [*As. Res.* vi, 1.

Chambers, William.—Some Account of the Sculptures and Ruins at Mavalipuram, a place few miles north of Sadras, and known to seamen by the name of the Seven Pagodas. [*As. Res.* i, 145.

Champion, Capt. — Notice on the *Coleoptera* of Hong-Kong. [*Jl.* xvii, pt. ii, 206.

Chandra, Jaya.—Note on a Copper Land-Grant. [*Jl.* x, 98.

Chapman, Dr. H.—Meteorological Register kept at Darjíling for the months of April, May, June and July, 1837. [*Jl.* vi, 700.

Meteorological Register kept at Darjíling for August, 1837. [*Jl.* vi, 888.

Chapman. J. S.—Notes on the Gems found at Beghram. [*Jl* x, 613.

Charagh Ali.—*See* **Wade, Capt. C. M.**

Chatterjee, Chunder Seekur.—On Whirlwind at Pandooah. [*Proc.* 1865, 124.

Chinese Map of India. [*Jl.* xvii, pt. ii, 60.

Christian, J.—Prashnotaramálá, or Catechetical Dialogue of Sook. Translated. [*Jl.* xvi, 1228.

Christie, A. T.—On Porcelain Clay found at Mangalore. [*Jl.* x, 967.

Clarke, Hyde.—Assyro-Pseudo-Sesostris. [*Jl.* xxxv, pt. 1, 87.

Clayton, Serjeant C.—Description of the Tomb of an Ahom Noble, in a letter to Major S. F Hannay. [*Jl.* xvii, pt. i. 473.

Clint, L.—A Tale by Inshá Allah Khán. [*Jl.* xxi, 1.

Coal Beds of Assam. Report upon the. (Submitted to Government by the Committee appointed to investigate the Coal and Iron resources of the Bengal Presidency, as a supplement to their first printed Report.) [*Jl.* vii, 948.

Coal Committee, Report of the. [*Jl.* ix, 198.

Coal Field of Tenasserim, Papers relative to the new. [*Jl.* viii. 385.

Coal, Note on the, discovered at Khyúk Phyú, in the Arracan District. [*Jl.* ii, 595.

Coal, Table of Indian, analyzed at the Calcutta Assay Office, including those published in the Gleanings in Science. September 1831, arranged according to localities; extracted from the Report of the Coal Committee. [*Jl.* vii, 197.

Cockburn, John.—Notes on Stone Implements from the Khasi Hills, and the Banda and Vellore Districts. [*Jl.* xlviii. pt. ii, 133.

Exhibition of Stone Implements by. [*Proc.* 1882, 6.

Exhibition of a Panchamukha Lingam. [*Proc.* 1882, 47.

Note on Torsion in the Awns of Spear grass. [*Proc.* 1882, 49.

Remarks on Earthen Vessels, &c., from Mahesar. [*Proc.* 1882, 105.

Cockburn, John (*contd.*) — On a case of Polydactylism in a horse. [*Proc.* 1882, 115.

On an Abnormality in the horns of the Hog-deer, *Axis porcinus*, with an amplification of the theory of the evolution of antlers in Ruminants. [*Jl.* li. pt. ii, 45.

On the Habits of a little-known Lizard, *Brachysaura Ornata.* [*Jl.* li. pt. ii, 50.

On the Recent Existence of *Rhinoceros Indicus* in the North-Western Provinces; and a Description of a tracing of an archaic rock painting from Mirzapur representing the hunting of this animal. [*Jl.* lii, pt. ii, 56.

Cole, Capt. R. A.—On Cromlechs of, in Coorg. [*Proc.* 1868, 151, 184, 243; 1869, 54.

Extract from a Report on Cromlechs in Southern India. [*Proc.* 1869, 202.

Memorandum on certain Copper Grants found in the Malnád, with translations of the inscriptions. [*Proc.* 1872, 193.

Colebrooke, Henry Thomas.—On the Duties of a Faithful Hindu Widow. [*As. Res.* iv, 209.

Enumeration of Indian Classes. [*As. Res.* v, 53.

On Indian Weights and Measures. [*As. Res.* v, 91.

On the Religious Ceremonies of the Hindus, and of the Bráhmens especially. [*As. Res.* v, 345; vii. 232, 288.

Translation of one of the Inscriptions on the Pillar at Dehlee, called the Lát of Ferroz Shah. [*As. Res.* vii, 175.

On the Sanscrit and Prácrit Languages. [*As. Res.* vii, 199.

On the Origin and Peculiar Tenets of certain Muhammedan Sects. [*As. Res.* vii, 338.

On the Védas, or Sacred Writings of the Hindus. [*As. Res.* viii, 369.

Description of a Species of Ox named Gayal. [*As. Res.* viii, 487.

Observations on the Sect of Jains. [*As. Res.* ix. 287.

On the Indian and Arabian Divisions of the Zodiack. [*As. Res.* ix, 323.

On Olibanum or Frankincense. [*As. Res.* ix, 377.

On Sanscrit and Prácrit Poetry. [*As. Res.* x, 389.

On Ancient Monuments containing Sanscrit Inscriptions. [*As. Res.* ix, 398.

On the Sources of the Ganges in the Himádri or Emodus. [*As. Res.* xi, 429.

Colebrooke, Henry Thomas (*contd.*) — On the Notions of the Hindu Astronomers concerning the Precession of the Equinoxes and Motions of the Planets. [*As. Res.* xii, 209.

On the Height of the Himálaya Mountains. [*As. Res.* xii, 251.

On the *Dryobalanops Camphora*, or Camphor-tree of Sumatra. [*As. Res.* xii, 535.

Colebrooke, Major R. H.—On the Islands Nancoury and Comarty. [*As. Res.* iv, 129.

Astronomical Observations made on a Voyage to the Andaman and Nicobar Islands. [*As. Res.* iv, 317.

Astronomical Observations made on a Survey through the Carnatic and Mysore Country. [*As. Res.* iv, 321.

On the Andaman Islands. [*As. Res.* iv, 385.

On Barren Island and its Volcano. [*As. Res.* iv, 397.

On the Course of the Ganges through Bengal. [*As. Res.* vii, 1.

Coleopterous Insects, Instructions for collecting and preserving. [*Jl.* i, 324.

Colvin, A. — Translations from the Táríkh-i-Fírúz Sháhí. The Reign of Ghiásuddín Tughluq. [*Jl.* xl, pt. i, 217.

Colvin, Colonel—On the Restoration of the Ancient Canals in the Delhi Territory. [*Jl.* ii, 105.

Catalogue of a Second Collection of Fossil Bones presented to the Asiatic Society's Museum. [*Jl.* v, 179.

Horary Observations taken at Dádúpur. in conformity with Sir John Herschel's Circular. [*Jl.* v, 299.

Conolly, Capt. Arthur. — Extracts from Demi-Official Reports on a Mission into Khorasan. [*Jl.* x, 116.

Conolly, Lieut. Edward.—Observations upon the past and present condition of Oujein or Ujjayani. [*Jl.* vi, 813.

Note of Discoveries of Gems from Khandahar. [*Jl.* ix, 97.

Sketch of the Physical Geography of Seistan. [*Jl.* ix, 710.

Notes on the Eusofzye Tribes of Afghanistan. [*Jl.* ix, 924.

Journal kept while travelling in Seistan. [*Jl.* x, 319.

Cooper, T. T. — Notes on Western China. [*Proc.* 1869, 143.

Cope, Henry.—Letter to the Editor, on Lichens in the Himalayas. [*Jl.* x, 828.

Cope, Henry (*contd.*) — A Connected View of the species of Lichens, with their Botanical relationship existing between them and the Indian productions. [*Jl.* x, 888.

Memorandum regarding the recently discovered Ruins of Ranode in Scindeah's Dominions. [*Jl.* xvi, 1079.

Public Inscriptions at Lahore. [*Jl.* xxvii, 308.

Cope, Henry; and Lewis, Henry.—Some Account of the Town and Palace of Feerozabad, in the vicinity of Delhi, with Introductory Remarks on the Sites of other Towns. [*Jl.* xvi, 971.

See **Lewis, Lieut. Henry.**

Corse, John.—An Account of the Method of Catching Wild Elephants at Tipura. [*As. Res.* iii, 229.

Costello, Dr. C. P. — Observations on the Geological Features, &c., of the country in the neighbourhood of Bunnoo and the Sanatorium of Shaikh Boodeen. [*Jl.* xxxiii. 378.

Costley, W. C.—On Fall of Aerolite at Shergotty. [*Proc.* 1865, 194.

Coulthard, Capt. S. — The Trap formation of the Ságor district, and of those districts westward of it, as far as Bhopalpur on the banks of the river Newas, in Omatwara. [*As. Res.* xviii, pt. i, 47.

Court, A.—Further Information on the Topes of Manikyála, being the translation of an Extract from a Manuscript Memoir on Ancient Taxila. [*Jl.* iii, 556.

Conjectures on the March of Alexander. [*Jl.* v, 387.

Extracts translated from a Memoir on a Map of Peshâwar and the Country comprised between the Indus and the Hydaspes, the Peucelaotis and Taxila of ancient geography. [*Jl.* v, 468.

Collection of Facts which may be useful for the comprehension of Alexander the Great's exploits on the western banks of the Indus. [*Jl.* viii, 304.

Cowell, E. B.—On the Swayamvara of the Ancient Hindús, and its traces in the ancient world generally. [*Jl.* xxviii, 31.

On certain Mediæval Apologues. [*Jl.* xxix, 10.

Attempts of Asiatic Sovereigns to establish a Paper Currency [*Jl.* xxix, 183.

On a Passage in the Tenth Book of the Sáhitya Darpana. [*Jl.* xxix, 217.

Cowell, E. B. (*contd.*) — The Kiránus-Sa'dain of Mír Khusrau. [*Jl.* xxix, 225.

Gyges' ring in Plato and Nizámí. [*Jl.* xxx, 151.

The Chárváka System of Philosophy. [*Jl.* xxxi, 371.

On Toles of Nuddea. [*Proc.* 1867, 87.

Cowie, W. G.—Notes on some of the Temples of Kashmir, especially those not described by General A. Cunningham in his Essay published in the Journal of the Asiatic Society of Bengal for September. 1848. [*Jl.* xxxv, pt. i, 91.

Cowles, Capt. C.—Description of the Anglometer, an instrument for working Lunar Calculations. [*Jl.* i, 551.

Cox, Capt. Hiram.—An Account of the Petroleum Wells in the Burmha Dominions, extracted from journal of a voyage from Ranghong up the river Erai-Wuddey to Amarapoorah, the present capital of the Burmha Empire. [*As. Res.* vi, 127.

On the Burmha Game of Chess; compared with the Indian, Chinese, and Persian Game of the same denomination. [*As. Res.* vii, 486.

Cracroft, William.—Notes relative to the Collection of some Geological Specimens in the Kasia Hills between Assam and Nanklow. [*Jl.* iii, 293.

On the Measurement of the Ilahy Guz of the Emperor Akber. [*Jl.* iii, 360.

Table of Multipliers for ascertaining the Deviation of a Transit Instrument from the Meridian, &c. [*As. Res.* xv, vi.

Cracroft, W.; and Prinsep, J.—Latitude of the Hindu Observatory at Benares. [*As. Res.* xv, 1.

Crawfurd, John.—On the Existence of the Hindu Religion in the Island of Bali. [*As. Res.* xiii, 128.

The Ruins of Prambanan in Java. [*As. Res.* xiii, 337.

Crisp, John.—An Account of the Inhabitants of the Poggy or Nassau Islands, lying off Sumatra. [*As. Res.* vi, 77.

Cruttenden, Lieut. C. J.—Note on the Mijjertheyn Somalees. [*Jl.* xiii, 319.

Cunningham, General Alexander.—Correction of a Mistake regarding some of the Roman Coins found in the Tope at Manikyála opened by M. Court. [*Jl.* iii, 635.

Notice of some Counterfeit Bactrian Coins. [*Jl.* ix, 393.

Notes on Captain Hay's Bactrian Coins. [*Jl.* ix, 531.

Cunningham General Alexander (*contd.*)—Description of, and Deductions from, a consideration of some new Bactrian Coins. [*Jl.* ix, 867.

Note to be appended to the Account of the Coins of Mayas, in the preceding article on "Some New Bactrian Coins." [*Jl.* ix, 1008.

Second Notice of some forged Coins of the Bactrians and Indo-Scythians. [*Jl.* ix, 1217.

Abstract Journal of the Route to the Sources of the Punjab rivers. [*Jl.* x, 105.

Description of some Ancient Gems and Seals from Bactria, the Punjab and India. [*Jl.* x, 147.

A Sketch of the second Silver Plate found at Badakshân. [*Jl.* x, 570.

Second Notice of some new Bactrian Coins. [*Jl.* xi, 130.

Notice of some unpublished Coins of the Indo-Scythians. [*Jl.* xiv, 430.

Journal of a Trip through Kulu and Láhul, to the Chu Mureri Lake, in Ladák, during the months of August and September, 1846. [*Jl.* xvii, pt. i, 201.

Memorandum detailing the Boundary between the territories of Maharaja Guláb Singh and British India, as determined by the Commissioners P. A. Vans Agnew, Esq., and Capt. A. Cunningham. [*Jl.* xvii, pt. i. 295.

Verification of the Itinerary of Hwan Thsang through Ariana and India, with reference to Major Anderson's hypothesis of its modern compilation. [*Jl.* xvii, pt. i, 476.

Proposed Archæological Investigation. [*Jl.* xvii, pt. i, 535.

Verification of the Itinerary of the Chinese Pilgrim Hwan Thsang, through Afghanistan and India, during the first half of the seventh century of the Christian era. [*Jl.* xvii, pt. ii, 13.

An Essay on the Arian Order of Architecture, as exhibited in the Temples of Kashmír. [*Jl.* xvii, pt. ii, 241.

Coins of Indian Buddhist Satraps, with Greek Inscriptions. [*Jl.* xxiii 679.

Memorandum on the Irawadi river, with a monthly register of its rise and fall from 1856 to 1858, and a measurement of its minimum discharge. [*Jl.* xxix, 175.

Remarks on the Bactro-Pali Inscription from Taxila. [*Jl.* xxxii, 139, 172.

Archæological Survey Report for 1861-62. [*Jl.* xxxii (Supp. No.), 1.

Note on the Bactro-Pali Inscription from Taxila. [*Jl.* xxxiii, 35.

Cunningham, General Alexander. (*contd.*)—Remarks on the Date of the Pehewa Inscription of Raja Bhoja. [*Jl.* xxxiii, 223.

On the Pehoa Inscription of Raja Bhoja. [*Jl.* xxxiii., 229.

Archæological Survey Report for 1863-64 [*Jl.* xxxiii (Supp. No.), 1

On Antiquities of Bairat, etc. [*Proc.* 1865, 97.

Coins of the Nine Nâgas, and of two other Dynasties of Narwar and Gwalior. [*Jl.* xxxiv, pt. i, 115

Report of the Proceedings of the Archæological Surveyor to the Government of India for the Season of 1862-63. (Part II.) [*Jl.* xxxiv, pt. i, 155.

Report of the Proceedings of the Archæological Surveyor to the Government of India for the Season of 1862-63. [*Jl.* xxxiv, pt. i, 195.

Memorandum on the Operations of the Archæological Survey for season 1873-74. [*Proc.* 1874, 108.

Notes on the Gold Coins found in the Ahin Posh Tope. [*Proc.* 1879, 205.

Remarks on Bactrian and South Indian Coins. [*Proc.* 1880, 117.

Letter on some Antiquities exhibited at previous meetings. [*Proc.* 1881, 138.

Note on Coin of Shams-ud-din Kaimurs. [*Proc.* 1881, 158.

Relics from Ancient Persia in Gold, Silver, and Copper. [*Jl.* l, pt. i, 151.

Note on Coin from Mahanada. [*Proc.* 1882, 104.

Remarks on Coins from Toomluk. [*Proc.* 1882, 113.

On a Gold Gupta Coin sent by Mr. H. Rivett-Carnac. [*Proc.* 1883, 144.

Relics from Ancient Persia, in Gold, Silver, and Copper. [*Jl.* lii, pt. i, 64,258.

See **Broome, Lt. A ; Burt, Capt. T. S.**

Cunningham, Capt. J. D.—Notes on Moorcroft's Travels in Ladakh and on Gerard's Account of Kunáwar, including a general Description of the latter district. [*Jl.* xiii, 172, 223.

Notes on the Antiquities of the Districts within the Bhopal Agency, &c. [*Jl.* xvi, 739.

On the Ruins at Putharee. [*Jl.* xvii, pt. i, 305.

Cunningham, Capt. J. D. (*contd.*)—Notes on the Limits of Perpetual Snow in the Himalayas. [*Jl.* xviii, 694.

On the Embankments of Rivers, and on the Nature of Overflowing Rivers in Diluvial Plains. [*Jl.* xviii, 697.

Curnin, John.—A Catalogue of Stars to be observed with the Moon in March and April, with the view of determining the difference of longitude of the places whereat they may be observed. [*Jl.* iii, 94.

Curran, R. H.—Note on Gold and Silver Pieces found under the skin of a Burmese convict. [*Proc.* 1868, 115.

Cust, R. N.—On the Non-Aryan Languages of India. [*Proc.* 1877, 6.

On the Languages of the Indo-Chinese Peninsula and the Indian Archipelago. [*Proc.* 1877, 205.

DaCosta, Lewis.—On the Properties ascribed in Native medical works to the Acacia Arabica. [*Jl.* vi, 392.

Da Cunha, Dr.—On some Portuguese Inscriptions discovered on the walls of the fort of Mombassa. [*Proc.* 1875, 214.

Dagoberti Caroli de Daldorff Scarabaeorum (*i. e.*, Insectorum, quae sub nomine Generis Superioris Scarabaeus militaverunt in Fabricii Entomologia Systematica em : et auct :) distributio in genera proxima, (id est naturalia) divisiones, subdivisionesque, instrumentis cibariis, larvarum imaginumque; victu et oeconomia, aliisque insecti perfecti partibus consultis, No. 1. [*As. Res.* vii, 455.

Daji, Dr. Bhau.—On Ancient Sanskrit Numerals. [*Jl.* xxxii, 161.

Dall, Rev. C. H.—Remarks on the Remeasurement of Mt. St. Elias (Alaska). [*Proc.* 1876, 1.

Dall, W. H.—Extracts from a letter on the Operations of the U. S. Coast Survey, 1874. [*Proc.* 1874, 245.

Dalton, Col. Ed. Tuite.—Report of a Visit to the Hills in the neighbourhood of the Soobanshiri river. [*Jl.* xiv, 250.

On the Meris and Abors of Assam. In a letter to Major Jenkins. [*Jl.* xiv, 426.

Visit to Dewangari. [*Jl.* xviii, 66.

Earthquakes experienced in Assam in the latter end of Jan. 1849. [*Jl.* xviii, 173.

Notes on the "Mahápurushyas," a sect of Vaishnavas in Asám [*Jl.* xx, 455.

Dalton, Col. Ed. Tuite (*contd.*)—Account of a Visit to the Jugloo and Seesee rivers in Upper Assam; together with a Note on the Gold Fields of that Province. by Major Hannay. [*Jl.* xxii, 511.

Notes on Assam Temple Ruins. [*Jl.* xxiv. 1.

Notes of a Tour made in 1863-64 in the Tributary Mehals under the Commissioner of Chota-Nagpore, Bonai, Gangpore, Odeypore and Sirgooja. [*Jl.* xxxiv, pt. ii, 1.

Notes on a Tour in Manbhoom in 1864-65. [*Jl.* xxxv, pt. i, 186.

The "Kols" of Chota-Nagpore. [*Jl.* xxxv, pt. ii. Extra No., 153.

Brief Vocabulary of the Moondah and Cognate Languages of the Kolarian type. [*Jl.* xxxv, pt. ii, Extra No., 266.

Rude Stone Monuments in Chutiá Nágpúr and other places [*Jl.* xlii, pt. i, 112.

Letter on a large Picture representing the Conquest of Palámau in 1660 by Dáúd Khán Aurangzíb's General. [*Jl.* xliii, pt. i, 240.

Damant, G. H.—Notes of Sháh Ismá'íl Ghází, with a Sketch of the contents of a Persian MS., entitled "Risálat ush-Shuhadá," found at Kántá Dúár, Rangpúr. [*Jl.* xliii, pt. i, 215.

Letter on Manipúri Alphabet. [*Proc.* 1875, 17.

Notes on Manipuri Grammar. [*Jl.* xliv, pt. i, 173.

Note on the Old Manipuri Character. [*Jl.* xlvi, pt. i, 36.

Dames, M. Longworth.—A Grammar and Vocabulary of the Balochi Language. [*Jl.* xlix, pt. i. Extra No., 1.

Note on Durrani Coins. [*Proc.* 1883, 96.

Darjiling, on the Climate of. [*Jl.* vi, 308.

Das, Sarat Chandra.—Contributions on the Religion, History, &c., of Tibet.

I.—The Bon (Pon) Religion. [*Jl.* l, pt. i, 187.

II.—Dispute between a Buddhist and a Bonpo Priest for the possession of Mount Kailása and the Lake Mánasa, [*Jl.* l, pt. i, 206.

III.—Part I. Early History of Tibet. [*Jl.* l, pt. i., 211.

Part II. Tibet in the Middle Ages. [*Jl.* l, pt. i, 235.

IV.—Rise and Progress of Buddhism in Tibet. [*Jl.* li, pt. i, 1.

Das, Sarat Chandra.—(*contd.*)

V.—The Lives of the Panchhen-Rin-pochhes or Tasi Lamas. [*Jl.* li, pt. i, 15.

VI.—Life and Legend of Tson Khapa (Lo-ssan-tagpa), the Great Buddhist Reformer. [*Jl.* li., pt. i. 53.

VII.—Rise and Progress of Buddhism in Mongolia (Hor). [*Jl.* li, pt. i, 58.

VIII. — Rise and Progress of Jin or Buddhism in China. [*Jl.* li. pt. i, 87.

IX.—Ancient China: its Sacred Literature. Philosophy and Religion as known to the Tibetans. [*Jl.* li, pt. i, 99.

X.—Life and Legend of Nágárjuna [*Jl.* li, pt. i, 115.

XI.—Detached Notices of the different Buddhist Schools of Tibet. [*Jl.* li, pt. i, 121.

Dashwood, T.—Abstract of a Meteorological Register kept at Mozafferpur in Tirhut. [*Jl.* iii. 79.

Datta, Narasinha.—The Zafarnámah: a Dialogue between Aristotle and Buzurjmihr. Translated from the Persian. [*Jl.* xx, 426.

Davids, T. W. Rhys.—The Conquest of South India in the Twelfth Century by Parákráma Báhu. the great King of Ceylon. [*Jl.* xli, pt. i, 197.

Davidson, Major. — Note on the Habits of the Coel, and on the Discovery of Isinglass. [*Jl.* viii, 684.

Davis, Samuel.—On the Astronomical Computations of the Hindus. [*As. Res.* ii, 225.

On some Roman Coins found at Nelore. [*As. Res.* ii, 331.

On the Indian Cycle of Sixty Years. [*As. Res* iii, 209.

Davy, Dr. J.—Analysis of the Snake-Stone. [*As. Res.* xiii, 317.

Dawe, William.—Memorandum of the progress of sinking a Well in the Bunds of Chandpur, near the foot of the hills. [*Jl.* vi, 52.

Dawson, Rev. James.—List of Gondi Words and Phrases. [*Jl.* xxxix, pt. i, 108.

Additional Gondi Vocabulary. [*Jl.* xxxix. pt. i, 172.

Day, Dr. Francis.—Notes on the Andamanese. [*Proc.* 1870, 153.

Notes on the genus Hara. [*Jl.* xxxix, pt. ii, 37.

On Hamilton-Buchanan's Original Drawings of Fish in the library of the Asiatic Society of Bengal. [*Proc.* 1871, 195.

Day, Dr. Francis. (*contd.*)—Monograph of Indian *Cyprinidæ* (Part I). [*Jl.* xl, pt. ii, 95.

Monograph of Indian *Cyprinidæ* (Part II). [*Jl.* xl, pt. ii, 277.

Monograph of Indian *Cyprinidæ* (Part III). [*Jl.* xl, pt. ii, 337.

On the Identity of the Siluroid genera *Erethistes* and *Hara.* [*Proc.* 1872, 122.

Monograph of Indian *Cyprinidæ* (Part IV). [*Jl.* xli, pt. ii, 1.

Monograph of Indian *Cyprinidæ* (Part V). [*Jl.* xli, pt. ii, 171.

Notes on Fish collected by Dr. Stoliczka in Kachh. [*Jl.* xli, pt. ii, 258.

Monograph of Indian *Cyprinidæ* (Part VI). [*Jl.* xli, pt. ii, 318.

Remarks on some Indian Fishes. [*Jl.* xliii, pt. ii, 31.

Dean, Serjeant Edmund.—On the Strata of the Jumna Alluvium, as exemplified in the Rocks and Shoals lately removed from the bed of the river; and of the sites of the Fossil Bones discovered therein. [*Jl.* iv, 261.

Notice of the Temple called Seo Byjnauth (Siva Vaidyanátha) discovered on the 3rd December, 1834, on the Hill of Unchápahar, in the Shekáwati Territory. [*Jl.* iv, 361.

On the Fossil Bones of the Jumna river. [*Jl.* iv. 495.

De la Hoste, Captain E. P.—Memoranda respecting the existence of Copper in the territory of Luz near Bela. [*Jl.* ix, 30.

Report on the Country between Kurrachee, Tatta, and Sehwan, Scinde. [*Jl.* ix, 907.

Delmerick, J. G.—Notes on Archæological Remains at Sháhki Dherí, and the Site of Taxila. [*Jl.* xxxix, pt. i, 89.

A History of the Gakk'hars. [*Jl.* xl, pt. i, 67.

Letter on a unique Tetradrachma of Plato the Illustrious, a new Bactrian King. [*Proc.* 1872, 34.

On Arabic and Persian Inscriptions from Sonpat. [*Proc.* 1873, 95.

Note on a new Gold Coin of Mahmúd Sháh bin Muhammad Sháh bin Tughluq Sháh, of Dihlí. [*Jl.* xliii, pt. i, 97.

Lists of Rare Muhammadan Coins.—No. I. Coins of the Kings of Dihlí and Jaunpúr. [*Jl.* xliv, pt. i, 126.

List of Rare Muhammadan Coins.—No. II. Coins of the Kings of Dihlí, Málwah, Bengal, Kulbarga, and Kashmír. [*Jl.* xlv, pt. i, 291.

Delmerick, J. G. (*contd.*)—On a Silver Coin of Shams-uddin Kaimurs. [*Proc.* 1881, 157.

De Nice'ville, Lionel.—Description of a new species of Butterfly belonging to the genus *Dodona.* [*Proc.* 1881, 121.

A List of Butterflies taken in Sikkim in October 1880, with Notes on habits, &c. [*Jl.* l, pt. ii, 49.

Second List of Butterflies taken in Sikkim in October 1882, with Notes on habits, &c. [*Jl.* li, pt. ii, 54.

Description of a new species of the Rhopalocerous, genus *Cyrestis*, from the Great Nicobar. [*Jl.* lii. pt. ii. 1.

On new and little-known *Rhopalocera* from the Indian Region. [*Jl.* lii, pt. ii, 65.

Third List of Butterflies taken in Sikkim in October 1883, with Notes on habits, &c [*Jl.* lii, pt. ii, 92.

See **Marshall, G. F. L.**; **Wood-Mason, J.**

Denison, Sir W.—Notes on the Didunculus Strigirostris, or Tooth-Billed Pigeon of the Navigator Islands—the nearest living ally to the extinct Dodo.—Communicated. [*Jl.* xxxiii, 373.

Depree, Capt. G. C.—On a Pali Inscription. [*Proc.* 1866, 117.

Desgodins Abbe.—On the Eastern Frontier of Thibet. [*Proc.* 1880, 197.

See **Waterhouse, Major J.**

Des Granges, Baron Otto.—*See* **Granges, Baron Otto des.**

Diard and Duvaucel.—On the *Sorex Glis.* [*As. Res.* xiv, 471.

Dias, J.—Daily Register of the Tides at Singapore, from the 1st September 1834 to the 31st August 1835, inclusive. [*As. Res.* xix, pt. i, 201.

Distant, W. L. — Description of a new Homopterous Insect belonging to the genus *Cosmoscarta.* [*Jl.* xlvii, pt. ii, 194.

Hemiptera from Upper Tenasserim. [*Jl.* xlviii, pt. ii, 37.

D'Mazure, Very Rev. Thomine.—Memorandum on the Countries between Thibet, Yunân and Burmah. With Notes and a Comment by Lieut.-Col. H. Yule. [*Jl.* xxx, 367.

Doab Canal, Description of the Regulating Dam-Sluices of the. [*Jl.* i, 44.

Dobson, Dr. G. E. On new species of Malayan bats. [*Proc.* 1871, 105.

Notes on the new species of Indian and Indo-Chinese *Vespertilionidæ*, with Remarks on the synonymy and classification of some other species of the same family. [*Proc.* 1871, 210.

Dobson, Dr. G. E. (*contd.*)—On a New Species of Vespertilio. [*Jl.* xl, pt. ii, 186.

Description of four new species of Malayan Bats from the collection of Dr. Stoliczka. [*Jl.* xl, pt. ii, 260.

On a New Genus and Species of *Rhinolophidæ*, with description of a new species of *Vesperus*, and notes on some other species of insectivorous bats from Persia. [*Jl.* xl, pt. ii, 455.

Notes on the Asiatic Species of the genus *Taphozous*, Geoff. [*Proc.* 1872, 151.

Notes on some Species of *Chiroptera* collected by W. Theobald, Esq., in Barmah. [*Proc.* 1872, 154.

Notes on some Bats collected by Capt. W. G. Murray, in the N. W. Himalaya. [*Proc.* 1872, 208.

On the Osteology of Triænops persicus. [*Jl.* xli, pt. ii, 136.

On the Osteology of some species of Bats. [*Jl.* xli, pt. ii, 334.

Brief Descriptions of five new species of Rhinolophine Bats. [*Jl.* xli, pt. ii, 336.

Description of a new species of *Molossus* from Johore in the Malay Peninsula. [*Proc.* 1873, 22.

On the Genera *Murina* and *Harpyiocephalus* of Gray. [*Proc.* 1873, 107.

On the *Pteropidæ* of India and its Islands, with descriptions of new or little known species. [*Jl.* xlii, pt. ii, 194.

Description of a new species of *Vespertilio* from the North-Western Himalaya. [*Jl.* xlii, pt. ii, 205.

On the Asiatic Species of *Molossi*. [*Jl.* xliii, pt. ii, 142.

List of *Chiroptera* inhabiting the Khasia Hills, with description of a new species. [*Jl.* xliii, pt. ii, 234.

Descriptions of new species of *Chiroptera* from India and Yunan. [*Jl.* xliii, pt. ii, 237.

Postscript to the List of *Chiroptera* inhabiting the Khásia Hills. [*Proc.* 1875, 85.

Notes on a Collection of *Chiroptera* from India and Burma, with description of new species. [*Jl.* xlvi, pt. ii, 310.

Douglas, J. C.—The use of Silver Films in Improved Instruments of the Camera Lucida class. [*Proc.* 1880, 73.

Exhibition of Gower Bell Telephone. [*Proc.* 1881, 39.

The Phenomenon commonly called the "Cry of Tin." [*Proc.* 1881, 42.

Douglas, J. C. (*contd.*)—Some Observations on the Standing of Animals. the Perching of Birds and the Walking Pace of Man. [*Proc.* 1881, 53.

Dowson, Professor J.—Remarks on the Taxila Inscription. [*Jl.* xxxii, 421.

Drummond, Capt. H.—Report on the Copper Mines of Kumaon. [*Jl.* vii, 934.

On the Mines and Mineral Resources of Northern Afghanistan. [*Jl.* x. 74.

Drury, Capt.—Remarks on some lately discovered Roman Gold Coins. [*Jl.* xx, 371.

Duka, Dr.—On Knyahinya Meteorite. [*Proc.* 1867, 21.

Dunbar, Dr. W.—Discovery of Coal in a new site. [*Jl.* x, 300.

Duncan, Jonathan.—Historical Remarks on the Coast of Malabar, with some description of the Manners of its Inhabitants [*As. Res.* v, 1.

An Account of two Fakeers, with their Portraits [*As. Res.* v, 37.

An Account of the Discovery of two Urns in the vicinity of Benares. [*As. Res.* v, 131.

Dunkin, Sir William.—Extract from a Diary of a Journey over the great desert, from Aleppo to Bussora. in April, 1878 [*As. Res.* iv, 401.

Durand, Lieut. H. M.—Specimens of the Hippopotamus and other Fossil Genera of the Sub-Himálayas in the Dádúpur Collection. [*As. Res.* xix, pt. 1, 54.

See **Baker, Lieut. W. E.**

Duthoit, W.—On Muhammadan Silver Coins. [*Proc.* 1874, 239.

Duvaucel, A.—On the Black Deer of Bengal. [*As. Res.* xv, 157.

See **Diard.**

Dye-stuffs, Correspondence regarding samples of, of Indian growth and of Tusser and other Silks. [*Proc.* 1875, 128.

Earthquake felt in Sind. 28th October, 1870, Notice of an. [*Proc.* 1871, 56.

Earthquake of the 26th August, 1833. [*Jl.* ii, 438.

Earthquakes in Assam, record of the occurrence of, during the years 1874—80. [*Jl.* xlvi, pt. ii. 294; xlvii, pt. ii, 4; xlviii, pt. ii, 48; l; pt. ii, 61.

Earthquake in Murwut. [*Proc.* 1869, 163.

East, Sir Edward Hyde.—Abstract of an Account containing the particulars of a boring made near the river Hooghly, in the vicinity of Calcutta, from May to July 1814, inclusive, in search of a spring of pure water. [*As. Res.* xii, 542.

Eastwick, Capt. J. B.—A Vocabulary of the Scindee Language. [*Jl.* xii, 1.

Economic Geology, Correspondence respecting the Society's Museum of. [*Jl.* xi, 326.

Edgeworth, M. P.—Register of the Weather at Futtehgurh (Lat. 27° 21′ N., Long. 79° 3′ E.) from April 1832 to October 1833. [*Jl.* iii. 46.

Register of the Thermometer at Ambála, for 1834. [*Jl.* iv, 405.

Botanico-Agricultural Account of the Protected Sikh States. [*Jl.* vii, 751.

Grammar and Vocabulary of the Cashmiri Language. [*Jl.* x, 1038.

Note to the Botanico-Agricultural Account of the Protected Sikh States. [*Jl.* xi, 26.

Observations on the Genus Spathium. [*Jl.* xi, 145.

A Couple of Hours' Herborization at Aden. [*Jl.* xvi, 1211.

Report on the Statistics of Banda. [*Jl.* xix, 89.

Catalogue of Plants found in the Banda district, 1847—49. [*Jl.* xxi, 24.

Catalogue of Plants found in the Banda district, 1847—49 [*Jl.* xxi, 151.

Abstract of a Journal kept by Mr. Gardiner during his travels in Central Asia; with a Note and Introduction. [*Jl.* xxii, 283.

Description of Mohzarkhala in the Kohistan of the Western Huzara, extracted from the Journal of Mr. A. Gardiner. [*Jl.* xxii, 383.

Notes on the Sources of the Abi Mai, or Amoo or Oxus, extracted from the Journal of Mr. E. Gardiner. [*Jl.* xxii, 431.

Egerton, R. E.—Note on Earthquake in Murwut. [*Proc.* 1869, 163.

Elephant, The Osteology of the. (From India Sporting Review.) [*Jl.* xiii, 915.

Eliot, John.—Observations on the Inhabitants of the Garrow Hills, made during a Publick Deputation in the years 1788 and 1789. [*As. Res.* iii, 17.

Ellis, Francis.—Account of a Discovery of a modern imitation of the Védas, with Remarks on the genuine works. [*As. Res.* xiv, 1.

Ellis, R. R. M.—On Recorded Solar Eclipse. [*Proc.* 1867, 172.

Elliot, Walter—On Bos Gaurus. [*Jl.* x, 579.

Observations on the Language of the Goands, and the identity of many of its terms with words now in use in the Telugu, Tamil and Canarese. [*Jl.* xvi, 1140.

Comparative List of Upanishads. [*Jl.* xx, 607.

Elliott, H. M.—Reports upon His Majesty the King of Oude's Observatory at Lucknow. Communicated. [*Jl.* xvii, pt. 1, 507.

Elliott, J. B.—Note on an Inscription found near the Kesariah Mound, in Tirhut. [*Jl.* iv, 286.

Elmslie, Dr. W. J.—List of Words and Phrases to be noted and used as test words for the discovery of the radical affinities of languages and for easy comparison, drawn up by Mr. Justice Campbell. Translated into Kashmírí. [*Jl.* xxxix, pt. i, 95.

Emmott, J.—Extracts from a Journal kept while visiting the Sapan Forests. [*Jl.* i, 544.

Erhardt, Rev.—Letter regarding so-called Wolf-children in the Secundra Orphanage. [*Proc.* 1873, 155.

Euphrates, A general statement of the Labors and Proceedings of the Expedition to the, under the command of Colonel Chesney. [*Jl.* v, 675.

Evans, Dr. George.—Examination of a Mummy Head supposed to be brought from Egypt by Lieutenant Archbold. [*Jl.* iv, 322.

Note on a Specimen of the Bos Gaurus. [*Jl.* vi, 223.

Note on a Species of Arctonix from Arracan. [*Jl.* vii, 732.

Note on the New Zealand Caterpillar. [*Jl.* vii, 787.

Note on the Dissection of the Arctonix Collaris, or Sand Hog. [*Jl.* viii, 408.

Evans, Lieut.—*See* **Keatinge, Lieut.**

Evaporation in Calcutta, Daily rate of. [*Jl.* xvii, pt. i, 236.

Everest, Captain G. — On the Formulæ for calculating Azimuth in Trigonometrical Operations. [*As. Res.*, xviii, pt. ii, 93.

On the Compensation Measuring Apparatus of the Great Trigonometrical Survey of India. [*As. Res.* xviii, pt. ii, 189.

Everest, Rev. Robert.—Memorandum on the Fossil Shells discovered in the Himalayan Mountains. [*As. Res.* xviii, pt. ii, 107.

Note on Indian Saline Deposits. [*Jl.* i, 149.

Some Observations on the quantity of earthy matter brought down by the Ganges river. [*Jl.* i, 238.

Remarks on a late Paper in the Asiatic Journal on the Gypsum of the Himalaya. [*Jl.* i. 450. [*As. Res.* xviii, pt. ii, 107

Some Additional Observations on the quantity of earthy matter brought down by the Ganges, its depth and velocity, made during the rainy season of 1832, at Gharjpur. [*Jl.* i, 549.

Some Geological Remarks made in the country between Mirzapúr and Ságar, and from Ságar northwards to the Jamna. [*Jl.* ii, 475.

On the Climate of the Fossil Elephant. [*Jl.* iii, 18.

On the Influence of the Moon on Atmospherical Phenomena. [*Jl.* iii, 345.

Further notice of the Influence of the Moon on Atmospherical Phenomena. [*Jl.* iii, 631.

On the Amount of Rainfall at Calcutta, as affected by the Declination of the Moon. [*Jl.* iv, 207.

On the Temperture of Deep Wells to the West of the Jamna. [*Jl.* iv, 229.

Comparison of the Heights of the Barometer, with the distance of the Moon from the Celestial Equator. [*Jl.* iv, 252.

Geological Observations made in a Journey from Mussooree (Masúrí) to Gungotree (Gangautrí). [*Jl.* iv, 690.

On the Revolution of the Seasons. [*Jl.* v. 281.

Continuation of a Paper (Journal, May 1835), on the Heights of the Barometer as affected by the position of the Moon. [*Jl.* v, 585.

On the Revolution of the Seasons. [*Jl.* vi, 303 ; vii, 192.

Remarks upon the Rain and Drought of the last eight seasons in India. [*Jl.* viii, 313.

Ewer, Walter.—An Account of the Cootub Minar and the Inscriptions in its vicinity. [*As. Res.* xiv, 480.

Fairbank, Rev. S. B.—The Ravages of Rats and Mice in the Dakhan during the Harvest of 1878-79. [*Jl.* xlviii, pt. ii, 143.

Falconer, Dr. Hugh.—On the Aptitude of the Himalayan Range for the Culture of the Tea Plant. [*Jl.* iii, 178.

Note on the Occurrence of Fossil Bones in the Sewalik Range, eastward of Hardwar. [*Jl.* vi, 233.

On Additional Fossil Species of the order Quadrumana from the Sewálik Hills. [*Jl.* vi, 354.

Letter to the Secretary of the Asiatic Society on the Cataclysm of the Indus. [*Jl.* x, 615.

Falconer, Dr. Hugh ; and Cautley, Capt. P. T.

Sivatherium Giganteum, a new Fossil Ruminant Genus from the valley of the Markanda, in the Siválik Branch of the Sub-Himálayan Mountains. [*As. Res.* xix, pt. i, 1.

Note on the Fossil Hippopotamus of the Siválik Hills. [*As. Res.* xix, pt. i, 39.

Note on the Fossil Camel of the Siválik Hills. [*As. Res.* xix, pt. i, 115

Note on the Felis Cristata, a new Fossil Tiger from the Siválik Hills. [*As. Res.* xix, pt. i, 135.

Sivatherium Giganteum, a new Fossil Ruminant Genus from the valley of the Markanda in the Siválik Branch of the Sub-Himalayan Mountains [*Jl.* v, 38.

See **Cautley, Capt. P. T.**

Farquhar, Major W.—Account of a new species of Tapir found in the Peninsula of Malacca. [*As. Res.* xiii, 417.

Fasson, J. H.—A Report on a Whirlwind which occurred in the Maimansingh district, on the 26th March. [*Proc.* 1875, 103.

Fattapoer and Sjatterapoer, Note on the (probable) identity of, in Van den Broucke's Map of Bengal, with Fathpur and Jatrapur, in the Jessore District. [*Proc.* 1874, 19.

Fayrer, Dr. J.—On proposed Ethnological Exhibition. [*Proc.* 1866, 81.

Fedden, F.—On Fire-flies. [*Proc.* 1866, 19.

Remarks on Shells found at Káthiáwár. [*Proc.* 1881, 124.

Feistmantel, Dr. Ottokar. — Contributions towards the knowledge of the Indian Fossil Flora. On some Fossil Plants from the Dumúdar Series in the Ránígani Coalfields, collected by Mr. J. Wood-Mason. [*Proc.* 1876, 223.

A Sketch of the History of the Fossils of the Indian Gondwana System. [*Jl.* l, pt. ii, 168.

Fell, Capt. E.—Sanscrit Inscriptions, with remarks by H. H. Wilson. [*As. Res.* xv, 436.

Fenwick, Capt.—Journal of a passage down the Nerbudda, from Chikuldah to Baroach, with notices of the most important obstructions to the Navigation. [*Jl.* xviii, 461.

Journey of the Passage from the Dharee Falls to the Hirnphal. [*Jl.* xvii, pt. ii, 210.

Ferrar, M. L.—Letter regarding the Birthplace of Todar Mall. [*Proc.* 1871, 178.

Letter on further particulars regarding Rájah Todar Mall. [*Proc.* 1872, 35.

Finnis, Lieut. John.—A Summary Description of the Geology of the country between Hoshungabad on the Nerbudda, and Nagpoor, by the direction of Baitool. [*Jl.* iii, 71.

Firuz Sháh Zafar, son of Fírúz Sháh of Delhi, Note on a Gold Coin bearing the name of Prince. [*Jl.* xl, pt. i, 160.

Fisher, F. H.—Geological Sketch of Masúrí and Landour, in the Himalaya; together with an abstract of the Thermometrical Register kept at Landour during the year 1831. [*Jl.* i, 193.

Fisher, Capt.—Memoir of Sylhet. Kachar, and the adjacent districts. [*Jl.* ix, 808.

Fleming, Dr. John. — A Catalogue of Indian Medical Plants and Drugs, with their Names in the Hindustání and Sanscrit languages. [*As. Res.* xi, 153.

Flemming, Dr. Andrew.—Report on the Salt Range, and on its Coal and other Minerals. [*Jl.* xvii, pt. ii. 500.

Diary of a Trip to Pind Dadun Khan and the Salt Range. [*Jl.* xviii, 661.

Report on the Geological Structure and Mineral Wealth of the Salt Range in the Punjaub. [*Jl.* xxii, 229. 333, 444.

Notes on the Iron Ore of Korana in the Jetch Dooab of the Punjab, with a qualitative analysis of the same. [*Jl.* xxiii. 92.

Floyd, J. — Account of the Hurricane or Whirlwind of the 8th April, 1838. [*Jl.* vii, 422.

Foley, Capt. Wm. — Journal of a Tour through the Island of Rambree, with a Geological Sketch of the Country, and Brief Account of the Customs, &c., of its Inhabitants. [*Jl.* iv, 20.

Foley, Capt. Wm. (*contd.*)—Journal of a Tour through the Island of Rambree, with a Geological Sketch of the Country and Brief Account of the Customs, &c., of its inhabitants. [*Jl.* iv, 82.

Journal of a Tour through the Island of Rambree (Rámrí; Sans. Ramavati), on the Arracan Coast. [*Jl.* iv, 199.

Notes on the Geology, &c., of the Country in the neighbourhood of Maulamyeng (vulg. Moulmein). [*Jl.* v, 269.

Note on a Remnant of the Hun Nation. [*Jl.* v, 813.

Fontana, Nicolas.—On the Nicobar Isles and the Fruit of the Mellori. [*As. Res.* iii, 149.

Forbes, Capt. J.—Notes on the Buddhas from Ceylonese Authorities, with an attempt to fix the dates of the appearance of the last four; being those of the Mahá Bhadra Kalpa (or present age) [*Jl.* v, 321.

Forbes, L. R.—Letter regarding the Mughul Invasions of Palámau. [*Jl.* xl, pt. i, 129.

Ford, Major.—Report on Barren Island. [*Proc.* 1866, 212.

Forlong, Capt. J. G.—*See* **Fraser, Capt. Alex.**

Forrest, R. E.—On Rock Inscriptions near Khalsi. [*Proc.* 1865, 199.

Foster. J. M.—Note on Ghargáon, Asám. [*Jl.* xli, pt. i, 32.

The Temple of Jayságar, Upper Asám. [*Jl.* xliii, pt. i, 311.

Foulkes, Rev. Thomas. — Extracts from letters regarding three sets of Copper Sasanams discovered in the Vizagapatam district. [*Jl.* xxxix, pt. i, 153.

Fowke, Francis.—On the Víná, or Indian Lyre. [*As. Res.* i, 295.

Franklin, Capt. James. — On the Geology of a portion of Bundelkhand, Boghelkhand, and the districts of Ságar and Jebelpur. [*As. Res.* xviii, pt. i, 23.

On the Diamond Mines of Panna in Bundelkhand. [*As. Res.* xviii, pt. i, 100.

Franklin, Lieut. William. — An Account of the present state of Delhi. [*As. Res.* iv, 419.

Fraser, Capt. Alex.; and Forlong, Capt. J. G.—Report on a Route from the mouth of the Pakchan to Krau, and thence across the Isthmus of Krau to the Gulf of Siam. [*Jl.* xxxi, 347.

Fraser, James B. — Account of a Journey to the Sources of the Jumna and Bhágírathí rivers. [*As. Res.* xiii, 171.

Fraser, Hugh.—Further particulars regarding the Dandapur Meteorite. [*Proc.* 1878, 190.

Folklore from Eastern Gorakhpur (N. W. P.). [*Jl.* lii, pt. i, 1.

Fraser, O. L. — Note on the Occurrence of a partially ossified Nasal Septum in *Rhinoceros Sondaicus.* [*Jl.* xliii, pt. ii, 10.

Freeling, George H. — Coin Collections lost during the Rebellion. [*Jl.* xxvii, 169.

Account of Pergunnah Mahoba, Zillah Humeerpore, Bundelcund [*Jl.* xxviii, 369.

Fryer, Col. G. E. — A Contribution to our knowledge of Pelagic Mollusca. [*Jl.* xxxviii, pt. ii, 259.

On Burmese Celts. [*Proc.* 1872, 46.

Note on an Arakanese Coin. [*Jl.* xli, pt. i, 201.

On the Khyeng People of the Sandoway district, Arakan. [*Jl.* xliv, pt. i, 39.

Pali Studies.—No. 1, Analysis and Text of the Subodhálankára, or 'Easy Rhetoric,' by Sangharakkhita Thera. [*Jl.* xliv, pt. i, 91.

Pali Studies.—No. 2, Vuttodaya (Exposition of Metre), by Sangharakkhita Thera. [*Jl.* xlvi, pt. i, 369.

Letter on the Pali Language, being the original language. [*Proc.* 1879, 155.

Letter forwarding copies of two Buddhist Inscriptions. [*Proc.* 1879, 201.

Note on the Páli Grammarian Kachcháyana. [*Proc.* 1882, 119.

Fuller, Major A. R. — Translations from the Táríkh i Fírúz Sháhí. [*Jl.* xxxviii, pt. i, 18; xxxix, pt. i, 1.

Fulljames, Lieut. George.—Section of the Strata passed through in an experimental boring at the town of Gogah, on the Gujerat Peninsula, Gulph of Cambay. [*Jl.* vi, 786.

Note on the black and brown Floriken of Guzerat. [*Jl.* vi, 789.

See **Hugel, Baron.**

Furdoonjee, Nowrozjee.—*See* **Nowroyjee Furdoonjee.**

Fytche, Colonel A. — Papers relating to the Aborigines of the Andaman Islands, communicated by the Govt. of India. [*Jl.* xxx, 251.

On the Panthays of Yunan. [*Proc.* 1867, 176.

Gardiner.—*See* **Edgeworth, M. P.**

Gauja Agrahar and Koppa Gadde Sásanas, Sanskrit Transcripts of. [*Proc.* 1873, 75.

Geddes, Surgeon W.—On the Climate of Nagpúr. [*Jl.* ii, 239.

Gerard, Lieut. A.—Narrative of a Journey from Soobathoo to Shipke, in Chinese Tartary. [*Jl.* xi, 363.

Gerard, Dr. J. G.—Observations on the Spiti Valley and circumjacent country within the Himálaya. [*As. Res.* xviii, pt. ii, 238.

Memoir on the Topes and Antiquities of Afghanistan. [*Jl.* iii, 321.

See **Burnes, Lieut. A.**

Gerard, Capt. Patrick—Observations on the Climate of Subathu and Kotgerh. [*As. Res.* xv. 469.

Abstract of a Meteorological Journal kept at Kotgarh (Lat. 31° 11′ 45″ N. Long. 77° 27′·49″ E.), Subathu, and the intermediate places in the Himálaya Mountains for 1819-20. [*Jl.* ii, 615.

A Vocabulary of the Koonawur Languages. [*Jl.* xi, 479.

A general Statement of the Weather at Kotgurh and Soobathoo, for 1819-20-21. [*Jl.* xii, 749.

Ghosha, Pratapachandra.—The Adjustment of the Hindoo Calendar. [*Jl.* xxxvii, pt. ii, 181.

Text and Translation of a Bulandshahar Inscription. [*Jl.* xxxviii, pt. i, 21.

Remarks on Jayanti Coins, presented by Mr. Belletty. [*Proc.* 1870, 260.

Notes on Vernacular Lexicography. [*Jl.* xxxix, pt. i, 131.

The Vástu Yága and its bearing upon Tree and Serpent Worship in India. [*Jl.* xxxix, pt. i, 199.

Notes on, and Translation of, two Copper-plate Inscriptions from Bámanghátí. [*Jl.* xl, pt. i, 161.

Note on several Asám Coins. [*Proc.* 1872, 2.

Transcript of the Pála Inscription of the Buddal Pillar, Dínájpúr, by Pandit Harachandra Chakravartí. With an annotated translation. [*Jl.* xliii, pt. i, 356.

Notes on, and Translation of, three Copper-plate Inscriptions from Sumbalpur. [*Jl.* xlvi, pt. i, 173.

Gibbs, Hon. James.—Exhibition of a Gold Ramtinki. [*Proc.* 1882, 47.

Note on Coins of the Andhrabhritya Dynasty. [*Proc.* 1882, 58.

Gibbs, Hon. James (*contd.*)—
Exhibition of a Drawing and Estampage of two enormous Gold Coins. [*Proc.* 1883, 3.
Exhibition of some rare Muhammadan Coins. [*Proc.* 1883, 4.
Exhibition of some Gold Ramtinkis, and note thereon. [*Proc.* 1883, 76.

Gilchrist, John. — Account of the Hindustanee Horometry. [*As. Res.* v, 81.

Gill, Major.—Extracts from Notes on Hemadpauti Temples, &c., made during a tour through a portion of West Berar in 1868, 1869 and in May, 1871. [*Proc.* 1873, 66.

Girdlestone, C. E. R.—Letter forwarding a copy of the plan of encampment used at the Installation of the Dalai Lama. [*Proc.* 1879, 275.
On Medal sent by Mr. Gennoe. [*Proc.* 1880, 172.

Giuseppe, Father.—An Account of the Kingdom of Nepal. [*As. Res.* ii, 307.

Glasfurd, Capt. C.—Extract from a Report of the Dependency of Bustar. [*Jl.* xxxiii, 44.

Glasfurd, Lieut. John.—Report on the Progress made up to the 1st May 1839, in opening the experimental Copper Mine in Kumaon. [*Jl.* viii. 471.

Godwin-Austen, Lt.-Col. H. H.—
On the System employed in Outlining the Figures of Deities and other Religious Drawings, as practised in Ladak, Zaskar, &c. [*Jl.* xxxiii, 151.
Description of a Mystic Play, as performed in Ladak, Zaskar, &c. [*Jl.* xxxiv, pt. i. 71.
Notes on the Sandstone Formation, &c., near Buxa Fort, Bhootan Dooars. [*Jl.* xxxiv, pt. ii, 106
A Vocabulary of English, Balti and Kashmiri. [*Jl.* xxxv, pt. i, 233.
Notes on the Pangong-lake, district of Ladakh, from journal made in 1863. [*Jl.* xxxvii, pt. ii, 84.
Figures of the species of *Diplommatinæ* Benson, hitherto described as inhabiting the Himalayas, Khasi Hills and Burmah, etc. [*Jl.* xxxvii, pt. ii, 83.
Notes on Geological Features of the country near foot of hills in the Western Bhootan Dooars. [*Jl.* xxxvii, pt. ii, 117.

Godwin-Austen, Lt.-Col. H. H. (*contd.*)—Notes to accompany a Geological Map of a portion of the Khasi Hills near Longitude 91° E. [*Jl.* xxxviii, pt. ii, 1.
Notes from Assaloo, North Cachar, on the great earthquake, January 10th, 1869. [*Proc.* 1869, 91.
Notes on the Geology and Physical Features of the Jaintia Hills. [*Jl.* xxxviii, pt. ii, 151.
Descriptions of New Species of *Diplommatinæ* from the Khasi Hills. [*Jl.* xxxix. pt. ii, 1.
A List of Birds obtained in the Khasi and North Cachar Hills. [*Jl.* xxxix, pt. ii, 91.
Second List of Birds obtained in the Khasi and North Cachar Hill ranges, including the Garo Hills and country at their base in the Mymensing and Sylhet districts. [*Jl.* xxxix, pt. ii, 264.
Descriptions of the Species of *Alycæinæ* known to inhabit the Khasi Hill ranges. [*Jl.* xl, pt. ii, 87.
Third List of Birds obtained in the Khasi and Garo Hill ranges, with some corrections and additions to the former lists. [*Jl.* xli, pt. ii. 142.
On the Ruins at Dímápúr on the Dunsirí river, Asám. [*Jl.* xliii, pt. i, 1.
Descriptions of New Species of Mollusca of the genera *Helix* and *Glessula* from the Khasi Hills and Manipur. [*Jl.* xliii. pt. ii, 1.
Descriptions of four New Species of Mollusca belonging to the family *Zonitidæ* from the N. E. Frontier of Bengal, with drawings of *Helicarion gigas*, Benson, and of a variety of the same. [*Jl.* xliii, pt. ii. 4.
Descriptions of New Operculated Landshells belonging to the genera *Craspedotropis*, *Alycæus*, and *Diplommatinæ*, from the Naga Hills and Assam. [*Jl.* xliii, pt. ii, 7.
Notes on the Geology of part of the Dafla Hills, Assam; lately visited by the Force under Brigadier-General Stafford. [*Jl.* xliii. pt. ii, 35.
Descriptions of nine Species of *Alycæinæ* from Assam and the Naga Hills. [*Jl.* xliii, pt. ii, 145.
Fourth List of Birds principally from the Naga Hills and Munipur, including others from the Khasi, Garo, and Tipperah Hills. [*Jl.* xliii, pt. ii, 151.
Exhibition of a Celt found at Shillong. [*Proc.* 1875, 158.
The Evidence of past Glacial Action in the Nágá Hills, Assam. [*Jl.* xliv, pt. ii, 209.

Godwin-Austen, Lt.-Col. H. H. (*contd.*)—List of the Birds collected on the Expedition into the Dafla Hills, Assam; together with those obtained in the adjacent Darrang Terai. [*Jl.* xlv, pt. ii, 64.

On the *Cyclostomacea* of the Dafla Hills, Assam. [*Jl.* xlv, pt. ii, 171.

Remarks on Himâlayan Glaciation. [*Proc.* 1877, 4.

Some Notes on the *Genera Pellorneum* and *Pomatorhinus*, with a description of a variety of *Chleuasicus ruficeps*, Blyth. [*Proc.* 1877, 146.

Descriptions of three new Species of Birds of the Genera *Pellorneum*, *Actinura*, and *Pomatorhinus*; lately collected in the neighbourhood of Saddya, Assam, by Mr. M. J. Ogle, of the Topographical Survey. [*Jl.* xlvi, pt. ii. 43.

Sixth List of Birds from the Hill Ranges of the North-East Frontier of India. [*Jl.* xlvii, pt. ii, 12.

On new species of the Genus *Plectopylis* of the Family *Helicidæ*. [*Jl.* xlviii, pt. ii, 1.

Notes on, and Drawings of, the Animals of various Indian Land Mollusca (*Pulmonifera*). [*Jl.* xlix, pt. ii, 151.

Notes on, and Drawings of, the Animals of various Indian Land Mollusca (*Pulmonifera*). [*Jl.* li. pt. ii, 68.

Gold Dust from the Sand of the Ningthee River, on the frontier of Manipur, Mode of extracting the. [*Jl.* i, 148.

Goldingham, J.—Some Account of the Cave in the Island of Elephanta. [*As. Res.* iv, 409.

Some Account of the Sculptures at Mahabalipoorum usually called the Seven Pagodas. [*As. Res.* v, 69.

Golubief, Capt.—Observations on the Astronomical Points determined by the brothers Schlagintweit in Central Asia. [*Jl.* xxxv, pt. ii, 46.

Goodwyn, Major Henry.—Memoir on the application of Asphaltic Mastic to Flooring, Roofing, and Hydraulic works in India. [*Jl.* xii, 534.

A Resultant System for the Construction of Iron Tension Bridges. [*Jl.* xvii, pt. ii, 412.

Goojrat District in 1858, Table of the Coins of former Governments more or less current in the Bazars of the. [*Jl.* xxxiii, 434.

Gordon, Dr. C. A.—Report on the Dust Whirlwinds of the Punjab. [*Jl.* xxiii, 364.

Notes on the Topography of Murree. [*Jl.* xxiii, 461.

Gordon, G. J.—Memorandum of an Excursion to the Tea Hills which produce the description of Tea known in commerce under the designation of Ankoy Tea. [*Jl.* iv, 95.

Journal of an attempted Ascent of the river Min, to visit the Tea Plantations of the Fuhkin Province of China. [*Jl.* iv, 563.

Gowan, Capt. W. E.—Geographical information regarding the Kirghiz Steppes and Country of Turkistan afforded by the Book of the Great Survey. Translated from the Russian. [*Proc.* 1879, 222.

Graham, Capt.—Report on the Agricultural and Land Produce of Shoa. [*Jl.* xiii, 253.

Report on the Manners, Customs and Superstitions of the people of Shoa, and on the History of the Abyssinian Church. [*Jl.* xii, 625.

Grange, E. R.—Extracts from the Narrative of an Expedition into the Naga Territory of Assam. [*Jl.* viii, 445.

Grange, Lieut.—Extracts from the Journal of an Expedition into the Naga Hills on the Assam Frontier. [*Jl.* ix, 947.

Granges, Baron Otto des.—Short Survey of the Countries between Bengal and China, showing the great Commercial and Political importance of the Burmese town of Bhanmo, on the Upper Irawady, and the practicability of a direct trade overland between Calcutta and China. [*Jl.* xvii, pt. i, 132.

Grant, Capt. F. T.—Progress of the Boring for Coal at Jamutra in Cutch. [*Jl.* iii, 40.

Extract from a Journal kept by Captain F. T. Grant, of the Manipur Levy, during a Tour of Inspection of the Manipur Frontier, along the course of the Ningthee river, &c., in January, 1832. [*Jl.* iii, 124.

Grant, Capt. P. W.—On a new Method of determining the Longitude, from the observed Interval between the Transit of the Moon's Enlightened Limb, and that of the Sun, or of one or more Stars. [*As. Res.* vi, 235.

Gray, J. J.—On a simple Method of Manipulation in the Calotype process. [*Jl.* xxiv, 287.

Greenlaw, C. B.—Note to accompany a Map of the Isle St. Martin's. [*Jl.* xi, 309.

Grierson, George A.—Are Kálidása's Heroes monogamists? [*Jl.* xlvi, pt. i, 39.

Notes on the Rangpur Dialect. [*Jl.* xlvi, pt. i, 186.

On the Rungpuri Genitive. [*Proc.* 1878, 64.

The Song of Mánik Chandra. [*Jl.* xlvii. pt. i, 135.

Some Further Notes on Kálidása. [*Jl.* xlviii, pt. i, 32.

An Introduction to the Maithili Language of NorthBihár, containing a Grammar, Chrestomathy and Vocabulary, Part I. [*Jl.* xlix, pt. i, Extra No., 1.

Manbodh's Haribans. [*Jl.* li, pt. i, 129.

An Introduction to the Maithili Language of North Bihár containing a Grammar, Chrestomathy and Vocabulary, Part II. [*Jl.* li, pt. i, Extra No., 1.

Essays on Bihárí Declension and Conjugation. [*Jl.* lii, pt. i, 119.

Griffith, R. T. H.—Indian Idylls, No. I. [*Jl.* xxx, 110.

Griffith, Dr. William.—Description of two genera of the Family of *Hamamelideæ*, two species of *Podostemon* and one species of *Kaulfussia*. [*As. Res.* xix, pt. i. 94.

Description of some Grasses which form part of the vegetation in the Jheels of the district of Sylhet. [*Jl.* v, 570.

Some Remarks on the Development of Pollen. [*Jl.* v, 732.

Remarks on a Collection of Plants made at Sadiyá, Upper Assam, from April to September, 1836. [*Jl.* v, 806.

Journal of a Visit to the Mishmee Hills in Assam. [*Jl.* vi, 325.

Report on the Caoutchouc Tree of Assam. [*Jl.* vii, 132.

Journal of the Mission which visited Bootan, in 1837-38, under Captain R. Boileau Pemberton. [*Jl.* viii, 208, 251.

Extracts from a Report on subjects connected with Affghanistan. [*Jl.* x, 797, 977.

Tables of Barometrical and Thermometrical Observations, made in Affghanistan, Upper Scinde and Kutch Gundava, during the years 1839-40. [*Jl.* xi, 49.

Some Account of the Botanical Collection brought from the eastward in 1841, by Dr. Cantor. [*Jl.* xxiii, 623.

Grote, Arthur.—A Memoir of the late Mr. Ed. Blyth, C.M.Z.S., and Hon. Member, Asiatic Soc. of Bengal. [*Jl.* xliv. pt. ii, Extra No., iii.

Growse, F. S.—Some Objections to the Modern Style of Official Hindustani. [*Jl.* xxxv, pt. i, 172.

On the Transliteration of Indian Alphabets in Roman Characters. [*Jl.* xxxvi, pt. i, 136.

On the village of Paindhat, Mainpuri. [*Proc.* 1868, 62.

Further Notes on the Prithirajráyasa. [*Jl.* xxxviii, pt. i, 1.

The Poems of Chand Barday. [*Jl.* xxxvii, pt. i, 119.

Translations from Chand. [*Jl.* xxxviii, pt. i, 161.

Rejoinder to Mr. Beames. [*Jl.* xxxix, pt. i, 52.

The Country of Braj. [*Jl.* xl, pt. i, 34.

The Tírthas of Vrindá-vana and Gokula [*Jl.* xli, pt. i, 313.

Note on the Proportion of the Muhammadan and Hindu Population of the village of Dotána near Mathurá. [*Proc.* 1873, 81.

A Metrical Version of the opening Stanzas of Chand's Prithiráj Rásau, [*Jl.* xlii, pt. i, 329.

The Etymology of Local Names in Northern India, as exemplified in the district of Mathurá. [*Jl.* xliii, pt. i, 324.

Supposed Greek Sculpture at Mathurá. [*Jl.* xliv, pt. i, 212.

The Prologue to the Rámáyana of Tulsi Dás. A specimen translation. [*Jl.* xlv, pt. i, 1.

Srí Swámí Hari Dás of Brindában. [*Jl.* xlv, pt. i, 312.

Mathurá Notes. [*Jl.* xlvii, pt. i, 97.

The Sect of the Prán-náthis. [*Jl.* xlviii, pt. i, 171.

Bulandshahr Antiquities. With a Note by Dr. Rájendralála Mitra. [*Jl.* xlviii, pt. i, 270.

Note on a Photograph of a Buddhist Sculpture found at Bulandshahr. [*Proc.* 1881, 112.

Note on some Curiosities found at Bulandshahr. [*Proc.* 1881, 113.

On a Wax Impression of an old Seal of baked clay found at Bulandshahr. [*Proc.* 1881, 120.

Note on the word "Nuthar," or "Nisar." [*Proc.* 1883, 99.

The Town of Bulandshahr. [*Jl.* lii, pt. i, 270.

Gubbins, Charles.—Mode of Manufacture of the Salumba Salt of Upper India. [*Jl.* vii, 363.

Daily Register of Temperature during a part of 1850, at Meeruth, in the Upper Doab. [*Jl.* xxi, 562a.

Notes on the Ruins at Mahábálipuram on the Coromandel Coast. [*Jl.* xxii, 656.

Gurdyal Singh Sirdar.—Memorandum on the Superstitions connected with Child-birth, and precautions taken and rites performed on the occasion of the birth of a child among the Jats of Hoshiyarpur in the Panjab. [*Jl.* lii, pt. i, 205.

Haidinger, Dr. W.—Report on the Shalka, Futtehpore, Pegu, Assam, and Segowlee Meteorites sent from the Asiatic Society of Bengal (Calcutta) to the Imperial Museum of Vienna. [*Jl.* xxx, 129.

Haines, Capt. S. B.—Ancient Inscription found at Aden. [*Jl.* xi, 958.

Haldar, Rakhal Das.—On Temples near the Barakar river [*Proc.* 1866, 73.

Notes on a Copper-plate Inscription in the possession of certain Kols. [*Proc.* 1869, 203.

An Introduction to the Mundárí Language. [*Jl.* xl, pt. i, 46.

Notes on three Inscriptions on stone found in Chutiá Nágpúr. [*Jl.* xl, pt. i, 108.

Hall, Dr. Fitz-Edward.—Hindí and Urdú-Hindí Tazkiras. [*Jl.* xvii, pt. i, 541.

A Passage in the life of Válmíki. [*Jl.* xxiii, 494.

Of two Edicts bestowing Land, recorded on plates of copper. [*Jl.* xxvii, 217.

A few Remarks on the first Fasciculus of Professor Wilson's Sanskrit Dictionary, as "extended and improved" by Dr. Goldstucker. [*Jl.* xxvii, 301.

Decipherment of a Sanskrit Inscription dated in the fourteenth century, with a translation and notes. [*Jl.* xxviii, 1.

Fragments of three early Hindu Dramatists, Bhasa, Ramila, and Somila. [*Jl.* xxviii 28.

The S'ri-súkta, or Litany to Fortune; text and commentary with translation. [*Jl.* xxviii, 121.

Two Letters on Indian Inscriptions. [*Jl.* xxix, 18.

Hall, Dr. Fitz-Edward (*contd.*)—Of two Land-grants, issued by king Hastin, bearing date in the years 156 and 163 after the Subversion of the Guptas. [*Jl.* xxx, 1.

The Inscriptions of Erikaina, now Eran, re-deciphered and re-translated. [*Jl.* xxx, 14.

Note on Budhagupta. [*Jl.* xxx, 139.

A Donative Inscription of the Tenth Century; the Sanskrit Original and its Substance in English: with Remarks on the later Kings of Dhárá in Málava. [*Jl.* xxx, 195.

Decipherment of an Inscription from Chedi, with a brief Statement of the Historical and other Indications therefrom derived. [*Jl.* xxx, 317.

Letter to the Secretary of the Asiatic Society of Bengal, on some Recent Statements touching certain of the Gupta Kings and others. [*Jl.* xxx, 383.

Vestiges of Three Royal Lines of Kányakubja, or Kánouj; with Indications of its Literature. [*Jl.* xxxi, 1.

Three Sanskrit Inscriptions: Copies of the Originals, and Prefatory Observations. [*Jl.* xxxi, 111.

Rávana's Commentary on the Rig Veda. [*Jl.* xxxi, 129.

Notes on the Eran Inscription, being extracts from a letter to the Editor. [*Jl.* xxxiv, pt. i, 38.

Halstead, Ed. P.—Report on the Island of Chedooba. [*Jl.* x, 349.

Report on the Island of Chedooba. [*Jl.* x, 419.

Hamilton, Lieut. Charles.—A Description of the Máhwah Tree. [*As. Res.* i. 300.

Hamilton, G.—A short Description of Carnicobar. [*As. Res.* ii, 337.

Hamilton, R. N. C.—Note on the Transport of Coal from the pits at Sonadeh to Bombay, by the Nerbudda. [*Jl.* xviii, 594.

Hamilton, Sir R.—Table of Heights and Distances along the proposed line of Railway from Surat to Agra. [*Jl.* xxv, 221.

Hammer, Baron Joseph Von.—Extracts from the Mohit, that is the Ocean, a Turkish Work on Navigation in the Indian Seas. [*Jl.* iii, 545; v, 441; vi, 805; vii, 767; viii, 823.

Hannay, Lieut.-Col. S. F.—Further information on the Gold Washings of Assam. [*Jl.* vii, 625.

A Short Account of the Moa Morah Sect, and of the Country at present occupied by the Bor Senaputtee. [*Jl.* vii, 671.

Hannay, Lieut.-Col. S. F. (*contd.*) —Memoranda of Earthquakes and other remarkable Occurrences in Upper Assam, from January 1839 to September 1843. [*Jl.* xii, 907.

On the Assam Petroleum Beds. [*Jl.* xiv, 817.

Notes on Ancient Temples and other Remains in the vicinity of Suddyah, Upper Assam. [*Jl.* xvii, pt. i, 459.

Brief Notice of the Sil Háko or stone bridge in Zillah Kámrúp. [*Jl.* xx, 291.

Notes on the Iron Ore Statistics and Economic Geology of Upper Assam. [*Jl.* xxv, 330.

See DALTON, COL. E. T.; PEMBERTON, CAPT. R. B.

Hannyngton, Major J. C.—Barometrical Observations taken to ascertain the Altitude of the Station of Purulia, in the Ramghur district. [*Jl.* xii, 226.

Comparative Tables of the Law of Mortality, the Expectation of Life, and the Values of Annuities in India and England. [*Jl.* xii, 1057.

Note on a Method of determining the Neutral Point of Barometers having small circular cisterns. [*Jl.* xvii, pt. i, 533.

Tables of Mortality according to the experience of the Bengal Civil Service, with the values of Annuities, Assurances, &c. [*Jl.* xix, 250.

Tables for determining Heights by the Barometer. [*Jl.* xix, 394.

Hardie, James. — Remarks on the Geology of the Country on the Route from Baroda to Udayapur, *viâ* Birpur and Salambhar. [*As. Res.* xviii, pt. i, 82.

Sketch of the Geology of Central India, exclusive of Malwa. [*As. Res.* xviii, pt. ii, 27.

Explanation of the Sketch giving a Geological Section of the Strata from Nimach to Merta, published in the Asiatic Researches, Vol. XVIII, page 92. [*Jl.* iii, 238.

Harding, Chas. — Memorandum on the diurnal Variation of Atmospheric Pressure at the Sandheads. With a Prefatory Note by Henry F. Blanford [*Jl.* xlvi, pt. ii, 339.

Hardwicke, Major-Genl. Thomas. —Description of species of Meloë, an insect of the 1st or Coleopterous order in the Linnean system: found in all parts of Bengal, Behar and Oudh, and possessing all the proper ties of the Spanish Blistering Fly or Meloë vesicatorius. [*As. Res.* v, 213.

Hardwicke, Major-Genl. Thomas (*contd.*)—Description of a Zoophyte commonly found about the coasts of Singapore Island. [*As. Res.* xiv, 180.

Description of a substance called Gez. or Manna, and the Insect producing it. [*As. Res.* xiv, 182.

Narrative of a Journey to Sirinagur. [*As. Res.* vi, 309.

Harington, John Herbert.—A Description of a Cave near Gya. [*As. Res.* i, 276.

The Plan of a Common-Place Book. [*As. Res.* iii, 249.

Remarks upon the Authorities of Mosulman Law. [*As. Res.* x, 475.

Harishchandra. — Extracts from a letter on a new Hindi Book—Dristokutá of Sur Dás. [*Proc.* 1879, 5.

Harman, Lieut. H. J.—On the Operations for obtaining the Discharges of the large Rivers in Upper Assam, during Season 1877-78. [*Jl.* xlviii, pt. ii, 4,

Harris, Captn. J. C.—Notes on the Rainfall in the Basin of the river Mahanuddy and the Floods consequent thereupon. [*Jl.* xxx, 216.

Hart, Capt. N. — Some Account of a Journey from Kurrachee to Hinglaj, in the Lus territory, descriptive of the intermediate country, and of the port of Soumeanee. [*Jl.* ix, 134.

Letter from Capt. Hart, forwarding a Map of the Route to Hinglaj. [*Jl.* ix, 615.

General Notice of the tribe of Kujjukzyes (Upper Sinde). [*Jl.* ix, 1214.

Note on the Brahooees. [*Jl.* x, 136.

Haughton, Col. J. C. — Memorandum on the Geological Structure and Mineral Resources of the Singhbhoom Division, South-West Frontier Agency. [*Jl.* xxiii, 103.

Account of a Meteor in Cooch Behar, April 30th, 1869. [*Proc.* 1866, 169.

Hay, Capt. W. C. — Account of Coins found at Bameean. [*Jl.* ix, 68.

Notes on the Wild Sheep of the Hindoo Koosh, and a species of Cicada. [*Jl.* ix, 440.

Fossil Shells discovered by Capt. Hay. [*Jl.* ix, 1126.

Note on a Bird, Native of the Eastern Islands, undescribed (?). [*Jl.* x, 573.

Report on the Valley of Spiti; and facts collected with a view to a future Revenue Settlement. [*Jl.* xix, 429.

Heatly, S. G. Tollemache.—On the Theory of Angular Geometry. [*Jl.* xi, 23

Heatly, S. G. Tollemache (*contd.*)—
A Note on Capt. Shortrede's Remarks on the Theory of Angular Geometry in No. CXXIII (Page 240) of this Journal. [*Jl.* xi, 782.
Contributions towards a History of the development of the Mineral Resources of India. [*Jl.* xi, 811.
On the Treatment of Geometry as a branch of Analysis. [*Jl.* xii, 110.
Contributions towards a History of the Mineral Resources of the development of India. [*Jl.* xii, 542.

Hekekyan Bey.—Notice of the Cave Temples and Emerald Mines of Sakeyt, in the eastern desert of Egypt. [*Jl.* xvi, 1138.
Notes on the Eastern Desert of Egypt, from Gebel Afrit, by the ancient Porphyry Quarries of Gebel Dukhan, near to the old station of Gebel Gir; with a brief account of the Ruins at Gebel Dukhan. [*Jl.* xvii, pt. ii 584.
Note on the Strata cut through in excavating for Coal in Wádi Araba, eastern desert of Egypt. [*Jl.* xix, 139.
Note on the Formations and Lead Mines of Kohel at Teráfeh, Eastern desert of Egypt. [*Jl.* xix, 217.

Helfer, Dr. John William.—On the Indigenous Silkworms of India. [*Jl.* vi, 38.
Report on the Coal discovered in the Tenasserim provinces. [*Jl.* vii. 701.
Note on the Animal Productions of the Tenasserim Provinces. [*Jl.* vii, 855.
Third Report on Tenasserim—the surrounding Nations,—Inhabitants, Natives and Foreigners—Character, Morals and Religion. [*Jl.* viii, 973.
Fourth Report on the Tenasserim Provinces, considered as a resort for Europeans. [*Jl.* ix, 155.

Henderson, Capt. H. B. Results of an Enquiry respecting the Law of Mortality, for British India, deduced from the Reports and Appendices of the Committee appointed by the Bengal Government in 1834, to consider the expediency of a Government Life Assurance Institution. [*As. Res.* xx, pt. i, 190.

Henderson, Capt. W.—Memorandum on the Nature and Effects of the Flooding of the Indus on 10th August, 1858, as ascertained at Attok and its neighbourhood. [*Jl.* xxviii, 199.

Hendley, Dr. T. H.—An Account of the Maiwár Bhils. [*Jl.* xliv, pt. i, 347.

Hennessey, J. B. N.—Letter on an Outburst of Sunspots. [*Proc.* 1881, 153.

Hennessey, Sir John Pope.—On Chinese Bank-Notes. [*Proc.* 1882, 77.

Herbert, Capt. J. D. — An Account of a Tour made to lay down the Course and Levels of the river Setlej or Satúdrá, as far as traceable within the limits of the British Authority, performed in 1819. [*As. Res.* xv, 339.
On the Zehr Mohereh, or Snake-Stone. [*As. Res.* xvi, 382.
Notice of the Occurrence of Coal, within the Indo-Gangetic Tract of Mountains. [*As. Res.* xvi, 397.
Notice of the Occurrence of Gypsum in the Indo-Gangetic tract of Mountains. [*As. Res.* xviii, pt. i, 216.
On the Mineral Productions of that part of the Himálaya Mountains lying between the Satlaj and the Káli (Gágra) rivers; considered in an economical point of view; including an account of the Mines, and methods of working them, with suggestions for their improvement. [*As. Res.* xviii, pt. i, 227.
Report of the Mineralogical Survey of the Himalaya Mountains lying between the rivers Sutlej and Kalee. Illustrated by a Geological Map. [*Jl.* xi (suppl.) i.
Journal of Captain Herbert's Tour from Almorah in a N. W., W., and S. W. direction, through parts of the province of Kumaon and British Gurhwal, chiefly in the centre of the Hills, *vide* No. 66, Indian Atlas. Edited by J. H. Batten. [*Jl.* xiii, 734.
Geological Map. [*Jl.* xiii, pt. i, 171.
See HOGSON, CAPT. J. A.

Herschel, W.—Description of the Chandrarekhágurh near Sashtanee, Pergunnah Nyegur, Zillah Midnapore. [*Jl.* xxxv, pt i, 111.
Description of a Hindu Temple converted into a Mosque at Gaganesvar, Zila Medinípur. [*Jl.* xxxvii. pt. i, 78.

Hesselmeyer, Revd. C. H. — The Hill Tribes of the Northern Frontier of Assam [*Jl.* xxxvii, pt. ii, 192.

Hildebrant, Chev. Hans.—Memorandum on Swedish Remains and the Indian Prehistoric Tumuli and Markings. [*Proc.* 1880, 89.

Hill, S. A.—On the Measurement of Solar Radiation by means of the black-bulb Thermometer in vacuo. [*Jl.* lii, pt. ii, 3.

Hill, S. A. (*contd.*)—Hindu Antiquities, Photographs of, in Java. [*Proc.* 1873, 153.

Hindu Coins, Ancient, from Jyonpur and Oojein. [*Jl.* vii, 1052.

Hiranand Pandit. — *See* KITTOE, CAPT. M.

Hislop, Revd. Stephen.—On the age of the Coal Strata in Western Bengal and Central India. [*Jl.* xxiv, 347.

Hodgson, B. H. — Notices of the Languages, Literature and Religion of the Bauddhas of Nepal and Bhot. [*As. Res.* xvi, 409.

Route from Cathmandu in Nepal to Tāzedx, on the Chinese Frontier, with some occasional allusions to the manners and customs of the Bhotiahs, by Amir, a Cashmiro-Bhotiah by birth, and by vocation an interpreter to the traders on the route described. [*As. Res.* xvii, 513.

On a New Species of *Buceros.* [*As. Res.* xviii, pt. i, 178.

On a Species of *Aquila circæetus* and *Dicrurus.* [*As. Res.* xviii, pt. ii, 13.

On the Migration of the *Natatores* and *Grallatores*, as observed at Kathmandu. [*As. Res.* xviii, pt. ii, 122.

The Wild Goat, and the Wild Sheep, of Nepal. [*As. Res.* xviii, pt. ii, 129.

On the Ratwa Deer of Nepal. [*As. Res.* xviii, pt. ii, 139.

Description of the *Buceros Homrai* of the Himalaya. [*As. Res.* xviii, pt. ii, 169.

Description of the Wild Dog of the Himalaya. [*As. Res.* xviii, pt. ii, 221.

Indication of a New Genus of the Carnivora, with description of the species on which it is founded. [*As. Res.* xix, pt. i, 60.

Description of Three New Species of Paradoxurus, inhabiting the Southern, Central, and Northern Regions of Nèpál respectively, with notices of the habits and structure of the Genus. [*As. Res.* xix, pt. i, 72.

Notices of the Ornithology of Nèpál. [*As. Res.* xix, pt. i, 143.

On the Administration of Justice in Nepál, with some account of the several Courts, extent of their jurisdiction, and modes of procedure. [*As. Res.* xx, pt. i, 94.

On the Native Method of making the Paper, denominated in Hindustan, Nipalese. [*Jl.* i, 8.

Further Illustrations of the Antelope Hodgesonii, [*Jl.* i, 59.

Hodgson, B. H. (*contd.*) — Note relative to the account of the Cervus jarâi, published in the *Gleanings*, No. 34 [*Jl.* i, 66.

On the Mammalia of Nepal. [*Jl.* i, 335.

Origin and Classification of the Military Tribes of Nepal. [*Jl.* ii, 217.

Note on the Chiru Antelope. [*Jl.* iii, 138.

Classification of Néwárs or Aborigines of Népál Proper, preceded by the most authoritative Legend relative to the Origin and Early History of the Race. [*Jl.* iii. 215.

European Speculations on Buddhism. [*Jl.* iii, 382.

Further Remarks on M. Remusat's Review of Buddhism. [*Jl.* iii, 425.

Notice of some Ancient Inscriptions in the Characters of the Allahabad Column. [*Jl.* iii, 481.

Remarks on M. Remusat's Review of Buddhism. [*Jl.* iii, 499.

Account of a Visit to the Ruins of Simroun, once the capital of the Mithila province. [*Jl.* iv, 121.

Remarks on an Inscription in the Ranja and Tibetan (Uchhén) Characters, taken from a Temple on the confines of the valley of Nepal. [*Jl.* iv, 196.

Further Note on the Inscription from Sárnáth. [*Jl.* iv, 211

Description of the Bearded Vulture of the Himálaya. [*Jl.* iv, 454.

On the Red-billed Erolia. [*Jl.* iv, 458, 701.

Synopsis of the Thár and Ghorál Antelopes. [*Jl.* iv, 487.

On the Wild Goat and Wild Sheep of Himálaya, with remarks on the genera, capra and ovis [*Jl.* iv, 490.

Specific Description of a new species of Cervus. [*Jl.* iv, 649.

Synopsis of the *Vespertilionidæ* of Nipal. [*Jl.* iv, 699.

Description of the little Musteline animal, denominated Káthiah Nyul in the Catalogue of the Nepálese Mammalia. [*Jl.* iv, 702.

Postscript to the Account of the Wild Goat of Nepal. [*Jl.* iv, 710.

Quotations from original Sanscrit authorities in proof and illustration of Mr. Hodgson's Sketch of Buddhism. [*Jl.* v, 28, 71.

Description of a new species of Columba. [*Jl.* v, 122.

Summary description of some new species of *Falconidæ.* [*Jl.* v, 227.

Hodgson, B. H. (*contd.*)—Synoptical description of sundry new animals, enumerated in the Catalogue of Nepálese Mammals. [*Jl.* v, 231.

Description of two new species belonging to a new form of the Meruline Group of Birds, with indication of their generic character. [*Jl.* v, 358.

On a new genus of the *Meropidæ.* [*Jl.* v, 360.

On a new Piscatory genus of the Strigine Family. [*Jl.* v, 362.

Postscript to the account of Ursitaxus, printed in the 19th volume of Researches As. Soc. [*Jl.* v, 671.

Note on Zoological Nomenclature. [*Jl.* v, 751.

Additions to the Ornithology of Népal. [*Jl.* v, 770.

On three new genera or sub-genera of long-legged Thrushes, with description of their species. [*Jl.* vi, 101.

Description of three new species of Woodpecker. [*Jl.* vi, 104.

Indication of a new genus of Insessorial Birds. [*Jl.* vi, 110.

On a new genus of the *Sylviadæ*, with description of three new species. [*Jl.* vi. 230.

On some new genera of *Raptores*, with remarks on the old genera. [*Jl.* vi, 361.

New species of *Scolopacidæ*, Indian Snipes. [*Jl.* vi, 489.

On a new genus of *Plantigrades.* [*Jl.* vi, 560.

Note on the Primary Language of the Buddhist writings. [*Jl.* vi, 682.

On the Bibos, Gauri Gau, or Gauríká Gan of the Indian Forests. [*Jl.* vi, 745.

On a new species of Pheasant from Tibet. [*Jl.* vii. 863.

On a new genus of the Fissirostral Tribe. [*Jl.* viii, 35.

Two new species of Meruline Birds. [*Jl.* viii, 37.

On Cuculus. [*Jl.* viii. 136.

On three new species of Musk (Moschus) inhabiting the Himalayan districts. [*Jl.* viii, 202.

Summary Description of four new species of Otter. [*Jl.* viii, 319.

A Cursory Notice of Nayakote. [*Jl.* ix, 1114.

On the Common Hare of the Gangetic Provinces and of the Sub-Himalaya; with a slight notice of a strictly Himalayan species. [*Jl.* ix, 1183.

Three new species of Monkey; with remarks on the genera Semnopithecus et Macacus. [*Jl.* ix, 1211.

Hodgson, B. H. (*contd.*)—Classical Terminology of Natural History. [*Jl.* x, 26.

On the two Wild Species of Sheep inhabiting the Himalayan region, with some brief remarks on the craniological character of Ovis, and its allies. [*Jl.* x, 230.

Note on the Cervus Elaphus (?) of the Sal Forest of Nepâl, Hodie, C. Affinis nob. [*Jl.* x, 721.

Notice of the Marmot of the Himálaya and of Tibet. [*Jl.* x, 777.

On a new Organ in the Genus Moschus. [*Jl.* x, 795.

Of a new species of Lagomys inhabiting Nepal, (with Plate)—Lagomys Nepalensis, Nob. [*Jl.* x, 854.

Notice of a new form of the Glaucopinæ, or Rasorial Crows, inhabiting the Northern region of Nepal—Conostoma Æmodius (Nobis type). [*Jl.* x, 856.

Classified Catalogue of Mammals of Nepal (corrected to the end of 1841, first printed in 1832). [*Jl.* x, 907.

Notice of the Mammals of Tibet, with descriptions and plates of some new species. [*Jl.* xi, 275.

Description of a new genus of Falconidæ. [*Jl.* xii, 127.

Translation of the Naipália Devuta Kalyána, with Notes. [*Jl.* xii, 400.

Notice of two Marmots inhabiting respectively the plains of Tibet and the Himálayan Slopes near to the Snows, and also of a Rhinolophus of the central region of Nepal. [*Jl.* xii, 409.

Additions to the Catalogue of Nepal Birds. [*Jl.* xii, 447.

On a new species of Cervus, Cervus Dimorphé. [*Jl.* xii, 897.

Summary Description of two new species of Flying Squirrel. [*Jl.* xiii, 67.

Description of a new species of Tibetan Antelope; with Plates. [*Jl.* xv, 334.

On a new form of the Hog kind, or Suidæ. [*Jl.* xvi, 423.

On the Hispid Hare of the Saul forest. [*Jl.* xvi, 572.

Postscript on the Pigmy Hog of the Saul forest. [*Jl.* xvi, 593.

On Various Genera of the Ruminants. [*Jl.* xvi, 685.

On the Tibetan Badger, Taxidia leucurus, N. S. [*Jl.* xvi, 763.

On a new species of Porcupine. [*Jl.* xvi, 771.

On the Charj, or Otis bengalensis. [*Jl.* xvi, 883.

Hodgson, B. H. (*contd.*)—The Slaty-blue Magaderme; Magaderma schistacea, N. S. [*Jl.* xvi, 889.

On a new species of Plecotus. [*Jl.* xvi, 894.

On the tame Sheep and Goats of the sub-Himálayas and of Tibet. [*Jl.* xvi, 1003.

On the Cat-toed Subplantigrades of the sub-Himálayas. [*Jl.* xvi, 1113.

On the Aborigines of the sub-Himálayas. [*Jl.* xvi, 1235.

Comparative Vocabulary of the several Languages or Dialects of the Eastern sub-Himálayas, from the Káli or Ghógrá, to the Dhansri, with the written and spoken Tibetan for comparison. [*Jl.* xvi, 1245.

Addenda et Corrigenda of the Paper on the Aborigines of the sub-Himálayas, in the December No. of the Journal. [*Jl.* xvii, pt. i, 73.

Ethnography and Geography of the sub-Himálayas. [*Jl.* xvii, pt. i, 544.

Tibetan type of Mankind. [*Jl.* xvii, pt. ii, 222.

Relics of the Catholic Mission in Tibet. [*Jl.* xvii, pt. ii, 225.

Anatomy of Ailurus, Porcula, and Stylocerus, in continuation, with sundry miscellaneous emendatory Notes. [*Jl.* xvii, pt. ii, 475.

The Aborigines of Central India. [*Jl.* xvii, pt. ii, 550.

Addendum on the Anatomy of Ailurus. [*Jl.* xvii, pt. ii, 573.

Route from Káthmándú, the capital of Nepal, to Darjeeling in Sikim, interspersed with remarks on the people and country. [*Jl.* xvii, pt. ii, 634.

Memorandum relative to the seven Cósis of Nepal. [*Jl.* xvii, pt. ii, 646.

On the Chépáng and Kúsúnda Tribes of Népál. [*Jl.* xvii, pt. ii, 650.

A Brief Note on Indian Ethnology. [*Jl.* xviii, 238.

Aborigines of Southern India. [*Jl.* xviii, 350.

The Polecat of Tibet, N. S. [*Jl.* xviii, 446.

On the Aborigines of North-Eastern India. [*Jl.* xviii, 451.

On the Origin, Location, Numbers, Creed, Customs, Character and Condition of the Kóoch, Bodo and Dhimál People, with a general description of the climate they dwell in. [*Jl.* xviii, 702.

On the Physical Geography of the Himálaya. [*Jl.* xviii, 761.

On the Aborigines of the Eastern Frontier. [*Jl.* xviii, 967.

Hodgson, B. H. (*contd.*)—On the Tákin of the Eastern Himálaya; Budorcas Taxicolor mihi, N. G. (With three Plates). [*Jl.* xix, 6.

Aborigines of the North-East Frontier. [*Jl.* xix, 309.

Aborigines of the South. [*Jl.* xix, 461.

On the Shou or Tibetan Stag. [*Jl.* xix, 466.

Additional Notice of the Shou or Tibetan Stag. [*Jl.* xix, 518.

On the Shou or Tibetan Stag, Cervus Affinis, mihi. (With two Plates). [*Jl.* xx, 388.

On the Indo-Chinese Borderers. and their connexion with the Himálayans and Tibetans. [*Jl.* xxii, 1.

On the Mongolian Affinities of the Caucasians. [*Jl.* xxii, 26.

Sifán and Hórsók Vocabularies, with another special exposition in the wide range of Mongolidan affinities and remarks on the lingual and physical characteristics of the family. [*Jl.* xxii, 121.

Catalogue of Nipalese Birds, collected between 1824 and 1844. [*Jl.* xxiv, 572.

Aborigines of the Nilgiris. [*Jl.* xxv, 31.

On a new Perdicine Bird from Tibet. [*Jl.* xxv. 165.

Route of two Nepalese Embassies to Pekin, with remarks on the water-shed and Plateau of Tibet. [*Jl.* xxv, 473.

Aborigines of the Nilgiris, with remarks on their Affinities. [*Jl.* xxv. 498.

On a new Lagomys and a new Mustela inhabiting the north region of Sikim and the proximate parts of Tibet. [*Jl.* xxvi, 207.

Comparative Vocabulary of the Languages of the broken Tribes of Nepal. [*Jl.* xxvi, 317, 429 ; xxvii, 393.

Description of a new species of Himálayan Mole, Talpa Macrura. [*Jl.* xxvii, 176.

Hodgson, B. H., and Blyth, E.—Catalogue of Nepalese Birds presented to the Asiatic Society, duly named and classified. Revised by Ed. Blyth. [*Jl.* xii, 301.

Hodgson, B. H., and Campbell, A.—Illustrations of the Genera of the Bovinæ.—Part I. Skeletons of Bos Bibos, and Bison, the individuals examined being the Common Bull of Nepal, the Gowri Gao of Nepal and the Yak. [*Jl.* x, 449.

Hodgson, C. K.—Memorandum on Earthquakes in January 1849, at Burpetah, Assam. [*Jl.* xviii, 174.

Hodgson, Capt. J. A.—Latitudes of Places in Hindustan and the Northern Mountains, with observations of Longitude in the Mountains, according to Immersions and Emersions of Jupiter's Satellites. [*As. Res.* xiv, 153.

Memorandum on the Differences of the Meridian of the Observatory at Madras, and the Flag-staff of Fort William, and of the Cantonment of Futtehghur in the Doab. [*Jl.* ix, 75.

Hodgson, Lt.-Col. J. A.—Journal of a Survey to the Heads of the rivers, Ganges and Jumna. [*As. Res.* xiv, 60.

Hodgson, Lt.-Col. J. A., and Blossville, M. de.—Observations on the Inclination and Declination of the Magnetic Needle. [*As. Res.* xviii, 1.

Hodgson, Lt.-Col. J. A., and Herbert, Lt. J. D.—An Account of Trigonometrical and Astronomical Operations for determining the Heights and Positions of the principal Peaks of the Himálaya Mountains. [*As. Res.* xiv, 187.

Hoernle, Revd. Dr. A. F. Rudolf.—On the term Gaurian as a name for the Sanskritic Vernaculars of North India. [*Proc.* 1872, 177.

Essays in aid of a Comparative Grammar of the Gaurian Languages. [*Jl.* xli, pt. i, 120; xlii, pt. i, 59; xliii, pt. i, 22.

A new Prakrit Grammar by Chaṇḍa. [*Proc.* 1878, 178.

Exhibition of a Prakrit Grammar of Vararuchi. [*Proc.* 1879, 79.

Exhibition of facsimiles of Inscriptions sent by Mr. H. Rivett-Carnac, C. I. E. [*Proc.* 1879, 122.

Description of the Gold Coins found in the Ahin Posh Tope near Jelalabad. [*Proc.* 1879, 122.

Exhibition of four Coins presented to the Society by Mr. F. S. Growse. [*Proc.* 1879, 173.

Remarks on Coins found in the Ahin Posh Tope. [*Proc.* 1879, 210.

Exhibition of ten Copper Coins of the Mitra Dynasty, and description of the same by A. C. Carlleyle. [*Proc.* 1880, 7.

Exhibition of a copy of a Pali Inscription sent by Mr. A. M. Markham. [*Proc.* 1880, 55.

Hoernle, Revd. Dr. A. F. Rudolf (*Contd.*)—Exhibition of the Impression and Sketch of a Gold Medal sent by Mr. T. A. M. Gennoe. [*Proc.* 1880, 100.

Exhibition of a MS. of an unknown Prakrit Grammar. [*Proc.* 1880, 101.

Exhibition of Brass Coins sent by Mr. H. Rivett-Carnac. [*Proc.* 1880, 102.

Remarks on Roman Indo-Scythian and Gupta Coins sent by Mr. H. Rivett-Carnac. [*Proc.* 1880, 118.

A Collection of Hindí Roots, with Remarks on their Derivation and Classification. [*Jl.* xlix, pt. i, 33.

Exhibition of Coins belonging to Mr. R. Nicholson. [*Proc.* 1881, 39.

Exhibition of Coins of the later Delhi Emperors. [*Proc.* 1881, 40.

On Coins, &c., from Khokhrakote. [*Proc.* 1811, 71.

Exhibition of Relics from Buddha Gaya. [*Proc.* 1881, 88.

A new Find of Early Muhammadun Coins. [*Jl.* l, pt. i, 53.

Exhibition of three Coins found near Mahanad, forwarded by the Rev. K. S. Macdonald. [*Proc.* 1882, 91.

Second Exhibition of a Coin from Mahanada, with Note by General Cunningham. [*Proc.* 1882, 104.

Exhibition of a Birch Bark MS. from Bakhsháli. [*Proc.* 1882, 108.

Exhibition of Coins and Clay Figures from Toomluk. [*Proc.* 1882, 111.

Exhibition of ten Silver Coins from Chhindwara. [*Proc.* 1882, 114.

Exhibition of three Clay Seals from Mr. Carr-Stephen. [*Proc.* 1880, 114.

Remarks on the Pali Grammarian Kachchayana. [*Proc.* 1882, 125.

Exhibition of Coins from Midnapur. [*Proc.* 1883, 59.

Note on Gold Coin sent by Mr. W. Campbell. [*Proc.* 1883, 143.

Note on Gold Coins forwarded by Mr. H. Rivett-Carnac. [*Proc.* 1883, 143.

Note on Bihári Declension and Conjugation. [*Jl.* lii, pt. i, 159.

A new Find of Muhammadan Coins of Bengal (Independent Period). [*Jl.* lii, pt. i. 211.

Holmboe, Prof.—*See* MITRA, RAJENDRALALA.

Homfray, J. — A Description of the Coal Field of the Damoodah Valley and the Adjacent Countries of Beerbhoom and Poorooleah, as applicable to the present date, 1842. [*Jl.* xi, 723.

Honigberger, Dr. Martin.—Journal of a Route from Dera-Ghazi-Khan, through the Veziri country, to Kabul. [*Jl.* iii, 175.

Hooker, Dr. J. D. — Observations made when following the Grand Trunk Road across the hills of Upper Bengal. Parus Nath, &c., in the Soane Valley; and on the Kymaon branch of the Vindhya Hills. [*Jl.* xvii, pt. ii, 355.

Notes, chiefly Botanical, made during an excursion from Darjeeling to Tongló, a lofty mountain on the confines of Sikkim and Nepal. [*Jl.* xviii, 419.

Horne, Charles.—On punched silver bits. [*Proc.* 1865, 149.

On Temple of Boodh Gya. [*Proc.* 1865, 162, 150.

Notes on Boodh Gaya. [*Jl.* xxxiv, pt. i, 278.

On Immunity from Wasp-stings. [*Proc.* 1866, 238.

On Fireflies. [*Proc.* 1866, 239.

Notes on Atranji Khera or Pi-lo-shan-na of General Cunningham. [*Jl.* xxxv. pt. i, 165.

Notes on the Jumma Masjid of Etáwáh. [*Jl.* xxxvi, pt. i, 74.

Notes on Buddhist Remains near Mynpoorie. [*Jl.* xxxvi, pt. i, 105.

Notes on the Carvings on the Buddhist Rail-posts at Budh Gayá. [*Jl.* xxxvi, pt. i, 107.

Notes on Ancient Remains in the Mainpuri District. [*Jl.* xxxvi, pt. i, 157.

Notes on the Age of the Ruins chiefly situate at Banaras and Jaunpur. [*Jl.* xlii, pt. i, 160.

See SHERRING, REVD. M. A.

Hoste, Capt. De la. — *See* DE LA HOSTE, CAPT.

Hough, Revd. G. H.—Translation of an Inscription on the Great Bell of Rangoon, with Notes and Illustrations. [*As. Res.* xvi, 270.

Howison, James.—Some Account of the Elastic Gum Vine of Prince of Wales' Island, and of experiments made on the milky juice which it produces; with hints respecting the useful purposes to which it may be applied. [*As. Res.* v, 157.

Huffnagle, Charles.—On the 'Electrotype.' [*Jl.* x, 478.

Hugel, Baron.—Notice of a Visit to the valley of Cashmir in 1836. [*Jl.* v, 184.

Hugel, Baron, and Fulljames, Geo.—Recent Discovery of Fossil Bones in Perim Island in the Cambay Gulf. [*Jl.* v, 288.

Hughes, Geo.—Are there Tenses in Arabic? [*Proc.* 1883, 129.

Hughes, Capt. W. G. — Copperplate Inscription found at Karenee. [*Proc.* 1872, 138.

Hughes, Rev. T. P.—Abstract of an Account of a Visit to Kafiristan. [*Proc.* 1883, 105.

Hugon, Thomas. — Remarks on the Silkworms and Silks of Assam. [*Jl.* vi, 21.

Human Race, Queries respecting the, to be addressed to Travellers and others. Drawn up by a Committee of the British Association for the advancement of Science, appointed in 1839, and circulated by the Ethnographical Society of London. [*Jl.* xiii, 919.

Humboldt, Baron Von. — What to observe on the Himálayas. [*Jl.* xvii, pt. i, 324.

Hume, Allan O.—Letter on certain Birds. [*Proc.* 1870, 265.

Additional Observations regardng some species of Birds noticed by Mr. W. T. Blanford, in his "*Ornithological Notes from Southern, Western and Central India.*" [*Jl.* xxxix, pt. ii, 113.

Note on a few species of Burmese Birds. [*Proc.* 1872, 70.

New species of Birds exhibited and characterised. [*Proc.* 1874, 106.

Note on two apparently undescribed species of Goat from Northern India, and a new species of Dove from the Nicobar Islands. [*Proc.* 1874, 240.

On a supposed new Sheep from the Central Hills of Kelat. [*Jl.* xlvi, pt. ii, 327.

Hunter, Dr. William.—On the Plant Morinda and its uses. [*As. Res.* iv, 35.

Astronomical Observations made in the upper parts of Hindustan, and on a Journey thence to Oujein. [*As. Res.* iv, 141.

Astronomical Observations. [*As. Res.* iv, 359.

Some Account of the Astronomical Labours of Jayasinha, Rajah of Ambhere, of Jayanagar. [*As. Res.* v, 177.

Astronomical Observations made in the Upper Provinces of Hindustan. [*As. Res.* v, 413.

Hunter, Dr. William (*contd.*)—
Narrative of a Journey from Agra to Oujein. [*As. Res.* vi, 7.
Remarks on the species of Pepper which are found on Prince of Wales' Island. [*As. Res.* ix, 383.

Hurry, W. C.—Note on the "Trochilus and Crocodile" of Herodotus. [*Jl.* viii, 590.

Hutton, Capt. Thos.—On the Habits of the Paludinœ. [*Jl.* i, 411.
Notes in Natural History. [*Jl.* i, 474, 554.
On the Nest of the Tailor Bird. [*Jl.* ii, 502.
On the Land Shells of India. [*Jl.* iii, 81, 520.
Account of the Bearded Vulture of the Hymálaya. [*Jl.* iii, 522.
Extracts from a Journal kept during a Voyage from England to Calcutta in 1831. [*Jl.* iv, 167.
Observations on an Article in Loudon's Magazine of Natural History, on the subject of the Albatross. [*Jl.* iv, 106.
Nest of a Bengal Vulture (Vultur Bengalensis); with Observations on the power of scent ascribed to the Vulture Tribe. [*Jl.* vi, 112.
On the "Indian Boa," "Python Tigris." [*Jl.* vi, 528.
Geometric Tortoises, "Testudo Geometrica." [*Jl.* vi, 689.
Journal of a Trip to the Burenda Pass, in 1836. [*Jl.* vi, 901.
Notice of the Himálayan Vulture Eagle. [*Jl.* vii, 20.
Journal of a Trip through Kunawur, Hungrung, and Spiti, undertaken in the year 1838, under the patronage of the Asiatic Society of Bengal, for the purpose of determining the geological formation of those districts. [*Jl.* viii, 901; ix, 489, 555.
Wool and Woollen Manufactures of Khorassan. [*Jl.* ix, 327.
Geological Report on the Valley of the Spiti, and of the Route from Kotghur. [*Jl.* x, 198.
On Galeodes (vorax?) [*Jl.* xi, 857.
On the Wool of the Bactrian, or two-humped Camel (Camelus Bactrianus), being a copy of an unpublished Paper forwarded to the Royal Asiatic Society of London. [*Jl.* xi, 1182.
Note on the "Flata Limbata," and the White Wax of China. [*Jl.* xii. 898, 1011.
Observations on the Ovis Ammonoides of Hodgson. [*Jl.* xvi, 568.

Hutton, Capt. Thos. (*contd.*)—
Rough Notes on the Ornithology of Candahar and its neighbourhood. [*Jl.* xvi, 775.
Notes on the Nidification of Indian Birds. [*Jl.* xvii, pt. ii, 3, 681.
Notes of some Land and Fresh-water Shells occurring in Afghanisthan. [*Jl.* xviii, 64.
Remarks on the Snow Line in the Himálaya. [*Jl.* xviii, 954.

Hutton, Capt. Thos., and Benson, W. H.—On the Land and Fresh-water Shells of the Western Himálaya. [*Jl.* vii, 211.

Hutton, Capt. Thos., & Blyth, Edward.—Rough Notes on the Zoology of Candahar and the Neighbouring Districts. With Notes by Ed. Blyth. [*Jl.* xiv, 340; xv, 135.

Hutton, Capt. Thos., and Smith, Lieut. J.—Report on some Inscriptions found at Hammam on the Southern Coast of Arabia, 1835. [*Jl.* iv, 533.

Hyde, Col. H.—Observations on the effect of a Thunderstorm on a Self-registering Indicator. [*Proc.* 1870, 269.
Exhibition of two specimens of Wrought-iron showing Crystalline Structure. [*Proc.* 1874, 73.

Ibbetson, D.—Letter asking for information regarding the Ethnology of the Panjab. [*Proc.* 1882, 157.

Impey, Major H. B.—Notes on the Garját States of Patna. [*Jl.* xxxiv, pt. i, 101.

Impey, Dr.—Description of a Colossal Jain Figure, nearly 80 feet high, cut in relief, discovered on a Spur of the Satpoorah Range, in the district of Burwanie, on the Nerbudda. [*Jl.* xviii, 918.

Index to the Indian Geological, Mineralogical and Palæontological Papers and Analysis in the Journal of the Asiatic Society. [*Jl.* xx, 409.

India. Computation of the Area of the Kingdoms and Principalities of. [*Jl.* ii. 488.

"Indian Oak," Narrative of facts attending the Wreck of the Transport on the Loochoo Islands. [*Jl.* ix, 916.

Indus and **Ganges** rivers, Comparison of the [*Jl.* i, 20.

Inscriptions, Ancient (*see* also PRINSEP, JAMES). [*Jl.* vii, 1055.

Iron Foundry at Kasipur, near Calcutta, Roof of the New. [*Jl.* iv, 111.

Iron in the Kasya Hills, Smelting of [*Jl.* i, 150.

Irvine, Dr. — On the Cotton called "Nurma." [*Jl.* xi, 311.

Irvine, Dr. R. H.—A few Observations on the Probable Results of a Scientific Research after Metalliferous Deposits in the sub-Himalayan range around Darjeeling. [*Jl.* xvii, pt. i, 137.

Irvine, William.—The Bangash Nawabs of Farrukhabad—A Chronicle (1713—1857.) [*Jl.* xlvii, pt. i, 259; xlviii, pt. i, 49.

Irwin, Lieut.—Memoir on the Climate. Soil, Produce and Husbandry of Afghanistan and the Neighbouring Countries. [*Jl.* viii, 745, 779, 869, 1005; ix, 33, 189.

Ivory.—Mr. Ivory's Tables of Mean Astronomical Refractions, revised and augmented by Major J. T. Boileau. [*Jl.* xiv, 1.

Jackson, Welby.—On the Iron-works of Beerbhoom. [*Jl.* xiv, 754.

Notice of two Heads found in the Northern Districts of the Punjab. [*Jl.* xxi, 511.

Jackson, Dr.—On the Cultivation of Roses and the Manufacture of Rose-Water and Utur at Ghazeepore. [*Jl.* viii, 411.

On the Native Mode of preparing the Perfumed Oils of Jasmine and Bela. [*Jl.* viii, 496.

Jacquet, Eugene. — Notice of the Vallabhi Dynasty of Saurashtra; extracted from the Buddhist records of the Chinese. [*Jl.* v, 685.

Jaeschke, Revd. H. A.—Note on the Pronunciation of the Tibetan Language. [*Jl.* xxxiv, pt. i, 91.

On N. Himalayan Languages. [*Proc.* 1866, 190.

James, J. O. N.—Memorandum on the Thunderstorm of June 8th. 1871. [*Proc.* 1871, 142.

Jameson, Dr. Wm.—On the Distribution of European Birds. [*Jl.* viii, 21.

Report on the Museum of the Asiatic Society. [*Jl.* viii, 241.

On the Geographic Distribution of the Vulturidæ, Falconidæ, and Strigidæ; being the first of a series of Memoirs intended to illustrate the Geographic Distribution of the Ornithological Kingdom. [*Jl.* viii, 321.

Remarks on the Geology, &c., of the Country extending between Bhar and Simla. [*Jl.* viii, 1037.

Jameson, Dr. Wm. (*contd.*)—First Report by Dr. Jameson of his Deputation by Government to examine the effects of the great Inundation of the Indus. [*Jl.* xii, 183.

Jarrad, Lieut. F. W.—Letter regarding future Deep-sea Dredging Operations. [*Proc.* 1878, 85.

Jarrett, Major H. S.—Note on Inscription from Kashmir. [*Proc.* 1880, 54.

Note on an Inscription on an Ancient Mosque in Koh Inám, Zillah Allahabad, sent by Mr. A. M. Markham. [*Proc.* 1880, 72.

Note on an Inscription found upon a stone lying near the ruins of a Masjid on Lanka Island, Wular Lake, Kashmir. [*Jl.* xlix, pt. i, 16.

Jeffreys, Julius.—An Inquiry into the Laws governing the two great powers, Attraction and Repulsion as operating on the Aggregation and Combination of Atoms. [*Jl.* ii, 441, 506.

Jenkins, Major F.—An Account of some Minerals collected at Nagpore and its vicinity, with Remarks on the Geology. &c., of that part of the Country. [*As. Res.*, xviii, pt. i, 195.

Further Discovery of Coal Beds in Assam. [*Jl.* iv, 704.

Interpretation of the Ahom extract published as Plate IV of the January number of the sixth volume of the Journal. [*Jl.* vi, 980.

Paper on Ancient Land Grants on Copper, discovered in Assam. Communicated by Major F. Jenkins, Governor General's Agent, N. E. Frontier. [*Jl.* ix, 766.

Jenkins, H. L.—Notes on the Burmese Route from Assam to the Hookoong valley. [*Proc.* 1869, 67.

Notes on a Trip across the Patkoi Range. [*Proc.* 1870, 230.

Jenkins, R. — Account of Ancient Hindu Remains in Chattisgher, with translations and remarks by H. H. Wilson. [*As. Res.* xv, 499.

Jerdon, T. C.—Catalogue of Reptiles inhabiting the Peninsula of India. [*Jl.* xxii, 462; 522.

Notes on some new species of Birds from the N. East Frontier of India. [*Proc.* 1870, 59.

Notes on Indian Herpetology. [*Proc.* 1870, 66.

Jessop & Co.—Note on the Smelting of the Iron Ore of the district of Burdwan. [*Jl.* viii, 683.

John, Revd. Dr.—A Summary Account of the Life and Writings of Avyar, a Tamul Female Philosopher. [*As. Res.* vii. 345.

Johnson, W. H.—On Journey to Khotan. [*Proc.* 1866, 182.

On Hindu Tartars. [*Proc.* 1866, 236.

Johnstone, Lieut. J.—Note on elephants. [*Proc.* 1868, 127.

Johnstone, Lt.-Col. J. W. H.—Awans resident in the Salt Range. [*Proc.* 1881, 50.

Joinville.—On the Religion and Manners of the People of Ceylon. [*As. Res.* vii, 399.

Jones, Sir William.—Discourse on the Institution of a Society for enquiring into the History, Civil and Natural, the Antiquities, Arts, Sciences and Literature of Asia. [*As. Res.* i, ix.

Dissertation on the Orthography of Asiatic Words in Roman Letters. [*As. Res.* i, 1.

On the Gods of Greece, Italy and India, written in 1784, and since revised. [*As. Res.* i, 221.

A Conversation with Abram, an Abyssinian, concerning the City of Gwender and the Sources of the Nile. [*As. Res.* i, 383.

The Second Anniversary Discourse. [*As. Res.* i, 405.

The Third Anniversary Discourse. [*As. Res.*, i, 415.

The Fourth Anniversary Discourse. [*As. Res.* ii, 1.

The Fifth Anniversary Discourse. [*As. Res.* ii, 19.

The Sixth Discourse; on the Persians. [*As. Res.* ii, 43.

Remarks on the Island of Hinzuan or Johanna. [*As. Res.* ii, 77.

On the Chronology of the Hindus. [*As. Res.* ii, 111.

On the Indian Game of Chess. [*As. Res.* ii, 159.

On the Second Classical Book of the Chinese. [*As. Res.* ii, 195.

On the Antiquity of the Indian Zodiac. [*As. Res.* ii, 289.

The Design of a Treatise on the Plants of India. [*As. Res.* ii, 345.

The Seventh Anniversary Discourse. [*As. Res.* ii. 365.

A Supplement to the Essay on Indian Chronology. [*As. Res.*, ii, 389.

On the Spikenard of the Ancients. [*As. Res.* ii, 405.

The Eighth Anniversary Discourse. [*As. Res.* iii, 1.

On the Musical Modes of the Hindus. [*As. Res.* iii, 55.

Jones, Sir William (*contd.*)—Translation of Royal Grant of Land in Carnata. [*As. Res.* iii, 39.

On the Mystical Poetry of the Persians and Hindus. [*As. Res.*, iii, 165.

The Lunar Year of the Hindus. [*As. Res.* iii, 257.

Discourse the Ninth, on the Origin and Families of Nations. [*As. Res.* iii, 479.

The Tenth Anniversary Discourse. [*As. Res.* iv, 1.

Additional Remarks on the Spikenard of the Ancients. [*As. Res.* iv, 109.

On the Loris, or slowpaced Lemur. [*As. Res.* iv, 135.

Discourse the Eleventh. On the Philosophy of the Asiaticks. [*As. Res.* iv, 165.

A Catalogue of Indian Plants, comprehending their Sanscrit, and as many of their Linnœan Generic, names, as could, with any degree of precision, be ascertained. [*As. Res.* iv, 229.

Botanical Observations on select Indian Plants. [*As. Res.* iv, 237.

Jones, Mr.—Description of the North-West Coal District, stretching along the river Damoda, from the neighbourhood of Jeria, or Juriagerh, to below Sanampur in the Pergunnah of Sheargerh, forming a line of about sixty-five miles. [*As. Res.* xviii, pt. i, 163.

Jones, Lieut.—Journal of a Steam Trip to the North of Baghdad, in April 1846, with Notes on the various objects of interest met with. [*Jl.* xvi, 301.

Julien, Stanislas. — M. Stanislas Julien on the Study of the Chinese Language. Translated by Henry Piddington. [*Jl.* xii, 816.

Jupiter's Satellites, Eclipses of. [*Jl.* i, 504, 550; ii, 41.

Kalikishen Bahadur, Raja.—On the Indications of the Pulse according to the Hindus. Translated from the 2nd section of the Oushudha Valí, a Medical Treatise in the Bhaka language. [*Jl.* i, 553.

Specimens of some Ornamental Forms of Persian Writing. [*Jl.* ii, 613.

Description of an Indian Balance, called Tula. [*Jl.* ii, 615.

Karr, W. Seton.—Note on the course of study pursued by Students in the Sanskrit College, Calcutta. [*Jl.* xiv, 135.

Kashinath.—Notes on Rájá Todar Mall. [*Proc.* 1872, 141.

Kater, Lieut. Henry.—Description of a very sensible Hygrometer. [*As. Res.* ix, 24.

Description of an improved Hygrometer. [*As. Res.*, ix, 394.

Kay, Rev. W.—On the Connection of the Dative and Accusative Cases in Bengali and Hindustani. [*Jl.* xxi, 105.

Kean, Dr.—Note on Dr. Stewart's Table of Mortality among Hindu Females. [*Jl.* viii, 704.

Keatinge, Lieut., and Evans, Lieut.—Report on a Passage made on the Nurbudda river, from the Falls of Dharee to Mundlaisir, by Lieut. Keatinge, and of a similar passage from Mundlaisir to Baroach, by Lt. Evans. (Communicated by the Government of the N. W. Provinces.) [*Jl.* xvi, 1104.

Keene, H. G.—Notes on a Map of the Mughal Empire. [*Proc.* 1878, 152.

On the Revenues of the Mughal Empire. [*Jl.* l. pt. i, 99.

Keir, Archibald.—Of the Method of Distilling as practised by the Natives at Chatra in Ramgur and in the other Provinces, perhaps, with but little variation. [*As. Res.* i, 309.

Khan Ali.—Second Paper on a march between Mhow and Sagur. On the Huli in Malwa. [*Jl.* ix, 311.

Khanikof, de.—Notes on Samarqand. [*Proc.* 1870, 226.

Khash Alee Shekh.—Account of the Esafzai-Affghans inhabiting Sama (the plains,) Swat, Bunher and the Chamla Valley, being a detail of their clans, villages, chiefs and force, and the tribute they pay to the Sikhs. By Shekh Khash Alee, a follower of the fanatic Synd Ahmed. Prepared in 1837, under the instructions of Major R. Leech. [*Jl.* xiv, 736.

Khwajah Ahmud Shah Nakshbundee Syud. — Narrative of the Travels of Khwajah Ahmud Shah Nakshbundee Syud, who started from Cashmere on the 28th October 1852, and went through Yarkund, Kokan, Bokhara and Cabul, in search of Mr. Wyburd. Communicated by the Government of India. [*Jl.* xxv, 344.

King, Dr. George.—On the Lion of Aboo. [*Proc.* 1868, 198.

On the Birds of the Goona District. [*Jl.* xxxvii, pt. ii, 208.

Notes on the Famine Foods of Marwar. [*Proc.* 1869, 116.

King, L. B. B.—Letter on the present state of the Ruins of Gaur, Bengal. [*Proc.* 1875, 93.

King, Wm.—Notice of a pre-historic Burial Place with Cruciform Monoliths, near Mungapet in the Nizam's Dominions. [*Jl.* xlvi, pt. i, 179.

King, W.—Letter regarding Prof. Schaffhausen's Ethnological Queries. [*Proc.* 1880, 2.

Kittoe, Major Markham.—Extracts from the Journal of Lieut. Markham Kittoe. Ruins and Pillar at Jajipur. [*Jl.* vii, 53.

Section of a Hill in Cuttack supposed to be likely to contain Coal. [*Jl.* vii, 152.

Extracts from the Journal of Lieut. Markham Kittoe, submitted to the Asiatic Society at the meeting of the 6th Oct. 1836.—Ruins and Pillar at Jajipur. [*Jl.* vii, 200.

Sketch of the Sculptured Images, on the Temple of Grámeswara, near Ratrapur. [*Jl.* vii, 660.

Journal of a Tour in the Province of Orissa. [*Jl.* vii, 679, 1060.

Sketch of the Temple to Durga at Badeswur, &c. [*Jl.* vii, 828.

Report on the Coal and Iron Mines of Talcheer and Ungool, &c.. &c. [*Jl.* viii, 137.

Account of a Journey from Calcutta *via* Cuttack and Pooree to Sumbulpur, and from thence to Mednipur through the Forests of Orissa. [*Jl.* viii, 367.

Proposed Publication of Plates of Hindu Architectural Remains. [*Jl.* viii, 384.

Account of a Journey from Sumbulpur to Mednipur, through the Forests of Orissa. [*Jl.* viii, 474, 606, 671.

Note on a Pillar found in the Ganges near Pubna and of another at Kurra near Allahabad. [*Jl.* viii, 681.

Note on an Image of Buddha found at Sherghatti, &c. [*Jl.* xvi, 78.

Notes on the Viharas and Chaityas of Behar. [*Jl.* xvi, 272.

Note on the Sculptures of Bôdh Gyah. [*Jl.* xvi, 334.

Instructions how to take Correct Facsimiles of Inscriptions. [*Jl.* xvi, 366.

Hints on the Easiest Method of taking and preparing Drawings for Lithograph. [*Jl.* xvi, 368.

Notes on the Caves of Burabur. [*Jl.* xvi, 401.

On the Temples and Ruins of Oemga. [*Jl.* xvi, 656.

Kittoe, Major Markham (*contd.*)—
Notes on Places in the Province of Behar, supposed to be those described by Chy-Fa-Hian, the Chinese Buddhist Priest, who made a pilgrimage to India, at the close of the fourth century A. D. [*Jl.* xvi, 953.
Inscription at Oomgá, and Notes on the same. [*Jl.* xvi, 1220.
Extract of a letter from Capt. Kittoe. [*Jl.* xvii, pt.. i, 536.
Note on an Inscription, engraved upon a brick, found some years ago in a field near a village in the Jaunpur district, with a transcript from the original by Hiranand Pandit, and a translation by James Ballantyne. [*Jl.* xix, 455.
Memo on some ancient Gold Coins found near Benares, in 1851. [*Jl.* xxi, 390.
See BALLANTYNE, DR.; POSTANS, LIEUT.

Knighton, William.—On the Ruins of Anuradhapura, formerly the capital of Ceylon. [*Jl.* xvi, 213.
On the Rock Temples of Dambool, Ceylon. [*Jl.* xvi, 340.

Koppa Gadde Sásana, Sanskrit transcript of, [*Proc.* 1873, 75.

Korosi, Alexander Csoma.—Analysis of the Dulva, a portion of the Tibetan work entitled the Kah-Gyur. [*As. Res.* xx, pt. i, 41.
Notices on the Life of Shakya, extracted from the Tibetan Authorities. [*As. Res.* xx, pt. ii. 285.
Analysis of the Sher-Chin—P'hal-ch'hen — Dkon-Séks — Do-Dé — Nyáng-Dás and Gyut. Being the 2nd, 3rd, 4th, 5th, 6th, and 7th divisions of the Tibetan Work, entitled the Kah-Gaur. [*As. Res.* xx, pt. ii, 393.
Abstract of the Contents of the Bstan-Hgyur. [*As. Res.* xx, pt. ii, 553.
Geographical Notice of Tibet. [*Jl.* i, 121.
Translation of a Tibetan Fragment. [*Jl.* i, 269.
Note on the origin of the Kala-Chakra and Adi-Buddha Systems. [*Jl.* ii. 57.
Translation of a Tibetan Passport, dated, A. D. 1688. [*Jl.* ii, 201.
Origin of the Shákya race, translated from the ऌ (La), or the 26th volume of the *m* Do class in the Ká-gyur, commencing on the 161st leaf. [*Jl.* ii. 385.
Extracts from Tibetan Works, translated by [*Jl.* iii, 57.

Korosi, Alexander Csoma (*contd.*)
—Analysis of a Tibetan Medical Work. [*Jl.* iv, 1.
Interpretation of the Tibetan Inscription on a Bhotian Banner. taken in Assam, and presented to the Asiatic Society by Captain Bogle. [*Jl.* v, 264.
Notices on the different systems of Buddhism, extracted from the Tibetan authorities. [*Jl.* vii. 142.
Enumeration of Historical and Grammatical works to be met with in Tibet. [*Jl.* vii, 147.

Koros, Csoma de.—A brief Notice of the Subháshita Ratna Nidhi of Sáskya Pandita, with extracts and translations. [*Jl.* xxiv, 141, xxv, 257.
See LLOYD, MAJOR, F. H. A.

Kosumbha, Correspondence relating to the Monolith of, in the Allahabad District. [*Proc.* 1870, 291.

Kuhn, Prof. A.—On myths connected with Sunrise. [*Proc.* 1868, 226.

Kumbhupatias, Communication regarding the, a Sect of Hindu Dissenters. [*Proc.* 1881, 154.
Note on the origin and growth of the Sect of the. [*Proc.* 1882, 2.

Kurz, S.—On Pandanophyllum and allied genera, especially those occurring in the Indian Archipelago. [*Jl.* xxxviii, pt. ii, 70.
Remarks on the species of Pandanus. [*Jl.* xxxviii, pt. ii, 145.
On some new or imperfectly known Indian Plants. [*Jl.* xxxix, pt. ii, 61 ; xl, pt. ii, 45.
A fourth List of Bengal Algae. [*Proc.* 1870, 257.
Gentiana Jæschkei re-established as a new genus of Gentianaceæ, (with Plate XIII). [*Jl.* xxxix, pt. ii, 229.
New Burmese Plants, Part I. [*Jl.* xli, pt. ii, 291.
New Burmese Plants, Part II. [*Jl.* xlii, pt. ii, 59.
New Burmese Plants, Part III (with Plates XVIII, XIX). [*Jl.* xlii, pt. ii, 227.
Contributions towards a knowledge of the Burmese Flora, Part I. [*Jl.* xliii, pt. ii, 39.
Descriptions of a few Indian Plants. [*Jl.* xliii, pt. ii, 181.
Enumeration of Burmese Palms. [*Jl.* xliii, pt. ii, 191.
Contributions towards a knowledge of the Burmese Flora, Part II. [*Jl.* xliv, pt. ii, 128.
Notes on a few new Oaks from India, (with Plates XIV). [*Jl.* xliv, pt. ii, 196.

Kurz, S. (*contd.*)—Description of a new species of *Tupistra* from Tenasserim. [*Jl.* xliv, pt. ii, 198.

Descriptions of new Indian Plants. [*Jl.* xliv, pt. ii, 199.

A Sketch of the Vegetation of the Nicobar Islands. [*Jl.* xlv, pt. ii. 105.

Contributions towards a knowledge of the Burmese Flora. [*Jl.* xlvi, pt. ii, 49.

Kyd, James.—Tables exhibiting a Daily Register of the Tides in the River Hooghly at Calcutta, from 1805 to 1828, with observations on the results thus obtained. [*As. Res.* xviii, pt. i, 259.

Lafont, Fr. E.—A Letter with reference to the erection of a Spectroscopic Observatory. [*Proc.* 1875, 58.

Exhibition of Crookes' Radiometer. [*Proc.* 1876, 171.

Exhibition of two Microphones. [*Proc.* 1878, 152.

Exhibition of some of W. Crookes' High Vacuum Tubes. [*Proc.* 1879, 279.

Exhibition of one of Crookes' Electrical Radiometers. [*Proc.* 1880, 61.

Laidlay, J. W.—On Catadioptric Microscopes. [*Jl.* iii, 288.

Analysis of Raw Silk. [*Jl.* iv, 710.

Observations on the rate of Evaporation on the Open Sea; with a description of an Instrument used for indicating its amount. [*Jl.* xiv, 213.

On the Coins of the Independent Muhammadan Sovereigns of Bengal. [*Jl.* xv, 323.

Note on a Sanskrit Inscription from Behar [*Jl.* xvii, pt. i, 498; xviii, 498.

Note on the Inscriptions from Singapur and Province Wellesley, forwarded by the Hon. Col. Butterworth, C. B., and Col. J. Low. [*Jl.* xvii, pt. ii, 66.

Notice of a Chinese Geographical Work. [*Jl.* xviii, 137.

On preparing Fac-similes of Coins, &c. [*Jl.* xviii, 976.

Lal, Munshi Mohan.—A Brief Description of Herat. [*Jl.* iii, 9.

Further information regarding the Siah Posh Tribe, or reputed descendants of the Macedonians. [*Jl.* iii, 76.

A brief account of Masud, known by the name of Faríd Shakarganj, or Shakarbár. [*Jl.* v, 635.

Description of Uch-Sharíf. [*Jl.* v, 796.

Account of Kála Bágh on the right bank of the Indus. [*Jl.* vii, 25.

Lal, Munshi Mohan (*contd.*)—A brief Account of the Origin of the Dáúd Putras, and of the power and birth of Baháwal Khán their chief, on the bank of the Ghara and Indus. [*Jl.* vii, 27.

Lamb, Dr. G. W.—Register of the Fall of Rain, in inches, at Dacca, from 1827 to 1834. [*Jl.* iv, 405.

Abstract of Temperature and Fall of Rain kept by Medical Officers in different parts of India. [*Jl.* xxi, 383.

Lamb, Major.—Note on an Earthquake at Kámrúp on the 19th December 1872. [*Proc.* 1873, 65.

Lambton, Lieut.-Col. William.—Observations on the Theory of Walls, wherein some particulars are investigated which have not been considered by writers on fortification. [*As. Res.* vi, 93.

On the Maximum of Mechanic Powers and the effects of Machines when in motion. [*As. Res.* vi, 137.

An account of a method for extending a Geographical Survey across the Peninsula of India. [*As. Res.* vii, 312.

An Account of the measurement of an Arc on the Meridian on the Coast of Coromandel, and the length of a degree deduced therefrom in the latitude 12° 32′. [*As. Res.* viii, 137.

An Account of the Trigonometrical Operations in crossing the Peninsula of India and connecting Fort St. George with Mangalore. [*As. Res.* x, 290.

An Account of the measurement of an Arc on the Meridian, comprehended between the latitudes 8° 9′ 38″ 39‴ and 10° 59′ 48″ 93‴ north, being a continuation of the grand Meridional Arc commenced in 1804, and extending to 14° 6′ 19″ North. [*As. Res.* xii, 1.

An Account of the measurement of an Arc on the Meridian extending from Latitude 10° 59′ 49″ to 15° 6′ 0″ 65‴ north. [*As. Res.* xii, 286.

An Account of the measurement of an Arc on the Meridian, extending from Latitude 15° 6′ 0″ 2‴ to Latitude 18° 3′ 45″, being a further continuation of the former Arc, commencing in Latitude 8° 9′ 38″. [*As. Res.* xiii, 1.

Landour, Accident from Lightning at. [*Proc.* 1879, 139.

Lassen, Christian.—Objects of Research in Afghanistan. [*Jl.* viii, 145.

Points in the History of the Greek and Indo-Scythian Kings in Bactria, Cabul, and India, as illustrated by decyphering the ancient legends on their coins. [*Jl.* ix, 251, 331, 449, 627, 733.

Latter, Capt. T. — Remarks on a Boodhist Coin or Medal, sent to the Society through Captain Macleod, Assistant Commissioner, Tenasserim, by H. H. the Prince of Mekkara. [*Jl.* xiii, 571.

On the Buddhist Emblems of Architecture. [*Jl.* xiv, 623.

A Note on some Hill Tribes on the Kuladyne River, Arracan. [*Jl.* xv, 60.

The Symbolical Coins of Arakan. [*Jl.* xv, 238.

Layard, Capt. F. P.—Nooks and Corners of Bengal.—No. I. The Tomb of Meer Muddan Khan, Commander-in-chief of the Nuwab Sooraj-ood-Dowlah's Army at the Battle of Plassey. [*Jl.* xxi, 148.

The Mausoleum of the Nuwabs Aliverdi Khan and Sooraj-ood-Dowlah, at Khooshbagh, near Moorshedabad. [*Jl.* xxi, 504.

The Ancient City of Kansonapuri, now called Rungamutty. [*Jl.* xxii, 281.

Lea, Isaac.—Characters of three new species of Indian Fresh-water Bivalves. [*Jl.* iv, 450.

Le Beck, Henry J.—An Account of the Pearl-Fishery in the Gulph of Mannar in March and April 1797. [*As. Res.* v, 393.

Lee, J. Bridges.—Remarks on Atmospheric Absorption. [*Proc.* 1883, 47.

A New Meteorological Instrument for determining the quantity of dew deposited on clear nights. [*Proc.* 1883, 66.

Leech, Major Robert.—Epitome of the Grammars of the Brahuiky, the Balochky and the Panjabi Languages with Vocabularies of the Baraky, the Pashi, the Laghmani, the Cashgari, the Teerhai, and the Deer Dialects. [*Jl.* vii, 538, 608, 711, 780.

A Grammar of the Pashtoo or Afghanee Language. [*Jl.* viii, 1.

Brief History of Kalat, brought down to the Deposition and Death of Mehrab Khan, Braho-ee. [*Jl.* xii, 473.

Notes on, and a short Vocabulary of, the Hinduvee Dialect of Bundelkhand. [*Jl.* xii, 1086.

Leech, Major Robert (*contd.*)—A Description of the Country of Seisthan. [*Jl.* xiii, 115.

A Grammar of the Cashmeeree Language. [*Jl.* xiii, 397, 553.

Route from Derá Ghazee Khan to Candahar, through the Sakhee Sarwar Pass and Buzdar, with other routes. [*Jl.* xiii, 527.

An Account of the early Ghiljáees. [*Jl.* xiv, 306.

A Supplementary Account of the Hazarahs. [*Jl.* xiv, 333.

Notes on the Religion of the Sikhs, being a Notice of their Prayers, Holidays, and Shrines. [*Jl.* xiv, 393.

An Account of the Early Abdalees. [*Jl.* xiv, 445.

See ABDUN NUBEE; HAJEE AGHA ABBAS; ALEEM-ULLA, FULLA; KHASH ALEE, SHEKH; RAIAH KHAN.

Lees, Capt. W. Nassau. — On the application of the Characters of the Roman Alphabet to Oriental Languages. [*Jl.* xxxiii, 345.

On Mahomedan Conquest of Arabia. [*Proc.* 1865, 100.

On the Igbál Námeh-i-Jahangiri and other authorities for the reign of the Emperor Jehángir. [*Proc.* 1865, 114.

On Double Currency. [*Proc.* 1865, 210.

On Oriental College at Lahore. [*Proc.* 1866, 129.

On Scientific Technology. [*Proc.* 1866, 163, 175.

On the Maásir i 'Álamgírí and Kháfí Khan. [*Proc.* 1868, 114.

Leigh, Capt. R. T.—Notes on Jumera Pát, in Sirgooja. [*Jl.* xxvi, 226.

Leitner, Dr. G. W.—Photograph of Indo-Aryans sent by. [*Proc.* 1880, 141, 171.

Lemesurier, M. H. P.—On Chambered Tumuli near Chunar. [*Proc.* 1867, 164.

Leonard, G. S.—The Mythic History of the God Viráj. [*Jl.* xlvi, pt. i, 126.

"Further Proofs of the Polygamy of Kálidása's Heroes." [*Jl.* xlvi, pt. i, 160.

Leonard.—On the Earthquake of 1869 in Cachar. [*Proc.* 1869, 102.

Lepper, C. H.—Notes on the Singpho and Kampti Country, North-Eastern Frontier. [*Proc.* 1882, 64.

Leslie, Matthew.—On the Pangolin of Bahar. [*As. Res.* i, 376.

Lethbridge, W. C.—On some old Dutch Records at Chinsura. [*Proc.* 1871, 85.

Leupolt, J. C.—Remarks on Earthen Medallions found in the Gorakhpur District. [*Proc.* 1869, 246.

Lewis, Lt. Henry, & Cope, Henry.—Some Account of the "Kalán Musjeed," commonly called the "Kalee Musjeed," within the new town of Dehli. [*Jl.* xvi, 577.
See COPE, HENRY.

Lewis, J.—On a mass of iron. [*Proc.* 1865, 77.

Lewis, Dr. T. R.—Remarks regarding the Hæmatozoa found in the stomach of Culex Mosquito. [*Proc.* 1878, 89.
Remarks on a Nematoid Hæmatozoon discovered by Dr. Griffith Evans in a Camel. [*Proc.* 1882, 63.

Lewis, Dr. T. R., and McConnell, Dr. J. F. P.—Amphistoma Hominis: A new Parasite affecting Man. [*Proc.* 1876, 182.

Leyden, Dr. J.—On the Languages and Literature of the Indo-Chinese Nations. [*As. Res.* x, 158.
On the Rosheniah Sect, and its founder Báyezíd Ansárí. [*As. Res.* xi, 363.

Liebig, Dr. G. Von.—Discussion of some Meteorological Observations made on Parasnath Hill. [*Jl.* xxvii, 1.
Account of a Cyclone in the Andaman Sea, on the 9th and 10th April, 1858. [*Jl.* xxvii, 323.
Accountof a Visit to Barren Island in March 1858. [*Jl.* xxix, 1.

Lightning, Accident from, at Landour. [*Proc.* 1872, 139.
Note regarding a fall of, at Morar. [*Proc.* 1872. 170.
Memorandum of Information required in cases of Accidents from. [*Proc.* 1877, 132.

Limrick, Rev. Paul.—Demonstration of the 12th Axiom of the First Book of Euclid. [*As. Res.*, vii, 449.

Liston, D.—Notice of a Colossal Alto-Relievo, known by the name of Mata Koonr situated near Kussía Tannah, in Pergunnah Sidowa, Eastern Division of Gorakhpur District. [*Jl.* vi, 477.
Translation of a Servitude-Bond granted by a Cultivator over his Family, and a Deed-of-Sale of two Slaves. [*Jl.* vi, 950.

Lloyd, M.—On Supposed Tea. [*Proc.* 1866, 79.

Lloyd, Capt. R.—A Short Notice of the Coast-line, Rivers and Islands adjacent, forming a portion of the Mergui Province, from a late survey. [*Jl.* vii, 1027.

Lloyd, Major T. H. A., and Korosi, Alex. Csoma.—Note on the White Satin embroidered Scarfs of the Tibetan Priests. With a translation of the motto on the margin of one presented to the Asiatic Society. [*Jl.* v, 383.

Lloyd, Lieut.-Col., and Campbell, A.—Further Notes respecting the late Csoma de Körös. [*Jl.* xiv, 823.

Lockett, Col.—Hints to Students of Arabic; extracted from a letter. [*Jl.* xvi, 373.

Loewenthal, Revd. Isidor.—Is the Pushto a Semitic Language? [*Jl.* xxix, 323.
On the Antiquities of the Peshawur District. [*Jl.* xxxii, 1.
Some Persian Inscriptions found in Srinagar, Kashmir. [*Jl.* xxxiii, 278.

Logan, J. R.—On the Local and Relative Geology of Singapore, including Notices of Sumatra, the Malay Peninsula, &c. [*Jl.* xvi, 667.
On the Local and Relative Geology of Singapore, including Notices of Sumatra, the Malay Peninsula, &c. [*Jl.* xvi, 519.

Lohar, Chhedi.—Barometrical Elevations taken on a Journey from Katmandhu to Gosainsthán, a place of pilgrimage in the mountains of Nipal. [*Jl.* vi, 696.

Long, Revd. James.—Tables of Comparative Philology, shewing specimens of the affinity of the Greek, Latin and English Languages, with the Sanskrit, Persian, Russian, Gaelic, Welsh, Lithuanian, German, Hebrew, and Anglo-Saxon. [*Jl.* xii, 837.
Queries on the Archæology of India. [*Jl.* xvi, 285.
Analysis of the Bengali Poem Ráj Málá, or Chronicles of Tripurá. [*Jl.* xix, 533.
Notice of a Ruin in Singhbhúm. [*Jl.* xx, 283.
Analysis of the Raghu Vansá, a Sanskrit Poem of Kálidása. [*Jl.* xxi, 445.
Notes and Queries suggested by a Visit to Orissa in January, 1859. [*Jl.* xxviii, 185.
On Recent Russian Researches. [*Jl.* xxix, 197.
On Scientific Technology. [*Proc.* 1866, 154.

Lord, Dr. P. B.—Some Account of a Visit to the Plain of Koh-i-Daman, the mining district of Ghorband, and the Pass of Hindu Kúsh, with a few general observations respecting the structure and conformation of the country from the Indus to Kábul. [*Jl.* vii, 521.

Louis, Most Revd. Jean.—Note on the Geography of Cochin China. [*Jl.* vi, 737.

Additional Notice on the Geography of Cochin China [*Jl.* vii, 317.

Low, Lieut.-Col. James.—Observations on the Geological Appearances and General Features of portions of the Malayan Peninsula, and of the Countries lying betwixt it and 18° North Latitude. [*As. Res.* xviii, pt. i, 128.

On the Government of Siam. [*As. Res.* xx, pt. ii, 245.

On Siamese Literature. [*As. Res.* xx, pt. ii, 338.

Excursions to the Eastward. No. 1. Extracts from the Journal of a Political Mission to the Rája of Ligor in Siam. [*Jl.* vii, 583.

Gleanings in Buddhism; or, Translations of Passages from a Siamese version of a Pali work, termed in Siamese "Phrâ Pat'hom," with passing observations on Buddhism and Brahmanism. [*Jl.* xvii, pt. ii, 72.

An Account of several Inscriptions found in Province Wellesley on the Peninsula of Malacca. [*Jl.* xvii, pt. ii, 62.

A Few Gleanings in Buddhism. [*Jl.* xvii, pt. ii, 591.

General Observations on the contending claims to antiquity of Brahmans and Buddhists. [*Jl.* xviii, 89.

On an Inscription from Keddah. [*Jl.* xviii, 247.

Lush, Dr. Charles.—Geological Notes on the Northern Conkan and a small portion of Guzerat and Kattawár. [*Jl.* v, 761.

Lushington, G. S.—On the Marriage Rites and Usages of the Játs of Bharatpúr. [*Jl.* ii, 273.

Report on the Government experimental working of the Copper Mines of Pokree, in Ghurwal, with notices of other Copper Mines. [*Jl.* xii, 453, 769.

Lyall, C. J.—The Mo'allaqah of Lebîd, with the Life of the poet as given in the Kitâb-el-Aghânî. [*Jl.* xlvi, pt. i, 61.

Three Translations from the Hamâseh. [*Jl.* xlvi, pt. i, 178.

Lyall, C. J. (*contd.*)—Translations from the Hamâseh and the Aghânî. [*Jl.* xlvi, pt. i, 437.

The Mo'allaqah of Zuheyr, rendered into English, with an Introduction and Notes. [*Jl.* xlvii, pt. i, 1.

Translations from the Hamâseh. [*Jl.* l, pt. i, 107.

Lydekker, Richard.—Exhibition of a portion of the lower Jaw of Tetraconodon Magnum, Falconer, from the Siwaliks. [*Proc.* 1876, 172.

Notes on the Mammalian Fauna of the Wardwán and Upper Chináb Valleys. [*Jl.* xlvi, pt. ii, 283.

Exhibition of the Palate of an Anthropoid Ape found in the Siwaliks of the Punjab. [*Proc.* 1878, 191.

Aberrant Dentition of Felis Tigris. [*Jl.* xlvii, pt. ii, 2.

Great Snow-fall in Kashmir. [*Jl.* xlvii, pt. ii, 177.

On the Occurrence of the Musk-Deer in Tibet. [*Jl.* xlix, pt. ii, 4.

Note on some Ladák Mammals. [*Jl.* xlix, pt. ii, 6.

A Sketch of the History of the Fossil Vertebrata of India. [*Jl.* xlix, pt. ii, 8.

On the Zoological Position of the Bharal, or Blue-Sheep of Tibet. [*Jl.* xlix, pt. ii, 131.

Notes on the Dentition of Rhinoceros. [*Jl.* xlix, pt. ii, 135.

Macaire, J.—Analysis of the Chinese Varnish. [*Jl.* i, 183.

M'Cann, H. W.—Remarks on an Outburst of Sunspots. [*Proc.* 1881, 154.

McClintock.—On Chinese Grass-cloth. [*Proc.* 1867, 103.

McCosh, J.—Account of the Mountain Tribes on the extreme N. E. Frontier of Bengal. [*Jl.* v, 193.

Macdonald, John.—On the Gold of Limong in Sumatra. [*As. Res.* i, 336.

On three Natural Productions of Sumatra. [*As. Res.* iv, 19.

Macdonald, Major J.—On the Eclipse of 18th August 1868. [*Proc.* 1868, 215.

Macgowan, Dr. D. J.—An Inscription from a Tablet in a Buddhist Monastery at Ningpo in China. [*Jl.* xiii, 113.

Examination of some Atmospheric Dust from Shanghae, forwarded to the Asiatic Society of Bengal. [*Jl.* xvi, 193.

Remarks on Showers of Sand in the Chinese Plain. [*Jl.* xx, 192.

McGregor, Lieut. A. Murray.—An improvement on Irrigation. [*Jl.* xi, 39.
A Geographical Notice of the Valley of Jullalabad. [*Jl.* xi, 117.

MacGregor, Capt. G. H.—A Geographical Notice of the Valley of Jullalabad. [*Jl.* xiii, 867.

MacGregor, W.—Abstract of a Paper on the Prevention of Accidents from Lightning. [*Proc.* 1876, 104.

Mackay, Revd. Dr. W. S.—The Great Comet of 1861. [*Jl.* xxx, 279.

Mackenzie, Col. Colin.—Account of the Pagoda at Jerwuttum. [*As. Res.* v, 303.
Remarks on some Antiquities on the West and South Coasts of Ceylon. [*As. Res.* vi, 425.
View of the principal Political Events that occurred in the Carnatic, from the dissolution of the Ancient Hindoo Government in 1564, till the Mogul Government was established in 1687, on the Conquest of the Capitals of Beejapoor and Golconda. Compiled from various Authentic Memoirs and Original MSS. collected chiefly within the last ten years, and referred to in the Notes at the bottom of each page. [*Jl.* xiii, 421, 578.

Mackenzie, Capt. H.—On the Antiquities of Guzerat. [*Jl.* xxxiii, 402.

Mackenzie, Dr. — An Account of Venomous Sea Snakes on the Coast of Madras. [*As. Res.* xiii, 329.

Mackeson, Major F. — Journal of Captain C. M. Wade's Voyage, from Lodiana to Mithankot by the river Sutlaj, on his mission to Lahore and Bahawalpur in 1832-33. [*Jl.* vi, 169.
Report on the Route from Seersa to Bahawulpore. [*Jl.* xiii, 297.

Mackintosh, Capt.—On an Indian method of Constructing Arches. [*As. Res.* xiv, 476.

Maclagan, Major-General R.—Fragments of the History of Mooltan, the Derajat, and Bahawulpore, from Persian MSS. [*Jl.* xvii, pt. ii, 559.
List of Arabic Works preserved in a library at Aleppo. [*Jl.* xxiii 44.
On Early Asiatic Fire Weapons. [*Jl.* xlv, pt, i, 30.

M'Clelland, Dr. John.—Indian Cyprinidæ. [*As. Res.* xix, pt. ii, 217.
Notice of some Fossil Impressions occurring in the Transition Limestone of Kemaon. [*Jl.* iii, 628.

M'Clelland, Dr. John (*contd.*)—Description of the (so-called) Mountain Trout of Kemaon. [*Jl.* iv, 39.
Catalogue of Geological Specimens from Kemaon presented to the Asiatic Society. [*Jl.* vi, 653.
On the Difference of Level in Indian Coal-fields, and the causes to which this may be ascribed. [*Jl.* vii, 65.
Observations on six new species of Cyprinidæ, with an outline of a new classification of the family. [*Jl.* vii 941.
On the genus Hexaprotodon of Dr. Falconer and Captain Cautley. [*Jl.* vii, 1038.
On Isinglass in *Polynemus sele*, Buch, a species which is very common in the Estuaries of the Ganges. [*Jl.* viii, 203.
Memoranda on the Museum of the Asiatic Society. [*Jl.* viii, 415.
Extracts from Mr. M'Clelland's paper on Indian Cyprinidæ. [*Jl.* viii, 650.
Extracts from a letter to Government on Capt. G. B. Tremenheere's report on the tin of Mergui. [*Jl.* xi, 25.
Note on the Discharge of Water by the Irrawaddy [*Jl.* xxii, 480.

McLeod, Col. D.—Abstract Report of the Proceedings of the Committee appointed to superintend the Boring Operations in Fort William, from their commencement in December, 1835, to their close in April, 1840. [*Jl.* ix, 677.

Macleod, Sir D. F.—On Oriental College at Lahore. [*Proc.* 1866, 118.

McLeod, D. W.—Memorandum regarding specimens from Seoni, Chupara. [*Jl.* vi, 1091.

McLeod, Capt. T. E.—Abstract Journal of an Expedition to Kiang Hung on the Chinese Frontier, starting from Moulmein on the 13th December, 1836. [*Jl.* vi, 989.
Note on the Map attached to the Report of the Coal Committee in the 98th Number of the Journal of the Asiatic Society. [*Jl.* ix, 582.

McMaster, Lieut.-Col. A. C.—Notes on Birds observed in the neighbourhood of Nagpore and Kamptee, (Central Provinces), Chikalda and Akola in Berar. [*Jl.* xl, pt. ii, 207.

Macnamara, Dr. C.—On the intimate structure of Muscular Fibre. [*Jl.* xxxvii, pt. ii, 71.

Macpherson, Lieut. S. Charters.—On the Geology of the Peninsula. [*As. Res.* xviii, pt. ii, 115.

Macrae, John.—Account of the Kookies or Lunctas. [*As. Res.* vii, 183.
Case of the Bite of a Poisonous Snake successfully treated. [*As. Res.* xi. 309.

MacRitchie, J.—Abstract of Meteorological Tables kept at Bancoora for 1830 and 1831. [*Jl.* i, 154.
Meteorological Register for 1833, kept at Bancoora. [*Jl.* iii, 190.

Madden, Major Edward.—Diary of an Excursion to the Shatool and Boorun Passes over the Himalaya, in September, 1845. [*Jl.* xv, 79.
Notes of an Excursion to the Pindree Glacier, in September, 1846. [*Jl.* xvi, 226, 596.
The Turaee and Outer Mountains of Kumaon. [*Jl.* xvii, pt. i. 349, 563.
Supplementary Notes to "The Turaee and Outer Mountains of Kumaon;" Journal of Asiatic Society, Bengal, May and June, 1848. [*Jl.* xviii, 603.

Mahommed, Ismail Moulvi.—Notice of the peculiar Tenets held by the followers of Syed Ahmed, taken chiefly from the "Sirat-ul-Mústaím," a principal Treatise of that Sect. [*Jl.* i, 479.

Mahony, Capt. — On Singhala or Ceylon, and the Doctrines of Bhooddha, from the Books of the Singhalais. [*As. Res.* vii, 32.

Maingay, Dr. A. C.—On rare Malayan Animals. [*Proc.* 1868. 194.

Mainwaring, Col. G. B.—Remarks on the term Mun, Mwon or Món [*Proc.* 1873, 133.

Maisey, Lieut. F.—Description of the Antiquities at Kalinjar. [*Jl.* xvii, pt. i, 171.
Appendix to the Account of the Antiquities of Kalinjar. [*Jl.* xvii, pt. i. 313.

Malcolm, Brigadier-General John.—Translations of two Letters of Nadir Shah, with Introductory Observations. [*As. Res.* x, 526.
Sketch of the Sikhs. [*As. Res.* xi, 197.

Malcolmson, J. G.—Note on Saline Deposits in Hyderabad. [*Jl.* ii, 77.
Notes explanatory of a Collection of Geological Specimens from the Country between Hyderabad and Nágpur. [*Jl.* v, 96.

Malet, Sir C. W.—Description of the Caves or Excavations on the mountain about a mile to the eastward of the town of Ellora, or as called on the spot Verrool, though therein there appears inaccuracy, as the foundation of the town is attributed to Yelloo, or Elloo rajah, whose capital is said to have been Ellichpore. [*As. Res.* vi, 389.

Mallet, F. R.—Exhibition of a Meteorite received from Mr. H. Fraser. [*Proc.* 1878. 174.

Man, E. H.—List of Words of the Nicobar Language as spoken at Camorta, Nancowry, Trinkutt, and Katschal. [*Jl.* xli, pt. i, 1.

Mandara Hill, near Bhagelpore, Note on an Inscription on the. [*Jl.* iv, 166.

Manger, O.—Specimen of the Language of the Goonds as spoken in the District of Seonee, Chuparah; comprising a Vocabulary, Grammar, &c. [*Jl.* xvi. 286.

Mangosteen on the Kukumb-ka-tel, or Concrete Oil of the Wild. [*Jl.* ii. 592.

Manson, Capt. — Captain Manson's Journal of a Visit to Melum and the Oonta Dhoora Pass in Juwahir. Edited by J. H. Batten. [*Jl.* xi. 1157.

Marcadieu, M.—Report on the Kooloo Iron Mines and on a portion of the Mannikurn Valley. (Communicated by the Government of India.) [*Jl.* xxiv, 191.

Maritime Surveys, Progress of Indian. [*Jl.* i, 327.

Marsden, William.—On the Traces of the Hindu Language and Literature extant amongst the Malays. [*As. Res.* iv, 221.

Marsh, Capt. H. C.—Description of a Trip to the Gilgit Valley, a dependency of the Maharaja of Kashmír. [*Jl.* xlv, pt. i, 119.

Marshall, Capt. G. T.—Translation of an Inscription on a Stone in the Asiatic Society's Museum, marked No. 2. [*Jl.* vi, 88.

Marshall, Major G. F. L.—Notes on the Butterflies of India. [*Proc.* 1882, 142.
Some New or Rare Species of Rhopalocerous *Lepidoptera* from the Indian regions. [*Jl.* li. pt. ii. 37.
A New Species of *Hipparchia* (*Lepidoptera Rhopalocera*) from the N. W. Himálayas. [*Jl.* li, pt. ii. 67.

Marshall, Major G. F. L., and De Niceville, L.—Some New Species of Rhopalocerous *Lepidoptera* from the Indian region. [*Jl.* xlix, pt. ii. 245.

Martens, Dr. G. Von.—A third list of Bengal Algæ. [*Proc.* 1870, 9.
Notes on Javanese, Algæ. [*Proc.* 1870, 182.
A fifth list of Bengal Algæ [*Proc.* 1871, 170.
List of Algæ collected by Mr. S. Kurz, in Burma and adjacent Islands. [*Jl.* xl, pt. ii, 461.

Martin, Lieut.-Col. Claude.—On the Manufacture of Indigo at Ambore. [*As. Res.* iii, 475.

Martin, J. W. B.—On the Archæological Remains of Barantpur in Zila' Bhágalpúr. [*Proc.* 1872, 175.

Martin, W. B.—Letter forwarding an Inscription found at Srinagar near Madhipurah. [*Proc.* 1875, 107.

Letter regarding Buddhist Remains in North Bhágalpur. [*Proc.* 1875, 128.

On Hindi Inscriptions from near Monghyr. [*Proc.* 1881, 42.

Mas, Sinbaldo de.—On the Egyptian System of Artificial Hatching. [*Jl.* viii, 38.

See PIDDINGTON, H.

Mason, Rev. Dr. Francis.—On the Gamboge of the Tenasserim Provinces. [*Jl.* xvi, 661.

The Land Shells of the Tenasserim Provinces. [*Jl.* xvii, pt. i, 62.

The Liquidamber tree of the Tenasserim Provinces. [*Jl.* xvii, pt. i, 532.

The Gum Kino of the Tenasserim Provinces. [*Jl.* xviii, pt. ii, 223.

The Pine tree of the Tenasserim Provinces. [*Jl.* xviii, 73.

Notes of the Karen Language. [*Jl.* xxvii, 129.

A Sketch of Toungoo History. [*Jl.* xviii, 9.

Religion, &c., among the Karens. [*Jl.* xxxiv, pt. ii, 173.

Religion, Mythology, and Astronomy among the Karens. [*Jl.* xxxiv. pt. ii, 195.

Physical Characters of the Karens. [*Jl.* xxxv, pt. ii, 1.

On Dwellings, Works of Art, Laws, &c. of the Karens [*Jl.* xxxvii, pt. ii, 125.

Mason, James Wood—*See* WOOD-MASON, JAMES.

Masson, Chas.—Memoir on the Ancient Coins found at Beghrám, in the Kohistán of Kábul. [*Jl.* iii, 152.

Extracts from Mr. Masson's Letter to Dr. J. G. Gerard, on the Excavation Topes, dated Tattung, 22nd March 1834. [*Jl.* iii, 329.

Second Memoir on the Ancient Coins found at Beghrám, in the Kohistán of Kábul. [*Jl.* v, 1.

Note on an Inscription at Bámián. [*Jl.* v, 188.

Third Memoir on the Ancient Coins discovered at the site called Beghrám in the Kohistán of Kábul. [*Jl.* v, 537.

Masson, Chas. (*contd.*)—Notes on the Antiquities of Bámián. [*Jl.* v, 707.

Suggestions on the Sites of Sangala and the Altars of Alexander: being an extract from Notes of a Journey from Lahore to Karychee, made in 1830. [*Jl.* vi, 57.

Masters, J. W.—Flora of the Naga Hills. [*Jl.* xiii, 707.

Extract from a Memoir of some of the Natural Productions of the Angami Naga Hills and other parts of Upper Assam. [*Jl.* xvii, pt. i, 57.

Masters, W.—Summation of Polynomial Co-efficients. [*Jl.* i, 187.

On the Trisection of Angles. [*Jl.* i, 501.

On November Meteors. [*Proc.* 1867, 17, 20.

Ma-twanlin. — Chinese Account of India, Translated from the Wanhëen-t'hung-Kaou, or 'Deep Researches into Ancient Monuments.' [*Jl.* vi, 61.

Mazuchelli, Rev. F. F.—On an Iron Cage. [*Proc.* 1868, 79.

Mazure, Thomine d'.—*See* D'MAZURE THOMINE.

Medlicott, Henry B.—On the Sub-Himálayan Rocks between the Ganges and the Jumna. [*Jl.* xxx, 22.

Note relating to Sivalik Fauna. [*Jl.* xxxiv, pt. ii, 63.

On the Action of the Ganges. [*Proc.* 1868, 232.

On a Celt from the Ossiferous "Pliocene" deposits of the Narbadá Valley. [*Proc.* 1873, 138.

Record of the Khairpur Meteorite of 23rd September, 1873. [*Jl.* xliii, pt. ii, 33.

Exhibition of a Meteorite from Raipur. [*Proc.* 1876, 115.

Exhibition of Meteorites recently fallen in India, with remarks upon them. [*Proc.* 1876, 221.

Remarks on Himalayan Glaciation. [*Proc.* 1877, 3.

Note on Mr. J. F. Campbell's Remarks on Himálayan Glaciation. [*Jl.* xlvi, pt. ii, 11.

Exhibition of the new Geological Map of India. [*Proc.* 1878, 124.

Exhibition of some Geological Specimens from Afghanistan. [*Proc.* 1880, 3.

Exhibition of a specimen of Rocksalt from the Chakmani territory. [*Proc.* 1880, 123.

Note on Chloromelanite. [*Proc.* 1883, 80.

Melville, Capt. W. R.—Note on some Buddhist Ruins at Doob Koond. [*Jl.* xxxv, pt. i, 168.

Metcalfe, C. T. — *See* MITRA, DR. RAJENDRALALA.

Meteor, Extraordinary, observed at the Nicobars. [*Proc.* 1874, 156.

Meteorological Observations, Abstract of the, taken at Gangaroowa, near Kandy, Ceylon. [*Jl.* xxxiii, 1; xvii, lxi; xxxiv, pt. ii, xvii; xxxv, pt. ii, lxii.

Meteorological Observations kept at Rangoon. [*Jl.* xxi. 520, 622; xxii, 113, 317, 421, 502, 596; xxiii (1).

Meteorological Register kept at Lucknow. [*Jl.* xxiii, (77); xxiv, xlix, lv, lxiv, lxvii.

Meteorological Register kept at the Surveyor-General's office, Calcutta. [*Jl.* i, 23. 40, 80, 120, 168, 216, 264, 326, 374, 430, 478, 534, 574; ii, 56, 104, 160, 216, 272, 328, 383, 384, 440, 496, 560, 608, 615, 641, 660; iii, 56, 104, 152. 208, 256, 312, 368, 424, 480, 544, 600, 656; iv, 64, 120, 184, 240, 296, 360, 412, 476, 532, 588, 652, 716; v, 60, 128, 192, 256, 320, 376, 440, 520, 600, 684, 760, 836; vi, 80, 160, 245, 324, 404, 500, 620, 712, 804. 900, 988, 1100; vii, 92, 172, 286, 370, 468, 582, 67', 750, 838, 918, 990, 1064; viii. 76, 158, 250, 346. 442, 621, 692, 777, 867, 917, 1069; ix, 95, 217; xvi, 850, 1002, 1094, 1182, 1278; xvii, pt. i, 86, 170, 256, 347, 458, 562; pt. ii, 125, 238, 353, 475, 591, 707; xviii, 88*a*, 182*a*, 286*a*, 418*a*, 552*a*, 649. 759. 866, 981; xix, 89, 189, 269, 349, 429, 499, 573; xx, 112, 217, 289, 369, 449, 535, 635; xxi. 103, 193, 280, 363, 443, 555, 643; xxii, 117, 508, 599, 687; xxiii, (9), (29), (41), (49), (57); xxiv (i), (xxv), (xxxix), (lxxi); xxv (i), (xxix), (xli), (lvii), (lxxxi), (xcix); xxvi, i, ix, xvii, xlix, lvii; xxvii, xlix, lvii; xxviii, i, xli; xxix, i, xxv, xlix, lvii; xxx, i, xxv, xlix, lxv; xxxi, i, xvii, xlix, lxxiii, xcvii; xxxii, i, xxv, xlix, lxxiii; xxxiii, i, xxv, xlix; xxxiv, pt. ii, i, ix, xxv, xxxiii; xxxv, pt ii, i, lvii; xxxvi, pt. ii, xvii, xxxiii, xli; xxxvii, pt. ii, i; xxxviii, pt. ii, i, lxix; xxxix, pt. ii, i, lxxxiii; xl, pt. ii, lxxxiv.

Meteorological Register kept at the office of the Secretary to Government, N. W. P., Agra. [*Jl.* xxii, 217, 325, 424, 705; xxiii (17), (34), (46), (54), (73), (81); xxiv, xvii, xxi; xxv, xl, li, lxxv, xciii, cxxv; xxvi, xxii.

Meteorological Register kept at the Surveyor General's Office, Calcutta. Monthly Means of Maximum and Minimum Pressures for 1841 to 1849, taken from the. [*Jl.* xx, 528.

Diagram of Monthly Mean Curves of Barometer and Thermometer, wet and dry bulb, and of Rainfall, Calcutta, 1856—1865. [*Jl.* xxxvii, pt. ii.

Table of Mean Monthly Readings and Hourly Variations of Barometer, Calcutta, 1856—1865. [*Jl.* xxxvii, pt. ii.

Meteorological Register kept on Ross Island, for December, 1859. [*Jl.* xxx, 32.

Meteorological Observations in the Punjab, Correspondence regarding. [*Proc.* 1871, 120.

Mhow and Saugor, 1839, March between. [*Jl.* viii, 805.

Michell, R.—*See* VENUIKOFF, W.

Middleton, J. — On the Meteors of August 10th, 1839. [*Jl.* viii, 495.

Description of an Astronomical Instrument presented by Rajah Ram Sing of Khota to the Government of India. [*Jl.* viii. 831.

Description of a Persian Astrolabe, submitted to the Asiatic Society by Major Pottinger. [*Jl.* x, 759.

On the Specific Gravity of Sea Water. [*Jl.* xiii, 766.

Influence of the Moon on the Weather. [*Jl.* xx, 275.

Mignan, Capt. Robert. — A brief Sketch of the present state of Georgia, now a Russian Province. [*Jl.* iii, 232.

Journal of Tour through Georgia, Persia, and Mesopotamia. [*Jl.* iii, 271, 332, 456, 576; iv, 602.

Miles, Lieut. R. H.—Some Remarks upon the Country to the south-west of Hoshungabad, and of the soil, cultivation, &c., of that part of the Valley of the Nerbudda situated between Hoshungabad and the Fort of Mokrai, in the lower range of the Kali-bheet Hills. [*Jl.* iii, 61.

Miles, Lt.-Col. S. B.—Translation of extracts from an Arabic work relating to Aden. [*Proc.* 1875, 218.

Miles, Lt.-Col. S. B. (*contd.*)—On the Route between Sohár and el-Bereymí in 'Oman, with a Note on the Zatt, or gipsies, in Arabia. [*Jl.* xlvi, pt. i, 41.

Mill, Revd. Dr. W. H.—Restoration of the Inscription, No. 2, on the Allahabad Column. [*Jl.* iii, 257.

Supplement to the Historical Remarks on the Allahabad Inscription, No. 2. [*Jl.* iii, 339.

Restitution and Translation of the Inscription found in the Ruins of the Mountain Temple of Shekáwati. [*Jl.* iv, 367.

Restoration and Translation of the Inscription on the Bhitárí Lát, with critical and historical remarks. [*Jl.* vi, 1.

Minas, Peter A.—A short Sketch of the Tribes of Bhutteanah and Hurrianah. [*Jl.* xxxvii, pt. ii, 171

Mino, Dr. J. E. — Memoir on the Regeneration and Actual State of Medicine in Egypt. [*Jl.* viii, 393.

Mitchell, Capt. J.—Additions to the knowledge of Silk. [*Jl.* xxxvii, pt ii, 169.

Mitra, Dr. Rajendralala. — Translation of a Mithraic hymn from the Vijaya Mandir at Udayapúr. [*Jl.* xvii, pt, ii, 69.

Translation of Copperplate Inscription, presented to the Society by Brigadier Stacy. [*Jl.* xvii, pt. i, 71.

Note on an Inscription from Oujein. [*Jl.* xix, 475.

Note on three ancient Coins found at Mohammadpur, in the Jessore district. [*Jl.* xxi, 401.

Note on an ancient Inscription from Tháneswar. [*Jl.* xxii, 673.

On the Peculiarities of the Gáthá Dialect. [*Jl.* xxiii, 604.

Notes on ancient Inscriptions from the Chusan Archipelago and Pesháwur. [*Jl.* xxiv, 324.

Buddhism and Odinism, their similitude; illustrated by Extracts from Professor Holmboe's Memoir on the "Traces de Buddhisme en Norwége." [*Jl.* xxvii, 46.

On the Identity of the Toramánas of Eran, Gwalior and Kashmir. [*Jl.* xxx, 267.

Translation of a Bactrian Inscription from Wardak in Afghanistan. [*Jl.* xxx, 337.

On some Bactro-Buddhist Relics from Ráwal Pindi. [*Jl.* xxxi, 175.

Vestiges of the Kings of Gwalior. [*Jl.* xxxi, 391.

Mitra, Dr. Rajendralala (*contd.*)—Bhoja Rájá of Dhár and his Homonyms. [*Jl.* xxxii, 91.

Note on Major-General A. Cunningham's Remarks on the Bactro-Pali Taxila Inscription. [*Jl.* xxxii, 151.

Two Ancient Sanskrita Inscriptions from Central India; texts, translations and comments. [*Jl.* xxxii, 273.

On the Ruins of Budha Gayá. [*Jl.* xxxiii, 173.

On a Land Grant of Mahendrapála Deva of Kanauj. [*Jl.* xxxiii, 321.

On the Buddhist Remains of Sultánganj. [*Jl.* xxxiii, 360.

On the Origin of the Hindví Language and its relation to the Urdu Dialect. [*Jl.* xxxiii, 480.

On Amen and Om. [*Proc.* 1865, 46.

On the Sena Rájás of Bengal as commemorated in an Inscription from Rájsháhi, decyphered and translated by C. T. Metcalfe, Esq., C. S. [*Jl.* xxxiv, pt. i, 128.

On Cashmir. [*Proc.* 1866, 65.

On Oriental College at Lahore. [*Proc.* 1866, 103, 125.

On Scientific Technology. [*Proc.* 1866, 148, 157.

On "Om" and "Amen." [*Proc.* 1866, 208.

Note on a Copperplate Inscription from Sambhalpur. [*Jl.* xxxv, pt. i, 195.

Notes on Gupta Inscriptions from Aphsar and Behar. [*Jl.* xxxv, pt. i, 268.

On Arian Alphabets. [*Proc.* 1867, 35.

On Sanscrit MSS. [*Proc.* 1868, 43.

On Coins of Antimachos and Azelisas. [*Proc.* 1868, 164.

Letters addressed to Babu R. Mitra. By Babu R. Mitra. [*Proc.* 1899, 188.

Extracts from letters from Prof. Holmboe. [*Proc.* 1869, 188.

Inscription from Mr. Beames. [*Proc.* 1870, 4.

Remarks on the relation of Urya to other modern languages. [*Proc.* 1870, 201.

Remarks on two Inscriptions received from Babu Rashbihari Bose. [*Proc.* 1870, 294.

Notes on Sanskrit Inscriptions from Mathurá. [*Jl.* xxxix, pt. i, 117.

On the Funeral Ceremonies of the Ancient Hindús. [*Jl.* xxxix, pt. i, 241.

Style of Dress in Ancient India. [*Proc.* 1871, 100.

Mitra, Dr. Rajendralala (*contd.*)—
Notes on the Allah Upanishad. [*Proc.* 1871. 140.
Report for 1870-71. regarding the cataloguing of Sanscrit MSS. that are found in the Libraries of Bengal. [*Proc.* 1871, 277.
The Alla Upanishad, a spurious chapter of the Atharva Veda, text, translation, and notes. [*Jl.* xl. pt. i, 170.
Electrotypes of two ancient Seals. [*Proc.* 1872, 140.
Remarks on the term Gamian. [*Proc.* 1872, 180.
Notes on two Inscriptions from Banka, Zilah Bhaghalpur. [*Proc.* 1872, 198.
Beef in Ancient India. [*Jl.* xli, pt. i, 174.
A Picnic in Ancient India. [*Jl.* xli, pt. i, 340.
Translation of, and Remarks on, Mr. Delmerick's Sanskrit Inscriptions from the neighbourhood of Delhi. [*Proc.* 1873. 102.
Spirituous Drinks in Ancient India. [*Jl.* xlii. pt. i, 1.
Postscript to the Paper on Spirituous Drinks in Ancient India. [*Jl.* xlii, pt. i. 58.
On two Copperplate Inscriptions (Kanauj). [*Jl.* xlii. pt. i, 314.
Note on the Pálam Báolí Inscription. [*Jl.* xliii, pt. i, 104.
On the supposed Identity of the Greeks with the Yavanas of the Sanskrit writers. [*Jl.* xliii. pt. i, 246.
On a Copperplate Inscription of the time of Skanda-Gupta (with a plate). [*Jl.* xliii. pt. i, 363.
Note on a Copperplate Inscription of the time of Skanda Gupta. [*Proc.* 1875. 45.
Report on Sanskrit MSS. [*Proc.* 1875, 63.
Translations of Inscriptions from Benares. [*Proc* 1875, 82.
Reply to enquiry regarding the mention of Leprosy by ancient Hindu writers. [*Proc.* 1875, 160.
Remarks on a letter from Mr. E. Thomas, on a Coin of Kunanda. [*Proc.* 1875, 165.
Letter pointing out a mistake in his paper on the Skanda Gupta Inscription from Anupshahr. [*Proc.* 1875, 163
On supposed Greek Sculpture at Mathura. [*Proc.* 1875, 165.
On a Coin of Kunanda from Karnál. [*Jl.* xliv, pt. i, 82.

Mitra, Dr. Rajendralala (*contd.*)—
Remarks on a letter from Dr. Burnell on the Invasion of Bengal by the Chola King Kulottunga. [*Proc.* 1875, 106. 108.
Translations of Inscriptions from Rohtas. [*Proc.* 1876. 100.
Remarks on a Copperplate Grant of Govind Chundra of Kanauj. presented to the Society by Mr. F. S. Growse. [*Proc.* 1879, 130.
On Human Sacrifices in Ancient India. [*Jl.* xlv, pt. i, 76.
An Imperial Assemblage at Delhi three thousand years ago. [*Jl.* xlv, pt. i, 368.
On a Copperplate Inscription from Pandukesvar. [*Proc.* 1877. 71.
Remarks on a Collection of Pottery from Baluchistan. [*Proc.* 1877, 160.
Exhibition of Plaster Casts of the Hathigumpha Inscription at Udayagiri. with a revised reading and translation. [*Proc.* 1877, 163.
Exhibition of, and Remarks on. a Copperplate Inscription received from Mr. W. R. Davies, of Bhagalpur. [*Proc.* 1877, 257.
Researches at Buddha Gaya. [*Proc.* 1877, 258.
On forged Pali Inscription. [*Proc.* 1877, 266.
Remarks on the Early Life of Asoka. [*Proc.* 1878. 8.
Silver Coins from Burmah, with Remarks on. [*Proc.* 1878, 102.
Discovery of a New Era. [*Proc.* 1878, 103.
Remarks on Photograph of a Sculpture group in Garalmandar Temple at Pathari, Central India. [*Proc.* 1878, 123.
Remarks on a new Coin of Toramana. [*Proc.* 1878. 191.
Remarks on a Hindi MSS. from Jaipur. [*Proc.* 1878, 194.
On Representations of Foreigners in the Ajantá Frescoes. [*Jl.* xlvii, pt. i, 62.
A Copperplate Grant from Bandá. [*Jl.* xlvii, pt. i, 73.
On the Pála and the Sena Rájás of Bengal. [*Jl.* xlvii, pt. i, 384.
Description of Gold and Silver Sitarami Coins received from H. Rivett-Carnac. [*Proc.* 1879, 64.
Notes on a Donative Inscription from Rajaurgarh, near Alwar. [*Proc.* 1879, 157.
Translation of a Copperplate Inscription from Nirmand. in Kulu. with a note on the same. [*Proc.* 1879, 212.

Mitra, Dr. Rajendralala (*contd.*)—
Note on an Inscription from the Gate of the Krishna Dvaraka Temple at Gaya. [*Proc.* 1879, 218.
Exhibition of a Collection of Native Paintings. [*Proc.* 1879, 276.
Remarks on Hindi Roots. [*Proc.* 1879, 281.
Exhibition of some very old Palm-leaf MSS., and some Ancient Coins. [*Proc.* 1880, 4.
Remarks on Copper Coins of the Mitra dynasty. [*Proc.* 1880, 8.
Note on Arakan Coins. [*Proc.* 1880, 53.
Remarks on a Pali Inscription from Bharhat. [*Proc.* 1880, 58.
Transcripts and Translations of two Inscriptions from Buddha Gaya. [*Proc.* 1880, 76.
Note on Coins, &c., from Lieut. R. C. Temple. [*Proc.* 1880, 89.
On Medal sent by Mr. T. A. M. Gennoe. [*Proc.* 1880, 100.
Note on a Palm-leaf MSS. of the Setubundha, 672 years old. [*Proc.* 1880, 119.
Exhibition of a facsimile of a Chinese Inscription from Buddha Gaya. [*Proc.* 1880, 138.
Exhibition of two Copperplate Inscriptions from Sylhet. [*Proc.* 1880, 139.
Remarks on Paper on the Calcutta watersupplies, past and present. [*Proc.* 1880, 153.
On Budha Gaya Inscriptions. [*Proc.* 1880, 172.
On Coins sent by Raja Udayaprotapa Sinha. [*Proc.* 1881, 41.
On Hindi Inscriptions from near Monghyr. [*Proc.* 1881, 42.
On the Origin of the Myth about Kerberos. [*Proc.* 1881, 91.
Note on a MS. of the Bhatti Kávya. [*Proc.* 1881, 134.
Note on a Copperplate Grant from Cuttack. [*Proc.* 1882, 9.
Exhibition of a Collection of Coins of Shah Kings of Saurashtra, with remarks. [*Proc.* 1882, 41.
Exhibition of four Silver Coins from Mr. Cockburn. [*Proc.* 1882, 47.
On three Clay Seals sent by Mr. Carr-Stephen. [*Proc.* 1882, 114.
Remarks on Clay Figures from Toomluk. [*Proc.* 1882, 114.
Note on a Kutila Inscription from Monghyr. [*Proc.* 1883, 46.
Reading and Translation of a Sankrit Inscription from Deoghar. [*Proc.* 1883, 59.
Remarks on Paper on History of Orissa. [*Proc.* 1883, 69.

Mitra, Dr. Rajendralala (*contd.*)—
Note on a Sanskrit Inscription from the Lalitpur District. [*Jl.* lii, pt. i, 67.
On the Temples of Deoghar. [*Jl.* lii, pt. i, 164.
On Gonikáputra and Gonardíya as Names of Patanjali. [*Jl.* lii, pt. i, 261.
See GROWSE, F. S.

Mollendorf, O. F. von.—On a Collection of Japanese *Clausiliæ* made by Brigade Surgeon R. Hungerford in 1881. [*Jl.* li, pt. ii, 1.
Clausilia nevilliana, a new species from the Nicobars. [*Jl.* li, pt. ii, 11.
Descriptions of some new Asiatic *Clausiliæ.* [*Jl.* li, pt. ii, 12.

Moneeram.—Native Account of washing for gold in Assam. [*Jl.* vii, 621.

Money, D.—An Account of the Temple of Triveni, near Hugli. [*Jl.* xvi, 393.

Montgomerie, Major T. G.—Memorandum on the Nanga Parbat and other Snowy Mountains of the Himálaya Range adjacent to Kashmir. [*Jl.* xxvi, 266.
Memorandum on the great flood of the river Indus which reached Attok on the 10th August, 1858. [*Jl.* xxix, 128.
Memorandum in answer to the five questions proposed by Major Becher regarding the flood of the Indus in 1858. [*Jl.* xxix, 132.
Memorandum drawn up by the order of Colonel A. Scott Waugh, Engineers, Surveyor General of India, on the progress of the Kashmir Series of the Great Trigonometrical Survey of India; with map and observations on the late Conquest of Gilgit and other incidental matters. [*Jl.* xxx, 99.
Narrative Report of the Trans-Himalayan Explorations made during 1868. [*Jl.* xxxix, pt. ii, 47.
See THUILLIER, MAJOR H. L.

Moon and Moon-culminating Stars at Seháranpur, Nasírabad, and Dholeswar, with the longitudes deduced, Observations of the. [*Jl.* iii, 297.

Moor, Capt. Edward.—Account of an Hereditary Living Deity, to whom devotion is paid by the Brámens of Poona and its neighbourhood. [*As. Res.* vii, 383.

Moorcroft, William.—A Journey to Lake Mánasaróvara in Undés, a Province of Little Tibet. [*As. Res.* xii, 375.

Morany, S.—Qualitative Examination of the Native Copper found on Round Island in the Cheduba group, south-east of Ramree, and forwarded to the Society by Captain Campbell. *See* Proceedings Asiatic Society for April 1843. [*Jl.* xii, 904.

Morar, Fall of Lightning at. [*Proc.* 1872, 170.

Morrieson, Lieut. Nasmyth.—Trisection of an Angle. [*Jl.* ii, 71.

Morton, Revd. W. — Remarks on "A Comparison of Indo-Chinese Languages, &c." [*Jl.* vii, 56.

Mouat, Dr. J.—Meteorological Register kept at Bangalore. [*Jl.* v, 296.

Meteorological Observations, taken every hour, at Bangalore, in the Hospital of H. M. 13th Dragoons, from 6 A.M. of the 21st to 6 P.M. of the 22nd March 1836, inclusive, in conformity with Sir W. Herschel's instructions. [*Jl.* v. 298.

Muir, J.—On the Genuine Character of the Horá Sástra, as regards the use of Greek terms. [*Jl.* xiv, 809. *See* ROTH RODOLPH.

Muller, Max.—On the Introduction of Writing into India. [*Jl.* xxviii, 136.

Mukerjea, Upendra Chandra.—The Bhádú and the Báuris. [*Proc.* 1873, 202.

Mulheran, J. — On Cromlechs and Crosses in India. [*Proc.* 1868, 115, 147.

Munro, Capt.—Report on the Timber Trees of Bengal. [*Jl.* xvi, 1095.

Munroe, Dr. W.—Requesting information regarding the mention of Leprosy by ancient Hindu writers. [*Proc.* 1875, 160.

Muqbura at Hailan, Inscription on the. [*Jl.* xxxiii, 549.

Murray, Lieut. W. G.—On a mass of Iron. [*Proc.* 1865, 76.

Murwut, Earthquake in. [*Proc.* 1869, 163.

Murshedabad, Census of the Population of the city and district of, taken in 1829. [*Jl.* ii, 567.

Mussi at Hyderabad, New Bridge over the [*Jl.* i, 17.

Nagarjuni Cave, Translation of the Inscription in the [*Jl.* xvi, 594.

Narayan Ram.—Translation of the Ayodhyá-Máhátmya, or Pilgrimage of Ayodhyá. [*Jl.* xliv, pt. i, 130.

Nash, D. W.—On Progressive Development in the cold-blooded Vertebrata. [*Jl.* ii, 465.

Natural History, Report on a Collection of objects of [*Jl.* ii, 588.

Nepal and Assam, Report of the Society of Arts on specimens of Rice, Wool, &c., from. [*Jl.* v. 365.

Neufville, Capt. John Bryan.—On the Geography and Population of Assam. [*As. Res.* xvi, 331.

Nevill, Geoffrey.—On the Land-Shells of Bourbon, with descriptions of a few New Species. [*Jl.* xxxix, pt. ii, 403.

List of the *Mollusca* brought back by Dr. J. Anderson, from Yunnan and Upper Burma, with descriptions of New Species. [*Jl.* xlvi, pt. ii, 14.

New Species of Brackish-water Mullusks. [*Jl.* xlix, pt. ii, 159.

New or little-known *Mollusca* of the Indo-Malayan Fauna. [*Jl.* l, pt. ii, 125.

Description of a New Species of *Rostellaria*, from the Bay of Bengal. [*Jl.* l, pt. ii, 262.

Nevill, G. & H.—On some new Marine Gastropoda from the Southern Province of Ceylon. [*Jl.* xxxviii, pt. ii, 65.

Descriptions of Marine Gastropoda from Ceylon, &c. [*Jl.* xxxviii, pt. ii, 157.

Descriptions of New Marine *Mollusca* from the Indian Ocean. [*Jl.* xliii, pt. ii, 21.

Descriptions of new *Mollusca* from the Eastern Regions. [*Jl.* xl, pt. ii, 1.

Descriptions of New Marine *Mollusca* from the Indian Ocean. [*Jl.* xliv, pt. ii, 83.

Nevill, H.—*See* NEVILL, G.

Note on *Onchidium verruculatum*, Cuv., from Ceylon. [*Proc.* 1870, 304.

Newall, Lieut.-Colonel D. F. — A Sketch of the Mahomedan History of Cashmere. [*Jl.* xxiii, 409.

Notes on Pilgrimages in the Country of Cashmere. [*Jl.* xxxv, pt. i, 219.

Some Observations on the Temples of "Razdan" or "Razdoing" in the "Lar" Pergunnah, Cashmere (with three Plates.) [*Jl.* xxxviii, pt. i, 177.

Some Account of the Rishis or Hermits of Kashmir. [*Jl.* xxxix, pt. i, 265.

Newbold, Capt. J. T.—A Visit to the Gold Mine at Batting Moring and summit of Mount Ophir, or "Gunong Ledang," in the Malay Peninsula. [*Jl.* ii, 497.

Some Account of the Territory and Inhabitants of Naning, in the Malayan Peninsula. [*Jl.* iii, 601.

Sketch of the four Menángkábowe States, in the interior of the Malayan Peninsula. [*Jl.* iv, 241.

Newbold, Capt. J. T. (*contd.*)—On the Government and History of Naning in the Malay Peninsula. [*Jl.* iv, 297.

Account of Súngie Ujong, one of the States in the Interior of Malacca. [*Jl.* iv, 537.

Account of Rumbówe, one of the States in the Interior of Malacca. [*Jl.* v, 61.

Johóle and its former Dependencies of Jompóle Gominchi. [*Jl.* v, 257.

Note on the States of Pérak, Srímenanti, and other States in the Malay Peninsula. [*Jl.* v, 505.

Sketch of the State of Múar, Malay Peninsula. [*Jl.* v, 561.

Outline of Political and Commercial Relations with the Native States on the Eastern and Western Coasts. Malay Peninsula. [*Jl.* v, 626.

Note on the Occurrence of Volcanic Scoria in the Southern Peninsula. [*Jl.* v, 670.

Notes, principally Geological, on the Tract between Bellary and Bijapore. [*Jl.* xi, 929.

Notes, principally Geological, from Bijapore to Bellary, *viâ* Kannighirri. [*Jl.* xi, 941.

Geological Specimens offered to the Asiatic Society of Bengal. [*Jl.* xi, 1131.

Note on a recent Fossil Fresh-water Deposit in Southern India, with a few remarks on the origin and age of the Kunker, and on the supposed decrease of Thermal Temperature in India. [*Jl.* xiii, 313.

Note on the Osseous Breccia and Deposit in the Caves of Billa Soorgum, Lat. 15° 25′, Long. 78° 15′, Southern India. [*Jl.* xiii, 610.

Notice of the Ajaib-al-Mukhlukat. [*Jl.* xiii, 632.

Notes, chiefly Geological, across the Peninsula from Masulipatam to Goa, comprising remarks on the origin of the Regur and Laterite; occurrence of Manganese veins in the latter, and on certain traces of aqueous denudation on the surface of Southern India. (With a Plate.) [*Jl.* xiii, 984.

On the Alpine Glacier, Iceberg, Diluvial and Wave Translation Theories; with reference to the deposits of Southern India, its furrowed and striated Rocks, and Rock basins. [*Jl.* xiv, 217.

Newbold, Capt. J. T. (*contd.*)—Notes, principally Geological, on the South Mahratta country—Falls of Gokauk—Classification of Rocks. [*Jl.* xiv, 268.

Notes, chiefly Geological, across the Peninsula of Southern India, from Madras, Lat. N. 13° 5′ to Goa, Lat. N. 15° 30′ by the Baulpilly Pass and Ruins of Bijanugger. [*Jl.* xiv, 497.

Notes, principally Geological, across the Peninsula of Southern India, from Kistapatam, Lat. 14° 17′ at the Embouchure of the Coileyroo River, on the Eastern Coast, to Honawer, Lat. 14° 16′ on the Western Coast, comprising a visit to the Falls of Gairsuppa. [*Jl.* xiv, 398.

Notes, chiefly Geological, across the Peninsula, from Mangalore, in Lat. N. 12° 49′, by the Bisly Pass to Madras, in Lat. N. 13° 4′. [*Jl.* xiv, 641.

Notes chiefly Geological, across South India from Pondicherry, Lat. N. 11° 56′, to Beypoor, in Lat. N. 11° 12′, through the great gap of Palghautcherry. [*Jl.* xiv, 759.

Notes, chiefly Geological, on the Coast of Coromandel, from the Pennaur to Pondicherry. [*Jl.* xv, 204.

Notes, chiefly Geological, on the Western Coast of South India. [*Jl.* xv, 224.

Notes, chiefly Geological, from Seringapatam, by the Hegulla Pass, to Cannanore. [*Jl.* xv, 315.

Notes, chiefly Geological, from Koompta on the Western Coast (S. India) by the Devamunni and Nundi Cunnama Passes, easterly to Cumbum, and thence southerly to Chittoor; comprising a notice of the Diamond and Lead Excavations of Buswapúr. [*Jl.* xv, 380.

Notes, chiefly Geological, from Gooty to Hydrabad, South India, comprising a brief notice of the old Diamond Pits at Dhone. [*Jl.* xvi, 477.

Niceville, L. de.—*See* DE NICEVILLE, L.

Nicobars, Extraordinary Meteor observed at the. [*Proc.* 1874, 156.

Nietner, John. — Entomological Papers, being descriptions of new Ceylon Coleoptera, with such observations on their habits as appear in any way interesting. [*Jl.* xxv, 381, 523.

Entomological Papers. [*Jl.* xxvi, 132.

Nipalese Zoology, Illustrations of, [*Jl.* iv, 521.

Nizamut Palace of Moorshedabad,—Extracts from official records, with descriptive details regarding the new;—erected by Colonel D. McLeod, Chief Engineer of Bengal. [*Jl.* viii. 552.

Nock.—Report on the Road from Sinde, from Subzul to Shikarpoor. [*Jl.* xii. 59.

Noton, Ben.—Table showing the Rise of Spring Tides in Bombay Harbour, during night and day, for the year 1832. [*Jl.* ii. 247.

N. W. Frontier. Note and Tabular Statement. [*Jl.* x. 476.

N. W. Frontier, Trade with Afghanistan. On Tabular Returns of the [*Jl.* x. 251.

Nowrozjee, Furdoonjee.—Report on the Weights, Measures, and Coins of Cabul and Bukhara. [*Jl.* vii, 892.

Oakes, Col.—Letter relating the discovery of Flint Implements at Jubbulpore. [*Proc.* 1869, 51.

Obbard, J.—On the Translation of Waves of Water with relation to the great flood of the Indus in 1858. [*Jl.* xxix, 266.

O'Donel, J. H.—Notes on the Tribes of the Eastern Frontier, Nos. 1 & 2. *See* Reynolds, H. J. [*Jl.* xxxii, 400, 404.

O'Donnell, C. J.—Note on Mahásthán near Bagurá (Bogra), Eastern Bengal. [*Jl.* xliv, pt. i, 183.

O'Kinealy, J. — Translation of an Arabic pamphlet on the history and doctrines of the Wahhábís, written by the grandson of Abdul Wahháb, founder of the sect. [*Jl.* xliii, pt. ii, 68.

Oliver, Lieut.-Col. Thos.—Abstract of Observations of the Temperature, Pressure, and Hygrometrical State of the Air in the Vicinity of Delhi. [*Jl.* i, 506.

Abstracts of Observations of the Temperature, Pressure, and Hygrometrical State of the Air at Nasirabad. [*Jl.* ii, 128.

Culminating Stars observed with the Moon at Násirabád. [*Jl.* ii, 432.

Latitude of the Church Bungalow at Nasírábad, by Altitudes (170) of Polaris out of the Meridian, observed with a Troughton's 18-inch Altitude and Azimuth Circle. [*Jl.* iii, 243.

Longitude of Nasírabad by Lunar Transits and by Observations of Moon-culminating stars. [*Jl.* iv, 52.

Oldham, Thomas.—Notes upon the Geology of the Rajmahal Hills; being the result of Examinations made during the cold season of 1852-53. [*Jl.* xxiii. 263.

Note on the Fossils in the Society's Collection reputed to be from Spiti. [*Jl.* xxxiii. 232.

On Stone Implements from Madras. [*Proc.* 1865, 206.

On Meteorite from Klein Menow. [*Proc.* 1868, 203, 208.

On Copper Implements found in Mainpuri. [*Proc.* 1868. 251.

Notes on the Earthquake of January 10th. 1869. [*Proc.* 1869, 113.

Notes on the Remains found in a Cromlech at Coorg. [*Proc.* 1869, 226.

Observations on Paper on the Normal Rainfall of Bengal. [*Proc.* 1870, 225.

Oldham, W.—On a Shower of Earth. [*Proc.* 1868. 182.

Memorandum on the action of the Ganges. [*Proc.* 1868, 229. *See* Baker, Major W. E.

Ommanney, Capt. E. L.—Note on Patna Boulders. [*Jl.* xix, 136.

Ophir, Note on the Botanical Specimens from Mount. [*Jl.* iii, 48.

Ord, Capt.—Extract from a Meteorological Journal kept at Kandy, Island of Ceylon. [*Jl.* iv, 709.

O'Reiley, E.—Remarks on the "Lake of Clear Water" in the district of Bassein, British Burmah. [*Jl.* xxxiii, 39.

Osborne, George.—Report of a Visit made to the supposed Coal-Field at Bidjeegurh (Vijayagadah). [*Jl.* vii, 839.

O'Shaughnessy, Dr. W. B.—On the Detection of Arsenical Poisons, &c., &c. [*Jl.* viii, 147.

Memoranda relative to experiments on the communication of Telegraph Signals by Induced Electricity. [*Jl.* viii, 714.

Extract from a Memoir on the Preparations of the Indian Hemp or Gunjah (*Cannabis Indica*), their effects on the Animal System in Health, and their utility in the Treatment of Tetanus and other Convulsive Diseases. [*Jl.* viii, 732, 838.

Memorandum on the Explosion of Gunpowder under Water by the Galvanic Battery; with a notice of the successful destruction of the "Equitable" at Pultah Reach. [*Jl.* viii, 351.

O'Shaughnessy, Dr. W. B. (*contd.*) —Official Correspondence on the attaching of Lightning Conductors to Powder Magazines. [*Jl.* ix. 277.

On Lightning Conductors to Powder Magazines. [*Jl.* x, 6.

Experiments and Papers, principally by W B. O'Shaughnessy, relating to the effects of Sea-water on Iron. [*Jl.* xii, 1066.

Memoranda on Explosive Cotton. [*Jl.* xvi, 177.

On the Refinage, on a large scale, by means of Nitre, of brittle or understandard Silver, for coinage purposes, and a ready mode of approximative assaying of silver. [*Jl.* xvi, 557.

O'Shaughnessy and Sutherland, J. J. C.—Notice of a Grant engraved on copper, found at Kumbhi in the Saugor Territory. [*Jl.* viii. 481.

Sanscrit Inscription on the Slab removed from above the Kothoutiya gate of the Fort Rohtas. [*Jl.* viii, 693.

Ouseley, Lieut.-Col. J. R.—Notice of two beds of Coal discovered. [*Jl.* iv, 648.

Note on the Process of Washing for the gold dust and diamonds at Heera Khoond. [*Jl.* viii, 1057.

On the Course of the river Nerbudda, [*Jl.* xiv, 354.

On the Antiquities of Sargujá and its neighbourhood. [*Jl.* xvii, pt. 1, 65

Ouseley, Major R.—On Peat in Pertabgurh. [*Proc.* 1865, 85.

Palestine, Notes of a Tour through. [*Jl.* iv, 438.

Pandit, Prannath.—Note on the Chittagong Copperplate, dated Sáka 1165, or A. D. 1243, presented to the Society by A. L. Clay, Esq., C. S. [*Jl.* xliii, pt. i, 318.

Krishna-cultus in the Brhat Samhita. [*Jl.* xliv, pt. i. 15.

Morals of Kálidása. [*Jl.* xlv, pt. i, 352.

See SMITH, V. A.

Parish, Revd. C. — Botanical Notes made during a month's tour from Moulmein to the three Pagodas and in the Shan States, in the month of February, 1859. [*Jl.* xxviii, 457.

Notes of a Trip up the Salween. [*Jl.* xxxiv, pt. ii, 135.

Parish, Lieut. William Hawtayne. —A Report of the Kohistan of the Jullundhur Doab. [*Jl.* xvii pt. i, 281.

Parish, Lieut. William Hawtayne (*continued*).—A Journal of a Trip through the Kohistán of the Jullundhur, undertaken at the close of the year 1847, and commencement of 1848, under the orders of the Supreme Government of India, for the purpose of determining the Geological formation of that district. [*Jl.* xviii, 360.

On the Influence of Forests on Climate. [*Jl.* xviii, 791.

Parry, J. W.—Notes on the Nángís: a religious sect. [*Proc.* 1883, 100.

Memorandum on a Couple of Stones found in the Cumbum Taluq of the Kurnul District. [*Proc.* 1883, 165.

Patterson, J. D.—Of the Origin of the Hindu Religion. [*As. Res.* viii, 44.

On the Grámas, or Musical Scales of the Hindus. [*As. Res.* ix, 445.

Paton, Charles.—Historical and Statistical Sketch of Aracan. [*As. Res.* xvi, 353.

Paul, A. W.—Inscribed Stones, &c., from Chittagong. [*Proc.* 1872, 191.

Paula, Ratna.—Translation of an Inscription in the Pali and Burma Languages on a Stone Slab from Ramavati (Ramree Island) in Aracan, presented to the Asiatic Society by H. Walters. [*Jl.* iii, 209.

Note on an extraordinary Flood in Upper Assam. [*Proc.* 1869, 264.

Nágá method of climbing trees. [*Proc.* 1872, 135.

Peal, S. E.—Notes on a Visit to the Tribes inhabiting the Hills south of Sibsagar, Assam. [*Jl.* xli, pt. i, 9.

A Vocabulary of the Banpará Nágás. [*Jl.* xlii, pt. i, xxx, app.

Extract of a letter on the subject of wild pigs eating fish. [*Proc.* 1876, 92.

Extracts from three letters relative to Pot-holes, the Geological Structure of Goalpara Hill, and movements of the clouds in Upper Assam. [*Proc.* 1877, 260.

A peculiarity of the River Names in Assam and some of the adjoining countries. [*Jl.* xlviii, pt. i, 258.

Note on the old Burmese Route over Patkai via Nongyang (viewed as the most feasible and direct route, from India to China). [*Jl.* xlviii, pt. ii, 69.

Report on a Visit to the Nongyang Lake, on the Burmese Frontier, February 1879. [*Jl.* l, pt. ii, 1.

Peal, S. E. (*contd.*)—Notes of a Trip up the Dihing basin to Dapha Pani &c., January and February, 1882. [*Jl.* lii, pt. ii, 7.

Pearse, G. G.—Letter relating to Ancient Structures near Rewah. [*Proc.* 1869, 108.

On some Bactrian and South Indian Coins. [*Proc.* 1880, 115.

Pearse, Col. Thomas D.—Astronomical Observations in Fort William, and between Madras and Calcutta. [*As. Res.* i, 57.

On two Hindu Festivals, and the Indian Sphinx. [*As. Res.* ii, 333.

Pearson, Dr. J. T.—Note on the Eurinorynchus Griseus. [*As. Res.* xix, pt. i, 169.

A Method of Preparing Strychnia. [*Jl.* ii, pt. i, 42.

Note on the Genus Spiraculum. [*Jl.* ii, 590.

Memorandum on the Fœtus of the Squalus Maximus. [*Jl.* iv, 324.

Hints for the Preservation of Objects of Natural History. [*Jl.* iv, 462.

Note on Thylacinus Cynocephalus. [*Jl.* iv, 572.

Memorandum on the Gaur and Gayal. [*Jl.* vi, 225.

A letter to Dr. Helfer, on the Zoology of Tenasserim and the neighbouring provinces. [*Jl.* vii, 357.

Observations on the "Report on the Museum of the Asiatic Society, by Dr. Wm. Jameson." [*Jl.* viii, 419.

On the Bora Chung, or the Ground Fish of Bootan. [*Jl.* viii, 551.

Zoological Catalogue of the Museum of the Asiatic Society. [*Jl.* ix, 514.

Catalogue of the Birds in the Museum of the Asiatic Society. [*Jl.* x, 628.

Catalogue of Mammalia in the Museum of the Asiatic Society. [*Jl.* x, 660.

Peat, Capt. A. C.—Various Routes in Scinde from Official Documents from Bombay, of March 1840. [*Jl.* xii, 11.

Pedler, Alexander.—Note on the Composition of the Calcutta Coal Gas. [*Proc.* 1874, 183.

Note on the Use of the Radiometer as a Photometer. [*Proc.* 1876, 187.

On the Past and Present Water-supplies of Calcutta. [*Jl.* xlix, pt. ii, 85.

Peer Mungul or Munga or Mungear, Temperature of the Hot Springs at, or Munga, or Mungear. [*Jl.* xvii, pt. ii, 230.

Pellew, F. H.—Letter on the Barisal Guns. *Proc.* 1870, 289.

Note on some Specimens of Wood and Soil dug out near Baddibati, Hughli district. [*Proc.* 1873, 78.

Pemberton, Capt. R. Boileau.—Abstract of the Journal of a Route travelled by Capt. S. F. Hannay, of the 40th Regiment Native Infantry. from the Capital of Ava to the Amber Mines of the Húkong Valley on the south-east frontier of Assam. [*Jl.* vi, 245.

See GRIFFITH. W.

Peppe, Mr. J. F.—On Antiquities of Gya. [*Proc.* 1865, 80, 150, 152.

Letter regarding the Antiquities of Bihár. [*Proc.* 1871, 251.

Peppe, W.—Rough Notes on some of the Antiquities in the Gayá district. [*Jl.* xxxv, pt. i, 49.

Pershad, Durga.—On Coins and Antiquities from Khokhrakote. [*Proc.* 1881, 69.

Phayre, Major-General Sir Arthur P.—Account of Arakan. [*Jl.* x, 679.

On the History of Arakan. [*Jl.* xiii 23.

The Historical Coins of Arakan. [*Jl.* xv 232.

Original Text and Translation of a scroll of Sílver in the Burmese language. found in a Buddhist Pagoda at Prome. [*Jl.* xxv, 173.

On the History of the Shwe Dagon Pagoda at Rangoon. [*Jl.* xxviii. 473.

Remarks upon an ancient Buddhist Monastery at Pu-gân, on the Irrawaddy [*Jl.* xxix, 346.

Remarks on a Stone Inscription from the ruins of Pu-gán on the Irrawaddy river. [*Jl.* xxxii, 267.

Memorandum on some Medals and Coins in the Museum of the Asiatic Society, found near Mergui on the Tenasserim Coast. [*Jl.* xxxii. 271.

On the History of the Burmah Race. [*Jl.* xxxiii, 1; xxxvii, pt. i, 73; xxxviii, pt. i, 29.

Memorandum upon some ancient Tiles obtained at Pugán in Burma. [*Jl.* xxxiii, 57.

Note on a Circle of Stones in the District of Yúsufzaí. [*Jl.* xxxix, pt. i, 58.

Letter regarding Gold Coins found on the Island of Cheduba. [*Proc.* 1872, 3

On the History of Pegu. [*Jl.* xlii, pt. i, 23, 120; xliii, pt. i, 6.

Letter on Stone Weapons from Burma. [*Proc.* 1876, 3.

Phear, Hon. J. B.—Note on North Westers. [*Proc.* 1870, 88.

Observations on Buddhist Heads. [*Proc.* 1870, 217.

Phear, Hon. J. B. (*contd.*)—Remarks on Paper on normal Rainfall of Bengal. [*Proc.* 1870, 223.

Exhibition of Barometric Curves. [*Proc.* 1871, 14.

Physical Class of the Asiatic Society of Bengal. Note on the Zoology of the 2nd Part of the Transactions of the [*Jl.* ii, 417.

Piddington, Henry.—Examination and Analysis of some Specimens of Iron Ore from Burdwan. [*As. Res.* xviii, pt. i, 171.

On the Fertilising Principles of the Inundations of the Hugli. [*As. Res.* xviii, pt. i, 224.

Notice of an Extraordinary Fish. [*Jl.* iv, 218.

Examination of a Mineral Exudation from Gazni. [*Jl.* iv, 696.

Researches on the Gale and Hurricane in the Bay of Bengal on the 3rd, 4th. and 5th of June, 1839; being a First Memoir with reference to the Theory of the Law of Storms in India. [*Jl.* viii, 559.

Researches on the Gale and Hurricane in the Bay of Bengal on the 3rd, 4th, and 5th of June, 1839; with reference to the Theory of the Law of Storms in India. [*Jl.* viii. 631.

On Camel Litters for the Wounded. [*Jl.* viii, 702.

A Second Memoir with reference to the Theory of the Law of Storms in India; being Researches relating to the Storm of the 19th to the 21st Sept. at the head of the Bay of Bengal; to the Great Hurricane at Coringa on the 16th November, 1839; and to another off the Island of Preparis on the 22nd November. [*Jl.* ix, 107.

A Second Memoir on Indian Tempests, with reference to the Theory of the Law of Storms. [*Jl.* ix, 397.

A Third Memoir with reference to the Theory of the Law of Storms in India; being Researches relating to the Hurricane in the Bay of Bengal and at Cuttack. from 27th April to 1st May, 1840. [*Jl.* ix, 1009.

Memoranda on the 'Chulchulheera' of the Hills, and on some Lichens from the Himálayas in the Collection of the Asiatic Society. [*Jl.* x, 377.

Examination and Analysis of a Soil brought from the Island of Chedooba. by Capt Halsted, of H. M. S. 'Childers.' [*Jl.* x, 436.

Piddington, Henry (*contd.*)—Report on the Soils brought from Chedooba, by H. M. S. 'Childers.' [*Jl.* x, 447.

Examination of some decayed Oriental Works in the Library of the Asiatic Society. [*Jl.* x, 576.

Note on the Fossil Jaw, sent from Jubbulpore, by Dr. Spilsbury. [*Jl.* x, 620.

Memorandum on Nurma Cotton. [*Jl.* x, 716.

Report on some Articles of Trade sent by Lieut. Postans from Khorassan. [*Jl.* x, 718.

Fourth Memoir on the Law of Storms in India, being remarks and documents relative to the loss of the Ship *Golconda* in the Tyfoons of 22nd to 24th September, 1840, in the China Sea. [*Jl.* x, 895.

Report to the Secretary of the Board of Customs, Salt and Opium, on the Salts, called Puckwah and Phool-Kharee; with a process for detecting the adulteration of Government Salt; estimates of the qualities of both Salts annually produced, and of the amount of loss which the revenue may sustain through the production of these two articles. [*Jl.* x, 939.

A Fifth Memoir with reference to the Theory of the Law of Storms in India; being Researches about the Madras Storm of May 16th, 1841, and an Account of a Whirlwind experienced by the French Ship "*Paquebot des Mers du Sud*," Capt. P. Saliz, off the Cape. [*Jl.* xi, 6.

Museum of Economic Geology of India [*Jl.* xi, 322.

Sixth Memoir on the Law of Storms in India; being Storms in the China Seas, from 1780 to 1841. [*Jl.* xi, 606.

A Seventh Memoir on the Law of Storms in India; being the Calcutta Hurricane of 3rd and 4th June, 1842. [*Jl.* xi, 971.

An Eighth Memoir on the Law of Storms in India; being Researches relative to the Storm in the Bay of Bengal, at Madras, and in the Arabian Sea, of 22nd to 31st October, 1842, with two Charts. [*Jl.* xii, 339.

On an improved Simpiesometer, "The Tropical Tempest Simpiesometer," just received in Calcutta. [*Jl.* xii, 451.

Piddington, Henry (*contd.*)—A Ninth Memoir on the Law of Storms in India; being the Pooree and Cuttack Storms of 2nd, and the Gya and Patna Storms of 5th and 6th October, 1842. [*Jl.* xii, 771.

Examination of a remarkable Red Sandstone from the junction of the Diamond Limestone and Sandstone at Nurnoor, in the Kurnool Territory, Southern India. Received for the Museum of Economic Geology, from Capt. Newbold, M. N. I., Assistant Commissioner, Kurnool. [*Jl.* xiii, 336.

Tenth Memoir on the Law of Storms in India; being the Madras and Masulipatam Storm of 21st to 23rd May, 1843. [*Jl.* xiii, 69.

Chemical Examination of an Ærolite which fell at the village of Manicgaon near Eidulabad in Khandesh. [*Jl.* xiii, 884.

An Eleventh Memoir on the Law of Storms in India; being the Storms in the Bay of Bengal and Southern Indian Ocean, from 26th November to 2nd December, 1843. [*Jl.* xiv, 10.

Twelfth Memoir on the Law of Storms in India; being the Storms of the Andaman Sea and Bay of Bengal, 9th to 14th November, 1844. [*Jl.* xiv, 357.

A Notice of the Alphabets of the Philippine Islands, Translated from the "Informe sobre el Estado de las Islas Filipinas," of Don Sinibaldo de Mas, Madrid, January 1843. Vol. I. p. 25. [*Jl.* xiv, 603.

A Thirteenth Memoir on the Law of Storms in the Indian and China Seas; being the *Charles Heddle's* Hurricane in the Southern Indian Ocean, 22nd to 27th February, 1845. [*Jl.* xiv, 703.

A Fourteenth Memoir on the Law of Storms in India; being the Bay of Bengal, Ceylon, Malabar Coast, and Arabian Sea Storms of 29th November to 5th December, 1845. [*Jl.* xiv, 878.

Notice of Tremenheerite, a new carbonaceous mineral. [*Jl.* xvi, 369.

On a new kind of Coal, being Volcanic Coal, from Arracan. [*Jl.* xvi, 371.

Notice on the Ferruginous Spherules imbedded in Sandstone from Lullutpore, in Bundlecund, by Dr. G. G. Spilsbury [*Jl.* xvi, 711.

Notice of the Deo Monnees, or sacred beads of Assam. [*Jl.* xvi, 713.

Piddington, Henry (*contd.*)—Note to accompany a Chart of the Bay of Bengal, with the average courses of its Hurricanes from A. D. 1800 to 1846. [*Jl.* xvi, 847.

Description and Analysis of the new Mineral Newboldite, sent from Southern India by Captain Newbold. [*Jl.* xvi, 1129.

A Fifteenth Memoir on the Law of Storms; being (Part I.) the Buckinghamshire and H. Co.'s Steamer *Cleopatra's* Hurricane on the Malabar Coast and Arabian Sea, of April 1847. The Hurricane of the H. C. S. *Essex* in June 1811, and (Part II.) some considerations on the loss of the *Cleopatra* Steamer, and for Steamers navigating the Eastern Seas in general. [*Jl.* xvii, pt. i, 27.

Examination and Analysis of the BALL COAL of the Burdwan Mines. [*Jl.* xvii, pt. i, 59.

A Notice of a remarkable Hot Wind in the Zillah of Purneah. [*Jl.* xvii, pt. i. 144.

On the Great Diamond in the possession of the Nizam. [*Jl.* xvii, pt. i, 151.

A Sixteenth Memoir on the Law of Storms; being the Hurricanes of the *Maria Somes* and other ships, in the Southern Indian Ocean, in March 1846. [*Jl.* xvii, pt. i, 517.

Description and Analysis of a large mass of Meteoric Iron, from the Kurruckpore hills, near Monghyr, presented to the Museum of the Asiatic Society by Captain W. S. Sherwill. [*Jl.* xvii, pt. ii, 538.

A Seventeenth Memoir on the Law of Storms in India; being Storms of the China Seas from 1842 to 1847, and some of the Northern Pacific Ocean, from 1797. [*Jl.* xviii, 1.

On a spontaneous combustion of Coal wetted with salt water, on board the ship *Sir Howard Douglas*, Capt. Ogilby. [*Jl.* xviii, 167.

A Supplementary Note on Captain Sherwill's Meteoric Iron. [*Jl.* xviii, 171.

A Notice of a remarkable local deviation of the Compass near Saugor in Bundlecund, communicated by Captain J. H. Campbell. [*Jl.* xviii, 410.

Further remarks on the Ball Coal of the Burdwan Mines. [*Jl.* xviii, 412.

An Eighteenth Memoir on the Law of Storms in India; being the Cyclone of 12th to 14th October 1848 in the Bay of Bengal. [*Jl.* xviii, 826.

Piddington, Henry (*contd.*)—A third Notice on the Ball Coal of the Burdwan Mines. [*Jl.* xix, 75.

Examination and Analysis of an orange-yellow Earth brought from the Sikkim Territory, by Dr. Campbell, Darjeeling, and said to be used there as a cure for Goitre. [*Jl.* xix, 143.

On Calderite, an undescribed Siliceo-Iron-and-Manganese Rock, from the district of Burdwan. [*Jl.* xix, 145.

Memorandum relative to the Storms of Wind experienced in Tartary, with suggestions relative to them, for the Mission proceeding there. [*Jl.* xix, 242.

A Nineteenth Memoir on the Law of Storms in the Indian and China Seas; being the Cyclones of the *Sir Howard Douglas* and of H. M. Brig *Jumna* in the Southern Indian Ocean. January to April, 1848. [*Jl.* xix, 349.

Examination of the New Mineral Haughtonite (a compound of Carbonate of Lead and Sulphate of Barytes). [*Jl.* xix, 452.

Detailed Report on the Copper Ores of the Deoghur Mines. [*Jl.* xx, 1.

A Twentieth Memoir on the Law of Storms in the Indian and China Seas; being the April Cyclone of the Bay of Bengal, 23rd to 28th April, 1850. [*Jl.* xx, 13.

On the Rates of Chronometers, as influenced by the Local Attraction of Ships and by Terrestrial Magnetism. [*Jl.* xx, 61.

On a Series of Calderite Rocks. [*Jl.* xx, 207.

On the Comparative Action of the Marine and Aneroid Barometers and Simpiesometer in Cyclones. [*Jl.* xx, 219.

Examination and Analysis of the *Shalka Meteorite* (Zillah West Burdwan). [*Jl.* xx, 299.

Second Notice on the Argentiferous Ores of Deoghur. [*Jl.* xxi, 74.

On Hircine, a new Resin. [*Jl.* xxi, 76.

A Table of Analyses of Indian Coals. [*Jl.* xxi, 270.

A Twenty-first Memoir on the Law of Storms in the Indian and China Seas; being the Cyclone of H. M. S. *Fox*, in the Bay of Bengal, 30th April to 6th May, 1851. [*Jl.* xxi, 283.

Apparatus for distilling off the Mercury from an Amalgam of Gold or Silver. [*Jl.* xxi, 403.

Piddington, Henry (*contd.*) — On Filtering the Waters of Tanks, in large quantities, for the use of Towns. [*Jl.* xxi, 473.

On a Geometrical Measurement of the distances from Crest to Crest of the Barometric Waves in a Cyclone. [*Jl.* xxii, 77.

Supplementary Notice on the new Mineral Resin, Hircine. [*Jl.* xxii, 279.

A Twenty-second Memoir on the Storms of the Indian and China Seas; Cyclones and Tornadoes of the Bay of Bengal, from 1848 to 1852. [*Jl.* xxiii, 1.

On Nepaulite: a new Mineral from the neighbourhood of Kathmandoo. [*Jl.* xxiii, 170.

On the Quantity of Silt held in suspension by the waters of the Hooghly at Calcutta in each month of the year. [*Jl.* xxiii, 283.

Examination and Analysis of four Specimens of Coal from the neighbourhood of Darjeeling, forwarded by A. Campbell, Esq., Supdt. [*Jl.* xxiii, 381.

Examination and Analysis of Dr. Campbell's Specimens of Copper Ores obtained in the neighbourhood of Darjeeling. [*Jl.* xxiii, 477.

A Twenty-third Memoir on the Law of Storms in the Indian and China Seas; being the Peninsular and Oriental Steam Navigation Company's ship *Precursor's* Cyclone of October, 1851. [*Jl.* xxiii, 505.

Examination and Analysis of two Specimens of Coal from Ava. [*Jl.* xxiii, 714.

Memorandum on an unknown Forest Race (of Indian Vedas?) inhabiting the Jungles south of Palamow; and on the deserted city of Dhoolmee in Manbhoom. [*Jl.* xxiv, 207.

Memorandum on the Kunkurs of Burdwan as a flux for smelting the Iron Ores, and on some smeltings of Iron Ores by Mr. Taylor, of that district. [*Jl.* xxiv, 212.

Report on two Specimens of Cuttack Coal from the Talcheer Mine, forwarded by E. A. Samuells, Esq., Commissioner of Cuttack. [*Jl.* xxiv, 240.

Examination and Analysis of a Coal from Cherra Punji, received from Messrs. *Gilmore* and *McKilligan*. [*Jl.* xxiv, 283.

Piddington, Henry (*contd.*) — A Twenty-fourth Memoir on the Law of Storms; being the *Calcutta* and *SunderbundCyclone* of 14th and 15th May, 1852. [*Jl.* xxiv, 397.

A second Series of Experiments to ascertain the mean quantity of Silt held in suspension by the waters of the Hooghly in various months of the year; as also the quantity carried out to sea. With an Appendix on its sectional Area and average Discharge. [*Jl.* xxv, 151.

Examination of three Specimens of Bengal Mineral Waters. [*Jl.* xxv, 190.

A Twenty-fifth Memoir on the Law of Storms in India; being the H. Company's Steamer *Pluto's* Cyclone in the Gulf of Martaban, 23rd and 24th April, 1854. [*Jl.* xxvii, 177.

See CAMPBELL, DR. A.; JULIEN, STANISLAS.

Pigou, Lieut.—On the Topes of Darounta and Caves of Bahrabad. [*Jl.* x, 381.

Piplianagar—Translation of a Támba Patra, which was found in a field of the village of, in the Shujálpur Parganá, by a *krisan* engaged in ploughing, and presented to Mr. L. Wilkinson, the Political Agent at Bhopál, by the Jagirdár. [*Jl.* v, 377.

Playfair, John.—Questions and Remarks on the Astronomy of the Hindus. [*As. Res.* iv, 159.

Pogson, N. R.—Discovery of the New Planet "*Asia*." [*Jl.* xxx, 291.

Polier, Lieut.-Col.—The Process of making Attar, or Essential Oil of Roses. [*As. Res.* i, 332.

Postans, Lieut. J.—Account of the Ruins and Site of Old Mandaví in Raepur, and legend of Vikramádityá's son in Cutch. [*Jl.* vi, 648.

Account of the Expedition of Chach (Chacha), extracted from the Chach Námeh, and extracts from the Tôhfat-ul-Khwán. [*Jl.* vii, 93.

Extracts from the Tôhfat-ul-Kiram, and the Chach Námeh, translated. [*Jl.* vii. 297.

An Account of the Jain Temple at Badrasir, and Ruins of Badránagiri in the province of Cutch. [*Jl.* vii, 431.

Memorandum on the Silk Trade between Shikarpore and Khorassan, and on the Produce of Indigo in Sinde. [*Jl.* ix, 843.

Memorandum on the Trade between the Towns of Shikarpore and Candahar. [*Jl.* x, 12.

Postans, Lieut. J. (*contd.*)—Memorandum on the city of Shikarpore, in Upper Sindh. [*Jl.* x, 17.

Of the early History of Sindh, from the "Chuch Namuh" and other authorities. [*Jl.* x, 183, 267.

Report on Upper Sindh and the Eastern portion of Cutchee, with a Memorandum on the Beloochee and other Tribes of Upper Sindh and Cutchee, and a Map of part of the Country referred to. [*Jl.* xii, 23.

Translation of the Toofut-ul-Kiram. a History of Sindh. [*Jl.* xiv, 75, 155.

Postans, Lieut., and Kittoe.—Notes of a Journey to Girnâr in the province of Kattywâr, for the purpose of copying the ancient Inscriptions upon the rock near that place.—Undertaken by order of the Bombay Government, with two Notes on Somnáth, one by Mr. Kittoe. [*Jl.* vii, 865.

Powel, Lieut. T.—Description of Heavandoo Pholo, the Northern Atoll of the Maldive Islands. [*Jl.* iv, 319.

Prasadh, Surodha Pundit.—Literal Translation of the Vasanta-Gurh Inscription. [*Jl.* x, 819.

Pratt, Ven'ble Archdeacon J. H.—Observations on the Herat Astrolabe, described in No. 118 of the Journal. [*Jl.* xi, 720.

Memoir upon the Quantity of Iron necessary in a Tension Chain Bridge. [*Jl.* xvii, pt. i, 1.

Note on Iron Tension Bridges. [*Jl.* xviii, 249.

On the Influence of Mountain-Attraction on the determination of the relative heights of Mount Everest, near Darjeeling, and the lofty peak lately discovered near Kashmir. [*Jl.* xxviii, 310.

The Great Indian Arc of Meridian, and the Figure of the Earth. [*Jl.* xxvii, 201.

A second Letter on the Indian Arc. [*Jl.* xxviii, 22.

On the Physical Difference between a rush of Water like a torrent down a channel and the transmission of a Wave down a river—with reference to the Inundation of the Indus, as observed at Attock, in August 1858. [*Jl.* xxix, 274.

On Colebrooke's determination of the Date of the Vedas. [*Jl.* xxxi, 49.

Memorandum showing the final result of calculations regarding the effect of Local Attraction upon the operations of the Great Trigonometrical Survey of India. [*Jl.* xxxi, 146.

Pratt, Ven'ble Archdeacon J. H. (*contd.*)—On Local Attraction. [*Proc.* 1865, 88.
On the Degree of uncertainty which Local Attraction, if not allowed for, occasions in the Map of a country, and in the Mean Figure of the Earth, as determined by Geodesy; a method of obtaining the Mean Figure free from ambiguity by a comparison of the Anglo-Gallic, Russian and Indian Arcs; and Speculations on the constitution of the Earth's Crust. [*Jl.* xxxiv, pt. ii, 34.
See TENNANT, J. F. (OR F. P.)

Pratt.—Extract of a Letter on a recent Destructive Storm in the neighbourhood of Ishwarganj. [*Proc.* 1875, 128.

Precious Minerals, Oriental Accounts of the. [*Jl.* i, 353.

Precious Stones, Short Description of the Mines of, in the district of Kyatpyen, in the kingdom of Ava. [*Jl.* ii, 75.

Presgrave, Col. D.—Application of Iron Rods, proposed to compensate for the strain occasioned by the tension of the strings upon Piano-Fortes, thereby to prevent warping, and to render them more durable and better adapted to keep longer in tune. [*Jl.* iv, 643.

Price, Lieut. W.—Translation of a Sanscrit Inscription on a stone found in Bundelc'hund. [*As. Res.* xii, 357.

Prichard, Dr.—Tibetan Type of Mankind. [*Jl.* xvii, pt. ii, 580.

Prideaux, Major W. F.—On the Coins of Charibael, king of the Homerites and Sabæans. (With a Plate.) [*Jl.* l, pt. i, 95.

Prinsep, G. A.—Abstracted Results of Marine Observations. [*As. Res.* xv, 15.
On the Temperature and Saltness of the River Húglí, from Calcutta to the Sea. [*Jl.* i, 104.
On a remarkable Heat observed in masses of Brine kept for some time in large reservoirs. [*Jl.* vii, 207.
On the spontaneous heating of Brine. [*Jl.* vii, 1014.

Prinsep, H. T.—Estimate of the Risk of Life to Civil Servants of the Bengal Presidency, in each year of their Residence in India. [*Jl.* i, 277.
Corrected Estimate of the Risk of Life to Civil Servants of the Bengal Presidency. [*Jl.* vi, 341.

Prinsep, H. T. (*contd.*)—Table of Mortality for Ages from birth to twenty years, framed from the Registers of the Lower Orphan School, Calcutta. [*Jl.* vii, 818.
Account of Tamba Patra Plates dug up at Baroda, in Goojrat; with Facsimile and Translation. [*Jl.* viii, 292.
Note on the Passes into Hindoostan from the West and North-west, and the use made of them by different conquerors. [*Jl.* xi, 552.

Prinsep, James.—Meteorological Journal. [*As. Res.* xv, 7.
Description of a Pluviometer and an Evaporometer constructed at Benares. [*As. Res.* xv, 13.
Analysis of a Mineral Water. [*As. Res.* xv, 14.
Census of the Population of the city of Benares. [*As. Res.* xvii, 470.
Note on the Discovery of Platina in Ava. [*As. Res.* xviii, pt. ii, 279.
Examination of Minerals from Ava. [*Jl.* i, 14.
Note on the Magic Mirrors of Japan. [*Jl.* i, 242.
On the Ancient Roman Coins in the Cabinet of the Asiatic Society. [*Jl.* i, 392.
Observations of the Transit of Mercury. [*Jl.* i, 408.
Note on the Jabalpúr Fossil Bones. [*Jl.* i, 456.
On the Greek Coins in the Cabinet of the Asiatic Society. [*Jl.* ii, 27.
Determination of the Constant of Expansion of the Standard 10-feet Iron Bar of the Great Trigonometrical Survey of India; and Expansion of Gold, Silver and Copper by the same Apparatus. [*Jl.* ii, 130.
Table for Ascertaining the Heights of Mountains from the boiling point of Water. [*Jl.* ii, 194.
Description of a Compensation Barometer, and Observations on Wet Barometers. [*Jl.* ii, 258.
Note on Lieut. Burnes' Collection of Ancient Coins. [*Jl.* ii, 310.
Bactrian and Indo-Scythic Coins. [*Jl.* ii, 405.
Note on the extraordinary fall of the Barometer during the Gale of the 21st May last. [*Jl.* ii, 427.
Chemical Analyses. [*Jl.* ii, 434.
Additional Note on the Climate of Nagpúr. [*Jl.* ii, 542.
Note on the Fossil Bones discovered near Jabalpúr. [*Jl.* ii, 583.

Prinsep, James (*contd.*)—Note on Inscription No. 1 of the Allahabad Column. [*Jl.* iii, 114.

Experiments on the Preservation of Sheet Iron from Rust in India. [*Jl.* iii, 191.

Note on the Coins found by Captain Cautley at Behat. [*Jl.* iii, 227.

On the Coins and Relics discovered by M. Chevalier Ventura, General in the service of Mahá Rájá Ranjit Singh, in the Tope of Manikyála. [*Jl.* iii, 313.

Note on the Fossil Bones of the Nerbudda Valley, discovered by Dr. G. G. Spilsbury near Nersinhpúr, &c. [*Jl.* iii, 396.

Continuation of Observations on the Coins and Relics, discovered by General Ventura in the Tope of Manikyala. [*Jl.* iii, 436.

Note on the Mathiah Lath Inscription. [*Jl.* iii, 483.

Second Note on the Bhilsa Inscription. [*Jl.* iii, 488.

Inscription on the Iron Pillar at Delhi. [*Jl.* iii, 494.

Note on the Coins discovered by M. Court. [*Jl.* iii, 562.

Note on the Brown Liquid, contained in the Cylinders, from Manikyala. [*Jl.* iii, 567.

Further particulars of the Sarun and Tirhoot Laths, an Account of two Buddha Inscriptions found, the one at Bakhra, in Tirhut, the other at Sarnath, near Benares. [*Jl.* iv, 124.

Further Notes and Drawings of Bactrian and Indo-Scythic Coins. [*Jl.* iv, 327.

Note on the Fossil Bones of the Jumna River. [*Jl.* iv, 500.

Chemical Analyses. [*Jl.* iv, 509.

Horary Meteorological Observations made at Calcutta on the 21st to 22nd September. [*Jl.* iv, 514.

Analysis of Copper Ore from Nellore: with Notice of the Copper Mines at Ajmír and Singhána. [*Jl.* iv, 574.

On the connection of various Ancient Hindu Coins with the Grecian or Indo-Scythic series. [*Jl.* iv, 621.

Notice of Ancient Hindu Coins. [*Jl.* iv, 668.

Various Ancient Inscriptions. [*Jl.* v, 340, 482, 554, 657, 724. 795; vi, 218, 278, 663, 869; vii, 33, 901, 966.

Experimental Researches on the Depressions of the Wet-bulb Hygrometer. [*Jl.* v, 396.

Prinsep, James (*contd.*)—New Varieties of Bactrian Coins engraved from Mr. Masson's Drawings and other sources. [*Jl.* v, 548.

New Varieties of the Mithraic or Indo-Scythic Series of Coins and their imitations. [*Jl.* v, 639.

New Types of Bactrian and Indo-Scythic Coins. [*Jl.* v, 720.

Note on the Nautical Instruments of the Arabs. [*Jl.* v, 784.

A Comparative View of the daily range of the Barometer in different parts of India. [*Jl.* v, 816.

Postscript to the Memoir on the Depression of the Wet-bulb Thermometer published in the July number. [*Jl.* v, 828.

Specimens of Hindu Coins descended from the Parthian type, and of the Ancient Coins of Ceylon. [*Jl.* vi, 288.

The Legends of the Saurashtra group of Coins deciphered. [*Jl.* vi, 377.

Note on the Facsimiles of Inscriptions from Sanchi near Bhilsa, taken for the Society, by Captain Ed. Smith, Engineers; and on the Drawings of the Buddhist Monument presented by Captain W. Murray at the meeting of the 7th June. [*Jl.* vi, 451.

Interpretation of the most ancient of the Inscriptions on the pillar called the Lát of Feroz Shah, near Delhi, and of the Allahabad, Radhia and Mattiah Pillar, or Lát, Inscriptions which agree therewith. [*Jl.* vi, 566.

Account of an Inscription found by Mr. H. S. Boulderson in the neighbourhood of Bareilly. [*Jl.* vi, 777.

Further elucidation of the Lát or Silasthambha Inscriptions from various sources. [*Jl.* vi, 790.

Note on the Facsimiles of the various Inscriptions on the ancient column at Allahabad, retaken by Captain Edward Smith. [*Jl.* vi, 963.

Note on Inscription at Udayagiri and Khandgiri, in Cuttack, in the lát character. [*Jl.* vi, 1072.

Discovery of the name of Antiochus the Great, in two of the Edicts of Asoka, king of India. [*Jl.* vii, 156.

On the Edicts of Piyadasi, or Asoka, the Buddhist monarch of India, preserved on the Girnar rock in the Gujerat Peninsula, and on the Dhauli rock in Cuttack; with the discovery of Ptolemy's name therein. [*Jl.* vii, 219.

Prinsep, James (*contd.*)—Examination of the Inscriptions from Girnar in Gujerat, and Dhauli in Cuttack. [*Jl.* vii, 334.

On the Application of a New Method of Block-printing, with examples of unedited Coins printed in facsimile. [*Jl.* vii, 414.

Examination of the separate edicts of the Aswastama Inscription at Dhauli in Cuttack. (Plate.) [*Jl.* vii, 434.

More Dánams from the Sanchi tope near Bhilsa, taken in impression by Capt T. S. Burt. Translated. [*Jl.* vii, 562.

Translation of Inscription in the Society's museum. [*Jl.* vii, 557.

Additions to Bactrian Numismatics and discovery of the Bactrian Alphabet. [*Jl.* vii, 636.

Coins and Relics from Bactria. [*Jl.* vii, 1047.

See CRACROFT, W.

Proceedings of the Asiatic Society of Bengal, [*Jl.* I, 35, 74, 116, 157, 209, 248, 298, 363, 415, 472, 512, 559; II, 43, 91, 149, 203, 262, 323, 367, 546, 645; III, 49, 96, 141, 193, 244, 300, 362, 410, 475, 524, 590; IV, 53, 177, 232, 287, 348, 407, 472, 516, 585, 650; V, 52, 124, 189, 245, 302, 369, 433, 509, 587, 672, 753, 823; VI, 77, 154, 238, 317, 397, 490, 612, 704, 797, 890, 984, 1092; VII, 87, 167, 283, 364, 456, 567, 663, 742, 829, 915, 983; VIII, 72, 150, 245, 341, 429, 526, 687, 863, 953, 1059; IX, 90, 215, 334, 444, 552, 624, 726, 859, 941, 1055, 1129; X, 31, 165, 500, 589, 674, 751, 833, 917; XI, 91, 196, 271, 439, 573, 786, 863, 876, 964, 1198, 1204; XII, 62, 129, 248, 314, 415, 513, 622, 729, 821, 910, 1012, 1107; XIII, i, xiii, xxi, xxix, xliii, liii, lxii, lxxiii, lxxxv, xcvii, cxxi, cxxxiii; XIV, i, xvii, xxxi, xxxix, lv, lxvii, lxxxix, cxi, cxxi; XV, i, xvii, xxiii, xxvii, xxxiii, xli, xlvii, lxvii, lxxix, lxxxv, ciii; XVI, 81, 201, 375, 497, 499, 716, 850, 987, 1089, 1247, 1263; XVII, p. i, 79, 159, 237, 325, 451, 551, p. ii. 121, 233, 472, 588, 697; XVIII, 76, 179, 283, 414, 542, 645, 754, 858, 979; XIX, 83, 149, 187, 264, 341, 346, 421, 481, 493, 497, 560, 563, 568; XX, 78, 211. 285, 359. 433, 437, 442, 445; XXI, 80. 188, 275, 337, 431, 536, 631; XXII, 82, 202, 307, 407, 494, 576, 680; XXIII. 97, 199, 303, 394, 502, 617, 727; XXIV, 53, 170, 244, 354, 364, 467 537, 702, 725, 730; XXV, 79, 167, 224, 227, 236, 359, 370, 419, 450, 462, 570, 579; XXVI, 65, 154, 227, 275; XXVII, 70, 196, 261, 365; XXVIII. 50, 156, 254. 389. 505; XXIX, 46, 202, 310. 405; XXX, 49, 159, 294, 395; XXXI, 53, 206, 300, 429, 533; XXXII, 21, 173, 288, 431; XXXIII, 61, 210, 335, 442, 573.

Pughe, Robertson.—Exhibition of a Collection of Sonthál, Bhootea, Gáro and Naga Weapons, &c.. sent by. [*Proc.* 1880, 105.

Pullan, Lieutenant Ayrton.—Remarks on some Ancient Hindu Ruins in the Garhwal Bhatur. [*Jl.* xxxvi, pt. i, 154.

Raffles, Thomas.—On the Malayan Nation, with a Translation of its Maritime institutions. [*As. Res.* xii, 102.

Rainey, H. J.—Note on three Maps of the Sundarban. [*Proc.* 1869, 219.

Letter on the 'Barisal Guns.' [*Proc.* 1870, 243. 290.

Letter on the probable origin of the scientific appellation of the common Striped Squirrel (*Sciurus palmarum*, Linn.) [*Proc.* 1875, 159.

A Legend regarding the origin of the name Chháyápati, or "Lord of the Shadows," a small táluk in Pargana Hoglá, Zila Jessore. [*Proc.* 1878, 105.

Note on certain peculiarities observed in Hailstones which fell at Khulna, Jessore, on the 31st March 1878. [*Proc.* 1878, 125.

Note on the absence of a Horn in the Female of the Sundarban Rhinoceros and Javanese Rhinoceros (*C. Rh. Javanicus*, Cuv.) [*Proc.* 1878, 139.

Rajah Khan.—Account of the Panjkora Valley, and of Lower and Upper Kashkar, by Rajah Khan of Cabool. Translated by Major R. Leech, C. B., late Political Agent, Candahar, at whose request it was drawn up in 1840. [*Jl.* xiv. 812.

Ramalochan Pandit.—A Royal Grant found at Tana. [*As. Res.* i, 357.

Raper, Captain, F. V.—Narrative of a Survey for the purpose of discovering the sources of the Ganges. [*As. Res.* xi, 446.

Ravenshaw, E. C.—Translation of various Inscriptions found among the Ruins of Vijayanagar. [*As. Res.* xx, pt. i.

Notice of Inscriptions in Behar. [*Jl.* viii, 347.

Ravenshaw, E. C. (*contd.*)—Notice of an Inscription in Behar. [*Jl.* ix, 65.

The Avatars of Vishnoo. An Abstract Translation from the Pudma Pooran. [*Jl.* xi, 1112.

Memorandum on the Construction of a Portable Meridian. [*Jl.* xii, 437.

Memorandum on the Ancient Bed of the River Soane and Site of Palibothra. [*Jl.* xiv, 137.

Raverty, Lieutenant H. G.—Some remarks on the origin of the Afghan People and Dialect, and on the connexion of the Pushto language with the Zend and Pehlavi and the Hebrew. [*Jl.* xxiii, 550.

Account of a Visit to the Shrine and Town of Sakhi Sarwar in the Lower Deráját; with a Notice of the Annual Melá or Fair held there. [*Jl.* xxiv, 329.

Notes on Kokan, Kashghar, Yarkand, and other places in Central Asia. [*Jl.* xxvi, 257.

An Account of the Mountain District forming the western boundary of the Lower Deráját, commonly called *Roh*, with Notices of the Tribes inhabiting it. [*Jl.* xxvi, 177.

Notes on Kafiristan. [*Jl.* xxviii, 317.

An Account of Upper and Lower Suwat, and the Kohistan, to the source of the Suwát River, with an Account of the Tribes inhabiting those valleys. [*Jl.* xxxi, 227.

An Account of Upper Kásh-kár and Chitral, or Lower Kash-kar, together with the Independent Afghan State of Panj-korah, including Talásh. [*Jl.* xxxiii, 125.

On the Language of the Si-ah-pos'*h* Kafirs, with a short list of words; to which are added specimens of Kohistani and other dialects spoken on the northern border of Afghanistan, &c. [*Jl.* xxxiii, 267.

Who were the "Patan" or "Pathan" Sultans of Dehli? [*Jl.* xliv, pt. i, 24.

Reply to several passages in Mr. Blochmann's "Contributions to the History and Geography of Bengal," No. III. [*Jl.* xlv, pt. i, 325.

Memoir of the Author of the Tabakát-i-Násirí. [*Jl.* li, pt. i, 77.

Rawlins, John.—On the Manners, Religion and Laws of the Cúcís, or the mountaineers of Tiperah. [*As. Res.* ii, 187.

Rebellion, Report of a Trial for, held at Moulmein by the Commissioner of Tenasserim. Communicated by the Sudder Dewanny Adawlut. [*Jl.* xiv, 747.

Receipt Book — Extracts from a Native. [*Jl.* i, 155.

Ráya, Kumára Chundranáth, on an Inscription found in Rájshahi. [*Proc.* 1868, 163.

Reckendorf Siegmund.—Notes on the Pokree and Dhanpoor Copper Mines in Gherwal. [*Jl.* xiv, 471.

Rees, Ludwig E.—*See* Roth, Dr. R.

Reid, Lieutenant-Colonel.—A Note on the Winds as influencing the Tracks sailed by Bermuda Vessels; and on the advantage which may be derived from sailing on Curved Courses when meeting with Revolving Winds. [*Jl.* xii, 1104.

Reynolds, Captain C. S.—A Narrative of our Connexions with the Dusannee and Cheannee Garrows, with a short Account of their Country. [*Jl.* xviii, 45.

Reynolds, H. J.—Notes on the Tribes of the Eastern Frontier, No. III. *See* O'Donel. J. H. [*Jl.* xxxii, 407.

Rhodes, Dr. W.—Climate of Chirra Púnji. [*Jl.* i, 297.

Richardson, Captain David.—An Account of the Bazeegurs, a sect commonly denominated the Nuts. [*As. Res.* vii, 457.

Richardson, Dr. D.—Journal of a March from Ava to Kendat, on the Khyen dwen River, performed in 1831 under the orders of Major H. Burney, the Resident at Ava. [*Jl.* ii, 59.

The History of Labong from Native Records. [*Jl.* vi, 55.

Abstract Journal of an Expedition from Moulmein to Ava through the Kareen country, between December 1836 and June 1837. [*Jl.* vi, 1005.

Journal of a Mission from the Supreme Government of India to the Court of Siam. [*Jl.* viii, 1016; ix, i, 219.

See Blundell, E.A.

Rigby, Lieutenant.—Memorandum on the usual Building Materials of the district of Cuttack, forwarded to the Museum of Economic Geology, with a set of Specimens. [*Jl.* xi, 836.

Rivett, Carnac H.—Remarks on Rude Stone Monuments in Chutiá Nágpúr. [*Proc.* 1873, 131.

Rivett, Carnac H. (*contd.*)—Rough Notes on some Ancient Sculpturings on rocks in Kamaon, similar to those found on monoliths and rocks in Europe. [*Jl.* xlvi, pt. i, 1.

Figure of Buddha recently found at Sarnath. [*Proc.* 1878, 66.

On 3 Hindoo and 3 Muhammadan Coins. [*Proc.* 1879. 64.

Memorandum on administrative rules for the Protection of Indian Antiquarian Remains. [*Proc.* 1879, 65.

2nd Memorandum on the Preservation of Antiquarian Remains. [*Proc.* 1879, 153.

Description of some Stone Carvings, collected in a Tour through the Doab, from Cawnpore to Mainpuri. [*Proc.* 1879, 189.

Prehistoric Remains in Central India. [*Jl.* xlviii, pt. i, 1.

The Snake Symbol in India, especially in connection with the worship of Siva. [*Jl.* xlviii, pt. i, 17.

Exhibition of a Metal Celt sent by. [*Proc.* 1880, 70.

Memorandum on Buddhist Copper Coins and Coins of the Sunga Dynasty. [*Proc.* 1880, 71.

Memorandum on Clay Discs, Spindle Whorls, &c. [*Proc.* 1880, 115.

Exhibition of Roman. Indo-Scythian and Gupta Coins, belonging to Col. Berkeley, and sent by. [*Proc.* 1880, 118.

On Coins from Jellalabad and Rewah. [*Proc.* 1880. 170.

Memorandum on Coins of the Sunga Dynasty. (With three Plates.) [*Jl.* xlix, pt. i, 87.

Memorandum on Clay Discs called "Spindle Whorls" and Votive Seals found at Sankisa, Behar, and other Buddhist ruins in the North-Western Provinces of India. [*Jl* xlix, pt. i, 127.

Note on some Copper Buddhist Coins. [*Jl.* xlix, pt. i, 138.

Exhibition of Stone Implements by. [*Proc.* 1882, 6.

Memorandum on a Brass-casting of the Arms of the old East India Company. [*Proc.* 1883, 79.

Note on some Geological Specimens received from Prof. Dr. Fischer. [*Proc.* 1883, 79.

Note forwarding some Relics from Er-Lannig, and a Memorandum on the same by the Count de Limur. [*Proc.* 1883, 110.

Exhibition of a Clay Seal, sent by. [*Proc.* 1883, 113.

Rivett, Carnac H. (*contd.*)—On Stone Implements from the North-Western Provinces of India. [*Jl.* lii, pt. i, 221.

Roberts, Major R. E.—Specimen of the Language of the People inhabiting the Hills in the vicinity of Bhagulpoor. [*As. Res.* v, 127.

Robinson, Capt. G. H.—Meteorological Register kept at Kathmandoo for the month of March 1834, Valley of Nepal. [*Jl.* xii, 768.

Robinson, Wm.—Notes on the Languages spoken by the various Tribes inhabiting the valley of Assam and its mountain confines. [*Jl.* xviii, 183, 310.

Notes on the Dophlás and the peculiarities of their Language. [*Jl.* xx, 126.

Notes on the Languages of the Mishmis. [*Jl.* xxiv. 307.

Rodgers, C. J.—Note on the Death of Humáyun. [*Jl.* xl, pt. i, 133.

Coins of Khusrau Sháh and Kharran Malik, the Ghaznavi Kings of Lahore. [*Proc.* 1879. 178.

The Copper Coins of the old Mahárájás of Kashmír. [*Jl.* xlviii. pt. i, 277.

The Copper Coins of the Sultans of Kashmír. [*Jl.* xlviii. pt. i. 282.

The Coins of the Mahárájahs of Kángra. [*Jl.* xlix, pt i. 10.

Coins supplementary to Thomas' "Chronicles of the Pathan Kings of Delhi." [*Jl.* xlix, pt. i, 81. 207.

A find of Coins struck by Gazni Sultans in Lahore. [*Proc.* 1881, 4.

Copper Coins of Akbar. [*Jl.* xlix, pt. i, 213.

On the Coins of the Sikhs. [*Jl.* l, pt. i, 71.

Notes on a List of Silver Coins of Aurangzeb Alamgir. [*Proc.* 1883, 11.

"Nisár" Coins sent by. [*Proc* 1883. 59.

Note on a "Nisár" of Shah Jahan in the Delhi Museum. [*Proc.* 1883, 112.

Coins supplementary to Thomas' "Chronicles of the Pathan Kings of Delhi," No. III. [*Jl.* lii, pt. i, 55.

The Rupees of the Months of the Iláhi Years of Akbar. [*Jl.* lii, pt. i, 97.

Roepstorff, F. A. de.—A short List of Andamanese Test-words. [*Proc.* 1870, 178.

Notes on the Inhabitants of the Nicobars. [*Proc.* 1876, 142; 1881, 7, 104.

Roer, Dr. E.—Report made by J. Mohl in the General Meeting of the Asiatic Society of Paris, 31st May, 1841, on the labours of the Committee during the six last months of 1840, and the six first months of 1841, translated from the French. [*Jl.* xi, 411.

Descriptive List of some Coins lately received from the University of Christiana by the Asiatic Society. [*Jl.* xii, 443.

Bháscaræ Achárya Siddhánta Shirómáni sic dicti operis pars tertia, Gunitadhiam, sive astronomiam continens. Latine vertit notasque adjacit, E. Roer. [*Jl.* xiii, 53.

Index to History of the Toorks, by Baron Hammer Von Purgstall. [*Jl.* xiii, 550.

Védánta-Sara, or Essence of the Védánta. An Introduction to the Védánta Philosophy by Sadenanda Parivrájakácharya, translated from the original Sanscrit. [*Jl.* xiv. 100.

Review of L'histoire du Buddhism Indien, par E. Burnouf. [*Jl.* xiv, 783.

Bhásha Parichéda, or Division of Language. A logical Treatise, translated from the Sanscrit. [*Jl.* xvi, 157.

Review of "A Lecture on the Sánkhya Philosophy, embracing the text of Tattwasamása," by Dr. J. R. Ballantyne, Mirzapore, 1850. [*Jl.* xx, 397.

Bibliographical Notes on the published Upanishads, with suggestions upon the publications of those which remain unedited. [*Jl.* xxiv, 38.

Rogers, Capt. T. E.—Correspondence regarding the Coal Beds in the Namsang Nago Hills. [*Jl.* xvii, pt. 1, 489 ; xviii, 489.

Roman Alphabet on the adaptation to the Orthography of oriental languages. [*Jl.* iii, 281.

Ross, Capt. D.—Memoranda regarding the Difference between Morning and Evening Altitudes for ascertaining the Apparent Time on board-ship. [*Jl.* i, 202.

Ross, Lt.-Col. E. C.—An Account of tenets of the Ibádhi sect of 'Omán. [*Proc.* 1873, 2.

Annals of Oman, from early times to the year 1728 A.D. From an Arabic MS. [*Jl.* xliii, pt. i, 111.

Ross, Dr. E. M.—On Ethnology of Travancore and Cochin. [*Proc.* 1866, 242.

Roth, Dr. Rudolph.—On the Literature and History of the Veda. Three Treatises, by Rudolph Roth, Ph. Dr., Stuttgart, 1846. (Translated by J. Muir, Esq., C. S.) [*Jl.* xvi, 812.

The most ancient Grammar of the Vedas, or the "Prâtiákhyasutren." Translated from the German by Ludwig E. Rees. [*Jl.* xvii, pt. i, 6.

Route Protraction, A method of rectifying a. [*Jl.* i, 19.

Row, Dr. J.—Geological Remarks during the March from Benares (Old Road), *via* Hazareebaugh, Bankoora, and Burdwan to Barrackpoor. [*Jl.* xiii, 862.

Rowlatt, Lieut. E. A.—Report of an Expedition into the Mishmee Hills to the north-east of Sudyah. [*Jl.* xiv, 477.

Roxburgh, Dr. William.—Flora Indica, or Descriptions of Indian Plants. [*Jl.* i, 131.

On the Lacshá, or Lac Insect. [*As. Res.* ii, 361.

A Description of the Plant Butea. [*As. Res.* iii, 469.

A Description of the Jonesia. [*As. Res.* iv, 355.

Prosopis aculeata. Kœnig. Pstramic of the Hindus in the Northern Sircars. [*As. Res.* iv, 405.

Botanical Observations on the Spikenard of the ancients, intended as a Supplement to the late Sir William Jones's paper on that plant. [*As. Res.* iv, 433.

A Botanical Description of Urecola elastica, or Caout-chouc Vine of Sumatra and Pullo-pinang, with an Account of the properties of its inspissated juice, compared with those of the American Caout-chouc. [*As. Res.* v, 167.

An Account of a new Species of Delphinus, an inhabitant of the Ganges. [*As. Res.* vii, 170.

A Botanical and Economical Account of Bassia Butyracea, or East India Butter Tree. [*As. Res.* viii, 477.

Descriptions of several of the monandrous Plants of India, belonging to the natural order called *Scitamineæ* by Linnæus, *Cannæ* by Jussien, and *Drimyrhizæ* by Ventenant. [*As. Res.* xi, 318.

Royle, Dr. J. Forbes.—Account of the Honorable Company's Botanic Garden at Seháranpur. [*Jl.* i, 41.

Royle, Dr. J. Forbes (*contd.*)—Extracts from Explanatory Address on the Exhibition of Dr. Royle's Collections in Natural History at the Meeting of the Asiatic Society on the 7th March. [*Jl.* i, 96.

List of Articles of Materia Medica obtained in the Bazars of the Western and Northern Provinces of India. [*Jl.* i, 458.

Illustrations of the Botany and other Branches of the Natural History of the Himálayan Mountains and of the Flora of Kashmír. [*Jl.* iii, 530.

Observations on the Graphite or Plumbago of Kumaon and of Travancore. (Communicated by the Government of India.) [*Jl.* xxiv, 203.

St. Barbe, H. L.—Pali Derivations in Burmese. [*Jl.* xlviii, pt. i, 253.

St. John, H. C.—Remarks on Winds, Typhoons, &c., on the south coast of Japan. [*Proc.* 1872, 205.

St. John, R. F.—Letter relative to some Burmese and Arracanese Celts. [*Proc.* 1871, 83.

St. Peter's Church in Fort William, On the method employed to remove the Vaulted Roof of. [*Jl.* v, 208.

Sale, Lt., on Spheres of Sandstones found in Cachar. [*Proc.* 1868, 90.

Samuells, E. A.—A Visit to the Rock-cut Temples of Khandgiri. [*Jl.* xxv, 222.

Notes on a Forest Race called Puttooas or Juanga, inhabiting certain of the Tributary Mehals of Cuttack. [*Jl.* xxv, 295.

Samuells, J. H.—Notice of Old Temples near Harchoka. [*Proc.* 1871, 57.

Samuells, Capt. W. L.—Letter on Two Copper Axes. [*Proc.* 1871, 231.

Letter on the Rock and Temples at Harchoka, Chutiá Nágpur. [*Proc.* 1871, 236.

The Rock-cut Excavations at Harchoka, discovered by Capt. W. L. Samuells when employed as Boundary Commissioner on the Rewah and Chutiá Nágpúr Frontier, season 1870-71. [*Jl.* xl, pt. i, 177.

The Legend of Bághesar, a deified spirit held in great reverence by the Kúsrú, Súri, Markám, Netiá, and Sársún clans of the Gond Tribe. [*Jl.* xli, pt. i, 115.

Sanders, Capt. Edw.—Route from Candahar to Herat. From the Political Secretariat of the Government of India. [*Jl.* xiii, 121.

Sarel, Lieut.-Col.—Notes on the River Yang-tse-Kiang from Hankow to Pingshan. [*Jl.* xxx, 223.

Sarman, Radhacanta.—Inscriptions on the staff of Fírúz Shah. [*As Res.* i, 379.

Sarnath.—Correspondence relating to the Exploration of the Ruins of. [*Jl.* xxv, 395.

Sastri, Prof. Bapudeva—On recorded Solar Eclipse. [*Proc.* 1867, 174.

Satlaj.—Table shewing the breadth of the river and the rate of its current at different stages, from Harríke Pattan to its junction with the Indus at Mithankot. [*Jl.* v, 814.

Saxton, Colonel.—Letter regarding the fall of an Aerolite at Nidigullam, Vizagapatam district. [*Proc.* 1870, 64.

Schaffhausen, Prof.—Ethnological Queries. [*Proc.* 1879, 200.

Schlagintweit, Adolphe.—Report on the Progress of the Magnetic Survey, and of the Researches connected with it. from November 1855 to April 1856. [*Jl.* xxvi, 97.

Schlagintweit, Adolphe and Robert.—Report upon the Progress of the Magnetic Survey of India and of the Researches connected with it in the Himálaya Mountains, from April to October 1855. [*Jl.* xxv, 105.

Schlagintweit, Hermann.—Report on the Progress of the Magnetic Survey and the Researches connected with it in Sikkim, the Khasia Hills and Assam, April to December 1855. [*Jl.* xxv, 1.

Report on the Proceedings of the Magnetic Survey, from January to May 1856. [*Jl.* xxv, 554.

Schlagintweit, Robert de.—Report on the Progress of the Magnetic Survey and of the Researches connected with it, from November 1855 to April 1856. [*Jl.* xxvi, 54.

Report on the Proceedings of the Officers engaged in the Magnetic Survey of India. [*Jl.* xxvi, 208.

Enumeration of the Hot Springs of India and High Asia. [*Jl.* xxxiii, 49.

Comparative hypsometrical and physical Tableau of High Asia, the Andes, and the Alps. [*Jl.* xxxv, pt. ii, 51.

See SCHLAGINTWEIT, ADOLPHE.

Schlegel, Professor.—Mode of expressing numerals in the Sanskrit and Tebetan language. [*Jl.* iii, 1.

Schomburgh, Sir Robert H.—A Visit to Xiengmai, the principal city of the Laos or Shan States. [*Jl.* xxxii, 387.

Schwendler, Louis—On a Practical Method for detecting bad Insulators on Telegraph Lines. [*Proc.* 1871, 71.

On the Discharge of long Overland Telegraph Lines. [*Jl.* xl, pt. ii, 78.

On 'Insulator Detector.' [*Proc.* 1872, 92.

On Differential Galvanometers. [*Jl.* xli. pt. ii, 144 ; xlii, pt. ii, i.

Exhibition of a Crow's Nest made of telegraph wire. [*Proc.* 1874, 74.

On the General Theory of Duplex Telegraphy, [*Jl.* xliii, pt. ii, 1,218 ; xliv, pt. ii, 47 ; xlv, pt. ii, 1.

On Ailurus fulgens, or "Cat-bear." [*Proc.* 1875, 98.

Exhibition of Hooper's Telegraph Core penetrated by Grass. [*Proc.* 1875, 158.

Précis of a Report on Electric Light Experiments. [*Proc.* 1879, 81.

On a new Standard of Light. [*Jl.* xlviii, pt. ii, 83.

Zoological Notes. [*Proc.* 1880, 55.

On some Experiments instituted to supply all the Lines terminating at the Calcutta Telegraph Office with Currents tapped from the Main Current produced by a Dynamo-electric Machine. [*Proc.* 1880, 173.

On a Simple Method of using an Insignificant Fraction of the Main Current produced by a Dynamo-electric Machine for Telegraph purposes. [*Jl.* xlix, pt. ii, 1.

On some Experiments instituted to supply all the Lines terminating at the Calcutta Telegraph Office with Currents tapped from the Main Current produced by a Dynamo-electric Machine. [*Jl.* xlix, pt. ii, 167.

Science in England, State of. [*Jl.* i, 198.

Scott, John.—On the Reproductive Functional Relations of several Species and Varieties of Verbasca. [*Jl.* xxxvi, pt. ii, 143.

Scully, Dr. J.—*See* SHAW, R. B.

Seals of the E. I. Company, three old silver. [*Proc.* 1872, 172.

Semenof, M.—Notes on Central Asia, by M Semenof. [*Jl.* xxxiv, pt. ii, 113.

Sen, Gopenath.—Monthly Mean of the principal Meteorological Elements and actual Rainfall, recorded at the Calcutta Observatory for twelve years, from 1856 to 1867. [*Jl.* xxxviii, pt. ii.

Sen, Gopenath (*contd.*)—Tabular Statement shewing the Monthly Rainfall, from January 1837 to November 1868, and the Monthly Quinquennial Average for each month during that period, as taken at the Surveyor-General's Office, Calcutta. [*Jl.* xxxviii, pt. ii.

Sen, Ram Comul.—A Short Account of the Charak Púja Ceremonies, and Description of the Implements used. [*Jl.* ii, 609.

Seringapatam—Climate of, Latitude 12° 45′ N.; Longitude 76° 51′ E. [*Jl.* iii, 138.

Shakespear, A.—Note on the Navigation of the River Nurbudda. [*Jl.* xiii, 495.

Shakespeare, John.—Observations regarding Badhiks and Thegs ; Extracted from an official report. [*As. Res.* xiii, 282.

Sharp, D.—Preliminary Diagnoses of new Coleopterous Insects belonging to the families Dytiscidæ, Staphylinidæ, and Scarabæidæ, obtained by the late Dr. F. Stoliczka, during the 2nd mission to Yarkand under Sir Douglas Forsyth. [*Jl.* xlvii, pt. ii, 169.

Shaw, R. B.—Letter on Yarkand Antiquities. [*Proc.* 1875, 92.

On the Ghalchah Languages (Wakhí and Sarikolí). [*Jl.* xlv, pt. i, 139.

On the Shighni (Ghalchah) Dialect. [*Jl.* xlvi, pt. i, 97.

A Grammar of the Language of Eastern Turkistan. [*Jl.* xlvi, pt. i, 242.

Stray Arians in Tibet. [*Jl.* xlvii, pt. i, 26.

A Vocabulary of the Language of Eastern Turkistan. With two Turki Vocabularies of Birds and Plants by Dr. J. Scully. [*Jl.* xlvii, pt. i, Extra No. 1.

Shaw, Lieut. Thomas.—On the Inhabitants of the Hills near Rájamahal. [*As. Res.* iv, 45.

Shastri, Bapu Deva.—Bhaskára's Knowledge of the Differential Calculus. [*Jl.* xxvii, 213.

Sherring, Revd. M. A., & Horne, C.—Description of the Buddhist Ruins at Bakariya Kund, Benares. [*Jl.* xxxiv, pt. i, 1.

Some Account of Ancient Remains at Saidpúr and Bhitari. [*Jl.* xxxiv, pt. i, 80.

Sherring, Revd. M.A., & Horne, C. (*contd.*)—Descriptions of Ancient Remains of Buddhist Monasteries and Temples, and of other buildings, recently discovered in Benares and its vicinity. [*Jl.* xxxv, pt. i, 61.

Sherwill, Major J. L.—Journal of a Trip undertaken to explore the Glaciers of the Kanchunjingah Group in the Sikkim Himálaya, in November 1861. [*Jl.* xxxi, 457.

Sherwell, Capt. S. R.—The Kurrukpur Hills. [*Jl.* xxi, 195.

Sherwill, Major Walter Stanhope.—Note on a curious Sandstone Formation at Sasseram, Zillah Shahabad. [*Jl.* xiv, 496.

Note on the Geological Features of Zillah Behar. [*Jl.* xv, 55.

Geological Notes on Zillah Shahabad, or Arrah. [*Jl.* xvi, 279.

Note on the Bird-devouring Habits of a species of Spider. [*Jl.* xix, 474.

A short Notice of an Ancient Colossal Figure carved in Granite on the Mandár Hill in the district of Bhágálpur. [*Jl.* xx, 272.

A Sketch of the Behar Mica Mines. [*Jl.* xx, 295.

Notes upon a Tour through the Rájmahal Hills. [*Jl.* xx, 544.

Notes upon a Tour in the Sikkim Himálaya Mountains, undertaken for the purpose of ascertaining the Geological Formation of Kunchinjinga and of the perpetually snow-covered Peaks in its vicinity. [*Jl.* xxii, 540, 611.

Notes upon some Atmospherical Phenomena observed at Darjeeling in the Himálaya Mountains during the summer of 1852. [*Jl.* xxiii, 49.

Notes upon some remarkable Water-spouts seen in Bengal between the years 1852 and 1860. [*Jl.* xxix, 366.

Sherwood, Dr.—Of the Murderers called Phánsígárs. [*As. Res.* xiii, 250.

Shore, Sir John.—Translation of an Inscription in the Mega language engraved on a Silver Plate found in a Cave near Islámabád. [*As. Res.* ii, 383.

A Discourse delivered at a Meeting of the Asiatick Society on the 22nd May 1794. [*As. Res.* iv, 181.

On some Extraordinary Facts, Customs, and Practices of the Hindus. [*As. Res.* iv, 331.

Shortrede, Captn. Robert.—Scheme of a Table for all Time. [*Jl.* x, 595.

Table of Proportional Logarithms. [*Jl.* x, 713.

On Equations of Condition for a Quadrilateral, common or re-entrant. [*Jl.* xi. 28, 207.

Compendious Logarithmic Tables. [*Jl.* xi, 40.

Remarks on the Essay "On the Theory of Angular Geometry." [*Jl.* xi, 240.

On an Ancient Magic Square, cut in a Temple at Gwalior. [*Jl.* xi, 292.

Comparison of the Areas of Plane and Spherical Triangles. [*Jl.* xi, 776.

Meteors observed at Allahabad on the 10th of August 1842. [*Jl.* xi, 959.

A Perpetual Moon Table. [*Jl.* xii, 103.

A Companion on the Moon Table. [*Jl.* xii, 231.

Account of a luminous Meteor seen at Charka, lat. 24° 06′, long. 81° 02′, on the morning of the 11th April 1842. [*Jl.* xii, 235.

Remarks on some of the Disturbing Causes in Barometric Observations. [*Jl.* xii, 293.

On Barometric Heights. [*Jl.* xii, 298.

Showers, Lieut.-Col. St. G. D.—Translation of an Inscription on a Gun at Moorshedabad, with remarks. [*Jl.* xvi, 589.

On the Meenas, a wild Tribe of Central India. [*Proc.* 1869, 238.

Sickdhar, Radhanath.—An Account of the Table used for reducing Barometrical Observations to 32° Fahrenheit, taken in the Surveyor-General's Office, Calcutta. [*Jl.* xi, 329.

Siddons, Lieut. H.—Observations of the Tides at Chittagong, made in conformity with the Circular of the Asiatic Society. [*Jl.* vi, 949.

Siddons, Lieut. G. R.—Translation of one of the Granthas, or sacred books of the Dadupanthi Sect. [*Jl.* vi, 480.

Extracts translated from the Granthas, or sacred books of the Dadupanthi Sect. [*Jl.* vi, 750.

Translation of the "Vichitra Nátak," or "Beautiful Epitome,"—a fragment of the Sikh Granth entitled "the Book of the Tenth Pontiff." [*Jl.* xix, 521 ; xx, 314, 487.

Simpson, W.—Exhibition of Gold Coins from the Ahin Posh Tope near Jelalabad, found by. [*Proc.* 1879, 77.

Simson, A.—Letter descriptive of Hail-storm at Shamnagar. [*Proc.* 1883, 58.

Sinclair, P. G.—Table of the Times of High Water at the principal places between Calcutta and Point Palmiras. [*Jl.* iii. 408.

Sind, Earthquake in. [*Proc.* 1871, 56.

Singapúr Climate of. [*Jl.* ii, 428.

Sivatnerium, Additional fragments of the. [*Jl.* vi, 152.

Sjatterapoer, On the identity of, with Jatrapur. [*Proc.* 1874, 19.

Slater, Revd. S.—A Tale by Inshá Alláh Khaán, translated. [*Jl.* xxiv, 79.

Sleeman, Capt. W. H.—History of the Gurha Mundala Rajas. [*Jl.* vi, 621.

Smith, A.—On Earthquakes at Chittagong. [*Proc.* 1866, 39.

Smith, Dr. D. Boyes, on Andamanese. [*Proc.* 1865, 182.

Smith, Capt. E.—Notes on the Specimens of the Kankar Formation, and on Fossil Bones collected on the Jamna. [*Jl.* ii, 622.

Smith, Frederick.—List of *Hymenoptera* obtained by Mr. Ossain Limborg east of Moulmain, Tenasserim Provinces, during the months of December 1876, January, March and April 1877, with Descriptions of new Species. [*Jl.* xlvii, pt. ii, 167.

Smith, J.—Specimen of the Burmese Drama. [*Jl.* viii, 535.

Smith, Lieut. J.—*See* HUTTON, T. G.

Smith, Lewis Ferdinand.—A Chronological Table of the Moghul Emperors, from Umeer Tymoor to Alumgeer II, the father of the present Emperor Shah Alum, being from A. H. 736 to 1173, or A. D. 1335 to 1760. [*As. Res.* vii, 447.

Smith, Lieut. R. Baird.—The Galvanic Battery in its various Practical Applications as an Igniting Agent. [*Jl.* ix, 1149.

Memorandum on the Organization of a Museum of Economic Geology for the North-Western Provinces of British India, to be established at Agra. [*Jl.* x, 779.

Notes on the Recent Earthquakes on the North-Western Frontier. [*Jl.* xi, 242.

Memoir on Indian Earthquakes. [*Jl.* xii, 258, 1029; xiii, 964.

Register of Indian and Asiatic Earthquakes for the year 1843. [*Jl.* xiv, 604.

Smith, Vincent A.—Popular Songs of the Hamírpur District in Bundelkhand, N. W. P. [*Jl.* xliv, pt. i, 389; xlv, pt. i, 279.

Notes on the Bhars and other Early Inhabitants of Bundelkhand. [*Jl.* xlvi, pt. i, 227.

Notes on two Ancient Copper-plate Inscriptions found in the Hamírpúr District, N. W. P. With a Note by Prannath Pandit. [*Jl.* xlvii, pt. i, 80.

Exhibition of Coins sent. by [*Proc.* 1880, 118.

Contributions to the History of Bundelkhand. [*Jl.* l, pt. i, 1.

Letter regarding a Catalogue of the Gold Coins of the Gupta Dynasty. [*Proc.* 1883, 110.

The Sáliváhana Era. [*Proc.* 1883, 144.

Smith, V. A., and Black, F. C.—Observations on some Chandel Antiquities. [*Jl.* xlviii, pt. i, 285.

Smythe, Prof. Piazzi—On Stone for Standard Measures. [*Proc.* 1867, 53.

Snake discovered in the Doad, On a new Species of. [*Jl.* iv, 217.

Somnath, Documents relating to the Gates of. [*Jl.* xii, 73.

Spilsbury, Dr. George G.—Geological Section across the Valley of the Nerbudda from Tendukhérí to Bittoul. [*Jl.* iii, 388.

Notice of new Sites of Fossil Deposits in the Nerbudda Valley. [*Jl.* vi. 487.

On Fifteen Varieties of Fossil Shells found in the Saugor and Nerbudda territories. [*Jl.* viii, 708.

Notes on various Fossil Sites on the Nurbudda; illustrated by Specimens and Drawings. [*Jl.* viii, 950.

On Bos Gaurus. [*Jl.* ix, 551.

Notes of a March from Brímhan Ghat on the Nerbudda to Umurkuntuk, the source of that river. [*Jl.* ix, 889.

Notes on Fossil Discoveries in the valley of the Nerbudda. [*Jl.* x, 626.

Notes on Nerbudda Fossils. [*Jl.* xiii, 765.

Sprenger, Dr. A.—As-Soyúti's work on Earthquakes, called Kashf as Salsalah 'an wasf Azzal-zalah, *i.e.*, removing the noisefrom the description of the Earthquakes (or clearing up the description of Earthquakes.) Translated from the Arabic. [*Jl.* xii, 741.

Some original passages on the Early Commerce of the Arabs. [*Jl.* xiii, 519.

Sprenger, Dr. A. (*contd.*)—Notices of some copies of the Arabic work entitled "Rasáyil Ikhwánal-çafá." [*Jl.* xvii. pt. i, 501.
Notice of the Ikhwân-al-çafâ. [*Jl.* xvii, pt. ii, 183.
Ballamy's Translation of the History of Tabary, and Ghazzály's History of the Prophets. [*Jl.* xvii, pt. ii, 437.
A passage from Ibn Qotaybah's Adab al Kátib' on Arabic Astronomy. [*Jl.* xvii, pt. ii, 659.
Notice of a copy of the fourth volume of the original text of Tabary. [*Jl.* xix, 108.
On the Ghassánite Kings. [*Jl.* xix, 469.
Foreign words occurring in the Qorân. [*Jl.* xxi, 109.
Observations on the Physiology of the Arabic Language. [*Jl.* xx, 115.
The initial letters of the Nineteenth Súrah of the Qorân. [*Jl.* xx, 280.
Chronology of Makkah and the Hijâz before Mohammad, chiefly founded upon Genealogy. [*Jl.* xx, 349.
On the Earliest Biography of Mohammad. [*Jl.* xx, 395.
Has Sády of Shyráz written Rékhtah Verses? [*Jl.* xxi, 513.
Mohammad's Journey to Syria, and Professor Fleischer's Opinion thereon. [*Jl.* xxi, 576.
The first volume of the original text of Tabary. [*Jl.* xxii, 195.
Early Hindústány Poetry. [*Jl.* xxii, 442.
Catalogues of Oriental Libraries. [*Jl.* xxii, 535.
Manuscripts of the late Sir H. Elliot, K.C.B. [*Jl.* xxiii, 225.
Notes on Alfred von Kremer's edition of Wakidy's Campaigns. [*Jl.* xxv, 53, 199.
Notices on the دوارا القلوب of Mohásaby, being the earliest work on Súfism as yet discovered, and on an Arabic Translation of a work ascribed to Enoch. [*Jl.* xxv, 133.
The Copernican System of Astronomy among the Arabs. [*Jl.* xxv, 189.
On the Origin and Progress of writing down historical facts among the Musalmans. [*Jl.* xxv. 303, 375.
Remarks on Barbier de Meynard's edition of Ibn Khordádbeh and on the Land-tax of the Empire of the Khalyfs. [*Jl.* xxxv, pt. i, 124.

Sprenger, Dr.—On Mahomedan Conquest of Arabia. [*Proc.* 1865, 100.

Spry, Henry Harper.—Note on Indian Saline Deposit. [*Jl.* i, 503.
Note on the Fossil Palms and Shells lately discovered on the Table-land of Sagár in Central India. [*Jl.* ii, 639.

Stacy, Major D. L.—Note on two Coins of the same species as those found at Behat, having Greek Inscriptions. [*Jl.* iii, 431.

Stacy, Lieut.-Col. L. R.—Note on the Discovery of a Relic of Grecian Sculpture in Upper India. [*Jl.* v. 567.

Stars to be observed with the Moon in May 1834, Catalogue of. [*Jl.* iii, 139.

Steel, Lt. E. H.—On an Earthquake in Upper Assam. [*Proc.* 1870, 222.
Letter on Jade Celts found in Assam. [*Proc.* 1870, 267.

Stephenson, J.—On the Saline Nature of the Soil of Ghazipoor and Manufacture of Common Salt, as practised by the Natives of the villages of Tuttulapoor. Ratouly, Sahory, Chilar and Becompoor. [*Jl.* iii, 36.
On the Efflorescence of Khari Nún, or Sulphate of Soda, as found native in the soil of Tirhut and Sarun in the province of Behar. [*Jl.* iii, 188.
Excursions to the Ruins and Site of an Ancient City near Bakhra, 13 cos north of Patna, and six north from Singhea. [*Jl.* iv, 128.
Note on the Vegetable Impressions in Agates. [*Jl.* iv, 507.
Specimens of the Soil and Salt from the Sámar, or Sambhur Lake Salt Works. Collected by Lieut. Arthur Conolly. [*Jl.* v, 798.

Stevenson, J.—On the Manufacture of Saltpetre as practised by the Natives of Tirhút. [*Jl.* ii, 23.
Notice of a Native Sulphate of Alumina from the Aluminous Rocks of Nipal. [*Jl.* ii, 321.
Notice of a Native Sulphate of Iron from the Hills of Behar, and used Native Dyers' of Patna. [*Jl.* ii, 321.
Notice of Analysis of the Ashes of four Indian Plants. [*Jl.* ii, 322.
Restoration and Translation of some Inscriptions at the Caves of Carlí. [*Jl.* iii, 495.

Stevenson, Capt. J. F.—Account of a Visit to the Hot Springs of Pai in the Tavoy District. [*Jl.* xxxii, 383.

Stewart, Dr. Duncan.—Statistical Record of the duration of diseases in 13,019 fatal cases in Hindoos—Extraordinary mortality among Lying-in Women. [*Jl.* viii, 316.

Stewart, Dr. J. L.—Memoranda on the Peshawur Valley, chiefly regarding its Flora. [*Jl.* xxxii, 219.

Notes of Observations on the Boksas of the Bijnour District. [*Jl.* xxxiv, pt. ii, 147.

On Carnivorous Habits of Bears. [*Proc.* 1867, 115.

Stewart, Lieut. R.—Notes on Northern Cachar. [*Jl.* xxiv, 582.

A slight Notice of the Grammar of the Thadou or new Kookie language. [*Jl.* xxv, 178.

Stirling, Andrew.—An Account, Geographical. Statistical and Historical, of Orissa Proper, or Cuttack. [*As. Res.* xv. 163.

History of the Rájas of Orissa. from the reign of Rája Yudhistira. Translated from the Vansávali. [*Jl.* vi. 756.

Stirling, Edward.—Price of Grain at Allygurh, near Delhi, from the year 1804 to 1832 inclusive. [*Jl.* iii, 620.

Notes on the Manners and Habits of the Torkoman Tribes, with some Geographical Notices of the Country they occupy. [*Jl.* x, 290.

Stoliczka, Dr. Ferd.—Note on *Lagomys Curzoniæ*, Hodgson. [*Jl.* xxxiv. pt. ii, 108.

On *Nanina pollux* and *Helix propinqua.* [*Proc.* 1868, 263.

On *Sagartia Schilleriana* and *Membranipora Bengalensis.* [*Proc.* 1868. 263.

On the Eclipse of 18th August 1868. [*Proc.* 1868, 275.

Ornithological Observations in the Sutlej Valley, N. W. Himálaya. [*Jl.* xxxvii, pt. ii. 1.

On the Anatomy of *Sagartia Schilleriana* and *Membranipora Bengalensis*, a new Coral and a Bryozoon living in brackish water at Port Canning. [*Jl.* xxxvii, pt. ii, 28.

Observation regarding the changes of organs in certain Mollusca. [*Proc.* 1869, 187.

The Malacology of Lower Bengal and the adjoining provinces. [*Jl.* xxxviii, pt. ii, 86.

Contribution towards the knowledge of Indian Arachnoidea. [*Jl.* xxxviii, pt. ii, 201.

Observations on *Chamæleo vulgaris.* [*Proc.* 1870, 1.

Stoliczka, Dr. Ferd. (*contd.*)—Note on the Kjokkenmoddings of the Andaman Islands. [*Proc.* 1870, 13.

Note on a few Species of Andamanese Land-shells. [*Proc.* 1870, 86.

Note on Three Species of Batracchia from Moulmein. [*Proc.* 1870, 272.

Observations on some Indian and Malayan Amphibia and Reptilia. [*Jl.* xxxix. pt. ii, 134, 159.

A Contribution to Malayan Ornithology. [*Jl.* xxxix, pt. ii, 277.

Observation on Indian and Malayan *Telphusidæ.* [*Proc.* 1871, 84.

On the Anatomy of *Cremnoconchus.* [*Proc.* 1871, 108.

Notes on Terrestrial Mollusca from the neighbourhood of Moulmein (Tenasserim Provinces), with Descriptions of new Species. [*Jl.* xl, pt. ii, 143, 217.

Notes on some Indian and Burmese Ophidians. [*Jl.* xl, pt. ii, 421.

Notes on the Reptilian and Amphibian Fauna of Kachh. [*Proc.* 1872, 71.

Notes on Reptiles, collected by Surgeon F. Day in Sind. [*Proc.* 1872, 85.

Observations on Indian Batracchia. [*Proc.* 1872, 101.

Notes on some new Species of Reptilia and Amphibia, collected by Dr. W. Waagen in North-Western Panjab. [*Proc.* 1872, 124.

Note on a few Burmese Species of Sauria, Ophidia and Batrachia. [*Proc.* 1872, 143.

Notes on various new or little-known Indian Lizards. [*Jl.* xli, pt. ii, 86, 117.

Postscript to the Monograph of Himálayan and Burmese *Clausiliæ.* [*Jl.* xli, pt. ii, 207.

Notice of the Mammals and Birds inhabiting Kachh. [*Jl.* xli, pt. ii, 211.

On the Land-shells of Penang Island, with Descriptions of the Animals and Anatomical Notes; *part first*, Cyclostomacea. [*Jl.* xli, pt. ii, 261.

On the Land-shells of Penang Island, with Descriptions of the Animals and Anatomical Notes; *part second*, *Helicacea.* (with Pls. I-III.) [*Jl.* xlii, pt. ii, 11.

Notes on some Species of Malayan Amphibia and Reptilia. [*Jl.* xlii, pt. ii, 111.

Notes on the Indian Species of *Thelyphonus.* [*Jl.* xlii, pt. ii, 126.

Stoliczka, Dr. Ferd. (*contd.*)—Contribution towards a Monograph of the Indian Passalidæ. [*Jl.* xiii, pt. ii, 149.

Note on some Andamanese and Nicobarese Reptiles, with the Description of three new Species of Lizards. [*Jl.* xlii, pt. ii, 162.

Descriptions of two new Species of Indian Land-shells. [*Jl.* xlii, pt. ii, 169.

See THEOBALD, W.

Stoliczka, Dr. F., and Blanford, H. F.—Catalogue of the Specimens of Meteoric Stones and Meteoric Irons in the Museum of the Asiatic Society of Bengal, Calcutta, corrected up to January 1866. [*Jl.* xxxv, pt. ii, 43.

Stoney, R. V.—Letter on a Specie of Calcareous Tufa. [*Proc.* 1870, 135.

Strachey, Edward—On the Early History of Algebra. [*As. Res.* xii, 159.

Strachey, Lt. Henry.—Narrative of a Journey to Cho Lagan (Rákas Tal), Cho Mapan (Manasarówar), and the valley of Pruang in Gnari, Hundés, in September and Oct. 1846. [*Jl.* xvii, pt. ii, 127.

Narrative of a Journey to Cho Lagan (Rákas Tal). Cho Mapan (Manasarówar), and the valley of Pruang in Gnari (Hundés), in September and October 1846. [*Jl.* xvii, pt. ii, 327.

Explanation of the Elevations of places between Almorah and Gangri. [*Jl.* xvii, pt. ii, 527.

Note on the Construction of the Map of the British Himálayan Frontier in Kumaon and Gurhwál. [*Jl.* xvii, pt. ii, 532.

Strachey, Colonel R.—Note on the Motion of the Glacier of the Pindur in Kumaon. [*Jl.* xvii. pt. ii. 203.

A Description of the Glaciers of the Pindur and Kuphilee Rivers in the Kumaon Himálaya. [*Jl.* xvi, 794.

On the Snow-line in the Himálaya. [*Jl.* xviii, 287.

Notice of a Trip to the Nití Pass. [*Jl.* xix, 79.

Notice of Lieut. Strachey's Scientific Enquiries in Kumaon. [*Jl.* xix, 239.

Memorandum on Mr. Blyth's paper on the Animals known as Wild Asses. [*Jl.* xxix, 136.

On Barometric and other Curves. [*Proc.* 1871, 64.

Observation on the Causes of the Daily Maxima and Minima of Barometric Pressure. [*Proc.* 1871, 15.

Strutt, Major C. H.—On Coins of Sophytus. [*Proc.* 1867, 106.

Stubbs, Major F. W.—Letter regarding Inscriptions, &c., found at Attock. [*Proc.* 1870, 241.

Letter on Counterfeit Coins. [*Proc.* 1870, 302.

Letter on a new Coin. [*Proc.* 1871, 97.

Stulpnagel, C. R.—Coins of Ghiás-ud-dín and Mu'az-ud-dín bin Sám. [*Jl.* xlix, pt. i, 29.

Sutherland, J. C. C.—Sisupala Badha, or Death of Sisupala by Mágha. Translated with Annotations. [*Jl.* viii, 16.

See O'SHAUGHNESSY, DR. W. B.

Swiney, Dr. J.—On the Explanation of Indo-Scythic Legends of the Bactrian Coins, through the medium of the Celtic. [*Jl.* vi, 98.

Swinhoe, Robert.—Ornithology of Amoy. [*Jl.* xxix, 240.

Swynnerton, Rev. Chas.—On a Celt of the Palæolithic type, found at Thandiani. Punjab, September 10th, 1880, by Charles Massy-Swynnerton. [*Proc.* 1880, 175.

Note on a Specimen of Yusafzai Sculpture. [*Proc.* 1880, 196.

Folktales from the Upper Punjab. [*Jl.* LII, pt. I. 81.

Sydenham, Capt. G.—An Account of Bíjapúr in 1811. [*As. Res.* xiii, 433.

Sykes, Col. W. H.—Catalogue of Mammalia observed in the Dukhun. [*Jl.* i, 161.

Catalogue of Birds of the Raptorial and Insessorial Orders. (systematically arranged,) observed in the Dakhan. [*Jl.* iii, 418.

Catalogue of Birds of the Insessorial Order in the Dakhan. [*Jl.* iii, 536.

Catalogue of Birds (systematically arranged,) of the Rasorial, Grallatorial, and Natatorial Orders, observed in the Dakhan. [*Jl.* iii, 597, 639.

Specimens of Buddhist Inscriptions, with Symbols, from the west of India. [*Jl.* vi, 1038.

Symes, Capt. Michael—Of the City of Pegue, and the Temple of Shoemadoo Praw. [*As. Res.* v, 111.

Tagore, G. M.—On Translation of Technical Terms. [*Proc.* 1866, 145, 172.

Tanner, Capt. H.—Note on the Asurhár of the Rájmahal Hills. [*Jl.* iv, 707.

Tanner, Major H. C. B.—Remarks on the Eclipse of 18th August 1868. [*Proc.* 1868, 209.

Extract from a Letter on the Kafir Language. [*Proc.* 1879, 75.

Tawney, C. H.—Remarks on Fire Sticks. [*Proc.* 1881, 74.

Exhibition of a rare Coin of Sophytes. [*Proc.* 1881, 104.

Taylor, Dr. James.—Remarks on the Sequel to the Periplus of the Erythrean Sea, and on the country of the Seres, as described by Ammianus Marcellinus. [*Jl.* xvi, 1.

Taylor, Lieut. G. J.—A Brief Account of the System adopted by Divers in the Deccan, for the Recovery of Valuables lost in the Tanks and Rivers of that Province. [*Jl.* iii, 45.

Taylor, R., Esq.—On Changes of Madras Coast. [*Proc.* 1866, 51.

Taylor, T. G.—Determination of the Errors of Division of the Mural Circle at the Madras Observatory. [*Jl.* iii, 403.

Collimation Error of Astronomical Instruments. [*Jl.* iv, 258.

Observations of the Magnetic Dip and Intensity at Madras. [*Jl.* vi, 374.

Taylor, Major T. M.—Progress Report of the Boring Experiment in Fort William. [*Jl.* vi, 234.

Taylor, Revd. William.—Examination and Analysis of the Mackenzie Manuscripts deposited in the Madras College Library. [*Jl.* vii, 105, 173.

Second Report on the Examination and Restoration of the Mackenzie Manuscripts. [*Jl.* vii, 371, 469.

Tea Plant, Discovery of the Genuine, in Upper Assam. [*Jl.* iv, 42.

Temple, Capt. R. C.—The Lokaníti, translated from the Burmese Paraphrase. [*Jl.* xlvii, pt. i, 239.

Rough Notes on the Distribution of the Afghan Tribes about Kandahar. [*Jl.* xlviii, pt. i, 181.

Notes on the Formation of the Country passed through by the 2nd Column Tal Chotiali Field Force during its march from Kala Abdullah Khan in the Khôjak Pass to Lugárí Bárkhán. Spring of 1879. [*Jl.* xlviii, pt. ii, 103.

Letter regarding an Inscription at Sultanpur. [*Proc.* 1880, 10.

Exhibition of Afghan Helmet. [*Proc.* 1880, 171.

Remarks on the Afghâns found along the Route of the Tal Chotiali Field Force in the spring of 1879. [*Jl.* xlix, pt. i, 91, 143.

Some Hindú Folksongs from the Panjáb. [*Jl.* li, pt. i, 151.

Tennant, Col. J. F.—Reply to Mr. Pratt's Letter to the Asiatic Journal on the Indian Arc of Meridian. [*Jl.* xxviii, 17.

Tennant, Col. J. F. (*contd.*)—Results deducible from Eclipse of August 1868. [*Proc.* 1868, 273.

Memorandum on the Total Eclipse of December 11, (12), 1871. [*Proc.* 171, 128.

Suggestions for Visitors to the Total Eclipse on 12th December 1871. [*Proc.* 1871, 150.

On some Experiments made at H. M.'s Mint in Calcutta on Coining Silver into Rupees. [*Jl.* xlviii, pt. ii, 56.

Letter regarding Newcomb's Astronomical Papers. [*Proc.* 1880, 41.

Account of the Verification of some Standard Weights, with considerations on Standard Weights in general. [*Jl.* xlix, pt. ii, 41.

Table of Predictions of the Eclipse of the Sun, May 16th, 17th, 1882. [*Proc.* 1881, 88.

Photographs of Terra del Fuego Savages, forwarded by. [*Proc.* 1881, 152.

Theobald, W.—Indian Oology. Notes on the Nidification of some of the commoner Birds of the Salt Range, with a few additional, from Kashmir. [*Jl.* xxiii, 589.

Notes on the Geology of the Panjab Salt Range. [*Jl.* xxiii, 651.

Indian Oology. [*Jl.* xxiv, 520.

Notes on the Distribution of some of the Land and Fresh-water Shells of India. Part I. [*Jl.* xxvi, 245; xxvii, 313.

Descriptions of some new Burmese and Indian Helicidæ, with Remarks on some previously described species. [*Jl.* xxviii, 305.

Notes of a Trip from Simla to the Spiti Valley and Chomoriri (Tshomoriri) Lake during the months of July, August and September, 1861. [*Jl.* xxxi, 480.

Notes on the Distribution of Indian terrestrial *Gasteropoda*, considered with reference to its bearing on the origin of species. [*Jl.* xxxii, 354.

Notes on the variation of some Indian and Burmese Helicidæ, with an attempt at their re-arrangement, together with descriptions of new Burmese *Gasteropoda*. [*Jl.* xxxiii, 238.

Theobald, W.—On Stone Implements. [*Proc.* 1865, 126.

Observations on certain Strictures by Mr. H. F. Blanford on W. Theobald's Paper on the Distribution of Indian *Gasteropoda*. [*Jl.* xxxiv, pt. ii, 60.

Theobald, W. (*contd.*)—Notes on a Collection of Land and Fresh-water Shells from the Shan States. Collected by F. Fedden, Esq., 1864-65. [*Jl.* xxxiv, pt. ii. 273.

On *Nesokia Indica.* [*Proc.* 1866, 239.

Catalogue of Reptiles in the Museum of the Asiatic Society of Bengal. [*Jl.* xxxvii, pt. ii, extra No.

Descriptions of some new Land Shells from the Shan States and Pegu. [*Jl.* xxxix, pt. ii, 395.

Notes on Stone Implements of Burma. [*Proc.* 1869, 181.

Note on some Agate Beads from North-Western India. [*Proc.* 1869, 253.

Remarks on a Stone Implement from Burmah. [*Proc.* 1870, 220.

Note regarding certain Type Specimens of Batrachia in the Asiatic Society's Museum. [*Proc.* 1873. 110.

Descriptions of new Species of *Unionidæ.* [*Jl.* xlii, pt. ii, 207.

Observations on some Indian and Burmese Species of *Trionyx.* [*Proc.* 1874, 75.

Letter forwarding two Perforated Stone Implements found at Kharakpur, in the Monghyr District. [*Proc.* 1875, 102.

Observations on some Indian and Burmese Species of *Trionyx*, with a Rectification of their Synonymy and a Description of two new Species. [*Proc.* 1875, 170.

Descriptions of some new Land and Fresh-water Shells from India and Burmah. [*Jl.* xlv, pt. ii, 183.

Remarks on Mr. Campbell's Paper on Himalayan Glaciation in the Journal A. S. B., No. 1, Part II, 1877. [*Proc.* 1877, 137.

Notes on the *Land* and *Fresh-water Shells* of *Kashmir*, more particularly of the Jhilum valley below Srinagar and the Hills north of Jamu. [*Jl.* xlvii, pt. ii, 141.

List of *Mollusca* from the Hills between Mari and Tandiani. [*Jl.* l, pt. ii, 44.

Theobold, W., and Stoliczka, Dr. F.—Notes on Burmese and Arakanese Land Shells, with Descriptions of a new Species. [*Jl.* xli, pt. ii, 329.

Thibaut, Dr. G.—On the S'ulvasútras. [*Jl.* xliv, pt. i, 227.

Contributions to the Explanation of the Jyotisha-Vedánga. [*Jl.* xlvi, pt. i, 411.

On the Súryaprajńapti. [*Jl.* xlix, pt. i, 107, 181.

Thomas, Edward—On Sassanian Coins. [*Jl.* xx, 525.

An Account of eight Kúfic Silver Coins. [*Jl.* xx, 537.

Note on Col. Stacey's Ghazni Coins. [*Jl.* xxi, 115.

Note on the present state of the Excavations at Sárnáth. [*Jl.* xxiii, 469.

On the Epoch of the Gupta Dynasty. [*Jl.* xxiv, 371.

On the Coins of the Gupta Dynasty. [*Jl.* xxiv, 483.

Ancient Indian Numerals. [*Jl.* xxiv. 551.

Catalogue of the Coins in the Cabinet of the late Col. Stacy, with the estimated prices attached. [*Jl.* xxvii, 251.

On Ancient Indian Weights. [*Jl.* xxxiii, 251 ; xxxiv. pt. i, 14, 151.

On Double Currency. [*Proc.* 1865, 208.

On Arian Alphabets. [*Proc.* 1866, 138.

On Arian Alphabets. [*Proc.* 1867, 33.

The Initial Coinage of Bengal. [*Jl.* xxxvi, pt. i, 1 ; xlii, pt. i, 343.

On a Coin of Plato. [*Proc.* 1872, 174.

Readings of rare Bengal Coins. [*Proc.* 1872, 199.

On a Coin of Kunanda. [*Proc.* 1875, 163.

Note on Jainism. [*Proc.* 1879, 1.

The Revenues of the Mughal Empire. [*Jl.* l, pt. i, 147.

Thomason, J.—Report on the Settlement of the Ceded District of Azimgurh, commonly called Chaklah-Azimgurh. [*Jl.* viii, 77.

Thompson, Capt. W. B.—Note on the Báigás of Bálághát. [*Proc.* 1872, 172.

Thomson, Capt. J.—Rules for calculating the Lengths of the Drop-bars of Suspension Bridges, the Length and Deflection of the Chain, Rise of the Roadway, &c. [*Jl.* iv, 222.

Table shewing the Weight or Pressure which a Cylindrical Wrought-iron Bolt will sustain when supported at the ends, and bonded in the middle of its length. [*Jl.* iv, 225.

A Table of the Scantlings of Beams of Teak or of Saul Wood, to sustain a Terrace Roof not exceeding seven inches in thickness ; the deflection not to exceed one-fortieth of an inch for each foot of length. [*Jl.* v, 227.

Thomson, Thos.—Notes on the Herbarium of the Calcutta Botanic Garden, with Especial Reference to the completion of the Flora Indica. [*Jl.* xv, 405.

Thuillier, Genl. H. E. L.—A Tabular view of the fall of Rain and other remarkable Meteorological Phenomena in Calcutta from 1829 to 1847. [*Jl.* xvii, pt. i, 349.

Meteorological Summary for 1847. [*Jl.* xvii, pt. i, 550.

Memorandum on the Survey of Kashmir in progress under Capt. T. G. Montgomerie, and the Topographical Map of the valley and surrounding mountains, with Chart of the Triangulation of the same executed in the Field office, and under the superintendence of Lieut.-Colonel A. Scott Waugh, Surveyor-General of India, Dehra-Dun, May 1859. [*Jl.* xxix, 20.

Remarks on the connection of the Brahmaputra and Sanpú. [*Proc.* 1878, 26.

Thurburn, Capt.—Report on the Turan Mall Hill. addressed to R. N. C. Hamilton, Esquire, Resident at Indore. [*Jl.* xx. 502.

Tibetan Frontier, Correspondence of the Commissioners deputed to the. [*Jl.* xvii, pt. i, 89.

Tickell, Lieut.-Colonel S. R.—List of Birds collected in the Jungles of Borabhúm and Dholbhúm. [*Jl.* ii, 569.

Memoir on the Hodesum (improperly called Kolehan). [*Jl.* ix, 694, 783.

Grammatical construction of the Ho Language. [*Jl.* ix, 997.

Vocabulary of the Ho Language. [*Jl.* ix, 1063.

Supplementary Note to the Memoir on the Hodésum. [*J.* x, 30.

Notes on the Bendkar, a People of Keonjur. [*Jl.* xi, 205.

Manis Crassicaudata., (Auct.) M. Pentadactyla, (Ibid). Short-tailed or thick-tailed Manis. In Hindustan, generally called "Bujjerkeet."—Orissa, "Bujjer Kepta" and "Sooruj Mookhee."—By the Lurka Koles, "Armoo." [*Jl.* xi, 221.

Notes on a curious Species of Tiger or Jaguar, killed near the Snowy Range, north of Darjeeling. [*Jl.* xii, 814.

On the Oology of India: a Description of the Eggs, also Nests, of several Birds of the plains of India, collected chiefly during 1845, '46. [*Jl.* xvii, pt. i, 297.

Tickell, Lieut.-Col. S. R. (*contd.*)—Notes on the Heumá or "Shendoos," a Tribe inhabiting the Hills north of Arakan. [*Jl.* xxi, 207

Description of a new Species of Hornbill. by Capt. S. R. Tickell, Principal Assistant Commissioner, Tenasserim Provinces. [*Jl.* xxiv, 285.

Itinerary, with Memoranda, chiefly Topographical and Zoological, through the southerly portions of the district of Amherst, province of Tenasserim. [*Jl.* xxviii, 421.

Order Chelonia. [*Jl.* xxxi, 367.

Memoranda relative to three Andamanese in the charge of Major Tickell, when Deputy Commissioner of Amherst, Tenasserim, in 1861. [*Jl.* xxxiii, 162.

Note on the Gibbon (Hylobates lar), of Tenasserim. [*Jl.* xxxiii, 196.

Description of a supposed new genus of the Gadidæ, Arakan. [*Jl.* xxxvii, pt. ii, 32.

Grammar of the Ho Language. (Kolarian Aborigines.) [*Jl.* xxxv, pt. ii, *Extra No.* 268.

Tide, Register of the Rise and Fall of the, at Prince of Wales Island and Singapore. [*Jl.* xi, 149, 263, 359.

Tides, Results of the Observations made on the. at Madras, from the 31st May to the 10th October 1821, by means of a Tide-gauge fixed near the north-east angle of the Fort. [*Jl.* iv, 325.

Tides, Succinct Review of the Observations of the, in the Indian Archipelago, made during the year 1839, by order of his Excellency the Governor-General of His Netherlandish Majesty's possessions, 20th October 1838, No. 3. [*Jl.* x, 302.

Todd, Major.—Report of a Journey from Herat to Simla, *via* Candahar, Cabool and the Punjaub, undertaken in the year 1838, by order of His Excellency John McNeill, Esquire, H. B. M. Envoy Extraordinary and Minister Plenipotentiary at the Court of Persia. [*Jl.* xiii, 339.

Tolbort, T. W. H.—The District of Lúdiáná. [*Jl.* xxxviii, pt. i, 83.

The District of Dehra Ismail Khan. Trans-Indus. [*Jl.* xl, pt. i, 1.

Authorities for the History of the Portuguese in India. [*Jl.* xlii, pt. i, 193.

On the Portuguese Settlements in India. [*Proc.* 1874, 128.

Torrens, Henry.—Remarks on M. Schlegel's Objections to the restored editions of the Alif Leilah, or Arabian Nights' Entertainments. [*Jl.* vi, 161.
Note on Bameean Coins. [*Jl.* ix, 70.
Note on Discoveries of Gems from Kandahar. [*Jl.* ix, 100.
Note on an Inscription from Oodeypore near Sagur. [*Jl.* ix, 545.
On the Gem and Coins, figured as Nos. 7 and 8 in the preceding Plate, and on a Gem belonging to the late Edward Conolly. [*Jl.* xi, 137.
On a Cylinder and certain Gems, collected in the neighbourhood of Herat by Major Pottinger. [*Jl.* xi, 316.
On Native Impressions regarding the Natural History of certain Animals. [*Jl.* xviii, 788.
Some Conjectures on the Progress of the Bráhminical Conquerors of India. [*Jl.* xix, 1.
Note, with a Specimen of Iron from the Dhunakar hills, Birbhum. [*Jl.* xix, 77.
Translation of some uncertain Greek legends on Coins of the Indo-Scythian Princes of Cabul. [*Jl.* xx, 137.

Tounghoo, Dy. Com. of—On the Gyeikki country. [*Proc.* 1866, 80.

Towers, Captain John.—Observations on the Alphabetical System of the Language of Awâ and Ràc'hain. [*As. Res.* v, 143.

Trail, Henry.—A Meteorological Diary kept at Calcutta. [*As. Res.* ii, 419.

Traill, George William.—Statistical Sketch of Kamaon. [*As. Res.* xvi, 137.
Statistical Report on the Bhotia Mehals of Kamaon. [*As. Res.* xvii, 1.

Trant, Lieut. T. A.—Notice of the Khyĕn Tribe, inhabiting the Yúma Mountains, between Ava and Aracan. [*As. Res.* xvi, 261.
Report on a Route from Pakung Yeh in Ava, to Aeng in Aracan. [*Jl.* xi, 1136.

Tregear, Vincent.—Notice of an Ancient Mahal or Palace near Jaunpur, in which some Hindu Coins were lately dug up. [*Jl.* iii, 617.
Note on the River Goomtee, with a Section of its Bed. [*Jl.* viii, 712.
Mode of taking Facsimiles of Coins. [*Jl.* x, 158.
A few Instructions for Insect Collectors. [*Jl.* xi, 473.

Tremenheere, Captn. G. B.—Letters forwarding a Paper on the Formation of the Museum of Economic Geology of India. [*Jl.* ix, 973.
Report on the Tin of the Province of Mergui. [*Jl.* x, 845; xi, 24, 289.
Report on the Manganese of the Mergui Province. [*Jl.* x, 852.
Second Report on the Tin of Mergui. [*Jl.* xi, 839.
Report of a Visit to the Pakchan River, and of some Tin Localities in the southern portion of the Tenasserim Provinces. [*Jl.* xii, 523.
Report, &c., with information concerning the price of Tin Ore of Mergui, in reference to Extract from a Despatch from the Honorable Court of Directors, dated 25th October 1843, No. 20. [*Jl.* xiv, 329.
On Thamman Tank. [*Proc.* 1866, 109.

Tremlett, J. D.—Notes on Old Delhi. [*Jl.* xxxix, pt. i, 70.

Trotter, Robert.—Notes regarding the Meteorology and Climate of the Cape of Good Hope. [*Jl.* xi, 211.

Troyer, Captn. A.—Remarks upon the Second Inscription of the Allahabad Pillar. [*Jl.* iii, 118.

Turner, Lieut. Samuel.—An Account of a Journey to Tibet. [*As. Res.* i, 207.
Copy of an Account given by Mr. Turner of his Interview with Teeshoo Lama at the Monastery of Terpaling, enclosed in Mr. Turner's Letter to the Honorable the Governor-General. [*As. Res.* i, 199.
Description of the Yàk of Tartary, called Soora-Goy, or the Bushy-tailed Bull of Tibet. [*As. Res.* iv, 351.

Turnour, Hon'ble George.—Examination of some points of Buddhist Chronology. [*Jl.* v, 521.
An Examination of the Páli Buddhistical Annals. [*Jl.* vi, 501, 713; vii, 686, 789, 919, 991.
Account of the Tooth Relic of Ceylon, supposed to be alluded to in the opening passage of the Feroz Lát Inscription. [*Jl.* vi, 856.
Further Notes on the Inscriptions on the columns at Delhi, Allahabad, Betiah, &c. [*Jl.* vi, 1049.

Turpentine, On the Native Manufacture of. [*Jl.* ii, 248.

Tusser and other Silks, Correspondence regarding Samples of. [*Proc.* 1875, 128.

Tween, A.—On Analysis of Peat. [*Proc.* 1865, 86.

Twemlow, Brigadier G.—On Modes of obtaining Important Results by Simple Means. [*Jl.* i, 68, 105.
On Artificial Fuel. [*Jl.* xii, 228.

Tytler, J.—Essay on the Binomial Theorem as known to the Arabs. [*As. Res.* xiii, 456.
An Essay on the Extraction of the Roots of Integers, as practised by the Arabs. [*As. Res.* xvii, 51.

Tytler, Lieut.-Col. R. C.—Account of further Intercourse with the Natives of the Andaman Islands. [*Jl.* xxxiii, 31.
Description of a new Species of Paradoxurus from the Andaman Islands. [*Jl.* xxxiii, 188.
Observations on keeping Salt-water Fish alive for a considerable time. [*Jl.* xxxiii, 534.
Observations on a few Species of Geckos alive in the possession of the Author. [*Jl.* xxxiii, 535.

Tytler, Lieut.-Col. R. C.—On supposed new Species of Rats. [*Proc.* 1865, 76.
Description of new Species of *Spizætus.* [*Proc.* 1865, 112.
Vulter Monachus. [*Proc.* 1866, 74.
On Drymoipus Verreauxi. [*Proc.* 1868, 200.

Ujfaboy, Ch.—*See* WATERHOUSE, MAJOR J.

Uma, The Birth of—a Legend of Himalaya by Cálidása. [*Jl.* ii, 329.

Ure, Dr. A.—Analysis of Iron Ores from Tavoy and Mergui, and of Limestone from Mergui. [*Jl.* xii, 236.

Ushruff Khan.—*See* ABBOTT, CAPT. J.

Vansittart, Henry—On the Descent of the Afghans from the Jews. [*As. Res.* ii, 67.
A Description of Assam by Mohammed Cazim. [*As. Res.* ii, 171.

Venuikoff, W.—Statistical Data on the Area of Asiatic Russia, translated from No. III, 1865, of the Notes of the Imperial Russian Geographical Society, by Mr. R. Michell. [*Jl.* xxxix, pt. ii, 41.

Verchere, Dr. Albert M.—Notes to accompany a Geological Map and Section of the Lowa Ghur or Sheen Ghur Range in the district of Bunnoo, Punjab: with Analyses of the Lignites. [*Jl.* xxxiv, pt. ii, 42.

Verchere, Dr. Albert M. (*contd.*)—
Kashmir, the Western Himálaya and the Afghan Mountains, a Geological Paper, with a Note on the Fossils by M. Edouard de Verneuil. [*Jl.* xxxv, pt. ii, 89, 159; xxxvi, pt. ii, 9, 83, 201.
Kashmir, the Western Himalaya and the Afghan Mountains, a Geological Paper, with a Note on the Fossils by M. Edouard de Verneuil. [*Jl.* xxxv. pt. ii, 159.
Kashmir, the Western Himálayas and the Afghan Mountains, a Geological Paper, with a Note on the Fossils by M. Edouard de Verneuil. [*Jl.* xxxvi, pt. ii, 9.
Kashmir, the Western Himálaya and the Afghan Mountains, a Geological Paper, with a Note on the Fossils by M. Edouard de Verneuil. [*Jl.* xxvi, pt. ii, 83.
Kashmir, the Western Himalaya and the Afghan Mountains, a Geological Paper, with a Note on the Fossils by M. Edouard de Verneuil. [*Jl.* xxxvi, pt. ii, 201.

Vermilion—On Chinese. [*Jl.* i, 151.

Vernueil, Edouard de.—*See* VERCHERE, DR. ALBERT M.

Vicary, Capt. N.—List of Specimens from Bilwar. [*Jl.* iv, 571.
Note on the Scapes of Xanthorhæa and Fossil Stems of Lapidodendra [*Jl.* viii, 685.
Notes on the Botany of Sinde. [*Jl.* xvi, 1152.

Vigne, G. J.—Some Account of the valley of Kashmir, Ghazni, and Kabul. [*Jl.* vi, 766.

Voysey, Dr. H. W.—Description of the Native Manufacture of Steel in Southern India. [*Jl.* i, 245.
On the Diamond Mines of Southern India. [*As. Res.* xv, 120.
On the Building Stones and Mosaic of Akberabad or Agra. [*As. Res.* xv, 429.
On the Geological and Mineralogical Structure of the Hills of Sitábald, Nágpur, and its immediate vicinity. [*As. Res.* xviii, pt. i, 123.
On some Petrified Shells found in the Gawilgerh Range of Hills in April 1823. [*As. Res.* xviii, pt. i, 187.
Report on the Geology of Hyderabad. [*Jl.* ii, 298.
Second Report on the Geology of Hyderabad. [*Jl.* ii, 392.
Vocabulary of Goand and Cole Words. [*Jl.* xiii, 19.

Voysey, Dr. H. W. (*contd.*)—Extracts from Dr. Voysey's Private Journal when attached to the Trigonometrical Survey in Southern and Central India. [*Jl.* xiii, 853; xix, 190, 269.

Wade, Capt. C. M.—Notes taken in 1829, relative to the Territory and Government of Iskárdoh, from information given by Charágh Ali, an agent deputed to him in that year by Ahmad Sháh, the Gelp or ruler of that country. [*Jl.* iv. 589.

Note on the Hot Spring of Lohand Khad. [*Jl.* vi, 153.

See MACKESON, LIEUT. F.

Walden, Arthur, Viscount.—*See* BLYTH, E.

Waldie, D.—On Burmese Paraffine. [*Proc.* 1866, 72.

On Iron Pseudomorphs. [*Proc.* 1866, 136.

On Scientific Technology. [*Proc.* 1866, 175.

Experimental Investigations connected with the supply of water from the Hooghly to Calcutta. [*Jl.* xxxv, pt. ii, 203.

On Calcutta Water-supply. [*Proc.* 1867, 166.

Experimental Investigations connected with the supply of water from the Hooghly to Calcutta, Part II, being supplementary observations. [*Jl.* xxxvi, pt. ii, 1.

Experimental Investigations connected with the supply of to water Calcutta, Part III [*Jl.* xxxvi. pt. ii, 115.

Analysis of the Khettree Meteorite. [*Jl.* xxxviii, pt. ii, 252.

Analysis of a new Mineral from Burmah. [*Proc.* 1870, 279.

Remarks on the Filtration of Hughli water during the rainy season. [*Proc.* 1873, 162.

On the Muddy Water of the Hughli during the rainy season, with reference to its Purification and to the Calcutta Water-supply. [*Jl.* xlii, pt. ii, 210.

Walker, Dr. A. M.—Report on Productions and Manufactures in the district of Hunumkoondah. in the dominions of H. H. the Nizam of Hyderabad. [*Jl.* x, 386.

On the Geology, &c., &c., of Hunumkoondah (H. H. the Nizam's territory). [*Jl.* x, 471.

On the Natural Products about the Pundeelah River, H. H. the Nizam's territory. [*Jl.* x. 509.

Notes and Observations in continuation. [*Jl.* x, 725.

Walker, H.—Notice of the Kiang. [*Jl.* xvii, pt. ii, 1.

Walker, Major-Gen. J. T.—The Trigonometrical Survey of India. [*Jl* xxxi, 32.

Progress of the Trigonometrical Survey, being Extracts from a Report to the Secy. to the Govt. of India, Military Department. [*Jl.* xxxii, 111.

Extract from Report of the Operations of the Great Trigonometrical Survey of India during the year 1862-63. [*Jl.* xxxiii. 381.

Russian Geographical Operations in Asia. [*Jl.* xxxv, pt. ii, 77.

On Port Blair. [*Proc.* 1868, 91.

Recent Trans-Frontier Explorations. [*Jl.* xlvii. pt. i, 78.

Exploration of the Great Sanpo River of Thibet, during 1877, in connection with the Operations of the Survey of India. [*Proc.* 1879. 203.

The Evidence afforded by the Indian Pendulum Observations on the Constitution of the Earth's Crust and on Geodesy. [*Proc.* 1879, 246.

On the Eastern Frontier of Thibet. [*Proc.* 1880, 200.

Remarks on the Singpho and Kampti Country. [*Proc.* 1882, 7.

The Spirit Levelling Operations executed in connection with the Tidal Observations of the Indian Survey Department. [*Proc.* 1882, 78.

An Account of the return of explorers from Thibet. [*Proc.* 1882. 159.

On the Earthquake of the 31st December 1881. [*Proc.* 1883, 60.

Walker, W.—Memoir on the Coal found at Kotah, &c., with a Note on the Anthracite of Duntimnapilly (H. H. the Nizam's dominions). [*Jl.* x, 341.

Wallich, Dr. N.—Descriptions of two new Species of Sarcolobus, and some other Indian Plants. [*As. Res.* xii, 566.

Descriptions of some rare Indian Plants. [*As. Res.* xiii, 369.

An Account of a new Species of a Camellia growing wild at Nepal. [*As. Res.* xiii, 428.

List of Indian Woods collected by. [*Jl.* ii, 167.

Observations on the Burmese and Munipoor Varnish Tree. [*Jl.* viii, 70.

Walters, Henry.—Journey across the Pandua Hills near Sylhet in Bengal. [*As. Res.* xvii, 499.

Census of the City of Dacca. [*As. Res.* xvii, 535.

Ward, G. E.—On Budhist Remains. [*Proc.* 1866, 97.

Ward, T.—Short Sketch of the Geology of Pulo-Pinang and the neighbouring Islands, with a Map and Sections. [*As. Res.* xviii, pt. ii, 149.

Ward, Major.—Some Account of the Hill Tribes of the Piney Hills in the Madura District. Communicated by Capt. T. J. Taylor. [*Jl.* iv, 664.

Warlow, W.—Systematically arranged Catalogue of the Mammalia and Birds belonging to the Museum of the Asiatic Society, Calcutta. [*Jl.* ii, 96.

Warren, Capt. John.—An Account of Experiments made in the Mysore country, in the year 1804, to investigate the effects of Terrestrial Refraction. [*As. Res.* ix, 1.

An Account of Astronomical Obvervations taken at the Honorable Company's Observatory, near Fort St. George in the East Indies, in the years 1806 and 1807. To which are added some Remarks on the Declination of certain Stars and of the Sun, when near the zenith of that place. [*As. Res.* x, 513.

An Account of the Petrifactions near the village of Treevikera in the Carnatic. [*As. Res.* xi, 1.

An Account of Experiments made at the Observatory, near Fort St. George, for determining the length of the simple pendulum beating seconds of time at that place; to which are added Comparisons of the said Experiments, with others made in different parts of the globe, and some Remarks on the ellipticity of the earth, as deduced from these operations. [*As. Res.* xi, 293.

An Account of Observations taken at the Observatory, near Fort St. George in the East Indies, for determining the obliquities of the Ecliptic, in the months of December 1809, June and December, 1810. [*As. Res.* xii, 192.

Observations on the Golden Ore, found in the Eastern Provinces of Mysore, in the year 1802. [*Jl.* iii, 463.

Warth, Dr. H.—Preliminary Report on Comparative Observations of air-temperature and humidity at different elevations above the ground-surface. [*Proc.* 1883, 80.

Waterhouse, Major J.—On a new Photo-callographic Printing Process. [*Proc.* 1871, 239.

Waterhouse, Major J. (*contd.*)—On the Application of Electro-deposition to the Correction of Engraved Copperplates. [*Proc.* 1874, 2.

Exhibition of Photographs showing the extreme Red Rays of the Solar Spectrum. [*Proc.* 1875, 198.

Photography in connection with the Observation of the Transit of Venus at Roorkee, December 9th (Civil), 1874. [*Jl.* xliv, pt. ii, 64.

On the Influence of Eosin on the Photographic Action of the Solar Spectrum upon the Bromide and Bromoiodide of Silver. [*Proc.* 1876, 12.

Translations of Extracts of letters from M. Ch. Ujfalvy and the Abbé Desgodins, descriptive of recent Geographical researches in Turkestan and Tibet, published in the October number of the Bulletin de la Société de Géographie. [*Proc.* 1878, 21.

Exhibition of a Photograph by M. Janssen of a part of the Sun's disc. [*Proc.* 1878, 119.

Exhibition of a photograph of a sculptured group in the Garalmandal Temple at Pathári, Central India. [*Proc.* 1878, 122.

An Account of the Tidal Observations in the Gulf of Cutch, conducted by the Great Trigonometrical Survey, under the superintendence of Col. J. T. Walker, C.B., R.E., during the years 1873-74-75. Compiled from the Great Trigonometrical Survey Report. [*Jl.* xlvii, pt. ii, 26.

The Application of Photography to the Reproduction of Maps and Plans by Photo-mechanical and other processes. [*Jl.* xlvii, pt. ii, 53.

Remarks on Coins, &c., from Ahin Posh Tope. [*Proc.* 1879, 79.

Note on the Fourth Edition of General Walker's Map of Turkestan, in four Sheets. [*Proc.* 1879, 186.

Notes on the Survey Operations in Afghanistan, in connection with the Campaign of 1878-79. Compiled from Letters and Diaries of the Survey Officers. [*Jl.* xlviii, pt. ii, 146.

Water-mill.—Description of the Panchaki or Native. [*Jl.* ii, 359.

Wathen, W. H. — Memoir on the U'sbek state of Kokan, properly called Khokend (the Ancient Ferghana), in Central Asia. [*Jl.* iii, 369.

Wathen, W. H. (*contd.*)—Note on a Pilgrimage undertaken by an U'sbek and his two sons from Khokend, or Kokan, in Tartary, through Russia, &c., to Mecca. [*Jl.* iii, 379.

Account of the Inscriptions upon two sets of Copperplates, found in the Western part of Gujerat. [*Jl.* iv, 477.

Memoir on Chinese Tartary and Khoten. [*Jl.* iv, 653.

A Grammar of the Sindhi Language. [*Jl.* vi, 347.

Watson, Lieut.-Col. T. C.—Chirra Punji, and a detail of some of the favourable circumstances which render it an advantageous site for the erection of an Iron and Steel Manufactory on an extensive scale. [*Jl.* iii. 25.

Waugh, Lieut.-Col. A. Scott.—*See* THUILLIER, H. L.

Webb, Capt. W. S.—Memoir relative to a Survey of Kumaon, with some Account of the principles upon which it has been conducted. [*As. Res.* xiii, 293.

Weights of England and India, On the Standard. [*Jl.* i. 442.

Weller, Lieut. J. A.—Extract from the Journal kept on a Trip to the Bulcha and Oonta Dhoora Passes, with an Eye-sketch. [*Jl.* xii. 78.

Wellsted, Lieut. J. R.—Account of some Inscriptions in the Abyssinian character, found at Hassan Ghorab, near Aden, on the Arabian Coast. [*Jl.* iii, 554.

Report on the Island of Socotra. [*Jl.* iv, 138.

Westland, J.—Remarks on an Afghan Helmet. [*Proc.* 1880, 171.

Exhibition of Old Maps of Calcutta and Bengal. [*Proc.* 1881, 89.

Westmacott, E. V.—Letter on the Identification of Ancient Towns in Bengal. [*Proc.* 1874, 57.

Note on the Site of Fort Ekdalah. District Dinajpur. [*Jl.* xliii, pt. i, 244.

A Copperplate containing a grant of land by Lakshman Sen of Bengal, found near Torpon-dighi in the District of Dinajpur, 1874. [*Jl.* xliv, pt. i, 1.

On Traces of Buddhism in Dinajpur and Bagura (Bogra). [*Jl.* xliv, pt. i, 187.

Letter on a Kutila Inscription from Monghyr. [*Proc.* 1883, 45.

See BLOCHMANN, H.

Westmacott, Capt. G. E.—Some Account of a Sect of Hindu Schismatics in Western India, calling themselves Ramsanèhi, or Friends of God. [*Jl.* iv, 65.

Description of Ancient Temples and Ruins at Chárdwár in Assam. [*Jl.* iv, 185.

A short Account of Khyrpoor and the Fortress of Bukur, in North Sind. [*Jl.* ix. 1090.

A short Account of Khyrpoor and the Fortress of Bukur, in South Sind. [*Jl.* ix. 1187.

Roree in Khyrpoor; its Population and Manufactures. [*Jl.* x. 393, 479.

Whalley, P.—Translations from the Táríkh í Fírúz Sháhí. The reign of Mu'izzuddín. [*Jl.* xl, pt. i, 185.

Translations from the Díwán of Zíb-un-nisá Begum, poetically styled 'Makhfí,' daughter of the Emperor Aurangzib. [*Jl.* xlv, pt. i. 308.

Metrical Translations from the Quatrains of 'Umar Khayyám. [*Jl.* xlvi, pt. i, 158

White, Lieut. Charles—On the Dhanésa, or Indian Buceros. [*As. Res.* iv, 119.

Whitty, I. J.—Note on a Case of Death from Lightning in a Mine. [*Proc.* 1877, 102.

Wilcox, Lieut. R.—Memoir of a Survey of Assam and the neighbouring Countries, executed in 1825-6-7-8. [*As. Res.* xvii, 314.

Wilford, Colonel Francis.—Remarks on the City of Tagara. [*As. Res.* i, 369.

On Egypt and other Countries adjacent to the Cálí River, or Nile of Ethiopia, from the Ancient Books of the Hindus. [*As. Res.* iii, 295.

A Dissertation on Semiramis, the Origin of Mecca, &c., from the Hindu Sacred Books. [*As. Res.* iv, 363.

Account of some Ancient Inscriptions. [*As. Res.* v, 135.

On the Chronology of the Hindus. [*As. Res.* v. 241.

Remarks on the Names of the Cabirian Deities, and on some words used in the Mysteries of Eleusis. [*As. Res.* v, 297.

On Mount Caucasus. [*As. Res.* vi, 455.

An Essay on the Sacred Isles in the West, with other Essays connected with that work. [*As. Res.* viii, 245; ix, 32; x, 27; xi, 11.

Wilford, Colonel Francis (*contd.*)—
On the Ancient Geography of India. [*As. Res.* xiv, 373.
An Essay on the Comparative Geography of Ancient India. [*Jl.* xx, 227, 470.

Wilkins, Charles.—A Royal Grant of Land, engraved on a Copperplate, bearing date twenty-three years before Christ, and discovered among the Ruins of Mongueer. [*As. Res.* i. 123.
An Inscription on a Pillar near Buddal. [*As. Res.* i, 131.
Translation of a Sanscrit Inscription, copied from a Stone at Booddhā-Gaya by Mr. Wilmot. 1785. [*As. Res.* i, 284.
On the Sic'hs and their College. [*As. Res.* i, 288.
Two Inscriptions from the Vindya Mountains. [*As. Res.* ii. 167.

Wilkinson, Lancelot—On the use of the Siddhántas in the Work of Native Education. [*Jl.* iii. 504.
Discovery of the Rekhá Ganita, a Translation of the Elements of Euclid into Sanskrit by Samrát Jagannátha, under the orders of Rája Siwái Jaya Sinha of Jaipur. [*Jl.* vi, 938.
Translation of an Inscription on a Támba Patra found in the village of Pipliánagar, in the Shujalpur Pergana, and presented to the Political Agent, Bhopal, by the Jagirdár. [*Jl.* vii, 736.

Williams, Dr. C.—Extract from Journal of a Trip to Bhamo. [*Jl.* xxxiii, 189.
Memorandum on the Question of British Trade with Western China *viâ* Burmah. [*Jl.* xxxiii, 407.

Williams, John.—On the Cure of persons bitten by Snakes. [*As. Res.* ii, 323.

Williamson, Lieut. W. J.—A Vocabulary of the Garo and Konch Dialects. [*Jl.* xxxviii, pt. i, 14.

Willson, W. G.—Observations on Mr. Blanford's Paper on the Normal Rainfall of Bengal. [*Proc.* 1870, 225.
An Account of the Occurrence of a Whirlwind in the neighbourhood of Calcutta. [*Proc.* 1872, 96.

Wilson, Horace Hayman.—An Essay on the Hindu History of Cashmir. [*As. Res.* xv, 1.
A Sketch of the Religious Sects of the Hindus. [*As. Res.* xvi, 1; xvii, 169.
Sanskrit Inscriptions at Abu. [*As. Res.* xvi. 284.

Wilson, Horace Hayman (*contd.*)—
Notice of three Tracts received from Nepal. [*As. Res.* xvi, 450.
Description of Select Coins, from Originals or Drawings, in the possession of the Asiatic Society. [*As. Res.* xvii, 559.
Remarks on the portion of the Dionysiacs of Nonnus relating to the Indians. [*As. Res.* xvii, 607.
Abstract of the Contents of the Dulvá, or first portion of the Kah-gyur. [*Jl.* i, 1.
Analysis of the Puránas. [*Jl.* i, 81, 217.
Analysis of the Kah-gyur. [*Jl.* i, 375.
Analysis of the Vishnu Purána. [*Jl.* i, 431.
Analysis of the Váyu Purána. [*Jl.* i, 535.

Wilson, Revd. John.—Address read before the Bombay Branch of the Royal Asiatic Society on the 27th January 1836. [*Jl.* v, 304.

Wilson, Revd. Dr.—Address on the Prospects of Indian Research. [*Proc.* 1869. 109.

Wilson, R. H.—On Earthquakes of Chittagong. [*Proc.* 1866. 40.

Wilson, W. L.—On Chipped Implements of Saugor District. [*Proc.* 1867, 142.

Wise, Dr. James.—Notes on Sunárgáon, Eastern Bengal. [*Jl.* xliii, pt. i, 82.

Wise, Dr. J.—On the Bárah Bhúyas of Eastern Bengal. [*Jl.* xliii, pt. i, 197 ; xliv, pt. i, 181.
See BLOCHMANN, H.

Wise, Dr. T. A.—An Experimental Inquiry into the means employed by the Natives of Bengal for making Ice. [*Jl.* ii, 80.
Peculiarities and Uses of the Pillar Towers of the British Islands. [*Jl.* xxxiii, 552.

Withecombe, Dr. J. R.—Mean Temperature and fall of rain at Darjiling, Sikkim, Himâlayah, 1848 to 1855. [*Jl.* xxvi 63.

Wood, Browne.—Extracts from a Report of a Journey into the Naga Hills, in 1844. [*Jl.* xiii, 771.

Wood, Lieut.—Report on the River Indus (Sections 1 to 5). [*Jl.* x, 518.

Wood-Mason, James.—On Polydactylism in a Horse. [*Proc.* 1871, 18.
Contributions to Indian Carcinology.—On Indian and Malayan Telphusidæ. Part I. [*Jl.* xl, pt. ii, 189, 201, 449.

Wood-Mason, James (*contd.*)—Remarks on Mr. Peal's Account of several Naga Tribes in Asám. [*Proc.* 1872, 49.

On *Nephropsis Stewarti*, a new Genus and Species of Macrurous Crustaceans, dredged in deep water off the Eastern Coast of the Andaman Islands. [*Proc.* 1872, 151.

Note on certain Species of *Phasmidæ*, hitherto referred to the genus *Bacillus*. [*Proc.* 1873, 148.

Remarks on a Specimen of *Carcinus Mænus*, Pennant. [*Proc.* 1873, 172.

On *Nephropsis Stewarti*, a new Genus and Species of Macrurous Crustaceans. [*Jl.* xlii, pt. ii, 39.

On new or little-known Species of *Phasmidæ*, Part I,—Genus Bacillus. [*Jl.* xlii, pt. ii, 45.

On *Rhopalorhynchus Kröyeri*, a new Genus and Species of *Pycnogonidi*. [*Jl.* xlii, pt. ii, 171.

On a new Genus and Species (*Hylæocarcinus Humei*) of Land Crabs from the Nicobar Islands. [*Jl.* xlii. pt. ii. 258.

Abstract of Remarks on Drawings of Blind Crustaceans. [*Proc.* 1874, 180.

Note on *Trictenotoma Childrenii*, Gray. [*Proc.* 1874, 181.

On the Occurrence of a Superorbital Chain of Bones in the *Arboricolæ* (Wood-Partridges) (Plate II). [*Jl.* xliii, pt. ii, 254.

Remarks on Measurements of Crania of Mongoloid races. [*Proc.* 1875, 97.

Exhibition of a Gigantic Stridulating Spider. [*Proc.* 1875, 197.

Exhibition of Photographs of *Rhinoceros Sondaicus* and *R. Indicus*. [*Proc.* 1875, 229.

Exhibition of new Crustaceans of the genera *Paratelphusa*, *Astacus*, *Coronis*, *Gonodactylus*, *Squilla*, and *Clorida*. [*Proc.* 1875, 230.

On new or little-known Species of *Phasmidæ*, with a brief Preliminary Notice of the Occurrence of a Clasping Apparatus in the males throughout the family. [*Jl.* xliv, pt. ii. 215.

Exhibition of Specimens of new or little-known Phasmideous Insects and of new fresh-water *Astacidæ* from New Zealand. [*Proc.* 1876, 3.

Description of a new Rodent from Central Asia. [*Proc.* 1876, 80.

Wood-Mason, James (*contd.*)—Exhibition of forms of *Arthropoda* new to India, and of some remarkable Species of *Mantidæ*; with Remarks on the use of the femoral brushes of the *Mantidæ*. [*Proc.* 1876, 174.

Description of a new Species of *Phasmidæ*. [*Jl.* xlv. pt. ii, 47.

Description of a new Species of *Cetoniidæ*. [*Jl.* xlv. pt. ii, 52.

Descriptions of new Species of *Blattidæ* belonging to the Genus *Panesthia*. [*Jl.* xlv. pt. ii. 189.

Exhibition of a Specimen of a Newt from Sikkim. [*Proc.* 1877. 53.

Exhibition of Specimens of new and little known Insects collected by Mr. Limborg in Upper Tenasserim. [*Proc.* 1877, 160.

Notes on *Phasmidæ*. [*Jl.* xlvi. pt. ii, 342.

Description of a new Lepidopterous Insect belonging to the Genus *Thaumantis*. [*Jl.* xlvii, pt. ii, 175.

Exhibition of a Head of *Ovis poli*. [*Proc.* 1879. 280.

Preliminary Notice of a new Genus (*Parectatosoma*) of *Phasmidæ* from Madagascar, with brief Descriptions of its two Species. [*Jl.* xlviii, pt. ii, 117.

Exhibition of Butterflies from the Andamans. [*Proc.* 1880, 102.

Exhibition of some Butterflies from the Andamans, from Mussoorie, and from Sibsagar. [*Proc.* 1880, 123.

Synopsis of the Species of *Choeradodis*, a remarkable Genus of *Mantodea* common to India and Tropical America. [*Jl.* xlix. pt. ii, 82.

Description of a new Species of Diurnal Lepidoptera belonging to the genus *Hebomoia*. [*Jl.* xlix pt. ii. 134

On a new Species of *Papilio* from South India, with Remarks on the Species allied thereto. [*Jl.* xlix. pt. ii, 144.

Description of the Female of *Hebomoia Roepstorffii*. [*Jl.* xlix, pt. ii. 150.

On the Lepidopterous Genus *Æmona*, with the Description of a new Species. [*Jl.* xlix. pt. ii, 175.

Description of a new *Papilio* from the Andaman Islands. [*Jl.* xlix, pt. ii, 178.

Description of *Parantirrhœa Marshalli*, the Type of a new Genus and Species of Rhopalocerous Lepidoptera from South India. [*Jl.* xlix, pt. ii, 248.

Wood-Mason, James (*contd.*)—On some Lepidopterous Insects belonging to the Rhopalocerous Generaia *Euripus* and *Penthema* from India and Burmah. [*Jl.* l, pt. ii, 85.

Description of a new Species of the Lepidopterous Genus *Euripus* from North-Eastern India. [*Jl*, l, pt. ii, 21.

On new and little-known *Mantodea*. [*Jl.* li, pt ii, 272

Wood-Mason, J., & Dr. Niceville, Lionel.—List of Diurnal *Lepidoptera* from Port Blair, Andaman Islands, with Descriptions of some new or little-known Species and of a new Species of *Hestia* from Burmah. [*Jl.* xlix, pt. ii, 223.

List of Diurnal *Lepidoptera* inhabiting the Nicobar Islands. [*Jl.* l, pt. ii. 224

Second List of Rhopalocerous *Lepidoptera* from Port Blair, Andaman Islands, with Descriptions of, and Notes on, new and little-known Species and Varieties. [*Jl.* l, pt. ii, 243.

Second List of Diurnal *Lepidoptera* inhabiting the Nicobar Islands. [*Jl.* li, pt. ii, 14.

Wrede, F.—Account of the St. Thomé Christians on the Coast of Malabar. [*As. Res.* vii, 364.

Wroughton, Capt. R.—Statistical, Agricultural, and Revenue Return of Muthra District, made up to 1st October 1835. [*Jl.* v, 216.

Account and Drawing of two Burmese Bells now placed in a Hindu temple in Upper India. [*Jl.* vi, 1064.

Wyat.—Letter *on a Shoal of Dead Fish.* [*Proc.* 1872, 43.

Wynne, A. B.—Notes on the Earthquake in the Punjab of March 2nd, 1878. [*Jl.* xlvii, pt. ii, 131.

Yarkand Mission, Memorandum of Subjects for scientific observation for the Members of the. [*Proc.* 1873, 123.

Yates, Rev. William.—Essay on Sanskrit Alliteration. [*As. Res.* xx. pt. i, 135.

Review of the Naishadha Charita, or Adventures of Nala Rájá of Naishadha; a Sanskrit Poem, by Shrí Harsha of Cashmir, with a Commentary by Prema Chandra. Published by the Asiatic Society, 1836. [*As. Res.* xx, pt. ii, 318.

Yezd to Herat, Itinerary from. [*Jl.* xxii, 827.

Young, Capt. C. B.—A few Remarks on the subject of the Laterite found near Rangoon. [*Jl.* xxii, 196.

Yule, Lieut.-Col. Henry.—Notes on the Iron of the Kasia Hills, for the Museum of Economic Geology. [*Jl.* xi, 853.

Notes on the Kasia Hills and People. [*Jl.* xiii. 612

A Canal Act of the Emperor Akbar, with some Notes and Remarks on the History of the Western Jumna Canals. [*Jl.* xv, 213.

An Account of the Ancient Buddhist Remains at Pagán on the Iráwádi. [*Jl.* xxvi, 1.

A few Notes on Antiquities near Jubbulpoor. [*Jl.* xxx, 211.

Notes of a Brief Visit to some of the Indian Remains in Java. [*Jl.* xxxi, 16. *See* D'MAZUZE VERY REV. THOMINE.

Yunan Expedition, Suggestions for the. [*Proc.* 1875, 2.

Zeller, Dr. G.—Algarum Species in India Orientali Centrali a S. Kurz collectas determinavit. [*Proc.* 1875, 96.

Algæ collected by Mr. S. Kurz in Arakan and British Burmah, determined and systematically arranged. [*Jl.* xlii, pt. ii, 175.

CENTENARY REVIEW

OF THE

ASIATIC SOCIETY OF BENGAL

From 1784—1883.

PART II.

ARCHÆOLOGY, HISTORY, LITERATURE, &c.

BY

DR. A. F. RUDOLF HOERNLE.

Published by the Society.

PREFACE.

The subjects which were set apart for the investigation of the Literary Section of the Society are "Literature, Philology, History, Antiquities, Religion, Manners and Customs, and whatever is comprehended under the general term of Literature." Among these, History and Antiquities are very closely connected with one another, the latter being subservient to a correct knowledge of the former. Hence the two first chapters of this Review are devoted to a survey of the results of antiquarian and archæological enquiry which are set out under the two heads of Antiquities, including ancient monuments, inscriptions, etc., and Coins. Next follows a chapter, giving a historical sketch of the two greatest discoveries to which the Society can lay claim, and which are directly based on its archæological researches, those of the decipherment of the Indian Páli and the Arian Páli alphabets. The next in order is a chapter containing a statement of the discoveries in Indian History, which were the natural result of the successful reading of the ancient inscriptions on stones, copper-plates and coins. The last chapter gives the results of the investigations into the Language and Literature of India and its multifarious races.

In compiling the several chapters, the writer has attempted to take as his model one of the best specimens of a review of this kind which forms the Introduction to the well-known *Ariana Antiqua* of Professor H. H. Wilson, than whom the Society perhaps possessed no better writer. One portion, indeed, of that Introduction, reviewing the history of coin-discovery during the earlier half of the century, up to the year 1840, has been, as far as possible, adopted into the chapter on coins, the fresh portion of which mainly consists in continuing Professor Wilson's review through the remaining half of the century.

The system of transliteration is very imperfect. This is to be regretted; for various reasons—one of them being the want of the necessary type—it was found to be impossible to carry through a more perfect one.

R. H.

CONTENTS.

CHAPTER I. PAGE

ANTIQUITIES 1

CHAPTER II.

COINS 28

CHAPTER III.

ANCIENT INDIAN ALPHABETS 50

CHAPTER IV.

HISTORY 82

CHAPTER V.

LANGUAGE AND LITERATURE 137

LIST OF ERRATA AND ADDENDA 198

APPENDIXES (*to the Chapter on History*)—

No. I 199

No. II 203

CLASSIFIED INDEX (*of Papers and Notices*) 217

I—Antiquities ... ... i and xciii

II—Coins, Gems, Weights and Measures ... xxxv „ xcviii

III—History ... ...xlviii „ ci

IV—Language and Literature ... ... lx „ cii

V—Religion, Manners and Customs, etc. lxxxiii „ ciii

Centenary Review

OF THE

ASIATIC SOCIETY OF BENGAL

From 1784 to 1883.

Part II.

ARCHÆOLOGY, HISTORY, LITERATURE, Etc.

CHAPTER I.

ANTIQUITIES.

[Ancient Monuments: topes, temples, monoliths, etc. — Caves — Sculptures — Inscriptions on rocks, pillars, stone-slabs, copperplates, etc. — Votive objects — Pottery, etc. — Prehistoric remains, etc.]

THE Antiquities of India were certain to become one of the first objects of attention to the members of the Asiatic Society. They possess the twofold advantage of appealing to the natural curiosity of man and furnishing an incentive to the speculation of the learned. Their importance with regard to the elucidation of History was well described by Mr. H. T. Colebrooke in an early volume of the Asiatic Researches: "In the scarcity of authentic materials," he writes,[1] "for the ancient, and even for the modern, history of the Hindu race, importance is justly attached to all genuine monuments, and especially inscriptions on stone and metal, which are occasionally discovered through various accidents. If these be carefully preserved and diligently examined, and the facts ascertained from them be judiciously employed towards elucidating the scattered information, which can be yet collected from the remains of Indian literature, a satisfactory progress may be finally made in investigating the history of the Hindus."[1]

This remark is illustrated by the very first two ancient monuments, the discovery of which is recorded in any of the publications of the Society, and which, as it happened, have proved of very great consequence. For they led, as will be shown in a later place, one to the decipherment of the so-called Kutila, the other to the discovery of the so-called Gupta, characters. The former monument was the well-known monolith pillar of Buddal, the other were the celebrated Nágárjuní caves near Buddha Gaya, both described in 1785 in the first volume of the Asiatic Researches by Mr. Charles Wilkins and Mr. John Herbert Harrington respectively.[2] Curiously enough it was nearly a century afterwards, in 1874, that a transcript of the text of the Buddal Pillar inscription was for the first time published in the Journal by Babu Pratapa Chandra Ghosh.[3]

In the first volume of the Researches there is also a brief account by Mr. William Chambers of some sculptures and ruins at Mavalipuram (Mahábalipuram) on the Coromandel Coast in South India,[4] the ancient inscriptions on which were a few years afterwards brought to notice by Mr. J. Goldingham,[5] and which, much later, in 1853, were re-described by Mr. C. Gubbins in the Journal.[6] The former also

---

[1] As. Res., Vol. IX, p. 398. [2] As. Res., Vol. I, pp. 131, 276; Vol. II, p. 167; republished in J. A. S. B., Vol. XVI, p. 594. [3] J. A. S B., Vol. XLIII, p. 356. [4] As. Res., Vol. I, p. 145. [5] *Ibid.*, Vol. V, p. 69. [6] J. A. S. B., Vol. XXII, p. 656.

communicated some account of the well-known caves in Elephanta and the sculptures contained in them.[1]

About the same time, in 1795, the Society's attention was first directed to the famed monuments of antiquity on the site of old Dehli, the best known of which, the Qutab Minár, was measured and described by Ensign James T. Blunt.[2] His sketch of the Minár made in 1794 has a peculiar interest, as it shows that tower still crowned by the Sultan Fírúz Sháh's old cupola of red granite, which was thrown down in 1803 by an earthquake. Copies of the Persian inscriptions on the Minár were afterwards, in 1822, supplied by Mr. Walter Ewer.[3] A general description of old Dehli as it appeared in 1793 was contributed by Lieutenant William Franklin.[4] On the opposite side of India, the ancient city of Pegu and its chief temple were briefly noticed in 1798 by Captain Michael Symes,[5] and the ancient pagoda of Perwattum with its sculptures in South India, by Major Kirkpatrick, from the journals of Captain Colin Mackenzie.[6]

But the most interesting communication of this period is Mr. Jonathan Duncan's account of the discovery of two urns in a so-called tope or stúpa at Sárnáth, about four miles from Benares.[7] This is the first mention of a monument of that class, which thenceforth was destined to prove one of the most important factors in opening up the ancient history of India through the coins, inscriptions, and other objects found in them. "In 1794, a native, digging for stones from extensive ruins at this spot, discovered, twenty-seven feet below the surface, a stone urn, of the size and shape of the Barberini vase enclosing one also

---

[1] As. Res., Vol. IV, p. 409. [2] *Ibid.*, p. 313. [3] *Ibid.*, Vol. XIV, p. 480. [4] *Ibid.*, Vol. IV, p. 419. [5] *Ibid.*, Vol. V, p. 111. [6] *Ibid.*, p. 303. [7] *Ibid.*, p. 131.

of stone, within which were human bones, pearls, gold-leaves, and jewels of no value. A statue of Buddha was also found, bearing an inscription, which stated that a monastery and lofty shrine had been built or rather repaired here in Samvat 1083 (A.D. 1026). The inscription terminated with a stanza, which is now well-known as the "Buddhist creed," and which was also found, when the building was opened in 1835 by Lieutenant (now Major-General) A. Cunningham, upon a stone slab in the interior of the edifice."[1] "A few years afterwards, the visits of Colonel Mackenzie and Mr. Harrington to Ceylon added to the knowledge of the peculiar form of these Buddhist stúpas or topes. At Devendar, or Dondera, the former noticed a low temple, of a circular shape, of about one hundred and sixty feet in circumference, erected on a platform. The structure, it was said, was solid and had one of the teeth of the sacred elephant enshrined in it. Mr. Harrington described a dahgopa at Kalaní as a solid mass of earth and brickwork sixty feet high, and shaped somewhat like a dome with a cupola above. This monumental temple was said to contain twenty images of Buddha buried underneath it. These accounts were published in 1799."[2] In the same year, 1799, was published the first detailed account, with measurements and drawings, of the celebrated caves, and the sculptures they contain, near Ellora, from the pen of Mr. C. W. Malet.[3]

About this time the materials commenced being collected, which a generation afterwards led to the great discovery of Mr. J. Prinsep; for in 1801, Mr. J. H. Harington published a "Book of Drawings and Inscriptions" prepared under the

[1] See Ariana Antiqua, p. 29. As. Res., Vol. IX, p. 203; Vol. X, p. 130. J. A. S. B., Vol. IV, pp. 132, 211, 712. [2] As. Res., Vol. VI, pp. 425, 438, 448. See Ariana Antiqua, pp. 29, 30. [3] As. Res., pp. 382, 389.

direction of Captain James Hoare, and presented by him to the Society, among which the most important were copies of the inscriptions on the celebrated pillars of Dehli and Allahabad.[1] Both were about thirty years afterwards, in 1834 and 1837, republished in a more complete form by Mr. J. Prinsep, in the third and sixth volumes of the Journal, from drawings and copies prepared by Lieutenant T. S. Burt.[2] In 1807, Mr. H. T. Colebrooke published a series of inscriptions on stone and copper of subordinate value. They had been presented to the Society from time to time, and came from Tripura, Gorakhpur, Chitradurg, Kurugode, Kurrah, Dinájpur, Nidigal, Goujda, and Benares.[3] In the same year also were published for the first time by Major C. Mackenzie figures, with inscriptions, of some celebrated Jain statues, especially of the gigantic image of Gomatesvara Svámi near Belligola.[4] A Sanskrit stone inscription of the Chandel Rájas was communicated in 1813 by Lieutenant W. Price, who had found it at the foot of a rocky hill in the vicinity of the town of Mow, about ten miles from Chatterpur.[5] It was the first authentic notice of that line of mediæval princes of Bundelkhand, on whose history subsequent discoveries of inscriptions have thrown so much light.[6]

In 1816, Mr. John Crawford presented to the Society an account of the Buddhist temple ruins situated about Prambanan in Java,[7] and Captain G. Sydenham, of the stately Muhammadan architecture in Bijapur, called "the Palmyra of the Dekkan" by Sir James Mackintosh.[8] In

---

[1] As. Res., Vol. VII, p. 175. [2] J. A. S. B., Vol. III, pp. 105, 114, 118, see also p. 257; and Vol. VI, p. 566, see also p. 963. [3] As. Res., Vol. IX, pp. 398. 401, 406, 412, 421, 422, 432, 434, 438, 441. [4] *Ibid.*, pp. 256, 264, 272. [5] *Ibid.*, Vol. VII, p. 358. [6] J. A. S. B., Vol. VIII, p. 159; Vol. XXXII, p. 273; Vol. XLVII, pp. 73, 80. [7] As. Res., Vol. XIII, p. 337. [8] *Ibid.*, p. 431.

1825, Professor H. H. Wilson published some Sanskrit inscriptions, translated by Captain E. Fell, from Garha Mandela, Hansí, and Benares, which gave a "tolerably satisfactory idea of the series of princes who reigned at Kanauj and Delhi" about the time of the Muhammadan conquest.[1] In the same year, Mr. R. Jenkins presented an account of the ancient Hindu remains in Chattisgarh, together with some copperplate inscriptions, written in the square box-headed characters; a variety of monumental writing first made public on that occasion.[2] Mr. A. Stirling also drew attention to the ancient temples and other antiquities of Orissa. Among the latter is specially noteworthy his copy of a portion of the famous Khandagiri rock inscription in the Asoka characters, then first made known.[3] It was republished in the Journal, in 1837, in a more complete form, by Mr. J. Prinsep, from copies prepared by Lieutenant Kittoe.[4] In the following volume of the Asiatic Researches, in 1828, the Rev. G. H. Hough made known an inscription engraved on the Great Bell of Rangoon.[5] In the same volume Professor H. H. Wilson again published a large series of forty-three Sanskrit inscriptions found on Mount Abú, many of which are of much interest, because "they throw considerable light upon the religious and political history of a place which is of high consideration in the west of India, and elucidate the early career of different Rájpút dynasties," such as the Chalukyas, Pramaras, Guhilas, Chauháns, etc.[6] The Jain temples on Mount Abú, in which some of these inscriptions occur, were described in the Journal of 1833 by Lieutenant Burnes.[7]

---

[1] As. Res., Vol. XV, pp. 436, 437, 443, 446, 460. [2] *Ibid.*, pp. 499, 506.
[3] *Ibid.*, pp. 163, 306, 313, 329, 330, 337. [4] J. A. S. B., Vol. VI, p. 1080.
[5] As. Res., Vol. XVI, p. 270. [6] *Ibid.*, pp. 284, 317. [7] J. A. S. B., Vol. II, p. 161.

The most important event of this time was the opening of the great tope at Manikyála, which had been already observed and described by Elphinstone in 1808.[1] It was effected by General Ventura in 1830. An account of it in French was forwarded by the General to Calcutta and published by Professor H. H. Wilson in the Asiatic Researches in 1832,[2] and republished later, in 1834, in an English version, by Mr. J. Prinsep, in the Journal.[3] Lieutenant Alexander Burnes, who afterward visited the opened tope, made known in 1833 some further particulars concerning it,[4] and so did Major J. Abbot on a much later visit in 1853.[5] A good deal more information on this tope, as well as on some others in the Panjab and in Afghanistan which were opened by General Court and Messrs. Honigberger and Masson respectively, was made public in the Journal for 1834 by Dr. Gerard and Mr. J. Prinsep, derived from the letters and journals of the original discoverers.[6]

The Journal of the year 1834 is particularly rich in the record of discoveries. Thus Captain P. T. Cautly announced the important discovery by him of the remains of an ancient town at Behat, near Saharanpur, seventeen feet below the present surface of the country and upwards of twenty-five below that of the modern town of Behat. Various relics were found, and one hundred and seventy coins, all of very ancient date (Indo-Scythian and early Buddhist), fixing the age of the town in the earliest centuries of our era.[7] Mr. B. H. Hodgson communicated the discovery of three *láths* or monumental pillars, with inscriptions in the Asoka characters on them.

---

[1] See Ariana Antiqua, p. 31. [2] As. Res., Vol. XVII, pp. 563, 600. [3] J. A. S. B., Vol. III, p. 315. [4] *Ibid.*, Vol. II, p. 308. [5] *Ibid.*, Vol. XXII, p. 570. [6] *Ibid.*, Vol. III, pp. 321, 329, 556. [7] *Ibid.*, pp. 43, 221, 227.

Among them were the now well-known Radhiah and Mathiah Pillars. Two of the pillars, those at Bakhrah in Tirhut and Radhiah in Sárun, had been already noticed in 1784 by Mr. Law, and later by Mr. Stirling; and of the Mathiah Pillar Mr. Hodgson himself had sent a notice already ten years previously; but at that time these notices appear to have attracted no attention. Their importance, however, was now recognized by Mr. J. Prinsep, who, seeing at once that the inscriptions they bore were identical with those on the pillars of Allahabad and Dehli, published them in full.[1] At the same time, his attention having been recalled by Mr. Hodgson to the famous Sanchi Tope and its inscriptions near Bhilsa, he reprinted a description of them from the Calcutta Journal of the 11th July, 1819, where it had been published by Captain E. Fell, the original discoverer of the Tope.[2] Several of the inscriptions taken by Captains Smith and Burt, and drawings of the monuments and its sculptures prepared by Captain Murray, were published by Mr. J. Prinsep later on, in the sixth and seventh volumes of the Journal, in 1837 and 1838.[3] They led to important results, enabling Mr. Prinsep, as will be related in another place, to extend his discoveries and to complete the deciphering of the ancient alphabet and inscriptions on the staff of Firoz Shah, on the Buddhist coins of Behat, and on the rocks in Orissa and Guzerat.[4] An important link, however, in the chain of events, which led to these discoveries, was the publication by Mr. W. H. Wathen, in 1835, of two Vallabhi copperplate grants found in the

---

[1] J. A. S. B., Vol. III, pp. 481, 483; and Vol. IV, p. 124. [2] *Ibid.*, Vol. III, pp. 488, 490. [3] *Ibid.*, Vol. VI, pp. 451ff.; Vol. VII, pp. 562ff. [4] See Ariana Antiqua, pp. 33, 34.

western part of Guzerat, and written in an alphabet intermediate between that of Asoka and the Guptas.[1]

In the Journal of the same year, 1835, various ancient ruins were described ; those of Simraun, once the capital of the Mithila Province, by Mr. B. H. Hodgson ;[2] those of an ancient city near Bakhra, north of Patna, by Mr. J. Stephenson ;[3] those at Chárdwár in Assam, by Captain G. E. Westmacott ;[4] and those of the Baijnáth Temple at Harsha in Shekáwati, by Sergeant E. Dean.[5] A long inscription of the tenth century was found in the latter place and published by Dr. W. H. Mill.[6] In the following year, 1836, Mr. C. Masson contributed some notes on the antiquities of Bámián, especially of its caves and colossal idols, which had already been noticed in 1833 by Lieutenant Alexander Burnes.[7] Mr. L. Wilkinson made known a copperplate grant found at Piplianagar in the Shujalpur Perganah, which turned out to be of some importance as it supplemented the list of Rájas of Malva by four hitherto unknown names.[8] Colonel H. Burney reported the discovery of some Buddhist images at Tagoung, the ancient capital of Burma, which were inscribed with the well-known Buddhist creed in Gupta characters and in the Pali language.[9]

By this time copies of such a large number of inscriptions of diverse kinds, which had been discovered from time to time, had been accumulating in the hands of the Society, that it was feared that they might be mislaid or lost sight of, before anyone was found with sufficient leisure to decipher them completely, unless they were at once com-

---

[1] J. A. S. B., Vol. IV, p. 477. [2] *Ibid.*, p. 121. [3] *Ibid.*, p. 128. [4] *Ibid.*, p. 185. [5] *Ibid.*, p. 361. [6] *Ibid.*, p. 367. [7] *Ibid.*, Vol. V, p. 707 ; see also Vol. II, p. 561. [8] *Ibid.*, Vol. V, p. 378 ; see also Vol. VII, p. 736, for another grant. [9] *Ibid.*, Vol. V, p. 157.

mitted to print. Accordingly, Mr. J. Prinsep published in 1836, in the fifth volume of the Journal, a long series of facsimiles of ancient inscriptions, including those from Wara in South Konkan, from the Damatha Cavern near Maulmain, from the fort of Chunár near Benares, from Barahat in Garhwál, from Iskardo in Little Tibet,[1] from the caves of Ajunta,[2] from Asírgarh, from Peshawar (on a bronze image), from Kumaon (on bronze tridents at Barahat and Gopesvara),[3] from Trincomalee and other places in Ceylon,[4] from Buddha Gaya,[5] from Seoni (five copperplates), and a few from unknown places.[6] This series of facsimiles was continued in the volumes for 1837 and 1838, which contain the following inscriptions: from the Amrávati Tope (from Colonel Colin Mackenzie's manuscripts),[7] from Kalanjar in Bundelkhand, from Gumsar (three copperplates), from the Nágárjuní Caves near Gaya, from a rock at Singapur,[8] from Illahabas in the Bareilly District (found by Mr. H. S. Bouldeson in 1826 or 1827), from Mullaye (three copperplates), from Hund near Attock, from Jayanagar in Bundelkhand,[9] from Gorakhpur (on the Kuhaon pillar), from Bakerganj in Eastern Bengal (copperplate), from Ajmir (on a Jain image),[10] from Cuttack (Brahmesvara temple),[11] from Warangal, from Kaira in Guzerat (copperplates),[12] from Bageswar near Almora in Kumaon,[13] and again a few from unknown places.[14]

Early in 1837, the Rev. Dr. W. H. Mill made known a new Gupta inscription, copied by Lieutenant (now Major General) A. Cunningham from the newly-discovered Bhitari

---

[1] J. A. S. B., Vol. V, pp. 340, 341, 347, 348. [2] *Ibid.*, pp. 348, 556. [3] *Ibid.*, pp. 482, 484, 485; see also Vol. VII, p. 39. [4] *Ibid.*, Vol. V, pp. 454, 456. [5] *Ibid.*, p. 657. [6] *Ibid.*, p. 724. [7] *Ibid.*, Vol. VI, p. 218. [8] *Ibid.*, pp. 665, 667, 671, 680; see also Vol. XVII, Part I, p. 154; Part II, p. 66. [9] *Ibid.*, Vol. VI, pp. 869, 876, 887. [10] *Ibid.*, Vol. VII, pp. 33, 40, 51. [11] *Ibid.*, p. 557. [12] *Ibid.*, pp. 901, 908, 966. [13] *Ibid.*, p. 1056. [14] *Ibid.*, Vol. VI, pp. 278, 663.

Lath (or Pillar) in the Ghazipur District,[1] while a little later, Mr. J. Prinsep republished the Gupta inscription on the Allahabad Pillar from impressions taken by Captain Edward Smith.[2] He also published two collections of smaller inscriptions in the most ancient characters, which had been newly made, one by Major Kittoe from the caves at Udayagiri and Khandagiri in Cuttack[3] (Eastern India), the other by Colonel W. H. Sykes from the caves (Karle, Sainhadri) of Western India.[4] In the following year, 1838, he crowned his labours in this direction by the publication of copies of the celebrated great rock inscriptions at Dhauli and Girnar (of Asoka and Chandragupta), together with detailed descriptions of their localities, the materials for which had been supplied to him by Major Kittoe, Captain Lang, Lieutenant Postans, and the Rev. Dr. J. Wilson.[5] To these he added the smaller, though no less important, Gupta inscriptions at Delhi and Eran, taken in ectype by Capt. T. S. Burt.[6] Of the latter, those at Eran were later on, in the year 1861, re-deciphered and re-translated by FitzEdward Hall.[7]

As already mentioned, for much of his information Mr. Prinsep was indebted to Major Kittoe, who had been deputed by the Coal and Mineral Committee to explore the supposed coal-fields of Orissa. He left "with a determination to make the most of his time and journey, also of the small pecuniary allowance made for the purpose, in antiquarian and other research beyond the mere exploring of the coal localities." The results of these antiquarian researches were communicated, in 1838, in the seventh volume of the Journal, including descriptions and drawings of caves

[1] J. A. S. B., Vol. VI, p. 1. [2] *Ibid.*, p. 969. [3] *Ibid.*, p. 1072. [4] *Ibid.*, p. 1038. [5] *Ibid.*, Vol. VII, pp. 219, 334, 434, 865. [6] *Ibid.*, p. 629. [7] *Ibid.*, Vol. XXX, p. 14; see also Vol. XXXIV, p. 38.

(Udayagiri), temples (Gramesvara, and others), pillars (at Jájipur), inscriptions, etc.[1] In the same volume is published an inscription in Burmese and Talain "with an admixture of Pali at the commencement and termination," engraved on a large Arracan Bell, which was taken by Captain Wroughton. This bell was then at Nadrohighat, in the Aligarh District, but had originally belonged to the Gaudama Mani temple in Arracan. The somewhat romantic story of how it was carried off from there by a native non-commissioned officer after the war in 1825 is related in the sixth volume of the Journal.[2] The inscription happens to contain "a scrap of history of no small interest in its way."[3]

With the year 1838 the era of great discoveries may be said to have closed. Not much was done in 1839, but the joint editors of the Journal published a new Chandel inscription discovered and copied by Captain T. S. Burt from a slab in the temple of Lálaji at Khajráo in Bundelkhand,[4] a Chera copperplate grant dug up at Baroda in Guzerat,[5] a Kulachúri copperplate grant dug up at Kumbhi in the Sagar territory,[6] and a Tomára inscription on a slab originally at the fort of Rohtas in Behar.[7] The latter had been brought to their notice by Mr. E. L. Ravenshaw, who also contributed some account of various other antiquities (Persian and Sanskrit inscriptions) in Behar.[8]

The following year, 1840, was again signalised by a small, though most important, discovery. It was that of a new specimen of an Asoka edict, which was found by Captain Burt engraved on a rock near Bairat or Bhabra.[9] Another small contribution was made by Captain Burt, in

---

[1] J. A. S. B., Vol. VII, pp. 53, 660, 679, 828; see also Vol. XXV, p. 222.
[2] *Ibid.*, Vol. VI, p. 1064. [3] *Ibid.*, Vol. VII, p. 287. [4] *Ibid.*, Vol. VIII, p. 159.
[5] *Ibid.*, p. 292. [6] *Ibid.*, p. 487. [7] *Ibid.*, p. 693. [8] *Ibid.*, p. 347. [9] *Ibid.*, Vol. IX, p. 616.

an inscription from Udayapur near Sagar, which deserves particular mention, because the date is given in three eras of Vikramáditya, Saliváhana, and Udayáditya,[1] the last of which was new. Of some importance is also a very ancient inscription from the fort of Behar, communicated by Mr. Ravenshaw, written in badly-formed characters of the Gupta style.[2] Major Jenkins made known an ancient Assamese land grant on three copperplates, dug up near Tezpore in the Durrang Division.[3] Another copper land grant, of the Rathor Prince Jaya Chandra of Kanauj, found near Fyzabad in Oudh, was made known in the following year 1841.[4] But a far more interesting publication of that year was the account of the opening of the ancient topes at Kanheri near Bombay, and at Damuta in Afghanistan, by Dr. James Bird and Lieutenant Pigon respectively. The usual relics, consisting of inscriptions, coins, jewels, etc., were found in them.[5] Lieutenant Alexander Cunningham published a sketch of the second silverplate found by Dr. Lord in Badakshan, a drawing of the first patera having been already given in 1838 in the seventh volume of the Journal.[6] Two inscriptions from the neighbourhood of Mount Abú (Vasantagarh), dated in Samvat 1099 and 1053, both discovered and taken by Captain T. S. Burt, were also made known by the editors of the Journal.[7]

The period including the years 1842 to 1846 is one of the most barren of discoveries, so far as recorded in the pages of the Society's Journal. But the only two communications,—one, in 1842, of an ancient Himaritic stone inscription found near Aden,[8] the other, in 1844, of a

---

[1] J. A. S. B., Vol. IX, p. 545; see also Vol. VII, p. 1056. [2] *Ibid.*, Vol. IX, p. 65; see also Vol. VIII, p. 347. [3] *Ibid.*, Vol. IX, p. 766. [4] *Ibid.*, Vol. X, p. 98. [5] *Ibid.*, pp. 94, 381. [6] *Ibid.*, p. 570; and Vol. VII, p. 1047. [7] *Ibid.*, Vol. X, pp. 664, 819, 821. [8] *Ibid.*, Vol. XI, p. 958.

Chinese inscription on a wooden tablet in a Buddhist monastery at Ningpo,[1]—have at least the interest of illustrating the wide sphere embraced by the researches of the Society.

With the year 1847 a new period of archæological activity commenced, worthily introduced by Captain M. Kittoe, who supplied much fresh information on the numerous antiquities in Behar,[2] especially on the caves and their inscriptions at Barábar,[3] the sculptures at Buddha Gaya, etc.,[4] and the temples and inscriptions at Oomga.[5] Mr. D. Money contributed an account of the ruined old temple of Tribeni near Hughli;[6] Captain J. D. Cunningham, of the antiquities in the districts within the Bhopal Agency, including the well-known topes near Bhilsa;[7] and Mr. Henry Cope, of the ruins of Ranode in the Chandorí District of Scindiah's dominions.[8] Captain James Abbott reported the discovery of some sculptures in the Panjab, showing traces of Greek influence.[9] A higher interest possess the contributions of Mr. William Knighton, who described the dagobahs (or topes) and viháras of Anuradhapura, the former capital of Ceylon, and the rock temples at Dambool, also in Ceylon.[10]

The volume of the following year, 1848, is again replete with descriptions of antiquities; thus, those of Sarguja and its neighbourhood, by Lieutenant-Colonel J. R. Ousley;[11] those at Kalinjar in Bundelkhand, by Lieutenant F. Maisey;[12] those in the vicinity of Suddyah in Upper Assam, by Major S. F. Hannay;[13] those at Pukarí, near Udayapur, by Captain J. D. Cunningham.[14] A few inscriptions were also pub-

[1] J. A. S. B., Vol. XIII, p. 113. [2] *Ibid.*, Vol. XVI, p. 272. [3] *Ibid.*, p. 401. [4] *Ibid.*, p. 334. [5] *Ibid.*, pp. 656, 1220. [6] *Ibid.*, p. 393. [7] *Ibid.*, p. 739. [8] *Ibid.*, p. 1079. [9] *Ibid.*, p. 664. [10] *Ibid.*, pp. 213, 340. [11] *Ibid.*, Vol. XVII, Part I, p. 65. [12] *Ibid.*, p. 171. [13] *Ibid.*, p. 459. [14] *Ibid.*, p. 305.

lished, one from the Vijaya Mandir in Udayapur, another of a copperplate grant,[1] and a third, a Buddhist one, of rather more interest, from the village of Pesserawa in Bihar.[2] Of still greater interest, however, were a few small inscriptions in the ancient Gupta characters, found on a granite rock at a place called Tokoon, almost directly east of Penang town in the peninsula of Malacca, and forwarded by Lieutenant-Colonel James Low.[3] In the following year, 1849, another similar inscription was sent by him from Keddah, near Buket Murriam.[4] In the same year, Captain James Abbott reported the discovery by him of remains of Greek sculptures in Potawar or the tableland between the Indus and Jelum in the Panjab;[5] and Dr. Impey announced the discovery of the famous colossal Jain figure on a spur of the Satpura Range in the district of Burwání on the Nerbada. It is a colossal rock image cut in relief, nearly 80 feet high, and second only in magnitude to the celebrated so-called Bhúts at Bamiyan,[6] and about twice as large as the colossal figures at Kassia in the Gorakhpur District[7] and at Belligola in Mysore.[8] Two years later another colossal figure, of a head only, near Bhagalpur, was made known by Captain W. S. Sherwell. It had been, however, already noticed by Dr. Buchanan in 1810.[9] The preceding year, 1850, had brought only two small inscriptions, one on a brick found in a field in the Jaunpur District by Captain M. Kittoe,[10] and another, a Malva land grant, on two copperplates dug out by Mr. R. N. C. Hamilton near Oujein and published by Babu Rájendralála Mitra.[11]

---

[1] J. A. S. B., Vol. XVII, Part I, pp. 68, 71. [2] *Ibid.*, p. 492. [3] *Ibid.*, Part II, pp. 62, 71. [4] *Ibid.*, Vol. XVIII, p. 247. [5] *Ibid.*, p. 131. [6] *Ibid.*, p. 918. [7] *Ibid.*, Vol. VI, p. 477. [8] As. Res., Vol. IX, p. 264. [9] J. A. S. B., Vol. XX, p. 272. [10] *Ibid.*, Vol. XIX, p. 454. [11] *Ibid.*, p. 475.

The following ten years were not much more fruitful, though each year brought some more or less important discovery. Thus in 1851 we have a very short notice of certain hitherto unvisited rockcut caves near the village of Marah in Singbhúm, which had been seen by the Rev. Mather in January, 1850;[1] and of a fine ancient stone bridge (Sil Hako) near Gowhatty in the Kamrup District.[2] In 1852, we have detailed descriptions by Mr. W. Jackson and Mr. (now Sir) E. C. Bayley of sculptures found in the Peshawur District and exhibiting traces of Greek influence.[3] In 1853 there is a notice of an inscription from Pehewa in the Thaneswar District found by Mr. Bowering and published by Babu Rájendralála Mitra.[4] The year 1854 brings us the two now well-known rock inscriptions found by Mr. E. C. Bayley on two large granite boulders about thirty yards apart, near the village of Khunniára in the Kángra District. Though exceedingly small, consisting of only two or three words, they are of extreme interest, seeing that they are duplicates in the ancient Arian Páli and Indian Páli characters respectively.[5] In the same year Mr. E. Thomas also published the result of the final excavations, so far as made by Captain M. Kittoe and himself, on the site of the well-known old tope and monastery at Sárnáth near Benares.[6] This report was continued, in the twenty-fifth volume of the Journal in 1856, from official papers communicated by the Government of the N. W. Provinces. In 1855 there is an important contribution by Captain E. Taite Dalton, giving a full description of the antiquities of Assam, especially its temples and sculptures (in Gow-

---

[1] J. A. S. B., Vol. XX, p. 283. [2] *Ibid.*, p. 291. [3] *Ibid.*, Vol. XXI, pp. 511, 606.
[4] *Ibid.*, Vol. XXII, p. 673; see also Vol. XXXII, p. 97; Vol. XXXIII, p. 223.
[5] *Ibid.*, Vol. XXIII, p. 57. [6] *Ibid.*, p. 469. [7] *Ibid.*, Vol. XXV, p. 395.

hatty, Tejpore, Seesee, and other places).[1] There is also a very meagre notice of the ruins of the deserted city of Dhúlme in Maubhúm by Mr. Henry Piddington.[2]

With 1857 begins a series of valuable contributions on the antiquities of Burma. It was commenced by Captain Henry Yule, on the ancient Buddhist remains, chiefly temples at Pugán on the Iráwadí,[3] and continued by Colonel (now Sir) A. P. Phayre, who, in 1860 added an account of an ancient Buddhist monastery, in 1863 of an old Burmese inscription, and in 1864 of some ancient tiles at the same place.[4] In 1858, Mr. FitzEdward Hall published two copper land grants of the Rathore Princes, Madanapála and Govinda Chandra of Kanauj, neither of very great importance;[5] and in the following year, 1859, he added a Sanskrit stone inscription, from Harsauda in the Hoshangabad District, of an unknown prince Devapála, recording the construction of a temple and a tank.[6] In the previous year, Mr. Henry Cope also made known a series of six Persian inscriptions, mostly of the earliest Moghul Emperors, all of which exist on certain public buildings in Lahor.[7]

With the year 1861 contributions describing archæological discoveries again began to become more numerous. Thus several very important land grants were made known in that year, among them especially two grants, on two and three copperplates respectively, of king Hastin, which, being dated in terms both of the Gupta era and the Jovian Cycle, are of extreme value for the determination of the initial year of that ancient era. They are said to have

---

[1] J. A. S. B., Vol. XXIV, p. 1. [2] *Ibid.*, p. 207. [3] *Ibid.*, Vol. XXVI, p. 1. [4] *Ibid.*, Vol. XXIX, p. 346; Vol. XXXII. p. 267; Vol. XXXIII, p. 57. [5] *Ibid.*, Vol XXVII, pp. 217, 241. [6] *Ibid.*, Vol. XXVIII, p. 1. [7] *Ibid.*, Vol. XXVII, p. 308.

been procured from Nagode in Bundelkhand, and are now deposited in the Benares College.[1] A third is a large stone inscription from Belhari, which throws much light on the old kingdom of Chedi and its Kulachúri princes.[2] A fourth is a Malava land grant on two copper-plates of the tenth century, found not far from Indore.[3] These four inscriptions were all made public by Mr. FitzEdward Hall. In the same year, it may be mentioned, Babu Rájendralála Mitra republished from Mr. E. Thomas's edition of J. Prinsep's Indian Antiquities[4] the important Arian Páli inscription, which had been discovered by Mr. Masson on a brass vase in one of the Wardak topes in Afghanistan.[5] The same made known in the following year, 1862, a number of relics and a small Arian Páli inscription found by Captain Stubbs not far from Ráwal Pindi in the Panjab, where they had been exhumed from the centre of some ruins.[6] Mr. FitzEdward Hall again published three more copper land grants of the Kulachúri princes of Chedi, one of which, however, had already appeared previously in the Journal of 1839.[7] The most valuable contribution, however, was one by Lieutenant-Colonel Henry Yule on the ancient Indian remains, both Buddhistic and Brahmanical, in the Island of Java, the existence of some of which was known from the earlier accounts of Messrs. Raffles and Crawfurd. The temples now described were those of Mundot, Boro Bodor, and Brambanan.[8] In 1863, there are an account by the Rev. J. Lœwenthal of some antiquities in the Peshawar

---

[1] J. A. S. B., Vol. XXX, p. 1; see also Genl. A. Cunningham's Arch. Report, Vol. X, Appendix. [2] J. A. S. B., Vol. XXX, p. 317. [3] *Ibid.*, p. 195. [4] See Ind. Ant.. Vol. I, p. 163. [5] J. A. S. B., Vol. XXX, p. 337. [6] *Ibid.*, Vol. XXXI, p. 175; see also *ibid.*, p. 184. [7] *Ibid.*, p. 111; see also Vol. VIII, p. 481. [8] *Ibid.*, Vol. XXXI, pp. 16, 20, 24.

District,[1] and some remarks on the Taxila and other Arian Páli inscriptions by Major-General A. Cunningham and Babu Rájendralála Mitra.[2] The latter also published two stone inscriptions, one a Chandel one from Kajráha in Bundelkhand, the other a Chedi one from Ratanpur in the province of Nágpur.[3] It may be mentioned here, that, in the volume of the Journal for the year 1863, General A. Cunningham's Archæological Survey Report was published for the first time as a 'supplementary number,' communicated by the Government of India. This practice was only continued, however, for three years, the Archæological Reports published in the three Journals being for the years 1861—1864.[4]

General Cunningham's operation undoubtedly gave a new stimulus to archæological researches; for, during the next following years, contributions on this subject to the Journal grew more and more numerous, so much so that some of the volumes are almost entirely taken up by them. For the most part, however, these contributions refer to remains, not of the highest antiquity, but of the middle ages, immediately before and after the Muhammadan conquest of India. Thus, in 1864, the Rev. J. Lœwenthal sent some Persian inscriptions recorded in the tombs and mosques of Srinagar in Kashmir.[5] Captain C. Glasfurd reported on the Hindu antiquities (temples, ruins, sculptures, and inscriptions) of Bustar, about eight hundred years old.[6] From Captain H. Mackenzie there is a short note on the antiquities of Guzerat, including some inscriptions from Hailan.[7] Babu Rájendralála Mitra published

---

[1] J. A. S. B., Vol. XXXII, p. 1. [2] *Ibid.*, pp. 139, 151; see also Vol. XXXIII, p. 35. [3] *Ibid.*, Vol. XXXII, pp. 273, 277. [4] *Ibid.*, p. i (for 1861-1862); Vol. XXXIII, p. i. (for 1863-1864); Vol. XXXIV, p. 295 (for 1862-1863). [5] *Ibid.*, Vol. XXXIII, p. 278. [6] *Ibid.*, p. 44. [7] *Ibid.*, pp. 402, 549.

a copper land grant of Mahendrapála Deva of Kanauj, found at Digheva Dúbanesar in the Sárun District.[1] He also described some ancient Buddhist remains of a monastery excavated by Mr. Harris in connection with the East Indian Railway at Sultanganj. In it, among other relics, a colossal copper figure of Buddha was discovered.[2]

It had all along been well known that Benares was in a sensethe "birthplace of Buddhism;" yet, strange to say, hitherto few or no Buddhist remains in the city proper had been discovered, but the reason of this was that they had never been sought after. It is true, extensive ruins had been found at Sárnáth, but they were three miles distant from the present city. Accordingly a search was made in the course of the year 1863 by the Rev. M. A. Sherring and Mr. C. Horne, jointly, with much success, and an account of the remains discovered at Bakaríyakund, Rájghát and other places, was communicated by them in 1865 and 1866.[3] They also reported on some ancient remains at Saidpúr and Bhitari, which hitherto had escaped notice.[4] Mr. C. Horne himself added a note on the already much discussed ruins of Buddha Gaya, on which subject there is also a note by Mr. W. Peppe in 1866, and by Babu Rájendralála Mitra in 1864.[5] The latter also published an important inscription of the Sena Rájas of Bengal, found by Mr. C. T. Metcalfe near Deoparah in Rájsháhi, which gave fresh information on the earlier members of that royal house.[6] In 1866, the Rev. W. G. Cowie described some of the temples of Kashmir, which had been left unnoticed by General A. Cunningham in

[1] J. A. S. B., Vol. XXXIII, p. 321. [2] *Ibid.*, p. 360. [3] *Ibid.*, Vol. XXXIV, p. 1; Vol. XXXV, p. 61; see also Vol. XLII, p. 160. [4] *Ibid.*, Vol. XXXIV p. 80. [5] *Ibid.*, p. 278; Vol. XXXV, p. 49; Vol. XXXIII, p. 173. [6] *Ibid.*, Vol. XXXIV, p. 128.

his Essay published in the Journal for 1848;[1] and three years later, in 1869, Lieutenant-Colonel D. F. Newall again added the description of a few more, those of Razdan in the Lar Pergunnah.[2] Captain W. R. Melville reported the discovery of some "totally new Buddhist ruins" of a temple, containing some sculptures and an inscription, situated at Dúb Kúnd in Eastern Rajputána.[3] Mr. W. J. Herschel described a very curious old fort and temple of Chandrarekhagarh, which he found in the jungle near Sashtaní in the Midnapúr District,[4] and Lieutenant-Colonel E. T. Dalton, some antiquities in Manbhúm, some of which had been already previously noticed.[5] Babu Rájendralála Mitra made known a copper land grant from Sambalpur,[6] and the important well-known inscriptions of the later Guptas from Aphsar and Bihar, one of which had been already before published in 1840.[7] In the Journal for 1867, Mr. C. Horne continued his antiquarian papers, one on the Jumma Masjid of Etawah, originally a Hindu temple, another on the Buddhist remains in the Mainpuri District, and a third on the carvings on the Buddhist rail-posts at Buddha Gaya.[8] A similar instance of a Hindu temple converted into a mosque was noted by Mr. W. Herschel in the following year, 1868, at Gaganesvar in the Midnapur District.[9] Babu Gaur Dass Bysack described the antiquities of Bágerhát, fifty miles south of Jessore, consisting of Muhammadan tombs and mosques, not more than four hundred years old;[10] and Lieutenant Ayrton Pullan, some ancient Hindu temple

---

[1] J. A. S. B., Vol. XXXV, p. 91; see also Vol. XVII, p. 241. [2] *Ibid.*, Vol. XXXVIII, p. 177. [3] *Ibid.*, Vol. XXXV, p. 168. [4] *Ibid.*, p. 181. [5] *Ibid.*, p. 186. [6] *Ibid.*, p. 195. [7] *Ibid.*, p. 268; see also Vol. IX, p. 65. [8] *Ibid.*, Vol. XXXVI, pp. 74, 105, 107, 157. [9] *Ibid.*, Vol. XXXVII, p. 73. [10] *Ibid.*, Vol. XXXVI, p. 126.

ruins and sculptures in the dense forest at the foot of the Himálayas between Gharwál and Rohilkhund.[1] From Dr. A. Bastian was received the translation of an inscription existing "inside the great temple at Nakhon Vat in Kambodia."[2] In 1869, Babu Pratap Chandra Ghosha published a copper land grant of the Dor Rájas at Manpur in the Bulandshahar District;[3] and in 1871, two other copper land grants found at Chaibása in Singbhúm.[4]

The year 1870 brought some more than usually interesting accounts of discoveries. Among these was the well-known Arian Páli copperplate inscription, found in a ruined Buddhist tower at Sue Vihár near Bhawalpur, which Mr. (now Sir) E. C. Bayley made known with a tentative reading, and of which a correct translation was published about ten years later by the writer of this Review.[5] No less important was the celebrated series of Mathura inscriptions, which Babu Rájendralála Mitra made public. They were engraved on the remains of Buddhist buildings and sculptures, dating from the time of the Indo-Scythian kings. These remains had been found already in 1862 by Mr. Best, the Collector of Mathura, and had been removed to Calcutta in 1863, but the inscriptions on them had, until now, not been published.[6] Of no inconsiderable interest was also the series of Arabic and Persian inscriptions scattered over Bengal, the publication of which was commenced by Mr. H. Blochmann in the same year 1870, and by the help of which it afterwards became possible to correct and supplement the Muhammadan historians of Bengal and construct a trustworthy history of that province under its Muham-

---

[1] J. A. S. B., Vol. XXXVI, p. 154. [2] *Ibid.*, p. 76. [3] *Ibid.*, Vol. XXXVIII, p. 21. [4] *Ibid.*, Vol. XL, p. 161. [5] *Ibid.*, Vol. XXXIX, p. 65; and Proceedings for 1881, p. 139. [6] *Ibid.*, Vol. XXXIX, p. 117; see also General A. Cunningham's Arch. Rep. in J. A. S. B., Vol. XXXIV, p. 155.

madan rulers. The inscriptions, together with notes on the buildings in which they occurred, which were made public by Mr. Blochmann in the year 1870, were from Tribeni, Mulla Simla, Sátgánw, Panduah, and Dínánáth in the Hughli District.[1] In 1871 followed inscriptions from Burdwan and Gaur, together with a few others not belonging to Bengal;[2] and in 1872, some from Dinájpúr, Dháká, Dhámrái, Badaon, and 'Alápúr.[3] Finally, from 1873 to 1875, came his well-known contributions to the geography and history of Bengal during the Muhammadan period, based partly on the inscriptions already published, partly on others which were now first made known.[4]

To return again to the year 1870, Mr. J. D. Tremlett described some of the ancient Hindu and Pathan buildings of historical or architectural interest situated in or around the site of old Dehli, which had been left unnoticed in the Archæological Reports of General Cunningham.[5] There are also some notes of lesser interest on the antiquities of the Nalti, the Assia and the Maháviṇayaka Hills of Cuttack by Babu Chandrasekhara Banurji,[6] supplemented afterwards, in 1875, by Mr. J. Beames, on the Alti Hills;[7] also some notice of the archæological remains at Shah-ki-Dheri and the site of Taxila in the Punjab by Mr. J. G. Delmerick,[8] and of three sets of coppor land grants discovered in the Vizagapatam District, by the Rev. T. Foulkes.[9] In 1871, there was an important report by Captain W. L. Samuells on the discovery of ruins of rock-cut temples of the

[1] J. A. S. B., Vol. XXXIX, pp. 280, 283, 291, 292, 300, 302. [2] *Ibid.*, Vol. XL, pp. 251, 256, 258. [3] *Ibid.*, Vol. XLI, pp. 102, 107, 109, 110, 112. [4] *Ibid.*, Vol. XLII, p. 209; Vol. XLIII, p. 280; Vol. XLIV, p. 275. [5] *Ibid.*, Vol. XXXIX, p. 70. [6] *Ibid.*, p. 158. [7] *Ibid.*, Vol. XLIV, p. 19. [8] *Ibid.*, Vol. XXXIX, p. 89, [9] *Ibid.*, p. 153.

ninth or tenth century at Harchoka on the Rewa and Chutiya-Nágpúr frontier.[1] There were also some less important notes on the antiquities of Jájpur in Orissa by Babu Chandrasekhara Banurji;[2] and on three rather modern inscriptions, one of them in Hindi verse, found in Chutiya-Nágpúr, by Babu Rakhal Das Haldar.[3] Mr. J. Beames also contributed notices of Buddhist ruins at Kopari in the Balasore District,[4] and in the following year, 1872, some more on the remains at Chhatiya near Katak.[5] In the same year the antiquities of the much-discussed and much-described home of Buddhism, Bihar, was once more treated very fully by Mr. A. M. Broadley.[6]

Hitherto the historic remains of ancient and mediæval India had almost entirely monopolised the attention of the Society, but now the so-called prehistoric remains also began to be drawn within the sphere of their research. One of the first moves in this direction had already been made in 1870 by Colonel Sir A. Phayre, who reported the discovery of a circle of tall, upright stones near Sung Butte in the district of Yusufzai in Afghanistan.[7] Col. E. T. Dalton now contributed, in 1873, a description of rude sepulchral stone monuments in Chutiya-Nágpúr and other places.[8] The subject was continued some years later, in a series of papers, by Mr. H. Rivett-Carnac, who described in 1877 the ancient sculpturings (cup-marks, circles, &c.) to be seen on rocks in Kumaon, similar to those found on monoliths and rocks in Europe;[9] in 1879, the prehistoric remains in Central India (Nágpúr, etc.);[10] and in 1883, stone implements from the N.-W. Provinces of India.[11]

---

[1] J. A. S. B., Vol. XL, p. 177. [2] *Ibid.*, p. 151. [3] *Ibid.*, p. 108. [4] *Ibid.*, p. 247. [5] *Ibid.*, Vol. XLI, p. 7. [6] *Ibid.*, p. 209. [7] *Ibid.*, Vol. XXXIX, p. 58. [8] *Ibid.*, Vol. XLII, p. 112. [9] *Ibid.*, Vol. XLVI, p. 1. [10] *Ibid.*, Vol. XLVIII, p. 1. [11] *Ibid.*, Vol. LII, p. 221.

Mr. W. King, also, noticed in 1877 a prehistoric burial-place with cruciform monoliths, near Mungapet in the Nizam's dominions.[1]

In the volume of 1873, Babu Rájendralála Mitra published copper land grants of the Rathore prince Govinda Chandra of Kanauj of the twelfth century A.D.;[2] and in the following year, 1874, two more inscriptions, one on stone, from the Pálam Báoli in the Dehli District,[3] of the thirteenth century, and another far more important one, on a copperplate, of the time of Chandragupta in the fourth century, discovered by General Cunningham at Indor near Anupshahar on the Ganges.[4] Another copper land grant found near Chittagong, of the thirteenth century, was made known by Babu Prannáth Pandit.[5] Dr. Wise noticed some Muhammadan antiquities about Sanargaon in Eastern Bengal;[6] and Colonel E. T. Dalton, a large Muhammadan picture, representing the conquest of Palaman in 1660 by Daud Khán, Aurangzib's General.[7]

The temple ruins of Assam, a subject which, though well worthy of research, had been neglected since 1855, was now taken up again by Major H. H. Godwin-Austen, who described the ruins at Dimápur,[8] and Mr J. M. Foster, who described those at Jayaságar.[9] In 1875, Mr. E. Vesey Westmacott noticed an inscribed pillar and other traces of Buddhism in Dinájpur and Bagura.[10] He also published a copper land grant of Lakhsman Sen found in a small tank at the former place.[11] Mr. F. S. Growse published some Bacchanalian sculptures which had been found in Mathurá in 1836, hitherto considered to be Grecian, but which he thought might be Buddhist or Brahmanic.[12] He

---

[1] J. A. S. B., Vol. XLVI, p. 179. [2] *Ibid.*, Vol. XLII, p. 314. [3] *Ibid.*, Vol. XLIII, p. 104. [4] *Ibid.*, p. 363. [5] *Ibid.*, p. 318. [6] *Ibid.*, p. 82. [7] *Ibid.*, p. 240. [8] *Ibid.*, p. 1. [9] *Ibid.*, p. 311. [10] *Ibid.*, Vol. XLIV, p. 187. [11] *Ibid.*, p. 1. [12] *Ibid.*, Vol. XLV, p. 212.

afterwards, in 1878, 1879 and 1883, followed up his researches by exhaustive notes on the antiquities of Mathurá and Bulandshahar.[1] In the volume for 1877, Babu Chandrasekhara Banurji also noticed some of the antiquities met with in the Kaimur Range;[2] and Babu Rangalála Banerji made known an important copper land grant, found in the Record Office of Katak, of the Kalinga prince Yayáti during the reign of Siva Gupta,[3] while Babu Pratapa Chandra Ghosha published another copper land grant (on three plates) of the same early period, dug out in the Tributary State of Patna in the Sambalpur District.[4] In 1878, three copper land grants of the Chandel Rájas were brought to notice by Dr. Rájendralála Mitra and Mr. V. A. Smith.[5] The latter followed this up in 1879, in conjunction with Mr. F. C. Black, by descriptions of some Chandel antiquities at Khajráho and Mahoba, which had not been fully noticed by General Cunningham in his Archæological Survey Reports.[6] In 1880, Major Jarrett noticed a small Persian inscription found upon a stone lying near the ruins of a mosque on Lanka Island in the Walar Lake in Kashmir, of the time of Sultan Zayn-úl-A'ábidin;[7] and Mr. H. Rivett-Carnac contributed some account of so-called "spindle whorls" and votive seals found at Sankisa, Behar, and other Buddhist ruins in the North-Western Provinces of India.[8]

In the following year, 1881, General A. Cunningham commenced a valuable series of descriptions of ancient Persian relics in gold, silver, and copper, mostly belonging to a large treasure found in 1877, on the north bank of the

---

[1] J. A. S. B., Vol. XLVII, p. 97; Vol. XLVIII, p. 270; and Vol. LII, p. 275.
[2] *Ibid.*, Vol. XLVI, p. 16. [3] *Ibid.*, p. 149. [4] *Ibid.*, p. 173. [5] *Ibid.*, Vol. XLVII, pp. 73, 80. [6] *Ibid.*, Vol. XLVIII, p. 285. [7] *Ibid.*, Vol. XLIX, p. 16.
[8] *Ibid.*, p. 127.

Oxus, near the town of Tahht-i-Kuwat.[1] He continued it in two memoirs in the volume for 1883.[2] In 1882, Mr. P. N. Bose reported the discovery by him of some earthen pots found in an ancient well at Mahesvara, similar to those found in the ancient town of Behat.[3] Dr. Rájendralála Mitra followed, in 1883, with a notice of a stone inscription of the fifteenth century found in the old Fort of Deogarh in the Lalitpur District,[4] and with an exhaustive description of the temples of Deogarh in the Santhal Pergunnahs.[5] The last year of the Society's century closes with the account, by Mr. R. Roskell Bayne, of the discovery of the very modern, though in some respects not the least interesting, remains of portions of the Old Fort William in Calcutta, as it existed towards the end of the last century.[6]

---

[1] J. A. S. B., Vol. L, p. 151. [2] *Ibid.*, Vol. LII, pp. 64, and 258. [3] *Ibid.*, Vol. LI, p. 226. [4] *Ibid.*, Vol. LII, p. 67. [5] *Ibid.*, p. 164. [6] *Ibid.*, p. 105.

CHAPTER II.

COINS.

[Roman and Greek — Bactrian — Indo-Scythian — Sassanian — Buddhist — Surashtrian — Arakanese — Ghaznavite — Gupta — Buddhist Satraps — Punch-coins — Nága, Mitra, Kunanda, &c. — Muhammadan, of Bengal, Dehli, Jaunpur, &c. — South Indian — Homerite and Sabæan — Persian and Greek.]

THE first notice on the subject of Numismatic research occurs as early as the year 1790 in the second volume of the Asiatic Researches. It refers to the discovery, near Nelor in Southern India, of a number of "Roman Coins and Medals of the second century," reported in a letter of Mr. Alexander Davidson.[1] After this "there is nothing of numismatic interest in the volumes of the Asiatic Researches, until some time subsequent to Colonel Tod's publication in the Transactions of the Royal Asiatic Society of a memoir upon Greek, Parthian, and Indian medals, illustrated by engravings. It must not be inferred, however, that the subject was one of easy prosecution, or that it had been entirely neglected. There were not many private individuals in India who had the means or opportunities of forming collections of coins, and it was long after the institution of the Asiatic Society, in 1814, that any attempt was made to form a museum in connection with it of any description."[2] Gradually, however, a small collection was formed, partly from coins given by various members from time to time, but princi-

[1] As. Res., Vol. II, p. 332. [2] J. A. S. B., Vol. I, p. 392; As. Res., Vol. XII, App., p. v.; Pref. Wilson's Ariana Antiqua, pp. 4, 6.

pally from duplicates presented by the Government ot Bengal, from the late Colonel Mackenzie's collection. From these, aided by a few others, Professor H. H. Wilson prepared an account of select Hindu coins in the Society's Cabinet in 1831.[1] The author was assisted in this undertaking by Mr. J. Prinsep, and the zealous interest which the latter thus learned to take in the subject of Indian numismatics did not cease with the occasion, and the continuance of his labours not only, but the stimulation of a similar interest in other parts of India, may be considered as the most important consequence of the publication of the paper in question.[2] The first fruits of Mr. J. Prinsep's new interest in coins was a description, in 1832, of the "Ancient Roman Coins in the Cabinet of the Asiatic Society,"[3] and in 1833, of the Greek coins in the same Cabinet.[4]

Not long before, in 1830, General Ventura had excavated the celebrated Manikyála Tope, in which he had found a number of unknown curious coins, now known as Indo-Scythian. In the beginning of 1832, Lieutenant Burnes, on his way to Bokhara, visited Manikyála and inspected General Ventura's operations. The Bactrian and Indo-Scythian coins which he found on that occasion were described by Mr. J. Prinsep in 1833, together with some others with which he had been supplied;[5] and it may be noted that on one of the former the now well-known name of Kanerkes was for the first time distinctly legible. To his description Mr. J. Prinsep added some remarks on the historical bearings of the coins, and some speculations as to the appropriations of such as were least known.

---

[1] As. Res., Vol. XVII, p. 560. [2] See Ariana Antiqua, p. 8. [3] J. A. S. B., Vol. I, p. 392. [4] *Ibid.*, Vol. II, p. 27. [5] *Ibid.*, Vol. III, p. 310.

He little anticipated at that time the extent to which materials were about to pour in upon him, or the important conclusions which he was consequently enabled to establish or suggest. Only two months later, in the same year, he was enabled to publish a description and engravings of eighteen coins, Bactrian and Hindu, chiefly from the collection of Dr. Swiney, amongst which were now made known, for the first time, some of the drachmae, no doubt spoken of by Arrian, those of Menander and Apollodotus. Some other coins, since known to belong to Indo-Scythic and Hindu princes, were also now, for the first time, delineated and described.[1]

An accession of unexpected extent was soon after, in 1834, made through Mr. Masson's explorations of the ancient topes in Afghanistan, especially at a place named Beghram, of which an account was communicated to the public through the Journal.[2] Mr. Masson continued his researches about Beghram during the four succeeding years, and collected in this interval above thirty thousand coins. A further account of these operations is given in the Journal for 1836.[3] Among the coins discovered by him are not only new ones of Greek princes already known, but also those of several whose names are not mentioned in history, as Antialkides, Lysias, Agathocles, Archebias, Pantaleon, and Hermæus. He also found the coins of the king whose titles only are specified as the Great King of Kings, the Preserver, and of others whose names, although assuming a Greek form, indisputably denote barbaric or Indo-Scythic princes—Undopherres, Azes, Azilises, Kadphises, and Kanerkes. The first great step in the series of

[1] J. A. S. B., Vol. II, pp. 37, 405. See Ariana Antiqua, pp. 9, 10. [2] J. A. S. B., Vol. III, p. 153. See Ariana Antiqua, p. 10. [3] J. A. S. B., Vol. V, p. 1. See Ariana Antiqua, p. 11.

Bactrian numismatic discovery was thus accomplished, and the great object of later investigations became only to complete and extend the structure, of which such broad foundations had been laid.[1]

In consequence of a remark made by Mr. J. Prinsep in the previous volume of the Journal,[2] intimating the hope that a more precise account of General Ventura's discoveries might be published in its pages, which remark was communicated to that officer, he immediately, with the most disinterested liberality, placed his collection at the disposal of Mr. Prinsep. The latter, in the Journal for 1834, devoted two memoirs to the description of the General's collection.[3] The coins were Sassanian and Indo-Scythic. The former added to their usual characteristic types and legends the peculiarity of a Nágarí inscription, which, though then unintelligible, was afterwards, in 1838, deciphered by Mr. Prinsep in its entirety as referring to Persian princes, though of unknown and uncertain appellations.[4] The Indo-Scythic coins were of the Kanerkes type, and, by comparison with some of the same kind sent by others, the legends on them, written in a barbarised form of Greek, were completely read by Mr. Prinsep.[5] In the same Journal the latter also described some coins found by Captain (afterwards General) Court in another tope at Manikyála, which he had opened himself;[6] a description which, in one point, was corrected by Lieutenant (now Major-General) A. Cunningham.[7]

---

[1] See Ariana Antiqua, p. 12. [2] J. A. S. B., Vol. II, p. 308. [3] *Ibid.*, Vol. III, pp. 313, 436. See Ariana Antiqua, p. 13. [4] J. A. S. B., Vol. VII, p. 418. [5] See Ariana Antiqua, p. 14. [6] J. A. S. B., Vol. III, p. 562. See also Captain Court's Memoir, *ibid.*, p. 556. [7] *Ibid.*, p. 635. See, however, Journal des Savants, February, 1836, p. 71; and Ariana Antiqua, p. 15.

The interest excited by the coins and relics of the Panjab and the districts beyond the Indus, stimulated persons less favourably circumstanced than the officers of Ranjit Singh to look around them for such remains of past times as India Proper might afford; and the search was not in vain. A curious discovery was made in 1833, by Captain Cautley, of the site of an ancient town near Behat in the Doab, which was seventeen feet below the surface of the soil.[1] It was laid bare in clearing out the bed of a canal, and, amongst other relics, a number of coins were found.[2] These were engraved and described by Mr. Prinsep in the Journal for 1834; some were rude specimens of Indo-Scythic coins, but others formed a new series distinguished by peculiar types and ancient Sanskrit characters.[3] Their publication soon produced others of a similar description. Two procured at Chitore were sent by Major Stacy; others were obtained by Lieutenant Conolly at Kanauj, and several were comprised in the Cabinet of Dr. Swiney. These were also described and delineated by Mr. Prinsep, who pointed out that the inscriptions on them were in the ancient Indian Pali alphabet.[4] Three years later, in 1837, after having discovered the key to that alphabet, he deciphered the inscriptions, when sufficiently distinct. From other specimens, since found in better preservation, it is now known that they belonged to ancient Hindu princes (Mitras, Dattas, Devas, Kunindas, Yaudheyanas), who, as shown by the symbols on the coins, professed the Buddhist faith, and who must have belonged to a period when Buddhism prevailed in Upper Hindustan.[5]

---

[1] J. A. S. B., Vol. III, p. 43. See Ariana Antiqua, p. 16. [2] J. A. S. B., p. 221. [3] *Ibid.*, p. 227. [4] *Ibid.*, pp. 431, 433. See Ariana Antiqua, p. 16. [5] See J. A. S. B., Vol. VI, p. 463; Vol. VII, pp. 1047, 1052.

At the same time another family of Indian coins was brought to notice — the coins of Kanauj. Some specimens had already appeared in 1832, in the seventeenth volume of the Researches,[1] but little was known of their appropriation. The legends on them were in the same characters as the second inscription on the celebrated Allahabad Pillar, and the decipherment of the latter by Dr. Mill, in 1834,[2] determined them as belonging to a dynasty of princes bearing the family designation of Gupta. Some of the Gupta coins found at Kanauj by Lieutenant Conolly were described and figured by Mr. Prinsep in the Journal,[3] and others were reported by Mr. Tregear as having been obtained at Jaunpur.[4]

Thus, by the end of 1834, or in less than two years from the first attempt made in Calcutta to describe and delineate the ancient coins of India, vast numbers of the Greek coins of Bactria had been obtained, many bearing the names of kings never heard of before; and equal numbers of the coins of the Indo-Scythic kings who succeeded the Greeks, and of the two families of the coins of Behat and Kanauj—acquisitions which would have lingered on unnoticed and unprofitable for an indefinite period, had not Mr. Prinsep, then the editor of the Society's Journal, been ever at hand to aid and encourage and make known the successful exertions of all who preceded or accompanied him in numismatic research.[5]

The next contribution to the subject by Mr. Prinsep constitutes an important epoch in its history. It had been all along observed that all the later Bactrian and earlier Indo-Scythian coins, while they presented Greek inscriptions on

---

[1] As. Res., Vol. XVII, p. 568, fig. 5, 7, 12, 13, 14, 16, 17, 18, 19. [2] J. A. S. B., Vol. III, p. 257. [3] *Ibid.*, p. 229. [4] *Ibid.*, p. 617. [5] See Ariana Antiqua, p. 18.

one face, offered on the reverse a legend in unknown characters. Having bestowed on these coins a deliberate investigation, Mr. Prinsep published another memoir, more fully descriptive of all which had been sent to him, or of which he had any knowledge up to the middle of the year 1835. The result of his investigation he stated to be, that it brought to light the names of several princes unknown to history; that it furnished him with a clue to the alphabet which is found on the reverse of many of these coins; and lastly, that it laid open a perfect link and connection between what had hitherto been called the Indo-Scythic coins with corrupted Greek inscriptions and the Hindu coins attributed, with reasonable certainty, to the Kanauj dynasties.[1] Of these three results the most important was the ascertainment of the unknown alphabet, the history of which will be detailed in another portion of this Review.[2] The other great object of Mr. Prinsep's conclusions was the connection that existed between the Indo-Scythic, the early Hindu, the Buddhist, the Surashtrian, the Gupta, the Rajput, and the early Muhammadan coins. He traced the connection through four memoirs, published in 1835, 1836 and 1837, illustrated with engravings, and in the course of them determined several curious and novel facts.[3] The Buddhist coins of the Behat group are supposed to have originated with the so-called punch coins, rude pieces of silver, with various symbols punched on them, which may be considered the earliest attempts of the Hindus to fabricate a national currency, and which have been found in all parts of India in considerable numbers.[4] At a later date they were more regularly formed, and when

---

[1] J. A. S. B., Vol. IV, p. 327; also Vol. VII, p. 636. See Ariana Antiqua, p. 18.
[2] See *infra*, p. 50. [3] J. A. S. B., Vol. IV, pp. 621, 668; Vol. V, p. 639; Vol. VI, p. 288. See Ariana Antiqua, p. 20. [4] As. Res., Vol. XVII, p. 596, fig. 101-108.

assuming Buddhist symbols, they were probably struck in the monasteries of the period. Those which offer imitations of the Indo-Scythic coins, of course followed the establishment of the princes of that nation. In a better style the type of the coins of these princes was also repeated on those of the Gupta princes of Kanauj ; and the latter again became the prototypes of the later coins of the various Rajput dynasties down to the time of the Muhammadan conquest.[1]

While prosecuting his comparative researches in Indian numismatics, Mr. Prinsep did not neglect his examination of the Bactrian coins with which he had been so abundantly supplied by Mr. Masson and others. In 1836 he published two memoirs on new varieties of these coins which he had discovered, and from which he brought to light the names of several new princes, among them Archebias, Amyntas, and the Queen Agathokleia.[2] Another and no less curious series of coins, however, which were being found in Suráshtra, and of which a few detached specimens only had been before published, also attracted Mr. Prinsep's attention at this time (1834). He noticed that they were imitations of Bactrian coins,[3] but the legends on them, which were to him at first unintelligible, he only succeeded in deciphering two years later, in 1836, as written in an ancient form of Nágarí and referring to a dynasty of rulers which, as shown afterwards, bore the title of Kshatrapa (Satrap), and of which eleven descents could be made out from the coins. At the same time the first discovery was made, which was amply confirmed afterwards, that these coins were dated in an ancient form of the Nágarí numerals.[4]

---

[1] See Ariana Antiqua, pp. 20, 21. [2] J. A. S. B., Vol. V, pp. 348, 720. [3] *Ibid.*, Vol. IV, p. 684. [4] *Ibid.*, Vol. VI, p. 377 ; Vol. VII, pp. 347, 348.

On the departure of Mr. Prinsep from India in November 1838, his researches into the Bactrian and Indo-Scythian coins were zealously continued by Captain (now Major-General) Alexander Cunningham, who all along had been the trusty coadjutor of Mr. Prinsep in his investigations.[1] His results Captain Cunningham communicated to the Society in 1840, 1842 and 1845, in three notices of some new Bactrian coins. In these he had the satisfaction of being able to add no less than nine new names to the already long list of Bactrian sovereigns; of which seven were pure Greek, and the other two genuine Parthian.[2] In a fourth notice on the same subject, in 1840, he described a number of Bactrian and Sassanian coins found by Captain Hay at Bameran.[3] The extensive demand for Bactrian coins, engendered by the eager interest widely taken in them consequent upon the researches of the Numismatists, led to the natural, though undesirable, result of attempts, made chiefly by native workmen, to supply it by means of forgeries. The experienced eye of Captain A. Cunningham, however, at once discovered them; and in two notices on counterfeit Bactrian and Indo-Scythian coins, he supplied the unwary collector with the much needed information.[4]

These two classes of coins, together with the Surashtrian and Sassanian, had hitherto concentrated on themselves the almost undivided attention of those engaged in Indian numismatic research. This was natural; for being the most ancient as well as the most obscure, they naturally offered the widest and most promising field for discoveries. But the harvest now began to grow exhausted, and the eyes

---

[1] J. A. S. B., Vol. V, p. 652. [2] *Ibid.*, Vol. IX, Pt. I, pp. 867, 1008; and Vol XI, Pt. I, p. 130; Vol. XIV, Pt. I, p. 430. [3] *Ibid.*, Vol. IX, Pt. I, pp. 68, 70, 531. [4] *Ibid.*, p. 393; Pt. II, p. 1217.

of the inquisitive began to turn in other directions. Still there were gleanings to be made, as fresh coins of those classes were constantly being found in various places. Thus Mr. Laidlay noticed, in 1848, eight Indo-Scythian gold coins found at Kussaraya in the Mungir District,[1] and Captain (now General) James Abbott, in 1853, a few Bactrian and Indo-Scythian coins, got from their old well-known find-place, the neighbourhood of Manikyalá;[2] while Mr. E. Thomas, in 1851, contributed a description of a curious new coin of the Sassanian type.[3] The most important later finds, however, were a silver coin of a new Bactrian king, Plato the Illustrious, reported by Mr. J. Delmerick in 1872,[4] and a deposit of twenty Indo-Scythian and Roman gold coins, excavated by Mr. W. Simpson from the Ahin Posh Tope at Jalálabád and described by the writer of this Review in the 'Proceedings' for 1879.[5] A small hoard of ten Surashtrian coins, found near Chhindwára in 1882 by Mr. J. W. Tawney, may also be noticed [6]

About this time an altogether different field, that of the Muhammadan coins of India, comes, for the first time, prominently into view. Some indications of this field had already been given by Mr. Prinsep[7] and the Hon'ble H. T. Colebrooke, the latter of whom described, in 1841, "a quantity of coins of the Musalman kings of Bengal found at Howrah," and presented to the Society by Mr. H. R. Torrens.[8] The latter species of coins, though now not uncommon, were in those days of such rarity that it was far easier to procure the coins of Alexander or his

---

[1] J. A. S. B., Vol. XVII, Part I, p. 454. [2] *Ibid.*, Vol. XXII, p. 573. See also *ibid.*, Vol. XX, p. 137. [3] *Ibid.*, Vol. XX, p. 525. [4] Proceedings for 1872, pp. 34, 174. [5] *Ibid.*, for 1879, pp. 77, 122, 210. [6] *Ibid.*, for 1882, p. 114; see also p. 41. [7] J. A. S. B., Vol. IV, pp. 679, 680. [8] *Ibid.*, Vol. X, Part I, p. 108.

successors in Bactria, than those of the Sultans of Bengal.[1] The Bengal coins of the Society's Cabinet, together with others which were in his own possession, received a careful examination at the hands of Mr. Laidlay, the result of which he communicated in the Journal for 1846, and by which he succeeded in throwing considerable light on the history of the independent kings of Bengal, until then very little known. The series of these kings he succeeded in tracing by the help of the coins, with tolerable continuity, from the first independent Sultan, Ilyás Sháh, down to the last Mahmúd Sháh, with whom the independence of the kingdom of Bengal was extinguished.[2] After Mr. Laidlay's first attempt, the subject of the Bengal coins remained entirely unnoticed till, upwards of twenty years afterwards, in 1867, when, as will be shown below, it was taken up in right earnest by Mr. E. Thomas and Mr. H. Blochmann, owing to the happy discovery of an extraordinary large hoard of Bengal coins.

In the meanwhile, investigations of no less interest and with equally important results were carried on in other, as yet almost, if not quite, untrodden fields of numismatic research. Thus, in 1846, the first information and delineation of the comparatively modern coins of Arakan of the seventeenth and eighteenth centuries was supplied by Captain (now General Sir) A. P. Phayre;[3] and at the same time it was supplemented by Lieutenant Thomas Latter by a description and delineation of another species of Arakan coins, bearing ancient Nágarí characters which he did not recognize,[4] but which were afterwards, in 1872, shown by Captain (now Colonel) G. E. Fryer to be coins of an ancient

---

[1] J. A. S. B., Vol. XV, p. 324. [2] *Ibid.*, p. 323. [3] *Ibid.*, p. 232. [4] *Ibid.*, p. 238.

Arakanese dynasty of the eighth and ninth centuries, A. D.;[1] a conclusion which, in 1878 and 1880, was confirmed by Dr. Rájendralála Mitra from a new find of similar coins.[2]

In 1852, Mr. E. Thomas, who had already successfully investigated the coins of the kings of Ghazni from the specimens in Mr. Masson's large collection,[3] contributed another no less valuable memoir on that subject in the pages of the Society's Journal, based on the Ghazni coins in Colonel Stacy's Cabinet. It described coins belonging to six sovereigns, including Subaktigin, Ismael, Mahmúd, Mas'aúd, Madúd, and Ibráhím; it incidentally also noticed a curious coin of the Rájpút Bull and Horseman type inscribed with 'Mas'aúd,' the name of one of these sovereigns.[4] In connection with this subject it may be mentioned that, in the year before, 1851, Mr. E. Thomas had published descriptions and delineations of eight specimens of Central Asiatic Kufic coinages of various dates and kingdoms.[5] A few years later, in 1855, he contributed a valuable memoir on a very different, as well as much more ancient, and for Indian history much more important, class of coins, those known by the name of the Gupta dynasty, of which two principal species had been met with, one in gold, the other in silver. These coins had already been noticed by Mr. J. Prinsep and correctly appropriated by him, though he was unable to read the legends on the second species of them.[6] Since his time coins of this class were repeatedly found in various places, and occasionally noticed in the Journal. Thus, in 1852, Major M.

---

[1] J. A. S. B., Vol. XLI, Part I, p. 201. [2] Proceedings for 1878, pp. 102, 103; and for 1880, pp. 53, 54. [3] See Journal of the Royal Asiatic Society for 1848. [4] J. A. S. B., Vol. XXI, p. 115. See also a later notice by Mr. C. J. Rodgers, in Proceedings for 1879, p. 78; and for 1881, p. 4. [5] J. A. S. B., Vol. XX, p. 537. [6] *Ibid.*, Vol. III, p. 230; and Vol. IV, p. 687.

Kittoe brought to notice a large hoard found at Benares, of which some were described and figured by Mr. (now Sir) E. C. Bayley;[1] and in the same year, Dr. Rájendralála Mitra described and delineated three curious coins found at Muhammadpur in the Jessore District, among which, however, only one is probably to be classed as a Gupta coin, while another is now known to belong to the Susanka series, and the third is a South Indian coin.[2] In the memoir of 1855, already alluded to, Mr. E. Thomas, who had the advantage of examining all these coins together with others in Colonel Stacy's and his own possession, successfully brought together and systematised all that had hitherto been ascertained regarding the gold and silver currency of the Guptas, adding at the same time much new information, especially with regard to their silver coinage.[3] Another class of coins, more ancient and hardly less important than those of the Guptas, but having their affinities rather with the Indo-Scythian coins, was brought to notice about the same time, in the Journal of 1854, by Major A. Cunningham. These are the so-called coins of the Indian Buddhist Satraps, of Mahigala, Jivanisa, and Rájabala, the peculiarity of which is that they exhibit for the first time pure Hindu names written in Greek characters. They are of the highest interest and value for the elucidation of Indian history just before the Christian era, as they afford a sure guide to the religious and political state of India at that particular period.[4]

At this time a long pause occurred; during the next ten years, from 1855 to 1864, the Journal contains not

---

[1] J. A. S. B., Vol. XXI, pp. 390, 392. [2] *Ibid.*, Vol. XXI, p. 401. [3] *Ibid.*, Vol. XXIV, p. 483. For some later notices of finds of Gupta coins of well-known types, see Proceedings for 1878, p. 191; for 1879, p. 174; for 1881, p. 39; for 1882, p. 112. [4] J. A. S. B., Vol. XXIII, p. 679.

a single numismatic contribution. But though there was no outward manifestation, the work of enquiring into the coinages of India was carried on with undiminished zeal, in the study and in the field. The first fruit of this laborious though quiet research was the publication by Mr. E. Thomas, in the Journal for 1864 and 1865, of three learned memoirs on "ancient Indian weights."[1] The substance of these memoirs had been originally prepared by him for insertion in the Numismatic Chronicle, but as a large proportion of their contents proved, in the progress of the enquiry, to relate to questions beyond the legitimate scope of that Journal, they were, in a revised and amplified form, published in the Society's Transactions. The attention of archæologists had, just then, been attracted to the weights and measures of ancient nations, by the elaborate work of M. Queipo, and the less voluminous but more directly interesting article of Mr. R. S. Poole (in Smith's Dictionary of the Bible) on the Babylonian and other early metrologies. Mr. E. Thomas's memoirs on the system of the ancient Indian weights is not the least valuable contribution to this enquiry. For "that system, in its local development, though necessarily possessing a minor claim upon the consideration of the European world, may well maintain a leading position in the general investigation, on the ground of its primitive and independent organization, and the very ancient date at which its terms were embodied and defined in writing; while to numismatists it offers the exceptional interest of possessing extant equivalents of the specified weights given in the archaic documentary record which Sanksrit literature has preserved in the text of the original Code of the Hindus."

[1] J. A. S. B., Vol. XXXIII, p. 251; Vol. XXXIV, pp. 14, 51.

In the course of his memoirs, the author proves the very early date of the employment of coined money in India, the earliest representatives of which were the so-called "punch-coins," already referred to in connection with the Behat discovery. These were "flat pieces of metal, some round, some square or oblong, adjusted with considerable accuracy to a fixed weight and usually of an uniform purity, seemingly verified and stamped anew with distinctive symbols by succeeding generations, which clearly represented an effective currency long before the ultimate date of the engrossment of the Laws of Manu."[1] These pieces may still be found all over Northern India in unusual numbers, though mostly in silver, while their more perishable and less esteemed copper equivalents are of very rare occurrence. Their appearance may be judged from the delineations on the two plates which accompany Mr. Thomas's memoirs.[2] At a later date the ancient Indian coinage shows distinct traces of Greek influence; notably in the case of the Surashtrian and Gupta coins.

Another class of coins of this type, though preserving more of a distinctively Indian character, was brought to notice by Major-General A. Cunningham, at the same time that Mr. Thomas's memoir on the earliest currency appeared. In the Journal for 1865, he described and delineated coins, mostly of great rarity, of three different dynasties which anciently held sway in Narwar and Gwalior, and the earliest of which, that of the so-called "nine Nágas," was contemporary with the Guptas, in the second century of the Christian era.[3] To the same type belong the coins of the Sunga or Mitra dynasty, which reigned in north Panchala, the modern Rohilkhand, and, like the Nágas,

---

[1] J. A. S. B., Vol. XXXIV, p. 15. [2] *Ibid.*, Plates ix and xi. [3] *Ibid.*, p. 115.

was contemporary with the great Guptas. Colonel Stacy's specimens of their coins, as well as of those of the Nágas, had been already noticed by Mr. J. Prinsep,[1] as long ago as 1837, since when little or nothing had been added to their knowledge. But, in 1879, Mr. H. Rivett-Carnac was so fortunate as to procure a considerable number and variety of them from the ruined site of the ancient town of Ahichhatra. They were placed by him in the hands of Mr. A. C. Carlleyle, who published a careful description and delineation of them in the Journal for 1880.[2] Later, in the same volume, Mr. Rivett-Carnac himself gave a large number of additional delineations of Mitra coins and others similar to them.[3] A few years previously, in 1873, the Hon'ble E. C. Bayley had published two other coins of the same class, found on the site of the ancient city of Kausambhí,[4] and in 1875 Dr. Rájendralála Mitra contributed some further elucidation of another well-known and often described kind of coin of the same type, that of Kunanda, of which a new specimen had been found at Karnal.[5] Two curious gold coins, of unknown attribution, but probably belonging to the same class, were described and delineated by the writer of this Review in 1881 and 1882.[6]

These were but gleanings on the field of the earlier Hindu coinages of India — a field which now, after the long continued and searching labours of General Cunningham and his co-workers, appears rapidly to become exhausted. But there was still a field on which,

---

[1] See J. A. S. B., Vol. VI, pp. 297, 298. [2] *Ibid.*, Vol. XLIX, p. 21. [3] *Ibid.*, Vol. XLIX, pp. 87, 138. See also, for a later find, Proceedings for 1881, p. 64. [4] J. A. S. B., Vol. XLII, pp. 109, 191. [5] *Ibid.*, Vol. XLIV, p. 82. See also Mr. Thomas's Description and Delineation in Vol. XXXIV, p. 65. [6] Proceedings for 1881, pp. 39, 138, and for 1882, pp. 91, 194.

though much had been already done, there remained yet very much more to be done by those of a later day, who took an interest in the numismatics of India. This field comprised the varied and, some of them, extensive classes of Muhammadan coins—the imperial coinage of Delhi as well as the provincial ones of Bengal, Gujarát, Malwa, and others. It included also the later Hindu coins of Kashmir, Kangra, &c., contemporary with, and subsequent to, the Muhammadan conquest. Here again, after a preliminary publication, in 1864, of a catalogue and delineations of Muhammadan coins current in the bazars of the Gujarat District in 1859, the experienced numismatist, Mr. E. Thomas, some of whose valuable contributions on a similar subject have been already noticed, took the lead. It was a remarkable discovery which afforded the occasion. In 1863, an extraordinarily large hoard of coins, numbering in all no less than 13,500 pieces of silver, was found in Cooch Bihar, in Northern Bengal. The autumnal fall of a river bank, not far removed from the traditional capital of Kanteswar Rája, a king of mark in provincial annals, disclosed to modern eyes the hidden treasure of some credulous mortal who, in olden time, entrusted his wealth to the keeping of an alluvial soil, carefully stored and secured in brass vessels specially constructed for the purpose, but destined to contribute undesignedly to an alien inheritance, and a disentombment at a period much posterior to that contemplated by its depositor. This accumulation, so singular in its numerical amount, is not less remarkable on account of its component elements, all the coins being, with a very few exceptions of imperial coins of Delhi, the unmixed produce of the provincial mints of Bengal, and embracing the records of no more than ten kings, ten mint cities, and one hundred and seven years up to the end of the fourteenth century. From this great store careful selections were made by Dr. Rájendralála Mitra for the Calcutta Mint, the Asiatic Society and Colonel C. S. Guthrie,[1] and these selections afforded to Mr. Thomas the leading materials for his invaluable monograph on "The Initial Coinage of Bengal," which was first published in the Journal of the Royal Asiatic Society of Great Britain and Ireland,[2] and afterwards in 1867 reprinted in the pages of the Journal of this Society.[3] After an introductory exposition of the Muhammadan system of coinage, the monograph proceeds to describe and delineate the coins of ten Bengal sovereigns, beginning with Ruknuddín Kai Kaus, and ending with Ghiyásuddin, 'Azam Sháh, noticing at the same time the imperial coins of Násiruddín Mahmúd Sháh and of Jalálatuddín Riziyah.

A careful examination of these coins enabled the author to throw considerable light on the hitherto little or obscurely known history of the early Muhammadan occupation of Bengal, extending over a century and a half. There still, however, remained much to be cleared up, especially regarding the course of events during those frequent rebellions to which the Governors of Bengal were tempted by the remoteness of their province from the centre of the empire. One of these residual obscurities, relating to the rebellion of the Bengal Governor, Ghiyásuddín 'Iwaz, Mr. Thomas himself was able to clear up some years later, owing to the discovery, near the fort of Bihar, of thirty-seven coins, among which were some of Ghiyásuddín, and others of the contemporary Delhi Emperor, Altamsh. Regarding these Mr. Thomas contributed to the Journal of 1873 a supplementary memoir

---

[1] J. A. S. B., Vol. XXXIII, p. 480. [2] See Journal, R. A. S., Vol. II, p. 1, (N. S.) [3] J. A. S. B., Vol. XXXVI, p. 1.

of the Initial Coinage of Bengal.[1] Still later in 1881, another of the residual obscurities, relating to the history of the rebellion of the Governor Mughísuddín Yuzbaq, was elucidated by a third discovery of a hoard of thirty-eight coins near Gauhati in Assam, which were described and delineated in the Journal of that year by the writer of the present Review.

In the meanwhile a large and varied number of Bengal coins of a somewhat later period had been accumulating in the Society's Cabinet. These, with some others in the possession of private individuals, were subjected to a careful examination by Mr. H. Blochmann, the late Philological Secretary of the Society, who brought to bear on them his extensive linguistic and historic experience. The result were three very valuable memoirs on "The Geography and History of Bengal," published in the Journals for 1873, 1874, 1875, in the course of which he described and delineated a large number of coins of eleven of the independent Sultans of Bengal, and by their aid settled many hitherto disputed or obscure points in their history.[2] Some additional information on the same subject was afforded by the Hon'ble E. C. Bayley, who, in 1873, contributed a notice and delineation of a rare coin of the independent Sultan of Bengal, Muzaffar Sháh;[3] and a little later by Mr. J. G. Delmerick, who, in 1876, noticed and delineated two new coins of Bahádur Sháh and Husain Sháh.[4] In the very last year of the century, 1883, a new find of coins of Mahmúd Sháh I. and Bárbak Sháh, which were described and delineated by the writer of the present Review, removed some further obscurities in the

---

[1] J. A. S. B., Vol. XLII, p. 343. [2] *Ibid.*, p. 209; Vol. XLIII, p. 280; Vol. XLIV, p. 275. [3] *Ibid.*, Vol. XLII, p. 311. [4] *Ibid.*, Vol. XLV, p. 295.

history of those two Sultans.[1] Thus, within the short space of seventeen years, the coins of Bengal, which formerly were hardly known at all, became one the richest and best ascertained of the Indian coinages.

While this active research in the coins of Bengal was going on, those of the great Delhi empire were not neglected. Already in 1847, Mr. E. Thomas, who had made the Muhammadan coins of India his particular study, had published a separate memoir on the "Coins of the Pathan Sultans of Hindustan;" to which he added a "Supplement" in 1851. But the rapidly increasing accumulation of new and very ample materials induced him to undertake a thorough revision of the whole subject, the result of which appeared in a masterly form in 1871, as "The Chronicles of the Pathan Kings of Delhi."[2] The work, at the time of its appearance, could rightly claim to be almost exhaustive. But the subject of the Pathan coins is so extensive, that it cannot be wondered that further research brought to light so many new coins as to render the want of a supplement much felt. This want Mr. C. J. Rodgers, whom zealous numismatic enquiries had fitted for the task, undertook to supply; and in the Journals for 1880 and 1883 he contributed three supplementary memoirs, in which he described and delineated a large number of hitherto unnoticed or newly found coins of the Pathan Empire.[3] A few isolated additions to Mr. Thomas's great work had been already previously made from time to time. Thus, in the Journal for 1871, Mr. E. C. Bayley described and delineated a rare coin of Sultan

---

[1] J. A. S. B., Vol. LII, p. 211. [2] See Preface to the *Chronicles of the Pathan Kings of Delhi.* [3] J. A. S. B., Vol. XLIX, pp. 81, 207; Vol. LII, p. 55.

Fírúz Sháh Zafar;[1] in 1873, he made known a unique gold coin of the usurper, Násiruddín Khusrau;[2] in 1876, the Rev. Mr. Carleton published an unique gold coin of Násiruddín Mahmúd Shah;[3] in 1878, Mr. H. Blochman, an unique gold coin of Jalal-uddín Fírúz Shah II;[4] in 1881, Mr. J. G. Delmerick, an unique silver coin of Shamsuddín Kaimurs;[5] and in 1880, Dr. C. R. Stulpnagel added a few new coins struck in the joint names of Ghiyásuddín and Muizzuddín bin Sám.[6] Mr. J. G. Delmerick, the same whose contribution of two supplementary Bengal coins has already been noted, also contributed descriptions and delineations of some new and rare Pathans in the Journals for 1874, 1875 and 1876.[7] In his second and third papers also occur the first more detailed notices, ever published in the Journal, of some of the Muhammadan provincial coinages, those of Jaunpur,[8] Malwa, Kulbarga, and Kashmir, as well as of coins of the Mogul Empire.[9] The researches into some of these provincial coins were pursued more especially by Mr. C. J. Rodgers, who has been just mentioned in connection with the Pathan coins. The Journals for 1879, 1880, 1801 and 1883 contain several valuable memoirs from him, on the coins of Akbar,[10] those of the Sultans and Maháríjas of Kashmir[11] and Kángra,[12] and those of the Sikhs.[13] The subject of the provincial coins of South India was, about the same time, taken up by Dr. G. Bidie, who contributed to

[1] J. A. S. B., Vol. XL, p. 160. [2] *Ibid.*, Vol. XLII, p. 311. [3] Proceedings for 1876, p. 91. [4] *Ibid.*, for 1878, p. 64. [5] *Ibid.*, for 1881, p. 157. [6] J. A. S. B., Vol. XLIX, p. 29. [7] *Ibid.*, Vol. XLIII, p. 97; Vol. XLIV, p. 126; Vol. XLV, p. 291. [8] *Ibid.*, Vol. XLIV, p. 126. See also Proceedings for 1881, pp. 40, 41. [9] J. A. S. B., Vol. XLV, p. 292. See also Proceedings for 1869, p. 266. [10] J. A. S. B., Vol. XLIX, p. 213; Vol. LII, p. 97. [11] *Ibid.*, Vol. XLVIII, pp. 277, 282. [12] *Ibid.*, Vol. XLIX, p. 10. [13] *Ibid.*, Vol. L, p. 71.

the Journal for 1883 a short monograph on the so-called Pagoda or Varáha coins.[1]

The last two contributions in the pages of the Society's Journal refer to countries beyond the confines of India proper. These are a memoir by Major W. F. Prideaux on the "Coins of Charibael, King of the Homerites and Sabaeans,"[2] and two others by Major-General A. Cunningham on "Relics of Ancient Persia in Gold, Silver, and Copper," in which, among other relics, he describes and delineates a large number of coins of Persian kings and satraps and of Greek kings and cities, discovered in 1877 on the north bank of the Oxus. Thus, with the close of the century, the researches in Indian numismatics, as represented in the Society's Journal, after having gradually brought the whole extent of India proper within their purview, returned once more to the earliest field of their enquiry beyond the Western frontiers of modern India.

---

[1] J. A. S. B., Vol. LII, p. 33. [2] *Ibid.*, Vol. L, pp. 95, 151; and Vol. LII, p. 64.

CHAPTER III.

ANCIENT INDIAN ALPHABETS.

[Indian Pali characters: the Kutila, the Gupta, the Asoka—Arian Pali characters.]

THE most interesting and important period of the Society's activity with regard to the reading and translation of Ancient Inscriptions lies between the years 1834 and 1839, and is mainly connected with the name of Mr. James Prinsep, the Society's secretary at that time. Within the short space of those few years, and through the labours, in the main, of *one* man, those great discoveries were made which form the foundation of our knowledge of the ancient art of writing, language, and history of India.

The modern Devanágarí characters are now known to have past, roughly speaking, through three previous stages of development,—the Kutila, the Gupta, and the Asoka. The last two are named, respectively, after the Gupta kings (between the 2nd and 4th centuries, A.D.), and king Asoka (in the 3rd century, B.C.); the first name is descriptive ('curved'), and was first noticed by Mr. J. Prinsep in an inscription from the Bareilly District.[1] The characters named Kutila very closely resemble the modern Devanágarí, and inscriptions written in them offered no very great

[1] J. A. S. B., Vol. VI, p. 779 (verse 36).

difficulty to the early decipherers. As early as 1785, Charles Wilkins published a transcript and translation of the Kutila inscription on the well-known Pillar at Buddal. In a letter dated 14th July, 1785, he thus refers to it: "I have lately been so fortunate as to decipher the character; and I have the honour to lay before the Society a transcript of the original in the modern writing, and a translation, and at the same time to exhibit the two impressions I took from the stone itself."[1] About the same time Pandit Radha Kanta Sarma communicated a translation of the Kutila inscription of Visala Deva on the famous Iron Pillar in Dehli,[2] which, about 1801, was retranslated and revised by Mr. Henry Colebrooke.[3]

The Gupta characters, the general appearance of which differs not inconsiderably both from the Kutila and the modern Nágarí, offered a much more serious difficulty. Yet about the same time the ingenuity of Mr. Charles Wilkins succeeded also in overcoming the difficulties of these peculiar characters. In the years 1785-1789, he deciphered and published readings and translations of three of the now well-known short inscriptions of the Varma Kings in the Nágárjuní caves near Buddha-Gaya. In a letter to the secretary, dated 17th March 1785, he says: "Having been so fortunate as to make out the whole of the very curious inscription you were so obliging as to lend me, I herewith return it, accompanied by an exact copy, in a reduced size, interlined with each corresponding letter in the modern Devanágarí character; and also a copy of my translation, which is as literal as the idioms would admit of to be. The character is, undoubtedly, the most ancient of any that have hitherto come under my inspection. It is

[1] As. Res., Vol. I, p. 131. [2] *Ibid.*, p. 379. [3] *Ibid.*, Vol. VII, p. 173.

not only dissimilar to that which is now in use, but even very materially different from that we find in inscriptions of eighteen hundred years ago. But though the writing be not modern, the language is pure Sanskrit."[1]

Notwithstanding the success, however, of Mr. Wilkins, it was a considerable interval of years before any practical application was made of his discovery to attempt a decipherment of the numerous inscriptions in the same character which came to be made known from time to time. Of the important Chandra Gupta inscription on the Sanchi Tope, Mr. James Prinsep still writes in 1834: "None of our Orientalists have yet been able to make anything of the Bhilsa or Sanchi inscription, although they are far from abandoning their attempts to decipher it;"[2] and it was only in 1837 that he himself published the first translation of it.[3] For some thirty years, the main interest of the Society in Indian researches had been turned into other channels; and when the study of ancient inscriptions was again taken up, there were difficulties that retarded progress. In the first place, it was only after repeated attempts at taking eye-copies or facsimiles that sufficiently serviceable copies of the most important inscriptions were obtained. What difficulties were encountered in this respect may be judged, for example, from what Mr. J. Prinsep says in 1838 with regard to the Dehli Pillar inscription: "I allude to the short inscription on the celebrated Iron Pillar at Dehli, of which I published, in 1834, an attempted copy taken by the late Lieutenant William Elliot, at the express request of the Revd. Dr. Mill; but it was so ingeni-

[1] As. Res., Vol. I, p. 279; and Vol. II, p. 167, reprinted in J. A. S. B., Vol. XVI, p. 594. See also J. A. S. B., Vol. IV, p. 691; and Genl. Cunningham's Archæological Reports, Vol. I, pp. 47-49. [2] J. A. S. B., Vol. III, p. 488. [3] *Ibid.*, Vol. VI, p. 455.

ously mismanaged, that not a single word could be made out."[1] Next, though Mr. Wilkins's successful decipherment had furnished a key to the reading of the Gupta characters, it required yet much careful handling of it before it would unlock all the mysteries of that system of writing. Referring to the Gupta inscription on the Pillar of Allahabad, of which he had taken a copy for the Society, Lieutenant T. S. Burt writes in 1834: "On examining all the eighteen volumes of the Asiatic Researches, I am happy to say I have found, or at least partly found, a key to the character No. 2[2] in the transcript and interpretation of an ancient inscription at Gaya, by Dr. Wilkins.[3] This will evidently serve as a guide by which nearly half of the letters can be made out."[4] What was still wanting, however, was now soon supplied by the joint labours of Captain A. Troyer, Dr. W. H. Mill, and Mr. James Prinsep, who successively and successfully examined and translated some of the most celebrated Gupta inscriptions. Thus, in 1834, Captain Troyer gave a partial translation of the Gupta inscription on the Allahabad Pillar.[5] Dr. Mill in the same year completed it; and, in 1837, added to it a translation of its companion inscription on the Bhitari Pillar.[6] Mr. James Prinsep, in 1837 and 1838, further added a translation of the inscriptions on the pillars at Delhi,[7] Kuhaun,[8] (Gorakhpur District), Eran (in Bhopal),[9] on the topes of Sanchi[10] and Amravati,[11] and on the rock of Junagarh.[12] To the names of these three pioneers should be added

---

[1] J. A. S. B., Vol. VII, p. 629. [2] This is the term used at that time to designate what are now commonly called the Gupta characters. [3] As. Res., Vol. I, p. 279. [4] J. A. S. B., Vol. III, p. 111. [5] *Ibid.*, p. 118. [6] *Ibid.*, pp. 257ff; and Vol. VI, pp. 1ff. [7] *Ibid.*, Vol. VII, pp. 629ff. [8] *Ibid.*, pp. 36ff. [9] *Ibid.*, pp. 633ff. [10] *Ibid.*, Vol. VI, pp. 455ff. [11] *Ibid.*, pp. 218ff. [12] *Ibid.*, Vol. VII, pp. 337ff.

that of Mr. W. H. Wathen, who, in 1835, contributed to the general result by his successful reading of some Gujaráti copper-plates written in a later variety of the Gupta characters.[1] There is no need to trace the history of the decipherment of the Gupta characters any further.

At first the age of this system of writing was greatly over-estimated. The general impression was that it belonged to the early centuries before the Christian era. This opinion seems to have originated from a casual remark of Dr. Charles Wilkins in the passage above quoted, as would appear from Mr. J. Prinsep's observation referring to it in 1831, that Dr. Wilkins had imagined the Gaya characters to be as ancient as the Christian era,[2] and from a similar remark of Lieutenant T. S. Burt, that the Allahabad pillar inscriptions, "from what the Doctor (Wilkins) says as applied to the Gaya inscription, will probably prove to be composed of pure Sanskrit and to be more than 1800 years old."[3] On what grounds Dr. Wilkins had formed his conjecture does not appear, for he can hardly have been aware of the principal argument which afterwards seemed to make in support of his view. This was the ascertainment of the name of Chandra Gupta in the Allahabad and its companion inscriptions, which there was a natural tendency at first to identify with the celebrated Maurya King Chandra Gupta or Sandracottus, whose date towards the end of the fourth century B. C. was well ascertained from being mentioned by Strabo and Arrian.[4] This identification was thought by many to be strongly confirmed by the information on the history of Sandracottus, derived by Mr. Turnour from the Mahavamso.[5] But Mr. J.

---

[1] J. A. S. B., Vol. IV, p. 476. [2] *Ibid.*, Vol. III, p. 115. [3] *Ibid.*, p. 111.
[4] *Ibid.*, pp. 266, 267. [5] *Ibid.*, Vol. VI, p. 15.

Prinsep, who in 1834 first suggested the identification, himself pointed out two of the difficulties of it, which lay in the two facts that the names of the Gupta dynasty in the inscription did not accord with those of the Maurya dynasty, and that the capitals of the two dynasties were different, *viz.*, Kanauj and Patna respectively.[1] Dr. Mill strongly supported these objections, adding to them two more, based on the difference of race and religious profession of the two dynasties, the Mauryas being of the Solar race, while the Guptas were of the Lunar race, and some of them held the late Sakti form of the Sivaite faith.[2] He himself proposed another date, which however erred as much in the opposite direction. Rightly identifying the Gupta dynasty with that mentioned in the Purânas, but miscalculating their age from the untrustworthy dates furnished by those pseudo-historical works, he suggested in 1837 the "age of Charlemagne in Europe," in the ninth century A. D., as the probable date of the Guptas and their inscriptions.[3] A similarly erroneous suggestion had been, already in 1834, made by Mr. J. Prinsep, who thought the similarity of the Gupta character with those of Tibet, known to have been brought there from India in the seventh century A.D., might be considered to favour the latter date.[4] In the meanwhile, however, the dated copper-plates from Gujrat were read by Mr. W. H. Wathen in 1835. Their dates and the striking similarity of their characters with those of the Gupta inscription finally led Mr. J. Prinsep to the discovery of the true date, the third century A. D., which he announced in 1838, and illustrated by a comparative table of the successive Indian alphabets.[5]

---

[1] J. A. S. B., Vol. III, p. 115. [2] *Ibid.*, p. 267; and Vol. VI, p. 9. [3] *Ibid.*, Vol. VI, p. 12. [4] *Ibid.*, Vol. III, p. 115. [5] *Ibid.*, Vol. VII, pp. 275, 629.

The most important achievement of Mr. James Prinsep, however, consists in his great discovery of the value of "the alphabet and the language of those ancient pillars and rock inscriptions which have been," as he says, "the wonder of the learned since the days of Sir William Jones."[1] The characters of these inscriptions are again as widely different from the Gupta characters, as the latter are from the modern Nágarí.[2] They appear to have been first made known to the Society about 1795 through some short inscriptions from the Ellora caves, forwarded to Sir W. Jones by Sir Charles Ware Mallet. They were submitted to Lieutenant Wilford, whose ingenuity did not fail him in providing a translation. "I have the honour to return," he writes to Sir W. Jones, "the facsimile of the several inscriptions with an explanation of them. I despaired at first of ever being able to decipher them; for as there are no ancient inscriptions in that part of India (Benares), we never had, of course, any opportunity to try our skill and improve our talents in the art of deciphering. However, after many fruitless attempts on our part, we were so fortunate as to find at last an ancient sage, who gave us the key, and produced a book in Sanskrit containing a great many ancient alphabets, formerly in use in different parts of India; this was really a fortunate discovery, which hereafter may be of great service to us."[3] Lieutenant Wilford's 'discovery' appears to have passed unquestioned for many years, for Mr. A. Sterling, writing about 1820 on the Khandagiri rock inscription, which is in the same character, says:—"A portion of the Ellora and Salsette inscriptions, written in the above character, has been deciphered by the learning and ingenuity of Major Wilford, aided by the discovery of

---

[1] J. A. S. B., Vol. VI, p. 452. [2] *Ibid.*, p. 566. [3] As. Res., Vol. V, p. 135.

a key to the unravelling of ancient inscriptions in the possession of a learned Brahmin; and it is to be regretted that the same has not been further applied to deciphering the Dehli and other characters."[1] Indeed a similar regretful reference to Lieutenant Wilford's discovery of the key was made by Mr. Prinsep himself in 1833, only about a year or two before he discovered the true key.[2] This regret is natural enough, but it can hardly surprise that no further practical application was made of the "learned Brahmin's" key, for it is much to be feared that, as in his other antiquarian researches, in this instance too, Lieutenant Wilford fell a victim to the astuteness of a designing pandit, who traded on his credulity. However that may be, it is certain that his so-called 'discovery' was a thorough delusion, for his texts are entirely imaginary readings of the original, while his translations are entirely imaginary interpretations of the imaginary texts—an unintelligible jargon which is supposed to relate the wanderings of Yudhisthira and the Pandavas through forests and uninhabited places. "They were precluded"—so Lieutenant Wilford conjectures—"by agreement from conversing with mankind. But their friends and relations, Vidura and Vyasa, contrived to convey to them such intelligence and information as they deemed necessary for their safety. This they did by writing short and obscure sentences on rocks or stones in the wilderness, and in characters previously agreed upon betwixt them."[3]

Subsequently some more and larger inscriptions in the same character were communicated to the Society, among

---

[1] As. Res., Vol. XV, p. 314. [2] J. A. S. B., Vol. II, p. 317. [3] As. Res., Vol. V, p. 136. The ascription to the Pandavas seems to have been a common Hindu conceit, for the Dehli Pillar, which exhibits the same character, is by them supposed to have been Bhim Sen's staff with which he used to grind his *bhang*: see J. A. S. B., Vol. III, p. 106.

them the celebrated Asoka inscriptions on the pillars of Dehli and Allahabad from Captain J. Hoare, and that on the Khandagiri Rock from Mr. A. Sterling.[1] But, after Lieutenant Wilford's failure, no further attempt was made to read them, and they remained to the European enquirers as great a mystery as they had been for ages to the natives of India, till Mr. J. Prinsep's efforts again brought them into prominent notice, and his genius succeeded in discovering the true key to their decipherment. In 1834, he prevailed on Lieutenant T. S. Burt to procure a good and complete facsimile of the inscription on the Allahabad pillar; and in the same year he received a copy of the inscription on the pillar of Mathiah, and in the following year (1835) one of that on the pillar of Radhiah, both through the assistance of Mr. B. H. Hodgson.[2] On comparing these three inscriptions with that on the Dehli pillar, which had been previously in the Society's possession, with a view to find any other words which might be common either to two or to all of them, Mr. Prinsep was led, as he tells us, "to the most important discovery that all four inscriptions were identically the same."[3] This was, indeed, an important discovery, as it afforded to him a fuller and more trustworthy means of comparing and classifying the symbols of the mysterious alphabet—a task which he had commenced not long before. Mr. A. Stirling, when communicating to the Society his copy of the Khandagiri rock inscription, had thought he could notice "a close resemblance of some of the letters to those of the Greek alphabet," instancing particularly "the Greek *ou*, *sigma*, *lambda*, *chi*, *delta*, *epsilon*, and a something closely resembling the figure of the *digamma*."[4] In doing so, however,

[1] As. Res., Vol. VII, pp. 175, 176; and Vol. XV, p. 312. [2] J. A. S. B., Vol. III, p. 483; and Vol. IV, p. 126. [3] *Ibid.*, Vol. III, p. 484; *Ibid.*, Vol. IV, p. 126. [4] As. Res., Vol. XV, pp. 313-314.

he merely repeated an observation which had occurred to others long before him, as noted by Father Tieffenthaler,[1] who says that those who held the Grecian theory believed that the Dehli pillar had been erected by Alexander the Great; and he adds that "this was an error." But Tieffenthaler's own explanation, that they were partly numerical figures, partly figurations of weapons of war, (the record, in fact, being merely a numerical list of arms,) was no better than Lieutenant Wilford's so-called discovery.

Curiously enough, the Greek theory received in 1834 what almost seemed to amount to proof from Major (afterwards Colonel) D. L. Stacy, who actually read the Greek word *soter* on two coins bearing an inscription in those unknown characters. Mr. J. Prinsep, however, at once suspected the fallaciousness of this reading, for he remarked that "the apparently Greek letters, when inverted, resembled closely the Dehli character; it would be wrong, therefore, to assume positively that they were Greek."[2] He felt convinced that the resemblance to Greek letters was "entirely accidental, and that the alphabet was really "of the Sanskrit family." It was for the purpose of determining this point that he undertook the trouble of minutely analysing and classifying all the symbols occurring in the Allahabad pillar inscription. Proceeding in this manner, he soon perceived that each radical letter was subject to five principal inflections, the same in all, corresponding in their nature and application with the five vowel marks of the ancient Sanskrit of the Gupta inscriptions which was already

[1] Description de l'Inde, Part I, p. 129 (French Edition). Mr. J. Prinsep, in J. A. S. B., Vol. III, p. 117, seems to have thought it an original observation of Mr. Stirling's; but the latter himself refers to Tieffenthaler. [2] J. A. S. B., Vol. III, p. 433.

well-known at that time. His result he exhibited in a well-arranged table showing the letters and their inflections, and thus clearly established his first point, that the letters were Sanskrit and not Greek.[1]

The next point to discover was the power, or signification of these unknown letters, that is, to determine to which of the Sanskrit characters of the well-known Nágarí system each of the unknown ancient Sanskrit symbols corresponded. The first mode which occurred to him was to count how often each radical symbol of the unknown system and of the modern Nágar respectively occurred in a page of the ancient inscription and in a page of a modern copy of some well-known Sanskrit work (he took the *Bhatti Kávya*), and then to compare the numbers thus obtained. The idea, of course, was that those symbols which were found to coincide in frequency in the two lists would prove to possess the same power of signification. Though Mr. Prinsep himself appears to have expected much from this process,[2] it led to no result, and with our present knowledge, it is easy to see that it could not possibly yield any result; the very preliminary conditions of a successful comparison were absent; for, as we now know, the subject-matter of the two writings compared is widely different, and what is more, the language of the inscription is not Sanskrit, but an ancient kind of Prákrit (Páli). The next method which Mr. Prinsep tried for the purpose of determining the value of the unknown letters was a much sounder one, and one which did actually lead a long way in the solution of the riddle. He set himself to compare carefully the forms of the unknown letters with those of the Gupta alphabet, the oldest till then known. In this manner he soon discovered

[1] J. A. S. B., Vol. III, p. 117, plate v; also *ibid.*, p. 487. [2] *Ibid.*, p. 484.

that certain letters of the two alphabets resembled one another, from which he further concluded that in all probability they were identical. And though no doubt some of his identifications ultimately turned out to be erroneous, he was correct in many others; for example, in those referred to by him in the following passage, written in October 1834:—"From the resemblance (of a certain subjoined letter) to the corresponding letter of the Gaya alphabet, I think a strong probability is established that this letter is equivalent to *y* of the Devanágarí alphabet. The other subjoined letter has a great analogy to the Sanskrit *v*. The letter with which those two are most frequently united may, with equal probability, be set down as equivalent to the Devanágarí *s*."[1] About the same time, encouraged by the earlier efforts of Mr. Prinsep, the Rev. J. Stevenson was induced to take up the same line of enquiry, and succeeded in adding a few more to the list of identified symbols, among them those for *k*, *j*, *th*, *p*, and *b*.[2]

With the help of these identifications attempts were at once made to translate the inscriptions, but with no satisfactory result; partly because the translators were still under the erroneous impression that their language was Sanskrit,[3] partly because of the most important letters some had been wrongly identified (*e.g.*, *n* as *r*), while others had not been identified at all (*e.g.*, *d*). One very striking and most interesting application, however, was made at this stage by Professor Lassen, of Bonn, who, in 1835 or 1836, successfully read the name of Agathocles on a Bactrian coin, inscribed with those ancient symbols.[4]

[1] J. A. S. B., Vol. III, p. 485. [2] *Ibid.*, p. 498. [3] *Ibid.*, pp. 487, 495.
[4] *Ibid.*, Vol. V, p. 723; and Vol. VI., 465.

But it was not till early in 1837 that Mr. Prinsep discovered by what cannot be described otherwise than a happy inspiration, that which proved to be the key to the whole mystery, the little word *dánam* meaning 'a gift.' This discovery will be best narrated in Mr. Prinsep's own words: "In laying open a discovery of this nature, some little explanation is generally expected of the means by which it has been attained. Like most other inventions, when once found, it appears extremely simple; and, as in most others, accident rather than study has had the merit of solving the enigma which has so long baffled the learned. While arranging and lithographing the numerous scraps of facsimiles for Plate XXVII, I was struck at their all terminating with the same two letters. Coupling this circumstance with their extreme brevity and insulated position, which proved that they could not be fragments of a continuous text, it immediately occurred that they must record either obituary notices, or more probably the offerings and presents of votaries, as is known to be the present custom in the Buddhist temples at Ava, where numerous *dwajas* or flagstaffs, images and small *chaityas*, are crowded within the enclosure, surrounding the chief cupola, each bearing the name of the donor. The next point noted was the frequent occurrence of the letter, already set down incontestably as *s*, before the final word of each record. Now this I had learnt from the Saurashtra coins, deciphered only a day or two before,[1] to be one sign of the genitive case singular, being the *ssa* of the Páli, or *sya* of the Sanskrit. 'Of so and so the gift' must then be the form of each brief sentence; and the vowel *á* and *anuswára* led to the speedy recognition of the word *dánam* (gift),

[1] J. A. S. B., Vol. VI, pp. 378ff.

teaching me the very two letters, *d* and *n*, most different from known forms, and which had failed me most in my former attempts. Since 1834 also my acquaintance with ancient alphabets had become so familiar that most of the remaining letters in the present examples could be named at once on re-inspection. In the course of a few minutes I thus became possessed of the whole alphabet, which I tested by applying it to the inscription on the Dehli column."[1]

Mr. Prinsep speedily applied his discovery not only to the decipherment of the Dehli pillar and Sanchi Tope inscriptions,[2] but, in rapid and regular succession, to every one of the groups of inscriptions, which till then had been made known,—those on the pillars of Allahabad, Dehli, Radhia, Mathiah,[3] on the rocks of Girnár and Dhauli,[4] in the caves of Barabar, Junir and Khandagiri,[5] and on the Buddhist coins.[6] His readings and interpretations, though by no means perfect,—indeed even after the revised readings of Messrs. Wilson, Burnouf, Kern, Senart, and others an entirely satisfactory translation is still a desideratum—at all events sufficed to demonstrate the genuineness of his discovery.

The discovery of the key to these ancient characters proved to be only the commencement of a series of discoveries, in some respects even more important, relating to the language and chronology of ancient India. Most of these, too, it was the good fortune of Mr. James Prinsep to make.

From the beginning it was suspected that the characters were of a very great age, and Mr. Prinsep in 1834 at

---

[1] J. A. S. B., Vol. VI, pp. 460, 461. [2] *Ibid.*, pp. 461ff, 467ff; and Vol. VII, pp. 562ff. [3] *Ibid.*, Vol. VI, pp. 566ff, and 963ff. [4] *Ibid.*, Vol. VII, pp. 156ff, 219ff, 434ff. [5] *Ibid.*, Vol. VI, pp. 676ff, 1042ff, 1072ff. [6] *Ibid.*, pp. 463ff.

once declared his belief that they were more ancient than the Gupta characters, which at the time were believed to be coeval with the commencement of the Christian era. He thought that this might be proved—"First, by the position the inscription occupied on the Allahabad columns as well as on that of Dehli; in both it was the principal, and, as it were, the original inscription, the others being subsequently added, perhaps on some occasion of triumph or visit to the spot. Secondly, the simplicity of the character and the limited number of radicals denoted its priority to the more complicated and refined system afterwards adopted; while, thirdly, the very great rarity of its occurrence on ancient monuments, and the perfect ignorance which prevailed regarding its origin in the earliest Persian historians who mentioned the lath of Feroz Shah, confirmed its belonging to an epoch beyond the reach of native research."[1] With the exception of the reference to the very great rarity of such inscriptions—for they really occur more frequently than it was known at that time—Mr. Prinsep's reasons still hold good. But the question was finally set at rest, and the truth of his surmise proved by the discovery, made mainly by Mr. Prinsep himself, of the mention in the inscription of the names of certain persons whose place in history was perfectly well ascertained. On applying his key to the pillar inscriptions, he soon discovered in 1837 that they contained edicts promulgated by a certain king called "Piyadasi, the beloved of the gods;"[2] and his discovery was carried a step further by the Hon'ble G. Turnour, who, a little later in the same year, succeeded, from information afforded by the historical works of the Buddhists in Ceylon, in identifying

[1] J. A. S. B., Vol. III, p. 116. [2] *Ibid.*, Vol. VI, pp. 470ff.

the Piyadasi of the inscriptions with the Indian king Asoka, a grandson of the well-known Chandra Gupta, of the Maurya dynasty.[1] In the following year, 1838, Mr. Prinsep crowned this series of discoveries by discovering that king Piyadasi in his edicts mentioned by name several Greek kings. Among them were an Antiochus and a Ptolemy. It is true that Turnour, whose view was adopted by Mr. Prinsep, misled by the inaccurate chronological system of the Ceylonese Buddhist works, fell into an error in calculating Asoka's date, making his long reign of forty-one years to fall at first into the last quarter of the fourth century B.C., and afterwards into the second half of the third century B.C.,[2] and accordingly identifying the Antiochus of the inscriptions with Antiochus III (the Great of Syria, 225-176 B.C.).[3] Later investigations have shown that the two names of Antiochus and Ptolemy mentioned in the inscriptions really referred to Antiochus II (Theos of Syria, 263-247 B.C.), and Ptolemy III (Philadelphus of Egypt, 281-247 B.C.), and that the correct date of Asoka's reign most probably is about 264-223 B.C.[4] But, though important as regards strict historical accuracy, after all the correction is too insignificant to detract anything from the honour due to Messrs. Prinsep and Turnour for the success of their original discovery.

The opinions of the early enquirers with regard to the language in which these ancient inscriptions were composed went through some curious alternations. The earliest view was that they were expressed in an ancient species of the vernacular of India, or, as we should now say, in a species of ancient Prákrit (or Páli). This was the

---

[1] J. A. S. B., Vol. VI, pp. 1054ff. [2] *Ibid.*, p. 1057. [3] *Ibid.*, Vol. VII, p. 162.

[4] See Genl. Cunningham's Corpus Inscriptionum Indicarum, preface, pp. iii, vii.

opinion of Lieutenant Wilford, who, writing about the year 1795 on the Ellora inscriptions, which he thought he had deciphered, says:—"They are written in an ancient vernacular dialect, and the characters, though very different from those now in use, are nevertheless derived from the original or primeval Sanskrit, for the elements are the same."[1] Lieutenant Wilford's opinion appears to have been generally acquiesced in, for Mr. A. Stirling, referring to the Khandagiri rock inscription, in 1823, writes:—"The natives of the district can give no explanation whatever on the subject. The Brahmins refer the inscription with shuddering and disgust to the *budh ka amel*, or time when the Buddhist doctrines prevailed. I have in vain also applied to the Jains of the district for an explanation. I cannot, however, divest myself of the notion that the character has some connection with the ancient Prákrit; and considering that it occurs in a spot for many ages consecrated to the worship of Parasnáth, which the Brahmins are pleased to confound with the Buddhist religion, and that the figure or characteristic mark which appears in company with it (the *swastika*) does, in some sort, seem to identify it with the former worship, I am persuaded that a full explanation is to be looked for only from some of the learned of the Jain sect."[2]

Mr. Stirling's opinion, though based more on conjecture than sound evidence, came really much nearer the truth than he at that time could know; but the discovery of it was not made by a "learned of the Jain sect," but by one of his own nation. Previously, however, the current of the general opinion regarding the language of the inscription underwent, for a time, an entire

---

[1] As. Res., Vol. V, p. 136. [2] *Ibid.*, Vol. XV, pp. 314, 315.

change. This may be inferred from a remark of Mr. James Prinsep in 1834:—"It is not yet ascertained whether the language this character expresses is Sanskrit."[1] The remark, it is true, occurs in an argument directed, not against the Prákrit, but the Greek theory of the inscription, and may therefore be thought not necessarily to exclude the former theory. But in the same year the Sanskrit theory was distinctly put forward by Mr. B. H. Hodgson in a letter addressed to Mr. J. Prinsep:—"When we consider the wide diffusion over all parts of India of these alphabetical signs, we can scarcely doubt their derivation from Devanágarí, and the inference is equally worthy of attention that the language is Sanskrit."[2] And in commenting on this communication, Mr. J. Prinsep expressed his acquiescence in Mr. Hodgson's suggestion:—"The new facts now brought to light will, I hope, tend to facilitate this object (the discovery of the language), and leave little doubt that the alphabet is a modification of Devanágarí and the language Sanskrit, as suggested by Mr. Hodgson."[3] Neither were Messrs. Hodgson and Prinsep singular in accepting this view; for it was also held by the Rev. J. Stevenson, on the Bombay side, as is evident from a remark he made in transmitting (in 1834) to Mr. Prinsep the result of his researches into the pillar inscriptions:—"I think the first thirteen letters on the Allahabad stone may, without much difficulty, be read as containing an address, probably to the sun, in pure Sanskrit."[4]

Of course, this view was at once abandoned, the moment that Mr. Prinsep made his great discovery of the key to the true reading of the ancient character which left no further doubt that the language was really an old vernacular, a kind

---

[1] J. A. S. B., Vol. VI, p. 116. [2] *Ibid.*, Vol. III, pp. 481, 482. [3] *Ibid.*, p. 487. [4] *Ibid.*, p. 495.

of ancient Prákrit. Communicating the first correct transcription of the opening sentence of the pillar inscription, after his discovery, Mr. Prinsep says:—"Here we perceive at once that the language is the same as was observed on the Bhilsa fragments"—which had just before furnished him with the 'key,'—"not Sanskrit but the vernacular modification of it, which has been so fortunately preserved for us in the Páli scriptures of Ceylon and Ava."[1] The last statement is not strictly correct. It is now known that the language of the Asoka inscriptions is not identical with the Páli of the Southern Buddhists, though it is very closely allied to that language. It cannot be expected, however, that such an intricate point of difference should be recognized at once; and as to the main issue, undoubtedly Mr. Prinsep's discovery was perfectly genuine.

Looking back on the series of discoveries, for which we are thus indebted to his genius, it is impossible not to sympathise heartily with the gratified tone of Mr. Prinsep's words, in which he, in 1837, shortly before he left the shores of India, summed up the results of his original researches. It was a particularly gratifying circumstance which afforded him the occasion of doing so. Some years previously, Colonel W. H. Sykes had forwarded to the Royal Asiatic Society of England a series of copies of inscriptions met with in Western India; but on learning, as he says, "the admirable and efficient use Mr. Prinsep had made in his able journal, of the ancient inscriptions and ancient coins found in various parts of India, he was induced to apply to withdraw all his copies from the hands of the Royal Asiatic Society with a view to offer them to Mr. Prinsep to make such use of as he might think proper."[2] As it happened,

---

[1] J. A. S. B., Vol. VI, p. 469.

[2] *Ibid.*, p. 1038.

the copies were not returned from England; but it was on the occasion of this offer of Colonel Sykes, the honor implied in which deeply touched him, that Mr. Prinsep recorded the summary above referred to :—" More than one great question is certainly involved in the solution of the cave inscriptions of Western India. To whom is to be attributed their construction? From what period have they existed? In what language and character are the records sculptured? 'Unknown to Colonel Sykes, the whole of these questions have been already solved as regards the pillar monuments on this side of India. They are of the third or fourth century anterior of our era; they are of Buddhist foundation; and the language is not Sanskrit, but a link between that grammatical idiom and the Páli of the Buddhist scriptures; and the alphabet appears to be the very prototype of all the Devanágarí and Dakshiní alphabets."[1]

Colonel Sykes, in the passage quoted above, speaks of the admirable and efficient use which Mr. Prinsep made of ancient coins. This brings us to another great discovery similar to, and hardly less important than, the discovery of the key to the Asoka alphabet—a discovery of which Mr. Prinsep at least laid the foundation, though others were destined to carry it to so much of its successful conclusion as has been at present attained.

Contemporaneously with the Asoka alphabet, the successful discovery of the key of which has been above related, another system was also in use in ancient India. This system is now commonly called the Bactrian or Arian Páli alphabet, to distinguish it from the Lath or Indian Páli. The area in which it flourished was the

---

[1] J. A. S. B., Vol. VI, p. 1043.

north-western portion of India, which anciently included the modern Panjáb as well as the modern Afghanistan, while to the east of this area the Indian Páli characters were current. It is now known that the celebrated edicts of king Asoka, which are seen in the Indian Páli characters on the rocks of Girnár, Dhauli and other places, are inscribed on a rock near Shahbazgarhi (or Kapurdigiri) to the west of the Indus, in the Arian Páli or Bactrian alphabet. This inscription was first observed by General Court, who very briefly refers to it in a communication to the Society in 1836:—"Quite close to this village (Kapurdigiri), I observed a rock on which there are inscriptions almost effaced by time, and out of which I could only decipher twenty-three characters."[1] It was not, however, till 1838 that the inscription was fully copied by Mr. Masson and recognised by Mr. Norris, as containing the edicts of Asoka and being engraved in Arian Páli characters.[2]

The existence of these characters, however, had been known for some years before, and even some progress had been made towards the recovery of their lost value. They had become known through the collections of Bactrian and Indo-Scythian coins, made by Colonel Tod,[3] who may be said to have commenced the development of this new branch of numismatology, and General Ventura, whose successful exploration of the famous Tope of Manikyala pointed out the track to Lieutenant (afterwards Sir Alexander) Burnes, Mr. Masson and others for their subsequent large collections acquired in their journeys through ancient Bactriana.[4] It was at once observed that numerous

[1] J. A. S. B., Vol. V, p. 481; see fig. 5 on plate xxviii. [2] See Genl. Cunningham's Corpus Inscriptionum Indicarum, Vol. I, p. 8. [3] J. A. S. B., Vol. III, p. 37; also pp. 28, 29. [4] *Ibid.*, Vol. II, p. 37; Vol. III, p. 313.

coins of this class bore inscriptions in two different characters, of which those on one side were unmistakeably Greek and easily read, while those on the other side were wholly unknown, both as regards their power of signification and the language which they expressed.

At first it was generally assumed that these unknown characters must belong to some kind of Sassanian or Pehlevi alphabet. Colonel Tod, describing an Indo-Scythian coin of Kadphises in 1824, in the first volume of the Transactions of the Royal Asiatic Society, says, that "on the reverse is the sacred bull with a man, perhaps the sacrificing priest, and the epigraphe is in the Sassanian character,"[1] and Mr. James Prinsep afterwards constantly refers to them as the Pehlevi characters: thus, in 1833, with regard to a coin of Apollodotos, "on the other side the inscription is in Pehlevi;"[2] again in 1834, "the inscriptions or legends on the reverses are invariably Pehlevi."[3] There is, however, good reason for believing that, in doing so, Mr. Prinsep was merely repeating an opinion then generally acquiesced in, rather than expressing a view at which he had arrived from personal enquiry. For, curiously enough, he appears from the beginning to have made a wide distinction between the characters inscribed on the reverses of the Indo-Scythian and those engraved on the reverses of the Bactrian coins. Though in reality they are both identical, Mr. Prinsep, while allowing the latter to be Pehlevi, declares the former to be an ancient type of the Nágarí, in fact closely allied to the well-known Asoka letters. Thus in 1833, after having described some Bactrian coins and mentioned that "on the other side (the

---

[1] As. Res., Vol. XVII, p. 578. [2] J. A. S. B., Vol. II, p. 313. [3] *Ibid.*, Vol. III, pp. 157, 158.

reverse) the inscription is in Pehlevi," he proceeds to distinguish the Indo-Scythian coins, and says "on some of them (the coins of Kadphises, which Mr. Prinsep at that time believed to be posterior to those of Kanerki) "we find the same kind of character which appears on the Dehli and Allahabad pillars, the same which is found at Ellora and in many ancient caves and temples of Central India, and is held in abhorrence by Brahmins as belonging to the Buddhist religion."[1] As an instance, he quotes the very coin above referred to, which Colonel Tod had described as having a Sassanian legend, and says:—"what he supposes to be Pehlevi characters on the reverse, I incline to think characters of the Dehli type."[2]

It is clear from this strange discrepancy that at that time Mr. Prinsep could not have given much examination to these characters; if he had done so, he could not possibly have failed to recognise that the characters on the two classes of coins, the Bactrian and Indo-Scythian, were identical, and that therefore they must all be either Pehlevi or Nágarí. Indeed, it is evident from the context in which his remarks occur, that the contradictory view which he then unwittingly held was based not so much on paleographic as on historical grounds. He had rightly enough come to the conclusion, that the Indo-Scythian kings were Buddhists, whence he, though wrongly, inferred that the alphabet they used must be the ancient Nágarí which he knew to have been used by the Buddhist King Asoka.

---

[1] J. A. S. B., Vol. II, pp. 313 and 316. In the latter part of the passage, he in referring to the remarks of Major Wilford in As. Res., Vol. V, p. 140, and of Mr. A. Stirling in As. Res., Vol. XV, p. 314 (above quoted, see p. 66.) [2] J. A. S. B., Vol. II, p. 317.

About twelve months later, in July 1834, he takes occasion to state once more his view of the Nágarí character of the alphabet. General Ventura, in excavating the Manikyála Tope, had found a brass reliquiary and a silver disk, both bearing short inscriptions in Arian Páli characters. Describing the former object he says:—"The character so strongly resembles an ancient form of Nágarí, such as might be used in writing, without the head lines of the book-letter, that sanguine hopes may be entertained of its yielding to the already successful efforts of our Vice-President (Rev. Dr. Mill) and Captain Troyer."[1] And similarly with regard to the silver disk: "The characters are precisely those of the lid of the outer brass cylinder; but their combination is different. There can be little doubt of their affinity to the Sanskrit, but the difficulty of deciphering them is enhanced by the substitution of the written-hand for the perfect Nágarí, which it is clearly proved from the coins discovered in the first box to have been known at the same period. The difference is such as is remarked between the Maháַjaní and the printed Nágarí of the present day."[2]

It is not difficult to read between the lines of this passage the progress which Mr. Prinsep, in the meanwhile, had made in his views. It is clear that he had applied himself to the discovery of the key of the new alphabet; on doing so, he had—as indeed could not be otherwise—recognized that the characters on the Bactrian and Indo-Scythian coins were identical; that the theory he had hitherto held regarding them was contradictory and untenable, and that the alphabet must be either wholly Pehlevi or wholly Nágarí; lastly

---

[1] J. A. S. B., Vol. III, p. 318; compare p. 118. [2] *Ibid.*, p. 319.

he had decided in his own mind that it must be wholly Nágarí. It should be remembered that just at that time Mr. Prinsep had been successful in proving his own view of the Sanskritic character of the Asoka alphabet against the upholders of the Grecian theory. It cannot surprise us, therefore, to find him similarly favouring a Sanskrit theory of the Arian Páli alphabet in opposition to the Pehlevi theory at that time generally accepted. His idea seems to have been that the Indian Páli and the Arian Páli characters would prove to be merely two forms of the same ancient Nágarí alphabet, the former being its *kalligraphic*, the latter its *cursive* form. And it may be assumed, with great probability, that he similarly expected the language expressed by the latter character would prove to be a kind of ancient Prákrit (or Páli). With regard to the letters he was undoubtedly in error, but in his expectation of the language being ancient Prákrit, the event proved him to have been correct.

In the meantime, he soon found reason to abandon his newly conceived Nágarí-Prákrit theory altogether in favour of a return to the old theory of the letters and language being some kind of Pehlevi. The first indication of this new change of front appears only six months later, toward the end of 1834. In the course of that year an Arian Páli inscription on a large slab of stone had been discovered in a tope opened by Captain (afterwards General) Court. Referring to this inscription, a copy of which had been sent to Mr. Prinsep, he says, that "it will probably prove to be in the same dialect of the Pehlevi as occurs on the cylinders;" and he adds: "although my progress in deciphering the character in which it is written does not yet enable me to transcribe the whole, still I see very distinctly in the second line the word *Malikao*, 'king,' in the very same characters that occur on the reverse of so many of the Bactrian coins."[1]

Among the circumstances which induced him to return to the older Pehlevi theory and which at the same time led him to discover the key of the unknown alphabet, one, and that not the least important, was contributed by Mr. Masson, well known through his antiquarian discoveries in Afghanistan. They are thus related by himself in 1835: After mentioning that he had received three large collections of Bactrian coins belonging to Shekh Keramut Ali, Dr. Geraud and General Ventura, he proceeds to say: "The careful examination of the whole (of these collections) has furnished me a clue to the Bactrian form (if we may so call it) of the Pehlevi character, which is found on the reverse of many of these coins; and it will better enable us to describe them, if we begin by explaining what we have been able to make of the alphabet of this native language, which, from its marked difference from other types of the same character, I have ventured to term the Bactrian Pehlevi. Mr. Masson first pointed out, in a note addressed to myself through the late Dr. Geraud, the Pehlevi signs, which he had found to stand for the words *Menandrou*, *Apollodotou*, *Ermaiou*, *Basileos* and *Soteros*. When a supply of coins came into my hands, sufficiently legible to pursue the enquiry, I soon verified the accuracy of his observation; found the same signs, with slight variation, constantly to recur; and extended the series of words thus authenticated to the names of twelve kings, and to six titles or epithets. It immediately struck me, that if the genuine Greek names were faithfully expressed in the unknown character, a clue would, through them, be

[1] J. A. S. B., Vol. III, pp. 557, 563.

formed to unravel the value of a portion of the alphabet, which might in its turn be applied to the translated epithets and titles, and thus lead to a knowledge of the language employed. Incompetent as I felt myself to this investigation, it was too seductive not to lead me to a humble attempt at its solution."[1]

The attempt at thus comparing the corresponding groups of Greek and Arian Páli letters led to two important results. In the first place, it showed Mr. Prinsep that the two groups differed in one important respect; while the Greek letters, as is well-known, are read from left to right, these Arian Pali letters, as he found, must be read from right to left. There could be no doubt on this point; for one thing, it followed "from the regular recurrence of certain letters at what must be the close of the words to which they belonged, as it was impossible that various names and epithets should begin with the same letter, although as taking the like inflections of gender and case, they would most probably end alike."[2] This important fact was sufficient at once to convince Mr. Prinsep that his idea of the unknown characters being Nágarí was wrong, and that they belonged to the Semitic class of letters, and, as had generally been inferred from various resemblances to Pehlevi, must be some form of the latter alphabet. In the second place, his comparison of the corresponding groups of Greek and Arian Páli letters enabled him to attempt a determination of a considerable number of Arian Páli equivalents of Greek letters. Unfortunately his prejudice—a very natural one under the circumstances—that since the alphabet had proved to be a kind of Pehlevi, the language expressed by it must be also referred to the same affinity, necessarily

---

[1] J. A. S. B., Vol. IV, pp. 327, 328, 329.

[2] See Wilson's Ariana Antiqua, p. 260.

betrayed him into many erroneous valuations. Thus finding the word *malaka* to express 'king' in the Pehlevi legends of Sassanian coins, he adopted it as the Arian Páli equivalent of the Greek *Basileos.*[1] The consequence was that he mistook the true value of the three letters *l*, *k*, *o*, the only correct identification being that of the initial letter *m*. Under these circumstances, it cannot be surprising that the result of this first attempt at decipherment was not generally accepted as satisfactory, for it was soon found that many groups of letters, which were well enough known according to Mr. Prinsep's valuation, would yield no intelligible Pehlevi words.

This difficulty led Dr. Swiney to look for the key to the unknown alphabet in an altogether different direction. In 1837 he announced what he believed to be a discovery of it in the Celtic language, the grounds for which he thus explained: "The key I propose is the Celtic—a name given to a language now only known by its remains, preserved to us by various hordes of men settled in Europe, it is true, but for whom the learned of every age have claimed an eastern descent and high antiquity. What advantages the Celtic may possess over the Zend and the Syriac in unravelling Bactrian terms, remains to be proved. It will be admitted, however, by the examples I am about to give that something more than a verbal coincidence of terms has been ascertained."[2] It is not necessary to quote these examples or further to notice this curiously abortive attempt at a Celtic identification, seeing that it laboured *ab initio* under the fatal defect of being based on a comparison of entirely imaginary words. There is the less need to do so, as Mr. Prinsep, who had himself been not

[1] J. A. S. B., Vol. IV, p. 335. [2] *Ibid.*, Vol. VI, p. 98.

the least dissatisfied with the result of his first attempt, was soon after led to seek the solution of the enigma in the true quarters, namely, the ancient Prákrit or Páli.

Early in 1838 his attention had been attracted by the occurrence of the well-known Asoka character in inscriptions and on some coins found within the limits of ancient Bactriana, whence he rightly argued that "a dialect mainly derived from the Sanskrit was anciently used in Bactria."[1] Applying this new light to the reading of the Bactrian coins, he soon discovered that it did indeed clear up the mystery. "When I look back," he writes, "at my attempt of 1835, I must confess it was very unsatisfactory even to myself. I was misled by the Nakshi Rustam trilingual inscription, wherein the title of king of kings has been uniformly read as *malakán malaká*, though I balanced between this and the term *maharáo*, having found *rao* on the Indo-Scythic series. But once perceiving that the final letter might be rendered as *sa*, which is the regular Páli termination of the genitive case, I threw off the fetters of an interpretation through the Semitic languages, and at once found an easy solution of all the names and the epithets through the pliant, the wonder-working Páli, which seems really to have held an universal sway during the prevalence of the Buddhist faith in India."[2] The new view thus opened out not only led to an almost entirely new re-valuation of the Bactrian symbols, but laid the foundation of that system of decipherment of Arian Páli inscriptions, the truth of which was increasingly confirmed by every new accession to our knowledge.

Among those who made the most extensive contributions to this knowledge was Lieutenant (now Major-General) A.

---

[1] J. A. S. B., Vol. VII, p. 638. [2] *Ibid.*, p. 643.

Cunningham. He was indeed from the first associated with Mr. James Prinsep in his discoveries, as may be seen from the following reference to his valuable assistance, which occurs in one of Mr. Prinsep's Essays as early as 1836 : "Henceforth my readers should understand, and they will, doubtless, soon perceive the fact, that my coin essays are joint productions, and that I have an auxiliary at my elbow, far better acquainted with the contents of, I may say, all the collections of coins in India than I have leisure to become. With his zealous aid in hunting out the unpublished varieties of every class, I hope to make these notices complete as far as discovery has yet proceeded, and to do fuller justice to the numerous contributions I continue to receive from my numismatic coadjutors in the interior."[1] It was Lieutenant Cunningham who, after the departure of Mr. Prinsep from India, mainly carried on the course of the recovery of the Arian Páli alphabet. He not only gradually succeeded in adding many more to the single letters already discovered by Mr. Prinsep,[2] so that in 1845 he was in a position to announce that "he believed he had found the Ariano-Páli equivalent for every letter of the Sanskrit alphabet,"[3] but he was also the first to identify some of the much more difficult compound symbols, especially the conjuncts of *r* (as *tr*, *rm*, *rv.*)[4]

In connection with this subject it would not be right to pass over altogether the name of Mr. Norris, who, together with Mr. Prinsep and General Cunningham, forms the triumvirate of Arian Páli discoverers ; though his contributions, being made through the Royal Asiatic Society, do not belong to the honour-roll of this Society.

---

[1] J. A. S. B., Vol. V, p. 652. [2] *Ibid.*, Vol. IX, pp. 871, 882, 883, 887-889 ; Vol. XXIII, p. 709. [3] *Ibid.*, Vol. XIV, p. 430. [4] *Ibid.*, Vol. IX, p. 868 ; Vol. XIV, p. 432 ; and Vol. XXIII, pp. 709, 710.

In the main, the discovery of the Arian Páli alphabet, as at present known, was completed about 1854. In that year the results then attained were thus summed up by Major A. Cunningham, at the end of an essay on coins of the Indian Buddhist Satraps, in which he had just announced some new identifications: "I cannot close this account without saying a few words in favor of my claim to the discovery of the true values of eleven letters or just one-third of the Ariano-Páli alphabet. The whole number of single-letters amount to thirty five, of which Mr. James Prinsep had assigned the true value to seventeen, or just one-half. To Mr. Norris is due the discovery of six single letters, of which two are the monumental forms of *ch* and its aspirate; and the form of one letter, *jh*, still remains unknown. Of the nine known vowels (five initial and four medial) seven were determined by Mr. James Prinsep, and two by me. Of the few compound letters which are at present known, the numismatic *anusvára* was discovered by Mr. James Prinsep, the monumental one by Mr. Norris, but the attached *r* in *kra*, *tra*, *dra*, and *stra*, the attached *t* in *st*, the attached *m* in *rm* are all due to myself. The single letters, of which I claim the discovery are *g*, *gh*, *ng*; *ch*, *cch*; *t*, *d*; *ph*, *b*, *bh*; *v*; all of which, with the exception of the fourth and fifth, were made known in this Journal before the publication of Mr. Norris's alphabet in the Journal of the Royal Asiatic Society for 1846."[1]

Though the determination of the Arian Páli alphabet, as it stands at present, is undoubtedly a very great step in advance, much yet remains to be done before its enigma can be said to be truly resolved. The very circumstance which first afforded a clue to the disco-

[1] J. A. S. B., Vol. XXIII, p. 714.

very—the equivalence of Greek and Arian Páli letters on the bilingual coins of ancient Bactriana—now acts to some degree as a hindrance; for there are far-reaching divergences between the language and symbols of the Arian Páli and the Greek. The alphabet which has yielded fairly satisfactory renderings of the bilingual Bactrian coins and very small Prákrit inscriptions has hitherto failed, with one exception, to render intelligible any of the larger Arian Páli records, though undoubtedly much of this failure is also due to the unsatisfactory character of the copies as yet available. The earliest of these attempts at reading any of the larger inscriptions was made by Sir E. C. Bayley on the record engraved on the Wardak vase; his rendering, with alterations and additions made by Dr. Rájendralála Mitra, was published in 1861.[1] Two years later, in 1863, General Cunningham published a preliminary reading of the inscription on the Taxila copper plate;[2] and again seven years later, in 1870, Sir E. C. Bayley gave a tentative reading of the copper plate inscription found in the Sue Vihár tower.[3] The last inscription is the one above referred to as being the only one which as yet has received an intelligible and satisfactory translation. This was done in 1881 by the writer of the present Review.[4]

---

[1] J. A. S. B., Vol. XXX, pp. 337ff, 347ff. [2] *Ibid.*, Vol. XXXII, pp. 130ff. [3] *Ibid.*, Vol. XXXIX, pp. 65ff. [4] Proceedings for 1881, p. 139; see also Indian Antiquary, Vol. X, pp. 324ff.

CHAPTER IV.

HISTORY.

[The Mauryas: Chandragupta, Asoka, Dasaratha — The Andhras — The Graeco-Bactrians and Indo-Bactrians — The Indo-Scythians: Kadphises, Kanishka, Hushka — The Surashtrians or Satraps — The Mitras or Sungas, the Dattas, the Devas, the Kunandas, the Nágas — The Guptas: their list, date and era — The Valabhis: their list and era — The Rathors of Kanauj — The earlier rulers of Kanauj — The Chandels of Mahoba — The Pálas of Bihár and Bengal — The Senas of Bengal — The Muhammadan rulers of Bengal — Miscellaneous historical and biographical contributions.]

ONE of the great merits of the Asiatic Society of Bengal is to have laid the foundation for a true history of Ancient India. Antecedently to the discoveries made through the researches of the Society in the antiquities of India, the history and chronology of that country down to the Muhammadan conquest was inextricable from a mist of more or less legendary tradition, a great part of which was incredible, and all of which was exaggerated or distorted both in regard to the actual events and to the dates at which they were said to have occurred. The only sources which, at that time, were available to the student of Indian history were the traditions, legends and myths, which had been gradually, in the course of many centuries, accumulated in the great epic poems, the Puranic cyclopædias and provincial chronicles, written for the most part in scholastic Sanskrit language by authors to whom history and fiction seem not to have appeared antagonistic. Indeed, the two most trustworthy of the provincial chronicles, the Rája-tarangini of Kashmir and the Mahavamsa of Ceylon, which make the nearest approach to historical narration, did not become sufficiently known, till after the first landmarks in ancient Indian history had been fixed through the discoveries of the Asiatic Society, when they rendered material assistance in filling in such details as could not be ascertained from other sources. The most important of these sources, without which indeed no history of ancient India would have been possible, are the antiquities of the country, its ancient monuments, inscriptions and coins, the discovery and interpretation of which are mainly due to the researches of the Society.

The unsatisfactory character of the knowledge of ancient Indian history, before those discoveries, is not without illustrations in the very pages of the earlier Transactions of the Society itself. The earlier volumes of the Asiatic Researches contain several lengthy dissertations by Lieutenant (afterwards Colonel) Francis Wilford on various subjects connected with the chronology and history of ancient India, published successively in the years 1792, 1795, 1798, 1805, 1807, 1808, 1810 and 1822.[1] They are perhaps unrivalled for the labour, learning and ingenuity bestowed on them, but they are no less unsafe as a guide to Indian history, both on account of the untrustworthiness of the sources relied on, and the extravagance of conjecture displayed in them. Belonging to the same early stage of

---

[1] As. Res., Vol. III, p. 295, "On Egypt and the Nile, from the Sanskrit;" Vol. IV, p. 363, "On Semiramis, the origin of Mecca, &c., from the Hindu Sacred Books;" Vol. V, p. 241, "On the Chronology of the Hindus;" Vol. VIII, p. 245, "On the Sacred Isles in the West;" Vol. IX, p. 32, "On the Sacred Isles in the West, including Essays on the Chronology of the kings of Magadha, and on the Eras of Vikramaditya and Salivahana;" Vol. X, p. 27, and Vol. XI, p. 11, "On the Sacred Isles in the West;" Vol. XIV, p. 373, "On the Ancient Geography of India;" J. A. S. B., Vol. XX, pp. 227, 470, "On the Comparative Geography of Ancient India."

historical enquiry, though of a much more sober character, are two contributions by Sir William Jones, one a "discourse on the Hindus," published in the first volume of the Researches (1788), the other a memoir on "the chronology of the Hindus" in the second volume (1790).[1] The conclusions possible on such data as were then available may be judged from the fact, that in these dissertations Sir W. Jones "fixes the time of Buddha in the year one thousand and fourteen before the birth of Christ, or two thousand seven hundred and ninety years ago."[2] He was not unconscious, however, of the unsatisfactory character of his sources, for summing up his results he confesses, "that though he has given a sketch of Indian history through the longest period fairly assignable to it, and has traced the foundation of the Indian empire above three thousand eight hundred years from the present time; still, on a subject in itself so obscure and so much clouded by the fictions of the Brahmans, who, to aggrandize themselves, have designedly raised their antiquity beyond the truth, we must be satisfied with probable conjecture and just reasoning from the best attainable data; nor can we hope for a system of Indian chronology, to which no objection can be made, unless the astronomical books in Sanskrit shall yield their unexceptional evidence."[3] Shortly afterwards some of this expected astronomical evidence was made available to Sir William Jones. On a careful consideration of it, he came to the conclusion, which he published in 1790 in a supplementary memoir, and which is still substantially correct, "that the dawn of true Indian history appears only three

[1] As. Res., Vol. I, p. 415, "The third Anniversary Discourse;" see especially p. 425; Vol. II, p. 111, "On the Chronology of the Hindus." [2] *Ibid.*, Vol. I, p. 425; Vol. II, p. 125. [3] *Ibid.*, Vol. II, pp. 145, 146.

or four centuries before the Christian era, the preceding ages being clouded by allegory or fable."[1]

In those days great results were expected from researches in the astronomical works of the Hindus, with regard to their ancient chronology. These expectations have been only very partially verified; but it was impossible for Sir William Jones, at that time, to foresee the remarkable discoveries that would be made in the antiquities of India and what a flood of light these would throw on its ancient history. Yet he himself was destined, not long afterwards, to announce the first in the long series of historical discoveries,—that of the identity of the Indian Chandra Gupta with the Greek Sandracottus. The announcement occurs in his tenth anniversary discourse on "Asiatic History, Civil and Natural," published in 1795 in the fourth volume of the Researches.[2] It may be given in his own words: "The jurisprudence of the Hindus and Arabs being the field which I have chosen for my peculiar toil, you cannot expect that I should greatly enlarge your collection of historical knowledge; but I may be able to offer you some occasional tribute, and I can not help mentioning a discovery which accident threw in my way; though my proofs must be reserved for an essay, which I have destined for the fourth volume of your Transactions.[3] To fix the situation of that Palibothra, which was visited and described by Megasthenes, had always appeared a very difficult problem; for though it could not have been Prayaga, nor Canyacubja, nor Gaur, yet we could not confidently decide that it was Pataliputra, though names and most cir-

---

[1] As. Res., Vol. II, p. 389; see especially p. 401. [2] *Ibid.*, Vol. IV, p. 1; see especially p. 11. [3] This essay was never published. Unfortunately Sir William Jones died on the 27th April 1794, only a year after the announcement of his great discovery.

cumstances nearly correspond, because that renowned capital extended from the confluence of the Sone and the Ganges to the site of Pátna, while Palibothra stood at the junction of the Ganges and Erannoboas, which the accurate M. D'Anville had pronounced to be the Yamuna: but this only difficulty was removed, when I found in a classical Sanskrit book near two thousand years old, that Hiranyabáhu, or "golden armed," which the Greeks changed into Erannoboas, or "the river with a lovely murmur," was in fact another name for the Sona itself, though Megasthenes, from ignorance or inattention, has named them separately. This discovery led to another of greater moment; for Chandra Gupta, who, from a military adventurer, became, like Sandracottus, the sovereign of upper Hindustan, actually fixed the site of his empire at Pataliputra, where he received ambassadors from foreign princes, and was no other than that very Sandracottus who concluded a treaty with Seleucus Nicator."[1] Sir William Jones' important discovery was at once accepted by Captain Francis Wilford, who adduced some further evidence in confirmation of it;[2] and though at first some scholars raised a few objections, mainly geographical, regarding the apparently different positions of the ancient Palibothra and modern Patna, which further enquiries dispelled, the identification was soon universally admitted to be indubitable, and nothing will ever shake its certainty. Its great importance lies in the fact, that it renders it possible to synchronize the history of India with that of Greece at one point; and as the chronology of Greece is well known and quite certain, we thus obtain a date in Indian chronology as a starting point, from which calculations may be made forwards and backwards with some degree of assurance. Sandracottus, namely,

---

[1] As. Res., Vol. IV, pp. 10, 11. [2] *Ibid.*, Vol. V, p. 262.

according to Justin, a Greek historian, had seized the throne of India after the prefects of Alexander had been murdered in 317 B. C. Seleucus found him as sovereign of India, when, after the taking of Babylon and the conquest of the Bactrians, he passed on into India. He did not, however, conquer Sandracottus, but, after concluding a treaty with him, marched on to make war against Antigonus. This must have taken place before the year 312 B. C., as in that year Seleucus had returned to Babylon. The accession of Chandra Gupta must, therefore, be placed about 315 B. C., or some time between 317 and 312.[1] This date, then, is the sheet-anchor of Indian chronology. Basing on it, and assisted by Indian chronicles or ancient inscriptions and coins, all calculations referring to the history of ancient India were henceforth made, backwards as well as forwards. The more important forward calculations will be noticed further on; of the backward calculations it will suffice to mention here the most important one—that referring to the date of Buddha's death. The most probable date for this event was ultimately ascertained in 1852 by Major (now Major-General) A. Cunningham, to be the year 477 or 478 B. C.[2]

Sir William Jones' identification of Chandra Gupta with Sandracottus had been suggested to him by the notices of that king which he met with in the Hindu Purános and in a Sanskrit drama, called Mudrá Rákshasa, which described his usurpation and coronation.[3] About forty years later, in 1836 and 1837, his discovery received a striking confirmation which the Hon'ble George Turnour was able to produce from the Buddhistic Annals of Ceylon.[4] Another item of

---

[1] See M. Muller's History of Ancient Sanskrit Literature, pp. 275, 278, 298, 300.
[2] J. A. S. B., Vol. XXIII, p. 704; see also Genl. Cunningham's Corpus Inscr. Ind., p. 4.
[3] As. Res., Vol. IV, p. 6; Vol. V, p. 262. [4] J. A. S. B., Vol. VI, p. 713.

evidence, however, which was produced about the same time and which, if true, would have been of far greater importance, because it would have been absolutely authentic and nearly contemporary, proved, in the course of further research, to be untenable. This is the occurrence of the name of Chandra Gupta in one of the ancient inscriptions on the pillar of Allahabad. It was thought at first by the early decipherers of those inscriptions, Captain A. Troyer and Mr. J. Prinsep, that this Chandra Gupta might be identical with the Chandra Gupta (Sandracottus) of the Maurya race, whose date had been already satisfactorily ascertained.[1] Further enquiry soon showed that this opinion was erroneous; but at the same time it also resulted, as will be shown further on, in a new discovery, which is only second in importance to that of Sandracottus himself.

This happened in the years 1834-1837, the brief period of great historical discoveries, in which the names of the Hon'ble G. Turnour and Mr. J. Prinsep are distinguished above all in the small band of enquirers and scholars who contributed to the great result. About this time the former had commenced a careful study and analysis of the Páli Buddhistical Annals of Ceylon. Some of the results of it he communicated, in a series of memoirs, to the Journal of the Society. The first of these memoirs, in the volume for 1836, was called forth by some disparaging remarks on the trustworthiness of Buddhistical as compared with Brahmanical chronology, into which Professor H. H. Wilson and Mr. J. Prinsep had been betrayed.[2] In the course of his reply he showed that the king Asoka of Kashmir, mentioned in the chronicles of that country, was the same Asoka

---

[1] J. A. S. B., Vol. III, pp. 119, 120; Vol. VII, p. 343. [2] *Ibid.*, Vol. V, pp. 525, 536.

whom the Buddhist annals relate to have been the grandson of Chandra Gupta of the Mauryan dynasty and to have ascended the throne of Magadha in the year 325 B. C.[1] A second and third memoir, published in 1837, are devoted to the elucidation of some of the chronological statements and difficulties occurring in those portions of the Buddhist annals which relate the history of Asoka and his dynasty. Mr. Turnour came to the conclusion that the only way to arrive at an agreement between the dates furnished by these annals and those of Europe was to admit in the former an error of about sixty years—an error which he thought was designedly committed by the Buddhist annalists.[2]

In the meanwhile, Mr. J. Prinsep had been zealously carrying on his attempts in deciphering the most ancient of the pillar inscriptions at Allahabad, Dehli and other places. In these, as already related in the preceding chapter of this Review, he was eminently successful. In the Journal for that very year, 1837, he published his first discovery, that those inscriptions professed to have been made by the order of a king Piyadassi; and having failed to identify this king with any prince mentioned in any of the Hindu genealogical tables with which he was acquainted, he suggested that Piyadassi, who called himself "the beloved of the Gods" (*devánam priya*), might be identical with a Ceylonese king, called Deveni Piatissa, who in the Buddhist annals of Ceylon is said to have succeeded his father in B. C. 307, and to have prevailed on the Indian king, Asoka of Magadha, to introduce Buddhism into that island. He pointed out that his suggestion was in agreement with the date of Asoka, as calculated from that of his grandfather Chandra Gupta, whose date had been determined by

[1] J. A. S. B., Vol. V, p. 521. [2] *Ibid.*, Vol. VI, pp. 501, 713.

Sir William Jones ;[1] and that further this proved that the pillars had been erected about three hundred years before the Christian era.[2] As he went on, however, deciphering the remainder of Piyadassi's inscriptions, he found reason to mistrust his identification of that king with the Ceylonese prince, and his doubts were converted into certainty when Mr. Turnour communicated to him his discovery that, according to the Buddhist annals, Piyadassi was no one else than the well-known Asoka of Magadha himself, who bore Piyadassi as a surname. Mr. Turnour's discovery Mr. Prinsep lost no time in communicating to the world in the pages of the Journal for 1837 ;[3] and a little later in the same year, Mr. Turnour himself, in the course of two further memoirs which he contributed to the pages of the Journal, gave a detailed account of his discovery of the identity of Piyadassi with Asoka in the Dipavamsa, a newly discovered ancient Buddhist chronicle ; and further confirmed it by the authority of another ancient chronicle, the Rasaváhiní.[4] In the Journal for the following year, 1838, Mr. Turnour pursued his researches into the Buddhist annals of Ceylon, which had yielded such happy results, through three additional memoirs, in one of which he communicated an analysis of the Dipavamsa.[5] In the same year, 1838, Mr. J. Prinsep had once more the happiness to announce the third and last of the discoveries connected with the name of king Asoka. It was the synchronism between that king and the kings Antiochus II Theos of Syria and Ptolemy Philadelphos of Egypt, who died in 247 B. C., and with whom Asoka is stated in his inscriptions to have

---

[1] J. A. S. B., Vol. VI. pp. 469ff. [2] *Ibid.*, pp. 566, 567. [3] *Ibid.*

[4] *Ibid.*, pp. 856 and 1050; see especially pp. 1054, 1056 ; see also Vol. VII, p. 156.

[5] *Ibid.*, Vol. VII, pp. 686, 789, 919, 991.

entered into treaty relations.[1] Thus three independent bases had now been found, from which it was possible to calculate the date of king Asoka's reign and fix it with certainty within very narrow limits,—*i. e.*, most probably from 264 to 223,—[2] a date which fully bore out Mr. Turnour's discovery of an error of about sixty years in the Buddhist chronology.[3]

The identification of Asoka immediately led to the verification of a third member of the Maurya dynasty, his grandson Dasaratha. The existence of this prince had been doubtful, as in some of the Puranic annals his name was omitted from the list of Maurya sovereigns. But, in 1837, Mr. J. Prinsep succeeded in deciphering his name in an inscription occurring in one of the Nágárjuní caves, near Gaya; and as the inscription is engraved in the characters of the time of Asoka and the very surname Devánam priya, which is borne by Asoka himself, is given in it to Dasaratha, there could be no longer any doubt as to the existence and identity of the latter.[4]

The discoveries connected with Asoka led to another identification which deserves a passing notice; for though at that time based on a fallacy, it has since been established on much more satisfactory grounds. In one of the inscriptions on the rock of Girnar, Mr. J. Prinsep discovered, in 1838, the name of a king Satakarni, who, as was known from the Hindu genealogical lists, belonged to a line of Andhra sovereigns. The exact date of these kings was not known, but in an essay on the kings of Magadha, published in the

---

[1] J. A. S. B., Vol. VII, pp. 156 (160), and pp. 219, 225. At first Mr. Prinsep had identified the Antiochus of the inscription with Antiochus the Great (VII, p. 160), but afterwards he corrected his mistake (VII, p. 225). [2] See General Cunningham's Corpus Inscr. Ind., pp. III-X. [3] See above, p. 89. [4] J. A. S. B., Vol. VI, pp. 676-678, 790; and Vol. VII, p. 156.

Asiatic Researches in 1807, it was conjecturally placed by Captain F. Wilford between the third and sixth centuries after Christ.[1] Mr. Prinsep, who ascribed the inscription to the age of the great Chandra Gupta and his grandson Asoka mentioned in it, concluded that the Andhra dynasty must have been contemporary with the Maurya dynasty.[2] Though his premises were wrong, his conclusion nevertheless, as already said, more recent researches have proved to be correct.

The discovery of a mention of Greek kings in the Asoka inscriptions, as entertaining treaty relations with an Indian sovereign, tended to intensify the interest, at that time already strongly excited, in researches into the history of the Greek and Indo-Greek kings of Bactria, which were at once sustained and stimulated by the enormous finds of Bactrian coins made within the few previous years. Previous to 1833, "the means of an acquaintance with the history of Bactria and Bactrian India were extremely circumscribed. It was known that, after the death of Alexander, Bactria became an independent principality under Greek sovereigns, and the names of a few of them were picked out with extraordinary labour and learning from the fragmentary notices of classical authors and one or two coins. It had also been ascertained from the same writers and from Chinese authorities that the Greek rule was overthrown by Scythian chiefs, whose sway extended to the mouth of the Indus.[3] These few leading facts were unaccompanied by details, and scantily occupied the interval that separated the Scythian conquest from the Macedonian invasion. Within the next seven years this deficiency was

---

[1] As. Res., Vol. IX, pp. 101-104, 110-112. [2] J. A. S. B., Vol. VII, pp. 346, 347.

[3] *Ibid.*, Vol. VI, p. 61. See also two papers by Mr. Johannes Avdall on Ancient Armenia and its relation to India, J. A. S. B., Vol. V, p. 331; Vol. VI, p. 81.

remedied, and the barrenness of events changed to abundance. Successful research not only corroborated all that was before imperfectly known, but filled up the meagre outline with circumstances and persons of historical truth and importance. The hitherto unnamed or unknown members of successive or synchronous dynasties came now into view as well-defined individuals and in connected order; and revolutions of a religious as well as of a political origin could be discerned, if not with all the minuteness one could wish, yet with a distinctness that still demands unquestioning reliance. The means by which these additions to our knowledge of the past were effected, were, as already said, the numerous coins which were found within those seven years in Turkistan, Afghanistan and the Panjáb."[1] A large number of zealous collectors and investigators co-operated in the researches: Lieutenant Burnes, Generals Court, Allard and Ventura, Doctors Gerard, Swiney, Lord, and Martin Honigberger, Shekh Karamat Ali and others.[2] But foremost amongst them all were Mr. James Prinsep, General Cunningham, and above all Mr. Masson. The latter "had resided some time in Afghanistan, and had been engaged either by himself or in co-operation with a medical officer in the service of Ranjit Singh, Dr. Honigberger, in examining the ancient monuments, the topes and tumuli of that country. In the course of these investigations some coins were obtained, but the chief site of Mr. Masson's discoveries was at a place named Beghram." "At an early period of his researches he proposed to the Government of Bombay to transfer his actual and all future collections to the East India Company, on condition of their defraying the cost of

---

[1] See Ariana Antiqua, pp. 2, 3. [2] See J. A. S. B., Vol. II, pp. 28, 37, 308, 311; Vol. III, pp. 175, 313, 320, 324, 436; Vol. IV, pp. 327, 328; Vol. V, p. 549; Vol. VII, pp. 637, 1047.

his operations. The proposal was favourably received, and from the year 1834 until 1837 Mr. Masson was sedulously employed in the pursuit, in which he had engaged with equal intelligence and zeal, on behalf and at the expense of the East India Company. In the course of time the collections which he had formed and which included above thirty thousand coins, were transmitted to England and deposited in the Company's museum."[1]

Antecedently to the discoveries made by Mr. Masson and his co-operators, no more than nine kings of Bactriana were known to the learned world. These were Theodotus I and II, Euthydemus, Demetrius, Eukratides, Heliokles, Antimachus, Menander and Apollodotus.[2] The last two had only been discovered a few years previously to 1833, by Colonel Tod, who, during twelve years of his residence in India, had conducted a zealous search after ancient coins, and in that interval had succeeded in accumulating no less than twenty thousand coins of all denominations. He published his discovery of Menander and Apollodotus in the Transactions of the Royal Asiatic Society for 1824.[3] In 1833 Mr. Masson's successful operations in Kabul commenced,[4] the results of which he made known in the pages of the Journal, in a series of most interesting memoirs. In the very first of these, published in 1834, he was able to announce the discovery of no less than six new Bactrian sovereigns, namely Antialkides, Lysias, Agathocles, Pantaleon, Hermæus and two others whom he called Unadpherras,[5] and Sotereages or Hegas. The latter name was immediately discerned by Mr. Prinsep to be a

---

[1] See Ariana Antiqua, pref., p. v, and pp. 10, 11. [2] J. A. S. B., Vol. II, pp. 37, 315; Vol. III, pp. 155, 156. See also Ariana Antiqua, pp. 3, 4. [3] J. A. S. B., Vol. II, pp. 29, 37. See also Transaction, R. A. S., Vol. I, p. 314; and Ariana Antiqua, p. 4. [4] J. A. S. B., Vol. III, p. 153. [5] *Ibid.*, pp. 162, 442; and Vol. IV, p. 327.

mislection for Megas "the Great," and to be the designation of an otherwise unnamed king.[1] One of this king's coins had already been noticed, as early as 1832 and 1833, though not recognized, in the Asiatic Researches and the Journal.[2] The other name Unadpherras was also afterwards corrected by Mr. Prinsep to Gondophares.[3] Most of the extensive collections made by Mr. Masson, Lieut. Burnes, and others had the good fortune of passing under the experienced eye of Mr. J. Prinsep in Calcutta, and from time to time, as he made new discoveries, they were communicated to the world in successive volumes of the Journal. Thus, in 1835, he announced the discovery of another batch of four new kings: Philoxenes, Azes, Azilises and Vonones.[4] The name of the last, however, was at that time read incorrectly as Nonus; and it may be added that one of his coins as well as three of Azes had been already described, though not recognized, by Mr. Masson in his memoir of the preceding year.[5] In 1836, the latter published a second memoir on the ancient coins of Beghram. In this, again, three new kings were added to those already discovered,—*viz.* Diomedes and two others,—whose names Mr. Masson read as Adelphortes and Palerkes.[6] In a third memoir, however, published a little later in the same year, 1836, he corrected the second of the two names into Spalirisus,[7] while Mr. Prinsep succeeded in finding the true name of the first king to be Spalyrius.[8] Here again, coins of these two kings had been noticed, but not recognized, much earlier; *viz.* Spalyrius in 1830 and Spalirisus

---

[1] J. A. S. B., Vol. III, pp. 162, 168; Vol. IV, 344, 345. [2] As. Res., Vol. XVII, pp. 575—577 (figs. 23—25); J. A. S. B., Vol. II, p. 38 (figs. 19, 20), p. 314 (fig. 113), p. 411 (figs. 9, 10). [3] J. A. S. B., Vol. IV, p. 346; and Vol. VII, p. 654. [4] *Ibid.*, Vol. IV, pp. 341-345. [5] *Ibid.*, p. 342; Vol. V, p. 25; also Vol. III, p. 172 (figs. 43, 45, 46, 47). See also Ariana Antiqua, p. 338 (No. 2). [6] J. A. S. B., Vol. V, pp. 1, 18, 19, 20, 24, and 25; see also p. 549. [7] *Ibid.*, p. 547; see also p. 551. [8] *Ibid.*, p. 551.

in 1834.[1] In the same memoir Mr. Masson succeeded in adding one more to his discoveries, *viz.* the king Achelius, or, as his name is now generally accepted to be, Archebius.[2] Only two months afterwards, in November 1836, the list of Bactrian sovereigns was again enriched, through Mr. Prinsep, with two new names, those of a king Amyntas and a queen Agathokleia,[3] and after a pause of nearly two years, in July 1838, one more was added by him, named Abagases (or Abalgases or Abdagases.)[4] Again two years later, in 1840, Lieutenant (now Major-General) A. Cunningham brought forward a new king Zoilus:[5] and after an interval of another two years, he had the satisfaction of announcing the discovery of no less than eight new names of Bactrian sovereigns. These were the kings Strato, Telephus, Hippostratus, Pakores, Arsaces, Dionysíus, Nikias, and the queen Kalliope.[6] With this last successful find the long series of discoveries in the regal history of Bactriana came, in the main, to an end. Only one more addition was made many years afterwards; it was that of a king Plato, who was discovered in 1872 by Mr. J. G. Delmerick.[7]

Besides the mere list of sovereigns of Bactriana, the coins afforded much additional information on the political, social, and religious condition of that country. This information was carefully collected by Mr. Masson, Professor Lassen, and Lieutenant A. Cunningham, and published by them in a series of memoirs contributed to the Journal during the years 1834 to 1840.[8] It would exceed, how-

---

[1] J. A. S. B., Vol. III, p. 172 (fig. 44); and Vol. IV, p. 342 (figs. 6, 9). [2] *Ibid.*, Vol. V, pp. 547, 548; see also Ariana Antiqua, pp. 279, 280 (No. 1). [3] J. A. S. B., Vol. V, pp. 720, 721. [4] *Ibid.*, Vol. VII, pp. 640, 645, 654; see also Vol. IX, p. 882. [5] *Ibid.*, Vol IX, p. 871. [6] *Ibid.*, Vol. XI, Part i, pp. 130-135. [7] Proceedings for 1872, pp. 34, 174. [8] J A. S. B., Vol. III, p. 153; Vol. V, pp. 537, 707; Vol. VI, p. 57 (Masson);—Vol. IX, pp. 251, 339, 449, 627, 933 (Lassen; translated by Dr. Roer);—Vol. IX, 867 (Cunningham).

ever, the proper limits of this Review to enter fully into this subject, which, moreover, in not a few points, is still a matter of doubt and difference, even at the present day. It will suffice to state, that the coins, from their characters, inscriptions, emblems, find-places and various other circumstances, clearly show, that the line of princes discovered through them did not form a continuous succession of sovereigns, but that many of them must have been contemporaneous rulers in a variety of independent Greek principalities, into which the whole of Bactriana was divided; that some of these principalities must have included Afghanistan and the Panjáb, and used the old western Páli—a language closely akin to Sanskrit; that by the side of the worship of Greek and Iranian divinities the Buddhist faith must have been current in the eastern portion of Bactriana; and that the period during which these Bactrian and Indo-Bactrian reigns lasted must have extended from about 250 to 120 before Christ, when they were subverted by an irruption of Scythian tribes from the centre of Asia.

It had long been known from the annals of Kashmir, an account of which was published by Professor H. H. Wilson in 1825 in the Asiatic Researches,[1] that, at an ancient period, a dynasty of Turkish or Indo-Scythian princes had conquered and held sway over that country. Three members of the dynasty were especially named—Kaniskha, Hushka and Yashka—whose date was supposed to be the fifth century before the Christian era.[2] It was about ten years later, that Mr. J. Prinsep first succeeded in verifying these Indo-Scythic princes and their true dates through their coins. The first specimens of these coins were made known in 1824 by Colonel Tod in the Transactions of the

[1] As. Res., Vol. XV, p. 1. [2] *Ibid.*, pp. 23, 24, 91, 92. J. A. S. B., Vol. II, p. 315.

Royal Asiatic Society,[1] and a year later, in 1825, by Professor H. H. Wilson in the Asiatic Researches of this Society.[2] They were, however, not fully recognized at that time, and it was not till 1833, when a well-preserved specimen was discovered by Lieutenant Burnes, that Mr. Prinsep was first enabled to decipher the name of king Kanishka on it. It is true, the name on the coin reads Kanerkou ; but Mr. Prinsep at once recognized it to be merely another form of the well-known Kanishka ;[3] and though a year later, in 1834, some mistaken evidence led him and Mr. Masson to feel uncertain as to this happy identification,[4] it soon gained the general assent of all numismatists and historians, while in 1845, some new Buddhistic coins of that king enabled Lieutenant A. Cunningham to "afford the last links in the chain of evidence to prove the identity of the Indo-Scythian Kanerki with the Buddhist prince Kanishka of Kashmir."[5] In the same year, 1845, Lieutenant Cunningham also proved that the Indo-Scythian king Oerki or Hoerki, many of whose coins had been found in the meanwhile, was the same as the king Hushka of the Kashmirian annals.[6] The existence of a third Indo-Scythian king, called Kadphises, had been already previously, in 1834, established from his coin by Mr. Masson.[7] A careful consideration of the types of the coins of these three kings clearly showed, that they succeeded each other in the following order—Kadphises, Kanerki, Hoerki,[8] and a com-

---

[1] See Transactions, R. A. S., Vol. I. [2] As. Res., Vol. XVII, pp. 562-566, 577-583 (figs. 1-4 and 26-42). [3] J. A. S. B., Vol. II, pp. 314, 315. [4] *Ibid.*, Vol. III, pp. 159, 449. [5] *Ibid.*, Vol. XIV, pp. 430, 440, 441. [6] *Ibid.*, p. 431, [7] *Ibid.*, Vol. III, pp. 160, 229, 443. At first the name was read wrongly, Mokadphises, by M. R. Rochette and M. Jacquet of Paris; see *ibid.*, Vol. V, p. 553, and Ariana Antiqua, p. 354. [8] J. A. S. B., Vol. IV, pp. 630, 631; Vol. XIV, p. 441; see Ariana Antiqua, pp. 353, 357, 373. At first Mr. Masson placed Kadphises after Kanerki; see J. A. S. B., Vol. III, pp. 173, 174.

parison of the coins of Kadphises with those of Hermæus, the last king of the Bactrian kingdom of Nysa, further showed that the latter must have been overthrown by an irruption of the Indo-Scythians under his leadership.[1] A clearly defined progress of imitation and modification traceable through the coins of Hermæus, Kadphises, Kanishka and Hushka left no reasonable doubt on this point ; and an additional confirmation was derived from the fact, that the find-spots of the coins pointed to Kabul,—where indeed the tomb of Kadphises was discovered by Dr. Martin Honigberger,—as the capital of the Indo-Scythian dynasty.[2] Moreover it was possible, from the coins, in combination with historical traditions, to determine approximately the period during which the Indo-Scythian empire lasted, *viz.*, from about the commencement of the first century before Christ, when the kingdom of Nysa was conquered, to about the end of the second century after Christ, when the reign of Vasudeva, the successor of Hushka, must have terminated. Indeed, there is every probability that the accession of Kanishka is coincident with the establishment of the celebrated Saka or Scythian era. According to the trustworthy Buddhist tradition of Tibet, Kanishka reigned upwards of 400 years after the death of Buddha. That event is now known to have taken place in 477 or 478 B.C., so that the accession of Kanishka in 78 A.D., the initial year of the Saka era, is quite probable. Calculations approaching this result had been made by MM. Prinsep, Masson and Cunningham ;[3] though it was reserved for much later researches by Dr. R. Mitra and others, founded upon the discoveries of inscriptions of Kanishka and his successor at

---

[1] J. A. S. B., Vol. III, pp. 159, 160. [2] *Ibid.*, pp. 159, 160, 173. [3] *Ibid.*, Vol. II, p. 316 ; Vol. III, pp. 159, 160 ; Vol. XIV, p. 441.

Mathura and other places, together with other considerations, to arrive at some sort of finality on the subject of the date of the Indo-Scythian kings.[1]

The comparative study of Bactrian numismatics led, at this time, to another important discovery. It was that of a line of sovereigns who, under the style of "Satraps," ruled the country of Suráshtra, on the North-western coast of India. No mention was made of them in any of the annals or chronicles of India; and if it had not been for their coins, their very existence would have remained unknown to the world.[2] A few specimens of these coins were first noticed in 1824 by Colonel Tod in the Transactions of the Royal Asiatic Society,[3] and again in 1835, by Mr. Prinsep, in the Journal of this Society. The latter examined a large number of them very carefully. The results of his examination he published in the volumes for 1835 and 1837.[4] He found that all the coins he had examined consisted of no more than nine varieties, of which several could be traced from father to son in regular succession. He was thus able to draw up a list of the sovereigns of Suráshtra, which contained the names of eleven kings, with only two breaks in the succession.[5] That their kingdom was Katch, or rather Suráshtra, he rightly judged from the fact that their coins were principally found in those regions;[6] and from the number of their list he concluded that their rule "ran through a space of just two centuries."[7] In the main, the correctness of his conclusion has been generally admitted. He himself discovered a new name, and modified his list of kings slightly a year after-

---

[1] Thus, *e. g.*, J. A. S. B., Vol. XXXIX, p. 126, in the year 1870; see also *ibid.*, p. 65. [2] J. A. S. B., Vol. VI, p. 383. [3] *Ibid.*, p. 685. [4] *Ibid.*, Vol. IV, p. 684; and Vol. VI, p. 377. [5] *Ibid.*, Vol. VI, pp. 380, 383. [6] *Ibid.*, p. 378. [7] *Ibid.*, p. 383.

wards, in 1838, when he discovered that the coins bore dates in an ancient form of numeration and of an unknown era.[1] The subsequent researches of Mr. Thomas in 1848 and Mr. Newton in 1862 have added no less than fourteen new names, so that the list of Surashtrian kings now consists of twenty-six names, with the modifications necessitated by their discovery.[2] With regard to the date of these kings, Mr. Prinsep gave expression to several different, and even contradictory, opinions. At one time he ascribed them to a period from the third to the seventh centuries after Christ;[3] at another time, misled by his erroneous view of the great age of the Girnar inscription, he thought they might be as old as the time of the great Chandra Gupta in the fourth century B. C.[4] By the side of these, however, he also expressed a third view, for which he himself produced the strongest evidence, and which, being most consistent with all the circumstances of the Surashtrian coins, is now universally accepted as the only correct one. These coins, namely, exhibit the clearest evidence of likeness, on the one hand, with the coins of the later Parthian rulers of Bactriana, especially of those of king Kodes, of which they are unmistakable imitations; on the other hand, with the coins of the Gupta kings of Magadha and Kanauj, of which they are the prototypes.[5] This determines the date of their period as extending from the first century before Christ to the third century after Christ, so that possibly the well-known (so-called) Vikramáditya or Samvat era, which commences in 56 B. C., may date from the accession of their dynasty. Another evidence

[1] J. A. S. B., Vol. VII, pp. 348, 351. [2] See Proceedings for 1882, p. 42. Mr. Newton's paper is in the Journal, Bom. As. Soc., Vol. VII, p. 30; and Mr. Thomas', in the Journal, Royal Asiatic Society, Vol. XII, p. 32, and in Dr. Burgess' Archæological Survey of Western India, Vol. I, p. 44. [3] J. A. S. B., Vol. VI, pp. 385, 386. [4] *Ibid.*, p. 388; and Vol. VII, pp. 343, 345, 347. [5] *Ibid.*, Vol. IV, pp. 684, 685; Vol. VI, p. 389; see also Vol. XXIV, p. 504.

to the same effect is derived from the form of the characters of the coin-legends, which is less ancient than that of the Asoka alphabet, while it is older than that of the Gupta characters.[1] Once again, their title Kshatrapa, which is the same as the Persian Satrap, brings them in immediate contact with the later Bactrian-Greek or Parthian kings in the second and first centuries before Christ.[2]

The numismatic researches which were so zealously and successfully conducted in those early years helped to verify, as contemporaries of the Indo-Scythian and Surashtrian sovereigns, another class of Indian rulers, some of whom, unlike the Surashtrian kings, were distinctly recorded in the Puranic chronicles of India. These were the various dynasties known by the names of the Mitras or Sungas, the Dattas, the Devas, the Kunandas, the Nágas and others. Most of them had one common characteristic—that their coins bore various sorts of Buddhist symbols. This circumstance by itself indicated that they might be safely ascribed to that period of Indian history during which Buddhism held most undisputed sway over the political and social life of the people, in the centuries immediately before and after Christ.[3] To Mr. Prinsep and the earliest collectors who so abundantly supplied him with their newly found treasures, these coins were very obscure, nor have subsequent researches sufficed to remove all the obscurity attaching to them. But so much Mr. Prinsep clearly discerned from the character of their emblems, the ancient form of their letters, and their more or less close resemblance to the

---

[1] J. A. S. B., Vol. VI, p. 378; Vol. VII, p. 348; see also Vol. XXIV, pp. 390, 504.

[2] *Ibid.*, Vol. VII, pp. 344, 345. At first, Mr. Prinsep read the title as "Kritrima;" see *ibid.*, Vol. VI, pp. 380, 388; Vol. VII, p. 344. The Skr. *kshatrapa* becomes in Western Prákrit *chhatrapa*, which corresponds to Satrap, just as Prákrit *Chandra Gupta* to *Sandracottus* (*s*= *ch* or *chh*). [3] See Ariana Antiqua, p. 17.

later Bactrian coinage, that they were to be ascribed to a very early date,[1] and that they were Buddhistic.[2] His opinion as to their character and age is sufficiently indicated by the names he gave them—Indo-Bactrian or Buddhist Satrap coins, &c.[3] Subsequently three distinct divisions among these early Hindu or Buddhist coins have had some more light thrown on them, in consequence of further discoveries of coins. These are the coinages of the Buddhist Satraps, the Nágas, and the Mitras. On the two first mentioned, Major (now Major-General) A. Cunningham contributed two memoirs to the pages of the Journal of 1854 and 1865.[4] Of the so-called Buddhist Satraps he verified three members of a dynasty, which he identified with those of a Maurya dynasty of Dehli, mentioned in the Hindu genealogies.[5] At the same time, on account of the style of the Greek letters, and the types which are imitated from those of the later Bactrian kings, he fixed the date of these Satraps to have been the first century before the Christian era.[6] In his memoir of 1865, Major Cunningham verified a dynasty of nine Nága princes, who, to judge from the character of their coins, must have been contemporary with the well-known Guptas in the first and second centuries of the Christian era, and who are all recorded in the Puranic annals of India.[7] Regarding the Mitra dynasty, which is also recorded in the Puranic annals, no more information was received till nearly the close of the century. In 1879, a large number of coins of that dynasty were discovered near Rámanagar, which enabled Mr. A. C. Carlleyle, in

---

[1] J. A. S. B., Vol. III, pp. 227, 228, 435; Vol. IV, pp. 621, 627, 628, 689; Vol. VI, p. 463; Vol. VII, p. 1052. [2] *Ibid.*, Vol. IV, pp. 625, 628; Vol. VI, pp. 463, 465. [3] *Ibid.*, Vol. VII, pp. 1051, 1052. [4] *Ibid.*, Vol. XXIII, p. 679; Vol. XXXIV, p. 115. [5] *Ibid.*, Vol. XXIII, pp. 681, 683. [6] *Ibid.*, p. 681; see also Vol. XXIV, p. 396. [7] *Ibid.*, Vol. XXXIV, pp. 116, 118, 119, 120.

two memoirs, published in the Journal of 1880,[1] to make an attempt to arrange the Mitra princes provisionally in an order of succession, consisting of fourteen members,[2] and to refer their date to a period from the second century before Christ to the second century after Christ.[3]

To return to the period of Mr. Prinsep's activity, his successful decipherment, in conjunction with Captain Troyer, Dr. Mill and others, of the ancient pillar and rock inscriptions in 1834 to 1836 has been already related in a preceding chapter. That decipherment led to a dicovery hardly less important for the history of India than that of the date of the great Chandra Gupta, half a century before, by Sir William Jones.

Early in 1834, Captain Troyer, who had succeeded in partially deciphering the second of the inscriptions on the pillar at Allahabad, noticed that it contained the names of four generations of princes, called Gupta. These names he thought were Chandra Gupta, Yagnakacha, Chandra Gupta, and Samudra Gupta; and the first named Chandra Gupta, he suggested, though doubtfully, might be the same as the great Sandracottus of the fourth century B. C.[4] Two months later, in May 1834, the Revd. Dr. Mill, who had subjected the inscription to a careful re-examination, discovered that the first two names had been misread by Captain Troyer, and should be Gupta and Ghatotkacha, respectively. He also showed that the suggested identification of Chandra Gupta was open to too serious objections to be accepted. He pointed out that the letters of the inscription were of a comparatively too modern form to suit the early date of Sandracottus;

[1] J. A. S. B., Vol. XLIX, pp. 21, 87. See also Proceedings for 1880, pp. 7, 92.
[2] J. A. S. B., Vol. XLIX, pp. 23, 28. [3] *Ibid.*, p. 89. Proceedings for 1880, p. 92. [4] J. A. S. B., Vol. III, pp. 119, 120; Vol. V, p. 644.

that the names of the Gupta dynasty discovered on the pillar were entirely different from those of the Maurya dynasty recorded in the Puranic genealogies; and that, moreover, the Gupta kings were said in the inscriptions to belong to the Solar race of Indian sovereigns, while in the Purânas the Mauryas were classed as members of the Lunar race.[1] In a later communication to the Journal, he added a fourth objection based on the difference of religion professed by the Guptas and Mauryas respectively, the former being worshippers of Siva, while the latter were followers of Buddha,[2] and though the Hon'ble George Turnour and Mr. Prinsep showed that one of these objections,—that referring to the difference of race,—was not unsurmountable,[3] Dr. Mill's rejection of the proposed identification was then, and is now, universally assented to.

In default of this reluctantly dismissed identification, various others were at first attempted, though not with any greater success. Both Dr. Mill and Mr. Prinsep carefully searched through the traditional genealogies of the numerous Rajput dynasties of the middle ages, but without succeeding in finding any names that would allow of identification with the Guptas of the inscription.[4] The more so, as both the possibility and difficulty of an identification had, in the meanwhile, been greatly increased by the successful decipherment in 1837 of another ancient pillar inscription at Bhitari, which enabled both Mr. Prinsep and Dr. Mill to add three further names, those of Chandra Gupta II, Kumâra Gupta and

[1] J. A. S. B., Vol. III, pp. 259, 266, 267. Curiously enough, Dr. Mill himself appears to have overlooked that he also corrected Capt. Troyer's Chandra Gupta I into Gupta, see p. 259; but the original erroneous reading rests also on the evidence of Mr. Prinsep, see Vol. III, p. 115. [2] J. A. S. B., Vol. VI, pp. 9, 15. [3] *Ibid.*, pp. 15, 275. [4] *Ibid.*, Vol. III, pp. 339; Vol. IV, 639.

Skanda Gupta (besides an unnamed infant successor of the last) to the list of Guptas already known from the Allahabad pillar.[1] To this it may be added, that in the following year, 1838, Mr. Prinsep was able, from the pillar inscription at Eran, to add one more name to the list, Buddha Gupta (perhaps the unnamed infant of the Bhitari pillar), who must have succeeded Skanda Gupta and with whom the list of the Gupta dynasty now consisted of eight names.[2] The disovery of these additional names led Dr. Mill to turn to the Puranic records, which mention a Gupta dynasty as reigning in the kingdom of Magadha. He proposed as a "far more plausible hypothesis" that these Guptas of the Puránas might be the same as the Guptas of the pillar inscription; and on this hypothesis he calculated that their date "could scarcely be fixed higher than the age of Charlemagne in Europe" in the ninth century of our era.[3] This identification with the Puranic Guptas had already previously in 1836 been suggested by Mr. Prinsep, who, however, feeling the incongruity of the assignment of such a late date to the Guptas, was rightly inclined to adopt the other alternative of "carrying back the chronology of the Puránas a few centuries."[4]

At this point, a very important light was thrown on the question of the true date of the Gupta dynasty, by the

---

[1] J. A. S. B., Vol. V, p. 644; Vol. VI, pp. 7, 8. [2] *Ibid.*, Vol. VII, p. 632. Two more names have since been noted, *viz.*, Nara Gupta and Bakrà Gupta. Of these the former may be the same as Buddha Gupta, while the latter is probably an erroneous reading for Chandra Gupta. See Dr. Burgess' Archæological Survey of Western India, Vol. I, pp. 39, 63, and General Cunningham's Archæological Survey Reports, Vol. IX, p. 23. [3] J. A. S. B., Vol. VI, pp. 9, 10, 12. [4] *Ibid.*, Vol. V, p. 644. The same feeling, it may be here mentioned, induced Mr. Prinsep about the same time to suggest the identification of Chandra Gupta with a prince Chandra Kanta in the 5th century A. D., mentioned in a Chinese account of India; see Vol. VI, pp. 65, 975. This suggestion was not followed up any further.

numismatic enquiries which had been, proceeding *pari passu* with the examination of the inscriptions. A curious kind of early Hindu coins, inscribed with letters in an ancient form of Nágarí and exhibiting striking resemblances to the Indo-Scythian coinage, had been observed as early as 1824, when Col. Tod published some in the Transactions of the Royal Asiatic Society.[1] Others were made known in 1825 by Professor Wilson in the Asiatic Researches, and in 1833 by Mr. J. Prinsep, in the Journal.[2] Their ascription was, however, not recognized till the following year, 1834, when both Mr. Prinsep and Dr. Mill observed that they bore not only the same type of letters as those on the second Allahabad inscription, but actually the same names, Ghatotkacha, Chandra Gupta and Samudra Gupta.[3] In the following year, 1835, their observation was fully confirmed by the discovery, on other similar coins, of the remainder of the Gupta names known from the Bhitari inscription, Kumára Gupta and Skanda Gupta.[4] It was evident, therefore, that the Guptas of the coins belonged to the same dynasty of princes as that which had caused the pillar inscriptions to be set up.[5]

Among the coins there were some which bore the name of Mahendra Gupta. It was thought by Mr. Prinsep, that their discovery added to the list of the dynasty a new name, not mentioned in any inscription.[6] His opinion was

---

[1] Ariana Antiqua, pp. 5, 6. Similar coins had been first discovered in 1783 near Calcutta, on the bank of the Hooghly. [2] As. Res., Vol. XVII, pp. 566, 568, 570-574 (figs. 5, 7, 12, 13, 14, 16-19); J. A. S. B., Vol. II, pp. 412-415 (fig. 15); see also J. A. S. B., Vol. III, p. 620, editorial note. [3] J. A. S. B., Vol. III, pp. 231, 267, 268 (see also p. 268 foot-note), 620; see also Vol. IV, pp. 634, 637, 642. [4] J. A. S. B., Vol. IV, pp. 634-643; Vol. V, p. 644. [5] *Ibid.*, Vol. III, p. 268; Vol. IV, p. 641. [6] *Ibid.*, Vol. V, p. 644. In Vol. IV, p. 643, Mr. Prinsep gives a list of 13 members of the dynasty, many of whom, however, have since proved to be the same persons.

long accepted as correct by every one,[1] but latterly it has been abandoned as untenable, it having been found that the appellation Mahendra Gupta was only another name of Kumára Gupta.[2]

All the coins hitherto examined had been of gold. The Gupta kings, however, possessed also a silver currency. Specimens of these silver coins had been published by Mr. Prinsep as early as 1834 and 1835.[3] On account of their striking resemblance to the Satrap coins of Suráshtra, they seem, at first, to have been looked upon as a variety of that class of coins. Gradually, however, as the legends on them were deciphered, it was found that they bore the names of some of the now well-known kings of the Gupta dynasty, and it was evident that they were simply the silver division of the Gupta currency. The names noticed on these silver coins were those of the later kings, Chandra Gupta II, Kumára Gupta, Skanda Gupta and Buddha Gupta. No name of an earlier king was ever met with. At length in 1835 the whole subject of the Gupta mintages, including both their gold and silver currencies, was reviewed by Mr. E. Thomas in a memoir published in the twenty fourth volume of the Journal, in which he gathered together and summed up all the numismatic information on the Guptas available at that time.[4]

The careful examination of the Gupta mintages established

---

[1] So in 1855, by Mr E. Thomas, in J. A. S. B., Vol. XXIV, pp. 383, 485; see also Prof. H. H. Wilson in Ariana Antiqua, p. 420, in 1841; and Lassen in his Indian Antiquities, Vol. II, p. 971. [2] J. A. S. B., Vol. XXX, p. 146; see also General Cunningham's Bhilsa Topes, p. 141; Mr. E. Thomas's edition of Prinsep's Indian Antiquities, Vol. I, p. 276; and the same in Dr. Burgess' Archæological Survey of Western India, Vol. I, p. 70. [3] J. A. S. B., Vol. III, p. 230 (fig. 20); Vol. IV, p. 687 (figs. 10-12). [4] *Ibid.*, Vol. XXIV, p. 483. A later summary in 1876, by the same author, is included in Dr. Burgess' Archæological Survey of Western India, Vol. I, p. 18.

two points of great historic importance, the extent of their empire and the date of their rule. Dr. Mill first suggested, in 1834, that the capital of the Gupta dynasty must have been Kanauj, on the ground that they were, as he fallaciously thought, "a branch of the Solar family." As an other, and a much better founded reason he referred to the fact, that their gold coins were most frequently found in the ruins of that ancient town.[1] On the latter ground his suggestion was generally accepted until latterly, when it has been shown that their capital lay probably much lower down the Ganges, in Magadha proper, on the site of modern Patna or ancient Pataliputra. Mr. Prinsep, with the rest, adopted Dr. Mill's suggestion regarding the kingdom of the Guptas at Kanauj;[2] but from the types and the find-spots of their silver coins, in Ujjain, Suráshtra and other places, he concluded that, though their capital was at Kanauj, the empire must have included a very large portion of North India, from Magadha in the East to the Suráshtra province in the West.[3] Further researches, bringing out other, and in some respects more trustworthy evidence, have since confirmed Mr. Prinsep's conclusions, and shown that the Gupta empire, at one time, under Chandra Gupta II, must have had an almost as wide extent as that of the Mauryas at their best time, under Asoka.

With regard to the date of their empire, the evidence of the coins and of the inscriptions coincided and was conclusive. The characters on the coins as well as on the inscription, it was at once observed, were of the same type, and that, a very ancient one; indeed, if any thing, those on the silver coins were rather more ancient than those

---

[1] J. A. S. B., Vol. III, p. 267. [2] *Ibid.*, Vol. IV, p. 640; Vol. VI, p. 975.
[3] *Ibid.*, Vol. IV, pp. 640, 641; Vol. VI, p. 975.

on the gold currency.[1] From a comparison of this type of letters with the more modern Kutila characters of the twelfth century after Christ, and with the more ancient alphabet employed by Asoka in the third century before Christ, Mr. Prinsep drew the conclusion that the Gupta characters may be placed about midway in the third or fourth century of our era.[2] This conclusion was confirmed by the coins in a remarkable way. While on the one hand the gold coins of the Guptas exhibited a striking resemblance to those of the great Indo-Scythian sovereigns, their silver coins showed an even more unmistakable likeness with the silver currency of the Satrap rulers of Suráshtra on the one side, and that of the Valabhi kings on the other. It was evident, therefore, that, on the testimony of their coins, the Guptas must have followed the Indo-Scythians and the Satraps, and must have preceded the Valabhis.[3] The date of the accession of the last mentioned rulers of Valabhi in Gujarat was accurately known to be the year 319 A.D. For that date, according to the trustworthy statement of the Arab historian Al-Biruni, was the initial year of their own era, which commenced with their accession to the throne. On the other hand, there were, as has been previously shown, good reasons for fixing the termination of the rule of the Indo-Scythians and the Satraps somewhere towards the end of the second century after Christ.[4] Moreover, from the number of names in the list of Gupta kings, eight of whom, at least, were known, it could be calculated with much probability, that their rule must have "filled a space in Indian history of nearly two centuries."[5] It followed from all these

---

[1] J. A. S. B., Vol. II, p. 413; Vol. III, p. 231; Vol. IV, p. 634; Vol. VI, p. 378; Vol. VII, pp. 275, 276, 337; Vol. XXIV, pp. 389, 390. [2] *Ibid.*, Vol. VI, p. 566; see also Vol. VI, pp. 629, 968. [3] *Ibid.*, Vol. XXIV, pp. 503, 504. [4] See above, pp. 99, 100, 101. [5] J. A. S. B., Vol. V, p. 644.

considerations that the period of the Gupta empire must be fixed within the limits reaching from a little after the middle of the second century up to the year 319 A. D. The final year being already accurately known, it only remained for future researches to determine, if possible, the initial year of the Gupta rule.

It must not be supposed that all this information was the result of the earliest researches of Mr. Prinsep and his coadjutors. They only generally fixed the age of the Guptas to be the third and fourth centuries after Christ.[1] The terminal date, the year 319 A.D., was first determined by Mr. E. Thomas, in 1848, in a memoir on the dynasty of the Sah kings of Suráshtra, which was published in the Journal of the Royal Asiatic Society. His determination was based on certain passages of the Arab historian, Abu Rihan Al-Biruni, which had been translated and published by Mr. Reinaud.[2] It is true, it was at first strongly contested by Major A. Cunningham, Mr. J. Fergusson and others, who attempted to establish that the Guptas were contemporaneous with the Valabhis, and reigned between the second and fifth or sixth centuries after Christ.[3] But the incongruity of this opinion with the clear evidence of the inscriptions and coins could not fail to assert itself in the course of time;[4] and the terminal date of the Gupta empire as determined by Mr. Thomas may now be considered as one of those great historical landmarks, the truth of which is admittedly no more open to question.

---

[1] J. A. S. B., Vol. VI, p. 566. [2] *Ibid.*, Vol. XXIV, pp. 371, 375. See Journal, R. A. S., Vol. XII, p. 32. [3] J. A. S. B., Vol. XVII, p. 488; Vol. XXIV, p. 375. See Major A. Cunningham's Bhilsa Topes, p. 138; and Mr. Fergusson in Journal, R. A. S., Vol. IV, p. 108; Lassen's Indian Antiquities, Vol. II, p. 751; Vol. III, pp. 652, 659, 660, quoted in J. A. S. B., Vol. XXX, pp. 140, 143. [4] J. A. S. B., Vol. XXX, pp. 145, 146, 149. Proceedings for 1875, p. 45.

The determination of the initial date of the Gupta empire was a matter of much greater difficulty. It was observed very early that the Gupta kings were in the habit of employing a certain era, in which they date many of their inscriptions and coins. Thus Mr. Prinsep, in 1837, discovered that Chandra Gupta II's inscription on the Sanchi Tope bore a figured date, though he was unable to read it fully.[1] It was afterwards deciphered to be 93. In 1838 he discovered and partially read a series of figured dates on the Surashtrian silver coins,[2] and in the same year he found that the inscription on a pillar at Eran stated that it was erected in the 165th year, during the reign of Buddha Gupta. In this case, there was no difficulty in reading the date, as it was expressed in words.[3] There were other difficulties, however, in the record, which led to its re-examination, in 1861, by Mr. Fitz Edward Hall,[4] who confidently, though no less erroneously, announced that by the date of the inscription he had determined that Buddha Gupta was reigning "in the year of our Lord one hundred and eight, new style."[5] A further date, recorded likewise in words, on the Kuhaon pillar, was also read by Mr. Prinsep in 1838; but he read it wrongly as 133 dating from the decease of Skanda Gupta.[6] It was partially corrected in 1861 by Mr. Fitz Edward Hall, who read it as 141, dating from the overthrow of Skanda's Gupta empire.[7] But it remained for Dr. R. Mitra, in 1874, to point out the true reading, that it was the year 141, dating in the Gupta era itself.[8] At the same time

---

[1] J. A. S. B, Vol. VI, pp. 452, 457. See also Vol. VII, p. 349. [2] *Ibid.*, Vol. VII, p. 348. [3] *Ibid.*, pp. 632, 634. [4] *Ibid.*, Vol. XXX, pp. 14, 139. [5] *Ibid.*, pp. 15, 139, 148. An earlier reference to this inscription by Mr. Thomas occurs in *ibid.*, Vol. XXIV, p. 515. Mr. Fitz Edward Hall's papers led to an acrimonious controversy between him and Babu R. Mitra, *ibid.*, Vol. XXX, p. 267; Vol. XXXIV, p. 58. [6] J. A. S. B., Vol. VII, pp. 37, 31. [7] *Ibid.*, Vol. XXX, p. 3. [8] *Ibid.*, Vol. XLIII, p. 365.

he published a newly found inscription of the same Skanda Gupta, dated in the year 146 of the Gupta era.[1] Some years previously, in 1861, Mr. Fitz Edward Hall had published two land grants of a king Hastin, which were dated in the years 156 and 163 of the Gupta era.[2] Thus a considerable number of dates, all reckoned in the era of the Gupta kings, was gradually accumulated. It seemed possible by careful examination and combination of them, to calculate, with some degree of certainty, what the initial date of the Gupta era era might have been. At first it was supposed that the so-called era of the Guptas might prove to be the same as the well-known Saka era. This was the opinion of Dr. R. Mitra, the Hon'ble E. C. Bayley and others.[3] But in 1880, Major-General A. Cunningham, who had at first himself inclined to the Saka theory, showed after a renewed and very carefully conducted examination of all the given dates and other evidences, that that theory was untenable, and that, in all probability, the initial year of the Gupta era was 166 A.D., being the year of the accession of Chandra Gupta I.[4] This view, or some modification of it, has every promise of ultimately meeting with universal assent, and being the final verdict of the historic researches, regarding the Gupta dynasty, continued through exactly one half of the century.

The investigation into the chronology of the Gupta kings, as has been already mentioned incidentally, was most intimately connected with the identification of another

[1] J. A. S. B., Vol. XLIII, p. 363. Proceedings for 1865, p. 45. [2] J. A. S. B., Vol. XXX, p. 1. A further date, the year 82, during Chandra Gupta II's reign, was published by Major A. Cunningham, in Bhilsa Topes, p. 151; also the dates 191 and 209 of the Gupta era, in his Archæological Survey Reports, Vol. IX, pp. 13, 15. [3] J. A. S. B., Vol. XLIII, p. 372. Proceedings for 1875, pp. 45-46. [4] See General A. Cunningham's Archæological Survey Reports, Vol. X, Appendix.

dynasty of kings and the determination of the exact period of their rule. These were the Valabhi kings, whose capital was Valabhipur, in Gujarat. The researches into their history and chronology have only recently been brought to what may be regarded, at least provisionally, as a final result; and for the most part they were carried on in no direct connection with the Asiatic Society of Bengal. But the latter may claim at least the credit of having laid the foundation of the enquiry and brought to light the first trustworthy materials for its successful prosecution by others.

The existence of a dynasty of Valabhi kings was already known, in 1829, through Colonel Tod, who, in his Annals and Antiquities of Rajasthan, had stated, on the authority of certain Jain records, that Gehlot Rajputs either founded or became possessed of the city of Valabhipur, some time after the middle of the second century after Christ. The only names of its princes, however, which he particularised, were Kanak Sen, said to be the founder of the dynasty, Vijaya, who for generations afterwards built several cities, and Saláditya, the last of the race, in whose reign Valabhipur was besieged and taken by barbarians,[1] most probably, as later enquiries have shown, some Muhammadan invaders. In 1835, Mr. W. H. Wathen published two sets of copper land grants, which had been found in the earth at Gujarat several years previously.[2] From these he was able to make known in their order of succession nearly the entire list of the dynasty, consisting of no less than sixteen members.[3] Three years later, in 1838, Mr. J. Prinsep (or rather his

[1] J. A. S. B., Vol. IV, p. 480. See Tod's Rajasthan, Vol. I, p. 216 (or p. 165 in the 2nd edition, reprinted in Calcutta, 1877); also Ariana Antiqua. p. 407.
[2] J. A. S. B, Vol. IV, p. 477. [3] *Ibid.*, pp. 486, 487. Mr. Wathen erroneously supposed there were 18.

editors) added one more name from a third copperplate, discovered by Dr. A. Burns at Kaira.[1] Quite recently in 1877 and 1878 two further names have been discovered by Dr. G. Bühler, which at present complete the list of Valabhi rulers and bring it up to the number of nineteen.[2] That list, as it stands now, is the following; the order of succession is indicated by numbers; the unnumbered individuals do not appear to have reigned; those marked with * and † were added by Mr. Prinsep and Dr. Bühler, respectively.

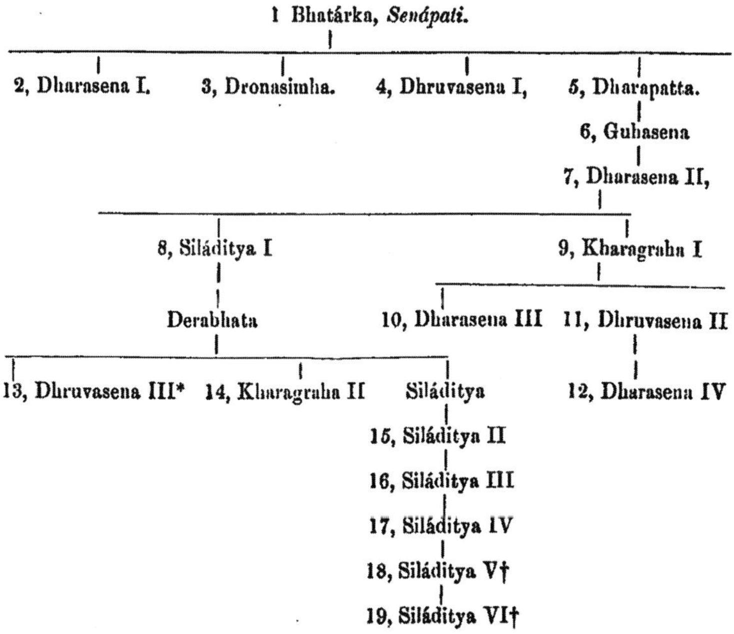

Mr. Wathen pointed out that it appeared from the terms of the land grants of these Valabhi rulers, that the two earliest members of the dynasty held only the position of a

---

[1] J. A. S. B., Vol. VII, p. 966. [2] See Indian Antiquary, Vol. VI, p. 17; Vol. VII, p. 80.

"*sénápati*, a general (or military governor) under a paramount sovereign by whom the province of Gujarat was committed to their charge," while the third on the list was the first of the dynasty who was "raised to the royal dignity by his sovereign, the great monarch, the sole sovereign of the entire world," meaning India.[1] Later researches have shown, that this great monarch, "in all probability was Chandra Gupta II of the well-known Gupta dynasty; and that the "royal dignity" in the case of many, if not of all, of the Valabhi rulers, amounted to no more than a nominal independence."[2]

Another, and far more important item of information afforded by the Valabhi land grants, of which a large number have been found since MM. Wathen and Prinsep's publications, are the contemparary dates with which all or nearly all the copperplates are furnished. Attempts to read and interpret them were made by both Mr. Wathen and Mr. Prinsep, though not altogether successfully.[3] They have since that time been fully read.[4] Much difficulty was experienced with regard to determining the particular era to which the dates of the land grants referred. Colonel Tod had stated in his Annals of Rajasthan that the Valabhi kings had instituted an era of their own, called the Valabhi Samvat, of which the initial year corresponded to A.D. 319. On this authority, Mr. Wathen considered that the dates of the land grants should be adjusted by the supposed Valabhi era.[5] This would have placed the Valabhi dynasty from the fourth to the eighth century after Christ, *i.e.* from A.D. 319 to at least A.D. 766, as the latest grant is dated

---

[1] J. A. S. B., Vol. IV, p. 480. [2] See Indian Antiquary, Vol. VI, p. 9. [3] J. A. S. B., Vol. IV, p. 481; Vol. VII, p. 349. [4] As to the value of the numeral figures, see especially Indian Antiquary. Vol. VI, p. 41, *et passim*. [5] J. A. S. B., Vol. IV, pp. 480, 481; Vol. VII, pp. 967, 968.

477.[1] On reconsidering the question in 1838, Mr. Prinsep came to the conclusion that the Valabhi dates must refer to the Vikramáditya Samvat, the initial year of which is B. C. 56. His reasons were, that the grants themselves did not name the Valabhi Samvat, and that hence the mere word *samvat* should, as usual, signify the samvat or era of Vikramáditya. Moreover, as his revised readings of the dates of the grants showed them to be of the third and fourth centuries, Mr. Prinsep seems to have thought, that, if calculated on the Valabhi era, they would bring the date of the Valabhi rulers much lower down than could be fairly assigned to them on other considerations.[2] Ten years later, on a renewed reconsideration of the question, in 1848, Mr. Thomas proposed to refer the Valabhi dates to the Saka era.[3] He was followed in this opinion by Dr. Bhaudaji in 1868,[4] and by Professor Bhandarkar, in 1872.[5] The main reasons were, that at the period of the Valabhi land grants the Saka era was known to have been used in other records; that the same era was used by the Satrap dynasty of Suráshtra; and that, therefore, it was most probable, that the Valabhi dynasty which superseded that of the Satraps, continued the use of the era which had been current under their predecessors.[6] Three years later, however, in 1875, Dr. G. Bühler proved from a newly found land grant, that the theory of the Valabhi grants being dated in the Saka era was untenable.[7] Another step in advance was made in 1878, when Dr. Bühler discovered from another newly recovered Valabhi land grant

---

[1] J. A. S B., Vol. IV, pp. 478, 497. See Indian Antiquary, Vol. VII, p. 80. [2] J. A. S. B., Vol. VII, pp. 354, 367, 368. [3] See Journal, R. A. S., Vol. XII. [4] See Journal, Bombay Branch R. A. S., Vol. VIII, pp. 232, 233. [5] See Indian Antiquary, Vol. I, pp. 45, 61. He abandoned this opinion two years later, see Vol. III, p. 304. [6] See Indian Antiquities, Vol. I, p. 61. [7] See Indian Antiquary, Vol. IV, p. 167.

that Şiláditya VI, the last in the present list, also bore the name of Dhruvabhata, under which name, as M. Eugene Jaquet had already pointed out more than forty years ago in 1836, that king was known to the Chinese traveller Hwen-thsang, when he visited him not long after A.D. 639.[1] The conclusion was inevitable that, as Siláditya VI's grant was dated 447, the initial year of the era of the plates must fall either shortly before or shortly after the year 200 A.D.[2] It has been stated previously,[3] that about this very time the investigation into the chronology of the Gupta dynasty had led to the conclusion, that the initial year of the Gupta era must be A.D. 166, or some year between that date and A.D. 200. On the whole, therefore, the opinion has the greatest probability in its favour, that the era in which the Valabhi plates are dated is the Gupta era, the use of which was naturally continued by the Valabhi rulers, after the fall of the Guptas under whom for a time they had been sub-kings. It is certain that the rule of the Valabhis embraces a period of at least two hundred and forty years, divisible among eleven generations, because the oldest known grant of Dhruvasena is dated 207, while the latest of Siláditya VI bears date 447. And it is in every way most probable that the period of the whole dynasty runs from the end of the second to the middle of the seventh century after Christ.

The close of the rule of the Valabhis carries us already well into the middle ages of Indian history. During those ages India was divided into a considerable number of principalities, of more or less extent and importance, and ruled by a variety of dynastic races which entertained the most changing relations to one another, sometimes of peace, sometimes of war, and generally of varying interdependence.

[1] J. A. S. B., Vol. V, pp. 685, 687. [2] See Indian Antiquary, Vol. VII, pp. 80, 81.
[3] See page 113.

Foremost amongst them, commencing in the west of India, are the Brahmanic rulers of Kabul and the Panjáb, the Utpala dynasty of Kashmir, the Mahárájas of Kángra, the Chauháns of Ajmir and Dehli, the Pramaras of Malwa, the Kachwáhas of Gwalior, the Chandel princes of Mahoba, the Rathor house of Kanauj, the Pála kings of Bihár and Bengal, and the Sena dynasty of Bengal. The main and only trustworthy source of information on the history of these races and dynasties and their mutual relations to one another are their inscriptions and their coins. The long genealogical lists of their members, which are preserved in chronicles and in the epics of bards, are only of subordinate and doubtful value. Though the diligent researches carried on through the whole of the century, with the help of those materials, have succeeded in reducing to some sort of order the confused and conflicting history of India's middle ages, there still remain many obscurities and discrepancies to be cleared away before that history can be said to be satisfactorily established. The Asiatic Society of Bengal contributed its share to those researches, nor was it a small one, at least with regard to four dynasties already named, the Rathors and their predecessors in Kanauj, the Chandels of Mahoba, and the Pálas and Senas of Bengal. With respect to the others, the contributions of the Society were much smaller, consisting rather in the supply of materials, than in establishing historical deductions from them, an operation which was left to the successful researches of other individuals and societies.

The kingdom of Kanauj was one of the first among the Hindu principalities of the middle ages to attract the attention of the Society through a copper land grant discovered about 1807. It was brought to the notice of Mr. H. T. Colebrooke, who published a translation in the Asiatic Researches.

It proved to be a grant, dated A. D. 1164, of Rája Vijaya Chandra of Kanauj, the father of Rája Jaya Chandra, who was already known from the Ain-i-Akbari to have lost his kingdom in the Muhammadan conquest of A. D. 1193. It also gave the whole ancestry of Rája Vijaya Chandra extending to six generations.[1] In 1825 Professor H. H. Wilson published another grant from Captain E. Fell's collection. This time it was a grant of Rája Jaya Chandra himself, dated A. D. 1177, and from it Professor Wilson was able to correct the first name of the Rája's ancestry, Yasovigraha, which, on the previous occasion, had been misread as Sripála.[2] The family whose genealogy consisting of seven generations had thus been recovered, belonged to the Rathor race of Rajputs, and the discovery of its true ancestry was all the more valuable, as the traditional one, known from Colonel Tod's Annals of Rajasthan,[3] differed entirely from it.[4] The truth of the ancestry, as given in the contemporary land grants, could, of course, not be questioned, but it was curiously confirmed by the discovery of coins, on which some of the names of the newly found Rathor line could be deciphered. These coins were found in great abundance, especially in the vicinity of the site of ancient Kanauj, but they were never noticed nor recognized till 1832, when Professor H. H. Wilson described and delineated two coins of Rája Govinda Chandra, the grandfather of Jaya Chandra, in the Asiatic Researches.[5] Three years later, in 1835, Mr. Prinsep not only confirmed Professor H. H. Wilson's discovery, but succeeded in verify-

---

[1] As. Res., Vol. IX, pp. 400, 441. See also the reprint: Miscellaneous Essays, Vol. II, p. 253. Mr. Colebrooke erroneously identified Vijaya Chandra with his son Jaya Chandra. [2] As. Res., Vol. XV, pp. 446, 453, 460, 461. [3] See Annals and Antiquities of Rajasthan, Vol. II, pp. 5-7 (pp. 4, 5 in the 2nd edition). See also As. Res.. Vol. XV, p. 461; J. A. S. B., Vol. III, pp. 339, 340. [4] J. A. S. B.. Vol. III, pp. 268, 341; Vol. IV, pp. 369, 392, 642, 669, 670. [5] As. Res., Vol. XVII, p. 585 (figs. 48, 50).

ing another name, that of Sri Chandra Deva himself. He also pointed out, that the ascription of these coins to the Rathor Rájas of Kanauj agreed with the comparatively very modern form of the Nágarí characters of their legends.[1] Subsequently to 1835, many more land grants of the Rathor princes have been discovered, every one of them confirming the genealogy already known from the earlier found grants. Thus in 1841, a grant of Jaya Chandra, of A. D. 1187, was published by Mr. H. Torrens;[2] and in 1858, two grants, one dated A. D. 1125, of Govinda Chandra, the other, dated A. D. 1097, of Madanapála, the grandfather and great grandfather, respectively, of Jaya Chandra, were made known by Mr. FitzEdward Hall.[3] All the later finds having been already fully noticed in an earlier portion of this Review,[4] there is no need of mentioning any of them here, except one of Govinda Chandra, published by Babu Rájendralála Mitra in 1873,[5] which fully confirmed an observation already previously made by Mr. Colebrooke, Professor H. H. Wilson and others,[6] that the two first members of the line, Yasovigraha and Mahi Chandra, were not kings of Kanauj, but that the third, Sri Chandra having conquered Kanauj, became its first king of the Rathor house. From the same inscription it also appeared, that the last member of the preceding dynasty was a certain Rája Bhoja, after whose death a period of disturbance ensued under a certain Rája Sri Karlla, and that during this period the Rathor prince Sri Chandra possessed himself of the

[1] J. A. S. B., Vol. IV, pp. 668-670 (figs. 7, 8). The coins have Ajaya Chandra, which may signify, as Mr. Prinsep thought, Jaya Chandra, but more probably the first king, Sri Chandra, who is called "Vijayi" in the inscription of 1873; see J. A. S. B., Vol. XLII, pp. 321, 322. [2] *Ibid.*, Vol. X, p. 98. [3] *Ibid.*, Vol. XXVII, p. 217. [4] See above, Chapter I. [5] J. A. S. B., Vol. XLII, pp. 314, 322. A counterpart of this inscription, dated A.D. 1111, and found at Ráhan in the Etawa district, was published by Dr. Mitra in the Proceedings for 1876, p. 130. [6] As. Res., Vol. IX, p. 441; Vol. XV, pp. 461, 462. J. A. S. B., Vol. XXVII, p. 218.

throne of Kanauj as the first of his dynasty of kings.[1] With the help supplied by all these land grants it was possible to fix accurately the period of the rule of the Rathor house of Kanauj as having extended from about A. D. 1050 to the year 1193.[2]

Between this period and that of the Gupta dynasty of Kanauj, the termination of which was known to have occurred about the middle of the fourth century of our era, there was a long gap of about eleven centuries.[3] It was very improbable that the renowned kingdom of Kanauj should have been in abeyance during this long period; yet for a long time no information was forthcoming which could afford any means of filling up the mysterious break in its history. It is true, it was known as early as 1825, through the researches of Professor H. H. Wilson in Sanskrit literature, that two kings, named Yasovarman and Sahasanka, reigned in Kanauj about the middle of the eighth and tenth centuries respectively.[4] Afterwards the researches of Mr. FitzEdward Hall, which were confirmed from the journal of the Chinese traveller Hwen-thsang, made known three members of a dynasty, Prabhákara, Rájya and Harsha, who were kings of Kanauj in the first half of the seventh century.[5] But these instances, isolated as they were, left untouched nearly one half of the chasm referred to above. It was not till 1862 that the history of this portion of the gap was supplied by Mr. FitzEdward Hall from a land

---

[1] The opening lines of this inscription have been misunderstood. The Vijayi, or 'Victorious King,' of verse 2, is Sri Chandra Deva himself. He is said to be the son of Mahiála (or Mahipála), another name of Mahi Chandra, see J. A. S. B., Vol. IV, p. 670, and to have belonged to the Rajput race of Gaharwálas, who are of the same family as the Rathors (see Elliot's Races of the N. W. Provinces of India, Vol. I, p. 121). [2] J. A. S. B., Vol. XXVII, p. 218; Vol. XXXI, p. 8; Vol. XXXIII, p. 232. [3] *Ibid.*, Vol. III, p. 339; Vol. IV, p. 640. [4] As. Res., Vol. XV, pp. 45, 86, 463; J. A. S. B., Vol. III, pp. 268, 339; Vol. XXXI, pp. 9, 10. [5] *Ibid.*, Vol. XXXI, p. 2; Vol. XXXIII, p. 231.

grant which had been published by Babu Rájendralála Mitra as early as 1848, but the attribution of which had not been recognized.[1] This inscription names a dynasty of Mahodaya or Kanauj, consisting of eight individuals.[2] Two years later, in 1864, Major A. Cunningham succeeded, with the help of another already known, but hitherto imperfectly read, inscription from Gwalior,[3] in determining the period of the rule of the newly found dynasty as extending from about the middle of the eighth to the middle of the tenth centuries.[4] This determination established a fairly continuous history of the kingdom of Kanauj from the eighth to the twelfth century, the only obscurity that has remained being the exact connection between the two dynasties whose rule fell within that period.[5]

Contemporaneously with the later kingdom of Kanauj there flourished a smaller kingdom at Mahoba, in the modern Bundelkhand, the rulers of which belonged to the Rajput clan of Chandels. It was first brought to the notice of the Society in 1813, when Lieutenant William Price found a large inscribed stone on a rocky hill in the vicinity of the town of Mau, about ten miles from Chattarpur, on which he noticed a Sanskrit inscription containing a genealogy of an unknown line of Hindu princes. A copy of this record he published in the Asiatic Researches. Unfortunately it was in a very mutilated condition; but what remained proved to contain the history of ten princes, with the names of their ministers.[6] It was not known at the time who these princes were; but from the comparatively very modern type of its characters and from the

[1] J. A. S. B., Vol. XVII, p. 71. [2] *Ibid.*, Vol. XXXI, p. 5. [3] *Ibid.*, Vol. XXII, p. 673; Vol. XXXII, p. 97. [4] *Ibid.*, Vol. XXXIII, p. 229. See also Vol. XXXII, p. 96. [5] See Appendix I. [6] As. Res., Vol. XII, p. 357; see also J. A. S. B., Vol. XXXII, p. 275; Vol. XLVII, pp. 73, 74.

mention in it of Jaya Chandra, the Rája of Kanauj, it was concluded that the inscription belonged to the time of the latter king. Subsequently, in 1838, another inscribed slab was discovered by Captain T. S. Burt at Kajráha, and published in the Journal. It was found to contain another genealogy of seven princes, and as it gave in addition the name of one of the princes, Jaya Varma Deva, mentioned in the previously discovered slab, it was doubtfully concluded that the two slabs together comprised the genealogy of two branches of a single line of princes, succeeding each other collaterally.[1] In 1848 Lieutenant F. Maisey published two other inscriptions from Kalinjar, mentioning some of the names of the same dynasty of princes, but affording no new information.[2] Unfortunately the last name of the list on the second slab had been read erroneously as Banga, instead of Dhanga. If it had been deciphered correctly, it would have been seen at once that the two slabs actually complemented each other; for the first name of the list on the first slab was known to be Dhanga. The error was discovered in 1860 by Colonel (now Major-general) A. Cunningham, who at the same time also ascertained the true date of the second record to be A. D. 999.[3] This discovery determined both the age of the dynasty and the whole list of its sixteen members; and the latter was fully verified by other inscriptions which were afterwards, in 1860, 1872 and 1878, found at Kajráha.[4] Not long afterwards, General Cunningham also succeeded in discovering from the great epic of Chand and other Annalists that the dynasty which is

---

[1] J. A. S. B., Vol. VIII, p. 160. [2] *Ibid.*, Vol. XVII, Part I, pp. 313, 317. [3] *Ibid.*, Vol. XXIX, p. 394. The date is given wrongly in J. A. S. B., Vol. XXXII, p. 275; Vol. XLVII, p. 74; Vol. XLVIII, p. 288. See also General Cunningham's Archæological Reports, Vol. II, p. 447. [4] J. A. S. B., Vol. XXIX, p. 395; Vol. XXXII, p. 272; Vol. XLVII, pp. 73, 80.

recorded in these inscriptions was that of the Chandel princes, who founded the town of Mahoba.[1] At the same time he was able to construct, mainly from the dates supplied by their inscriptions, a trustworthy chronological order of their succession, which showed that the period of the rule of the Chandel dynasty extended from the beginning of the ninth to the end of the twelfth century,[2] beginning with Nanika and ending with Paramardi Deva, who was defeated and expelled from Mahoba by Rája Prithiráj of Dehli in A. D. 1182. General Cunningham's deductions on the history and chronology of the dynasty were afterwards in 1879 and 1881 verified, and in some points revised, by Mr. V. A. Smith, who especially added whatever few and indistinct notices could be discovered of Rája Paramardi's obscure successors preceding the rise of the Bundel power in the fourteenth century.[3]

A third kingdom, contemporary with those of Mahoba and Kanauj, was that of Gaur in Bengal, ruled by a dynasty bearing the family name of Pála. This was the earliest of the kingdoms of the Indian middle ages, of which any notice occurs in the Transactions of the Society. As early as 1780, Mr. Charles Wilkins discovered in the vicinity of the town of Buddal an inscription engraved on a monumental stone pillar. He succeeded in translating it in 1785, and his translation was published in 1788 in the first volume of the Asiatic Researches.[4] It was found to record three members of the Pála dynasty which was then stated

---

[1] See General Cunningham's Archæological Reports, Vol. II, p. 448. [2] See *Ibid.*, p. 451. The Chandel chronology has also been discussed by Dr. R. Mitra in 1863 and 1878, but partially on erroneous data; see J. A. S. B., Vol. XXXII, p. 276; Vol. XLVII, p. 74. [3] J. A. S. B., Vol. XLVIII, p. 285; Vol. L, p. 1. [4] As. Res., Vol. I, p. 131. The text and a revised translation by Babu Pratapa Chandra Ghosh are published in the J. A. S. B., Vol. XLIII, p. 356.

to be reigning in Gaur or Bengal. The first of them, Deva Pála, was also stated to have made wide conquests in the South and West of India. About the same time, Mr. Wilkins discovered in the ruins of Mungír a copper land grant, a translation of which he also published, in 1788, in the same volume of the Researches.[1] This grant was also found to record three kings of the Pála dynasty, the last of whom, Deva Pála, whose conquests in the South and West of India were again prominently mentioned, was the same as the first in the list of the pillar inscription. It was noted also in this grant, that Deva Pála professed the Buddhist faith. The grant bore the date 33, which really referred to Deva Pála's reign, but which was misinterpreted by Mr. Wilkins as referring to the Vikramáditya era and thus placing the early Pálas in the first century before Christ. This error was afterwards rectified by Mr. H. T. Colebrooke, on the evidence of a third inscription discovered in 1794, in the ruins of Sárnáth, near Benares, and published by Mr. Jonathan Duncan in 1798.[2] This inscription not only added a new name, Mahi Pála, to the list already known, but also supplied his date Samvat 1083 equal to A. D. 1027, —the only chronological evidence hitherto come to light for fixing the true time of the Pála dynasty. A few years later, in 1807, Mr. H. T. Colebrooke made known another copper land grant, found in 1806 at Amgachhi, in the Dinájpur district of Northern Bengal. Unfortunately, this inscription was in a too mutilated condition to allow of a perfectly trustworthy translation. But it appeared to mention, in addition to the list already known, a few new names, among which that of Mahi Pála also occurred. The date of the latter being known from the Sárnáth inscription, Mr. Colebrooke

[1] As. Res., Vol. I, p. 123. See also J. A. S. B., Vol. XLVII, p. 385. [2] As. Res., Vol. V, p. 131.

fixed the eighth or ninth century of our era as the probable time of the earlier Pálas,[1] a result which was, some years later, in 1825, endorsed by Professor H. H. Wilson.[2] In 1835 the existence of king Mahi Pála was further confirmed by the discovery of one of his coins, which was published by Mr. J. Prinsep in the Journal.[3] Still later, in 1848, the discovery by Captain M. Kitto of a fifth inscription at Pesserawa verified the existence of Deva Pála, who is incidentally mentioned in it.[4] In 1872, the exertions of Mr. A. M. Broadley brought to light a considerable number of very small dedicatory inscriptions, which not only confirmed all the names already known, but added the names of a few more princes of the Pála dynasty. These latter must have reigned subsequently to Mahi Pála, as was shown by one of their inscriptions being dated A. D. 1175.[5] The information which had thus gradually accumulated from all these inscriptions, enabled Major-General A. Cunningham in 1873 to construct a chronological table of the Pála dynasty, according to which it appeared to have ruled from about the middle of the eighth to nearly the end of the twelfth century.[6] The discovery at Bhágalpur of a new inscription of Náráyana Pála, which was published by Dr. Rajendralála Mitra in 1878, afforded the latter the occasion of a reconsideration of the Pála chronology, the result of which was a reduction of the period of the Pála rule by nearly a hundred years, the

[1] As. Res., Vol. IX, p. 434; see also pp. 203ff, where Capt. F. Wilford, misled by the untrustworthy traditional lists, altogether confuses the chronology of the Pálas. Professor Wilson, in As. Res., Vol. XV, p. 464, corrects him.
[2] *Ibid.*, Vol. XV, pp. 464, 465. [3] J. A. S. B., Vol. IV, pp. 669, 670 (fig. 5). See also General Cunningham's Archæological Reports, Vol. XI, pp. 176, 177, where also coins of Vigraha Pála are published. [4] J. A. S. B., Vol. XVII, p. 492. [5] *Ibid.*, Vol. XLI, p. 209, see especially pp. 309-311. Some of these inscriptions, however, appear to have been known previously, see General Cunningham's Archæological Reports, Vol. XI. [6] See his Archæological Survey Reports, Vol. III, p. 134; see also Vol. XI, p. 181, where the period is reduced by 50 years at its beginning.

founder of the dynasty, Go Pála being placed in the middle of the ninth century.[1] There is still not a little obscurity attaching to the Pála chronology, and further research will probably show that a further reduction of about fifty years will have to be made, bringing the founder of the dynasty down to the commencement of the 10th century.[2]

It was well known that between the Pála dynasty of Bengal and its conquest by the Muhammadans intervened a line of rulers which bore the family name of Sena. Certain Muhammadan histories, the Ain-i-Akbari and others, had recorded what professed to be chronological lists of the Bengal kings of the Sena dynasty. But these could not be considered altogether trustworthy, seeing that they differed among themselves. It was in 1838 that the first reliable evidence was obtained through the discovery in Baqirganj of a copper land grant of one of the dynasty, Kesava Sena, which Mr. J. Prinsep published in the Journal of that year.[3] This grant verified the existence of five members of the dynasty, ascending from Kesava Sena to Vijaya Sena,[4] the reputed first Bengal king of the Sena family. About thirty years later, in 1865, a stone inscription was found in the Rájsháhí district, which carried the family list back for three more generations. It was translated by Mr. C. T. Metcalfe, and published by Babu Rájendralála Mitra in the Journal.[5] On examination it proved to record Vijaya Sena and three of his ancestors, among whom a certain Víra Sena was named as the founder of the family. In 1875, a third inscription, found in the Dinájpur district and published by Mr. E. V. Westmacott, strikingly confirmed the

[1] J. A. S. B., Vol. XLVII, p. 384. [2] See Appendix II. [3] J. A. S. B., Vol. VII. p. 40. [4] It actually recorded only four names, but that of the fifth, Mádhava Sena, was shown by Mr. Prinsep to have stood in it originally. [5] J. A. S. B., Vol. XXXIV, p. 128.

evidence of the two previously discovered inscriptions. It was a land-grant of Lakshmana Sena, and recorded four names, two of which, Vijaya and Hemanta, occurred in the Rájsháhí inscription, while three of them, Vijaya, Ballála and Lakshmana, were in the Bhágalpur grant. The evidence thus accumulated not only showed that the Vijaya Sena of the two first inscriptions was the same person and the father of the well-known Ballála Sena, but also that the joint regal and pre-regal lines of Senas as far as Kesava Sena consisted of seven members. The whole subject of the history and chronology of the Sena dynasty was carefully examined by Dr. Rájendralála Mitra in two papers contributed to the Journal in 1865 and 1878.[1] In the course of his enquiry he showed that the Sena family did not belong, as is now commonly believed, to the vaidya or medical caste, but that they were, as distinctly stated in their own inscriptions, members of the kshatriya or military caste. He also proved that Vijaya Sena was the same as Sukha Sena mentioned in the Muhammadan histories as the father of Ballála Sena and first Sena king of Bengal; that the Lakhmaniya, mentioned in the same histories as reigning at the time of the Muhammadan conquest, was the successor of Kesava Sena, and that the traditional Adisura, who introduced the five Brahmans and Kayasths into Bengal, was probably identical with Víra Sena,[2] the founder of the family. But the most important point which he was successful in establishing was the fact of the existence of an era, called after Lakshmana, and dating from A. D. 1106, the year of his accession. The mere fact of the existence of such an era had been already indistinctly

---

[1] J. A. S. B., Vol. XXXIV, p. 128; Vol. XLVII. p. 396. [2] Rather with Vijaya Sena, the founder of the regal portion of the family; see Appendix II.

recognized by Mr. Prinsep as early as 1836;[1] but his remarks had been no further noticed, and it was left to Dr. R. Mitra not only to prove distinctly its existence, but to determine accurately the year of its initiation.[2] With the fixed date thus supplied by that era, it was possible to calculate approximately the duration of the Sena family in Bengal. The final result arrived at on this point by Dr. R. Mitra was, that it covered a period extending from nearly the end of the tenth to about the middle of the twelfth century.[3]

The rule of the Sena dynasty in Bengal, though it dragged on an obscure existence for a little time longer, was practically put an end to by the Muhammadan conquest, early in the thirteenth century. The history and chronology of the Muhammadan rulers, who henceforth, down to the English conquest in the eighteenth century, governed Bengal, was fairly well-known from the comparatively accurate historians of their faith. Still there were not a few gaps in some places, and obscurities and contradictions in others. On all these points much unexpected light was thrown through the discovery of numerous inscriptions and coins, especially towards the end of the century under review. Speaking broadly, the history of Muhammadan Bengal may be divided into three great periods: first a period of dependence from Dehli, next a period of independence, and lastly another period of dependence from Dehli. The history of the first period of dependence was elucidated by Mr. E. Thomas in two memoirs contributed to the Jour-

---

[1] J. A. S. B., Vol. V, p. 659. [2] *Ibid.*, Vol. XLVII, p. 396. [3] As the date of Lakshmana's accession is A. D. 1106, *i.e.*, ten years less than that given by Abul Fazl (1116), the date of Ballála Sena should also be reduced by at least ten years, to 1056. This brings Vijaya down to 1036, or, as calculated in Appendix II, to about 1030.

nals for 1867 and 1873.[1] In these he was assisted mainly by the discovery of the great hoard of 13,500 coins, which has been already noticed in a previous portion of this Review.[2] His researches especially helped to clear up the confused chronology of the Bengal Governors Ghiyásuddín 'Iwaz, Kaikaus, Shamsuddín Fírúz, Shahábuddín Bughrah Sháh and Ghiyásuddín Bahádur Sháh. Subsequently, in 1881, another find of similar coins enabled the writer of the present Review to determine the hitherto equally confused chronology of the Governor Mughísuddín Yuzbaq.[3] The history of the remaining two periods of independence and dependence of Bengal was made the subject of careful enquiry by Mr. H. Blochmann in three memoirs published in the Journals of 1873, 1874, 1875. Mr. E. Thomas, also, in his first memoir mentioned above, had turned his attention to this portion of the history of Bengal. He was able to prove the reign of a Bengal Sultan, named Ikhtiyáruddín Gházi Sháh, from A. D. 1350-1352, who is entirely unnoticed in the histories, and whose very existence would have been unknown but for the fact of coins struck in his name having been found.[4] Similarly Mr. Blochmann succeeded in verifying the existence of another Sultan, 'Aláuddín Fírúz Sháh III, who, as shown by an inscription and a coin of his, must have reigned in A. D. 1532. As he is not mentioned in any of the Muhammadan histories except one, his existence, before Mr. Blochmann's verification in 1873, had been considered more than doubtful.[5] But, besides these direct discoveries, Mr. Blochmann's researches resulted in determining many hitherto

[1] J. A. S. B., Vol. XXXVI, p. 1. [2] See above, p. 44. [3] J. A. S. B., Vol. L, p. 53. [4] *Ibid.*, Vol. XXXVI, p. 54; Vol. XLII, p. 254. [5] *Ibid.*, Vol. XLI, p. 339; Vol. XLII, p. 297. See also Proceedings for 1872, p. 131; *Ibid.* for 1873, p. 42.

unknown or conflicting dates; such as the limits of the reigns of Fakhruddín Mubárak Sháh, Násiruddín Mahmúd Sháh I, Sikandar Sháh II, Saifuddín Fírúz Sháh II and others.[1] The general results of his chronological researches into the history of the independent Sultans of Bengal he exhibited in a comparative table, showing the names and dates of twenty-four Sultans, as reported in the Muhammadan histories and as determined by the inscriptions and coins of the Sultans themselves. The period of their collective rule was thus shown to cover exactly two centuries, from A. H. 739 to 944,[2] or A. D. 1338 to 1537.

So far those portions of the history of India have been noticed, in the investigation and establishment of which the Asiatic Society took a more prominent and extended part. It has been already mentioned, however, that there are many other portions of Indian history with respect to which the Society, at least, collected or supplemented materials for the prosecution of the researches of others enjoying better opportunities or a larger amount of leisure. To this category belong the genealogical tables published in 1835, by Mr. J. Prinsep, in the fourth volume of the Journal.[3] In the same volume he also made known a number of coins of the Hindu rulers of Kabul and of the Chohán and other Rajput princes, which were afterwards found to throw much light on the history of those dynasties.[4] In the following year, 1836, he made known a few coins of the Mahárájas of Kashmir. Though he pointed out their similarity to the earlier Indo-Scythian coins of the so-called Ardokro type, he

---

[1] J. A. S. B., Vol. XLII, pp. 252, 269, 281, 287. [2] *Ibid.*, pp. 308-310.
[3] *Ibid.*, Vol. IV, Appendix. [4] *Ibid.*, p. 674. See Mr. E. Thomas' and Sir E. Clive Bayley's papers on the Hindu kings of Kabul in the Numismatic Chronicle. See also J. A. S. B., Vol. IV, p. 367, for the Shekavati inscription published by Dr. Mill and referring to the Chohâns.

did not recognize their true attribution.[1] This was done some years afterwards, in 1843, by General A. Cunningham.[2] Some more information was added by Mr. C. J. Rodgers, in 1879, in the pages of the Journal.[3] Considerable help on this subject was rendered by Professor H. H. Wilson in 1825, and Lieutenant D. J. F. Newall in 1854, by publishing memoirs in the Asiatic Researches and the Journal on the Hindu and Muhammadan history of Kashmir.[4] In 1836 and 1838 Mr. L. Wilkinson published two copper land-grants of the Pramara Rájas of Malwa, which helped to adjust the order of succession of those princes.[5] In 1837 Mr. J. Prinsep published several coins of Buddhist Rájas of Ceylon, from which he was able to verify several of the royal names recorded in the Buddhist chronicles of that island and made known through the investigations of the Hon'ble G. Turnour.[6] In the same year Captain W. H. Sleeman contributed a short memoir on the history of the Garha Mandala Rájas.[7] In the Journal for 1845 there followed an account of the early Abdalís by Major R. Leech,[8] and in 1850 and 1851 two memoirs by Dr. A. Sprenger on the Ghassanite kings and the chronology of Mekkah and the Hijaz before Muhammad[9]—all based on Muhammadan histories. In 1863 Babu Rájendralála Mitra, in a paper on "Vestiges of the Kings of Gwalior," made known some inscriptions of the Kachwáha princes of that country.[10] The volumes for 1878 and 1879 contain a native chronicle of the Bangash Nawabs of Furrakhabad, translated

[1] J. A. S. B., Vol. V, p. 654. [2] See the Numismatic Chronicle on the Coinage of Kashmir. [3] J. A. S B., Vol. XLVIII, pp. 277, 282. [4] As. Res., Vol. XV, p. 1; and J. A. S. B., Vol. XXIII, p. 409. [5] J. A. S. B., Vol. V, p. 377; Vol. VII, p. 736. [6] *Ibid.*, Vol. VI, p. 298; see also p. 378. [7] *Ibid.*, p. 622. [8] *Ibid.*, Vol. XIV, p. 445. [9] *Ibid.*, Vol. XIX, p. 469; Vol. XX, p. 349. [10] *Ibid.*, Vol. XXXI, p. 391.

by Mr. Irvine.[1] In 1880 Mr. C. J. Rodgers published a few coins of the Maháréjas of Kángra, throwing further light on the history of those princes, which had been already investigated by General A. Cunningham in his Archæological Reports.[2]

Other contributions have more the character of biographies. To these belong the notices on the life of Buddha, published in 1836 in the Asiatic Researches by the well-known traveller, M. Alexander Csoma Korosi, from Tibetan authorities.[3] The Journal of the same year contains a memoir by Mr. Johannes Avdall on the life and writings of S. Nierses Clajensis, surnamed the Graceful, Pontiff of Armenia;[4] and in the Journal for 1838 there is a brief account by Munshi Mohan Lal of the origin of the Daud Putras, and of the power and birth of Bahawal Khan, their chief, on the Ghara and Indus.[5]

The Transactions of the Society also contain a number of monographs, on the history of various countries in India or nearly connected with India. The object of the authors was to reproduce, for the purposes of further investigation, whatever there appeared to be valuable in the native chronicles and annals of those countries. The help afforded by these contributions has, in several cases, proved invaluable. Particularly was this the case with regard to Professor H. H. Wilson's Essay on the history of Kashmir, which has been already mentioned in connection with the Kashmir coins,[6] and Mr. A. Stirling's account, geographical, statistical and historical, of Orissa Proper or Cuttack.[7] The latter memoir was partly based on a native chronicle,

---

[1] J. A. S. B., Vol. XLVII, p. 259; and Vol. XLVIII, p. 48. [2] *Ibid.*, Vol. XLIX, p. 10. See Archæological Reports, Vol. V, p. 165. [3] As. Res., Vol. XX, p. 285. [4] J. A. S. B., Vol. V, p. 129. [5] *Ibid.*, Vol. VII, p. 27. [6] As. Res., Vol. XV, p. 1. [7] *Ibid.*, p. 163.

a translation of which by Mr. A. Stirling was published, after his death, in the Journal of 1837.[1] On the history of Arakan, and of the countries of Further India generally, there are a considerable number of contributions, *viz.*: in 1828, a historical and statistical sketch of Arakan, by Mr. Charles Paton;[2] in 1835, a history of Naning in the Malay Peninsula, by Lieut. J. T. Newbold;[3] in 1837, a history of Labong, from the native records, by Dr. D. Richardson;[4] and some account of the wars between Burmah and China from Burmese documents, by Lieutenant-Colonel H. Burney.[5] Later, the history of Arakan was again made the subject of much careful investigation by Major-General Sir Arthur P. Phayre, who published his results in a series of papers and memoirs contributed to the Journal.[6] These are: in 1841, an account of Arakan; in 1844, a history of Arakan; in 1864, 1868 and 1869, a history of the Burma race; in 1873 and 1874, a history of Pegu. He also published in 1846 some coins of Arakan in illustration of his researches on its history;[7] the same was done by Lieut. Thomas Latter in the same year,[8] by Captain (now Colonel) G. E. Fryer in 1872,[9] and by Dr. Rájendrálala Mitra in 1880.[10] Some information on the ancient history of Ásám is contained in Captain G. E. Westmacott's description of ancient temples and ruins at Chardwar, published in 1835;[11] and on that of Kúch Bihar in Dr. Buchanan's account of Rangpur.[12] On the history of both Kúch Bihar and Ásám, Mr. H. Blochmann published a memoir in 1872, based on the Akbarnámah,

---

[1] J. A. S. B., Vol. VI, p. 756. [2] As. Res., Vol. XVI, p. 353. [3] J. A. S. B., Vol. IV, p. 297. [4] *Ibid.*, Vol. VI, p. 55. [5] *Ibid.*, pp. 121, 405, 542. [6] *Ibid.*, Vol. X, p. 679; Vol. XIII, p. 23; Vol. XXXIII, p. 1; Vol. XXXVII, p. 74; Vol. XXXVIII, p. 29; Vol. XLII, pp. 23, 120; Vol. XLIII, p. 6. [7] *Ibid.*, Vol. XV, p. 232. [8] *Ibid.*, p. 238. [9] *Ibid.*, Vol. XLI, p. 201. [10] Proceedings for 1880, p. 53. [11] J. A. S. B., Vol. IV, p. 185. [12] *Ibid.*, Vol. VII, p. 1.

Paḍishahnámah and the Fathiyah-i-'Ibriyah.[1] The early history of Sindh, as related in the Chachnámah and other Persian authorities, was treated by Lieutenant Postans in several papers inserted in the Jòurnals for 1838, 1841 and 1845.[2] On the history of South India from 1564-1687 there is a memoir by Colonel Mackenzie in 1844,[3] and in 1872 a short paper by Mr. T. W. Rhys David on the conquest of South India by Parákrama Bahu, the great king of Ceylon.[4] On the origion of the Afghan people Lieut. (now Major) H. G. Raverty contributed some remarks in 1854.[5] In the volume for 1871 there is a history of the Gakkhars, one of the Panjáb clans, by Mr. J. G. Delmerick.[6] The volumes for 1881 and 1882 contain a series of contributions on the history, religion, etc., of Thibet from Babu Sarat Chandra Das.[7]

---

[1] J. A. S.B., Vol. XLI, p. 49. [2] *Ibid.*, Vol. VII, p. 93; Vol. X, pp. 183, 267; Vol. XIV, pp. 75, 155. [3] *Ibid.*, Vol. XIII, pp. 421, 578. [4] *Ibid.*, Vol. XLI, p. 197. [5] *Ibid.*, Vol. XXIII, p. 550. [6] *Ibid.*, Vol. XL, p. 67. [7] *Ibid.*, Vol. L, pp. 187, 206, 211, 235; Vol. LI, pp. 1, 15, 53, 58, 87, 99, 115, 121.

CHAPTER V.

LANGUAGE AND LITERATURE.

[Sanskrit—Prakrit, Pali—Gaudian: Sindhi, Panjabi, Kashmiri, Hindi and Urdu, Bihari, Bengali, Gipsy,—Indo-Aryan: Kaffiri, Brahui, Baluchi, Pashtu, Chilas, Dardi, Galchah—Aboriginal: Dravidian, Kolarian, Tibeto-Birman, Indo-Chinese, Malayan —Arabic—Persian—General.]

Next to the classical countries of Greece and Rome, there is none which has rendered more important services to the science of Philology than India. It has presented that science, both, with a new classical literature, almost unbounded in its wealth, and with a new system which by its comparative method has gone far to revolutionize the science altogether. It has achieved this great result through its ancient language, the Sanskrit; and it has fallen to the proud lot of the Asiatic Society of Bengal to contribute the first step to its accomplishment.

It is now nearly one hundred years ago, that, in 1789, Sir William Jones, the founder of the Society, published his translation of the Sanskrit drama, the Sakuntalá. Of that work it may fairly be said that it was the starting point of Sanskrit philology.[1] At the same time, feeling how useful it would be to the learned and essential to the student and translator, he elaborated and published in 1788, in the first volume of the Researches, a system of transcribing Asiatic, and especially Sanskrit, words into Roman letters, in which he aimed at securing the double advantage of rendering Asiatic words letter for letter,

[1] See Professor Max Müller's History of Ancient Sanskrit Literature, p. 1.

while preserving their correct pronunciation.[1] His system, still known as the Jonesian, prevailed for a long time till it was superseded by others, which only excelled it by following out its principles in a simpler and more consistent manner.[2]

Having thus fairly started Sanskrit philology on its way, the Society was unable for some time to take any very active share in the further prosecution of its study. The opportunities and qualifications for such a task were much more abundantly present in Europe, and there were many other objects, natural and literary, connected with India, which more directly engaged the Society's attention and admitted of more easy investigation. Nevertheless, it did what lay in its power to further the study of Sanskrit and the publication of its literature. In 1806, it instituted the Bibliotheca Asiatica, in which it was intended "to publish, from time to time, as their funds would admit of it, translations of short works in the Sanskrit and other Asiatic languages, or extracts and descriptive accounts of books of greater length in those languages."[3] To this series of oriental publications contributions were invited from every quarter. For many years no response was made to the Society's invitations, and it was not until the year 1847 that it became possible to make an actual beginning of the series, under a new name and in a considerably modified form. In this series, which now received the name of the Bibliotheca Indica, it was intended to publish the texts, and, as far as practicable, translations of such oriental works as those of which manuscripts had become rare, or which, from the nature

---

[1] As. Res., Vol. I, p. 1. [2] See J. A. S. B., Vol. III, p. 281; and Proceedings for 1867, p. 80. [3] As. Res., Vol. XII, Appendix, p. vii.

of their subject-matter, could not be expected to be published by private enterprise.

The first work, the publication of which was taken into contemplation, was an edition of the whole of the Vedas; and an actual commencement was made in 1847 of the preparation of the Rig Veda Samhitá, under the editorship of Dr. Roer.[1] But as only a few months afterwards it became known "that the Court of Directors had sanctioned the immediate publication of the Rig Veda in London, to be edited by Professor Max Müller, with a translation by Professor Wilson," the Society's edition was at once abandoned in favour of that now well-known great edition,[2] and in its place it was resolved to publish an edition of the Upanishads, or the philosophical parts of the Vedas.[3] Their publication was entrusted to Dr. Roer, who commenced the series in 1849, with an edition of the text of eleven Upanishads,—*viz.*, the Aitareya, the Brihad Aranyaka, Taittiríya, Isa, Katha, Svetásvatara, Chhándogya, Kena, the Prasna, Mundaka, and Mandukya.[4] The first named of these Upanishads belonged to the Rig Veda; the next five to the Yajur Veda; the following two to the Sáma Veda, and the last three to the Atharva Veda. Their text was accompanied with the commentary (or bháshya) of Sankara Achárya and the gloss (or tíká) of Anandagiri in every case, except the Svetásvatara, of which Anandagiri's gloss could not be obtained. In the case of the Mandukya the explanation (or káriká) of Gaudapada was also given in addition to the other commentaries. All these Upanishads had been published before by others in a more

---

[1] J. A. S. B., Vol. XVI, pp. 496, 505, 1259. [2] *Ibid.*, pp. 1090, 1267. [3] *Ibid.*, p. 1268. [4] For a full statement of the titles, &c., of these and all other editions of the Bibliotheca Indica, referred to in the following pages, see Appendix C to the Historical Part of the Centenary Review.

or less complete form, but the commentary of Sankara to seven, and the gloss of Anandagiri to all of them, were now published for the first time.[1] These text editions Dr. Roer followed up soon afterwards, in 1852,[2] with translations; the only exception being the Chhándogya. A translation of this Upanishad was added by Babu Rájendralála Mitra in 1854. After an interval of a few years the series of Upanishad editions was continued, in 1861, by Professor E. B. Cowell, with the publication of the Kaushítakí Bráhmana, one of the oldest of that class of literature. He accompanied the text with the commentary of Sankara Ananda, as well as an English translation. In the following year, 1862, he followed it up with an edition and translation of the Maitrí or Maitráyaníya Upanishad, belonging to the Black Yajur Veda, to which he added the commentary of Rámatírtha. After another pause of ten years, the series of Upanishads was again continued by Pandit Rámamaya Tarkaratna, who in 1872 commenced the publication of a large collection of very small and very little known Upanishads of the Atharva Veda, which, however, was never completed.[3] Only one of these little philosophical treatises, the Rámatápaní, had been edited before by Professor Weber. The Pandit's text was accompanied by the commentary (or dípiká) of Náráyana, to which, in the case of the Kaivalya Upanishad, he was able to add also a commentary of San-

---

[1] See Preface to the Taittiríya Upanishad, p. viii. [2] The dates given with the works of Bibliotheca Indica refer only to the commencement of their publication. [3] The following Upanishads are comprised in this collection: Sira, Garbha, Nádavindu, Brahmavindu, Amritavindu, Dhyánavindu, Tejovindu, Yogasikhá, Yogatattva, Sannyása, Aruneya, Brahmavidyá, Kshuriká, Chuliká, Atharvasikhá, Brahma, Pránágnihotra, Nilarudra, Kanthasruti, Pinda, Atma, Rámapúrvatápani, Ramottaratápani, Hanumaduktaráma, Sarvopanishatsára, Hamsa, Paramahamsa, Jávála, Kaivalya, Garuda. The last named is left incomplete.

kara Ananda. Two other Upanishads of the Atharva Veda are the Nrisimha Tápaní and the Gopála Tápaní, both of which were published in 1870, the first by Pandit Rámamaya Tarkaratna, with the commentary of Sankara Achárya; the other by Pandits Hara Chandra Vidyábhúshana and Visvanátha Sastrí, with the commentary of Visvesvara.

Originally the Upanishads had their place in the Aranyakas and Bráhmanas. Several works belonging to the latter two classes of Vedic literature were edited in the Bibliotheca Indica. The publication of the Taittiríya Bráhmana of the Yajur Veda, with the commentary (or bháshya) of Savana Achárya, was commenced by Babu Rájendralála Mitra in 1855, and that of the Taittiríya Aranyaka of the same Veda in 1864. In the introduction to the latter edition he gave a complete analysis of the work in English, and the table of contents noticed the subjects of the mantras *seriatim*. In 1869, Pandit Ananda Chandra Vedántavágísa followed with the publication of the Tándya Mahábráhmana, the largest and most important of the Sáma Veda, containing the earliest speculations on the origin, nature, and purport of a number of Hindu sacrifices, rites, and ceremonies, and interspersed with a variety of anecdotes of great interest. In the following year, 1870, the publication of the Gopatha Bráhmana, the only extant one of the Atharva Veda, was entrusted to Pandit Hara Chandra Vidyábhúshana, who edited about one-half of it, and after his death, to Babu Rájendralála Mitra, who completed it and added a very full analytical introduction. Unfortunately, no manuscripts of any commentary being available, it was only possible to publish the text.[1]

---

[1] Proceedings for 1872, p. 14; see also Introduction to the Gopatha, p. 38.

In 1875, Dr. Rájendralála Mitra undertook the publication of the Aitareya Bráhmana of the Rig Veda, of the contents of which he supplied an abstract in an English introduction.

In the meanwhile the subject of the publication of the Vedic Samhitás had not been lost sight of. In the place of the Samhitá of the Rig Veda, the edition of which, as already mentioned, had to be abandoned, the Samhitá of the Black Yajur Veda was selected for publication, but the latter was not actually begun before 1854. The work comprises eight books, of which the first was edited by Dr. E. Roer, the second by Professor E. B. Cowell, the larger portion of the third by Pandit Ráma Náráyana Vidyáratna, and the remainder by Pandit Mahesa Chandra Nyáyaratna.[1] In 1871 a complete edition of the Samhitá of the Sáma Veda, with the commentary of Sayana, was undertaken by Pandit Satyavrata Sámasramí. "This Samhitá comprises four different works,—namely, the Grámageya Gána, Uha Gána, Uhya Gána, and Aranya Gána. These include all the hymns of the Sáma Veda set to music. Inasmuch, however, as the hymns with their musical notations were perfectly unintelligible, the words of the hymns were early separated into a distinct compilation, called 'Archika, or the verses of the Rig Veda, occurring in the Sáma Veda.' This compilation was commented upon by Sayana. A recension of it was published by the Oriental Translation Fund of London in 1842, and another by Professor Benfey in 1848. Both appeared under the name of the Samhitá of the Sáma Veda, but as they did not include those peculiarities which convert Rig verses into Sáma hymns, they were, in the

[1] Proceedings for 1872, pp. 13, 14; for 1873, p. 32; for 1874, p. 31.

form in which they appeared, not Sámas but Rig verses." In the edition of the Society "the Rig collection was adopted as the basis, and to every verse of it were added all the various transformations which it had undergone in changing from the Rig to the Sáma, including all the musical notations, as also the commentary of Sayana on the text. Thus, practically, the Society's edition comprised six different works,—namely, the Archika, the four Gánas, and the commentary of Sayana, and the bulk of the edition was necessarily greatly increased thereby; but it was hoped that it would afford to oriental scholars the most complete edition of the Sáma Samhitá. The plan adopted disturbed, in some places, the order in which the Gánas appear, in their respective collections, but this was unavoidable. To remedy the defect full indexes were supplied at the beginning of each volume." "The manuscripts used, all belonged to the North Indian recension, with prosodical marks differing in some respects from those which are current in Southern India, but the principal peculiarity, being the use of figures instead of letters to indicate the notes of the Gamut, is not of much importance."[1]

Next to the Vedas, the Vedángas, or the sciences subsidiary to them, claimed the greatest attention. These include phonology, grammar, prosody, glossary, rituals, and astronomy; the most important being the rituals or 'sútras.' They form a sort of exegesis of the Vedas, and it is impossible to understand the Vedic Mantras, and the most ancient laws, customs, and domestic rites of the Hindus without a careful study of these works. The attention of the Society was, therefore, early directed to collect materials for their publication.[2] This necessarily

[1] Proceedings for 1877, p. 35; for 1879, p. 26. [2] *Ibid.* for 1872, pp. 14, 15.

occupied considerable time; and it was not before 1864 that a commencement could be made with the Sútras or ritual works. These consists of two dfferent classes, the Srauta Sútras and the Grihya Sútras, treating of sacrificial and domestic ritual respectively. In 1864, the publication of the Srauta Sútras of Asvaláyana, belonging to the Rig Veda, was taken in hand by Pandit Ráma Náráyana Vidyáratna; and in 1866, that of the Grihya Sútra of the same author and the same Veda, by Pandit Ananda Chandra Vedántavágísa. The editors added to the text of both Sútras the commentary of Garga Náráyana, as well as elaborate indexes composed in Sanskrit by themselves.[1] The second of the two editors continued his labours in 1870, by the publication of the Srauta Sútra of Látyáyana, belonging to the Sáma Veda, to which he similarly added both the commentary (or bháshya) of Agnisvámin and an index of his own. In the following year, 1871, an edition was undertaken by Pandit Chandra Kánta Tarkálankára, of the Gobhilíya Grihya Sútra of the Sáma Veda, to which he added several appendixes (or parisishtas) containing the Sráddhakalpa, Sandhyá Sútra, and Snána Sútra of Gobhila himself, and the Grihya Sangraha of a son of Gobhila.[2] The commentary which the editor published with the text, he had compiled himself with the aid of two defective MSS. and the glosses on the Sútras of his Appendices.[3] Ten years later, in 1881, the publication of the Apastamba Srauta Sútra, belonging to the Black Yajur Veda, was commenced by Professor R. Garbe. This is a very rare and important ritual work, of which for a long time, till Mr. Burnell's successful researches, no complete manuscripts were available. To the text is

[1] Proceedings for 1870, p. 32. [2] *Ibid.* for 1878, p. 47. [3] *Ibid.* for 1877 pp. 35, 36.

added Rudra Datta's commentary, which, however, unfortunately does not extend to more than about two-thirds of the Sútra.[1]

On the Vedic prosody the leading work is the Chhandah Sútra of Pingala Achárya. Of this, as well as of a commentary on it by Haláyudha, an edition was published in 1871 by Pandit Visvanátha Sástrí.

Each Veda has its own separate system of phonology, or Prátisákhya. As the Society had already undertaken the publication of the Black Yajur Veda, it was resolved, in 1854, to print the Prátisákhya of that Veda, and the task was confided to Babu Rájendralála Mitra, the editor of the Taittiríya Bráhmana. Want of leisure, however, delayed the publication till 1871, when the text appeared together with its commentary, called the Tribháshyaratna.[2]

Vedic etymological lexicography is represented by *one* work, generally known by the name of Yáska's Nirukta. Professor Roth's well-known edition of this work having been long out of print, the Society, in 1880, entrusted the task of bringing out another edition to Pandit Satyavrata Sámasramí, who had just successfully brought to a close his edition of the Sáma Samhitá. His text of the Nirukta is accompanied by extracts from various commentaries.

Next to the literature of the Vedas, that connected with the six Darsanas, or philosophical schools of the Hindus, attracted the attention of the Society. The original text-books of all the six schools were gradually published.[3] The earliest to be edited were the Brahma Sútras, or the aphorisms of the Vedánta School, by Bádaráyana. They were published, together with the

---

[1] See Preface to the edition, p. 9. [2] Proceedings for 1872, pp. 15, 18.

[3] *Ibid.* for 1872, p. 15.

commentary of Sankara Achárya and the gloss of Govinda Ananda, in 1853, by Pandit Ráma Náráyana Vidyáratna. An English translation was commenced in 1870 by the Rev. K. M. Banerjea, but not continued much beyond the first section. Among the many commentaries extant on Sankara's exposition of the Vedánta aphorisms of Bádaráyana, the Bhámatí of Váchaspati Misra is held in high esteem by Indian scholars, and an edition of this work was undertaken in 1875 by Pandit Bála Sástrí.[1]

The peculiar form of the Vedánta doctrine which rejects the gnostic theory that knowledge is the one thing needful, and contends that knowledge is only the handmaid of faith, *i.e.*, the doctrine of the Bhaktimárga, is also represented in the Society's series, namely, by the aphorisms of Sándilya, which were edited by Dr. J. R. Ballantyne in 1861, and translated by Professor E. B. Cowell in 1878.[2] In this connection may be mentioned an edition, by Babu Rájendralála Mitra, in 1853, of the Chaitanya Chandrodaya Nátaka, the object of which is to inculcate in a dramatic form the peculiar tenets of the Bhaktimárga.

After the Vedánta followed, in 1860, the Kanáda Sútras, or the aphorisms of the Vaiseshika school. They were published by Pandit Jaya Náráyana Tarkapanchánana, who, in addition to the commentary of Sankara Misra, accompanied the text with a commentary of his own in Sanskrit. Two years later, in 1862, the Sankhyá aphorisms of Kapila were published by Dr. J. R. Ballantyne, together with an English translation of the text and many extracts from Vijnána Bhikshu's commentary. Another celebrated work of the Sankhyá philosophy, the Sankhyá Pravachana Bháshya, by Vijnána Bhikshu, had been already

---

[1] See Proceedings for 1876, p. 26. [2] See the Preface to the edition; also Proceedings for 1872, pp. 15, 16; for 1879, p. 26.

edited by Mr. FitzEdward Hall in 1854; and a third treatise, the Sankhyá Sára, also by Vijnána Bhikshu, was published by the same editor in 1865. The introduction prefixed to the later edition contains much valuable information on historic and literary questions connected with the Sankhyá philosophy. Next in order came the aphorisms of the Púrva Mímámsá school, by Jaimini, which, together with the commentary of Sávara Svámin, were edited in 1863 by Pandit Mahesa Chandra Nyáyaratna. In the following year, 1864, the Gotama Sútras, or the aphorisms of the Nyáya School, were published, together with the commentary of Vátsyáyana, by Pandit Jaya Náráyana Tarkapanchánana. Another of the most celebrated works of the Nyáya philosophy, the Bháshá Parichheda, had been already edited and translated, in 1850, by Dr. E. Roer. The Yoga Sútras of Patanjali were taken up by Dr. Rájendralála Mitra in 1880, who published them with the commentary of Bhoja Rájá and an English translation of both the text and commentary, and also with an English commentary compiled by the editor himself, including short extracts from the commentaries of Vyása, Vijnána Bhikshu, and Váchaspati Misra.

On the minor systems of philosophy two works were published by the Society,—the general philosophical summary of Mádhava Achárya, called the Sarvadarsana Sangraha, which was published in 1853 by Pandit Isvara Chandra Vidyáságara, and the polemical disquisitions of Sankara, called the Sankara Digvijaya, a work of Anandagiri, which was edited in 1864 by Pandit Jaya Náráyana Tarkapanchánana.

Next to the Vedas and Darsanas, the most important branch of Sanskrit literature, from the religious and social points of view, is represented by the Puránas. They form a distinct class, being a sort of Cyclopædia of Sanskrit literature, and have, of late, entirely superseded the religion of the Vedas. The attention of the Society was early turned to them, and four works were undertaken at different times.[1] Two of them, the Márkandeya Purána and the Náradapancharátna, were edited by the Rev. K. M. Banerjea in 1855 and 1861 respectively; the other two, the Agni Purána and the Vayu Purána, were edited by Dr. Rájendralála Mitra in 1870 and 1879 respectively.[2] The latter added to his edition of the Agni Purána an English introduction, which very fully describes the contents of that work, one of the most ancient of the Puránic class.

No work belonging to the Smriti or law literature of the Hindu was undertaken by the Society till 1871. But in that year a commencement was made by publishing the elaborate legal digest of Hemádri, entitled the Chaturvarga Chintámani. Its real author is generally believed to have been the celebrated grammarian Vopadeva, though the work is known by the name of its patron, and the fact of Vopadeva having quoted largely from several works, now accepted to be no more than two or three hundred years old, opens a new field of enquiry. The work is a very voluminous one, and is divided into five parts (or khandas), treating severally of fasts and penances (or vratas), gifts (or dánas), times (or kálas), funeral ceremonies (or sráddhá) and supplementary matters (or parisesbas). Manuscripts of it are very rare; indeed no manuscript of the complete work has yet been discovered. Fortunately the several

---

[1] Proceedings for 1872, p. 16. [2] The Agni Purána had been begun by Pandit Harachandra Vidyábhúshana, who died after bringing out three fasciculi. The Vayu Purána is still in course of publication.

portions of the work are practically independent of one another; and as the work is particularly valuable, because of the help it gives to the settlement of the dates of many treatises on Hindu law, and the light it throws on the state of Hindu society at the time when it was compiled and for some time previously, the Society resolved to proceed at once to the publication of those parts of the work of which manuscripts were already available, in the hope that by the time these were published, manuscripts of the remaining portions might be discovered. This hope has only partially been fulfilled. When the publication commenced in 1871, the only part of which sufficient manuscript material was at hand, was the second, treating of 'gifts' (or dánas) ; and the edition of this portion was entrusted to Pandit Bharata Chandra Siromani, who added an alphabetical index of the contents, as also of the names of the different authors quoted in the text. In the meanwhile sufficient manuscripts of the first part, on 'fasts and penances' (or vratas), had been procured ; and the edition of this portion was begun by the same editor in 1875, and after his death, continued by the Pandits Yogesvara Bhattá-chárya and Kámákhyánátha Tarkaratna. Soon after this portion was completed, sufficient manuscripts were found to be ready to proceed to the publication of the fifth or supplementary part (or parisesha khanda), which was done in 1881 by the joint editors of the previous portion. Of the fourth part, on the funeral ceremonies (or sráddhá), there are already three manuscripts available ; but of the fifth part, the Kála Khanda, there are still none known that are complete.[1] After the Chaturvarga Chintámani, the next work that was under-

[1] Proceedings for 1872, p. 16 ; for 1874, pp. 30, 31 ; for 1876, p. 26 ; for 1877 p. 35 ; for 1878, p. 47 ; for 1880, p. 27 ; for 1882, p. 28.

taken was the Vishnu Smriti. This work had been already printed in Calcutta some years previously, but in such an imperfect manner, that the Society thought itself justified in bringing out another more perfect edition. This was entrusted in 1881 to Professor J. Jolly,[1] who added to the text extracts from Nanda Pandita's commentary called the Vaijayantí, as also critical notes, an Anukramanika (or list of contents), an alphabetical list of words important for Sanskrit lexicography, and an index of the Vedic mantras quoted in the Vishnu Smriti. It may be added that an English translation of this law book had already been published by Professor Jolly, in 1880, in Professor Max Müller's series of "The Sacred Books of the East." In 1883 an edition of the Parásara Smriti, with the commentary of Mádhava Achárya, was commenced by Pandit Chandra Kánṭa Tarkálankára, who had just completed his able edition of the Gobhilíya Sútra, previously mentioned.[2]

The most important branch of Hindu physical science is astronomy; and on that subject three works have been published in the Bibliotheca Indica. Among these are the Súrya Siddhánta, edited in 1854 by Mr. Fitz Edward Hall, with the exposition (or Gúdhártha Prakása) of Ranganátha. An English translation of the latter work, by Pandit Bápúdeva Sástrí, was edited by the Ven. Archdeacon Pratt in 1860, and in the following year, 1861, the same editor published also an English translation of the Siddhánta Siromani prepared by Mr. L. Wilkinson and revised by Pandit Bápúdeva Sástrí.[3] In 1864, Professor H. Kern followed with an edition of the Brihat Samhitá of Varáha Mihira, to which he added a very valuable introduction on the astronomical literature of the Hindus. This

[1] Professor Jolly was afterwards elected Tagore Law Lecturer at the Calcutta University for the year 1882. [2] See above, p. 144. [3] Proceedings for 1872, p. 16.

work, however, is much more an astrological one, and as such partakes of a somewhat encyclopædic character, treating, among other things, of geography, architecture, sculpture, medicine, statecraft, etc.[1] In style and matter somewhat resembling it is another work, the Kámándakíya Nítisára, or the political maxims of Chánakya, the minister of Chandra Gupta, compiled by his disciple Kámandaki. It was edited, in 1849, by Dr. R. Mitra, with extracts from the commentary, entitled Upádhyáya Nirapekshá.[2]

The Hindu science of Medicine is represented in the Society's series by one work. This is the Susruta Samhitá, which, next to the Charaka, is the oldest and most important of the medical works of the Hindus. Of it Dr. Udoy Chánd Dutt commenced, in 1883, to publish an annotated translation.

Of works connected with Sanskrit rhetoric, the Bibliotheca Indica includes three. The first among them is the Sáhitya Darpana, or "Mirror of Composition," by Visvánátha Kavirája, which is admittedly the standard of taste among the learned Hindus. It had been printed in 1828 at Calcutta under the authority of the General Committee of Public Instruction, but a revised edition was brought out in 1850 in the Society's collection by Dr. E. Roer, and an English translation, together with an introductory analysis, was supplied by Dr. J. R. Ballantyne in 1865.[3] The second to be edited was the Kávyádarsa of Srí Dandin, which was published in 1861 by Pandit Prema Chandra Tarkabágísa, with a commentary prepared by himself. In the following year, 1862, Dr. FitzEdward Hall followed with the publication of the Dasarúpa by

[1] See Introduction to the edition, p. 27; and the translation in the Journal of the Royal Asiatic Society, Vol. IV (N.S.), pp. 437, 438. [2] See Weber's History of Ancient Sanskrit Literature, p. 271, foot-note. [3] See the "Advertisement" prefixed to the edition.

Dhanánjaya, a work which, though of but moderate antiquity, has long been the favourite authority among the Hindus for everything connected with the theatre. The introduction contains a good analysis of the Hindu canons of dramaturgy as enjoined in the Dasarúpa and similar works.

The Sanskrit grammatical science of the Hindus is only represented by one work. This is the Kátantra or Kálápa Vyákarana, commonly ascribed to Sarvavarman, of which Professor J. Eggeling published an excellent edition in 1874, with the commentary of Durgásimha and numerous notes and indexes. This grammar is important as the chief representative of the so-called Aindra school of grammarians, which has many points of difference from the standard school of Pánini.[1]

For the publication of the poetical portion of Sanskrit literature such ample provision was made on every side, that it was not thought necessary by the Society to take of it more than a passing notice. Only two works were published, but both standard works. One is the second part of Srí Harsha's great epic the Naishadha Charita, edited by Dr. E. Roer, in 1851; the other the Vásavadatta, a romance by Subandha, published, in 1855, by Mr. FitzEdward Hall, with the gloss of Sivaráma Tripáthin. In this connection may be also mentioned an English translation of the Kathá Sarit Ságara, which Mr. C. H. Tawney published in 1880. This work is the celebrated repository of Indian legends compiled from older sources by Somadeva of Kashmir toward the close of the eleventh century. The stories were illustrated by the translator with copious notes referring to similar legends current in other countries.

---

[1] See Dr. Burnell's Aindra School of Sanskrit Grammarians, p. 51.

Of Sanskrit works connected with Jainism, there is one in the Bibliotheca Indica. It is the Sthavirávali Charita, or Parisishta Parvan, an appendix of the Trishashti Sataka Purusha Charita by Hema Chandra, of which Professor Hermann Jacobi commenced an edition in 1883. It narrates the history of the first twelve Staviras, or patriarchs, from the death of Mahávíra, down to the last Srutakevalin of the Jain community.

Contrasted with the Society's Bibliotheca Indica, the pages of its Transactions could only receive philological contributions of small dimensions ; and as the energies of the Society were mainly devoted to the advancement of the former series with its far more important object of editing texts and translations of whole oriental works—a series[1] the quantity and quality of which indeed is sufficient by itself to establish the philological credit of the Society—it could not be expected that many of the smaller contributions to the Researches and the Journal should be of great or permanent value. Important contributions, in fact, only commenced to appear in the Society's Transactions when a new department of philology began to be opened up, and the attention of enquirers in India was turned from the study of the ancient Sanskrit to that of the numerous mediæval and modern vernacular languages and dialects.

Still Sanskrit philology did not remain entirely unrepresented. As early as 1789, there is in the first volume of the Researches a short essay on the Sanskrit literature of the Hindus by Govardhan Caul.[2] This is followed successively by three valuable dissertations from the pen of Mr. H. T. Colebrooke. The first, in 1801, treats of the Sanskrit and Prákrit languages, and is devoted mainly to an account of the

---

[1] As. Res., Vol. XII, Appendix, p. ii, Rule 5. [2] *Ibid.*, Vol. I, p. 340.

various native grammars and dictionaries, such as Pánini's and Amarasimha's works.[1] The second, published in 1805, discusses the Vedas or sacred writings of the Hindus; and in it the writer, after some introductory remarks on the traditional history of the Vedas, proceeds to give an analysis of the first, the Rig Veda.[2] The third, which appeared in 1808, treats on Sanskrit and Prákrit poetry, and is intended to exhibit the laws of Sanskrit versification, together with brief notices of the most celebrated poems, in which these have been exemplified.[3] In 1822, Mr. Francis Ellis gave an account of a curious modern imitation of the Vedas (Rik, Ezour, Cham and Odorba Veda) ascribed to the French Jesuit Missionary, Robert de Nobilis, in the first half of the seventeenth century.[4] Many years later, in 1871, a still more curious forgery of this kind was made known by Babu Rájendralála Mitra. It was the work of a Muhammadan at the court of the emperor Akbar, and professed to be the Allah Upanishad, a chapter of the Atharva Veda.[5]

The Puránas, another class of sacred writings of the Hindus, was made the subject of investigation by Professor H. H. Wilson, who, in 1832, contributed analyses of several of those works.[6] The Rev. William Yates, in 1836, wrote an essay on the employment of alliteration in Sanskrit poetry.[7] In the following year, 1837, Mr. Lancelot Wilkinson reported the discovery of the Rekhá Ganita, a translation of the Elements of Euclid into Sanskrit by Pandit Samrat Jagannátha, under the orders of Raja Siwai Jaya Singha of Jaipur.[8] Next follow several

---

[1] As. Res., Vol. VII, p. 199. [2] *Ibid.*, Vol. VIII, p. 369. [3] *Ibid.*, Vol X, p. 389. [4] *Ibid.*, Vol. XIV, p. 1. [5] J. A. S. B., Vol. XL, p. 170. [6] *Ibid.*, Vol. I, pp. 81 (Agnipurána), 217 (Brahma Vaivartta), 431 (Vishnu), 535 (Vayu). [7] As. Res., Vol. XX, p. 135. [8] J. A. S. B., Vol. VI, p. 938.

translations of extracts or of small Sanskrit works ; thus, in 1839, of a few of the opening stanzas of Magha's well-known poem, the Sisupála Badha, by Mr. J. C. C. Sutherland,[1] and of the Mahimnástava, or a hymn to Siva, by the Rev. Krishna Mohan Banerjee ;[2] in 1845, of the Vedánta Sára, an introduction into the Vedánta Philosophy, by Dr. E. Roer ;[3] in 1847, of the Prasnottara Málá, or catechetical dialogue of Suka, by Mr. J. Christian.[4] In the volume of the latter year, 1847, Dr. E. Roer also published a critical review of the leading ideas of the Nyáya and Vaiseshika systems of philosophy,[5] to which a few years later, in 1851, he added a few remarks on the Sankhyá philosophy, elicited by a lecture on that philosophy, from the pen of Dr. J. R. Ballántyne.[6]

At this time the study of the literature of the Vedas had attracted to itself the paramount interest of the scholars in Europe. In order to bring the result of their researches within the reach of Indian scholars, some of their best productions were translated and published in the Journal. Among these were three dissertations by Professor R. Roth, of Tübingen, on the hymn collections and the most ancient grammars of the Vedas, inserted in the Journals for 1847 and 1848.[7]

A no small portion of the Vedic literature consists of Upanishads or philosophical treatises. A large number of these were known to exist, through lists prepared by Mr. Colebrooke, Dr. Weber and others ; but in 1851, Mr. (now Sir) Walter Elliot was able to add considerably to these lists from information given him by Telingana Pandits. Some account of these additions and a synoptic view of this

---

[1] J. A. S. B., Vol. VIII, p. 16. [2] *Ibid.*, p. 355. [3] *Ibid.*, Vol. XIV, p. 100. [4] *Ibid.*, Vol. XVI, p. 1228. [5] *Ibid.*, p. 157. [6] *Ibid.*, Vol. XX, p. 397. [7] *Ibid.*, Vol. XVI, p. 812; Vol. XVII, p. 6.

whole class of literature, consisting now of 138 separate works, was prepared by Dr. Roer, and published in the volumes for 1851 and 1855.[1]

The Journal for 1852 again contains an analysis, prepared by the Rev. J. Long, of a Sanskrit poem, the famous Raghuvamsa of Kálidása, the chief of Sanskrit poets.[2] After a pause of some years the Journal for 1859 brings an edition and translation of the Vedic hymn, the Srí Sukta, or 'Litany to fortune,' by Mr. FitzEdward Hall.[3] In the following year, 1860, Professor E. B. Cowell contributed some remarks on the rhetoric forms of simile and metaphor as taught in the Sáhitya Darpana,[4] and in 1862, a review of the Chárváka, or atheistic system of Hindu Philosophy.[5] In the latter year Mr. FitzEdward Hall also made known some fragments of a commentary on the Rig Veda, by a certain Rávana, which he had extracted from a commentary on the Bhagavadgítá;[6] he likewise reported the discovery by him of a new and complete manuscript of the Nátya Sástra, by Bharata.[7] In the preceding year, 1861, Mr. R. T. H. Griffith published a verse translation of the story of Dilípa, an episode from Kálidása's celebrated poem, the Raghuvamsa.[8] In 1866, Professor G. Bühler, whose attention had been attracted to Hindu Law, contributed a translation of the chapter on Ordeals, from the Vyavahára Mayúkha, and a notice of the Saunaka Smriti, two books of which he had been successful in recovering.[9]

After another pause of about ten years, the Journal for 1875 contains a translation, by Pandit Ráma Náráyana, of

---

[1] J. A. S. B., Vol. XX, p. 606; Vol. XXIV, p. 38. [2] *Ibid.*, Vol. XXI, p. 446. [3] *Ibid.*, Vol. XXVIII, p. 121. [4] *Ibid.*, Vol. XXIX, p. 217. [5] *Ibid.*, Vol. XXXI, p. 371. [6] *Ibid.*, p. 129. [7] *Ibid.*, p. 51. [8] *Ibid.*, Vol. XXX, p. 111. [9] *Ibid.*, Vol. XXXV, pp. 14, 149.

the Ayodhya Mahátmya, a portion of the Skanda and Padma Puránas, describing the religious places of the holy city of Audh.[1] A far more important contribution in the same Journal is Dr. G. Thibaut's analysis of the Sulvasútras, which present us with the earliest beginnings among the Indians of geometrical and mathematical investigations arising from certain requirements of their sacrifices.[2] Dr. Rájendralála Mitra communicated a note in 1881 on a very old manuscript of the Bhattikávya, which afforded him the occasion of reviewing the question regarding its authorship, and deciding in favour of the proposition that Bhatti, the author of the poem, was a different person from Bartrihari to whom it is often ascribed.[3] The last contribution deserving notice is one by the same scholar in the Journal of 1883, on Gonikaputra and Gonardíya as names of the celebrated grammarian Patanjali, in which he addúces strong grounds for believing that they are not names of Patanjali, but of a much older grammarian referred to by Patanjali in the Mahábháshya.[4]

Besides the Sanskrit language, there were current in ancient India another class of languages, or dialects, of a more vernacular type, and designated collectively by the name of Prákrit. It was customary with Hindu dramatic writers to introduce specimens of these Prákrit languages into their plays. Hence it came to pass that the existence of them became known to the European world almost as early as that of the classical Sanskrit itself, for the ancient poetical literature of India was one of the earliest that attracted the attention of European enquirers. In Sir William Jones's translation of the Sakuntalá, previously mentioned as the starting point

---

[1] J. A. S. B., Vol. XLV, p. 130. [2] *Ibid.*, p. 227. [3] Proceedings for 1881, p. 134. [4] J. A. S. B., Vol. LII, p. 261.

of Sanskrit philology, the Prákrit language is already, though merely passingly, noticed in 1789. A much fuller notice of it was given by Mr. H. T. Colebrooke in his essay on the Sanskrit and Prákrit languages, published in 1801 in the seventh volume of the Researches.[1] In it he reviewed all the information at that time available on the subject of the various kinds of Prákrit and the literature in which it is used. It omitted, however, all mention of the most ancient forms of Prákrit, the Páli and the Gáthá, which had not yet become known ; and overlooking a distinction which was only a discovery of later days, it confused the modern forms of Prákrit (the Gaudians) with its mediæval forms (the Prákrits, commonly so called). The same subject, though from a particular point of view and with the same, at that time, natural defects, was continued by Mr. H. T. Colebrooke, in 1808, in his essay on Sanskrit and Prákrit poetry, in which he discussed the laws of Prákrit versification, and illustrated his remarks by numerous quotations from the vernacular literature.[2]

It was only about twenty years afterwards that the first knowledge of the Páli language, one of the oldest forms of the Prákrit, was obtained through the ancient Buddhist literature of Ceylon and Birma, which was composed in that language. Mr. B. Clough, in Colombo, and MM. E. Burnouf and Chr. Lassen, in Paris, were the first to study it more intimately and make it more generally known in 1824 and 1826.[3] About ten years later, the genuineness of the Páli, both with regard to its age and its being a natural product, received a striking confirmation through the discovery, by Mr. Prinsep

[1] As. Res., Vol. VII, p. 199. [2] *Ibid.*, Vol. X, p. 389. [3] See Mr. B. Clough's Compendious Páli Grammar in 1824, and Messrs. E. Burnouf and Chr. Lassen's Essay sur le Pali, in 1826.

and his coadjutors in 1837 and 1838, of ancient Prákrit dialects, more or less closely allied to the Páli, in which the rock and pillar inscriptions of Asoka and his contemporaries were composed.[1] From a cursory comparison of the language of these inscriptions with the Sanskrit of India and the Páli of Ceylon, Mr. J. Prinsep arrived at the conclusion, which later researches have proved to be substantially correct, that the language of the inscription is " intermediate between Sanskrit and Páli," and that it occurs in those inscriptions in two different dialects, one peculiar to the East, the other to the West of India.[2]

About the same time, the researches of Mr. B. H. Hodgson drew attention to a third kind of the ancient vernacular, in which the sacred works of the Northern Buddhists in Nepal were by him found to be composed. As this species of Prákrit exhibited in many ways a most curious resemblance to the well-known Sanskrit, it is not to be wondered that at first it was mistaken to be the latter.[3] It was not till many years later, when in 1853 Babu Rájendralála Mitra undertook to prepare an edition of a northern Buddhist work, the Lalita Vistara, for the Society's Bibliotheca Indica, that a more just appreciation of the language was formed.[4] It was then found that this Gáthá dialect, as it was called, was but another dialect like the Páli and the Mágadhí, possessing the closest affinities to Sanskrit.[5]

With the exception of these earlier contributions to the study of Prákrit philology, the latter did not engage

---

[1] J. A. S. B., Vol. VI, pp. 469, 686; Vol. VII, pp. 276, 563, *et passim*. [2] *Ibid.*, Vol. VII, p. 276. [3] *Ibid.*, Vol. VI, p. 682. [4] This work is a kind of "Memoirs" of the early life of Sákya Simha, the founder of Buddhism. An English translation of it was commenced by Dr. Mitra in 1881, also in the Bibliotheca Indica. See the list of the latter series in Appendix C to the Historical Part of the Centenary Review. [5] J. A. S. B., Vol. XXIII, p. 604.

the Society's attention during many years. Indeed, it was but comparatively lately that this branch of philological research has been more zealously cultivated even in Europe. A reflex of the new interest taken in it in Europe soon showed itself in India, its native country. The earliest was a translation, arranged on European models, of Kachcháyana's celebrated Páli grammar, which Dr. F. Mason published, in 1857, in the Bibliotheca Indica. In 1875, Major (now Lieutenant-Colonel) G. E. Fryer published a Páli study on the Ceylon grammarian Sangha Rakkhita Thera and on his treatise on Rhetoric, the Subodhálankára, the text of which he edited.[1] It was followed in 1877 by another study on the Páli text of the Vuttodaya, or 'exposition of metre,' by the same Sangha Rakkhita Thera, and to the text were added a translation and notes.[2] In 1878, the writer of the present Review made known a very old Prákrit grammar, called the Prákrita Lakshana, the work of a grammarian Chanda (or Chandra), and treating of the Arsha, or ancient Prákrit. An edition of it was published by him two years later, in 1880, in the Society's Bibliotheca Indica, together with a critical introduction and a comparative analysis of the grammars of the principal Prákrit idioms.[3] In 1879, Mr. H. L. St. Barbe contributed a short paper on Páli derivations in Burmese.[4] In the same year, the writer of this Review brought to notice a new manuscript of the well-known Prákrit grammar of Vararuchi, which was of some interest as giving several new readings, differing from those of the published text in Professor Cowell's edition.[5] In the following year, 1880,

[1] J. A. S. B., Vol. XLIV, p, 91. [2] *Ibid.*, Vol. XLVI, p. 369. [3] Proceedings for 1878, p. 178; for 1880, p. 88. See the list of the Bibliotheca Indica in Appendix C to the Historical Part of the Centenary Review. [4] J. A. S. B., Vol. XLVIII, p. 253. [5] Proceedings for 1879, p. 79.

the same made known a new and hitherto quite unknown Prákrit grammar, the Prákritánanda, by Raghunátha.[1] Lastly, in 1882, Lieutenant-Colonel G. E. Fryer communicated a note on the Páli grammarian Kachcháyana, in which he endeavoured to show that the true date of that grammarian, which had hitherto been placed before the Christian era, must be somewhere in or about the twelfth century after Christ—a proposition the establishment of which can only be expected from further research.[2]

Out of the ancient and mediæval Prákrit languages grew up, within the last six or seven centuries, the modern vernaculars of India. Of these, generally, eight are enumerated; namely, beginning in the North-West, the Kashmírí, Panjábí, Sindhí, Gujarátí, Maráthí, Hindí, Bangálí, Uriyá. Recent researches, as will be noticed further on, have shown that, in the area which is generally appropriated to Hindí, there exist in reality two distinct languages, the Hindí (properly so called), and the Bihárí. The correct number of modern vernaculars, therefore, is at least nine, which, moreover, possess a large number of dialectic varieties. It was the investigation of these languages and dialects of modern India to which the efforts of the Society were principally and most successfully directed. Curiously enough, the westernmost group of these languages, consisting of the Sindhí, Panjábí and Kashmírí, two of which, the Panjábí and Kashmírí, are at present among the least known, was the earliest to attract the Society's attention. Later on, various circumstances combined to concentrate the investigations of the Society on the central and eastern vernaculars, the Hindí, Bihárí, and Bangálí, regarding which our knowledge, in the present day, is most advanced.

[1] Proceedings for 1880, p. 100.

[2] *Ibid.* for 1882, pp. 116, 125.

Sindhí was brought under the notice of the Society, as early as 1837, by Mr. J. Prinsep, in a review, contributed by him to the Journal, of Mr. W. H. Wathen's grammar of that language.[1] A short vocabulary of it, drawn up by Captain J. B. Eastwick, was published a few years later in the Journal for 1843. It contained a promiscuous collection of words, followed by a particular list of names of different artificers and their implements; and a particularly valuable feature in it was that it gave the equivalents of every English word in two different Sindhí dialects, those of Sár and Lár.[2]

The first notice of the Panjábí occurs, almost as early as that of the Sindhí, in the Journal for 1838. It was communicated by Lieutenant R. Leech, whose position as an assistant on a Mission to Kabul gave him a welcome opportunity of acquiring some acquaintance with the various languages and dialects which he met on his route. He was thus enabled to furnish the Society with outline grammars and short vocabularies of no less than nine languages and dialects. One of the principal languages among them was the Panjábí, which he described as a "dialect of the Urdu or Hindustani, and differing from it chiefly in having those vowels short that the latter has long, and in having the Sanskrit *visarga* in the middle of words otherwise Hindustani." The latter observation he illustrated by the example of the Panjábí *attáhrán* for 'eighteen,' as compared with the Hindústání *athárá*. His essay contains an outline of the grammar, a short vocabulary and a series of sentences and dialogues.[3] In 1850 and 1851, Captain G. Siddons published a translation of the Vichitra Nátak, or 'Beautiful Epitome,' a fragment of the

---

[1] J. A. S. B., Vol. VI, p. 347. [2] *Ibid.*, Vol. XII, p. 1. [3] *Ibid.*, Vol. VII, p. 711.

Sikh Granth, entitled the "Book of the Tenth Pontiff."[1] Major (now General) J. Abbott followed in 1854 with a free translation of the Panjábí legend of Rasálú, to which he added copious explanatory notes.[2] Of a similar kind were the contributions of Lieutenant (now Captain) R. S. Temple in 1882, and Rev. C. Swynnerton in 1883. The latter published a collection of small folktales from the Upper Panjáb in an English translation. The former gave a number of Hindí folksongs from the same country, the usefulness of which was much increased by the grammatical and lexicographic remarks, with which Captain Temple accompanied the text and translation of his folk-songs. It should be noted, however, that much of the language from which all the foregoing translations were made, was not strictly Panjábí, but rather a species of Western Hindí.

The Kashmírí we find first noticed in 1841 in the tenth volume of the Journal. Mr. M. P. Edgeworth, finding himself stationed in Lúdiána, in the Panjáb, in the midst of a large colony of Kashmírí weavers, set to work to learn their language. The result he published in the Journal in the shape of a rudimentary grammar and short vocabulary.[3] A rather fuller grammar and vocabulary were published three years later, in 1844, by Major R. Leech.[4] Both these treatises labored under a serious disadvantage. They were not merely exceedingly meagre, but in addition they were avowedly founded upon the language of a small community of artisans, long expatriated from their native country, with whose language, moreover, the writers only became acquainted through the intervention of a Musalman. Under these circum-

---

[1] J. A. S. B., Vol. XIX, p. 521; Vol., XX, pp. 314, 487. [2] *Ibid.*, Vol. XXIII, p. 123. [3] *Ibid.*, Vol. X, p. 1038. [4] *Ibid.*, Vol. XIII, pp. 397, 553.

stances, the trustworthiness and usefulness of the information was necessarily very doubtful. This led the Hon'ble G. Campbell in 1866 to move the Society to request the Panjáb Government to take measures for obtaining an accurate knowledge of the Arian languages spoken in the territories of the Mahárája of Kashmir. During the discussion of Mr. Campbell's motion, some useful information regarding the affinities and the area of the Kashmírí language was elicited,[1] but beyond this the movement was not followed by any practical results. It is true, some lexicographic information was also given in 1866 by Captain H. H. Godwin-Austen, in a comparative collection of Kashmírí, Baltí and Kistwárí words;[2] and in 1870, by Dr. W. J. Elmslie, in a list of Kashmírí words drawn up according to Mr. Justice Campbell's "model vocabulary for the discovery of the radical affinities of languages and for easy comparison."[3] But both contributions, though proceeding from Kashmir itself, were too exceedingly meagre to be helpful in advancing the knowledge of Kashmírí. A complete and reliable grammar and dictionary of that language is still a desideratum, the supply of which must be hoped for from future researches.

Among all the modern vernaculars of North India, Hindí is one of the most important and prominent. Nevertheless, little notice of it, as distinguished from Bihárí, is found in the Society's Transactions. This fact, strange at first sight, is fully explained by the peculiar circumstances of that language. Unlike the other vernaculars of India, which before they were recognized and elevated under European influence, were more or less obscure

[1] Proceedings for 1866, pp. 46, 62, 191. [2] J. A. S. B., Vol. XXXV, p. 233.
[3] *Ibid.*, Vol. XXXIX, p. 95.

and uncultured provincial idioms; the Hindí, in its cultured form of Hindústání or Urdú, occupied an already acknowledged literary position under the Muhammadan Government of India. It possessed a well-known grammar and a not inconsiderable literature, and it was known and spoken, more or less purely and extensively, as an imperial *lingua franca*, by the educated population throughout the Muhammadan empire, the capital of which, Dehli, was also the stronghold of its language. This being so, the Hindí or Hindústání naturally offered no particular scope for original researches; and hence the investigation and cultivation of it was left by the Society to others, of whom there was no lack, who devoted themselves to the study of it with a view to the preparation of grammars, vocabularies or dictionaries, and translations.

There were two questions, however, connected with Hindí, to which the Society could still profitably turn its attention. One was the relation to one another of the two phases of Hindí, *viz.* Hindí proper and Urdú or Hindústání; the other was the relation of Hindí to its older dialects out of which it had grown up, and to its older literature. The former subject was hotly debated in several articles, published in the Journal, by MM. Beames and Growse in 1866 and 1867, the former being the champion of the Urdú and pleading for an ample admission of foreign, that is to say, Arabic and Persian words, into the Indian vernacular,[1] the latter taking the side of the Hindí and advocating the exclusion of all foreign elements, save such as had already won for themselves a secure position in popular speech.[2] A curious illustration, it may here be mentioned, of the practicability of writing in exclusive

[1] J. A. S. B., Vol. XXXV, p. 1; Vol. XXXVI, p. 145. [2] *Ibid.*, Vol. XXXV, p. 172.

Hindí had been furnished, some ten years previously, by the publication, in the Journals of 1852 and 1855, of a tale composed by Insha Allah Khan, the peculiarity of which professed to be that, "though pure and elegant Urdú, and fully intelligible even to the Musalmans of the court of Delhi or Lucknow, it did not contain one Persian word."[1] The dispute is one the settlement of which is yet a long way off, and which, though it cannot but be effected by 'academic' discussions of the learned, will ultimately rest with the writers of taste and culture among the people themselves.

As regards older Hindí literature, the earliest publication was that of the text, together with a translation, of one of the Granthas, or sacred books of the Dadupanthí sect, by Lieutenant G. R. Siddons, in 1837.[2] An account of the sect itself had been given in 1828 by Professor H. H. Wilson in the sixteenth volume of the Researches.[3] The language of the Grantha is the Eastern Rájpútání dialect of the Hindí of the seventeenth century. In 1852 and 1853, Dr. A. Sprenger published some stray specimens of early poetry in the 'Rekhtah idiom,' that is to say, in what is commonly called Urdú. They were verses traditionally ascribed, some to the celebrated Persian poet Sa'adi of Shiraz, others to Mír Khusrau of Delhi, others to Núrí, in the thirteenth, fourteenth and sixteenth centuries respectively.[4] He mentioned a still earlier Urdú poet, Ma'súd, of the twelfth century, but he was unable to produce any of his compositions, as unfortunately none were known to have been preserved.[5]

---

[1] J. A. S. B., Vol. XXI, p. 1, and Vol. XXIV, p. 79. The claim is not literally true, for about half a dozen foreign words do occur in it. [2] J. A. S. B., Vol. VI, p. 480. [3] As. Res., Vol. XVI, p. 79. [4] J. A. S. B., Vol. XXI, p. 513. [5] *Ibid.*, Vol. XXII, p. 442.

The researches into another ancient poem, also of the twelfth century, had a more happy result. This was a large epic poem, called the Prithiráj Rásau, the work of the famous bard Chand Bardáí, who lived at the court of the last Hindu ruler, Prithiráj, of Dehli, towards the end of the twelfth century. The poem describes, in sixty-six cantos, the family-history and personal exploits of Prithiráj, and the destruction of his empire by Muizzuddín Muhammad bin Sam, called Sahábuddín Gorí. It was written in an ancient species of Western Hindí, being a mixture of Eastern and Western Rájpútání. The attention of the Society was first called to this great Hindí epic by Mr. F. S. Growse in 1867, who suggested a search for manuscripts of it, with a view to an eventual publication.[1] This led to the gradual discovery of several manuscripts, among them one in the Agra College, and two others with the Rájas of Baidlah and Benares respectively.[2] Of the last mentioned manuscript, which showed considerable differences from the Agra manuscript, Mr. Growse gave some account in the Journal for 1868.[3] About the same time, Mr. J. Beames, whose offer to prepare an edition of the epic had been accepted by the Society, reported the discovery of three further manuscripts, two in the Royal Asiatic Society's Library in London, one of which had formerly belonged to Colonel Tod, and used by him in the compilation of his Annals of Rajasthan; the third in the Bodleian library at Oxford.[4] In the following year, 1869, the same scholar published, as an essay in translating the difficult work of Chand, a version and a portion of the text of

---

[1] Proceedings for 1868, p. 63. [2] *Ibid.*, p. 165. [3] J. A. S. B., Vol. XXXVII, p. 119. Proceedings for 1868, p. 245. See also J. A. S. B., Vol. XXXVIII, p. 1.
[4] Proceedings for 1868, p. 242; see also pp. 64, 165, 228. J. A. S. B., Vol. XXXVIII, p. 171.

the nineteenth canto of his poem.[1] This led to an acrimonious controversy between him and Mr. Growse regarding the proper method of editing and translating Chand's epic;[2] and was followed in 1872 and 1873 by rival translations of the same initial stanzas of the first canto, intended to illustrate their respective positions.[3] In the Journals of the same two years Mr. Beames also published a list of the books or cantos contained in Chand's poem,[4] and some valuable grammatical studies in the archaic language of that ancient bard.[5] At this time the plan of publishing in the Bibliotheca Indica an edition of Chand, which, as mentioned, had already received the Society's sanction some years previously, was actively taken up, and the work of editing it divided between Mr. Beames and the writer of this Review ; the former taking as his share the first twenty-two cantos of the epic, while the remaining forty-seven cantos were entrusted to the latter.[6] The first fasciculus of Mr. Beames's portion was published in 1873, after which unfortunately the pressure of official work compelled him to discontinue his edition. The first fasciculus of the second part was published in 1874, and was followed in the succeeding years[7] by three more fasciculi of the text, as well as one fasciculus of the translation.

Of a much later date than Chand's epic are the rhapsodies of Gambhír Rai, the bard of Núrpur. Mr. Beames had communicated to the Society a short notice of them in 1872 ;[8] but he afterwards published in the Journal for 1875 a portion of their text, together with a translation and

---

[1] J. A. S. B., Vol. XXXIX, p. 145. [2] *Ibid.*, Vol. XXXVIII, pp. 161, 171 ; Vol. XXXIX, p. 52. See also Proceedings for 1873, p. 122. [3] J. A. S. B., Vol. XLI, p. 42 ; Vol. XLII, p. 329. [4] *Ibid.*, Vol. XLI, p. 204. [5] *Ibid.*, Vol. XLII, p. 165. [6] Proceedings for 1874, p. 32. [7] *Ibid.* for 1875, p. 32. See the list of the Bibliotheca Indica in the Appendix C to the Historical Part of the Centenary Review. [8] Proceedings for 1872, p. 156.

explanatory notes. These songs are of the middle of the seventeenth century; their language is in the main Hindí, but full of Panjábí words and constructions,[1] and they relate the story of Rája Jagat Singh, lord of Núrpur, Mau and Pathan in the Kángrá district.

Of about the same age is a shorter epic, written by a bard Jodhráj in the Eastern Rájpútání dialect of Hindí. It is called the Hamír Rásá, and relates the story of Hamír, the Chohán lord of Rathambar, at the time when 'Aláuddín Muhammad Sháh was emperor of Dehli. An expurgated translation of this poem by Babu Brajanátha Bandyopádhyáya of Jaipur was published in the Journal for 1879.[2]

Until quite recently it was generally believed that the area of the Hindí language extended so far to the East as to be conterminous with that of the Bangálí. The error of this opinion was first prominently pointed out by the writer of this Review in 1872, who showed that that widely extended area was occupied by two entirely different classes of dialects, each of which classes constituted a distinct language, the boundary line being, roughly speaking, the 80th degree of longitude.[3] Among the western group of these dialects, one, the Braj Bháshá, had received a considerable amount of literary cultivation, and thus had gradually risen, in a somewhat modified form, to the position of the standard dialect of the group, under the name of Hindí. No corresponding process had taken place among the eastern group of those dialects; whence it had happened that their claim to constitute a separate language and bear a distinct name of their own had failed to be recognized. The want of such a distinctive and collective name, however, began to be strongly felt, as soon as the dialects belonging to

---

[1] J. A. S. B., Vol. XLIV, p. 192. [2] *Ibid.*, Vol. XLVIII, p. 186. See also Proceedings for 1878, p. 195. [3] J. A. S. B., Vol. XLI, pp. 121, 122.

the group were made the object of closer study. The desired name was at last supplied in 1883 by Mr. G. A. Grierson, who called the allied dialects of the group by the collective term of the Bihárí language—a term taken from the area of the most prominent of the dialects, the Maithilí, and recommending itself to general acceptance on the ground of the greatest convenience.

Besides the Maithilí, just mentioned, the following dialects belong to the Bihárí language: the Baiswárí or Bundelkhandí, the Bhojpúrí, and the Mágadhí. Among these the Bundelkhandí was noticed as a peculiar dialect, as early as 1843, by Major R. Leech, though its true relation to the Hindí was not at that time recognized. His paper gave merely a very meagre outline of its grammar and a very short vocabulary.[1] Nothing more was done till 1875, when Mr. V. A. Smith published the text, with translations and notes, of some popular songs of the Hamírpur district, in Bundelkhand, to which he added some more in 1876.[2] In the latter year, Mr. F. S. Growse also published, as a specimen translation, an English version of the prologue to the Rámáyan of the famous poet Tulsí Das. This vernacular rendering of Válmíki's celebrated epic is composed in the Baiswárí dialect, a variety of the Bundelkhandí.[3] Of the standard Bihárí dialect, the Maithilí, Mr. G. A. Grierson published in 1880-1882 a very full grammar, chrestomathy and vocabulary.[4] The chrestomathy, among other specimens of Maithilí literature, contained a complete edition of the genuine text of the poems of the well-known Bidyápati. To these specimens Mr. Grierson added, in 1882, an edition of the Haribans, a

[1] J. A. S. B., Vol. XII. p. 1086. [2] *Ibid.*, Vol. XLIV, p. 389; and Vol. XLV, p. 277. [3] *Ibid.*, Vol. XLV, p. 1. [4] *Ibid.*, Extra Numbers for 1880-1882.

poem of Manbodh or, as he is also called, Bholan Jhá.[1] The only specimens of the Bhojpúrí dialect of any extent hitherto published, are some folksongs from Eastern Gorakhpur, which were collected by Mr. Hugh Fraser, and edited by Mr. G. A. Grierson in 1883.[2] The latter added some valuable notes on certain dialectic peculiarities, which may be noticed in the songs.[3]

With regard to the Bangálí language, the earliest notice which occurs in the Journal is the analysis of a historical poem in Bangálí verse, called the Rájmálá, made by the Rev. James Long in 1850.[4] Of far greater importance is a contribution by Mr. G. A. Grierson in 1877 on the Northern Bangálí dialect of Rangpur. The fact is well-known that, beside the Nadíya dialect, which has afforded the basis for the modern literary or standard Bangálí, there are several dialects which in many respects exhibit considerable differences from that standard. The importance of the dialects from the philological point of view cannot be overestimated. But with the exception of the Rangpur dialect, their study has been hitherto almost entirely neglected. A brief outline of the grammar of that dialect was given by Mr. G. A. Grierson in 1877, together with a few specimens of Rangpurí folksongs;[5] and in 1878 he edited the longer 'Song of Manik Chandra,' with an English translation.[6]

Researches into the dialects of the Gaudian languages, with respect to their grammar, vocabulary and local extent, are of particular value from the point of view of comparative philology. Comparative studies accordingly commenced to be especially cultivated from the time that attention began to be more prominently directed to the investigation

---

[1] J. A. S. B., Vol. LI, p. 129. [2] *Ibid.*, Vol. LII, p. 1. [3] *Ibid.*, p. 20. [4] *Ibid.*, Vol. XIX, p. 533. [5] *Ibid.*, Vol. XLVI, 186. [6] *Ibid.*, Vol. XLVII, p. 135.

of the local and provincial dialects of North India. There are, however, a few notices of earlier attempts at a comparative study of the Gaudians. In the Journals for 1837, 1838, and 1849, there are short comparative vocabularies of the Bangálí and Assamese languages.[1] In the Journal for 1852 there is a short paper by the Rev. W. Kay on the identity of the dative and accusative cases when formed with a postposition in Bangálí and Hindústání.[2] In 1864, Babu Rájendralála Mitra contributed a paper on the origin of the Hindí language and its relation to the Urdú dialect. It was the first attempt in the Journal, though under the circumstances necessarily an imperfect one, to trace the grammar of modern Hindí to its Prákrit and Sanskrit sources.[3] A similar attempt with respect to the vocabulary of Bangálí was made in 1870 by Babu Pratapa Chandra Ghosha.[4] About this time the subject was taken up in right earnest by Mr. J. Beames, who communicated in 1870 a paper on the relation of Uriyá to the modern Aryan languages of India,[5] and afterwards prepared a comparative grammar of those languages, the first volume of which appeared early in 1872. In the Journal of the same year appeared the first three of a series of 'Essays in Aid of a Comparative Grammar of the Gaudian Languages,' contributed by the writer of the present Review.[6] A fourth essay followed in 1873,[7] and a fifth in 1874.[8] After some introductory remarks on the adoption of the term 'Gaudian' and the distinction between the 'Bihárí' and Hindí languages,[9]

[1] J. A. S. B., Vol. VI, p. 1023; Vol. VII, p. 56; Vol. XVIII, p. 183. [2] *Ibid.*, Vol. XXI, p. 105. [3] *Ibid.*, Vol. XXXIII, p. 489. [4] *Ibid.*, Vol. XXXIX, p. 131. [5] Proceedings for 1870, p. 192. [6] J. A. S. B., Vol. XLI, pp. 120, 124. [7] *Ibid.*, Vol. XLII, p. 59. [8] *Ibid.*, Vol. XLIII, p. 22. [9] The term 'Gaudian' was originally spelt 'Gaurian,' and its use evoked a small controversy; see Proceedings for 1872, pp. 98, 177. The terms originally used for 'Bihárí,' were 'Ganwárí' and 'Eastern Hindí.'

the essays proceeded to discuss the origin of the modern inflection of nouns from the Prákrit and Sanskrit. The continuation of the essays was interrupted by the departure from India of their author, who, some years later, in 1880, reviewed the whole subject of the affinities of the Gaudian languages to each other and their derivation from the Prákrit and Sanskrit in a separate volume treating on the comparative grammar of those languages. In the same year, 1880, he also contributed to the Journal a list of Hindí roots, with remarks on their derivation and classification.[1] Soon afterwards Mr. G. A. Grierson commenced a series of essays on the declension and conjugation of the Bihárí dialects, of which the first, containing some introductory remarks on the various dialects, and the second, treating of declension, were published in 1883.[2] On the latter subject some observations were added by the writer of this Review.[3] Some information of a comparative philological kind, it may be mentioned, was also contained in an earlier memoir by Mr. F. S. Growse, contributed in 1874, on the etymology of local names in Northern India, as exemplified in the district of Mathurá.[4]

In connection with the Gaudian languages may be mentioned the idiom of the Gipsies in Europe, whose connection with India as their original home was very early suspected. Thus, in 1801, Captain David Richardson published a memoir on the Indian 'Nats,' in which he pointed out various resemblances between their language and that of the Gipsies.[5]

The Gaudian vernaculars of India belong to the great stock of Indo-Aryan languages, the members of which

---

[1] J. A. S. B., Vol. XLIX, p. 33. [2] *Ibid.*, Vol. LII, p. 119. [3] *Ibid.*, p. 159. [4] *Ibid.*, Vol. XLIII, p. 324. [5] As. Res., Vol. VII, pp. 457, 481.

extend through Persia over the whole of Europe. As evidences of this connection there exist on the North-Western frontiers of India a number of languages, or dialects, which exhibit marks of a more or less close affinity to the North Indian vernaculars. These are the Káffirí, Brahúí, Balúchí, Pashtú, Dardí, Chilás and the Galchah ; and of each of these the Society's Journal contains shorter or longer notices. The earliest of the notices refer to the Káffirí, Brahúí and Balúchí, and occur in the seventh volume of the Journal of the year 1838. In that year Captain Alexander Burnes communicated a very short vocabulary of the Káffirí language;[1] and Lieutenant R. Leech, outlines of the grammar, together with short vocabularies, of the Brahúí (or Brahúiky) and Balúchí (or Balochky) languages.[2] An equally meagre list of words in Balúchí and Káffirí was given by Captain (now Major) H. G. Raverty in 1864.[3] In 1881, however, a sketch of the Northern Balúchí language was published by M. Longworth Dames, which contained a very serviceable grammar and vocabulary, together with specimens of that language.[4]

Of the Pashtú or Afghání language, Lieutenant R. Leech published, in 1839, an outline grammar and a short vocabulary.[5] Its exact affiliation as a Semitic or an Aryan language had long been a matter of dispute since Sir William Jones's unfortunate but excusable note as to its Chaldean affinity in the second volume of the Asiatic Researches.[6] Some remarks in reference to this subject were contributed by Lieutenant (now Major) H. G. Raverty in 1854,[7] but it was fully discussed and the Aryan affinity

---

[1] J. A. S. B., Vol. VII, p. 332. [2] *Ibid.*, pp. 538, 608. [3] *Ibid.*, Vol. XXXIII, p. 272. See also Proceedings for 1866, p. 63. [4] *Ibid.*, Extra Number for 1880. [5] *Ibid.*, Vol. VIII, p. 1. [6] As. Res., Vol. II, p. 76. [7] J. A. S. B., Vol. XXIII, p. 576.

of the Pashtú clearly shown by the Rev. Isidor Lœwenthal in 1860.[1]

On the language of Chilás some information was communicated by the Hon'ble G. Campbell in 1866.[2] It is spoken by the independent mountaineers on the Hazárah Frontier, thence throughout Chilás, which is the westerly hill-territory of the Mahárája of Kashmir, and in Ghilghit, another Central Asian acquisition of the Mahárája.

Closely allied to the Chilás language are the Dardí and Galchah languages. The latter language possesses several dialects, of three of which,—the Wakhí, Sarikolí and the Shighní,—Mr. R. B. Shaw published outline grammars and specimens in 1876 and 1877.[3] In the following year, 1878, he added a short account of the grammar of the Dardí dialects.[4]

Besides the Gaudian and Frontier languages of the Aryan stock, India possesses a large number of aboriginal languages, or dialects, of various classes. There are in the south the Drávidian, in the centre the Kolarian, in the north the Tibeto-Birman, in the east the Indo-Chinese languages. A large amount of information on all these languages and dialects is stored up in the Transactions of the Society, gathered together chiefly by the zealous enquiries of Mr. H. B. Hodgson, Rev. N. Browne, Mr. W. Robinson and others. It consists mainly of outline grammars and short comparative vocabularies, representing much valuable raw material, out of which, it may be hoped, a thorough and systematic knowledge of those multifarious languages and their mutual relations may be elaborated in the course of time.

---

[1] J. A. S. B., Vol. XXIX, p. 323. [2] Proceedings for 1866, pp. 42, 62, 191.
[3] J. A. S. B., Vol. XLV, p. 139; Vol. XLVI, p. 97. [4] *Ibid.*, Vol. XLVII, p. 38.

Of the principal members of the Drávidian family of languages,—the Tamil, Telugu, Tulu, Malayálam and Kanarese,—which have had much attention bestowed on them from other quarters, no more than a brief notice occurs in the Journal of the Society. It consists of a very small comparative vocabulary, contributed in 1849 by Mr. B. H. Hodgson.[1] Some of the Nílagiri dialects,—the Toda, Kota, Badaga, Kurumba, Irula,—were also noticed in that vocabulary, but a special list of words of these hill-dialects, together with some grammatical observations, was communicated by Mr. B. H. Hodgson in 1856.[2] Another hill dialect, the Pahárí, spoken in the Rájmahal Hills, in the vicinity of Bhagalpur, is the earliest of the Drávidian group ever mentioned in the Society's Transactions. A very small list of words of that dialect was communicated, as early as 1798, by Major R. E. Roberts in the Asiatic Researches.[3] A similar list was published much later, in 1848, by Mr. B. H. Hodgson, in a small comparative vocabulary, which also contained words of two other languages of the Drávidian group,—the Gondí and the Oráon.[4] A very small list of Gondí words had been already communicated in 1844 by Dr. Voysey,[5] and a somewhat larger one, together with a few grammatical notes and specimens, in 1847, by Dr. O. Manger.[6] A yet fuller grammar and vocabulary, though still too incomplete, was published by the Rev. James Dawson in 1870.[7]

The most prominent of the Kolarian family of aboriginal languages is the Mundárí, the language of the Kols

---

[1] J. A. S. B., Vol. XVIII, p. 350; see also Vol. XIX, p. 461, and Vol. XIII, p. 17.
[2] *Ibid.*, Vol. XXV, pp. 31, 39, 498. [3] As. Res., Vol. V, p. 127. [4] J. A. S. B., Vol. XVII, Part I, p. 553. [5] *Ibid.*, Vol. XIII, p. 19. [6] *Ibid.*, Vol. XVI, p. 286.
[7] *Ibid.*, Vol. XXXIX, pp. 108, 172.

or Hos. The first notice of it occurs in the Journal for 1840, in which Lieutenant Tickell published an outline of its grammar as well as a short vocabulary.[1] A very small list of words was also communicated in 1844, by Dr. Voysey;[2] and in 1848, by Mr. B. H. Hodgson, in his comparative vocabulary of aboriginal languages of Central India.[3] A much fuller vocabulary was contributed by Babu Rakhal Das Haldar in 1871.[4] Very closely allied to the Mundárí is the Sonthálí, of which a small list of words is also contained in Mr. B. H. Hodgson's comparative vocabulary, above mentioned.[5] A more subordinate dialect of the same class is the Juangí or Pattuáí, spoken by a savage race, "which inhabits the jungles of the Tributary Mehals to the south of Singhbhúm." A few words of this dialect were noted down by Mr. E. A. Samuells in 1856.[6]

On the southern ranges and at the foot of the Himalayan mountains, a very large number of languages, or rather dialects, are spoken, which are commonly classed together as the Sub-Himalayan, or Tibeto-Birman languages. They have received as yet very little accurate investigation; all that is at present known being more or less meagre comparative lists of words, and here and there some short grammatical observations. They have been provisionally divided into several groups: the Nepalese, the Sikhimí, the Assamese, the Manipurí, the Burmese, and the Trans-Himalayan. The affinity of all these Mongolian languages with those spoken in the Caucasus was discussed by Mr. B. H. Hodgson in a memoir contributed to the Journal of 1853.[7]

---

[1] J. A. S. B., Vol. IX, pp. 997, 1063. [2] *Ibid.*, Vol. XIII, p. 19. [3] *Ibid.*, Vol. XVII, Part I, p. 553. [4] *Ibid.*, Vol. XL, p. 46. [5] *Ibid.*, Vol. XVII, Part I, p. 553. [6] *Ibid.*, Vol. XXV, p. 302. [7] *Ibid.*, Vol. XXII, p. 26.

To the Nepalese group belong the Limbú and Murmí dialects, of which Mr. A. Campbell published, in 1840, small lists of words.[1] Another list of words was communicated by Mr. B. H. Hodgson, in 1847, as part of a comparative vocabulary, of the eastern Sub - Himalayan languages or dialects.[2] In the same vocabulary there are also lists of words of the Newár, Gurung, Magar, Sunwar and Kirantí dialects.[3] A much fuller vocabulary of the last mentioned dialects of the Kirantís, as well as of those of the Bahing and Váyu or Háyu tribes, was published by Mr. Hodgson in 1857;[4] and a grammar of the Bahing dialect was added in 1858.[5] In the Journal for 1857, Mr. Hodgson also published a short comparative vocabulary of a number of other small Nepalese dialects, the Daharí or Dahí, the Paharí or Pahí, the Denwar, Kuswar, Bramu, Pákhya, Táksya, Tharu, Kusunda and Chepang.[6] Of the last two dialects a very short list of words had been already communicated by him in 1848;[7] and on the language and literature of the Newárí there is some information by him as early as 1828 in the Asiatic Researches.[8]

There is only one language ascribed to the Sikhim group. It is the Lepcha, of which a list of words was given by Mr. B. H. Hodgson in 1847 in his above mentioned comparative vocabulary of the Sub-Himalayan languages.[9] A grammar of the language was afterwards published by Colonel Mainwaring.[10]

---

[1] J. A. S. B., Vol. IX, pp. 605, 613; see also Vol. XI, p. 4; and Vol. XXIV, p. 202, where there is a note on the Limbú alphabet. [2] *Ibid.*, Vol. XVI, p. 1235. [3] *Ibid.*, p. 1235. [4] *Ibid.*, Vol. XXVI, pp. 320, 333, 350, 372, 429, 486. [5] *Ibid.*, Vol. XXVII, p. 393. [6] *Ibid.*, Vol. XXVI, pp. 320, 327. [7] *Ibid.*, Vol. XVII, Part II, pp. 650, 655. [8] As. Res., Vol. XVI, p. 409. [9] J. A. S. B., Vol. XVI, p. 1235. [10] See the List of Publications in Appendix C of the Historical Part of the Centenary Review.

To the Assam group belong a large number of languages or dialects, of which the Rev. N. Brown published in 1837 a small comparative vocabulary. These are the Aka, Abor, Mishmi, Singpho, Jili and Garo.[1] Twelve years later, in 1849, MM. W. Robinson and B. H. Hodgson contributed short grammars and vocabularies of the last three of the dialects just mentioned, as well as of some new ones, *viz.*, the Kachárí or Bodo, Miri, Nága, Mikir, Dhimul.[2] Among these the Nága language is one of the most important, and possesses several distinct dialects. A small comparative vocabulary of these dialects was supplied by Mr. B. H. Hodgson in 1850.[3] The same was done in 1855 by Lieutenant R. Stewart, in a memoir on northern Kachár; and in 1872 and 1875, by Mr. S. E. Peal and Captain J. Butler in two memoirs on the Nága country. They also added the corresponding words from the Kachárí and Mikir dialects.[4] In the year 1851, Mr. W. Robinson also added to his previous contributions an outline grammar and vocabulary of the Dophla dialect;[5] and in 1855, he did the same for the Mishmi dialects.[6] In 1869, Lieutenant W. J. Williamson communicated a very small comparative vocabulary of the Garo and Konch dialects.[7]

In the Manipurí group the Manipurí language itself is the most important. A list of words belonging to it was communicated as early as 1837 by the Rev. N. Brown in his comparative vocabulary, mentioned in the remarks on the Nepalese group.[8] A somewhat fuller list, given in 1855, in Lieutenant R. Stewart's comparative vocabulary

---

[1] J. A. S. B., Vol. VI, pp. 1023, 1032. [2] *Ibid.*, Vol. XVIII, pp. 207, 456; pp. 318, 342, 969; pp. 215, 456; pp. 224, 969; pp. 323, 969; pp. 330, 342; p. 456. [3] *Ibid.*, Vol. XIX, pp. 309, 311. [4] *Ibid.*, Vol. XXIV, pp. 582, 656; and Vol. XLI, p. 29; Vol. XLII, Appendix; Vol. XLIV, pp. 216, 307, 333. [5] *Ibid.*, Vol. XX, p. 126. [6] *Ibid.*, Vol. XXIV, p. 307. [7] *Ibid.*, Vol. XXXVIII, p. 14. [8] *Ibid.*, Vol. VI, pp. 1023, 1033.

was added to his, also already mentioned, memoir on Northern Kachár.[1] Lastly, in 1875, some notes were contributed by Mr. G. H. Damant, on the grammar and very peculiar alphabetic characters of the Manipurí.[2] Closely allied to the latter language is the Kúki or Thádu. A small list of its words was also given in 1855 by Lieutenant R. Stewart in his comparative vocabulary;[3] and in 1856, he added a slight notice of its grammar.[4]

To the Birma group, of course, belongs the great Burmese language itself. Notices of it occur very early in the Asiatic Researches. In the fifth volume of 1798, there are some observations on the alphabetical system of the language of Ava and Arakan by Captain John Towers,[5] and a very small list of words of various Burmese dialects, by Dr. Francis Buchanan.[6] In the following year, 1799, the latter added some account of the literature of the Burmese.[7] Some further account of the Burmese language, together with a small vocabulary, was given by Dr. J. Leyden in 1808.[8] Another small list of Burmese words was given in 1837 by the Rev. N. Brown in his comparative vocabulary.[9] It was reprinted with many additions in 1849 by Mr. B. H. Hodgson.[10] In 1878, Lieutenant (now Captain) R. C. Temple published a translation of the Lokaníti from the Burmese paraphrase.[11] Another language of Birma, the Karen, was also noticed in 1837, by the Rev. N. Brown, in his comparative vocabulary.[12] But a much fuller list of words, together with some account of its grammar, was contributed by the Rev. Francis Masson in 1858.[13]

---

[1] J. A. S. B., Vol. XXIV, p. 656. [2] *Ibid.*, Vol. XLIV, p. 173; Vol. XLVI, p. 36; Proceedings for 1875, p. 17. [3] J. A. S. B., Vol. XXIV, p. 656. [4] *Ibid.*, Vol. XXV, p. 178. [5] As. Res., Vol. V, p. 143. [6] *Ibid.*, p. 224. [7] *Ibid.*, Vol. VI, p. 163. [8] *Ibid.*, Vol. X, pp. 222, 232. [9] J. A. S. B., Vol. VI, p. 1032. [10] *Ibid.*, Vol. XVIII, p. 969. [11] *Ibid.*, Vol. XLVII, p. 239. [12] *Ibid.*, Vol. VI, p. 1032. [13] *Ibid.*, Vol. XXVII, p. 129.

It may be added that, in 1845, Thomas Latter brought out a grammar of the language of Burmah, as a separate work, under the auspices of the Society.[1]

The leading language among the Trans-Himalayan group is the Tibetan. The first notice of it occurs in 1825, in the fifteenth volume of the Researches, which contains a small list of Tibetan (called there 'Tartar or Bhotia') words collected in 1819 by Captain J. D. Herbert.[2] The following volume of 1828 contains a memoir by Mr. B. H. Hodgson on the language and literature of Bhot or Tibet.[3] One of the earliest and best students, however, of the language and literature of Tibet, was the well-known Hungarian traveller, Alexander Csoma Körösi. His grammar and dictionary, published by the Society at the expense of the Indian Government in 1834,[4] were the first of their kind, and are deservedly held in high esteem. From his pen there also appeared at various times numerous analyses of Tibetan works; thus, in the Journal for 1832,[5] an abstract of the contents of the Dulva, or first portion of the Kahgyur; in that for 1834, some observations on Tibetan symbolical names used as numerals;[6] in that for 1835, an analysis of a medical work;[7] in the Researches for 1836, an analysis of the whole of the Kahgyur, including both the first and second portions of that voluminous work;[8] also notices of the life of Shakya, extracted from Tibetan authorities,[9] and an abstract of the contents of the Tangyur;[10] in the Journal for 1838, notices of the different systems of Buddhism, extracted

[1] See the List of Publications in Appendix C of the Historical Part of the Centenary Review. [2] As. Res., Vol. XV, p. 417. [3] *Ibid.*, Vol. XVI, p. 409. [4] J. A. S. B., Vol. III, p. 653. [5] *Ibid.*, Vol. I, pp. 1, 269, 375; Vol. II, p. 365; Vol. III, p. 57; see also Vol. II, p 367. [6] *Ibid.*, Vol. III, p. 6. [7] *Ibid.*, Vol. IV, p. 1. [8] As. Res., Vol. XX, pp. 41, 393. [9] *Ibid.*, p. 285. [10] *Ibid.*, p. 553.

from the Tibetan authorities,[1] and an enumeration of historical and grammatical works to be met with in Tibet.[2] So far the Tibetan language was treated by itself ; but in 1849, Mr. W. Robinson published some remarks on those points of its grammar "on which information appeared to be requisite to aid in instituting a comparison between this language and the dialects spoken by the adjoining tribes."[3] A very small list of words intended to subserve a similar purpose had been already communicated by Mr. S. W. Williams in 1838.[4] In 1865, the Rev. H. A. Jaeschke contributed a note on the pronunciation of the Tibetan language.[5] This language possesses a not inconsiderable number of dialects, two of which, the Changlo and the Baltí, have been noticed in the Journal. Of the former, Mr. W. Robinson supplied an outline grammar in 1849 ;[6] of the latter, Captain H. H. Godwin-Austen contributed a small vocabulary in 1866.[7]

Another language belonging to the Trans-Himalayan group is the Kunawarí, spoken in the territory of the Rája of Bussahir, in the Panjáb. It was noticed as early as 1825 in the fifteenth volume of the Researches by Captain J. D. Herbert, who, in 1819, collected a comparative list of Kunawarí and Tibetan words.[8] A much fuller vocabulary, comparing Tibetan with two distinct dialects of the Kunawarí,—*viz.*, the Milchan and the Tibarskad,—was published in 1842.[9]

Seven other languages classed in the same group,—the Thochu, Sokpá, Gyámi, Gyárúng, Horpa, Tákpa, and Manyak,—are only known from a small comparative vocabulary, published by Mr. B. H. Hodgson in 1853.[10]

---

[1] J. A. S. B., Vol. VII, p. 142. [2] *Ibid.*, p. 147. [3] *Ibid.*, Vol. XVIII, p. 194. [4] *Ibid.*, Vol. VII, p. 708. [5] *Ibid.*, Vol. XXXIV, p. 91. [6] *Ibid.*, Vol. XVIII, p. 202. [7] *Ibid.*, Vol XXXV, p. 233. [8] As. Res., Vol. XV, p. 417. [9] J. A. S. B., Vol. XI, p. 479. [10] *Ibid.*, Vol. XXII, pp. 121, 142.

On and beyond the eastern frontiers of India there exist a large number of languages or dialects which exhibit a distinct relationship to the language of China, and hence are commonly called Indo-Chinese. They may be divided provisionally into three families,—the Tay, the Mon-Anam, and the Khasi. The affinities of these with the Tibeto-Birman were discussed by Mr. B. H. Hodgson in a memoir published in 1853,[1] and again by Mr. R. Cust, in a pamphlet, originally inserted in the Transactions of the Philological Society, but afterwards, in 1877, reprinted in the Proceedings of the Asiatic Society.[2]

To the first named family belong the following languages: the Siamese, the Khamti, the Lao, the Shan, and the Ahom. Notices of them occur very early; the first in 1798, in the fifth volume of the Researches, in a comparative vocabulary prepared by Dr. F. Buchanan;[3] the second, in the tenth volume of 1808, in a memoir on the language and literature of the Indo-Chinese nations, by Dr. J. Leyden.[4] In 1836, Captain James Low published a memoir on Siamese literature;[5] and in 1837 the Rev. N. Brown, a small comparative list of Siamese and Khamti words.[6] The latter also contributed in the same year some account of the ancient Ahom language and its peculiar characters.[7] In 1849, Mr. W. Robinson published an outline grammar and a short vocabulary of the Khamti language;[8] and in the following year, 1850, Mr. B. H. Hodgson, a comparative vocabulary of the Siamese, Khámti, Laos and Ahom languages.[9]

To the Mon-Anam family belong the Anamese, the

[1] J. A. S. B., Vol. XXII, p. 1. [2] Proceedings for 1877, p. 205. [3] As. Res., Vol. V, p. 227. [4] *Ibid.*, Vol. X, pp. 240, 257. [5] *Ibid.*, Vol. XX, p. 338. [6] J. A. S. B., Vol. VI, p. 1031. [7] *Ibid.*, p. 17. [8] *Ibid.*, Vol. XVIII, pp. 311, 342. [9] *Ibid.*, Vol. XIX, p. 311.

Mon and the Khomen, some account of all of which was published in 1808 by Dr. J. Leyden in the tenth volume of the Researches.[1] A very small list of Anamese words was communicated by the Rev. N. Brown in 1837,[2] and of Mon words, by the Hon'ble G. Campbell in 1867.[3]

Of the Khasi language there is a very small list of words in the Journal for 1841, communicated by Mr. B. H. Hodgson.[4] In the following year, 1849, Mr. W. Robinson added an outline grammar and somewhat larger vocabulary, comparing Khasi words with those of the Tibeto-Birman languages.[5]

On the islands of the Indian Ocean there exist a number of languages, which belong to the Malayan stock. Many of these languages early attracted the notice of the Society, which, however, was afterwards almost entirely withdrawn, as was natural, in favour of the many subjects of interest lying nearer home. A small list of words of the Malayan language spoken in the Nicobar Isles was communicated, as early as 1792, in the third volume of the Researches, by Mr. Nicolas Fontana, in connection with a brief account of that group of islands.[6] A somewhat larger vocabulary was published eighty years later by Mr. E. H. Man in the Journal for 1872.[7] Another small list of words of the Malayan language spoken by the inhabitants of the Poggy (Pagai) or Nassau Islands lying off Sumatra, was communicated as early as 1799, in the sixth volume of the Researches, by Mr. John Crisp.[8] A little later, in 1808, Dr. J. Leyden gave some account of the Jawi, the Javanese, the Bugi, the Bima, the Batta, and the Gala or Tagala, of which the

---

[1] As. Res., Vol. X, pp. 239, 257, 261. [2] J. A. S. B., Vol. VI, p. 1031. [3] Proceedings for 1867, p. 51. [4] J. A. S. B., Vol. XVII, Part I, p. 547. [5] *Ibid.*, Vol. XVIII, pp. 336, 342. [6] As. Res., Vol. III, p. 157. [7] J. A. S. B., Vol. XLI, p. 1. [8] As. Res., Vol. VI, pp. 77, 90.

first mentioned is the namé of the written Malayan language, while the others are the names of the Malayan language as spoken in the islands of Java, Celebes, Sumbáwa, Sumatra, and the Philippines, respectively.[1] Some further information on these languages was communicated by Mr. Thomas Raffles, in 1816.[2] A specimen of the ancient Malayan language, called the Kawi, was communicated by Mr. John Crawfurd in 1820, in connection with an account of the island of Bali.[3] A short notice of the alphabets of the Philippine islands, with an illustrative plate, was published in 1845 by Mr. H. Piddington, who extracted it from a Spanish work of Don Sinibaldo de Mas.[4]

The Muhammadan conquest introduced the Persian and Arabic languages into India, and their knowledge and cultivation is still widely diffused among that portion of the population of India which professes the Muhammadan faith. It was natural, therefore, that, from the beginning the Asiatic Society extended its researches to the language and literature of Arabia and Persia. But, as in the case of the Sanskrit, the energies of the Society were principally directed to the publication of texts and translations of rare and valuable Arabic and Persian works in the Bibliotheca Indica.

All the earlier publications were Arabic works, except one, Nizámí's celebrated Sikandarnámah, of which however only about one half was edited in 1852 by Dr. Sprenger and Aghá Muhammad Shúshterí jointly.[5] The remaining portion was not published until 1869, when it was edited by Maulvi Aghá Ahmad 'Alí.[6] The same Maulvi also wrote an elaborate introduction to the Sikandarnámah, which was printed in 1874 as a separate work under the

---

[1] As. Res., Vol. X, pp. 163, 189, 192, 198, 202, 207. [2] *Ibid.*, Vol. XII, p. 102. [3] *Ibid.*, Vol. XIII, p. 162. [4] J. A. S. B., Vol. XIV, p. 603. [5] See the list of the Bibliotheca Indica in Appendix C to the Historical Part of the Centenary Review, for this and the other works mentioned hereafter. [6] Proceedings for 1870, p. 30.

name of Haft Asmán, and which was intended to give the history of the Masnaví or epic poetry of the Persians, in seven chapters; but owing to the death of the author, no more than the general portion and the first of the seven chapters could be published.[1]

The first Arabic publication was an Arabic Bibliography referring to sixty different subjects, treated by Shaikh-ul-Imám 'Abdullah Al Fákihí and Shaikh Shams-ud-dín As-Sakháwí. It was edited by Dr. A. Sprenger in 1849. Three years later, in 1852, Dr. Sprenger followed it up by an edition of As-Sayútí's Itqán on the Exegetic Sciences of the Qoran, which he prepared with the assistance of the Maulvis Saídud-dín Khán and Bashírud-dín. In the following year, 1853, Ensign (now Colonel) W. Nassau Lees undertook an edition of Al-Azdí's Fatúh-ush-Shám, in which the Moslem conquests in Syria are narrated. In the same year, he also published another work on the same subject,—the pseudo-Wáqidí's history of the conquest of Syria.[2] The publication of three other and larger works was also commenced in that year, 1853, the value of which to the students of Arabic philosophy and science and of the history of the first period of Islam cannot be overestimated. One of these was the Kashfu'z-Zunún, or "Dictionary of the technical terms used in the sciences of the Muhammadans," edited by the Maulvis Muhammad Wajíh and Gholam Qádir. Another is the Isábah fi-tamyíz-is-Sihábah, or "Bibliographical Dictionary of persons who knew Muhammad," edited by the same two Maulvis jointly with a third Maulvi, 'Abdul Haqq.[3] This

---

[1] See Proceedings for 1874, p. 34; and the Introduction to the edition written by Mr. Blochmann. [2] Proceedings for 1863, p. 26. [3] See Journal R. A. S., Vol. III (N. S.), p. 419.

is a voluminous work, of which manuscripts are only with great difficulty procurable. When the work, in 1853, was commenced, no complete manuscripts appear to have existed, and in 1856 it was dropped in the middle of the second volume for want of them. In 1864 it was determined to complete the dictionary as far as possible, and the fourth volume was published by Maulvi 'Abdul Hai. In 1873, unexpectedly three manuscripts of the second and third volumes turned up in the possession of Maulvi Kabíruddín Ahmad. These are now being published by Maulvi 'Abdul Hai, and there is every hope of completing this important work.[1] These two works were published under Dr. A. Sprenger's superintendence. The third, the Fihrisht-ut-Túsi, a descriptive list of Shiah works, was published by Dr. Sprenger himself, who also edited one of the Appendixes to the second named work, called the Risálah Shamsíyah and treating of the Logic of the Arabians. Two years later, in 1855, Mr. Alfred von Kremer prepared an edition of Al Wáqidí's Kitáb -ul-Maghází, which narrates the history of Muhammad's campaigns. It was made from a single manuscript discovered by the editor in Damascus in 1851, and, as unfortunatly the manuscript was a fragment, the edition could not be completed. Two complete manuscripts, however, have been procured not very long ago, and it may now be hoped that a new and complete edition of this important work will soon be published in Germany.[2]

In 1856 a change took place in the selection of works for publication in the Bibliotheca Indica. An objection having been raised by the Court of Directors to the selection being bestowed mainly on works in Arabic, it was resolved by the Society to devote the funds at its disposal

[1] Proceedings for 1874, pp. 32, 33. [2] *Ibid.* for 1881, p. 29.

to the institution of a Persian series which should contain chiefly works on the history of India,[1] giving the preference, when possible, to writers contemporary with the events which their histories chronicle.[2] The first work selected on this new plan was the Taríkh-í-Fírúz-Sháhí by Zíáuddín Barní, who brings the history of the Muhammadan sovereigns of India down to the sixth year of the reign of Fírúz Sháh, the nephew of Ghíyásuddín Tughlaq Sháh. The edition of his work was commenced in 1860 by Maulvi Sayyid Ahmad Khán, under the superintendence of Captain W. N. Lees.[3] The next work of the series was Abú'l Fazl Baihaqí's history of Ma'asúd, the son of Mahmúd of Ghazni, edited in 1861 by Mr. W. H. Morley. It is commonly styled the Taríkh-i-Baihaqí, but it is simply a portion of a very much larger work in several volumes, entitled the Taríkh-i-ál-i-Subuktagín, which relates the history of the descendants of Subuktagín, the father of Mahmúd the Great.[4] In 1863 followed the Tabaqát-i-Násirí by Minhájuddín Al Jurjání, edited by Captain W. Nassau Lees, in conjunction with Maulvis Khádim Husain and 'Abdul Hai. This work, however, is rather a book of dynasties than a history of any particular dynasty or number of reigns, with the exception of the author's contemporary, the emperor Násiruddín Mahmúd, of whose reign he gives a much fuller account. In his time Muhammadan India was divided into four kingdoms, those of Hindustan, Bengal, the Panjáb and Sindh; and the peculiar and important feature of the Tabaqát-i-Násirí is, that it gives a biographical sketch of the contemporary

---

[1] J. A. S. B., Vol. XXV, pp. 427, 455. See Journal R. A. S., Vol. III (N. S.), pp. 419, 420. [2] J. A. S. B., Vol. XXXIII, p. 465. See Journal R. A. S., Vol. III (N. S.), p. 420. [3] Proceedings for 1861, pp. 54, 55; for 1863, p. 31. See also Journal R. A. S., Vol. III (N. S.), pp. 441, 444. [4] See Journal R. A. S., Vol. III (N. S.), pp. 421, 422.

rulers of all these kingdoms, as also of the countries beyond the Indus.[1] An English translation of this important history, beginning with the seventh section of the original, was undertaken in 1873 by Major H. G. Raverty, who added numerous and valuable notes elucidatory of the text.[2] The fourth history of the Persian series is the Muntakhab-ut-Tawáríkh of 'Abdul Qádir, the Badáoní, which was edited in 1864 by Captain W. Nassau Lees in conjunction with Maulvis Kabíruddín Ahmad and Munshi Ahmad 'Alí, and which, as a history, is second to none in the whole range of historical works by Muhammadan authors. Though it professes to be simply an abridgment of Nizámuddín Ahmad's Tabaqát-i-Akbar Sháhí, its great value lies in its giving a view of the character of the great emperor Akbar from an opposition point, a somewhat rare qualification in a contemporary Muhammadan historian.[3] The next history in the series was the Iqbálnámah-i-Jahángírí by Mu'tamad Khán, the confidential secretary of the emperor Jahángír, by whose command he wrote that emperor's memoirs. No writer of the period was more competent or more favourably circumstanced for writing a history of the reign of Jahángír.[4] It was edited in 1865 by Maulvis 'Abdul Haqq and Ahmad 'Alí.

In the following year, 1866, the edition of two historics was commenced. These were Muhammad Qásim's Alamgírnámah, a court chronicle of emperor Aurangzíb's reign from its thirty-second year, edited by Maulvis Khádim Husain and 'Abdul Hai; and the Bádsháh-námah of

---

[1] See Journal R. A. S., Vol. III (N. S.), pp. 438, 439. [2] Proceedings for 1873, pp. 34, 38. [3] *Ibid.* for 1870, p. 30. See also Journal R. A. S., Vol. III (N. S.) pp. 451, 452, 455. [4] Proceedings for 1865, p. 114. See also Journal R. A. S., Vol. III (N. S.), p. 459.

'Abdul Hamíd Lahaurí, one of the principal authorities in the reign of the emperor Sháhjahán, edited by Maulvis Kabíruddín Ahmad and' Abdur Rahím.[1] In 1867 followed the Ain-i-Akbarí, or Institutes of Akbar, by the celebrated Abú'l Fazl, which some consider simply the third volume of the same author's Akbarnámah, but which is a large work in three volumes, complete in itself.[2] It was edited by Mr. H. Blochmann, who added an introductory English Biography of Abú'l Fazl. He also undertook, in the following year, 1868, an English translation accompanied with very valuable notes. Unfortunately, owing to the lamented death of the author, no more than one volume, about one-half of the whole, has been published. In the same year, 1868, the edition of another history of the reign of the emperor Alamgír was commenced, the Muntakhab-i-Lubáb, commonly called, from its author, the Táríkh-i-Kháfí Khán. It is the most comprehensive and most important of the histories of that period, being written by a person of singular capabilities for his task, who, moreover, was a contemporary with Aurangzíb for the greater portion of his reign.[3] It was edited by Maulvis Kabíruddín Ahmad and Ghulám Qádir. Two years later, in 1870, was added a third history of the same reign, the Maásir-i-Alamgírí by Muhammad Sáqí Musta'id Khán, edited by Maulvi Aghá Ahmad 'Alí. It is a small work, but its author had good opportunities of consulting the records of Government and of obtaining information regarding the events of Aurangzíb's reign.[3] The last of the Persian historical series, as yet published, was commenced in 1873. It is the celebrated Akbar-

---

[1] See Journal R. A. S., Vol. III (N. S.), pp. 462, 464. [2] *Ibid.*, p. 451.
[3] Proceedings for 1874, p. 33. See also Journal R. A. S., Vol. III (N. S.), pp. 464, 465, 466.

námah of Abú'l Fazl, which is pronounced by all competent judges to be an admirable history of the great emperor Akbar's reign, but from the most favourable point of view,—a memoir, in short, warranted to reflect only his virtues.[1] It was edited, at first, by Maulvi Aghá Ahmad 'Alí, after whose death it is being continued by Maulvi 'Abdur Rahím.[2]

Besides these historical works only two other works in Persian have been published. One is the Wís o Ramín, a romance of ancient Persia translated from the Pehlavi into Persian verse by Fakhruddín, the Jurjání. It was edited, in 1864, by Captain W. N. Lees and Munshi Ahmad 'Alí.[3] The other is the Farhang-i-Rashídí, an edition of which was commenced by Maulvi Zulfiqár 'Alí in 1870 and completed by Maulvi Azíz ur Rahman in 1875. This work is a dictionary of the Persian language, which was compiled in 1064 A. H. by Sayyid 'Abdur Rashíd of Tattá in Sindh, one of the best grammarians and lexicographers that India has produced. It is based on a critical examination of the numerous preceding dictionaries, and has itself been the basis of all later writers on Persian lexicography. The editors have added valuable notes from Surúrí, Jahángírí and the Siraj.[4]

Of Arabic works there are only two among the later editions included in the Bibliotheca Indica. These are the Nokhbat-ul-Fikr, with the commentary called Nozhat-un-Nazr, by Shahábuddín Ahmad Ibn Hajar al Asqalání, the author of the celebrated Isábah, previously mentioned; and an English translation of Jaláluddín As-Suyútí's Táríkh-ul-Khulfa or "History of the Caliphs." The former was

---

[1] Proceedings for 1873, p. 33. See also Journal R. A. S., Vol. III (N. S.), pp. 450, 451. [2] Proceedings for 1874, p. 34. [3] *Ibid.* [4] *Ibid.* for 1875, p. 32; and for 1876, pp. 24, 25.

edited in 1862 by Captain W. N. Lees, in conjunction with the Maulvis 'Abdul Haqq and Gholám Qádir; the latter by Major H. S. Jarrett, who introduced his translation with a short memoir of the author.

Besides these larger publications, a number of smaller contributions were published from time to time in the Transactions of the Society. As early as 1790, in the second volume of the Researches, there is an essay on the Arabic elements received into the Persian language.[1] This was followed in 1805 by another essay by Mr. Francis Balfour, in which he gave extracts from the Tahzíb-ul-Mantiq, or 'Essence of Logic,' as a small supplement to Arabic and Persian grammar, and with a view to elucidate certain points connected with Oriental literature.[2] In the Journal for 1834 was commenced, and continued in the following years, a translation, prepared by Baron Joseph von Hammer, of an Arabic work, the Mohit, on navigation in the Indian seas. The author of the original work was Sídí al Chelebi (Sídí 'Alí Capudán), Captain of the fleet of the Turkish Sultan Suleiman, who finished his book at Ahmedabad, the capital of Gujarát, in the year 1554.[3] In the volume for 1843, Dr. A. Sprenger published a translation of another Arabic work, Kashf-us-salsalah 'an wasf-uz-zalzalah, on earthquakes by Jaláluddín As-Sayútí.[4] The same contributed, in 1848, notices of some copies of the Arabic scientific work, entitled Rasáyil Ikhwán-us-safá, which, by the novelty of its ideas, the peculiarity of its style, and even of its language, had created considerable sensation.[5] In 1850, Sir Henry Elliot com-

[1] As. Res., Vol. II, p. 208. [2] *Ibid.*, Vol. VIII, p. 89. [3] J. A. S. B., Vol. III, p. 545; Vol. V, p. 441; Vol. VI, p. 805; Vol. VII, p. 767. [4] *Ibid.*, Vol. XII, p. 741. [5] *Ibid.*, Vol. XVII, Part I, p. 501.

municated, from Dr. Sprenger, a notice of a copy of the fourth volume of the original Arabic text of the history of Tabary which gives the life of Muhammad, and of which no other copy was at that time known to exist.[1] Dr. Sprenger himself contributed in 1851 some observations on the physiology of the Arabic language,[2] and on the initial letters of the nineteenth Súrah of the Qorán.[3] In the same year, Babu Nara Simha Datta published a translation of a Persian dialogue between Aristotle and Buzurjumihr on morals, called the Zafarnámah.[4] In 1852, Dr. Sprenger continued his contributions with a paper on foreign words occurring in the Qorán.[5] In the volumes for 1853 and 1854 were published several lists of Arabic and Persian works belonging to the libraries at Leyden, Aleppo and in the possession of Sir Henry Elliot.[6] In 1856, Dr. A. Sprenger again contributed notices on Mr. Alfred von Kremer's edition of Wáqidí's Campaigns,[7] and on the Dawá-ul-Qalúb of Mohásabí, the earliest work on Súfism yet discovered, and on an Arabic translation of a work ascribed to Enoch;[8] also an essay on the origin and progress of writing down historical facts among the Mussalmans.[9] In 1860, Professor E. B. Cowell communicated a paper on a few mediæval apologues[10] and an analysis of the Qírán-us-Sa'dain, a Persian poem by Mír Khusrau, describing the contemporary contest between the emperor Kaikobád and his father.[11] In 1863, Dr. A. Sprenger contributed some remarks on Barbier de Meynard's edition of Ibn Khordádbeh and on the land-tax of the empire of the Khalifs.[12] In 1868, Mr. H. Blochmann published some

[1] J. A. S. B., Vol. XIX, p. 108. See also Vol. XX, p. 195, for a short notice of a manuscript of the first volume in the Society's library. [2] *Ibid.*, Vol. XX, p. 115. [3] *Ibid.*, p. 280. [4] *Ibid.*, p. 426. [5] *Ibid.*, Vol. XXI, p. 109. [6] *Ibid.*, Vol. XXII, p. 535; Vol. XXIII, pp. 44, 225. [7] *Ibid.*, Vol. XXV, pp. 53, 199 [8] *Ibid.*, p. 133. [9] *Ibid.*, pp. 303, 375. [10] *Ibid.*, Vol. XXIX, p. 10. [11] *Ibid.* p. 225. [12] *Ibid.*, Vol. XXXV, p. 124.

contributions to Persian lexicography, in which he described a large number of Persian dictionaries compiled by natives of India.[1] In the following year, 1869, he added a memoir on the historian 'Abdul Qádir, called the Badáoní, and his works.[2] In the same year was also published the commencement of a translation from the Táríkh-i-Fírúz Sháhí, prepared by Major A. R. Fuller, which was continued in the two following years, 1870 and 1871, the last portion being by Mr. P. Whalley.[3] In 1874, Mr. J. O'Kinealy published a translation of an Arabic pamphlet on the history and doctrines of the Wahhábís, written by 'Abdullah, grandson of 'Abdul Wahháb, the founder of Wahhabism;[4] Mr. E. C. Ross, a translation of the annals of 'Oman from early times to the year 1728 A.D.;[5] and Mr. G. H. Damant, the Persian text of the Risálat-ush-Shuhadá, or "Book of Martyrs," containing an account of Ismá'il Ghází of Kántá Duár, in the Rangpur district.[6] In 1876, Mr. P. Whalley contributed some translations from the Diwan of Zíb-unnissá Begam, poetically styled Makhfí, daughter of the emperor Aurangzíb.[7] In 1877, Mr. C. J. Lyall published a translation of the fourth of the seven Mo'allaqát or "Suspended Poems," that of Lebíd, to which he added a notice of the life of that poet as given in the Kitáb-ul-Aghání.[8] In the following year he added a translation, together with the text, of the Mo'allaqah of Zuheyr.[9] In the volume of the previous year, 1871, he had also commenced to publish translations from the Hamáseh and the Aghání, which he continued in the volume for 1881.[10] There are also in the volume for 1877 some metrical trans-

---

[1] J. A. S. B., Vol. XXXVII, p. 1. [2] *Ibid.*, Vol. XXXVIII, p. 105. [3] *Ibid.*, p. 181; Vol. XXXIX, p. 1; Vol. XL, p. 185. [4] *Ibid.*, Vol. XLIII. p. 68. [5] *Ibid.*, p. 111. [6] *Ibid.*, p. 222. [7] *Ibid.*, Vol. XLV, p. 308. [8] *Ibid.*, Vol. XLVI, p. 61. [9] *Ibid.*, Vol. XLVII, p. 1. [10] *Ibid.*, Vol. XLVI, pp. 168, 437; Vol. L, p. 107.

lations from the quatrains of 'Umar Khayyám, contributed by Mr. P. Whalley.[1]

In connection with the Arabic language may be mentioned a report, by Lieutenant J. R. Wellsted, on the island of Socotra. In it he gives a small list of words of the language of the islanders, who appear to be immigrants from Arabia.[2]

The Asiatic Society, true to its name, did not limit its philological researches to the languages of India, or of countries nearly connected with India. Those of countries, more or less distant in geographical position or historical relation, like China, Armenia, Turkistan, also received an occasional notice. Thus, in the second volume of the Researches of the year 1790, Sir W. Jones published some account of the second classical book of the Chinese, the Shi-king, containing three hundred odes or short poems in praise of ancient sovereigns and legislators, or descriptive of ancient manners. Of one of these odes he added the original text, together with a literal and a free translation.[3] Much later in 1843, Mr. H. Piddington republished in the Journal the introduction to a paper on the study of the Chinese language written by Mr. Stanislas Julien.[4]

The first contribution on the language of Turkistan was made in 1835. In the Journal of that year Mr. H. Wathen published a memoir on Chinese Tartary and Khoten, to which he appended a small list of words of the Turkí dialect spoken at Yarkand.[5] Nothing more was done till 1877, when Mr. R. B. Shaw published a grammar of the language of Eastern Turkistan.[6] Three years later,

---

[1] J. A. S. B., Vol. XLVI, p. 158. [2] *Ibid.*, Vol. IV, pp. 138, 165. [3] As. Res., Vol. II, p. 195. [4] J. A. S. B., Vol. XII, p. 816. [5] *Ibid.*, Vol. IV, pp. 653, 663. [6] *Ibid.*, Vol. XLVI, p. 242.

in 1880, he added a fairly complete vocabulary of the same language, to which was appended a list of names of birds and plants prepared by Dr. J. Scully.[1]

On the literature of Armenia, there is one contribution in the Transactions of the Society. It occurs in the Journal for 1868, and is an account, by Mr. Johannes Avdall, of twenty-five authors of Armenian grammars from the earliest stages of Armenian literature up to that year.[2]

Besides the languages and literature of India, other matters more generally connected with the subject of philology found an occasional notice in the pages of the Journal. The volume for 1859 contains the well-known paper on the introduction of writing into India, by Professor Max Müller, which was afterwards printed in his History of Ancient Sanskrit Literature.[3] Some remarks on the ancient art of writing and the relation of the Indian to the Semitic alphabets by Mr. H. Blochmann and Babu Rájendralála Mitra were published in the Proceedings of 1865.[4] In the following two years the discussion of that subject, with respect to the origin and course of development of the Aryan alphabets, was continued by Mr. E. Thomas, the Hon'ble G. Campbell, Babu Rájendralála Mitra, and Rev. K. M. Banerjea.[5] Another subject closely connected with the ancient Indian alphabet is that of the ancient Indian numerals. A memoir on this subject was contributed in 1855 by Mr. E. Thomas, in which he revised and much extended the original discovery of those numerals made, as already alluded to in a former place,[6] by Mr. J. Prinsep as early as 1838.[7] Some years later,

---

[1] J. A. S. B., Extra Number for 1880. [2] *Ibid.*, Vol. XXXVII, p. 134. [3] *Ibid.*, Vol. XXVIII, p. 137. [4] Proceedings for 1865, pp. 171, 174. [5] *Ibid.* for 1866, p. 138; for 1867, pp. 33-51. [6] See p. 35. [7] J. A. S. B., Vol. XXIV, p. 551; see also Vol. VII, p. 348.

in 1863, another paper on the same subject was published by Dr. Bhau Daji of Bombay, whose successful decipherment of the numerical symbols occurring in the Násik cave inscriptions enabled him to greatly improve and consoldidate our knowledge of the ancient Indian method of expressing numbers in writing.[1]

The system of transliteration elaborated by Sir W. Jones has already been mentioned. This was a subject which would necessarily come to the front, from time to time, the more the study of oriental languages and literature progressed. Thus we find in the Journal for 1864 a paper on the application of the characters of the Roman alphabet to oriental languages, contributed by Captain W. Nassau Lees;[2] and another paper, in 1857, on the transliteration of Indian alphabets in the Roman characters, by Mr. F. S. Growse.[3] Somewhat analogous to the subject of transcribing oriental characters into those of Europe, is the question of translating European technical terms into oriental languages. Some discussions on this subject, initiated by the Hon'ble G. Campbell, took place in the Society in 1866, the substance of which is recorded in the Proceedings of that year.[4]

---

[1] J. A. S. B., Vol. XXXII, p. 161. [2] *Ibid.*, Vol. XXXIII, p. 345. [3] *Ibid.*, Vol. XXXVI, p. 136. [4] Proceedings for 1866, pp. 129, 131, 141, 159.

LIST OF ERRATA AND ADDENDA.

Page 35, line 21, *read* "1835" *for* "1834."
" 35, " 23, " "three" *for* "two."
" 35, " 24, " "1838" *for* "1836."
" 69, " 12, " "to our era" *for* "of our era."
" 79, " 27, " "form" *for* "forms."
" 113, " 10, " "era" *for* "era era."
" 121, " 26, " "Srίkarnna" *for* "Srί Karlla."
" 122, " 29, " "Mahiala" *for* "Mahiála."
" 122, " 30, " "Gaharwáras" *for* "Gaharwálas."
" 130, " 25, 26, " "upon" *for* "from."

On page 50, line 19, with regard to the name *kutila* it may be added, that a photo-zincographed copy of the Bareilly inscription is published in Vol. I of the Archæological Survey Reports of General Cunningham. The word *kutila* occurs in the last line. It is clearly not a mislection for *kumuda*, as erroneously stated in J. A. S. B., Vol. XXXIII, p. 226.

On page 130, add to footnote 2: "General Cunningham makes A.D. 1107 to be the initial year of the Sena era, see his Archæological Survey Reports, Vol. XV, p. 160."

Appendixes

To the Chapter on History.

No. I.

With regard to the events that led to the change of dynasty in Kanauj at the time of the accession of the (so-called) Raṭhors, I would venture to make a suggestion for further consideration. The Basáhí land-grant, published in the Journal A. S. B., Vol. XLII, p. 321, seems to me to throw light on this point. I do not think the significance of the historical notices contained in the opening verses of that grant has been quite correctly understood.

The *Vijayí* or 'victorious king' of the second verse is S'rí Chandra Deva himself, whose descent is described in that verse. The following verse (No. 3) relates the circumstances under which he obtained the throne of Kanauj. In this verse (No. 3) it is stated that after the death of a king S'rí Bhoja, there were troublous times under a king S'rí Karṇṇa,* to which S'rí Chandra Deva put an end by possessing himself of the country. The king Bhoja, I take to be Bhoja Deva II of the earlier Kanauj dynasty, who reigned about A. D. 925-950; for his father Mahendra Pála was still reigning in A. D. 921 (see Genl. Cunningham's Archæological Reports, Vol. IX, p. 85). Bhoja Deva II's son, Vinayaka Pála Deva, may, therefore, be put down to A. D. 950-975. About this time a Rájá Kokalla II, of the Kalachuri dynasty, was on the throne of Chedi (see *ibid.*, p. 85). He and his successors, Gángeya Deva and Karṇa Deva, carried on many successful wars. They must have invaded the territories of Mahoba and Kanauj; for Gángeya Deva is recorded to have died at Prayága, and his coins are found on the site of Kanauj. Karṇa Deva must have reigned about A. D. 1025-1050, as he is recorded to have been a contemporary of Bhíma Deva of Gujarát (A. D. 1022-1072) and of Bhoja Deva of Dhár (A. D. 1021-1042); see *ibid.*, p. 86. This makes him also a contemporary of S'rí Chandra Deva, the first Raṭhor king of Kanauj (about A. D. 1050). I take it, therefore, that the inscription refers to Karṇa Deva of Chedi.

* Not *S'rikarlla*, as given in the transcript, see the following footnote.

Further, in the second verse, Chandra Deva is called a son of Mahiala, which is either a mere provincialism or a clerical error for Mahítala. By the same name (Mahítala) Chandra Deva's father is called in the Ráhan land-grant of Govinda Chandra, published in the Proceedings for 1876, p. 131.* Usually his father is called Mahíchandra, while his son is always called Madanapála.† This fact shows that the term Chandra was by no means so distinctive, as is often thought, of the Kanauj royal family. Terms like chandra, tala, pála were interchangeable appendages to the actual name, and Mahíchandra might also call himself Mahítala or Mahípála. The Sáranáth inscription of Mahípála is dated A. D. 1026,—a date which synchronises with Chandra Deva's father Mahíchandra, *alias* Mahípála. The father of the Sáranáth Mahípála was Vigrahapála, while the father of Mahíchandra is called Yaśo-Vigraha. As Pála and Chandra are interchangeable, I take Vigrahapála and Mahípála of Benares as likelyto be the same as Yaśo-Vigraha and Mahíchandra (*alias* Mahípála), the ancestors of Chandra Deva. Dates and names favour the identification.

But more, the date of Vigrahapála and Mahípála is from A. D. 991

---

* The Basáhí plate spell's महिअल *mahiala*, but the Ráhan plate spells महीतल *mahítala*. The name Mahítala means 'the very earth.' It is an unusual name, and if it were not for the fact that it agrees with the metre (Upendravajrá) of the verse in which it occurs, one would be inclined to look upon it as one of the clerical errors (for Mahípála) with which this particular record abounds. The copper-plate is among the Society's collection, where I have examined it, and verified the correctness of the printed transcript of the second verse. As it is, 'Mahítala' evidently owes its origin merely to the exigencies of the metre. Of the other grant, published in the Journal for 1873, I have not seen the original, which appears to be in Allahabad. But I possess, through the kindness of Mr. J. F. Fleet, a very carefully prepared ink-impression, which clearly shows the name to be Mahiala, not Mahiála as published in the Journal. In all probability 'Mahiala' is aclerical error, apparently, for 'Mahitala,' but the latter is not required by the metre of the verse (No. 2), which is a śloka, and which admits of reading 'Mahípála' equally well. I may add here that the ink-impression clearly proves the name of the predecessor of Chandra Deva to be *Karṇṇa*, not *Karlla* as given in the transcript. The signs for ṇ and l, which often occur in the grant, are easily distinguishable from each other (ण and ल), and the sign of ṇṇ in the name is a distinct double ṇṇ (ण्ण).

† There may have been a special reason for Madana reverting to the ancestral title of 'Pála,' in the fact of his extending his kingdom over portions of the old Pála empire. For two inscriptions of his, dated in his 3rd and 19th years, have been found at Bihár and at Jayanagar near Lakhí Sarai respectively. (See Genl. Cunningham's Arch. Survey Rep., Vol. XV, p. 154.) The Madanapála of these inscriptions is usually placed among the later members of the proper Pála dynasty; but beyond the fact of the title of 'Pála' there is nothing in favor of that theory.

to 1058 (see Appendix, No. II, also J. A. S. B., Vol. XLVII, p. 394), which synchronises with the date of the Chedi rulers, Kokalla II, Gángeya and Karṇa. The Chedi rulers were of the Haihaya race (see Genl. Cunningham's Arch. Rep., Vol. IX, p. 77), and Vigrahapála is said to have married Lajjá, a princess of the Haihaya race (J. A. S. B., Vol. XLVII, p. 384). The Pálas of Benares and the Kalachuris of Chedi, therefore, were closely allied. Now Vinayakapála Deva of the earlier Kanauj line possessed Benares about A. D. 950-975 (J. A. S. B., Vol. XXXI, p. 5); but, according to the Sáranáth inscription, in A. D. 1026, Mahípála of the Bihár (and Bengal) line is in possession of Benares. The latter therefore must have changed hands in the interval. This must have occurred in the 'troublous times,' when the Chedi kings conquered Kanauj, while the Pálas (allied to them by marriage) conquered Benares.

I imagine the events to have occurred thus. Towards the end of the tenth century the Kalachuris and the Pálas, being allied, attacked the kingdom of Kanauj from the South and East; the former took Kanauj, the latter Benares; for Jayapála, the father of Vigrahapála, is recorded to have conquered Allahabad (see J. A. S. B., Vol. XLVII, p. 384). While the direct descendants of Mahípála continued to rule the Bihár and Bengal kingdom, including Benares, one of his younger sons, Chandra Deva, obtained for himself the kingdom of Kanauj, from the Kalachuri king Karṇa, and founded a new dynasty in Kanauj, which henceforth took from him its special name Chandra, in order, perhaps, to distinguish itself from the original stock of Pálas. Hence Vigrahapála and Mahípála, though named as the ancestors of Chandra Deva, are never included in the royal list of Kanauj.

But further, the Basáhí plate of 1873 distinctly states, that Mahípála and Chandra Deva were of the Gahaṛwár race of Rájpúts.* The same statement occurs in the land-grant, published in the Proceedings for 1876, p. 130. So far as I am aware, it does not occur in any of the land-grants of the Raṭhor kings of Kanauj, except these two. In all the other grants, I think, no information whatever is given regarding the particular Rájpút clan to which the kings professed to belong. The Raṭhor clan is not mentioned in any of them. It has always been taken for granted that the kings of Kanauj were of the Raṭhor clan. For this notion there appears to be no other ground than the tradition of the Raṭhor princes of Jodhpur

---

* The name is spelt गाहडवाड *gáhaḍawáḍa* in the grants; the modern spelling is गहड़वाड़ *gahaṛ'wáṛ* or (usually) गहरवार *gahaṛ'wár*. See Elliot's *Races of the N. W. Provinces*, Vol. I, p. 121.

in Márwár who affirm that Sivají, their ancestor, was a son of a child of Jaya Chandra of Kanauj. Now Jaya Chandra is a historical personage; he was the last of the Kanauj kings, who fell in battle with Shaháb-ud-dín Gorí, as testified by contemporary Muhammadan historians.* Sivají also is a historical personage, a real ancestor of the Márwár Raṭhor house. The connecting link between Sivají and Jaya Chandra is a child, otherwise unknown, who is said to have escaped the wreck of his father's house and reign. History, I believe, knows nothing about him; and the tradition about him suspiciously resembles similar traditions of princely houses, who claim ancient descent by the agency of some mysteriously born or preserved child. In any case, if the tradition is correct, it fails to account for the remarkable fact, how a family which was originally Gahaṛwár, as stated in their own grants, turned into Raṭhors. In a matter of this kind the evidence of a contemporary land-grant is of more value than a tradition. But, in fact, the traditions, confused and sometimes contradictory as they are, rather support the theory here put forward. It is said that "the Gahaṛwárs are of the same family as the Raṭhors, with whom they deem themselves on an equality and with whom it is said they never intermarry." The last statement, however, is only partially true. It does not appear that the (modern) Raṭhors can be traced further back than the Kanauj family; and Colonel Tod says that a doubt hangs over the origin of the Raṭhor race; by the bards they are held to be descendants of Kaśyapa.† In reference to the latter point, it may be noticed that the Gahaṛwárs are of the Káśyapa gotra or order, though the Raṭhors now profess to be of the S'áṇḍilya gotra. All these circumstances point to the conclusion that the so-called Raṭhors were an offshoot of the Gahaṛwárs; and it may well be that about the time of Mahípála a separation took place in the Gahaṛwár clan, possibly on religious grounds; for the Pálas professed Buddhism, while the Chandras were Brahmanists. The separation was marked by the secession of the latter to Kanauj, and by a change in their nomenclature (Chandra and Raṭhor, for Pála and Gahaṛwár). "The Gahaṛwárs are despised by the other Rájpút tribes," according to Tod (Rajasthán, Vol. I, p. 116). The original reason of this treatment may have been their heretical faith in the time of the Pálas. The Raṭhors would not be the only offshoot from the Gahaṛwár clan; the well-known Bundels (of Bundelkhaṇḍ) are another prominent instance of Gahaṛwár descent. Again: "the Gahaṛwárs assert that they were originally masters of Kanauj, local tradition confirms their

---

* See Major Raverty's Translation of the Ṭabaqát i Náṣirí, p. 470.

† See his Rajasthan, Vol. I, p. 88. (Reprint, pp. 67, 68.)

claims, and the Gautama Rájpúts attribute their own residence and possessions in the Lower Doáb to the bounty of a Gahaṛwár Rája of Kanauj." This tradition evidently refers to the Raṭhor rulers of Kanauj, and confirms the statement of their land-grants, that they were Gahaṛwárs. Again: "the present chief of the Gahaṛwárs resides at Kantit near Mirzapur, and tradition says, Gadan Deo, who by some is reckoned the son of Mánika Chandra, brother of Jayachandra, the Raṭhor, camę from Benares about the end of the 11th century, and settled at Kantit." This, as Sir Henry Elliot points out, is a confused tradition. Perhaps it points to the secession and emigration from Benares under Śrí Chandra, at the time of Mahípála. In any case, it clearly establishes the closest relationship between the Raṭhors and Gahaṛwárs. Again: "Benares is generally considered the original country of the Gahaṛwárs, who, it is often asserted, are descended from ancient kings of Benares;" and their chief seat is still in the Benares Division and in Bihár. This makes in support of the theory that the Pála kings of Bihár and Bengal, who also ruled in Benares, belonged to the Gahaṛwár clan, and consequently were closely related to the Raṭhors of Kanauj.* It is true, there is an indistinct tradition, which ascribes the Pála Rájas to the Bhúíhár race.† But there is no proof of it. In their inscriptions the Pálas make no mention of their caste. On the other hand, there are various incidental notices in them, which indicate their having been of a Rájpút caste. Thus Vigrahapála is said to have married the princess Lajjá of the Haihaya race (see App., No. II); this would hardly have occurred if the Pála Rájas had really belonged to a non-descript race, like the Bhúíhárs.

I only throw this out as a suggestion. It is by no means a new one; Mr. Prinsep already made it in J. A. S. B., Vol. IV, p. 670. But much additional information in support of it has since come to light.

No. II.

In computing the chronolgy of the Pála dynasty too much reliance is still placed on the Ámgáchhí inscription. But its mutilated state renders it practically useless unless where it is supported by other documentary evidence. Moreover, the description given by Mr. Colebrooke of its genealogy, which has hitherto been always relied on, is very inaccurate. He

---

* See the traditions, above quoted, of the Gahaṛwárs and Raṭhors in Elliot's *Races of the N. W. Provinces*, pp. 121-124; and Sherring's *Hindu Tribes and Castes*, Vol. I, pp. 140, 141, 175-177.

† See Gen. Cunningham's Arch. Survey Rep., Vol. XV, p. 147; Calcutta Review, Vol. LIX, p. 68. For an account of the Bhúíhárs see Elliot's *Races of the N. W. Provinces*, Vol. I, p. 21.

states (As. Res., Vol. IX, p. 435): "The first mentioned is Lokapála, and after him Dharmapála. The next name has not been deciphered: but the following one is Jayapála, succeeded by Devapála. Two or three subsequent names are yet undeciphered: one seems to be Náráyaṇa, perhaps Náráyaṇa-pála: they are followed by Rájapála,—Páladeva and Vigrahapála Deva, and subsequently Mahípála Deva, Nayapála and again Vigrahapála Deva."

The A'mgáchhi plate is in the Society's collection, where I have subjected it to a careful re-examination, with the following result. The first name is not Lokapála (which is mis-read for Lokanátha), but Gopála Deva (first word of the 5th line); then comes Dharmapála Nṛipa (middle of the 6th line). The next undeciphered name is Vákpála (near the beginning of the 7th line), called the Anuja or 'younger brother' of Dharmapála. The following name is Jayapála, succeeded by Devapála, his Púrvaja 'or elder brother' (both in the middle of the 8th line). The two subsequent, undeciphered names are Vigrahapála (1st word of the 9th line), and Náráyaṇa Prabhu (middle of the 10th line); there is no third undeciphered name. So far (that is, up to the 11th line) the record is nearly a duplicate of the Bhagalpur grant (J. A. S. B., Vol. XLVII, pp. 284, 404), with the exception of three laudatory verses which are omitted in the A'mgáchhí grant. Then follows the name Rájya-pála (last word of the 11th line), not Rájapála, as Mr. Colebrooke read it; and immediately afterwards (near the beginning of the 12th line) Lokapála, apparently qualifying Rájyapála. Next comes (1st word of the 13th line) an altogether illegible name (not Pála Deva), who is described as the son (*prasúta*) of a lucky queen (*bhágya-devyáḥ*) of (as it would seem) Rájyapála.* Then follows again Vigrahapála Deva (last word of the 14th line), then Mahípála Deva (middle of the 16th line), then Nayapála Narapati (middle of the 17th line), then again Vigrahapála Deva Nṛipati (end of the 18th line). So far extends Mr. Colebrooke's reading; and up to this place, that is from the 11th to the 20th line, the text of the A'mgáchhí grant is new. From the 21st line up to the end, the A'mgáchhí grant again almost verbally agrees with the Bhagalpur grant, excepting only the names of the

---

* The eleventh line closes with *S'rímá(n)*, which is the usual commencement of a name. Now the verse, of which *S'rímán* are the two initial syllables, is a 'Sragdhará' of 21 syllables, divided into three parts of 7 syllables each. The quantities of the first part, of 7 syllables, are — — — — ⏑ — —, of which the first two lengths are taken up by *S'rímán*. Into the remaining quantities — — ⏑ — — the name must be fitted; but *Vigrahapālo* will not do. Colebrooke read *pāladevo*, which, supposing it to be completed into *vākpāladevo* or the like, would do. But there are no traces of *deva* visible; if anything, the traces indicate *pálo* to have been the last two syllables of the title, so that the quantities — — ⏑ would remain for the real name.

donor, the donation (lines 24-26) and the donee (lines 36-40). The name of the donor is Vigrahapála Deva (middle of the 24th line), the successor (*pádánudhyáta*) of Nayapála Deva (end of the 23rd line). He is again named, at the end of the grant, as Vigrahapála Kshitipati-tilaka (middle of the 48th line). There is nothing to bear out Mr. Colebrooke's remark, that "in the making of the grant Nayapála likewise appears to have had some share."

Imperfectly as this grant can be read, it affords no ground for extending the Pála genealogy beyond Vigrahapála (so-called 'the first'). The grant to a very large extent verbally agrees with the Bhagalpur grant of Náráyaṇapála; its letters seem to be, if anything, of a rather older type; and there can be little doubt but that it is a grant of Náráyaṇa's father, Vigrahapála. The opening lines of it are identical with those of the Bhagalpur grant, down to Vigrahapála; but while the latter grant goes on to describe Náráyaṇapála as being on the throne and making a gift of land. the A'mgáchhí grant mentions Náráyaṇapála (or rather Náráyaṇa Prabhu) merely as a son of Vigrahapála, and the latter as making the gift of land. This points to the line of ruling kings ending, at the time of the A'mgáchhí grant, with Vigrahapála. It is true, after the first mention of Vigrahapála, there follow several names; *viz.*, Rájyapála (Mahípála ?), Vigrahapála, Mahípála, Nayapála, Vigrahapála, the last of these being the donor. As the record is not yet fully read, it is, of course, impossible to determine with absolute certainty the significance of this series of names. But the very order of repetition in which they follow, suggests that some of them are not new names. It is not an unprecedented feature in such land-grants, that, after giving the genealogical line, the writer once more recurs to some of the names already mentioned, for the purpose of giving further particulars; an instance in point is the grant of Govinda Chandra, published in the Proceedings for 1870, p. 131. Having brought the royal line down to Vigrahapála, the grantor, the record, before declaring the grant, apparently proceeds to add some particulars regarding the relation of Vigrahapála to Rájyapála, and Mahípála. That Rájyapála did not come after Vigrahapála and Náráyaṇapála is proved by the Mungir grant, published in the Asiatic Researches, Vol. I, p. 133, which states that he was the son and heir-apparent (*yuvarája*) of Devapála. He was, therefore, a brother of Vigrahapála. Mahípála's relation to him and to Vigrahapála is not intelligible from the imperfectly legible record; but he is clearly in some way cotemporary with Vigrahapála. As to Nayapála, he is evidently the same as Devapála; for in the genealogy Vigrahapála's predecessor is called Devapála, but afterwards in the statement of the grant he is called Nayapála.

There is a further point on which the A'mgáchhí grant throws light. It seems clear from this grant that Vigrahapála was not a nephew, but a son of Devapála; for the pronoun "his son" (*tat-súnuḥ*) must refer to the nearest preceding noun, which is Devapála. In the Bhagalpur grant this reference is obscured through the interpolation of an intermediate verse in praise of Jayapála, which makes it appear as if Vigrahapála were a son of Jayapála. The fact of this interpolation, by the way, shows that the version of the formula on the A'mgáchhí plate is the earlier and original one, on which the more fullsome writer of the Bhágalpur grant tried to improve, with the effect of obscuring the genealogy. This is an additional reason showing that the A'mgáchhí grant must be ascribed to Vigrahapála (the so-called 'first'), the father of Náráyaṇapála, the grantor of the Bhágalpur plate.

There is another name which has caused some difficulty. This is Súrapála. He seems to be supported by a short inscription which gives him at least thirteen years of reign (Gen. Cunningham's Arch. Rep., Vol. XI, p. 181). But what is more, he is mentioned in the Buddal inscription as the successor of Devapála (see J. A. S. B., Vol. XLIII, p. 356). It is true that, as has been already pointed out by others, that inscription did not intend to give a genealogy of the Pála kings, but only of their ministers; nevertheless, as a matter of fact, it *did* give the royal line; seeing that both lines, the royal and the ministerial, run side by side, it could not be otherwise. Moreover the events related in the inscription prove it. The sixth verse states that the minister of Devapála was Darbhapáṇí; the thirteenth verse states that Kedára Nátha Miśra, the grandson of Darbhapáṇí, was minister to a king who made successful conquests in the South and West of India; the fifteenth verse shows that Kedára Nátha was also the minister of Súrapála.* The Mungir inscription shows that the king who made those conquests was Devapála. Accordingly, Kedára Nátha was minister to two kings, Devapála and Súrapála: and it is therefore more than probable that Súrapála was the immediate successor of Devapála. On the other hand, the Bhagalpur grant says that the successor of Devapála was Vigrahapála. It seems evident, therefore, that Vigrahapála and Súrapála must have been the same person. There is nothing particular about this; Hindú kings are often known by different names; moreover the two names are nearly synonymous.

---

* That Devapála had three ministers, father, son and grandson, is explained by the fact that he had a very long reign, perhaps 40 years. The Mungir plate is dated in his 33rd year.

General Cunningham (Arch. Rep., Vol. XI, p. 178) says about Súrapála, that "he was the son and successor of Devapála Deva; and further it would appear that he had an elder brother named Rájyapála, who had been declared Yuvarája by his father." I do not know whether the statement is made on any direct documentary evidence, or whether it is merely an inferential combination. But if it is the former, it confirms my deduction, above given, that Vigrahapála, *alias* Súrapála, was a son of Devapála, and not of Jayapála. The same conclusion follows from the fact that the Buddal inscription in all probability mentions Náráyaṇapála as the immediate successor of Súrapála. The Bhagalpur grant says that Náráyaṇapála was the son and successor of Vigrahapála. Hence Súrapála and Vigrahapála are the same person.

The conclusion to which the evidence, such as it is, appears to point is, that Náráyaṇapála and Mahípala were contemporaries; the former being a son of Vigrahapála, and the latter being also a son of Vigrahapála, or perhaps his nephew and son of Rájyapála. Náráyaṇapála probably ruled the eastern portion (Bengal) of the Pála kingdom, while Mahípála reigned in the western half (Bihár, Benares). There is no direct evidence on the point; but there are some circumstantial indications. Viagrahapála was a stout Buddhist, so was Mahípála; but Náráyaṇapála was a Brahmanist. The latter fact is expressly stated in the Buddal inscription, and it is clearly implied both in the Bhagalpur grant and in the Gaya inscription No. 6 (Arch. Rep., Vol. III, p. 120), and his very name, Náráyaṇa, tends to prove it. That a division of the great Bengal and Bihár empire took place on account of religious differences is shown by the secession of the Sena family. It took place about the beginning of the 11th century, which, as will be presently seen, synchronises with the time of Náráyaṇapála.

Therefore, instead of thirteen or eleven ruling princes of the Pála family, as generally believed (Arch. Rep., Vol. XI, p. 181; J. A. S. B., Vol. XLVII, pp. 394, 401), there are only six (excepting the later Pálas), though there were altogether nine members of the Pála family, of whom, however, three did not actually reign.

Accordingly the genealogical table stands thus: reigning members are indicated by roman numerals; the numbers in round brackets give the highest *known* number of regnal years; the numbers in straight brackets give the *supposed* full numbers of regnal years; the dates are the calculated years of accession.

I, Gopála (7) [20] ... ... 906 A. D.

II, Dharmapála (26) [30] — Vákpála ... ... 926 „

III, Devapála (or Nayapála) (33) [35] — Jayapála .. ... 956 „

IV, Vigrahapála (or Súrapála) (13) [15] — Rájyapála ... 991 „

VI, Náráyaṇa (of Bengal) (17) [20] — V, Mahípála (of Benares) (48) [50] 1,006 „

The later Pálas (of Benares) — Chandra Deva (of Kanauj).

The date of Mahípála is known from the Benares inscription to be A. D. 1026. His contemporary Náráyaṇapála reigned at least seventeen years (Arch. Rep., Vol. XI, p. 181). Accordingly their accession may be dated about 1006. The highest known regnal number of Vigraha is 13; he may have succeeded in A. D. 991. The highest known regnal number of Devapála is 33; he may have succeeded in A. D. 956. The highest known regnal number of Dharmapála is 26 (Proceedings for 1880, p. 80); his date of accession will be A. D. 926. The highest known number of Gopála is 7, but all tradition agrees in giving him a very long reign of 45 or 55 years (Arch. Rep., Vol. XV, p. 150); a limit of 20 years, therefore, will be safe, and to him A. D. 906 may be given. Altogether this gives 120 years to five generations, which is certainly not too much. But there is a curious piece of evidence, which tends to confirm the date thus assigned to Devapála, *viz.*, A. D. 956-91. In the 'huge' Gwalior inscription noticed by Mr. FitzEdward Hall (J. A. S. B., Vol. XXXI, pp. 6-8), a king Devapála is mentioned, with the date Samvat 1025, corresponding to A. D. 968.* This exactly agrees with the date assigned to the Bengal Devapála, and as he is recorded to have made wide conquests towards the West, his mention in the Gwalior inscription would be accounted for. His warlike expeditions towards the West would bring him into contact with the Haihaya rulers of Chedi, and thus explain the statement in the Bhagalpur grant of the alliance of his son, Vigrahapála, with a Haihaya princess. Moreover, they would also explain the fact of the coins of Vigraha imitating the Sassanian type (see his coins in Arch. Rep., Vol. XI, pp. 176, 177). As to Mahípála, he is reported in Táránáth's History to have reigned 52 years—a statement which is borne out by two inscriptions found by Mr. J. E.

* Mr. Hall gives also the date 1005; but it must be a misprint, for his equivaluations A. D. 968 or A. D. 1103 (on p. 8) only agree with the other date 1025, given in the bottom line of p. 7.

Lincke at Imadpur (in the Muzaffarpur district) and dated in the 48th year of his reign.* Accordingly Mahípála's reign may be put down as having extended from A. D. 1006 to 1058.†

The history of the Pála empire about the turning of the 10th and 11th centuries, I imagine to have been thus: The empire included Bengal, Bihár and Audh (Gauṛ, Paṭna and Benares), and the Pála rulers were Buddhists. Towards the end of the 10th century a great disruption took place: Bengal under Náráyaṇapála became Brahmanic, while Bihár and Audh under Mahípála remained Buddhistic.‡ In the beginning of the 11th century another disruption took place,—Bihár under Mahípála's successors remained Buddhistic, while Audh under Chandra Deva, a son of Mahípála, who made Kanauj his capital, became Brahmanic. Bihár remained Buddhistic till the Muhammadan conquest destroyed the remnant of the ancient Pála kingdom. Náráyaṇa was probably assisted in the separation which he effected, by the Bengal Governors sprung from the Sena family, who were in charge of the province of Pauṇḍra Vardhana. The Sena family was intensely Brahmanic, and two of the earliest members of it, Samanta and Hemanta, synchronise with Náráyaṇa's date (A. D. 1006-1026). It was probably the successor of the latter, who was supplanted in the Bengal kingdom by Vijaya Sena (or Sukha Sena), the first Bengal king (though the fourth in descent) of the Sena family, whose date is about A. D. 1030. In the Baqirganj grant he is stated, in so many words, to have "rooted out those of the race of Bhúpála" (verse 6, see J. A. S. B., Vol. VII, pp. 43-47).§ Bhúpála is a

---

* See Proceedings for 1876, p. 98. The inscriptions, which are identical, are engraved below two groups of bronze figures, and the date runs as follows: श्रीमन्-अह्विपालदेवराजस समत्त् ४८ जेष्टदिन सुकलपच २।

† This is also Gen. Cunningham's conclusion in Arch. Survey Rep., Vol. XV, p. 153 (A. D. 1008—1060). In the Proceedings for 1876, p. 107, Dr. Burnell communicated an inscription of the Chola king Kulottunga, which gives Mahípála's date as A. D. 1093. As the date refers to the conquest of Bengal and Mahípála, perhaps it may be taken as the date of Mahípála's death in battle. It is difficult, however, to make this date harmonise with the Sáranátha date of A. D. 1026. The difference is 77 years, a period much too long to have been the reign of one person, even if we assume the traditional allowance of 52 years to fall short of the truth. It is clear that there is something wrong about one or the other of the two dates. But in any case, it is only a question of about 20 or 30 years, within which the above calculated dates of the Pála reigns may require adjustment.

‡ As Mahípála's reign was much longer than Náráyaṇa's, he may have temporarily regained possession of the whole of the ancestral empire, after Náráyaṇa's death.

§ Prinsep's Pandit translated "rooting out the families of the inimical royal lines." But *Vairi-Bhúpála-vaṃśyán* means simply "the inimical descendants of

well-known synonym of Gopála, the founder of the Pála dynasty. This is confirmed by the Bhagalpur inscription (J. A. S. B., Vol. XXXIV, p. 144), which says that Vijaya Sena overthrew the king of Gauḍa. It may be added that the tradition of Ádisúra, who appears to be the same as Vijaya Sena, the first of the Bengal kings (see J. A. S. B., Vol. XXXIV, pp. 139-140; Vol. XLIV, p. 4), having imported Kanauj Bráhmans, about the turning of the 10th and 11th centuries, coincides with the first disruption of the Pála kingdom and may be intimately connected with it.*

I append my reading of the Ámgáchhí plate, imperfect as it is. None, I believe, has ever been published, and though imperfect, my reading may prove helpful to others in fully deciphering the grant. I do not despair of the possibility of doing this, though I had too little leisure to do it myself: †

[1] Svasti || [1]Maitrí-káruṇya-ratna-pra(*seal*)mudita-hṛidayaḥ preyasíṃ sandadhánaḥ

[2] samyak-sambodhi-vidyá-sari(*seal*)d-amala-jala-kshálitájñána-pa-

[3] nkaḥ | jitvá yaḥ káma-ká(*seal*)ri-prabhavam abhibhavaṃ śáśvatí[ṃ]

[4] prápa śánti[ṃ] sa S'rímán Loka(*seal*)nátho jayati Daśabalo 'nyaś cha

[5] Gopála-devaḥ || [2]Lakshmí-janma-niketanaṃ samakaro voḍhu[ṃ] kshamaḥ kshmá-bharaṃ paksha-chchheda-bhayád upasthitavatám ekáśrayo bhúbhṛitáṃ | maryádá-paripálanaikaniratah (|) sau[r]yá-

[6] layo 'smád abhúd dugdhámbhodhi-vilása-hási-mahimá S'rí-Dha[r]-mapálo nṛipaḥ || [3]Rámasyeva gṛihíta-satya-tapasas tasyánurúpo guṇaiḥ Saumittrer udayádi-tulya-

---

Bhúpála." *Bhúpála* is here a proper name, not an appellative. If Mahípála, as suggested in the preceding footnote, regained possession of Bengal after Náráyaṇa's death, he may be referred to in that notice. *Bhúpála* and *Mahípála* are synonyms.

* The identification of Ádisúra with Vijaya Sena is supported by the genealogical tables, for the rate of "three generations a century" is too much. At the rate of four generations Ádisúra's date would be A. D. 1165, which is too low, as it would tend to identify him with Ballála Sena. A medium rate will suit best; it will make Ádisúra identical with Vijaya Sena. As to the names, Súra and Vijaya Sena are nearly synonymous, *ádi* indicates Vijaya Sena as the first king of the family. However, even if he be the same as Víra Sena, it does not materially affect the argument in the text.

† Doubtful portions are enclosed within round brackets. Restorations are within straight brackets. Syllables omitted are indicated by the number of dots, placed in their stead.

[7] mahimá Vákpála-námánujaḥ | yaḥ S'rímán naya-vikramaika-vasati[r] bhrátuḥ sthitaḥ śásane śúnyáḥ śatru-patákinibhir akarod eká-tapatrá diśaḥ [||] [4]Tasmád u-

[8] pendra-charitair jagatíṃ punánaḥ putro babhúva vijayí Jayapála-námá | dharmadvishá[ṃ] śamayitá yudhi Devapále yaḥ pú[r]vajo (?) bhuvana-rájya-sukhány avaishít || [5]S'rímá-

[9] n Vigrahapálas tat-súnur Ajátaśatrur iva játaḥ | śatru-vanitá-prasádhana-vilopi-vimalási-jaladháraḥ || [6]Dikpálaiḥ kshiti-pálanáya dadhataṃ dehe vibha-

[10] ktáḥ śriyaḥ S'rímantaṃ jana . . . ta tanayaṃ Náráyaṇaṃ sa prabhuṃ | yaḥ kshauṇí-patibhiḥ śiromaṇi-ruchásliśhṭáṃghi-píṭhopala[ṃ] nyáyopáttam ala[ṃ]chakára charitaiḥ

[11] svair eva dha[r]másanaṃ || [7]Tápá . . jaladhi-múla-gabhíra-garbhe deválayaiś cha kula-bhúta-ratna(sya) kakshaiḥ | vikhyáta-kírtir abhavat tanayaś cha tasya S'rí-Rájyapála i-

[12] . . . (ni) lokapálaḥ || [8]Tasya . va kshiti(vya)n nidhir iva mahasá rájyakúṭá . pe . pújyasyottunga-maule duhitari tanayo Bhágya-devyá prasútaḥ [|] S'rimá-

[13] n (*about one third of the line omitted*) bhavya . nnaikaratna . tikhavitavargaḥ si . vigráṃsukayoḥ || [9]yasváminarájyaguṇairatnanamásevâta .

[14] (*about one fourth omitted*) prabhuśakti lakshmíḥ púrvvíṃ sapatním iva śilapatra || [10]Tasmád babhúva savitur vasukoṭivardhí | kalena chandra-(. va)-Vigrahapáladeva[ḥ] ||

[15] [11] . . . . peṇa vimalena kalá(tpadena) | (á)váhitena panito bhuvanasya tápaḥ || [12]Bhava-sakala-vilakshaḥ sangare vá pradarpád anadhikṛita-vilagnaṃ rájyaṃ ásádya pitryaṃ [|]

[16] . . . . . ṇasadmábhúd . . . . vanipálaḥ S'ri-Mahípála-devaḥ || [13]Tyajan toshásanga[ṃ] śira(si) kṛitapádaḥ kshiti-bhútávivarṇṇe sarvváśáḥ prasabha-

[17] . . . . riva raviḥ [|] bhava . nnaḥ snigdha prakṛitir anurágo . vasati sma vá dhanyaḥ prakhyairajani Nayapálo narapatiḥ || [14]Pítaḥ sanganale (vanaiḥ) smara-ripoḥ pújá-

[18] . . . . . viśráme . . . dhikára-bhavanaḥ ka . kṛite vidvisháṃ | mantavyaṃ dvayam áśrayaḥ śivapasa . pengaga . ndavan (|) S'rímad-Vigrahapála-deva-nṛipatiḥ

[19] (*about three fourths omitted*) kṛityasándraikaru(prajahu)tágríkarair-

[20] (*about one half omitted*) sa khalu Bhágirathí-patha-pravarttamána-nánávidha-nau-váṭaka-sampádita-setubandha-vihita-

[21] śaila-śíkhara-śreṇí-vibhramát(|)nirati-śaya-ghana-ghanághana-ghaṭṭá-śyámáyamána-vásara-lakshmí-samárabdha-sannata-jalada-samaya-sandehát | udíchínáneka-

[22] narapati-prabhṛiti-kṛitáprameya-haya-váhiní-kharakhurotkháta-dhúli-dhusarita-digantarálát | Parameśvara-sevá-samáyátáśesha-Jambudwípa-bhúpálánanta-

[23] pádát bharanamadavaneḥ (S'rí-Mudgagiri)-samávásita-śrímaj-jaya-skandhávárát | parama-sogato Mahárá[já]dhirája-S'rí-Nayapála-deva-pádánudhyátaḥ parame-

[24] śvaraḥ (paramabhaṭṭárako Mahárá)jádhirájaḥ S'rímán Vigraha-pála-devaḥ kuśalí || S'rí Puṇḍavarddhana . kau Koṭívarshaṃ vishadháuuḥ páti . . . . .

[25] ma (*about one third omitted*) (petana dhaná ha)lakalita || Kákinín upádhikopamánadvayopeta .

[26] sa . . . . (ponnana) droṇa-dvaya-sameta || shaṭ(k)álya-pramáṇá-(ṭalu-ma)heśvara-sameta Vishamapuráṃśe samupagatáśe-

[27] sha-rá(já-purushán | rájara)náka | rájaputra | rájámátya | mahásándhivigrahika | mahákshapaṭalika | mahásámanta | mahásenapati | mahápratíhára |

[28] dauḥsádhasadhanika | mahádaṇḍanáyaka | mahákumárámátya | rájasthanoparika | dásáparádhika | chauroddharaṇika | dáṇḍika | daṇḍapásika | sau-

[29] lkika | (gaulmika) | kshetrapa | prántapala | koshapála | angaraksha | tadáyukta | viniyuktaka | hastyaśroshṭranauvalavyápṛitaka | kiśora | vaḍavá [|] gomahishyajá-

[30] vi(kályaksha | drutapesha)ṇika | gamágamika | abhitvaramáṇa | vishayapá | grámapati | tarika | goda | málava | khaśa | húṇa | kulika | kalláṭa | láṭa | cháṭa |

[31] (bhaṭa | sevakádín | anyáṃ-ś-chá)kírtitán | rájapádopájívina[ḥ] | prativásino bráhmaṇottarán | mahattamottama | ka . ma-puroga-maidándha-chaṇḍála-paryantán |

[32] (yathárhaṃ mánaya)ti | bodhayati | samádiśati cha | viditam astu bhavatá[ṃ] | yathoparilikhito 'rdhagrámaḥ | sva-símá-ṭriṇa-pratigochara-paryantaḥ | satalaḥ | so(ddeśaḥ) |

[33] (sámramadhúkaḥ) | sajala(sthalaḥ) | sagarttosharaḥ | sadaśo-pacháraḥ | sachauroddharaṇaḥ | paribhṛita-sarvapíḍaḥ | acháṭa-bhaṭa-praveśaḥ | akiñchit-pragráskaḥ | samasta-bhá-

[34] ga-bhoga-kara-hiraṇyádi-pratyáya(*seal*)sametaḥ | bhúmi-ch-chhidranyáyená-

[35] chandrárka-kshiti-samakálam (*seal*) mátápitror átmanaś (cha puṇya)-

[36] yaśo'bhivṛiddhaye bhagavantaṃ vṛi (*seal*) ddha-bhaṭṭárakaṁ uddiśya (śasaníkṛi-)

[37] tya sagotráya | S'áṇḍilya(*seal*)(maśiva | daiva) . . . ra

[38] harisa-brahmacháriṇe | S'ámave(*seal*)dine | Kauthumí-śákhádhyáyi-

[39] ne | Mímáṃsá-ṇyákaraṇa (*sic*)-tarkkavidyávide | kroḍákṛitinisaṃta-matsyávása-(vinirggatáya | . trágrámavástavyáya) | Vedántavikṛita . (hmivana)-devapautráya | maho-

[40] padhyáya . rkka-deva-putráya | (Khobhúta)-deva-śarmmaṇe | (s)onagráha-vidhi . . . angáya ('smat) sásaníkṛitya pradatto 'smábhiḥ | ato bhavadbhiḥ sarvair evánumanta-

[41] vyaṃ bhávibhir api bhúpatibhiḥ | bhúme[r] dána-phala-gauravát | apraharaṇena cha mahánaraka-páta-bhayát | dánam idam anumodyánumodyánupálaníyama patavási-

[42] . kshetrakaraiḥ || ájñá-śravaṇa-vidheyíbhúya yathákálaṃ samudita-bhága-bhota-kara-hiraṇyádi-pratyáyopanayaḥ kárya iti || samat | 2 | chaitradine 9 sarva-

[43] thátra dharmánusásinaḥ ślokáh || [1]bahubhi[r] vasudhá dattá rájabhiḥ Sagarádibhiḥ | yasya yasya yadá bhúmis tasya tasya tadá phala[ṃ] | [2]bhumi[ṃ] yaḥ pratigṛihṇáti yaś cha bhúmi[ṃ] pra-

[44] yachchhati | ubhau tau puṇyakarmmáṇau niyataṃ svargagáminau | [3]gám ekáṃ svarṇṇam ekañ cha bhúmer apy ekam angulaṃ | haran narakam áyáti yávad abhút asamplavaṃ || [4]shashṭivarsha-

[45] sahasráṇi svarge modati bhúmidaḥ | áksheptá chánumantá cha táneva narake vaset || [5]svadattáṃ paradattá[ṃ] vá yo hareta vasundharám | sa vistháyáṃ kṛimi[r] bhútvá pi-

[46] tṛibhiḥ saha pachyate || [6]sarván etán bhávinaḥ párthivendrá[n] bhúyo bhúyaḥ prá[r]thayaty esha rámaḥ | sámányo 'y[an dh]armasetur nṛipáṇá[ṃ] kále kále pálaníyaḥ krameṇa || [7]i-

[47] ti kamala-dalámbu-vindu-lolá[ṃ] śriyam anuchintya manushyajívitañ cha | sakalam idam udáhṛitañ cha buddhvá na hi purushaiḥ parakírtayo vilopyáḥ || [8]yau . .

[48] ví-kshama . . . . nidhi . brahma . . . dhanádhanye . . . . . . || S'rí-Vigrahapálaḥ kshitipati-tilako . . . . . . | S'rí-pra-

[49] hása-rá(ja)maka . . (nni)ṇam iha śasane bhútaṃ || Posalígrámaniryátá-Mahídhara-súnuná idaṃ śásanaṃ utkírṇṇaṃ S'aśideva . . . . . ||

Notes.

I have carefully re-examined the original plate of the Bhagalpur grant, which is in the Society's collection, for the purpose of the following notes:

Verse 1. The latter half of this verse in the Bhagalpur grant agrees with the A'mgáchhí grant, and reads as I have given it. The meaning is: "who having overcome the over-powering strength of desire has (now) obtained everlasting peace, may he, Gopáladeva, be prosperous, being another (*i. e.*, like) Daśabala (Buddha), the Lord of the world."

Verse 2. Both grants read distinctly °निकेतनंसमकरो बो° ; not वंशम् षकरोद् as given in the Bhagalpur transcript; the meaning is: "well able to sustain the weight of the earth, making it (the earth) to be like the native-place of Lakshmí, he became the only asylum of the princes who approached him (for protection) as if they were afraid that their wings might be clipt."—I may note here, that in the A'mgáchhí plate, the anuswáras and superscribed rephas are often wanting, whether from the engraver's carelessness or perhaps from the ravages of time, it is impossible to say. On the Bhagalpur plate they are always present. The repha, when it does appear on the A'mgáchhí plate, is often a minute stroke attached to the upper part of the left side of the letter.

Verse 3. This verse is, in the Bhagalpur grant, preceded by another, which is omitted in the A'mgáchhí grant.

Verse 4. The A'mgáchhí grant reads distinctly पूर्वजो (nom. sing.) If this should be correct, it would reverse the mutual relation of Jayapála and Devapála, making the former the elder brother of the latter. The context, however, certainly seems to confirm the reading of the Bhagalpur grant, which has equally distinctly पूर्व्वजे.—The A'mgáchhí plate has षवैषोत्, while the Bhagalpur plate has षनैषीत्, both equally distinctly. Both readings convey the same sense.

Verse 5. Another verse of the Bhagalpur grant is omitted here.

Verse 6. Here, again, a verse of the Bhagalpur grant is omitted.—The Bhagalpur grant has श्रियः, not श्रिय: as given in the transcript.—The latter part of the first half of this verse is different in the Bhagalpur grant, which reads *S'rí-Náráyaṇapáladevaṃ asṛijat tasyáṃ sa puṇyottaraṃ.*

Verse 7. Here commences the portion which is peculiar to the A'mgáchhí grant.

Line 20. In the middle of this line, with *sa khalu*, the identical portion of the two grants recommences.—The Bhagalpur plate has *váṭa* for *váṭaka.*

Line 23. The name of the capital should be S'rí-Mudgagiri. Though the number of the letters on the plate agrees with that name, their traces, which are only very faintly visible, hardly seem to do so.—The letters on the plate are only *Mahárádhirája*, the syllable *já* being omitted by mistake.

Line 24. From this line down to the end of line 26, the version of the Ámgáchhí grant is new. It mentions the donor, Vigrahapála, the province Puṇḍavardhana, and apparently a town Koṭívarsha.

Line 26. At the end of this line the two grants again coincide. There is a mention here of a place *Vishamapura.*

Line 28. The office of *mahákartákṛitika* is omitted in the Ámgáchhí grant.—To the title of *dauḥsádhasadhanika* the Bhagalpur grant prefixes *mahá*. द्दःसा॰ in the transcript of the latter grant is a misprint for द्दौःसा॰ as the original plate has it.—The Bhagalpur grant has *rájasthaníyoparika* for *rájasthánoparika;* also *dás'áparádhika, daṇḍapás'ika* and *s'aulkika*, with palatal श, while the Ámgáchhí plate spells with the dental स.

Line 29. *Prántapala* is clearly an error for *prántapála.*—The Bhagalpur plate has *tadáyuktaka* for *tadáyukta;* it also has *khaṇḍaraksha* instead of *angaraksha.*

Line 30. The Bhagalpur plate has *abhitvamáṇa* (not *abhitvamána*, as in the transcript), clearly an error for *abhitvaramáṇa.* It has also *vishayapati* for *vishayapá;* also *húṇa*, not *hraṇa*, as in the transcript.

Line 31. The Bhagalpur plate has *rájapadopajívinaḥ;* and it omits the imperfectly legible word *ka . ma* or *ke . ma.*

Line 32. The Bhagalpur grant has *matam* instead of *viditam.*—After *bhavatáṃ* it inserts two and a half lines containing particulars about Náráyaṇapála, which are omitted in the Ámgáchhí grant.

Line 33. After *sagarttosharaḥ*, the Bhagalpur grant inserts *soparikaraḥ.*—*Pragráskaḥ* is the correct reading in both grants, not *prayáskaḥ*, as given in the Bhagalpur transcript.

Line 35. The Bhagalpur grant inserts *yávat* after *samakálam.*

Line 36. From the middle of this line to the middle of the 40th line the Ámgáchhí text is new.

Line 40. The name of the donee is *khobhúta ?-deva.*—The Bhagalpur grant omits *asmábhiḥ;* and has *tato* for *ato.*

Line 41. Both grants have *bhúmer*, not *bhramair*, as the Bhagalpur transcript gives.—The Bhagalpur plate has only *apraharaṇe.*—This line in the Ámgáchhí plate is very carelessly written; *anumodya* is twice repeated, and the last words should evidently be *anupálaníyaṃ prativásibhiḥ.*

Line 42. The Bhagalpur plate has *samuchita* for *samudita.*—It inserts *sarva* before *pratyáya*, and omits it at the end of the line.—*Bhota* in the Ámgáchhí plate is clearly an error for *bhoga.*

Line 43. Both grants have *dattá*, not *bhúktá*, as given in the Bhagalpur transcript.—The Bhagalpur plate omits the second and third verses.

Line 45. *Táneva* is an error for *tányeva*, and *visthâyáṃ* for *víshṭháyáṃ*.

Line 46. *Ayarmasetur* is an error for *ayan dharmasetur*, the syllable न्ध *ndha* being omitted.

CLASSIFIED INDEX

TO THE

SCIENTIFIC PAPERS

IN THE SOCIETY'S PUBLICATIONS

FROM 1788 TO 1883.

I.

ANTIQUITIES.

[Abbreviations: A. = Ancient monuments: C. = Caves: Sc. = Sculptures: I. = Inscriptions: Cp. = Copperplates: V. = Votive objects: P. = Pottery: R. = Prehistoric Remains.]

As. Res.			
Vol. I. (1788.)	Cp.	A Royal Grant of Land on a Copper plate, dated 23 B. C.; discovered at Mungir. Translated by Charles Wilkins. (With 2 Plates)	123
	T.	An Inscription on a Pillar near Buddal. Translated by Charles Wilkins. (With a Plate)	131
		Remarks on the above two Inscriptions by Sir William Jones	142
	Sc. & A.	Some account of the Sculptures and Ruins at Mahavalipuram, a few miles north of Sadras and known as the seven Pagodas. William Chambers	145
	C. & I.	On a Cave with an Inscription near Gayá. John Herbert Harington. Translated by Charles Wilkins. (With a Plate)	276
	I.	Translation of a Sanskrit Inscription, on a stone at Buddha Gayá. Copied by Mr. Wilmot, translated by Charles Wilkins	284

As. Res. Vol.	Cp.		
I. (1788.)	Cp.	An Indian Grant of Land in 1018 A. D., found at Tanna, in Salset. Translated by Rámalochan Pandit. Communicated by General Carnac. (With a Plate)	357
	I.	Inscriptions on the Staff of Firúz Shah. Transl. by Rádhácánta Sarman. (With 2 Plates)	379
II. (1790.)	I.	Two Inscriptions from the Vindhya Mountains. Transl. by Charles Wilkins	167
	I.	Translation of an Inscription in the Maga language engraved on a silver plate, found in a cave near Islámabád. Communicated by John Shore.	383
	A.	Memorandum concerning an Old Building in the Hadjipore District, near the Ganduck River. Reuben Burrow...........	477
(III.) (1792.)	Cp.	A Royal Grant of Land in Carnáta. Transl. by Sir William Jones, communicated by Alexander Macleod. (With a Plate)....	39
IV. (1795.)	A.	A description of the Cuttab Minar. Ensign James T. Blunt. (With 2 Plates)	313
	A.	Extract from a Diary of a Journey over the Great Desert from Aleppo to Bussora in April 1782. Sir William Dunkin.	401
	C.	Some account of the Cave in the Island of Elephanta. J. Goldingham. (With 3 Plates)	409
	A.	An account of the present state of Delhi. Lieutenant William Franklin...........	419
V. (1798.)	Sc., I.	Some account of the Sculptures at Mahabalipuram, usually called the Seven Pagodas. J. Goldingham. (With copies of Inscriptions)	69
	A.	On the city of Pegue and the Temple of Shoemadoo Praw. Captain Michael Symes.	111

As. Res.			
Vol. V. (1798.)	V.	An account of the discovery of two Urns in the vicinity of Benares. Jonathan Duncan. (With a Plate)..............	131
	I.	Account of some ancient Inscriptions at Ellora. Sir Charles Ware Mallet. Taken by Mr. Wales; transl. by Lieut. F. Wilford. (With a Plate)	135
	A.	Account of the Pagoda at Perwattam. Captain Colin Mackenzie. Communicated by Major Kirkpatrick	303
VI. (1799.)	C. & Sc.	Description of the Caves or Excavations near Ellora. C. W. Mallet. (With 6 Plates)..	382
	A. & Sc.	Remarks on some antiquities on the West and South coasts of Ceylon. Captain Colin Mackenzie. (With 2 Plates)	425
VII. (1801.)	I.	Translation of the Inscriptions on the Pillar at Delhi, called the Lat of Firúz Shah. Henry Colebrooke. With introductory remarks by Mr. Harington. (With 13 Plates of Capt. James Hoare's drawings,)	176
VIII. (1805.)	A.	Extract from a Journal, during the late campaign in Egypt. Captain C. B. Burr	35
IX. (1807.)	I.	On Ancient Monuments, containing Sanskrit Inscriptions. H. T. Colebrooke. (With 2 Plates)	398
XII. (1816.)	I.	Translation of a Sanskrit Inscription on a Stone found in Bundelkhand. Lieutenant W. Price. (With Text)	357
XIII. (1820.)	A.	The Ruins of Prambanan in Java. John Crawfurd	337

As. Res. Vol.			
XIII.	A.	An account of Bijapur in 1811. Captain Sydenham. Communicated by Col. C. Mackenzie	433
XIV. (1822.)	A. & I.	An account of the Inscriptions on the Cootub Minar, and on the ruins in its vicinity. Walter Ewer. (With a Plate)	480
XV. (1825.)	I.	Sanskrit Inscriptions. Captain E. Fell. With observations by H. H. Wilson	436
	A. & I.	Account of ancient Hindu Remains in Chattisghar, R. Jenkins With translations and observations by H. H. Wilson. (With 2 Plates)	499
XVI. (1828.)	I.	Translation of an Inscription on the great bell of Rangoon, with notes and illustrations. Rev. G. H. Hough. (With Text and a Plate)	270
	I.	Sanskrit Inscriptions at Abú. Horace Hayman Wilson	284
XX. (1836-1839.)	I.	Translation of various inscriptions found among the Ruins of Vijayanagar. E. C. Ravenshaw. With preliminary observations by H. H. Wilson	1
	I.	Translation of an Inscription in the Burmese language, discovered at Buddha Gaya in 1833. Lieutenant-Colonel H. Burney. (With 2 Plates)	161
Journal Vol. II. (1833.)	A.	Account of the Jain Temples on mount Abú in Gujerat. Lieutenant Burnes	161
	A.	On the "Topes" and Grecian Remains in the Panjáb. Lieutenant A. Burnes	308
	Sc.	On the colossal Idols of Bamián. Lieutenant Alexander Burnes. (With a Plate)	561
	C.	Cave of Secanderiah near Tabriz	658

Journal			
Vol. III. (1834.)	A.	Discovery of an ancient town near Behut, in the Doab. Captain P. T. Cautley	43
	A.	A description with drawings of the ancient Stone Pillar at Allahabad, called Bhim Sen's Gada or Club, with accompanying copies of four inscriptions engraven in different characters upon its surface. Lieutenant T. S. Burt. (Wth a Plate)	105
	I.	Note on Inscription No. 1, of the Allahabad Column. James Prinsep. (With 2 Plates)	114
	I.	Remarks upon the second Inscription of the Allahabad pillar. Captain A. Troyer. (With a Plate)	118
	I.	Translation of an Inscription in the Páli and Burma languages on a stone slab from Ramávati (Ramree Island) in Arracan, presented by H. Walters. Ratna Paula. (With a Plate)	209
	I.	Translation of an Inscription in the Páli character and Burmese language, on a stone slab at Buddha Gaya, in Bihar. (With a Plate)	214
	A.	Further account of the Remains of an ancient town discovered at Behut near Saharanpur. Captain P. T. Cautley. (With a Plate)	221
	I.	Restoration of the Inscription, No. 2, on the Allahabad column. Rev. Dr. W. H. Mill. (With 2 Plates)	257
	A.	Memoir on the Topes and Antiquities of Afghanistan. Dr. J. G. Gerard........	321
	A.	Extracts from Mr. Masson's letter to Dr. J. G. Gerard on the Excavations of Topes, dated Tattung 22. March 1834.........	329
		Note on the locality of the Rajagriha, of the Town of that name, in Behar. By T. R. (Lieut. T. Renny?)	366
	I.	Notice of some ancient inscriptions in the characters of the Allahabad Column. B. H. Hodgson. (With a Plate)	481
	I.	Note on the Mathiah Láth Inscription. James Prinsep. (With a Plate)........	483

Journal.			
Vol. III. (1834.)	I.	Second note on the Bhilsa Inscription. James Prinsep. (With 2 Plates)	488
	T.	Inscription on the Iron Pillar at Delhi. James Prinsep. (With a Plate)	494
	C. & I.	Restoration and Translation of some Inscriptions at the Caves of Carli. Rev. J. Stevenson	495
	I.	Account of some Inscriptions in the Abyssinian character, found at Hassan Ghorab, near Aden, on the Arabian coast. Lieutenant Wellsted. (With a Plate)	554
	A.	Further information on the Topes of Manikyála, being a translation of an extract from a manuscript memoir on ancient Taxila by M. A. Court	556
	A.	Notice of an ancient Mahal or Palace near Jounpur in which some Hindu coins were lately dug up. V. Tregear	617
IV. (1835.)	A.	Account of a visit to the Ruins of Simraun, once the capital of the Mithila province. B. H. Hodgson. (With a Plate)	121
	I.	Further particulars of the Sarun and Tirhut Laths, and account of two Bauddha Inscriptions found the one at Bakhra, in Tirhut, the other at Sárnáth, near Benares. James Prinsep. (With a Plate)	124
	A.	Excursions to the Ruins and Site of an ancient city at Bakhra 13 cos north of Patna, and 6 north from Singhea. J. Stephenson	128
	I.	Note on the above by James Prinsep. (With a Plate)	131
	A.	Note on an Inscription on the Mandara Hill near Bhagulpur. James Prinsep. (With a Plate)	166
	I.	Description of ancient Temples and Ruins at Chărdwár in Assam. Captain G. E. Westmacott. (With a Plate)	185
	I.	Remarks on an Inscription in the Ranja and Tibetan (Uchhen) characters, taken from	

Journal.			
Vol. IV. (1835.)		a Temple on the confines of the valley of Nepal. B. H. Hodgson. (With a Plate)	196
	I.	Further note on the Inscription from Sárnath. B. H. Hodgson	211
	I.	Note on an Inscription found near the Kesariah Mound, in Tirhut. J. B. Elliott. (With a Plate)	286
	A.	Notice of the Temple called Seo Baijnáth, discovered by Sergeant E. Dean, on the Hill of Unchápahár, in the Shekawati Territory. (With 4 Plates and a Map)	361
	I.	Restitution and Translation of the Inscription found in the Ruins of the mountain Temple of Shekawati. Rev. Dr. W. H. Mill	367
	Cp.	Account of the Inscriptions upon two sets of Copper Plates, found in the western part of Gujerát. W. H. Wathen. (With 3 Plates)	477
	I.	Report on some Inscriptions found at Hammam, on the Southern coast of Arabia. T G. Hutton, and Lieut. J. Smith. (With 2 Plates)	533
	A.	Note regarding the Bhilsa monument. Dr. Spilsbury	712
	A.	Note on the Sárnáth Building. Baron Hügel	712
	I.	Note on the occurrence of the Bauddha formula. James Prinsep	713
V. (1836.)	Sc. & I.	Discovery of Buddhist images with Devanágari Inscriptions at Tagong, the ancient capital of the Burmese Empire. Colonel H Burney. (With a a Plate)	157
	I.	Note on an Inscription at Bamián. C. Masson. (With a Plate)	188
	I.	Interpretation of the Tibetan Inscription on a Bhotian banner, taken in Assam, and presented to the Asiatic Society by Captain Bogle. Alexander Csoma de Körös. (With a Plate)	264

Journal.			
Vol. V. (1836.)	I.	Facsimiles of various ancient inscriptions. James Prinsep. (With 8 Plates), 795, 724, 657, 554, 482,	340
	Cp.	Translation of a Támba patra, found near Piplianagar in the Shujalpur Parganá. L. Wilkinson	377
	A.	Extracts from a memoir on a map of Peshâwar and the countries between the Indus and the Hydaspes, the Peucalaotis and Taxila of ancient geography. A. Court. (With a Map)	468
	Sc.	Note on the discovery of a relic of Grecian Sculpture in Upper India. Lieut. Col. L. R. Stacy. (With a Plate)	567
	A.	Notes on the Antiquities of Bamian. C. Masson	707
	A.	Description of Uch-Sharif. Munshi Mohun Lál	796
VI. (1837.)	I.	Restoration and Translation of the Inscription on the Bhitári Lát with critical and historical remarks. Rev. Dr. W. H. Mill. (With a Plate)	1
	A.	Suggestions on the sites of Sangala and the altars of Alexander. C. Masson........	57
	A.	Chinese account of India. Translated from the Wan-heen-thung-kaon or "Deep researches into ancient monuments," by Matwanlin	61
	I.	Translation of an inscription on a stone in the Asiatic Society's Museum, marked No. 2. Captain G. T. Marshall. (With a Plate)	88
	I.	Facsimiles of ancient Inscriptions. James Prinsep. (With 15 Plates) .. 869, 663, 278,	218
	I. A.	Note on the Facsimiles of Inscriptions from Sanchi near Bhílsá, taken by Captain Ed. Smith, and on the drawings of the Buddhist monument, presented by Captain W. Murray. James Prinsep. (With 5 Plates)	451

Journal.	Sc.		
Vol. VI. (1837.)		Notice of a Colossal Alto-relievo, known by the name of Mata Koonr situated near Kussia Tannah, in Pargana Sidowa, in the Gorakhpur District. D. Liston	477
	I.	Interpretation of the most ancient of the inscriptions on the pillar called the lát of Firúz Shah, near Delhi and of the Allahabad, Radhia and Mattia pillar or lát inscriptions which agree therewith. James Prinsep	566
	A.	Account of the Ruins and Site of old Mandavi in Raepur, and legend of Vikramaditya's son in Cutch. Lieut. W. Postans	648
	I.	Account of an inscription found by Mr. H. S. Boulderson, in the neighbourhood of Bareilley. James Prinsep. (With a Plate)	777
	I.	Further elucidation of the Lát or Silasthambha inscriptions from various sources. James Prinsep. (With 2 Plates)	790
	A.	Observations upon the past and present condition of Oujein or Ujjayani. Lieutenant Edward Conolly. (With a Plate)	813
	I.	Note on the facsimiles of the various Inscriptions on the ancient column at Allahabad, retaken by Captain Edward Smith. James Prinsep. (With 2 Plates)	963
	I.	Specimens of Buddhist Inscriptions, with symbols from the West of India. Colonel W. H. Sykes	1038
		Note on Colonel Sykes' Inscriptions. James Prinsep. (With a Plate)	1042
	I.	Further notes on the inscriptions on the column at Delhi, Allahabad, Betiah, etc. Hon'ble George Turnour	1049
	V.	Account and drawing of two Burmese bells now placed in a Hindu temple in Upper India. Captain R. Wroughton. (With 2 Plates).........................	1064
	I.	Note on Inscriptions at Udayagiri and Khandagiri in Cuttack, in the láth character. James Prinsep. (With 2 Plates)	1072

Journal.		
Vol. VII. (1838.)	I.	Facsimiles of ancient Inscriptions (continued). James Prinsep. (With 8 Plates) 1058, 966, 901, 33
	A.	Ruins and Pillar at Jajipur, from Lieutenant Markham Kittoe's Journal. (With 2 Plates) 200, 53
	I.	Discovery of the name of Antiochus the Great, in two of the edicts of Asoka King of India. James Prinsep.............. 156
	I.	On the edicts of Piyadasi or Asoka, the Buddhist monarch of India, preserved on the Girnar rock in the Gujarat peninsula, and on the Dhauli rock in Cuttack; with the discovery of Ptolemy's name therein. James Prinsep. (With 3 Plates) 219
	I.	Restoration and Translation of the Inscription on the large Arracan Bell, now at Nadrohighat, Zillah Alligarh, described by Captain Wroughton. James Prinsep. (With a Plate) 287
	I.	Examination of the inscriptions from Girnar in Gujarat and Dhauli in Cuttack (continued). James Prinsep. (With 4 Plates) 334
	A.	Account of an ancient temple at Hissar, and of the ship model at that place. Captain Wm. Brown. (With a Plate).......... 429
	A.	An account of the Jain Temple at Badrasir; and ruins of Badranagari in the province of Cutch. Lieutenant W. Postans. (With a Plate) 431
	I.	Examination of the separate edicts of the Aswastama inscription at Dhauli in Cuttack. James Prinsep. (With 3 Plates).. 434
	J.	Translation of Inscriptions in the Society's Museum. (Continued). James Prinsep. (With a Plate) 557
	I.	More Dánams from the Sanchi Tope near Bhilsa, taken in impression, by Capt. T. S. Burt. Transl. by James Prinsep. (With a Plate.)......................... 562
	I.	Lithographs and translations of inscriptions taken in ectype by Captain T. S. Burt;

Journal.			
Vol. VII. (1838.)		and of one from Ghosi, taken by Captain A. Cunningham. James Prinsep. (With 3 Plates)	629
	Sc.	Sketch of the sculptured images, on the temples of Grámesvara near Rátrapur, from Lieut. Kittoe's Journal. (With 2 Plates).	660
	A.	Mr. Kittoe's Journal of his tour in the province of Orissa. (With 6 Plates)	679
	I.	Translation of an inscription on a Tambapatra, found at Piplianagar in the Shujalpur Purganá. L. Wilkinson	736
	A.	Sketch of the Temple to Durga at Baleswar, etc. from Lieutenant Kittoe's Journal. (With a Plate)	1060, 828
	I.	Notes of a Journey to Girnár in Kattyawar, for the purpose of copying the ancient Inscriptions upon the rock near that place. Lieut. Postans. With two notes on Somnáth, one by Mr. Kittoe. (With 5 Plates)	865
VIII. (1839.)	A.	Objects of Research in Afghanistan. Professor Lassen.	145
	I.	Notice of an Inscription on a Slab, discovered near Chatarpur, in Bundelkhand. Captain T. S. Burt.	159
	Cp.	Account of Tambapatra plates dug up at Baroda in Gujarat; with facsimile and translation. H. T. P. (H. T. Prinsep). (With a Plate)	292
	I.	Notice of Inscriptions in Bihar. Mr. Ravenshaw.	347
		Proposed publication of Plates of Hindu Architectural Remains.	384
IX. Part I. (1840.)	I.	Notice of an Inscription in Bihar. Mr. Ravenshaw. (With 4 Plates)	65
	I.	Note on an Inscription from Oodeypur near Sagur. H. Torrens. (With a Plate)	545
	I.	Inscription found near Bhabra. Captain Burt. With notes by H. Torrens and Capt. M. Kittoe. (With a Plate)	616

Journal.			
Part II.	I.	Paper on ancient Land-grants on Copper, discovered in Assam. Major F. Jenkins. (With a Plate)	766
X. Part I. (1841.)	A. & V.	Opening of the Topes at the caves of Kanari, near Bombay, and the Relics found in them. Dr. James Bird. (With a Plate)	94
	Cp.	Note on a Copper land grant of Jaya Chandra. H. Torrens	98
Part II.	A.	On the topes of Darunta and caves of Bahrabad. Lieut. Pigou. (With a Plate)	381
	V.	A sketch of the second silver plate found at Badakshan. Lieut. Alexander Cunningham. (With a Plate)	570
	I.	Inscription taken from a Baolee at Bussuntgurh, at the foot of the Southern range of Hills running parallel to mount Aboo. Captain T. S. Burt.	664
	I.	Literal translation of the Vasuntgurh Inscription. Pandit Surodaha Prasadh	819
	I.	Observations on a second inscription taken in facsimile from the neighbourbood of mount Aboo. Captain Burt	821
XI. Part I. (1842.)	I.	On an ancient Magic Square, cut in a temple at Gwalior. Captain Shortrede	292
Part II.	I.	Ancient Inscription found at Aden. S. B. Haines. (With a Plate)	958
XII. Part I. (1843.)	I.	Documents relating to the gates of Somnath. (With 4 Plates)	73
XIII. Part I. (1844.)	I.	An inscription from a Tablet in a Buddhist monastery at Ningpo in China. Dr. D. J. Macgowan. (With a Plate)	113
XIV. Part II. (1845.)	A.	On the Buddhist emblems of Architecture. Captain T. Latter. (With 2 Plates)	623

Journal.	Sc.		
Vol. XVI. Part I. (1847.)	Sc.	Note on an image of Buddha found at Sherghatti, etc. Captain Kittoe. (With a Plate)	78
	A.	On the Ruins of Anuradhapura, formerly the capital of Ceylon. William Knighton. (With 2 Plates)	213
	A.	Notes on the Viháras and Chaityas of Bihar. (With 2 Plates)	272
		Queries on Archæology of India. Rev. James Long	285
	Sc.	Note on the sculptures of Buddha Gaya. Captain M. Kittoe	334
	A.	The rock Temples of Dambool, Ceylon. William Knighton. (With a Plate)	340
		Instructions how to take correct facsimiles of Inscriptions. Captain Kittoe	366
		Hints on the easiest method of taking and preparing drawings for Lithograph. Captain Kittoe	368
	A.	An account of the Temple of Tribeni near Hooghly. D. Money	393
	C.	Notes on the caves of Burabur. Captain Kittoe. (With 3 Plates)	401
	A.	Some account of the "Kalán Musjeed," commonly called the "Kalee Musjeed," within the new town of Delhi. Lieutenant Henry Lewis. (With 5 Plates)	577
	I.	Translation of an Inscription on a Gun at Moorshedabad with Remarks. Major St. G. D. Showers	589
		Translation of an Inscription in the Nagarjuni Cave. (With a Plate)	594
	A.	On the Temples and Ruins of Oomga. Captain M. Kittoe	656
	Sc.	On a Sculpture from the site of the Indo-Greek city of Bucephalia. Captain James Abbott. (With 3 Plates)	664
Part II.	A.	Notes on the Antiquities of the Districts within the Bhopal Agency. Captain J. D. Cunningham. (With 2 Plates)	739
	A.	Some account of the Town and Palace of Firúzabad, near Delhi, with introductory re-	

Journal.			
		marks on the sites of other Towns. Henry Cope.	971
Vol. XVI. Part II.	A.	Memorandum regarding the recently discovered ruins at Ranode in Scindiah's Dominions. Henry Cope	1079
	I.	Inscription at Oomga and notes on the same. Captain Kittoe	1220
XVII. Part I. (1848.)	A.	On the antiquities of Sarguja and its neighbourhood. Lieutenant-Colonel J. R. Ousely. (With a Plate)	65
	I.	Inscriptions from Vijaya Mandir, Udayapúr, etc. Babu R. Mitra	68
	V.	Lingam at Bhojpur. Captain J. D. Cunningham	154
	I.	Inscription at Singapore. Captain J. D. Cunningham	154
	A.	Description of the Antiquities at Kalinjar. Lieut. F. Maisey. (With 19 Plates)	171
		Appendix to Ditto. (With a Plate)	313
	I.	Inscription from Penang. Colonel J. Low.	232
	A.	Antiquities of Orissa. Captain M. Kittoe	234
	A.	On the Ruins at Putharee. Captain J. D. Cunningham	305
	A.	Notes on ancient temples and other remains in the vicinity of Suddyah, Upper Assam. Major S. F. Hannay. Communicated by Mr. Seton Karr. (With 2 Plates)	459
	A.	Description of the Tomb of an Ahom noble. Sergeant C. Clayton. Communicated by Mr. Seton Karr. (With a Plate)	473
	I.	Sanskrit inscription from Behar, with a translation by Dr. Ballantyne and remarks by Captain M. Kittoe	492
		Note on the above by J W. Laidlay	498
		Proposed Archæological Investigation. Capt. A. Cunningham	535
XVII. Part II.	I.	An account of several inscriptions found in the Province Wellesley on the Peninsula of Malacca. Lieut.-Col. James Low. (With a Plate)	62

Journal.			
Vol. XVII. Part II. (1848.)	I.	Note on the Inscriptions from Singapur and Province Wellesley, forwarded by the Hon. Col. Butterworth. J. W. Laidlay. (With a Plate)	66
		Relics of the Catholic Mission in Tibet. B. H. Hodgson	225
	A.	An Essay on the Arian order of Architecture, as exhibited in the Temples of Kashmir. Captain A. Cunningham. Communicated by H. M. Elliot. (With 17 Plates)	241
XVIII. Part I. (1849.)	Sc.	Remains of Greek sculpture in Patowar. Captain James Abbott. (With 6 Plates)	131
	I.	On an Inscription from Keddah. Lieut. Col. Low. (With a Plate)	247
		Note on above. J. W. Laidlay	247
Part II.	Sc.	Description of a colossal Jain figure, nearly 80 feet high, cut in relief, discovered on a spur of the Satpura range in the district of Burwanie, on the Nerbudda. Dr. Impey..................................	918
XIX. (1850.)	I.	Note on an inscription on a brick, found in the Jounpur district by Captain M. Kittoe. Transl. by Dr. James Ballantyne........	454
	I.	Note on an inscription from Oujein. Babu Rájendralála Mittra	475
XX. (1857.)	Sc.	A short notice of an ancient colossal figure carved in granite on the Mandar Hill in the District of Bhágalpúr. Captain W. S. Sherwell. (With a Plate)	272
	A.	Notice of a Ruin in Singbhúm. Rev. J. Long	283
	A.	Brief notice of the Sil Háko or stone bridge in Zillah Kámrúp. Major S. T. Hannay. Communicated through Major F. Jenkins. (With a Plate)	291

Journal.			
Vol. XXI. (1852.)	A.	On the oriental character of certain Northern Antiquities. Dr. George Buist	127
	A.	Nooks and corners of Bengal. No. I, the Tomb of Meer Muddan Khan. Captain F. P. Layard	148
	A.	On the site of Nikaia and Boukephalon. Major James Abbott.................	214
	A.	The Mausoleum of the Nawabs Ali Verdi Khan and Soorajood Dowlah at Kooskbagh, near Moorshedabad. Captain F. P. Layard. (With 2 Plates)	504
	Sc.	Notice of two heads found in the Northern Districts of the Panjab, with drawings. W. Jackson. (With 2 Plates)	511
	Sc.	Note on some sculptures found in the district of Peshawar. E. C. Bayley. (With 11 Plates)	606
XXII. (1853.)	Sc.	Note on a sculpture in Alto-relievo sent by the Governor General to the Asiatic Society. Welby Jackson. (With a Plate)	193
	Sc.	The ancient city of Konsonapuri, now called Rungamutty. Captain F. P. Layard. (With a Plate)	281
	A.	Note on the ruins at Manikyála. Major James Abbott	570
	A.	Notes on the ruins at Mahábalipuram on the Coromandel Coast. C. Gubbins. (With 2 Plates)......................	656
	I.	Note on an ancient Inscription from Thaneswar. Babu Rájendralála Mitra......	673
XXIII. (1854.)	I.	Note on two inscriptions at Khunniara in the Kangra district. E. C. Bayley. (With a Plate)	57
		Gradus at Aornon. Major J. Abbott. (With a Map and 2 Plates)	309
		Indo-Grecian sculptures from the North Western Frontier. Major J. Abbott. (With a Plate)	394

Journal.			
Vol. XXIII. (1854.)	A.	Note on the present state of the excavations at Sarnáth. E. Thomas. (With 2 Plates.)	469
XXIV. (1855.)	A.	Notes on Assam Temple Ruins. Captain E. Taite Dalton. (With 11 Plates.)	1
	A.	Memorandum on the deserted city of Dhoolmee in Manbhoom. H. Piddington.	207
	I.	Notes on ancient inscriptions from the Chusan Archipelago and the Hazara country. Babu Rájendralála Mitra	324
XXV. (1856.)	V.	Original text and translation of a scroll of silver in the Burmese language, found in a Buddhist Pagoda at Prome. Major A. P. Phayre.	173
	C.	A visit to the Rock-cut temples of Khandgiri. E. D. Samuells.	222
	A.	Correspondence relating to the exploration of the ruins of Sarnáth.	395
XXVI. (1857.)	A.	An account of the ancient Buddhist remains at Pagán on the Iráwádi. Captain Henry Yule.	1
XXVII. (1858.)	Cp.	Of two edicts bestowing land, recorded on plates of copper. Fitz-Edward Hall.....	217
	I.	Public Inscriptions at Lahore. Henry Cope.	308
XXVIII. (1859.)	I.	Decipherment of a Sanskrit inscription, dated in the fourteenth century, with a translation and notes. Fitz-Edward Hall.......	1
XXIX. (1860.)	I.	Two letters on Indian Inscriptions. Fitz-Edward Hall..................	18
	A.	Remarks upon an ancient Buddhist monastery at Pagan on the Iráwády. Lieut.-Col. A. Phayre. (With 4 Plates.)	346

Journal.			
Vol. XXX. (1861.)	Cp.	Of two land grants, issued by king Hastin, bearing date in the years 156 and 163 after the subversion of the Guptas. Dr. Fitz-Edward Hall	1
	I.	The inscriptions of Erikaina, now Eran, redeciphered and retranslated by Dr. Fitz-Edward Hall	14
	Cp.	A donative Inscription of the tenth century; the Sanskrit original and its substance in English: with remarks on the later kings of Dhárá in Málana. Dr. Fitz-Edward Hall.	195
	A.	A few notes on antiquities near Jabalpur. Lieut.-Col. H. Yule. (With a Plate.) ..	211
	Cp.	Translation of a Bactrian Inscription from Wardak in Afghanistan. Babu Rájendralála Mitra. (With a Plate.)	337
		Note on the above. E. C. Bayley	347
	I.	Decipherment of an Inscription from Chedi, with a brief statement of the historical and other indications therefrom derived. Dr. Fitz-Edward Hall	317
XXXI. (1862.)	A.	Notes of a brief visit to some of the Indian Remains in Java. Lieut.-Col. Henry Yule. (With 9 Plates.)	16
	I. & Cp.	Three Sanskrit Inscriptions. Copies of the original and prefatory observations. Dr. Fitz-Edward Hall	111
	V.	On some Bactro-Buddhist relics from Rawal Pindi. Babu Rájendralála Mitra. (With a Plate.)	175
		Remarks on the above. E. C. Bayley. ..	184
XXXII. (1863.)	A.	On the antiquities of the Peshawar district. Rev. J. Loewenthal. (With a Plate.)....	1
	Cp.	Remarks on the Bactro-Pali Inscription from Taxila. Major General A. Cunningham..	139
		Note on the above. Babu Rájendralála Mitra	151

Journal.			
		Postscript to above. Major-General A. Cunningham.	172
Vol. XXXII. (1863.)	I.	Remarks on a stone inscription from the ruins of Pagán on the Iráwády river. Lieut.-Col. A. P. Phayre. (With a Plate.)	267
	I.	Two ancient Sanskrit Inscriptions from Central India; texts, translations, and comments. Babu Rájendralála Mitra.	273
	I.	Letter on the Taxila inscription from Professor J. Dawson.	421
		Colonel Cunningham's Archæological Survey Report for 1861-62, communicated by the Government of India.	i
XXXIII. (1864.)	Cp.	Note on the Bactro-Pali inscription from Taxila. Major General A. Cunningham..	35
	A.	Extract fron a Report on the Dependency of Bustar. Captain C. Glasfurd. (With 4 Plates.)	44
	V.	Memorandum upon some ancient Tiles obtained at Pagán in Burma. Lieut. Col. A. P. Phayre........................	57
		On the system employed in outlining the figures of deities, and other religious drawings, as practised in Ladak, Zaskar, etc. Captain H. H. Godwin Austen. (With 5 Plates.)	151
	Sc.	Memorandum on the life-sized statues lately exhumed inside the palace of Delhi. C. Campbell.	159
	A.	On the ruins of Buddha Gaya. Babu Rájenlála Mitra. (With a Plate.)	173
	I.	Some Persian inscriptions found in Srinagar Kashmir. Rev. J. Loewenthal	278
	Cp.	On a land-grant of Mahendrapála Deva of Kanauj. Babu Rájendralála Mitra. (With a Plate.)......	321
	Sc.	On the Buddhist Remains of Sultangunj. Babu Rájendralála Mitra. (With a Plate.)	360
	A.	On the Antiquities of Guzerat. Captain H. Mackenzie..........................	402

Journal.			
Vol. XXXIII. (1864.)	I.	Inscription on the Mugbara at Hailan.	549
	A.	Peculiarities and uses of the Pillar Towers of the British Islands. Dr. T. A. Wise. (With 2 Plates.)	552
		Colonel Cunningham's Archæological Survey Report for 1863-1864, communicated by the Government of India	i
XXXIV. (1865.)	A.	Description of the Buddhist Ruins at Bakariya Kund, Benares. Rev. M. A. Sherring, and Mr. C. Horne. (With 8 Plates.) ..	1
	I.	On some Siamese inscriptions. Dr. A. Bastian. (With a Plate.)	27
	I.	Notes on the Eran Inscription, being extracts from a letter to the Editor. Professor F. E. Hall	38
	A.	Some account of ancient remains at Saidpur and Bhitari. Rev. M. A. Sherring and Mr C. Horne. (With a Plate)	80
	A. & V.	Buddhist antiquities in the Hazara valley. Major Pearse.......................	111
	A.	Archæological Survey Reports for 1862-63. Major General A. Cunningham.	155, 195
		Notes on Buddha Gaya. C. Horne.	278
XXXV. (1866.)	A.	Rough notes on the Antiquities in the Gaya District. W. Peppe. (With 5 Plates.)..	49
	A.	Description of ancient remains of Buddhist Monasteries and Temples, and of other buildings, recently discovered in Benares and its vicinity. Rev. M. A. Sherring and Mr. Charles Horne. (With 5 Plates.)	61
	A.	Notes on some of the Temples of Kashmir, especially those not described by General A. Cunningham. Rev. W. G. Cowie. (With 4 Plates.)	91
		Notes on Atranji Khera or Pi-lo-Shan-na of General Cunningham. C. Horne. (With a Plate.)	165
	A.	Notes on some Buddhist ruins at Doob-Koond. Captain W R. Melville.	168

Journal.			
Vol. XXXV. (1866.)	A.	Description of the Chandrarekbágurh near Sashtání, Parganá Nyegur, zillah Midnapur. W. J. Herschel. (With a Plate.)..	181
	A.	Notes on a Tour in Manbhoom, in 1864-65. Lieut.-Col. E. T. Dalton...............	186
	Cp.	Notes on a copper plate Inscription from Sambhalpur. Babu Rájendralála Mitra..	195
	A.	Notes on the history and topography of the ancient cities of Delhi. C. J. Campbell. (With 3 Plates.)	199
	A.	Notes on pilgrimages in the country of Cashmere. Major D. F. Newall............	219
	I.	Notes on Gupta inscriptions from Aphsar and Behar. Babu Rájendralála Mitra. (With a Plate.)......................	268
XXXVI. (1867.)	A.	Notes on the Jumma Masjid of Etawah. C. Horne. (With a Plate.)	74
	I.	Translation of an Inscription copied in the Temple of Nakhon Vat, or the City of Monasteries, in Kambodia. Dr. A. Bastian..................................	76
	A.	Notes on Buddhist remains near Mynpoorie. C. Horne.	105
	Sc.	Notes on the Carvings on the Buddhist Railposts at Buddha Gaya. C. Horne. (With 3 Plates.)	107
	A.	The Pegu Pagoda. Captain H. A. Browne.	109
		The antiquities of Bagerhát. Babu Gourdass Bysack	126
	A.	Remarks on some ancient Hindu Ruins in the Garhwál Bhátur. Lieutenant Ayrton Pullan..............................	154
	A.	Notes on ancient remains in the Mainpuri District. C. Horne. (With 5 Plates.)..	157
XXXVII. (1868.)	A.	Description of a Hindu temple converted into a Mosque at Gaganesvar, zillah Midnapúr. W. Herschel.	73

Journal.			
Vol. XXXVIII. (1869.)	Cp.	Text and translation of a Balandshahar Inscription. Babu Pratapa Chandra Ghosha. (With a Plate.)	21
	A.	Some observations on the Temples of Razdan or Razdoing in the Lar Pargana, Cashmere. (With 3 Plates). Lieut. Col. D. F. Newall	177
XXXIX. (1870.)	R.	Note on a circle of stones in the District of Yusufzai. Colonel Sir A. Phayre. (With a Plate.)	58
	Cp.	Memorandum on and a tentative reading of the Sue Vihár Inscription from near Bháwalpúr. E. C. Bayley. (With 2 Plates.)	65
	A.	Notes on old Delhi. J. D. Tremlett	70
	A.	Notes on archæological remains at Sháh ki Dheri and the site of Taxila. J. G. Delmerick.	89
	I.	Notes on Sanskrit Inscriptions from Mathurá. Babu Rájendralála Mitra. (With 4 Plates.)	117
	Cp.	Three sets of Copper Sasanams discovered in the Vizagapatam District. Rev. T. Foulkes.	153
	A.	Notes on the Antiquities of the Nalti, the Assia, the Mahavinayaka hills of Cuttack. Babu Chandrasekhara Banerji	158
	A.	The Bonhara Temple, near Omerpore, Behar, and other antiquities of the place. Babu Rashbihári Bose	232
	I.	Facsimiles of autographs of Jahangir, Shahjehan and Prince Dárá Shikoh, with notes on the literary character and the capture and death of Dárá Shikoh. (With a Plate.)	271
	I.	Notes on Arabic and Persian Inscriptions, in the Húghli District. H. Blochmann. (With 5 Plates.)	279

Journal.			
Vol. XL. (1871.)	I.	Notes on three Inscriptions on stone found in Chutiá Nágpur. Babu Rakhal Das Haldar.	108
	A.	An account of the antiquities of Jajpur in Orisá. Babu Chandrasekhara Banerji....	151
	Cp.	Notes on, and translation of, two copper plate Inscriptions from Bhámangháti. Babu Pratapa Chandra Ghosha. (With 4 Plates.)	161
	C.	The rockcut excavations at Harchoka. Captain W. L. Samuells. (With 2 Plates.)..	177
	A.	The ruins at Kopari, Balasor District. J. Beames. (With 2 Plates)	247
	I.	Notes on several Arabic and Persian inscriptions. H. Blochmann. (With 4 Plates.)	251
XLI. (1872.)	A.	More Buddhist remains in Orisá. J. Beames.	7
	I.	Notes on Arabic and Persian inscriptions; No. II. H. Blochmann. (With a Plate)	102
	A.	The Buddhist remains of Bihar. A. M. Broadley. (With 9 Plates.)	209
		The Tirthas of Vrindávana and Gokula. F. S. Growse	313
(XLII.) (1873.)	R.	Rude stone monuments in Chutiá Nágpur and other places. Col. E. T. Dalton. (With 3 Plates)	112
	A.	Notes on the age of the Ruins chiefly situate at Benáres and Jounpur. Charles Horne	160
	I.	Contributions to the Geography and History of Bengal; from inscriptions. H. Blochmann. (With 3 Plates.)	209
	Cp.	Note on two copper plate inscriptions (Kanauj). Dr. Rájendralála Mitra	314
XLIII. (1874.)	A.	On the ruins at Dimápúr on the Dunsiri river, Asam. Major H. Godwin-Austin. (With 6 Plates.)	1

Journal.			
Vol. XLIII. (1874.)	A.	Notes on Sunárgáon, Eastern Bengal. Dr. James Wise. (With a Plan and a Plate)	82
	A.	Notes on the Pálam Báoli Inscription. Dr. Rájendralála Mitra. (With a Plate.)....	104
		Letter by Col. E. T. Dalton on a large picture representing the conquest of Palámau in 1660 by Daud Khán, Aurangzib's General.	240
	A.	Note on the site of Fort Ekdálah, District Dinajpúr. E. V. Westmacott. (With a Map.)	244
	A.	The Temple of Jayságar, Upper Asám. J. M. Foster. (With 4 Plates.)	311
	Cp.	Note on the Chittagong Copperplate dated Saka 1165 or A. D. 1243, presented by A. L. Clay. Pránnáth Pandit. (With a Plate.)	318
	I.	Transcript of the Pála inscription of the Buddal pillar, Dinajpur, by Pandit Hara Chakravarti. Communicated by E. V. Westmacott; transl. by Babu Pratapa Chandra Ghosha	356
	Cp.	Note on an inscription of the time of Skanda Gupta from Indor Khera Dr. Rájendralála Mitra. (With a Plate.)	363
XLIV. (1875.)	Cp.	A copper land grant of Lakshman Sen of Bengal, found near Torpondighi in the Dinajpur District. E. Vesey Westmacott. (With 2 Plates.)......................	1
	A.	The Alti Hills in Cuttack. J. Beames. (With 4 Plates.)	19
	A.	Note on Mahásthán near Bagura, Eastern Bengal. C. J. O'Donnell.	183
	A. & Sc.	On traces of Buddhism in Dinájpur and Bagura. E Vesey Westmacott. (With a Plate).	187
	Sc.	Supposed Greek sculpture at Mathura. F. S. Growse. (With 3 Plates.)	212

Journal.	Sc.		
Vol. XLVI. (1877.)		Rough notes on some ancient sculpturings on rocks in Kumaon, similar to those found on monoliths and rocks in Europe. H. Rivett-Carnac. (With 6 Plates.)	1
		The Kaimúr range. Babu Chandrasekhara Banúrji.	16
	Cp.	Note on a Copper plate grant found in the Record Office of the Cuttack Collectorate. Babu Rangalála Banerjea. (With a Plate.)	149
	A.	Note on Khánjá-Khán Garh in the District of Bardwán, Jahánábád. Babu Gour Das Bysack.	165
	Cp.	Notes on, and translations of, three Copper-plate inscriptions from Sambalpur. Babu Pratapa Chandra Ghosha	173
	R.	Notice of a prehistoric Burial place with cruciform Monoliths, near Mungapet in the Nizám's Dominions. William King. (With 2 Plates.).....................	179
XLVII. (1878.)	Cp.	A Copperplate grant from Banda. Dr. Rájendralála Mitra. (With a Plate.)....	73
	Cp.	Notes on two Copperplate inscriptions found in the Hamirpur District. V. A. Smith. With a note by Babu Pránnáth Pandit...	80
		The Antiquities of Bagura (Bogra). H. Beveridge.	89
XLVIII. (1879.)	R.	Prehistoric Remains in Central India. J. H. Rivett-Carnac. (With 5 Plates.)	1
	I. & Sc.	Bulandshahar Antiquities. F. S. Growse. (With 3 Plates). With a Note by Dr. Rájendralála Mitra.	270
	A. & I.	Observations on some Chandel Antiquities. V. A. Smith and F. C. Black. (With 6 Plates.)	285
XLIX. (1880.)	A.	Description of the Great Siva Temple of Gangai Kondapuram and of some other	

Journal.			
		places in the Trichinopoli District. Lieut.-Col. B. R. Branfill. (With a Plate.)	1
Vol. XLIX. (1880.)	R.	Rude Megalithic monuments in North Arcot. Lieut.-Col. B. R. Branfill. (With a Plate.)	8
	I.	Note on an inscription fourd upon a stone lying near the ruins of a Masjid on Lanka Island, Walar Lake, Kashmir. Major H. S. Jarrett.	16
	V.	Memorandum on Clay discs called spindle whorls and votive seals found at Sankisa, Bihar and other Buddhist ruins in the North-Western Provinces of India. H. Rivett-Carnac. (With 3 Plates.)	127
	V.	Supplementary Memorandum. By the same.	137
L. (1881.)		On the identity of Upello with Upaplava. Pandit Rishi Kesh Bhuttacharya.	103
	V.	Relics from Ancient Persia in Gold, Silver and Copper. No. I. Major-General A. Cunningham. (With 9 Plates.)	151
LI. (1882.)	P.	Note on some earthen pots found in the alluvium at Mahesvara (Mahesar). P. N. Bose. (With 2 Plates.)	226
LII. (1883.)	V.	Relics from Ancient Persia, in Gold, Silver, and Copper. No. II. Major-General A. Cunningham. (Wth 2 Plates.)	64
	I.	Note on a Sanskrit Inscription from the Lalitpur District. Dr. Rájendralála Mitra.	67
	A.	Notes on the Remains of old Fort William, discovered during the erection of the East Indian Railway Company's Offices. R. Roskell Bayne. (With 5 Plates.)	105
	A.	On the temples of Deoghar. Dr. Rájendralála Mitra. (With a Plate.)	164
	R.	On stone implements from the North Western Provinces. H. Rivett-Carnac. (With 3 Plates).	221
	Sc. & V.	The town of Bulandshahar. F. S. Growse. (With 2 Plates.)	270

Proceedings.			
(1865.)	I.	Inscription on a Baoli at Khasia. J. Beames.	66
	A.	Ruins in Manbhúm. Lieut. R. C. Beavan...	66
		Large mass of iron found under the ruins of a temple near Jubbalpore. Lieut. W. G. Murray and Mr. J. Lewis. (With a Plate.)	76
	R.	Flint arrow heads found in the Jubbalpore district. Lieut. Swiney.	77
	A.	Antiquities of Gaya. T. F. Peppe and C. Horne 80, 150,	162
	A.	Antiquities at Bairat, Ajmir, Gwalior, Khajuráha and Mahoba. Major-General A. Cunningham	97
	A.	Remarks on some temples in Kashmir. Bishop Cotton	165
	I.	Some remarks on the rock-inscriptions near Khalsi. R. E. Forrest................	199
(1866.)	R.	A perforated stone found on a "chabutra" at Jubbalpur. V. J. Carey. (With a Plate.)	135
(1867.)	R.	Stone implements found in India. W. T. Blanford, V. Ball and others	136
(1868.)		Note on the village of Paindhat in the District of Mainpuri. F. S. Growse	63
		An old relic in the shape of a human iron cage. Rev. F. F. Mazuchelli	79
	R.	Cromlechs of Central India. J. Mulheran. (With a Plate) 116,	148
	R.	Cromlechs in Coorg. Captain R. A. Cole. (With 2 Plates.).............. 151, 184,	243
	I.	Facsimile and sealing wax impression of an inscription found in Rájsháhí. Babu Kumára Chandranáth Raya............	163
	R.	Flint implements collected in the neighbourhood of Jabalpur. Col. R. E. Oakes....	51
	R.	Memorandum on Cromlechs found in Coorg. Lieut. R. E. Cole.	54

Proceedings.	Cp.		
(1869.)		Notes on a copperplate Inscription in the possession of certain Kols at Nágpur. Babu Bakhal Das Haldar.	203
	R.	Notes on the remains found in a Cromlech at Coorg. Dr. T. Oldham.	226
		Note on some Agate beads from North-Western India. W. Theobald. (With a Plate.)	253
(1870.)	I. & Sc.	Inscription on the back of a statuette found at Kopari, Zillah Balasore. J. Beames. (With a Plate.)	4
	I.	Observation on a Sanad, granted by Sháh Álam to Rája Pityámbar Mitra Bahádur. H. Blochmann.	6
	R.	Note on the Kitchen-middens of the Andaman Islands. Dr. F. Stoliczka.	13
	R. & P.	Iron implements, etc., found in a cromlech in the estate of Major Sweet, in the south of the Nilghery plateau. Col. G. H. Saxton.	52
	R.	Collection of stone implements from Central India. H. Rivett-Carnac.............	54
	V.	Silver and copper objects found near the village of Gungeria. A. Bloomfield. (With a Plate.)...........................	131
	R.	A stone implement from Prome. W. Theobald.	220
	I. & Sc.	A Sanskrit Inscription and several drawings of rude Carvings, near Attock. Major F. W. Stubbs	241
	R.	Stone implements from Dibrughar. Lieutenant E. H. Steel. (With 2 Plates.) ..	267
	A.	The Monolith at Kosumbha in the Allahabad District. C. A. Elliott.	291
	I.	Two inscriptions from Patna and the Mandar Hill. Dr. Rájendralála Mitra.......	294
	R.	On some North Arrakan Celts. St. John...	83
		On some old Dutch records of the settlement of Chinsurah. E. Lethbridge.........	85
	R.	Two copper axes. Captain W. L. Samuells.	231

Proceedings.			
(1871)	I.	Note on three Arabic Inscriptions by early Muhammadan Kings of Bengal, received from Mr. A. Broadley. H. Blochmann...	245
	A.	A set of photographs of temples, etc. in Behar. T. F. Peppe.	251
(1872.)	R.	A collection of Celts from Burma. Captain Fryer	46
	I.	Several Persian Inscriptions from Badáon. H. Blochmann.	47
	Cp.	A Copperplate Inscription found at Karenne, Hill Tracts. Arrakan. Captain W. G. Hughes.	138
	I.	Two Persian inscriptions from Sambhalherá, Muzaffarnagar, North Western Provinces; from A. C. Cadell. H. Blochmann.	165
	I.	Three Persian inscriptions from Kol, near Aligarh. From E. T. Atkinson. H. Blochmann.	166
	I.	Some Persian inscriptions from Miyan Mir. Major F. W. Stubbs	168
	A. & I.	On the Archæological remains of Basantpur in zillah Bhágalpur. J. W. B. Martin ..	175
	Cp.	Memorandum on Copper Grants found in the Malnad or Hill Tracts of the Nagar Division. R. Cole....................	193
	I.	Two inscriptions of Bhágalpur. Babu Rájendralála Mitra.......................	198
(1873.)	I.	A Persian inscription on the tomb of Shaikh Miná at Lukhnau, from Major F. W. Stubbs. H. Blochmann.	11
	I.	Persian and Hindustani inscriptions on buildings in the city of Mathura, from F. S. Growse. H. Blochmann...............	12
	I.	General Cunningham's Bengal Inscriptions (Muhammadan Period). H. Blochmman.	17
	A.	Extracts from Notes on Hemadpauti Temples, etc., in West Berar. Major R. Gill.	66
	Cp.	Transcripts in Sanskrit of the two Gunja Agrahár and Koppa Gadde Sásanas. (See Proc. for 1872, p. 193.)	75

Proceedings.			
(1873.)	I.	Persian Inscriptions from Sonpat and Pánipat. J. G. Delmerick.	94
	I.	Persian Inscriptions from Sambhal, Amrohah and Muradabad. Babu Gungá Pershad and Mr. H. Blochmann.	98
	I.	Sanskrit Inscriptions from Sárabala and Nádáyana. J. G. Delmerick and Dr. R. Mitra.	102
	I.	Persian Inscriptions from Jaunpur, Paniput and Muzaffarnagar. H. Blochmann.	129
	I.	Persian inscriptions from Ráprí, Mahobá, and Dihli. H. Blochmann.	156
	I.	Persian inscriptions from Biánah, Ajmir and Agrah. T. W. Beale	159
	I.	Persian inscriptions from Dihli, Badáon, Champanagar and Kanauj. H. Blochmann.	197
(1874.)		Identification of towns in Jessore. H. J. Rainey.	19
	I.	Persian inscriptions from Írich, Piparai, and Abúhar and Sirsá. H. Blochmann	69
	R.	On ancient perforated stone found in the Satpura Hills.	96
	I.	Persian inscriptions from Badáon, Dihli, Agra, Suján Deo, Benares, Sakít. H. Blochmann.	100
		Memorandum on operations of the Archæological Survey for the season 1873-74. Major General A. Cunningham	108
	A.	Memorandum on the remains at Garhwa, near Sheorájpur in the Allahabad District. E. T. Atkinson	123
	I.	Persian inscriptions from Agra, Fatehpur Sikri, Fírúzábád, Gwaliar; from Mr. T. W. Beale. H. Blochmann.	160
	I.	Persian Inscriptions from Agra, Sikandra and Nárnaul. H. Blochmann.	209
(1875.)	I.	Persian Inscriptions from Jaunpur and Tilbigrampur. H. Blochmann.	14

Proceedings.			
(1875.)	I.	Stone inscription near Toorsa, Aheri Zemindari, District Chanda, Central Provinces; from Captain R. Beavan. Hon'ble E. C. Bayley. (With a Plate.)	62
	I.	Sanskrit inscriptions from Benares. Dr. R. Mitra..	82
	A.	On the present state of the ruins of Gaur. L. B. B. King.	93
	I.	An inscription found at Srinagar near Madhipúra. W. B. Martin	107
	I.	Persian inscriptions from Kashmir and Agra. H. Blochmann.	113
	I.	Arabic and Persian Inscriptions from Dehli. H. Blochmann.	212
	I.	Portuguese Inscriptions from Mombassa. Dr. Da Cunha.	214
		Extracts from an Arabic work relating to Aden in former times.	218
(1876.)	R.	On stone weapons from Burma. Major General Sir A. P. Phayre....................	3
	I.	Arabic and Persian Inscriptions from Dehli, Rohtás and Sahasrám. H. Blochmann....	4
	I.	Sanskrit and Hindi inscriptions from Rohtás. Dr. R. Mitra.........	109
	R.	On an ancient Kitchen-Midden near Cuttack. V. Ball	120
	R.	On stone implements found in the Tributary States of Orissa.	122
	Cp.	Copper plate grant of Govinda Chandra of Kanauj. Dr. R. Mitra.	130
	A.	Ancient dwellings and Tombs in Baluchistan. Captain E. Mockler	172
(1877.)	Cp.	Copper land grant from Pandukeswar. Dr. R. Mitra. (With a Plate.)	71
	I.	Arabic and Persian inscriptions from Hisar Firúzah, Hánsi and Azamgarh. H. Blochmann.... 99,	117

Proceedings.			
(1877.)	P.	On ancient pottery, etc. from Baluchistan. W. T. Blanford. (With a Plate).	157
	I.	On the Háthigumpha Inscription. Dr. R. Mitra.	163
	I.	Persian Inscriptions from Jessore. H. Blochmann	256
	A.	Antiquities of Buddha Gaya. Dr. R. Mitra.	258
(1878)	Sc.	Figure of Buddha found at Sárnáth. H. Rivett-Carnac.	66
	Sc.	A Buddhist sculpture from Pathári. Captain J. Waterhouse and Dr. R. Mitra. (With a Plate.)	122
(1879)	I. & A.	Donative Inscription from Rajaurgarh. Dr. R. Mitra.	157
	Sc.	Description of stone carvings in the Doab. R. Rivett-Carnac. (With a Plate.)	189
	I.	Two small Buddhist Inscriptions, in Sandwé District, Arrakan Division. Lieut. Col. G. E. Fryer. (With a Plate.)	201
	Cp.	A copper plate inscription from Nirmand, in Kulu. Dr. R. Mitra.	212
		Note on an inscription from the Gate of the Krishna Dváraka Temple at Gaya. Dr. R. Mitra.	218
(1880.)	.	Old palm leaf Manuscripts, in Bengali characters and dated in the Sena era. Dr. R. Mitra.	4
		A rock-cut inscription near the falls of Keoti Kunda. Dr. A. F. Rudolf Hoernle.	55
		Remarks on a Pali inscription from Bárhut. Dr. R. Mitra.	58
		Note on an inscription on an ancient Mosque in Koh Inám, zillah Allahabad. Major H. S. Jarrett.	72
		Two inscriptions from Buddha Gaya. Dr. R. Mitra. (With a Plate.)	76
		Two Copper plate Inscriptions from Sylhet. Dr. R. Mitra.	141

Proceedings.			
(1880.)	R.	On a celt of the Palæolithic type, found at Thandiani, Panjab. Rev. Charles Swynnerton. (With a Plate.)	175
	Sc.	Specimen of Yusafzai Sculpture. Rev. Charles Swynnerton.	196
(1881.)	I.	Some old Hindi Inscriptions found in an Idgáh near Mungir. Mr. Martin and Dr. R. Mitra.	42
	P.	Some antiquities from Khokkra Kote, near Rohtak. Dr. A. F. Rudolf Hoernle. (With a woodcut.)	69
	Sc.	Some brass figures dug up near a mound called Jowhridi, in the Muzaffarpur District. J. E. Lineke.........................	98
	Sc.	Note on a Buddhist sculpture found at Bulandshahar. F. S. Growse.	112
	P.	Note on some curiosities found at Bulandshahar. F. S. Growse........................	113
	V.	Note on a curious old seal, found at Bulandshahar. F. S. Growse	120
	Cp.	A new reading of the Sue Vihára copper plate. Dr. A. F. Rudolf Hoernle.	139
(1882.)	R.	Stone implements from Banda. H. Rivett-Carnac.	6
	Cp.	Note on a copper plate grant from Cuttack. Dr. R. Mitra..	9
		On a Banknote of the Ming dynasty (1368 A. D.). Sir Pope Hennessy. (With a facsimile.)	77
		On a birch bark Manuscript found at Bakhshálí in the Yusufzai District. Dr. A. F. Rudolf Hoernle.	108
	V.	On three clay seals, found at Surat. Dr. R. Mitra.	114
(1883.)	A.	Excavations on the site of old Fort William. R. R. Bayne.	42

Pro-ceedings. (1873.)	I.	Note on a Kutila inscription from Mungir. W. E. Westmacott. (With a Plate.) ..	45
		Note on Mahisamati or Mahesvara (Mahesar) on the Narmadá, and the identification of Hiouen Thsang's Mahesvarapura. P. N. Bose.	127

N. B.—Some more notices of stone implements will be found in the Classified Index to the Scientific Papers of the Society, Chapter VI, Ethnology.

II.

COINS, GEMS, WEIGHTS AND MEASURES.

[Abbreviations: A. = Arakanese: B. = Bactrian: Bg. = Muhammadan, of Bengal: C. = Ceylonese: G. = Gupta: Gh. = Ghaznavite: Gr. = Greek: H. = Ancient Hindu or Buddhist: I. = Indo-Scythian: J. = Muhammadan, of Jaunpur: M. = Dehli Moghuls: P. = Dehli Pathan: R. = Roman: S. = Sassanian: Su. = Surashtrian.]

As. Res.			
Vol. II. (1790.)	R.	On some Roman Coins found at Nelore. Alexander Davidson	331
V. (1798.)		On Indian weights and measures. H. T. Colebrooke	91
XVII. (1832.)	B., I., Gr., etc.	Description of select coins, from originals or drawings in the possession of the Asiatic Society. H. H. Wilson. (With 5 Plates.)	559
Journal Vol. I. (1832.)	R.	On the ancient Roman Coins in the Cabinet of the Asiatic Society. James Prinsep. (With 4 Plates.)	392
	R.	Roman Coins in Upper India.	476
II. (1833.)	Gr.	On the Greek Coins in the Cabinet of the Asiatic Society. James Prinsep. (With 2 Plates.)	27
	Gr. & B.	Note on Lieutenant Burnes' Collection of Ancient Coins. James Prinsep. (With a Plate.)	310

Journal. Vol.	B., I., G., etc.		
II. (1833.)		Bactrian and Indo-Scythian coins (continued). James Prinsep. (With a Plate.)............	405
	G.	Note on the Inscription on the Hindu Coins. J. Prinsep..................................	649
(III.) (1834.)	B. & I.	Memoir on the ancient coins found at Beghram, in the Kohistan of Kabul. Chas. Masson. (With 6 Plates.)	153
	H. & G.	Note on the coins found by Captain Cautly at Behat. James Prinsep. (With a Plate.)............................	227
	I. & S.	On the coins and Relics delivered by M. le Chevalier Ventura, General in the service of Mahárája Ranjit Singh, in the Tope of Manikyála. James Prinsep. (With 2 Plates.)	313
	H.	Note on two coins of the same species as those found at Behat, having Greek inscriptions. Major D. L. Stacy. (With a Plate.)................................	431
	I., S., H.	Continuation of observations on the Coins and Relics discovered by General Ventura, in the Tope of Manikyala. J. Prinsep. (With a Plate.)	436
	R. & I.	Note on the Coins, discovered by M. Court. Jas. Prinsep. (With 2 Plates.)........	562
	R.	Correction of a mistake regarding some of the Roman Coins found in the Tope at Manikyala, opened by M. Court. Lieut. Alexander Cunningham...............	635
IV. (1835.)	B. & I.	Further notes and drawings of Bactrian and Indo-Scythic coins. James Prinsep. (With 8 Plates.)	327
	I. & G.	On the connection of various ancient Hindu Coins with the Grecian or Indo-Scythic Series. James Prinsep. (With 6 Plates.)	621
	H. & Su.	Notice of Ancient Hindu coins. James Prinsep. (With 4 Plates.)................	668

Journal.	B., I. & S.		
Vol. V. (1836.)		Second Memoir on the ancient coins found at Beghram, in the Kohistan of Kabúl. (With 3 Plates.)	1
	I.	Note on some Indo-Scythic Coins found by Mr. C. Masson at Beghram, in the Kohistan of Kabúl. Johannes Avdall.	266
		Third Memoir on the ancient coins, discovered at the site, called Beghram, in the Kohistan of Kabúl. Charles Masson. ..	537
	B.	New varieties of Bactrian coins from Mr. Masson's drawings and other sources. James Prinsep. (With a Plate.)	548
	I., G. & H.	New varieties of the Mithraic or Indo-Scythic series of coins and their imitations. James Prinsep. (With 3 Plates.)	639
	B. & I.	New types of Bactrian and Indo-Scythic coins. James Prinsep. (With a Plate.)	720
VII. (1837.)	I.	On the explanation of the Indo-Scythic legends of the Bactric coins through the medium of the Celtic. Dr. J. Swiney. ..	98
	S., H. & C.	Specimens of Hindu coins descended from the Parthian type, and of the ancient coins of Ceylon. James Prinsep. (With 3 Plates.)	288
	Su.	The legends of the Saurashtra group of coins deciphered. James Prinsep. (With a Plate.).............................	377
VII. (1838.)	S.	On the application of a new method of black-printing, with examples of unedited coins printed in facsimiles. James Prinsep. (With a Plate.)	414
	B.	Additions to Bactrian Numismatics and discovery of the Bactrian alphabet. James Prinsep. (With 3 Plates.)...........	636
		Report on the Weights, Measures and Coins of Cabul and Bukhara. Nowrozjee Furdoujee.	892

Journal Vol.			
VII. (1838.)	H.	Coins and Relics from Bactria. James Prinsep. (With 2 Plates.)	1047
	H.	Ancient Hindu Coins from Jaunpur and Oojein. James Prinsep. (With 2 Plates.)	1052
IX. Part I. (1840.)	B.	Account of Coins found at Bameean. Capt. Hay. (With a Plate.)	68
	B.	Note on Bameean Coins. H. Torrens	70
	B.	Note of discoveries of gems from Kandahar. Lieutenant Conolly.	97
	B.	Note on above. H. Torrens. (With 3 Plates.)	100
	B.	Notice of some counterfeit Bactrian coins. Captain Alexander Cunningham.........	543, 393
	B. & S.	Notes on Captain Hay's Bactrian coins. Capt. Alexander Cunningham. (With 4 Plates.)	531
Part II.	B.	Description of, and deduction from, a consideration of some new Bactrian coins. Lieut. Alexander Cunningham. (With a Plate.)	867
		Extract from Proceedings of the Numismatic Society of London on the mode of taking casts.	938
	B.	Note on the coins of Mayas. Lieutenant A. Cunningham...............	1008
	B. & I.	Second Notice of some forged coins of the Bactrian and Indo-Scythians. Lieutenant Alexander Cunningham.	1217
X. Part I. (1841.)	B. S. H.	Description of some ancient gems and seals from Bactria, the Panjab and India. Captain A. Cunningham. (With a Plate.) ...	147
		Mode of taking facsimiles of coins. Vincent Tregear.........	158
	Bg.	Muhammadan coins of Bengal, found at Howrah. Hon. H. T. Prinsep. (In the Proceedings.)................................	168
Part II.	B. & S.	Notes on the gems found at Beghram. J. S. Chapman. (With a Plate.)	613

Journal.			
Vol. XI. Part I. (1842.)	B.	Second notice of some new Bactrian Coins. Capt. A. Cunningham. (With a Plate.)	130
	B.	On some gems and coins. H. Torrens. (With a Plate.)................................	137
	S., etc.	On a cylinder and certain gems, collected from Herat by Major Pottinger. H. Torrens. (With a Plate.)......................	316
XII. Part I. (1843.)		Descriptive list of some coins lately received from the University of Christiana by the Asiatic Society. Dr. E. Roer..............	443
XIII. Part II. (1844.)	A.	Remarks on a Buddhist Coin or Medal, sent to the Society through Captain Macleod, by His Highness the Prince of Makkara. Captain T. Latter. (With a Plate.)	571
XIV. Part I. (1845.)	I.	Notice of some unpublished coins of the Indo-Scythians. Lieut. Alexander Cunningham. (With a Plate.)	430
XV. 1846.)	A.	The historical coins of Arakan. Captain A. P. Phayre. (With a Plate.)	232
	A.	The symbolical coins of Arakan. Lieut. T. Latter. (With a Plate.)	238
	Bg.	On the Coins of the independent Muhammadan Sovereigns of Bengal. J. W. Laidlay. (With 2 Plates.)	323
XVIII. Part II. (1849.)		On preparing facsimiles of coins, etc. J. W. Laidlay.	976
XX. (1851.)	I.	Translation of some uncertain Greek legends on coins of Indo-Scythian princes of Cabul. H. Torrens.	137

Journal.			
Vol. XX. (1851.)		An account of eight Kufic silver coins. E. Thomas. (With a Plate.)	537
	R.	Remarks on some lately discovered Roman gold coins. Captain Drury. Communicated by General Cullen through the Hon'ble W. Elliott.	371
	S.	On Sassanian Coins. Edward Thomas.	525
XXI. (1852.)	G.	Some ancient Gupta gold coins, found near Benares. Major M. Kittoe and E. C. Bayley. (With a Plate.)............ .	390
	G. & H.	Note on three ancient coins found at Muhammadpore, in the Jessore District. Babu Rájendrálála Mitra. (With a Plate.) ..	401
	Gh.	Note on Col. Stacy's Ghazni coins. E. Thomas. (With a Plate.)	115
XXIII. (1854.)	H.	Coins of Indian Buddhist Satraps, with Greek inscriptions. Major A. Cunningham. (With 2 Plates.)	679
XXIV. (1855.)	G.	On the coins of the Gupta dynasty. Edward Thomas.	483
XXVII. (1858.)		Catalogue of coins in the Cabinet of the late Col. Stacy, with the estimated prices attached. E. Thomas.	251
		Coin collections lost during the rebellion. George H. Freeling.	169
XXXII. (1863.)	A.	Memorandum on some medals and coins in the Museum of the Asiatic Society, found near Mergui on the Tenasserim Coast. Lieut. Col. A. P. Phayre. (With 6 Plates.)	271

Journal.			
Vol. XXXIII. (1864.)	H.	On ancient Indian Weights. E. Thomas....	251
		Table of the coins of former Governments more or less current in the Bazars of the Gujarát District in 1859. (With 4 Plates.)	434
XXXIV. (1865.)	H.	Ancient Indian Weights. E. Thomas. (With 2 Plates.)............................	51, 46, 14
	B.	Coin of Sophytes. General A. Cunningham.	46
	H.	Coins of the nine Nágas, and of two other dynasties of Narwar and Gwalior. Major-General A. Cunningham. (With a Plate.)	115
XXXVI. (1867.)	Bg. & P.	The inital coinage of Bengal. E. Thomas. (With 2 Plates)	1
XL. (1871.)	P.	Note on a gold coin of Prince Fírúz Sháh Zafar, son of Fírúz Sháh of Delhi. Hon'ble E. C. Bayley. (With a Woodcut.) ...	160
XLI. (1872.)	A.	Note on an Arakanese coin. Capt. G. E. Fryer. (With 3 Woodcuts.)	201
XLII. (1873.)	H.	Notes on two coins from Kausambhi. Hon'ble E. C. Bayley. (With a Woodcut.)	109
	H.	Further note on coins from Kausambhi. Hon'ble E. C. Bayley........................	191
	Bg.	Contributions to the History and Geography of Bengal; from unpublished coins. H. Blochmann. (With 2 Plates.)	209
	P. & Bg.	Note on two Muhammadan coins. Hon'ble E. C. Bayley....................................	311
	Bg.	The initial coinage of Bengal. Part II. E. Thomas. (With a Plate.)	343
XLIII. (1874.)	P.	Note on a new gold coin of Mahmúd Sháh bin Muhammad Sháh bin Tughlaq Sháh,	

Journal.			
		of Dihli. J. G. Delmerick. (With a Woodcut.)	97
Vol. XLIII. (1874.)	S.	Note on a hoard of 543 Sassanian coins in the possession of Colonel H. Hyde. Hon'ble E. C. Bayley. (With a Plate.)...	99
XLIV. (1875.)	H.	On a coin of Kunanda from Karnál. Dr. Rájendrálála Mitra. (With a Woodcut.)..	82
	P., M., J.	List of rare Muhammadan coins. J. G. Delmerick.	126
	Bg.	Contributions to the History and Geography of Bengal. From unpublished coins. H. Blochmann. (With a Plate.)	275
XLV. (1876.)	P., M., Bg., etc.	List of rare Muhammadan coins. No. II, (coins of the kings of Dilhi, Malwah, Bengal, Kulburga and Kashmir). J. G. Delmerick. (With 2 Plates.)..............	291
XLVIII. (1879.)	H.	The copper coins of the old Mahárájás of Kashmir. C. J. Rodgers. (With 2 Plates.)	277
		The copper coins of the Sultans of Kashmir. C. J. Rodgers. (With a Plate.)	282
XLIX. (1880.)	H.	The coins of the Mahárájas of Kángrá. C. J. Rodgers. (With a Plate.)	10
	H.	Coins of the Sunga or Mitra Dynasty, found near Rámanagar or Ahichhatra, the ancient capital of Panchála, in Rohilkhand. A. C. Carlleyle. (With a Plate.)	21
	P.	Coins of Ghiásuddín and Muizzuddín bin Sám. C. R. Stulpnagel. (With a Plate.)	29
	P.	Coins supplementary to Thomas' Chronicles of the Pathan Kings of Dehli. C. J. Rodgers. (With 4 Plates.)	207, 81

Journal.			
Vol. XLIX. (1880.)	H.	Memorandum on coins of the Sunga Dynasty by H. Rivett-Carnac. (With 3 Plates.) ...	87
	H.	Note on some copper Buddhist coins. H. Rivett-Carnac. (With 2 Plates.)	138
	M.	Copper coins of Akbar. Chas. J. Rodgers. (With 2 Plates.)	213
L. (1881.)	P. & Bg.	A new find of early Muhammadan coins of Bengal. Dr. A. F. Rudolf Hoernle. (With 4 Plates.)	53
	H.	On the coins of the Sikhs. Chas. J. Rodgers. (With 5 Plates.)	71
		On the coins of Charibael, king of the Homerites and Sabæans. Major W. F. Prideaux. (With a Plate.)	95
	G.	Relics from Ancient Persia in gold, silver and copper. Major-General A. Cunningham. (With 9 Plates.)	151
LII. (1883.)	H.	The Pagoda or Varáha coins of Southern India. Dr. G. Bidie. (With 3 Plates.)..	33
	P.	Coins supplementary to Thomas' Chronicles of the Pathan Kings of Delhi. No. III. Chas. J. Rodgers. (With 2 Plates.)	55
	M.	The Rupees of the months of the Iláhi years of Akbar. Ch. J. Rodgers. (With 2 Plates.)	97
	Bg.	A new find of Muhammadan coins of Bengal. (Independent period: Nasiruddin Mahmud II and Bárbak Shah). Dr. A. F. Rudolf Hoernle. (With 2 Plates.) ...	211
Proceedings. (1865.)		On double currency in India. E. Thomas and Major Lees......................	208
(1867.)	B.	A coin of Sophytes. Major C. H. Strutt. (With a Woodcut.)	106

Proceedings.			
(1868.)	B.	A rare tretradrachm of Antimachus Theos, and a coin of Azilises. H. F. Blanford. (With a Plate inserted as No. III in the Proceedings for 1869.)……	164
(1869.)	M.	Coins of Jahángír. H. Blochmann. (With a Plate.)…… 245,	255
		Note on a Malwah Gold Mohur. H. Blochmann. (With a Woodcut.)……	266
(1870.)	P. & J.	Muhammadan Copper coins, dug up near Partábgarh, presented by M. L. Ferrar. H. Blochmann. ……	151
	P. M.	Muhammadan Coins, sent by A. Carlleyle. E. C. Bayley. (With a Woodcut.)……	181
	P.	Counterfeit coins of obsolete Muhammadan mintages. Major F. W. Stubbs……	302
(1871.)	M.	On a coin of Muhammad Bedar Bakht. H. Blochmann. ……	97
	B.	A hoard of 74 Indo-Bactrian Hemidrachms in the Rawalpindi District. J. G. Delmerick. ……	276
(1872.)	H	Three large and three small Assam silver coins from Mr. J. M. Foster. Babu Pratápa Chandra Ghosha. ……	2
		Gold coins from the Island of Cheduba. Col. Sir A. Phayre. ……	3
	B.	A unique tetradrachm of a new Bactrian King, Plato the Illustrious. J. G. Delmerick. ……	34
	P.	A silver coin of Udaipur and of Alauddin Muhammad Sháh. Sirdar Attar Singh….	55
		Two Dakhin and one Bengal silver coins, exhibited by Col. H. Hyde. H. Blochmann……	118

Proceedings.			
(1872.)	B.	On the notice of the coin of Plato. E. Thomas.	174
	P. & Bg.	Readings of rare Bengal coins of Col. Guthrie. Hon'ble E. C. Bayley.	199
(1873.)	P.	Pathan Coins from Rupar. H. Blochmann.	155
(1874.)	P.	A gold coin of Mahmúd ibn Muhammad Shah ibn Tughluq Shah. J. G. Delmerick.	92
	Bg.	On a coin of Ghiyásuddin Azam Sháh. Hon. E. C. Bayley.	156
		On Col. H. Hyde's gold and silver coins. H. Blochmann.	207
	P.	On five Muhammadan silver coins.	239
(1875.)	H.	On a coin of Kunanda. E. Thomas and Babu R. Mitra.	163
(1876.)		Gold, Silver and Copper coins from Kashgar. H. Blochmann.	90
	P.	Unique gold coin of Nasiruddin Mahmúd Sháh. H. Blochmann. (With a Woodcut.)	91
	M.	On a silver coin of Shahjehán II.	139
(1877.)	Bg.	On a coin of Muhammad Adil Sháh. H. Blochmann.	156
(1878.)	P.	A unique gold coin of Jaláluddin Firúz Sháh II of Dihli. H. Blochmann. (With a Woodcut.)	65
	H.	On a coin of Toramána. Dr. R. Mitra. (With a Woodcut.)	191
(1879.)	I. & R.	Coins from the Ahin Posh Tope near Jalálábád, Afghánistán. Mr. Simpson and Captain Waterhouse.	77

Proceedings.	P. & Bg.		
(1879.)		Muhammadan coins of Delhi and Bengal. Dr. R. Mitra.	119
	I. & R.	Description of the coins found in the Ahin Posh Tope. Dr. A. F. Rudolf Hoernle. (With 3 Plates.)	122
	Gh.	Coins of Khusrau Sháh and Khusrau Malik, the Ghaznavi Kings of Lahore. C. J. Rodgers. (With a Plate.)	178
	I. & R.	Notes on the gold coins found in the Ahin Posh stúpa. Major-General A. Cunningham. (With 3 Plates.)	205
	I.	Remarks on the above. Dr. A. F. Rudolf Hoernle	210
(1880.)	H.	Coins of the Sunga or Mitra Dynasty. Dr. R. Mitra.	8
	A.	On Arakan coins. Dr. R. Mitra.	53
	B. & H.	On Bactrian and South Indian gold and silver coins. Major-Generals G. G. Pearse and A. Cunningham.	115
	R., I., G.	On eleven gold coins, Roman, Indo-Scythian and Gupta. Dr. A. F. Rudolf Hoernle	118
(1881.)	Gh.	On coins of Gazni Sultans. C. J. Rodgers.	5
	G., J., etc.	On some gold and silver coins, Gupta, Jaunpur, etc. Dr. A. F. Rudolf Hoernle. (With 2 Woodcuts.)	39
	H.	Two old Hindi silver coins from Sarnáth. Dr. A. F. Rudolf Hoernle. (With a Woodcut.)	41
	J.	Silver coins of the Jaunpúr Sultans. Dr. R. Mitra.	41
	H.	Some Copper coins dug out at Khokhrakote near Rohtak. Dr. A. F. Rudolf Hoernle. (With a Woodcut.)	71
	P.	On a silver coin of Shamsuddin Kaimurs. J. G. Delmerick and Major-General A. Cunningham. (With a Woodcut.)	157

Proceedings.			
(1882.)	Su.	On a collection of Surashtrian coins. Dr. R. Mitra.	41
	H.	On a gold Ramtinki coin. Hon'ble J. Gibbs.	49
	H.	On five Andhrabhritya coins. Hon'ble J. Gibbs.	59
	G.	On three gold Gupta coins. Dr. A. F. Rudolf Hoernle. (With a Woodcut.)	91, 104
	H.	On a number of Buddhist coins found at Toomluk. Dr. A. F. Rudolf Hoernle.	111
	Su.	On a number of Surashtrian silver coins. Dr. A. F. Rudolf Hoernle.	114
		A set of fifty-five specimen coins struck from the old dies in the Calcutta Mint. Col. J. Tennant.	139
(1883.)	M.	On two enormous gold coins of Sháh Jehán and Aurangzíb. Hon'ble J. Gibbs. (With a Plate.)	3
	M.	On some very rare Muhammadan coins. Hon'ble J. Gibbs. (With a Woodcut.)	4
	M.	On Mogul silver coins called *niṣárs*, etc. C. J. Rodgers. (With a Plate.)	11, 59
	Bg.	On some coins of Ilyás Sháh and Sikandar Sháh of Bengal. Dr. A. F. Rudolf Hoernle	59
	H.	Note on Ramtinkis. Hon'ble J. Gibbs	76
		On coins of the Durrani Dynasty. M. Longworth Dames.	96

III.

HISTORY.

[N. B. The entries marked with (*) are partly antiquarian; those marked with (†) partly philological.

As. Res.		
Vol. I.	Remarks on the city of Tagara. Lieut. Francis Wilford.	369
	A conversation with Abram, an Abyssinian, on the city of Gwender and the sources of the Nile. Sir William Jones.	383
II. (1790.)	† On the descent of the Afghans from the Jews. Henry Vansittart. With a note by Sir William Jones.	67
	On the Chronology of the Hindus. Sir William Jones.	111
	A Supplement to the Essay on Indian Chronology. Sir William Jones. (With a Plate.)	389
III. (1792.)	An account of the Battle of Paniput and of the events leading to it. Written in Persian by Cási Raja Pandit, who was present at the battle. Translated by James Browne.	88
	On Egypt and other countries adjacent to the Cáli river or Nile of Ethiopia, from the ancient Books of the Hindus. Lieutenant Francis Wilford.	295
	On the Origin and Families of Nations. The ninth anniversary Discourse. Sir William Jones.	479
IV. (1795.)	On Asiatick History, Civil and Natural. The tenth anniversary discourse. Sir William Jones.	1
	A dissertation on Semiramis, the origin of Mecca, etc., from the Hindu Sacred Books. Lieutenant Francis Wilford.	363

As. Res.		
Vol. V. (1798.)	Historical Remarks on the Coast of Malabar. Jonathan Duncan.	1
	On the Chronology of the Hindus. Captain Francis Wilford. (With a Table.)	241
VI. (1799.)	On Mount Caucasus. Captain Francis Wilford.....	455
VII. (1801.)	A Chronological Table of the Moghul Emperors, from Amir Timúr to Alamgir II, the father of the emperor Sháh Alam, being from A. H. 736 to 1173, or A. D. 1335 to 1760. Lewis Ferdinand Smith.	447
VIII. (1805.)	An Essay on the Sacred Isles in the West, with other Essays connected with that work. Captain F. Wilford. (With 3 Plates.)	245
IX. (1807.)	An Essay on the Sacred Isles in the West, with other Essays connected with that work. Captain F. Wilford. (With a Table.)	32
	Essay II. Anu-Gangam or the Gangetic Provinces and more particularly of Magadha. ..	32
	Essay III. of the Kings of Magadha, their Chronology.	82
	Essay IV. Vicramaditya and Salivahana; their respective Eras, with an account of the Bala-Rayas or Balhar Emperors.	117
X. (1808.)	An Essay on the Sacred Isles in the West, with other Essays, connected with that work. Captain. F. Wilford.	
	Essay V. Origin and Decline of the Christian Religion in India. (With 2 Plates.)	27
XI. (1810.)	An Essay on the Sacred Isles in the West, with other Essays connected with that work.	
	Essay VI. of Swetam or the White Island, called Sacam.	1
XIV. (1822.)	On the ancient Geography of India. Lieut.-Col. Francis Wilford.	373

As. Res.		
Vol. XV. (1825.)	An Essay on the Hindu History of Cashmir. Horace Hayman Wilson.	1
	Of the Pandæa Regio of the classical writers. H. H. Wilson.	95
	On the date of Yudhisthir, etc. H. H. Wilson.	97
	On the war between Jarasandha and Crishna. H. H. Wilson.	100
	On the Gandháras or Gandarii and other nations of the Panjab and North West of India. H. H. Wilson.	103
	On the ancient names of Cashmir in classical writers. H. H. Wilson.	115
	* An account, Geographical, Statistical and Historical, of Orissa proper or Cuttack. A. Stirling. (With 5 Plates.)	163
XVI. (1828.)	Historical and Statistical sketch of Aracan. Charles Paton.	353
XVII. (1832.)	Remarks on the portion of the Dionysiacs of Nonnus, relating to the Indians. H. H. Wilson.	607
Journal. Vol. II. (1833.)	On the reputed descendants of Alexander the Great, in the Valley of the Oxus. Lieut. Alexander Burnes.	305
III. (1834.)	Supplement to the Historical Remarks on the Allahabad Inscription, No. 2. Rev. W. H. Mill.	339
IV. (1835.)	Notice of Pugan, the ancient capital of the Burmese Empire. Lieut. Col. H. Burney.	400
V. (1836.)	Memoir of the Life and writings of St. Nierses Clajensis, surnamed the Graceful, Pontiff of Armenia. Johannes Avdall.	129

Journal.		
Vol. V. (1836.)	Notes on the Buddhas from Ceylonese authorities, with an attempt to fix the dates of the appearance of the last four, being those of the Mahábhadra Kalpa (or present age). Capt. J. Forbes.	321
	Memoir of a Hindu colony in Ancient Armenia. Johannes Avdall.	331
	Note on the origin of the Armenian era and the reformation of the Haican Kalendar. Johannes Avdall.	384
	Conjectures on the march of Alexander. M. Court.	387
	Examination of some points of Buddhist Chronology. George Turnour.	521
	A brief account of Masa'úd, known by the name of Farid Shakarganj or Shakarbár. Munshi Mohan Lál.	635
	Notice of the Vallabhi dynasty of Saurashtra; extracted from the Buddhist records of the Chinese. Eugene Jacquet.	685
	Note on a remnant of the Hun nation. Captain W. Foley.	813
VI. (1837.)	The history of Labong from the native records consulted by Dr. D. Richardson.	55
	Singular narrative of the Armenian King Arsaces and his contemporary Sapor, King of Persia; extracted from the Armenian Chronicles. Johannes Avdall.	81
	Some account of the wars between Burma and China together with the journals and routes of different embassies sent to Pekin by the King of Ava; taken from Burmese documents. Lieut. Col. H. Burney...........................	542, 405, 121
	An examination of the Pali Buddhistical Annals. Hon'ble George Turnour..................	713, 501
	History of the Garha Mandala Rajas. Captain W. H. Sleeman.	621
	History of the Rajas of Orissa from the reign of Raja Yudhishthira, translated from the Vansávali. Andrew Stirling.	756
	Account of the Tooth relic of Ceylon, supposed to be alluded to in the opening passage of the Feroz lát inscription. Hon'ble George Turnour.	856

Journal.		
Vol. VII. (1838.)	History of Cooch Behar, being an extract of a passage from Dr. Buchanan's account of Rangpur. Major F. Jenkins.	1
	Account of the expedition of Chach (Chacha) extracted from the Chach Nameh, and extracts from the Tohfat ul Khwán. Ensign Postans.	93, 297
	An examination of the Pali Buddhistical Annals. No. 3. Hon'ble George Turnour.	686, 789
	The same. No. 4.	919
	The same. No. 5.	991
VIII. (1839.)	Collection of facts which may be useful for the comprehension of Alexander the Great's exploits on the western banks of the Indus. M. Court. (With a Map.)............................	304
IX. Part I. (1840.)	Points in the history of the Greek and Indo-Scythian Kings in Bactria, Cabul and India, as illustrated by deciphering the ancient legends on their coins. Christian Lassen.	251, 339, 449
Part II.	The same. (Continued.)....................	627, 733
	On the historical Geography of Hindustan, and the origin of the social state among the Hindus. Jas. Bird.	884
	A short Memoir of Mechithar Ghosh, the Armenian legislator. Johannes Avdall.	967
X. Part I. (1841.)	Note on the Brahooees. Captain Hart.	136
	Of the early History of Sindh from the Chach Namah and other authorities. Lieut. Postans.	183, 267
XII. Part I. (1843.)	Brief history of Kelat, brought down to the deposition and death of Mehrab Khan, Brahoee. Major Robert Leech.	473
XIII. Part I. (1844.)	On the history of Arakan. Capt. A. P. Phayre.....	23
	View of the principal events in the Karnatic, between 1564 and 1687; compiled from various anthentic Memoirs and original manuscripts. Colonel Mackenzie.	578, 421
Part II.	Index to History of the Toorks by Baron Hammer Von Purgstall. Dr. E. Roer.	550

Journal.		
Vol. XIV. Part I. (1845.) Part II.	An account of the early Ghiljáees. Major R. Leech.	306
	An account of the early Abdalees. Major R. Leech.	445
	* Report of a trial for Rebellion, held at Moulmein by the Commissioner of Tenasserim. (With a Plate.)	747
	Further notes respecting the late Csoma de Körös. Lieut. Col. Lloyd and A. Campbell.	823
XVI. Part I. (1847.) Part II.	Remarks on the sequel to the Periplus of the Erythrean sea, and on the country of the Seres, as described by Ammianus Marcellinus. Dr. J. Taylor.	1
	* Notes on places in the province of Bihar, supposed to be those described by Chy-Fa-Hian, the Chinese Buddhist Priest, who made a pilgrimaga to India, at the close of the fourth century. A. D. Capt. M. Kittoe. (With 3 Plates.)..................	953
	An attempt to identify some of the places mentioned in the itinerary of Hiuan Thsang. Major William Anderson.	1183
XVII. Part I. (1848.)	Verification of the itinerary of Hwan Thsang through Ariana and India, with reference to Major Anderson's hypothesis of its modern compilation. Capt. Alexander Cunningham.	476
XVII. Part II. (1848.)	Verification of the itinerary of the Chinese Pilgrim, Hwan Thsang, through Afghanistan and India, during the first half of the seventh century of the Christian era. Capt. A. Cunningham. (With a Map.)	13
	Fragments of the history of Mooltan, Derajat and Baháwalpur, from Persian manuscripts. Lieut. R. Maclagan..................................	559
	* Some account of the battle field of Alexander and Porus. Capt. James Abbott. (With a Plate.) ..	619
XVIII. Part I. (1849.)	A narrative of our connexions with the Dusanee and Cheanee Garrows, with a short account of their country. Capt. C. S. Reynolds................	45

Journal.		
Vol. XVIII. Part I. (1849.)	General observations on the contending claims to antiquity of Brahmans and Buddhists. Lieut. Col. Low.	89
	Addendum on the Battlefield of Alexander and Porus. Capt. James Abbott.	176
	The Rajas of Sialkote. Capt. James Abbott.	177
XIX. (1850.)	Some conjectures on the progress of the Brahminical conquerors of India. Henry Torrens.	1
	On the Ghassanite Kings. Dr. A. Sprenger.	469
XX. (1851.)	A comparative Essay on the ancient geography of India. Col. F. Wilford.	470, 227
	Chronology of Makkah and the Hijaz before Muhammad, chiefly founded upon genealogy. Dr. A. Sprenger.	349
XXIII. (1854.)	* On the Ballads and legends of the Panjab. Major J. Abbott. (With a Plate.)	59
	A Sketch of the Mahomedan History of Cashmere. Lieut. D. J. F. Newall.	409
	† Some Remarks on the origin of the Afghan people and dialect. Lieut. H. G. Raverty.	550
XXIV. (1855.)	On the epoch of the Gupta dynasty. E. Thomas.	371
XXIX. (1860.)	Attempts of Asiatic sovereigns to establish a paper currency. E. B. Cowell	183
XXX. (1861.)	Note on Buddha Gupta. Dr. Fitz-Edward Hall.	139
	Letter on some recent statements touching certain of the Gupta kings and others. Dr. Fitz-Edward Hall.	383

Journal.		
Vol. XXXI. (1862.)	* Vestiges of three royal lines of Kanyakubja or Kanauj; with indications of its Literature. Dr. Fitz-Edward Hall.	1
	* Vestiges of the Kings of Gwalior. Babu Rájendralála Mitra. (With 4 Plates.)	391
XXXII. (1863.)	* Bhoja Raja of Dhár and his Homonyms. Babu Rájendralála Mitra. (With a Plate.)	91
	* Aornos. Lieut. Col. J. Abbott.	409
XXXIII. (1864.)	On the history of the Burmah Race. Lieut. Col. A. P. Phayre.	1
	Remarks on the date of the Pehewa inscriptions of Raja Bhoja. Major General A. Cunningham.	223
	Extract from a letter from Major General A. Cunningham.	229
XXXIV. (1865.)	Notes on the Gurjat States of Patna. Major H. B. Impey.	101
	* On the Sena Rájas of Bengal as commemorated in an inscription from Rajsháhi, deciphered and translated by C. T. Metcalfe. Babu Rájendralála Mitra.	128
XXXV. (1866.)	* Assyro-Pseudo-Sesostris. Hyde Clarke. (With a Plate.)	87
XXXVI. (1867.)	Note on Sirájuddaulah and the town of Murshidábád, taken from a Persian manuscript of the Táríkh i Mançúri. H. Blochmann.	85
XXXVII. (1868.)	On the history of the Burmah Race. Col. Sir A. Phayre.	74
XXXVIII. (1869.)	On the history of the Burmah Race. Col. Sir Arthur Phayre.	29
XXXIX (1870.)	A covenant of 'Ali, fourth Caliph of Baghdad. J. Avdall.	60

Journal.		
Vol. XL. (1871.)	* The district of Dera Ismáil Khan, Trans-Indus. T. W. H. Tolbort. (With a Map)	1
	A history of the Gakkhars. J. G. Delmerick.	67
	Notes from the Muhammadan historians on Chutia Nágpur, Pachet and Palámau. H. Blochmann. ..	111
	The Moghul invasions of Palámau. L. R. Forbes ...	129
	Note on the death of Humáyun. C. J. Rodgers. ..	133
	Note on the above. H. Blochmann.	136
XLI. (1872.)	Note on Ghargaon, Asám. J. M. Foster. (With a Plate.)	32
	Koch Bihár, Koch Hájo and Asám, in the 16th and 17th centuries, according to the Akbarnámah, the Padisháhnámah and the Fathiyah i 'Ibriyah. H. Blochmann.	49
	The conquest of South India in the 12th century by Parákrama Báhu, the great King of Ceylon. T. W. Rhys Davids.	197
	On a new king of Bengal and notes on the Husainí dynasty and their conquest of Chatgaon (Chittagong). H. Blochmann.	331
XLII. (1873.)	The history of Pegu. Major General Sir Arthur P. Phayre..................................	23, 120
	Authorities for the history of the Portuguese in India. T. W. H. Tolbort.	193
	* Contributions to the Geography and History of Bengal. Part II, historical. Based on inscriptions and unpublished coins. H. Blochmann. (With 6 Plates.)	209
XLIII. (1874.)	On the history of Pegu. Major General Sir A. P. Phayre (continued).	6
	Translation of an Arabic pamphlet on the history and doctrines of the Wahhábis, written by the grandson of Abdul Wahhab, founder of the sect. J. O'Kinealy.	68

Journal.		
Vol. XLIII. (1874.)	Annals of Omán, from early times to the year 1728 A. D. From an Arabic manuscript by Sheykh Sirhán bin Sa'íd bin Sirhán bin Muhammad of the Benú 'Alí tribe, of Omán. Transl. and annotated by E. C. Ross.	111
	On the Bárah Bhuyas of Eastern Bengal. Dr. James Wise. (With a Plate.)	197
	Notes on Sháh Ísmail Ghází, with a sketch of the contents of a Persian Manuscript, entitled "Risálat ush Shuhadá," found at Kántá Duár.	215
	On the supposed identity of the Greeks with the Yavanas of the Sanskrit writers. Dr. Rájendralála Mitra.	246
	* Contributions to the Geography and History of Bengal. No. II. H. Blochmann.	280
XLIV. (1875.)	Who were the Patan or Pathan Sultans of Dehli? Major G. H. Raverty........................	24
	The Bárah Bhuyas of Bengal. No. II. Dr. James Wise....................................	181
	* Contributions to the History and Geography of Bengal. No. III. H. Blochmann. (With a Plate.)	275
XLV. (1876.)	Were the Sundarbans inhabited in ancient times? H. Beveridge.	71
	The Bhars of Audh and Benares. Patrick Carnegy.	297
	Reply to several passages in Mr. Blochmann's "Contributions to the History and Geography of Bengal." No. III. Major H. G. Raverty..........	325
XLVI. (1877.)	Notes on the Bhars and other early inhabitants of Bundelkhand. Vincent A. Smith..............	227
XLVII. (1878.)	Note on Gorakshanáth and the Yogís. G. R. Grierson.	138
	The Pála kings of Rangpur. G. A. Grierson.	140
	The Bangash Nawábs of Farrukhabad. A chronicle (1713—1857). William Irvine. Part I.	259
	The Pála and the Sena Rájás of Bengal. Rájendralála Mitra.	384
XLVIII. (1879.)	The Bangash Nawábs of Farrukhábád. A chonicle. (1713—1857). William Irvine. Part II.	49

Journal.		
Vol. L. (1881.)	Contributions to the History of Bundelkhand. Vincent A. Smith.	1
	On the revenues of the Mughal Empire. H. G. Keene.	99
	The revenues of the Mughal Empire. Edward Thomas.	147
	Contributions on the Religion, History, etc. of Tibet. Babu Sarat Chandra Das.	211, 235
Extra-No.	On the genealogy of Bidyápati and the Rájas of Tirhut. G. A. Grierson. (In Introduction to Maithólí Language, Part II).	39
LI. (1882.)	Memoir of the Author of the Tabaqát-i-Násirí. Major H. G. Raverty.	77
LII. (1883.)	Notes on the history of Orissa. J. Beames.	2
Proceedings. (1865.)	Mahomedan conquest of India. Dr. A. Sprenger. (With a map.)	100
(1868.)	Queries regarding races of India. P. Carnegy.	86
(1869.)	Contributions to the Chronology of the reigns of Timúr and his descendants up to Shahjehán. No. I. H. Blochmann.	207
(1870.)	Notes on places of historical interest in the District of Húghly. H. Blochmann.	109
(1871.)	On the birth place of Todar Mall. M. L. Ferrar and H. Blochmann.	178
	A history of the Village of Arurá, Tahsil Jágráon, zillah Lúdhiáná. Attar Singh.	247
(1872.)	On the birthplace of Todar Mall. M. L. Ferrar and H. Blochmann.	35
	Note on Father Tieffenthaler. Lieut. Col. A. S. Allan.	59
	On Todar Mall's birthplace. Babu Kashináth.	141

Proceedings.		
(1875.)	On the Kanishka Dates. Hon'ble E. C. Bayley and Dr. R. Mitra.	45
(1876.)	Invasion of Bengal by Kullotunga, in the time of Mahipála. Dr. Burnell......................	107
(1878.)	On the early life of Asoka. Dr. Rájendralála Mitra.	1
	A legend regarding the origin of the name Chháyápati or "lord of the Shadows," a small Taluq in Pargana Hoglá, Zillah Jessore. H. James Rainey.	105
(1879.)	Note on Jainism. (Reprint). E. Thomas...	1
(1880.)	On the Lakshmana Sena Era. Dr. R. Mitra.	119
(1881.)	On the origin of the myth about Kerberos. Dr. R, Mitra.	91

IV.

LANGUAGE AND LITERATURE.

[Abbreviations: A. = Arabic: D. = Drávidian: G. = Gauḍian: I. A. = Indo-Aryan of the N. W. Frontier: I. C. = Indo-Chinese: K. = Kolarian: M = Malayan: P. = Páli: Pr. = Prákrit: Ps. = Persian: S. = Sanskrit: T. B. = Tibeto-Birman.]

As. Res.			
Vol. I. (1788.)		A dissertation on the Orthography of Asiatick words in Roman letters. Sir William Jones.	1
	S.	On the Literature of the Hindus. Goverdhan Caul.	340
II. (1790.)		On the second Classical Book of Odes of the Chinese. Sir William Jones. (With a Plate.)	195
	A.	On the Introduction of Arabic into Persian. (With two Tables.)	205
III. (1792.)	S. & Ps.	On the mystical poetry of the Persians and Hindus. Sir William Jones.	165
IV. (1795.)	S. & A.	On the Philosophy of the Asiaticks. The eleventh discourse, 20th Feby. 1794. Sir William Jones.	165
		On the traces of the Hindu Language and Literature, extract among the Malays. William Marsden.	221
	S.	Catalogue of Indian Plants comprehending their Sanskrit and as many of their Linnæan generic names as could with any degree of precision be ascertained. Sir William Jones.	229
		Specimen of the Andaman Language. Lieut. R. H. Colebrooke.	392

As. Res.			
Vol. V. (1798.)	D.	Specimen of the language of the people inhabiting the Hills in the vicinity of Bhagalpur. Major R. E. Roberts.	127
	T. B.	Observations on the Alphabetical System of the language of Ava and Aracan. Captain John Towers. (With 2 Plates.)	143
	T. B.	A comparative Vocabulary of some of the languages spoken in the Burma empire. Dr. Francis Buchanan.	219
		Remarks on the names of the Cabirian Deities and on some words used in the mysteries of Elensis. Captain Francis Wilford.	297
	S.	The Rudhirádhyáya or sanguinary Chapter, translated from the Cálicá Purána by W. C. Blaquiere.	371
VI. (1799.)	M.	Specimen of the language of the Poggy Islands. John Crisp.	77
VII. (1801.)	T. B.	Specimen of the Kookie language. John Macrae.	197
	S. & Pr.	On the Sanskrit and Prakrit languages. H. T. Colebrooke.	199
	D.	A summary account of the Life and writings of Asgar, a Tamul female philosopher. Rev. Dr. John.	345
	Gd.	A list of Gipsy and Hindustani words. Captain David Richardson.	481
VIII. (1805.)	A.	Extracts from the Tehzeebul Mantik or "Essence of Logic," as a Supplement to Arabic and Persian Grammar, and an elucidation of certain points of Oriental Literature. Francis Balfour	89
	S.	On the Vedas or Sacred Writings of the Hindus. H. T. Celebrooke............	369

As. Res.	M. & I. C.		
Vol. X. (1808)		On the Language and Literature of the Indo-Chinese Nations. D. J. Leyden.........	158
	S. & G.	On Sanskrit and Prakrit Poetry. H. T. Colebrooke.........................	389
	A.	Remarks upon the authorities of Musalman Law. J. H. Harington.........	475
	Ps.	Translations of two letters of Nadir Shah, with introductory observations. General John Malcolm.	526
XI. (1809.)	G. & S.	A catalogue of Indian Medical Plants and Drugs, with their names in the Hindustani and Sanskrit languages. Dr. John Fleming........................	153
XII. (1810.)	M.	On the Maláyu nation, with a translation of its maritime Institutions. Thomas Raffles.	102
XIV. (1822.)	S.	Account of a discovery of a modern imitation of the Vedas, with remarks on the genuine works. Francis Ellis.	1
XVI. (1828.)	T. B.	Notice of the Language, Literature and Religion of the Bauddhas of Nepál and Bhot (Tibet.) B. H. Hodgson. (With 3 Plates).	409
	T. B.	Notice of three Tracts received from Nepal. Horace Hayman Wilson. (With 3 Plates.)	450
XX. (1836-39.)	T. B.	Analysis of the Dulva, a portion of the Tibetan work entitled the Kah-Gyur. Alexander Csoma Körösi.....................	41
	S.	Essay on Sanscrit alliteration. Rev. William Yates.	135
	T. B.	Notices of the Life of Shákya, extracted from the Tibetan Authorities. Alexander Csoma Körösi.	285

As. Res.			
Vol. XX. 1836-39.	S.	Review of the Naishadha Charita, or adventures of Nala Rájá of Nishadha; a Sanscrit poem, by Sri Harsha of Cashmir, with a commentary by Prema Chandra, published by the Asiatic Society, 1836. Rev. William Yates.	318
	I. C.	On Siamese Literature. Captain James Low.	338
	T. B.	Analysis of the Sher-Chin-Phal-Chhen-Dkon Seks-Do De-Nyáng Dás and Gyut. Being the second Division of the Tibetan work, entitled the Kah-Gyur. Alexander Csoma Körösi.	393
		Abstract of the Contents of the *B*stan *H*gyur. Alexander Csoma Körösi.	553
Journal. Vol. I. (1832.)	T. B.	Abstract of the Contents of the Dulva, or first portion of the Kah-Gyur, from the Analysis of Mr. Alexander Csoma de Körös. H. H. Wilson.	1
	S.	Analysis of the Puránas. Agni Purána. H. H. Wilson.	81
		On the poetry of Madagascar. Rev. W. Baker.	86
	S.	Analysis of the Puránas; the Brahma Vaivartta Purána. H. H. Wilson.	217
	T. B.	Translation of a Tibetan fragment by Mr. Csoma de Körös, with remarks by H. H. Wilson. (With Text.)	269
	T. B.	Analysis of the Kahgyur. H. H. Wilson.	375
	S.	Analysis of the Vishnu Purána. H. H. Wilson.	431
	S.	Analysis of the Vayu Purána. H. H. Wilson.	535
II. (1833.)	T. B.	Translation of a Tibetan Passport, dated A. D. 1688. Alexander Csoma de Körös.	201
	S.	The birth of Umá, a legend of Himálaya, by Calidasa.	329
	T. B.	Origin of the Shákya race translated from the La or the 26th volume of the mDo class in the Kágyur, commencing on the 161st leaf. Alexander Csoma de Körös. ..	385

Journal.	Ps.		
Vol. II. (1833.)		Specimens of some ornamental forms of Persian writing. Mahárája Kali Kishen Bahádur. (With a Plate.)	613
III. (1834.)	S. & T. B.	Professor Schlegel's Enigma. Mode of expressing numerals in the Sanskrit and Tibetan languages.	1
	T. B.	Extracts from Tibetan works, translated by Alexander Csoma de Körös............	57
		On the adaptation of the Roman Alphabet to the Orthography of Oriental Languages. (With a Plate.)......................	281
	A.	Roman orthography of Oriental words.	413
		Extracts from the Mohit, that is, the Ocean, a Turkish work on Navigation in the Indian Seas. Translated by the Baron Joseph von Hammer.	545
	T. B.	Tibetan Grammar and Dictionary of M. Csoma de Körös.	653
IV. (1835.)	T. B.	Analysis of a Tibetan work. Alexander Csoma de Körös.	1
V. (1836.)	A.	Extracts from the Mohit (the Ocean), a Turkish work on Navigation in the Indian Seas. Joseph von Hammer. (continued.)	441
VI. (1837.)	I. C.	Alphabets of the Tai language. Rev. N. Brown. (With 3 Plates.)	17
	A.	Remarks on M. Schlegel's objections to the restored edition of the Alif Laila, or Arabian Night's entertainments. Henry Torrens.	161
	G.	A Grammar of the Sindhi language. W. H. Wathen. (With a Plate.)	347
	G.	Translation of one of the Granthas, or sacred books, of the Dadu-panthí sect. Lieut. G. R. Siddons.	750, 480

Journal.			
Vol. VI. (1837.)	S.	Note on the primary language of the Buddhist writings. B. H. Hodgson.	682
		Note on the above. James Prinsep.	686
	A.	Extracts from the Mohit (the Ocean), a Turkish work on Navigation in the Indian Seas. Translated by Joseph von Hammer. (continued.)	805
	S.	Discovery of the Rekhá Ganita, a translation of the Elements of Euclid into Sanskrit by Samrát Jagannátha under the orders of Rája Siwái Jaya Singha of Jaipúr. Lancelot Wilkinson. (With a Plate.)	938
	I. C.	Interpretation of an Ahom extract. Major F. Jenkins.........................	980
	I. C.	Comparison of the Indo-Chinese languages. Rev. N. Brown......................	1023
VII. (1838.)	I. C.	Remarks on "a comparison of Indo-Chinese languages, etc." Rev. W. Morton.......	56
	S. & D.	Examination and Analysis of the Mackenzie Manuscripts deposited in the Madras College library. Rev. William Taylor...	173, 105
	T. B.	Enumeration of Historical and Grammatical works to be met with in Tibet. Alexander Csoma Körösi..................	147
	S.	On the ancient Sanskrit Numerals. James Prinsep. (With a Plate.)	348
	I. A.	On the Siah Posh Kafirs with specimens of their language and costume. Captain Alexander Burnes.....................	325
	S. & D.	Second Report on the Examination and Restoration of the Mackenzie Manuscripts. Rev. William Taylor..............	371, 469
	I. A.	Epitome of the Grammars of Brahuiky, the Balochky and the Panjabi languages, with Vocabularies of the Baraky, the Pashi, the Laghmani, the Cashgari, the Teeshai and the Deer dialects. Lieut. R. Leech.	780, 711, 608, 538
		Comparison of Asiatic Languages.	707

Journal.			
Vol. VII. (1838.)	A.	Extracts from the Mohit (the Ocean), a Turkish work on navigation in the Indian Seas. Translated by Joseph von Hammer.	767
VIII. (1839.)	I. A.	A grammar of the Pashtú or Afghaní Language. Lieutenant Leech.	1
	S.	Sisupála Badha or death of Sisupála by Magha. Translated, with annotations, by J. C. C. Sutherland.	16
	S.	The Mahimnástava, or a Hymn to Shiva; with an English translation. Rev. K. M. Banerji..........................	355
IX. Part I. (1840.)	T. B.	Note on the Lepchas of Sikkim, with a Vocabulary of their language. A. Campbell.	379
	T. B.	Limboo Vocabulary. A. Campbell.........	605
Part II.	K.	Grammatical construction of the Ho Language. Lieut. Tickell.................	997
	K.	Vocabulary of the Ho Language. Lieut. Tickell..........................	1063
X. Part II. (1841.)	T. B.	Comparison of the languages spoken in Arakan and in the Hill Districts adjoining. Lieut. Phayre.	711
	G.	Grammar and Vocabulary of the Cashmiri language. M. P. Edgeworth...........	1038
XI. Part I. (1842.)	T. B.	A Vocabulary of the Koonawur languages...	479
Part II.	S.	The avatars of Vishnu. An abstract translation from the Padma Purána. E. C. Ravenshaw..........................	1112
XII. Part I. (1843.)	G.	A Vocabulary of the Scindee language. Capt. J. B. Eastwick.	1
	S.	Translation of the Naipalia Devata Kalyana, with notes. B. H. Hodgson.	400

Journal			
Vol. XII. Part I. (1843.)	A.	As-Suyúti's work on Earthquakes. Transl. by A. Sprenger.	741
		M. Stanislas Julien on the study of the Chinese language. Transl. by H. Piddington.	816
		Tables of comparative philology, shewing specimens of the affinity of the Greek, Latin and English languages with the Sanskrit, Persian, Russian, Gaelic, Welsh, Lithnanian, German, Hebrew and Anglo-Saxon. Rev. James Long.	837
	G.	Notes on, and a short Vocabulary of, the Hinduví Dialect of Bundelkhand. Major R. Leech.	1086
XIII. Part I. (1844)	K.	Vocabulary of Gond and Cole words. From Dr. Voysey's Manuscripts.	19
	S.	Bháscarae Acharyae Siddhánta Shiromani sic dicti operis pars tertia, Gunitadhiam sive astronomiam continens, latine vertit, notasque adjecit. E. Roer.	53
	G.	A Grammar of the Cashmeeree language. Major R. Leech.	553, 397
Part II.	A.	Some original passages on the early commerce of the Arabs. Dr. A. Sprenger.	519
	A.	Notice of the Ajáib ul Makhlúqát. Capt. Newbold.	632
XIV. Part I. (1845.)	A.	Translation of the Taufat ul Kiram, a History of Sindh. Lieut. Postans.	155, 75
	S.	Vedánta Sára, or Essence of the Vedanta, an introduction to the Vedanta Philosophy by Sadánanda Parivrajakácharya. Translated by E. Roer.	100
	S.	Note on the course of study pursued by Students in the Sanskrit College, Calcutta. W. Seton-Karr.	135
Part II.		On the invention of the Armenian Alphabet. Johannes Avdall.	522

Journal.			
Vol. XIV. Part II. (1845.)	M.	A notice of the Alphabet of the Philippine Islands, by Don Sinibaldo de Mas. Translated by H. Piddington. (With a Plate.)	603
	P.	Review of L'histoire du Buddhism Indien, par E. Burnouf. Dr. E. Roer.	783
	S.	On the genuine character of the Horá Sástra, as regards the use of Greek terms. J. Muir.	809
XV. (1846.)	T. B.	Comparative vocabulary of languages of Hill tribes in Arakan. Lieut. T. Latter.	66
	M.	Small vocabulary of the Nancowry Language. Rev. P. Barbe.	366
XVI. Part I. (1847.)	S.	Bháshá Parichheda or Division of Language. A logical treatise. Translated by Dr. E. Roer.	157
	K.	Specimen of the language of the Goonds, in the District of Seonee, Chuprah; comprising a Vocabulary, Grammar, etc. Dr. O. Manger.	286
	A.	Hints to students of Arabic. Col. Lockett.	373
	S.	Report on the Vedas.	505
Part II.	S.	Literature and History of the Vedas. Three treatises by Dr. R. Roth.	812
	S.	Prashnottaramálá or Catechetical Dialogue of Sook. Translated by J. Christian. ...	1228
	T. B.	Comparative Vocabulary of Sub-Himaláyan dialects. B. H. Hodgson.	1245
XVII. Part I. (1848.)	S.	The most ancient Grammar of the Vedas or the Prátisákhya Sûtra. Dr. R. Roth. ...	6
		Library at Jessalmere. A. Sutherland.	158
	A.	Notices of some copies of the Arabic work entitled Rasáyil Ikhwán us Safá. Dr. A. Sprenger. Communicated by H. M. Elliott.	501
	G.	Hindi and Urdú Tazkiras. F. Edward Hall.	541
	I. C.	Khas language. B. H. Hodgson.	547

Journal.			
Vol. XVII. Part II. (1848.)	A.	Notice of the Ikhwán us Safá. Dr. A. Sprenger. Communicated by H. M. Elliott. (Continued.)	183
	A.	Bal'amy's translation of the History of Tabary, and Ghazzály's History of the prophets. Dr. A. Sprenger.	437
	D. & K.	Comparative Vocabulary of the aboriginal languages of Central India. B. H. Hodgson.	553
	T. B.	Vocabulary of the language of Chepáng. B. H. Hodgson.	655
	A.	A passage from Ibn Qotaybah's Adab ul Kátib on Arabic Astronomy. Dr. A. Sprenger. Communicated by H. M. Elliott. ...	659
XVIII. Part I. (1849.)		Notice of a Chinese Geographical work. J. W. Laidlay.	137
	T. B.	Notes on the languages spoken by the various tribes inhabiting the Valley of Assam and its mountain confines. William Robinson.	183, 310
	R.	Aborigines of Southern India. B. H. Hodgson.	350
	T. B.	On the Aborigines of North Eastern India. B. H. Hodgson.	451
		Notes by M. Johannes Avdall, on the extracts proposed from the work of Moses Khorensis.	588
Part II.	T. B.	On the Aborigines of the Eastern Frontier. B. H. Hogdson	967
XIX. (1850.)	A.	Notice of a copy of the fourth volume of the original text of Tabary. Dr. A. Sprenger. Communicated by Sir Henry Elliot.	108
	T. B. & I. C.	Aborigines of the North East Frontier. B. H Hodgson.	309
	G. & D.	Aborigines of the South. B. H. Hodgson....	461
	G.	Translation of the "Vichitra Nátak" or "beautiful Epitome," a fragment of the Sikh Granth, entitled "the Book of the tenth Pontiff." Capt. G. Siddons.	521

Journal.			
Vol. XIX. (1850.)	G.	Analysis of the Bengali poem Rajmálá, or Chronicles of Tripurá. Rev. James Long.	533
XX. (1851.)	A.	Observations on the physiology of the Arabic language. Dr. A. Sprenger. (With a Table.)	115
	T. B.	Notes on the Dophlás and the peculiarities of their language. William Robinson. ...	126
	A.	The initial letters of the nineteenth Súrah of the Qoran. D. A. Sprenger....	280
	G.	Translation of the Vichitra Nátak. Captain Siddons.	487, 314
	A.	On the earliest biography of Muhammad. Dr. A. Sprenger.	395
	S.	Review of a lecture on the Sankhyá Philosophy, embracing the text of the Tattwa Samása, by J. R. Ballantyne. Dr. E. Roer.	397
	Ps.	The Zafarnámah, a dialogue between Aristotle and Buzurjumihr. Transl. by Babu Narasinha Datta.	426
	S.	Comparative list of Upanishads. E. Roer and Walter Elliott.	607
XXI. (1852.)	G.	A Tale by Inshá Allah Khan. Translated by L. Clint..	1
	G.	On the connection of the Dative and Accusative cases in Bengali and Hindustani. Rev. W. Kay.	105
	A.	Foreign words occurring in the Qoran. Dr. A. Sprenger.	109
	T. B.	Vocabulary of the Heuma or "Shendoos" language in Arakan. Capt. S. R. Tickell.	212
	S.	Analysis of the Raghu Vansa, a Sanskrit poem of Kalidása. Rev. J. Long.	445
	G.	Has Sády of Shiráz written Rekhtah verses? Dr. A. Sprenger.	513
	A.	Muhammad's Journey to Syria and Professor Fleischer's opinion thereon. Dr. A. Sprenger.	576

Journal.			
Vol. XXII. (1853.)	I. C. & T. B.	On the Indo-Chinese Borderers and their connexion with the Himalayans and Tibetans.	1
	T. B.	On the Mongolian affinities of the Caucasians. B. H. Hodgson.	26
	T. B.	Sifán and Horsok Vocabularies, with another special exposition in the wide range of Mongolidan affinities and remarks on the lingual and physical characteristics of the family. B. H. Hodgson. (With a Plate.)	121
	A.	The first volume of the original text of Tabary. Dr. A. Sprenger.	195
	G.	Early Hindustani poetry. Dr. A. Sprenger.	442
	A.	Catalogues of Oriental libraries. Dr. A. Sprenger.	535
XXIII. (1854.)	A.	List of Arabic works preserved in a library at Aleppo, communicated by Captain Maclagan.	44
	G.	On the Ballads and legends of the Panjab. Rifacimento of the legends of Russáloo. Major J. Abbott.	123
		Manuscripts of the late Sir H. Elliott. Dr. A. Sprenger.	225
	I. A.	Some remarks on the origin of the Afghan people and dialect and on the connection of the Pushto language with the Zend and Pehlevi and the Hebrew. Lieut. H. G. Raverty	550
	P.	On the peculiarities of the Gáthá dialect. Babu Rajendralála Mitra.	604
XXIV. (1855.)	S.	Bibliographical notes on the published Upanishads with suggestions upon the publication of those which remain unedited. E. Roer.	38
	G.	A tale by Inshá Allah Khan. Translated by the Rev. S. Slater. (Continued.)	79
	T. B.	A brief notice of the Subháshita Ratna Nidhi of Saskya Pandita, with extracts and translations by M. A. Csoma de Körös.	141

Journal.			
Vol. XXIV. (1855.)	T. B.	Note on the Limboo Alphabet of the Sikkim Himalaya. Dr. A. Campbell. (With a Plate.)................................	202
	T. B.	Notes on the languages spoken by the Mishmis. W. Robinson..................	307
	S.	Ancient Indian Numerals. Edward Thomas. (With 2 Plates.)......................	551
	T. B.	Comparative vocabulary of some of the various languages spoken on the Eastern frontier of Bengal. Lieut. R. Stewart...	658
XXV. (1856.)	D.	Aborigines of the Nilgris. B. H. Hodgson. (With a Plate.)	498, 31
	D.	Aborigines of the Eastern Gháts. B. H. Hodgson.	39
	A.	Notes on Alfred von Kremer's edition of Wakidy's campaigns. Dr. A. Sprenger.	199, 53
	A.	Notice on the earliest work on Sufism as yet discovered, and on an Arabic Translation of a work ascribed to Enoch. Dr. A. Sprenger.	133
	T. B.	A slight notice of the Grammar of the Thadon or new Kookie language. Lieut. R. Stewart......	178
	B.	A brief notice of the Subháshita Ratna Nidhi of Saskya Pandita, with extracts and translations by the late M. A. Csoma de Körös.	257
	D.	Vocabulary of the Juanga language. Lieut. R. Stewart.	302
	A.	On the origin and progress of writing down historical facts among the Musalmans. Dr. A. Sprenger.	303, 375
XXVI. (1857.)	T. B.	Comparative vocabulary of the languages of the broken tribes of Nepal.	317
	T. B.	Comparative vocabulary of the Kiranti dialects. B. H. Hodgson................	350
	T. B.	Vocabulary of the Vayu language. B. H. Hodgson.	372

Journal.			
Vol. XXVI. (1857.)	T. B.	Grammar of the Vayu language. B. H. Hodgson.	429
		Vocabulary of the Bahing language. B. H. Hodgson.	486
XXVII. (1858.)	T. B.	Notes on the Karen languages. Francis Mason.	129
	S.	A few remarks on the first fasciculus of Professor Wilson's Sanskrit Dictionary, as "extended and improved" by Dr. Goldstücker. Fitz-Edward Hall.	301
	T. B.	Comparative vocabulary of the languages of the broken tribes of Nepaul. B. H. Hodgson.	393
XXVIII. (1859.)	S.	Fragments of three early Hindu dramatists Bháca, Rámila and Somila. Fitz-Edward Hall.	28
		Memorandum on Education in China drawn up from information afforded by the Ex-imperial Commissioner, Yeh. C. Alabaster.	48
	S.	The Sri-Sukta or Litany to Fortune; text and commentary, with translation. Fitz-Edward Hall...	121
		On the introduction of writing into India. Professor Max Müller.	136
	S.	Notices of new works relating to Sanskrit Literature.	501
XXIX. (1860.)	Ps.	On certain mediæval apologues. E. B. Cowell	10
	S.	On a passage in the tenth Book of the Sáhitya Darpana. E. B. Cowell.	217
	P.	The Kírán-us-Sádain of Mir Khusrau. E. B. Cowell.	225
	I. A	Is the Pushto a Semitic language? Rev. Isidor Loewenthal.	323

Journal.			
Vol. XXX. (1861.)	S.	Notices of new works relating to Sanskrit Literature. Mánava Kalpa Sútra.	42
	S.	Indian Idylls, No. 1. R. T. H. Griffith. ..	111
	Ps.	Gyges' ring in Plato and Nizámi. E. B. Cowell.	157
XXXI. (1862.)	S.	Rávana's commentary on the Rig Veda. Dr. Fitz-Edward Hall.	129
	S.	Notice of the Kumára Sambhava, 8th Canto.	203
	S.	The Chárváka System of Philosophy. E. B. Cowell.	371
	S.	Notice of the Bhámini Vilása............	527
XXXII. (1863.)	S.	On ancient Sanskrit numerals. Dr. Bhau Daji.	160
XXXIII. (1864.)	I. A.	On the language of the Siahposh Kafirs, with a short list of words; to which are added specimens of Kohistani and other dialects spoken on the northern border of Afghanistan, etc. Captain H. G. Raverty.	267
		On the application of the character of the Roman Alphabet to Oriental Languages. Capt. W. Nassau Lees.	345
	G.	On the origin of the Hindui language and its relation to the Urdú dialect. Babu Rájendralála Mitra.	489
XXXIV. (1865.)	T. B.	Note on the pronunciation of the Tibetan Language. Rev. H. A. Jaeschke.	91
XXXV. (1866.)	G.	Outlines of a plea for the Arabic element in official Hindustani. J. Beames.	1
	S.	A translation of the chapter on ordeals from the Vyávahára Mayúkha. Professor George Bühler.	14
		Manuscripts in the Grantha characters. Dr. R. Rost.	60

Journal.			
Vol. XXXV. (1866.)	A.	Remarks on Barbier de Maynard's edition of Ibn Khordádbeh and on the land-tax of the empire of the Khalyfs. Dr. A. Sprenger.	124
	S.	A notice of the Saunaka Smriti. Professor George Bühler.	149
	G.	Some objections to the modern style of official Hindustani. F. S. Growse.	172
	G. & T.B.	A vocabulary of English, Balti and Kashmiri. H. H. Godwin-Austen.	233
XXXVI. (1861.)		On the transliteration of Indian Alphabets in Roman characters. F. S. Growse.	136
	G.	On the Arabic Element in official Hindustani. J. Beames.	145
	S.	Certain Sanskrit Manuscripts on Geography of which no notice has been met with since the time. Colonel Wilford.	176
XXXVII. (1868.)	Ps.	Contributions to Persian Lexicography. H. Blochmann.	1
	G.	The poems of Chand Bardáí. F. S. Growse.	119
		Authors of Armenian Grammars from the earliest stages of Armenian Literature up to the present day. J. Avdall.	135
XXXVIII. (1869.)	G.	Further notes on the Prithiráj Rásau. F. S. Growse.	1
	T. B.	A vocabulary of the Garo and Konch dialects.	14
	Ps.	Badaoni and his works. H. Blochmann.	105
	G.	The nineteenth book of the Gestes of Prithiraj, by Chand Bardáí, entitled "the Marriage with Padmavati," literally translated from the old Hindi. John Beames.	145
	G.	Translations from Chand. F. S. Growse.	161
	G.	Reply to Mr. Growse.	170
	Ps.	Translations from the Táríkh-i-Firúz Sháhi. Major A. R. Fuller. Communicated by T. W. H. Tolbort.	181

Journal.	Ps.	Translations from the Táríkh-i-Fírúz Sháhí. Major A. R. Fuller..............	1
Vol. XXXIX. (1870.)	G.	Rejoinder to Mr. Beames. F. S. Growse.	52
	G.	Kashmiri test words. W. J. Elmslie.........	95
	D.	Gondi Words and Phrases. Rev. James Dawson.	108, 172
	G. & Pr.	Contributions towards Vernacular Lexicography. Babu Pratapa Chandra Ghosha...	131
XL. (1871.)	K.	An introduction to the Mundári language. Rakhal Das Haldar.	46
	K. &. D.	Names of Birds, etc. in four of the aboriginal languages of Western Bengal. V. Ball...	103
	S.	The Alla Upanishad, a spurious chapter of the Atharva Veda. Text, translation and notes. Rájendralála Mitra.............	170
	Ps.	Translations from the Tárikh-i-Fírúz Sháhí. P. Walley and A. Colvin.	185, 217
XLI. (1872.)	M.	List of words of the Nicobar languages as spoken at Camorta, Nancowry, Trinkutt and Katschal. E. H. Man.............	1
	T. B.	Specimen of a Nága Vocabulary. S. E. Peal.	29
	G.	Translations of selected portions of Book I of Chand Bardai's Epic. John Beames.	42
	G. &. Pr.	Essays in aid of a Comparative Grammar of the Gaurian languages. Dr. A. F. Rudolf Hoernle.	120
	G.	List of books contained in Chand's poem, the Prithirája Ráso. John Beames.	204
XLII. (1873.)	G. & Pr.	Essays in aid of a Comparative Grammar of the Gaurian languages. Dr. A. F. Rudolf Hoernle.	59
	G.	Studies in the Grammar of Chand Bardái. John Beames.............................	165
	G.	A metrical version of the opening stanzas of Chand's Prithiráj Rásau. F. S. Growse.	329

Journal.	T. B.	A rough comparative vocabulary of some of the dialects spoken in the Nága Hills. Captain J. Butler. (Appendix.)........	I
Vol. XLII. (1873.)	T. B.	Vocabulary of the Banpará Nágás. S. E. Peal. Appendix.	XXX
XLIII. (1874.)	G. & Pr.	Essays in aid of a Comparative Grammar of the Gaurian languages. No. V. Dr. A. F. Rudolf Hoernle.	22
	A.	Translation of an Arabic pamphlet on the Wahhábis. J. O'Kinealy.	68
	A.	Translation of the Arabic Annales of 'Omán. E. C. Ross........................	111
	Ps.	Persian texts of the Risálah-ush-Sháhadá. ..	222
	G. & Pr.	The Etymology of local names in Northern India, as exemplified in the District of Mathurá. F. S. Growse...............	324
XLIV. (1875.)	P.	Páli Studies. No. 1, Analysis and Text of the Subodhálankára or "easy Rhetoric" by Sangharakhita Thera. Maj. G. F. Fryer.	91
	S.	Translation of the Ayodhya Mahátmya or Pilgrimage of Ayodhya. Ram Náráyan...	130
	T. B.	Notes on Manipuri Grammar. G. H. Damant...........................	173
	G.	The Rhapsodies of Gambhír Rái, the bard of Núrpur, A. D. 1650. John Beames.	192
	T. B.	A rough comparative Vocabulary of two more of the dialects spoken in the "Nágá Hills." Compiled by Captain John Butler.	216
	S.	On the Sulva sútras. Dr. G. Thibaut. (With 4 Plates.)	227
	T. B.	Rough notes on the Angami Nágás and their language. (With 7 Plates.)	307
	G.	Popular songs of the Hamirpur District in Bundelkhand. Vincent A. Smith.	389
XLV. (1876.)	G.	The prologue to the Rámáyana of Tulsi Dás. A specimen translation. F. S. Growse. ..	1

Journal.			
Vol. XLV. (1876.)	I. A.	On the Ghalchah languages, Wakhí and Sarikolí. R. B. Shaw.	139
	G.	Popular songs of the Hamirpur District in Bundelkhand, No. II. Vincent A. Smith.	279
	Ps.	Translations from the Diwán of Zíb-un-nisá Begam, poetically styled "Makhfí," daughter of the emperor Aurangzíb. P. Whalley.	308
	G.	Srí Swámí Hari Dás of Brindaban. F. S. Growse. (With one Plate.)...........	312
XLVI. (1877.)	T. B.	Note on the old Manipuri character. G. H. Damant. (With 2 Plates.)............	36
	A.	On the Mo'allaqah of Lebíd, with a life of the poet as given in the Kitáb el Aghání. C. J. Lyall.	61
	I. A.	On the Shighni (Ghalchah) dialect. R. B. Shaw.	97
	A.	Metrical translation from the quatrains of 'Umar Khayyám. P. Whalley..........	158
	A.	Three translations from the Ḥamáseh. C. J. Lyall.	178
	G.	Notes on the Rangpur dialect. G. A. Grierson..............................	186
	Ps.	An unpublished Ghazal by Háfiz. H. Blochmann.	237
		A grammar of the language of Eastern Turkistan. R. B. Shaw.	242
	P.	Páli studies. No. II. Vuttodaya (Exposition of Metre), by Sangharakhita Thera. Major G. E. Fryer.	369
	S.	Contributions to the explanation of the Jyotisha Vedánga. G. Thibaut.	411
	A.	Translations from the Ḥamáseh and the Aghání. C. J. Lyall.	437
XLVII. (1878.)	A.	The Mo'allaqah of Zuheyr, rendered into English, with an introduction and notes. C. J. Lyall.	1

Journal.	I. A.		
Vol. XLVII. (1878.)	I. A.	Some Grammatical forms of the Dárd dialects spoken by Brokpás of Dáh-Hanu and of Drás. R. B. Shaw.	38
	G.	The song of Mánik Chandra. G. A. Grierson..........	135
	T. B.	The Lokaníti, translated from the Burmese Paraphrase. Lieut. R. C. Temple...........	239
Extra Number.		Sketch of the Turkí language, as spoken in Eastern Turkistan. Vocabulary. R. B. Shaw.	
XLVIII. (1879.)	G.	Hamír Rása, or a History of Hamír, prince of Rathambar. Translated from the Hindí. Babu Brajanátha Bandyopádhyáya....... ..	186
	P. & T.B.	Páli Derivations in Burmese. H. L. St. Barbe.	253
	T. B.	A peculiarity of the River names in Ásám and some of the adjoining countries.	258
XLIX. (1880.)	G.	A collection of Hindí Roots, with remarks on their Derivation and Classification. Dr. A. F. Rudolf Hoernle. (With an Appendix: Index.)	53
Extra-Number.	Pr.	On the Súrya Prajnapti. Dr. G. Thibaut.	107, 181
	I. A.	Sketch of the Northern Balochí Grammar, Vocabulary and Specimens of the language. M. Longworth Dames.................	
L. (1881.)	A.	Translations from the Ḥamáseh. C. J. Lyall.	107
LI. (1882.)	G.	Manbodh's Haribans. G. A. Grierson.	129
	G.	Some Hindú folksongs from the Panjáb. Lieut. R. C. Temple...................	151
Extra-Number.	G.	Introduction to the Maithilí of North Bihar. Grammar, Chrestomathy and Vocabulary. G. A. Grierson.	

Journal.			
Vol. LII. (1883.)	G.	Folklore from Eastern Gorakhpur. Hugh Fraser.	1
	G.	Notes on dialective peculiarities in the above. G. A. Grierson.	20
	G.	Folktales from the Upper Panjáb. Rev. C. Swynnerton.	81
	G.	Essays on Bihárí Declension and Conjugation. G. A. Grierson.	119
	G.	Note on the preceding Essay. Dr. A. F. Rudolf Hoernle.	159
	S.	On Goṇikaputra and Gonardíya, as names of Patanjali. Dr. Rájendralála Mitra.	261
Proceedings. (1865.)	T. B.	Tibetan Publications. Dr. H. Cleghorn and Rev. H. A. Jäschke.	12
	S. & A.	Apparent community of Amen and Om. Dr. R. Mitra and H. Blochmann.	46
	Ps.	Note on the Iqbál Námah-i-Jahángírí and other authorities for the history of the reign of the emperor Jahángír. Captain W. N. Lees.	114
		Indian Palæography. H. Blochmann.	171
(1866.)	G. & I. A.	Arian languages spoken in the territories of the Mahárája of Cashmere. Hon'ble G. Campbell.	46, 62
	S. & A.	Apparent community of Amen and Om. J. Beames and H. Blochmann.	192, 208
(1867.)		On the derivation of Aryan alphabets. E. Thomas, R. Mitra, E. C. Bayley.	51
		The tales of Nuddea. E. B. Cowell.	87
(1868.)	S.	Note on a Manuscript English translation of the Mahábhárata belonging to the Society. Rájendralála Mitra.	43
	G.	On an edition of the Prithiráj Rásau of Chand Bardáí. F. S. Growse, Rev. J. Long, J. Beames and others.	242, 63

Proceedings.			
(1868.)	A.	Notes on an Arabic history of the Panthays, with translation, Maulvi Abdul Latif. ..	142
	G.	Manuscripts of the poems of Chand.	63, 165, 242
	Ps.	Notes on the poems of Prince A'zamuddín, a grandson of Tipú Sultán, and on three other Persian poets, known under the name of Sultán. H. Blochmann.	220
(1869.)	Ps.	A magnificent Persian Manuscript of the Khiradnámah-i-Sikandarí, with autographs of Jahángír and Sháhjehán; belonging to Babu Pratapa Chandra Ghosa. H. Blochmann.	190
(1870.)	Ps.	Note on a Persian manuscript entitled Mirát-ul-Quds, a life of Christ, compiled at the request of the Emperor Akbar by Jerome Xavier. H. Blochmann.	138
		A short list of Andamanese test words. F. A. de Roepstorff.	178
	G.	On the relation of the Uriyá to the other modern Aryan languages. John Beames. With remarks by Babu Rájendralála Mitra.	112
	S.	Notes on the Charaka Sanhitá. Dr. Mahendralal Sircar.	284
(1871.)	G.	On a Hindí work on Kharakpúr. Babu Rash Bihári Bose.	98
	Ps.	Observations on a Persian manuscript on the lives of the twelve apostles, by Jerome Xavier. H. Blochmann.	138
(1872.)	G.	The Rhapsodies of Gambhír Rái, the Bard of Núrpur. (A. D. 1650). J. Beames.....	156
	G.	On the term "Gaurian" as a name for the Sanskritic Vernaculars of North India. Dr. A. F. Rudolf Hoernle and Babu Rájendralála Mitra.	177

Proceedings.			
(1873.)	G.	On an edition of the Prithiráj Rásau of Chand Bardáí.	122
(1874.)	S.	Sanskrit manuscripts in Jesalmír. Dr. G. Bühler.	93
(1875.)	T. B.	On the Manipuri Alphabet. G. H. Damant. (With a Plate.)	17
	S.	Report on Sanskrit manuscripts. Dr. Rájendralála Mitra.	63
	Ps.	A Persian manuscript on the buildings in Agra in Akbar's time. T. W. Beale.	117
(1877.)		On the Non-Aryan languages of India. (Reprint.) R. N. Cust.	6
	S.	Catalogue of Sanskrit Manuscripts in the Society's Library. Dr. R. Mitra.	183
(1878.)	G.	Rangpurí genitive in *kere.* G. A. Grierson.	64
	Pr.	A new Prákrit grammar, by Chaṇḍa. Dr. A. F. Rudolf Hoernle.	178
(1879.)	G.	On Dṛishṭa Kúṭa of Sur Dás. Babu Harish Chandra.	5
	P.	Note on the Rúpa Siddhi. Lieut. Col. G. E. Fryer.	155
(1881.)	S.	Note on a Manuscript of the Bhaṭṭi Kavya. Dr. R. Mitra. (With a Plate.)	134
(1882.)	P.	On the Páli Grammarian Kachcháyana. Lieut. Col. G. E. Fryer.	116
	P.	Remarks on the above. Dr. A. F. Rudolf Hoernle.	125
(1883.)	A.	On Tenses in Arabic. George Hughes.	129

V.

RELIGION, MANNERS AND CUSTOMS, ETC.

[*N. B.*—The entries marked with (*) are partly philological, those marked with (†) partly historical.]

As. Res.		
Vol. I. (1788.)	Account of an Interview with Teeshoo Lama at the Monastery of Terpaling. Samuel Turner.	199
	On the gods of Greece, Italy and India. Sir William Jones. (With 14 Plates.)	221
	On the Sikhs and their College at Patna. Charles Wilkins.	288
	On the Viná or Indian Lyre. Francis Fowke. (With a Plate.)	295
	On the Trial by Ordeal among the Hindus. Ali Ibrahim Khan. Communicated by Warren Hastings.	389
	History, Science and Art of Asia. The second anniversary discourse. Sir William Jones.	405
	On the Hindus. The third anniversary discourse. Sir William Jones.	415
II. (1790.)	Remarks on the Island of Hinzuan or Johanna. Sir William Jones.	77
	On the Indian Game of Chess. Sir William Jones.	159
	A description of Assam by Muhammad Cazim, transl. by Henry Vansittart.	171
	On two Hindu Festivals (of Bhavání and Húli) and the Indian Sphinx. Colonel Pearse.	333
III. (1792.)	On the musical modes of the Hindus. Sir William Jones. (With 2 Plates.)	55

As. Res.		
Vol. IV. (1795.)	Discourse delivered by Sir John Shore, 22nd May 1794.	181
	On the duties of a faithful Hindu Widow. Henry Colebrooke.	209
	On some extraordinary facts, customs and practices of the Hindus. Sir John Shore.	331
V. (1798.)	Historical Remarks on the coast of Malabar with some descriptions of the manners of its inhabitants.	1
	An account of two Fakeers, with their portraits. Jonathan Duncan. (With 2 Plates.)	37
	Enumeration of Indian classes. H. T. Colebrooke.	53
	On the religious ceremonies of the Hindus and of the Brahmins specially. H. T. Colebrooke.	345
VI. (1799.)	On the religion and literature of the Burmas. Dr. Francis Buchanan.	163
VII. (1801.)	On Singhala or Ceylon, and the Doctrines of Buddha from the Books of the Singhalais. Captain Mahony.	32
	On the religious ceremonies of the Hindus and of the Brahmins generally, Essay II. H. T. Colebrooke.	232
	Ditto; Essay III.	288
	On the origin and peculiar tenets of certain Muhammadan sects. H. T. Colebrooke.	338
	Account of the S. Thome Christians on the coast of Malabar. F. Wrede.	364
	Account of an hereditary living deity at Poona. Captain Edward Moore.	383
	On the Religion and Manners of the people of Ceylon by Mr. Joinville.	399
	On the Burma game of Chess, compared with the Indian, Chinese and Persian game of the same denomination. Captain Hiram Cox.	486
VIII. (1805.)	On the origin of the Hindu Religion. J. D. Patterson. (With a Plate.)	44

As. Res.		
Vol. IX. (1807.)	Account of the Jains, collected from a priest of the Sect. Transl. by Cavelly Boria, Bráhmen, for Major C. Mackenzie. (With 4 Plates.)	244
	Observations on the sect of Jains. H. T. Colebrooke.	287
	On the Gramas or Musical Scales of the Hindus. J. D. Patterson.	446
X. (1808.)	Remarks on the state of Agriculture in the district of Dinajpur. W. Carey. (With a Plate.)......	1
XI. (1810.)	Sketch of the Sikhs. Brigadier General Malcolm...	197
	On the Rosheniah sect, and its founder Bayezid Ansari. Dr. J. Leyden.	363
XII. (1816.)	An account of the funeral ceremonies of a Burman Priest. Dr. Wm. Carey.	186
XIII. (1820.)	On the existence of the Hindu Religion in the Island of Bali. John Crawfurd.	128
	Of the Murderers, called Phánsigárs. Dr. Sherwood. Communicated by Colonel McKenzie.	250
	Observations regarding Badheks and Thegs. John Shakespear.	282
	Ceremonies at the coronation of a Hindu Rájá. Mr. Brown.	311
XV. (1825.)	Snake worship in Cashmir. H. H. Wilson.........	94
	Of the Buddha Religion in Cashmir. H. H. Wilson.	110
XVI. (1828.)	A sketch of the religious sects of the Hindus. Horace Hayman Wilson......................	1
	Notice of the language, literature and religion of the Bauddhas of Nepal and Bhat (or Tibet). B. H. Hodgson. (With 3 Plates.)	409
XVII. (1832.)	Sketch of the Religious Sects of the Hindus. Horace Hayman Wilson.	169

As. Res.		
Vol. XX. (1836-39.)	On the administration of Justice in Nepal, with some account of the several courts, extent of their jurisdiction, and modes of procedure. B. H. Hodgson.	94
	On the Government of Siam. Captain James Low.	245
Journal. Vol. I. (1832.)	Notice of the peculiar tenets held by the followers of Syed Ahmed, taken chiefly from the "Sirat ul Mustaqim," a principal treatise of that sect, written, by Maulavi Muhammad Ismail.	479
II. (1833.)	Note on the origin of the Kala-Chakra and Adi-Buddha systems. Alexander Csoma de Körös. (With a Plate of text.)	57
	A short account of the Charak Pújá ceremonies, and description of the implements used. Ram Comul Sen.	609
III. (1834.)	Memoir on the Usbek State of Kokan, properly called Khokend (the ancient Ferghana) in Central Asia. W. H. Wathen.	369
	European speculations on Buddhism. B. H. Hodgson.	382
	Further remarks on M. Remusat's Review of Buddhism. B. H. Hodgson.	425
	Remarks on M. Remusat's Review of Buddhism.	499
IV. (1835.)	Some account of a sect of Hindu Schismatics in Western India calling themselves Rámsanehí or Friends of God. Captain G. E. Westmacott.	65
	Sketch of the four Menángkábowe States, in the interiŏr of the Malayan Peninsula, Lieutenant J. T. Newbold. (With a Plate.)	241
	Memoir on Chinese Tartary and Khoten. W. H. Wathen.	653

Journal.		
Vol. V. (1836.)	Annotations from original Sanscrit authorities in proof and illustration of Mr. Hodgson's sketch of Buddhism. B. H. Hodgson.	28, 71
	Notice of a visit to the valley of Cashmir. Baron Hügel.	184
	Outline of the Political and Commercial Relations with the Native States on the Eastern and Western Coasts, Malay Peninsula. Lieut. T. J. Newbold.	626
VI. (1837.)	Translation of a Servitude bond, granted by a Cultivator over his family, and of a deed of sale of two slaves. D. Liston.	950
VII. (1838.)	Notices on the different systems of Buddhism, extracted from the Tibetan authorities. Alexander Csoma Körösi.	142
IX. Part II. (1840.)	Notice of Amulets in use by the Trans-Himalayan Buddhists. W. E. Carte. With a note. A. Csoma de Körös. (With 3 Plates.)	904
X. Part I. (1841.)	On the laws and lawbooks of the Armenians. Johannes Avdall.	235
	* Account of Arakan. Lieut. Phayre.	679
XII. Part I. (1843.)	Memorandum on the Beloochees and other tribes of Upper Scinde and Cutchee. Lieut. J. Postans. ..	23
Part II.	† Report on the Manners, Customs and Superstitions of the people of Shoa and on the history of the Abyssinian Church. Captain Graham	625
XIV. Part I. (1845.)	Note on the Religion of the Sikhs, being a notice of their prayers, holidays and shrines. Major R. Leech.	393
Part II.	On the tenures and fiscal relations of the owners and occupants of the soil in Bengal, Bihar and Orissa. James Alexander..................................	527

Journal.		
Vol. XV. (1846.)	* A note on some hill tribes on the Kuladyne River, in Arakan. Lieut. T. Latter. (With a Plate.)	60
XVII. Part II. (1848.)	Gleanings in Buddhism; or translations of passages from a Siamese version of a Páli work, termed in Siamese "Phrá Pathom." Lieut-Col. J. Low. ..	72
	A few Gleanings in Buddhism. Lieut.-Col. Low. ..	591
	* On the Chepang and Kúsúnda tribes of Nepal. B. H. Hodgson. (With a Plate.)	650
XX. (1851.)	Notes on the Maháparushyas, a sect of Vaishnavas in Asám. Capt. E. T. Dalton.	455
XXI. (1852.)	Notes on Eastern Tibet. Dr. A. Campbell. (With a Map.)	215
	Account of a visit to the shrine and town of Sakhi Sarwar in the lower Derajat; with a notice of the annual Mela or fair held there. Lieut. H. G. Raverty.	329
	Notes on northern Cachar. Lieut. R. Stewart.	582
XXVII. (1858.)	Notes on the Karens. Francis Mason.............	129
XXVIII. (1859.)	On the Swayamvara of the ancient Hindús, and its traces in the ancient word generally. E. B. Cowell	31
	Notes and queries suggested by a visit to Orissa in January 1859. Rev. J. Long	185
XXX. (1861.)	Papers relating to the Aborigines of the Andaman Islands. Captain J. C. Haughton and Lieut.-Col. Albert Fytche. (With a Plate.)	251
XXXIII. (1864.)	Account of further intercourse with the Natives of the Andaman Islands. Colonel Tytler........	31
	An account of Upper Kashkár, and Chitral or Lower Káshkár, together with the independent Afghan State of Panj-korah, including Tálásh. Captain H. G. Raverty...............................	125

Journal.		
Vol. XXXIV. (1865.)	Description of a mystic play as performed in Ladak, Zaskar, etc. Captain H. H. Godwin-Austen. (With 5 Plates.)	71
XXXVIII. (1869.)	The District of Lúdiáná. T. W. H. Tolbort.	83
XXXIX. (1870.)	The Vastuyága and its bearings upon tree and serpent worship in India. Babu Pratápa Chandra Ghosha.	199
	The funeral ceremonies of the ancient Hindus. Babu Rájendralála Mitra.	241
XL. (1871.)	A visit to Kharakpur, in Mungir, and several places in the Banka Sub-division (Bhagalpur). Rashbihárí Bose.	22
	The country of Braj. F. S. Growse.	34
	Legends and Ballads connected with persons deified or held in great veneration in Bhágalpur and the neighbouring districts. Rashbihárí Bose.........	138
XLI. (1872.)	Notes on a visit to the Tribes inhabiting the hills south of Sibságar, Asám. (With 5 Plates.)	9
	The legend of Bághesar, a deified spirit held in great reverence by the Kúsrú, Súrí, Markám, Netiá and Sársún clans of the Gond Tribe. Captain W. L. Samuells.	115
	Beef in ancient India. Babu Rájendralála Mitra. ..	174
	A Pioneer in Ancient India. Babu Rájendralála Mitra.	340
XLII. (1873.)	Spirituous drinks in ancient India. Babu Rájendralála Mitra.	1
	Postscript to the above.	58
XLIV. (1875.)	Krishna-cultus in the Bṛihat Samhitá. Prannath Pandit.	15
	On the Khyeng People of the Sandoway District, Arakan. Major G. E. Fryer..................	39

Journal.		
Vol. XLIV. (1875.)	Rough notes on the Angámí Nágas. (With two Plates.)	314
	An account of the Marwár Bhíls. Dr. T. H. Hendley. (With a Plate.)	347
XLV. (1876.)	On early Asiatic Fire weapons. Major-General R. Maclagan.	30
	On human sacrifices in Ancient India. Dr. Rájendralála Mitra.	76
	Description of a trip to the Ghilghit Valley, a dependency of the Máháraja of Kashmír. Captain H. C. Marsh. (With 4 Plates.)	119
	Morals of Kálidása. Prannáth Pandit.	352
	An imperial assemblage at Dehli three thousand years ago. Dr. Rájendralála Mitra.	368
XLVI. (1877.)	Are Kalidása's heroes monogamists. G. A. Grierson.	39
	On the route between Soḥár and el Bereymí in 'Omán, with a note on the Zaṭṭ or gipsies, in Arabic. Lieutenant-Colonel S. B. Miles. (With a Map.)	41
	The Mythic history of the god Viraj. G. S. Leonard.	126
	Further proofs of the polygamy of Kalidása's heroes. G. S. Leonard.	160
XLVII. (1878.)	Stray Arians in Tibet. R. B. Shaw. (With a Plate.)	26
	On representations of Foreigners in the Ajanta Frescoes. Dr. Rájendralála Mitra. (With 4 Plates.)	62
	Recent Trans-frontier Explorations, communicated by Col. J. T. Walker. (With a Map.)	78
	Mathurá Notes. F. S. Growse. (With 14 Plates.)	97
XLVIII. (1879.)	The Snake Symbol in India, especially in connection with the worship of Siva. J. H. Rivett-Carnac. (With 2 Plates.)	17
	Some further Notes on Kalidása. G. A. Grierson...	32
	The sect of the Prannáthis. F. S. Growse.	171
	Rough notes on the Distribution of the Afghan Tribes about Kandahar. Lieut. R. C. Temple.	181

Journal.	
Vol. XLIX. (1880.)	Remarks on the Afgháns found along the route of the Tal Chotiali field force, in the Spring of 1879. (With 3 Plates and a Map.) Lieut. R. C. Temple. 91, 143
L. (1881.)	Contributions on the Religion, History, etc. of Tibet. Babu Sarat Chandra Das. 187, 206
LII. (1882.)	Contributions on the Religion, History, etc. of Tibet. (Continued). Babu Sarat Chandra Dás. 1, 15, 53, 58, 87, 99, 115, 121
Proceedings. (1865.)	Ethnology of India. Hon'ble G. Campbell. ...... 142 On the Andamanese. Dr. Smith. 182
(1866.)	The Ram Thammám sect in the Panjab. J. D. Tremlett. 109
(1867.)	Memorandum on the Panthays of Yunan. Colonel A. Fytche.................................... 176
(1868.)	Notes on the Kherrahs, an aboriginal race living in the hill tracts of Manbhum. V. Ball. 190
(1872.)	On the Nágas of Asam. S. E. Peel. 135
(1873.)	An Account of the Tenets of the Ibádhí sect of 'Oman. E. C. Ross. .... 2 Notes on children found living with wolves in the North Western Provinces, and Oudh. V. Ball. .. 128 The Bhádu and the Báuris. Babu Upendra Chandra Mukerjea. 202
(1874.)	Description of a bachelor's Hall among the Mikir Tribes, Assam, with certain symbols connected therewith. C. Brownlow. (With a Plate.) 17

Proceedings.		
(1875.)	On leprosy in Ancient India. Babu Rájendralála Mitra.	160
	On Greek art in India. Babu RájendralálaMitra...	166
(1876.)	On human sacrifices in ancient India. Dr. Banerjea, Hon'ble E. C. Bayley, Dr. R. Mitra.	53
	Notes on the Inhabitants of the Nicobars. F. A. de Roepstorff.	142
(1879.)	On the installation of the Dalai Lama. C. Girdlestone. (With a Plate)	275
	Pictures of the Tírthankaras. Dr. R. Mitra......	276
(1881.)	Notes on the inhabitants of the Nicobars. F. A. de Roepstorff.	7, 104
	On a sect of Hindu dissenters, called Kumbhupatias.	155
(1882.)	On a sect of Hindu dissenters, followers of Alekh...	2
(1883.)	Notes on the Nangís, a religious sect. J. W. Parry.	100

N. B.—A number of contributions, belonging to this chapter, will be found noticed in the Classified Index to the Scientific Papers of the Society, under the Chapters V, VII, VIII on Geography, Ethnology, and Economic Science and Statistics.

INDEX OF NOTICES PUBLISHED IN THE PROCEEDINGS (1832-64).

I.

ANTIQUITIES.

Proceedings.			
(1832.)	Sc.	Image of Bhairava, presented through Dr. Twining, by General O'Halloran.	512
(1833.)	I.	Some Inscriptions, collected by Captain Forbes, in the Matele District, Ceylon. ..	548
	I.	An Arabic Inscription on a rock in the Fort of Chanderá. D. J. Tytler.	548
(1834.)	I.	Translation of an Inscription in Páli and Burmese from Arracan. H. Walters. ..	194
	I.	Inscription in Nágarí, Maráṭhi and Tamil characters, found at Benares. Munshi Pál Singh.	301
	Sc.	Image of Buddha, dug up near Kabul. Munshi Mohan Lal.	362
		An Egyptian mummy. Lieut. E. C. Archbold.	363, 477
		Collection of paintings, books and casts, belonging to the late R. Home, Esq., Lucknow, presented to the Society.	524, 570
(1835.)	A., Sc. & C.	Some singular ancient monuments near Hyderabad. Dr. S. G. Malcolmson.	180

Proceedings.			
(1836.)		A wooden standard taken from the Bhotian army, presented by Capt. Bagli.	248
	Sc.	Sculpture of Silenus or Bacchus, from Mathurá, sent by Col. Stacy.	517
	Sc.	Collection of statues and other specimens of Bauddha sculpture from Sarnáth. Presented by Captain A. Cunningham.	588
(1837.)	C. & I.	On the Caves and Inscription of Khandgiri. Lieut. M. Kittoe.	318, 986
(1838.)	I.	Inscription on a circular copper-plate. General Court.	366
(1840.)	I.	Inscription on a Chabútra at Devalghar in Ghurrawal. Captain Huddlestone.......	730
(1841.)	I.	Asoka Stone inscription, deposited in the Society's Rooms.	508
(1842.)	I.	Abstract of a Buddhist Inscription at Aurung in Chatisgaṛh. Major Thomas Wilkinson.	273
	Sc.	Burmese Images from Rangoon. Captain W. Macleod.	439
	Sc.	Antiquities in the Society's Museum. H. Torrens.	574
(1843.)	I.	Inscription on a brass image from Budh Gaya. E. C. Ravenshaw..............	1113
(1844.)		Antiquities and Coins from the Soonderbuns. John Mack.	lxxix

Proceedings.			
(1846.)	I.	Páli Inscription from Bihar. Mr. Latour...	xxviii
	A.	On a Hindu Temple, 460 years old, with Cufic inscriptions. Captain Kittoe.	liii
(1847.)	C.	Remarkable cave Temples in the Mirzapore district. W. M. Stuart.	83
	I.	Persian Stone Inscription in Cuttack. Capt. H. Rigby.	202
		On an ornamented Garrow korah or dish. S. Reynolds.	1253
(1848.)	I.	An Arabic Inscription, in Kufic characters, on a Jain temple near Ajmir. E. S. Braudreth.	553
	A.	List of antiquities, presented by Government. Captain M. Kittoe.	697
(1852.)		A Picture by a Burmese Artist. Dr. A. Thomas.	275
	A.	Antiquities at Gour in Bengal. Captain Layard.	276
		Description of a wrought iron gun from Burmah. Major Hugh Fraser and Lieut. E. C. S. Williams. (With a plate, in vol. for 1853).	631
(1853.)	I.	On a Sanskrit Inscription from Thánesar. L. Bowring.	204
	I.	On the Khanníarah Inscription. E. C. Bayley.	309
	I.	On two slabs of Basalt with Páli Inscriptions. Captain Layard.	577
	A.	On the antiquities of Singhbhoom. Captain J. C. Haughton.	579
(1854.)	Sc.	Indo-Grecian Sculptures from the N. W. Frontier. Major J. Abbott. (With a Plate)........................	394

Proceedings.			
(1855.)	Sc. & I.	Three bronze figures from Cuttack, with an inscription. R. P. Harrison.	730
(1856.)		On the Remains of the ancient Burmese Metropolis, called Pagan. Captain Yule.	572
(1857.)	P.	On a collection of old bricks, chiefly dug out of the oldest Hindu Forts and cities of the Mahabhárat period. C. Gubbins.....	154
(1858.)	A.	Description of the old Fort of Bilhari. Captain Vanrenen.....................	71
	Sc.	Note on a Stone Figure of a Bull from Buddha Gaya. Babu R. Mitra. (With a Plate.)............................	74
	Sc.	Note on a small Indo-Greek Sculpture. Colonel Abbott.	261
	P. & I.	Note on a brick bearing a Bengali Inscription. Babu Hori Shunker Dutt and Babu Gourdass Bysack......	370
(1859.)	V.	Note on four sepulchral alabaster Urns, found in Thebes, in 1846. D. T. Money.	163
		Note on two wooden guns, taken at the battle of Berhampur by Col. Duxeford, in October 1858. E. Samuells.	180
(1860.)	I.	An Arabic Stone Inscription from Mirzagunge, sent by J. H. Riley. Captain W. N. Lees.........................	406
(1861.)	R.	Note on twelve stone hatchets or celts, from Jabulpur. H. P. Le Mesurier.	81
	I.	Note on an Inscription on a stone at Sahibganj. T. Oldham and Babu R. Mitra. ..	171
		Account of a printing press discovered in the Fortress of Agra, in 1803. Lieut.-Col. H. Yule.	175
	Sc.	Account of some of the Sculptures in the Peshawer Museum. Rev. W. Loewenthal.	411
		Note on two small stone urns in the Peshawer Museum. G. D. Westropp........	413

Proceedings.			
		Memorandum* by Colonel A. Cunningham regarding a proposed investigation of the Archæological Remains of Upper India.	98
(1862.)	Sc. & I.	Notice of some sculptures and inscriptions from Muttra. E. C. Bayley.	300
	I.	On the Wardak and other Inscriptions. Colonel A. Cunningham.	303
	R.	Account of some celts, found in Bundelkhand. W. Theobald. (With two Plates.)	323
	A.	Account of the Buddhist discoveries at Sultanganj. Colonel A. Cunningham.......	452
(1863.)	Sc.	Memorandum regarding two life-size statues discovered in the Delhi Palace. Major-General A. Cunningham.	296
	I.	Note on the Bactro-Pali Inscription from Taxila and Wardak. Babu R. Mitra. ..	437
(1864.)	R.	On Stone implements from Madras. Mr. Oldham.	67
	Sc.	On four large slabs of wood carved with figures of Hindu idols, from the Kaiser Bagh, Lucknow.	114
	C.	Letter on the Caves of Ajunta and Ellora. J. Mulheran.	216
	I.	An Inscription on a rock at Taikal. L. B. Bowring.	573

II.

COINS, GEMS, ETC.

Proceedings.			
(1833.)	C.	Note on two Ceylonese Coins (gold and copper). H. H. Wilson.	45
	I.	Note on eleven coins from Manikyála. Lieut. A. Burnes.	153
	H. & M.	Hindu and Moghul coins presented to the Society.	204
(1834.)	H.	Twelve punch-coins dug up in the Sandarbans. W. Sturmer.	301
	B.	Catalogue of General Ventura's Bactrian Coins.	591
(1835.)	B.	Bactrian Coins and Relics from Afghanistan. W. Masson.	233
		Collection of Colonel S. P. Stacy's Coins...	295
(1837.)		Catalogue of Coins in the Society's Cabinet.	156
		Some ancient tin Coins from Singapur. T. Church.	896
(1839.)	B.	On some Bactrian Coins. Lieut.-Col. Stacy. (With two woodcuts.)	342
(1840.)		On an old Chinese coin. W. E. Sterling. ..	859
(1844.)	R., Gr., H.	Roman, Greek, and Kashmír Coins, from Lieut. A. Cunningham.	72
	H.	Note on Kashmír Coins. Lieut. A. Cunningham.	167
	Gr., R., H., M., P.	List of Coins presented to the Society by H. W. Torrens.	503
	P. & M.	Priced list of Pathan and Moghul Coins, purchased from Lieut. A. Cunningham...	505
(1842.)		List of English Coins purchased for the Society. Lieut. A. Cunningham.	787

Proceedings.			
(1843.)		Catalogue of Coins in the Society's Cabinet. Dr. E. Röer.	133
		List of Norwegian Coins, given to the Society. Dr. E. Röer.	515
		On two gold coins from Chedooba. Captain D. Williams.	520, 734
(1845.)	H.	On six gold coins from Heolee in the Malwar Talooka of the Ratnagarhi Collectorate. James Bird.	ix
	H.	Silver Coins found on the Sagar Island. H. Torrens.	xcv
(1848.)	I.	Eight gold Indo-Scythian Coins found at Kunaraya, in the Mungir District. J. W. Laidlay.	454
(1850.)	M.	Moghul Coins, presented by Mr. Gubbins. Babu R. Mitra.	346
(1852.)	Bg.	Silver and copper Coins from Gaur and Gangarampur. Capt. Layard.	337
(1853.)	H.	On the Mitra Coins. Capt. A. Cunningham.	309
(1854.)	H.	Copper and silver Coins of the Cheroo Rajas. Capt. Sherwill.	502
	Bg.	Silver Coins found at Gowhatty. Capt. E. T. Dalton.	616
(1856.)	Bg.	On a silver Coin from Mr. Downward at Precoond. Babu R. Mitra.	370
	B.	On some new Bactrian Coins (with two woodcuts). Capt. W. E. Hay.	433
	H.	On a silver coin of Cooch Bihar. Babu R. Mitra. (With a woodcut.)	457

Proceedings.			
(1856.)	B. & I.	On spurious Bactrian and Indo-Scythian coins. Major J. J. Bush.	465
(1857.)		A small number of copper coins, found in Sindh, near Hyderabad. W. H. Hoppner.	167
	I.	On an Indo-Scythian gold coin. Babu R. Mitra..............................	172
		Note on the collection of Coins in the Society's Cabinet. Mr. Freeling.	234
(1858.)	Su. & H.	Note on some Suráshtrian and punched coins. Babu R. Mitra......................	369
(1862.)	Gr.	Note on a small silver coin of Alexander the Great. E. C. Bayley.	206
	P.	Remarks on a rare silver coin of Altamsh, found at Kandi, in the Murshidabad District. E. C. Bayley.	207
	Bg.	On a Bengal Pathan coin, found at Rajsháhí. E. C. Bayley.	318
		On a collection of Muhammadan coins, procured from Capt. Stubbs. E. C. Bayley.	436
	P.	On two Delhi Pathan silver coins. A. Grote.	448
(1863.)	P.	Silver coins of Pathan Sultans of Delhi. E. C. Bayley........................	35
(1864.)	P. & Bg.	Note on the great hoard of Pathan Coins discovered in Kuch Behar. Babu R. Mitra.	579, 480
	M.	On Zodiacal rupees of Jehangír. Babu R. Mitra................................	483
		On the "saraffins" and their connection with the English "sovereign." Capt. W. N. Lees.	584

III.

HISTORY.

Proceedings.		
(1840.)	On the mythological connection between Artemis and Nana. Dr. W. E. Carte.	944
(1847.)	On the identification of the *Serica* of the Periplus. Capt. A. Cunningham.	989, 1254
(1853.)	On the Kotuck Kings of Kangra. E. C. Bayley. ..	204
(1863.)	A list of the Kings of Arakan. Lieut.-Colonel S. R. Tickell.	308
(1864.)	On the Muhammadan Historians of India. Capt. W. N. Lees.	484

IV.

LANGUAGE AND LITERATURE.

Proceedings.		
(1836.)	Catalogue of 352 valuable and useful Chinese books presented to the Society.	246
	Catalogue of Burmese and Talain Manuscripts, presented by Capt. W. Foley.	247
	Note on the Páli and Prákrit languages. Dr. W. H. Mill.	830
(1838.)	Manuscripts of the Lalita Vistara.	459
	On the North Indian Vernaculars.	743
	On the Bactrian Alphabet and Language. Prof Lassen.	831
(1839.)	A Jain Manuscript of the Samavaya. Col. Alves.	434
(1840.)	On the Jami-ut-Tawáríkh. W. Morley.	445
	The same. Professor Forbes.	1131
(1841.)	Language of the Hos or Kols. Capt. F. Jenkins and D. F. McLeod.	172
(1843.)	Identity of the Gond language with Canarese. Dr. F. McLeod.	132
(1846.)	On the Abom language. Major Jenkins and Capt. Brodie.	liv
(1863.)	On four valuable Persian Manuscripts. E. B. Cowell.	182
(1864.)	On the Romanising of Oriental Alphabets. Capt. W. N. Lees, Bishop Cotton and Mr. Heeley.	446
	On the Muhammadan Histories of India. Capt. W. N. Lees.	464
	On the origin of Hindi and its relation to the Urdu dialect. Capt. W. N. Lees.	469
	On the Derivation of the numismatic term "sovereign." Captain W. N. Lees.	589

V.

RELIGION, MANNERS AND CUSTOMS, ETC.

Proceedings.		
(1833)	On the marriage rites and usages of the Játs of Bharatpur. J. S. Lushington.	154
(1846.)	On a singular custom at Lahore. Major Kittoe. ..	liii
(1856.)	On the Coorumbas and other little known tribes of Central India. Lieutenant Macdonald.	436
(1864.)	Letter regarding a mystery play at the Hisnis Monastery between Leh and Ladak. Capt. A. B. Melville.	478

CENTENARY REVIEW

OF THE

ASIATIC SOCIETY OF BENGAL

From 1784—1883.

PART III.

NATURAL SCIENCE.

BY

P. N. BOSE.

Published by the Society.

ERRATA.

PART III.

Pages 28 to 47, for '*Strategraphical Geology*,' read '*Stratigraphical Geology*.'
Page 65, *for* 'T. Anderson,' *read* 'J. Anderson.'

Centenary Review

OF THE

ASIATIC SOCIETY OF BENGAL

From 1784 to 1883.

Part III.

NATURAL SCIENCE.

CHAPTER I.

MATHEMATICAL AND PHYSICAL SCIENCE.*

[§ 1. Introductory. § 2. Astronomical Observations and the Trigonometrical Survey — Burrow — Pearse — Colebrooke — Lambton — Warren — Hodgson and Herbert — Everest — Walker — Shortrede — Pratt — Taylor — Everest. § 3. Meteorology — Pearse — Trail — Prinsep — Boileau' — Schlagintweit — Shikdár — Blanford. § 4. Tidal Observations —Kyd — Waterhouse. § 5. Law of Storms — Piddington. § 6. Electrical Researches — O'Shaughnessy — Schwendler. § 7. Photography, Process of Coining, &c. — Waterhouse — Tenant. § 8. Mathematical Sciences of the Hindus — Davis — Jones — Burrow — Playfair — Bentley — Colebrooke — Hunter.]

§ 1.—*Introductory.*

When the Asiatic Society was formed, the Biological and Geological Sciences were in a transition state. The end of the eighteenth century was the beginning of the history of Modern Natural Science. The different branches of Mathematical Science, however, had then attained to a high degree of excellence. Mathematics had, for over

* See Index, pp. i—xxv.

a century, been a recognized branch of study in European Universities; and men who came out to India, especially in the scientific branches of the Military service, had mostly been well grounded in that subject. Among the earlier members of the Society, therefore, we find a number of mathematicians of no mean order; and down to 1828 the only scientific contributions of any importance received by the Society were connected with some branch or other of Mathematics, pure or mixed.

§ 2.—*Astronomical Observations and the Trigonometrical Survey.*

The first number of the Society's *Transactions* contains several articles by Reuben Burrow, an excellent mathematician. In 1787, he was requested by Colonel Call, the then Surveyor-General, to determine astronomically the position of the principal places in Bengal. Burrow went up the Ganges as far as Haridwár, and the results of his astronomical observations, communicated to the Asiatic Society, were published in the fourth volume of the *Researches*. He intended to give a detailed account of the manner in which the latitudes and longitudes were deduced; but did not live to accomplish his purpose.

R. Burrow. 1788—1795.*

Colonel Pearse, Commandant of Artillery, contributed to the first volume of the *Researches* a valuable record of astronomical observations made in Fort William and between Madras and Calcutta betweeen 1775 and 1784; and Lieutenant Colebrooke (the future Sur-

T. D. Pearse. 1788.

R. H. Colebrooke. 1795.

* These dates (which are mostly the dates of publication) have been given to facilitate reference to the accompanying Indices. When a contribution has appeared long after the date of communication, it has been ascertained, as approximately as possible, and inserted marginally, and the date of publication specially noted in the text.

veyor-General), who ably assisted Colonel Pearse, made observations of latitudes by meridian altitudes of stars, and of longitudes by eclipses of Jupiter's satellites on a voyage to the Andaman and Nicobar Islands in 1790, and subsequently in the Carnatic, and communicated them to the Society in two papers published in the fifth volume of its *Transactions*.

William Lambton. 1799—1820.

In the list of members appended to the sixth volume of the *Researches*, we find the name of Captain William Lambton, a remarkable man, the father of the great Indian Survey. He distinguished himself highly by his bravery and presence of mind in the memorable siege of Seringapatam. On the conclusion of the Maisúr campaign, "having long reflected on the great advantage to general Geography that would be derived from extending a survey across the Peninsula of India for the purpose of determining the positions of the principal geographical points; and seeing that by the success of the British arms during the late glorious campaign, a district of country is acquired which not only opens a free communication with the Malabar Coast, but from its nature affords a most admirable means of connecting that with the Coast of Coromandel by an uninterrupted series of triangles, and of continuing that series to an almost unlimited extent in every other direction," he communicated his ideas to the Governor of Madras, who approved of them and appointed him to conduct the measurements. The apparatus with which he was at first equipped consisted of a chain of blistered steel constructed by Ramsden, five coffers, twelve pickets of three-inch diameter, hooped and shod with iron, and a levelling telescope. With these instruments he measured a base line near Bangalúr, the particulars of which were communicated to the Society and published in the seventh volume of their *Transactions*.

In 1802, Lambton received, to use his own words. "a most complete apparatus," comprising steel chains, a theodolite, and zenith sector. It enabled him to make the first of that remarkable series of measurements which he carried on for upwards of twenty years with singular zeal and enthusiasm. The measurement in question was that of an arc of the meridian on the Coast of Coromandel, and the length of a degree deduced therefrom in Lat. 12° 32′. A paper containing the details of the measurement, and accompanied by a sketch of the triangles from which the meridional and perpendicular arcs were derived, appeared in the eighth volume of the *Researches*. Two years later we find in the pages of the same publication an account of the trigonometrical operations in crossing the Peninsula of India and connecting Fort St. George with Mangalúr, together with a general plan of the triangles; and in 1810, the Society received an account of the measurement of an arc on the meridian comprehended between latitudes 8° 9′ 38″.39 and 10° 59′ 48″.93 north, being a continuation of the grand meridional arc, commenced in 1804, and extending to 14° 6′ 9″ north. Lord Minto, in communicating this article, speaks of it as "containing matter of such high importance to the interests of science, and furnishing so many new proofs of the eminent endowments and indefatigable exertions which have long distinguished the character and labours of its respectable and meritorious author." By the year 1815, the arc had become one of the largest ever measured in any country, having an amplitude of 9° 53′ 45″; and the peninsula as high as 15° N. lat. had been covered with a network of triangles. "The whole of the Peninsula," says Lambton, writing about this time, "is now completed from Goa on the west to Masulipatam on the east, with all the interior country from Cape Comorin to the southern boundary of the Nizam's and

Mahratta's territories. In that great extent of country every object that could be of use in geography or in facilitating the detailed surveys of the provinces has been laid down with precision; all the great rivers sketched in a general manner, and all the great ranges of mountains slightly depicted."

The great "Trigonometrical Survey of India" was founded in January, 1818; and Lambton was appointed the first Superintendent. But the veteran surveyor did not live to complete the work he had sketched out Hard work and constant exposure had told seriously on his health, and he breathed his last at Hinganghât on the 20th of January, 1823.*

J. Warren. 1800—1815.

Lieutenant Warren, one of Lambton's chief assistants,† performed a number of interesting experiments in the Maisúr country in 1804, to investigate the effects of terrestrial refractions, which are summarized in the ninth volume of the *Researches.* He also instituted a series of valuable astronomical observations at Madras between 1805 and 1815, the results of which he regularly laid before the Society.

J. A. Hodgson and J. D. Herbert. 1815—1817.

Captain Hodgson and Lieutenant Herbert were appointed by Lord Hastings in 1815 to survey the country between the Sutlej and the Ganges; and in the fourteenth volume of the *Researches* we have a paper by the former on the "Latitudes of places in Hindusthan and the Northern Mountains; with Observations of the longitude in the mountains according to immersions and emersions of Jupiter's

---

* For a biographical sketch of Colonel Lambton, see "Gleanings in Science," Vol. II, p. 73.

† Lieutenant Henry Kater was another of Lambton's most distinguished colleagues. He became well-known afterwards for his scientific investigations in England. He invented and described in the ninth volume of the *Researches* a very sensitive hygrometer—an ingenious contrivance made of the bearded seed of a species of grass (*Andropogon Contortum*, Lin.)

Satellites." The same volume gives an account of the trigonometrical and astronomical operations undertaken by the surveyors to determine the heights and positions of the principal peaks of the Himálaya Mountains.

G. Everest. 1823—43.

George Everest, who came to Bengal as an Artillery Cadet in 1806, joined the Survey under Lambton in 1818. He succeeded his Chief as Superintendent of the Great Trigonometrical Survey in 1823. He was away in England from 1825—30, where he employed his time in studying the newest improvements and looking after the construction of instruments for the Survey on the latest and most approved principles. On his return to India, he delivered, before the Physical Class of our Society, a lecture, on the 11th of March, 1831, in illustration of the new measuring apparatus brought out by him. The substance of the discourse appears in the second part of the eighteenth volume of the *Researches.*

A. Waugh and J. T. Walker.

Everest, who combined in himself the appointments of Superintendent of the Great Trigonometrical Survey and Surveyor-General of India, retired in 1843, and was succeeded by Colonel (afterwards Sir) Andrew Waugh. A summary of the work done under his superintendence was communicated by Major (now Major-General) Walker, the present Surveyor-General, to the Asiatic Society in 1862. General Walker presented the Society with abstracts of the operations of the Trigonometrical Surveys down to 1864.

R. Shortrede. 1840—43.

Captain Robert Shortrede, who was appointed to superintend the Bombay Longitudinal Series in 1827, and was subsequently placed in charge of the Punjab Revenue Survey from 1849 to 1856, was an active contributor on mathematical subjects. In 1841, he constructed a table which showed at once, without calculation, the mean times of new and full Moon, &c., as also the Moon's age to the nearest day. It is published in the twelfth volume of the *Journal*, along with a Companion to the Moon Table, which was constructed in order to have the times of true as well as of mean new and full Moon.

J. H. Pratt. 1858—65.

The Venerable Archdeacon Pratt, one of the best mathematicians India has ever seen, was long and actively connected with the Society. The Notices of the Royal Astronomical Society for January 9, 1857, contained a paper by Lieutenant (now Major-General) J. F. Tennant, Bengal Engineers, on "An Examination of the Figure of the Indian Meridian as deduced by Archdeacon Pratt from the two Northern Indian Arcs; with a Proposition for testing that form by Astronomical Observations."

J. F. Tennant. 1857—.

This called forth a reply from the Archdeacon, which was published in the *Journal* for 1858. He concludes his communication with remarks on the position, at that time, of the question of the Himálayan attraction, as affecting the Great Trigonometrical Survey. Colonel Tennant communicated a counter-reply, which drew forth another article from Pratt. In this he reiterated his opinion that the Himálayan attraction was not to be trifled with and passed over. "The Himálayas are as great a tyrant," says he, "in the delicate problem of determining the curvature of the arc of the Meridian in Hindusthan as the planet Jupiter is in the Solar System." The Archdeacon explains the object of his writing to have been not to detect and expose flaws in the operations of the Great Trigonometrical Survey, but to assist in pointing out the sources of error, and the further observations and surveys which are necessary to remedy the evils which must inevitably follow if these sources of error are not attended to.

The discovery of a lofty peak near Káshmir by Major Montgomerie in 1859, only 724 feet lower than Mount Everest, led Mr. Pratt to write another paper on the influence of mountain attraction, which was read at the September meeting of the Society. He concludes by stating his persuasion, that when sufficient data were obtained to make the calculation complete, it would be found that mountain attraction, combined with deficiency of attraction of the ocean, so far affects the levelling of the instruments of observation as to cause the survey to bring out the height of the newly-discovered mountain near Káshmir too low by 150 or 200 feet relatively to Mount Everest. The last of his contributions appeared in the *Journal* for 1865, entitled "On the degree of uncertainty which local attraction, if not allowed for, occasions in the map of a country and in mean figure of the earth."

T. G. Taylor. 1831—1837.

Glanville Taylor, who was Astronomer in charge of the Madras Observatory from 1830 to 1848, contributed a paper to the *Journal*, in which he described a method of making "the telescope a collimator to itself, by viewing the image of the wires reflected from a basin of quicksilver at the same time that the direct image is viewed in the ordinary way through the eye-piece." To accomplish this, he showed it was only necessary "to exhibit a bright light behind the wires, so as not to interfere with the eye of the observer when applied to the eyepiece." In another article, published seven years later, he recorded the observations of the magnetic dip and intensity at Madras.

R. Everest. 1832—39.

The Rev. R. Everest was a frequent contributor. We shall have to speak of him later on in connection with Geological investigations. He is the author of a series of papers on the Revolution of the Seasons, the Influence of the Moon on

Atmospheric Phenomena, the Heights of the Barometer as affected by the position of the Moon, the Amount of Rainfall at Calcutta as affected by the declination of the Moon, &c. The last of his long list of contributions is contained in the eighth volume of the Society's *Journal*, in which he records his observations on the rain and drought in India from 1831 to 1838.

§ 3.—*Meteorology.*

T. D. Pearse. 1788.

Colonel Pearse, whose astronomical labours we have noticed before, kept a Meteorological Journal at Calcutta, between 1785 and 1788, which was printed in the first number of the *Asiatic Researches*. The earliest meteorological record extant in India, however, is that kept by Henry Trail from the 1st of February 1784 to the 31st of December 1785, which was published two years later in the next number of the same publication.

H. Traill. 1790.

J. Prinsep. 1820—39.

The illustrious James Prinsep, to whom this Society is so largely indebted for its success and prosperity, and whose name is so well and so widely known in connection with archæological researches, rendered no mean service in the cause of the Mathematical and Natural Sciences. His, like Sir W. Jones's, was a remarkably versatile genius. But the former had the advantage of having had a thorough scientific training in England before he came out to India. In 1819, at the age of twenty, he was appointed Assistant Assay Master at the Calcutta Mint, under Horace Hayman Wilson, the eminent orientalist. In the following year he went to Benares as Assay Master; while there he made a series of careful meteorological investigations, which he communicated to the Asiatic Society. He returned to Calcutta in 1830, and co-operated heartily with Major Herbert in starting a periodical called "Gleanings in Science." On the appointment of the latter as Astronomer in charge of the Nabáb of Oude's Observatory at Lucknow in 1831, Prinsep became the editor of the periodical; and on March 7th, 1832, changed its name to "The Journal of the Asiatic Society of Bengal." He was elected Secretary to the Physical Section of the Society on the 19th of August, 1830; and General Secretary on the 9th January, 1833.

The first volume of the *Journal* contains an account of Prinsep's Observations of the Transit of Mercury on the 5th of May, 1832, made with a 4-feet achromatic telescope, of 4-inch aperture, mounted equatorially and provided with a delicate wire micrometer. In March, 1833, he published the results of his experiments on the expansion of gold, silver, and copper, and two months later described a compensation barometer invented by him. One of the subjects to which Prinsep devoted a great portion of his time and attention was observation of the wet-bulb indications. He had with but little intermission registered daily observations since 1822. In July 1836, he contributed a paper to the *Journal*, entitled "Experimental Researches on the Depressions of the Wet-bulb Hygrometer."

The earlier volumes of the *Journal* contain a number of Meteorological Registers from various stations.* The most important of these were the "Term Observations" made in compliance with Sir W. Herschel's instructions. Horary

---

* Simlá, v. 825; Bijnúr, ii. 206; Bombay, v. 821; Kátmandu, v. 824, 889; and xii. 768; Tírhut, v. 822; Socotra, v. 821; Bangalúr, v. 296; Dárjiling, vi. 310, 700, 888; Rángun, xxii. 113, 317, 421, 502, 596; xxiii. (1); Bánkurá, i. 154; ii. 383; Chinsurá, ii. 86; Gházipur, ii. 604; Lucknow, xxiii. 76; Masúri, iv. 230; Kotgar, ii. 615; Chirápunji, i. 297; Canton and Macao, i. 303; Mozaffarpur, ii. 208; Nágpur, ii. 241, 543; Singápur, ii. 428; Nasirábád, iv. 49; Mauritius, iv. 715; Dádupur, v. 299; Umbálá, iv. 405.

observations of the barometer, thermometer, and wet-bulb thermometer were taken at Calcutta on the 21st and 22nd of December, 1835, and again on the 21st and 22nd of March, 1836, by Mr. H. Barrow, Mathematical Instrument-maker to the East India Company. Similar observations were taken at Bangalúr by Dr. J. Mouat, and at Dádupur by Colonel Colvin and Lieutenants Baker and Durand. All these records were printed in 1836 in the fifth volume of the *Journal.* The same volume also contains a paper by Prinsep on "A Comparative View of the Daily Range of the Barometer in different parts of India."

T. J. Boileau. 1841—45.

Major Boileau, author of a "New and complete set of Traverse Tables, showing the differences of latitude and the departure to every minute of the quadrant," and Superintendent of the Magnetic Observatory at Simlá, contributed the results of his physical investigations to the *Journal,* among which were tables for determining the elastic force of aqueous vapour in the atmosphere and the temperature of the dewpoint, by observations of a dry and wet-bulb thermometer, computed agreeably to Dr. Aphjohn's formula; and tables of mean astronomical refractions.

Messrs. Schlagintweit. 1854—58.

The Messrs. Schlagintweit, who conducted a Magnetic Survey from 1854 to 1858, published their reports in the pages of the *Journal.* These reports contain a great variety of observations—geographical, meteorological, geological, &c.

R. Shikdár. 1853—64.

The Meteorological observations taken at the Surveyor-General's Office have appeared regularly in the *Journal* and the *Proceedings* down to 1876. From 1853 to 1864, they were compiled by Rádhánáth Shikdár, who was for several years on the Physical Science Committee of the Society.

H. F. Blanford. 1870—.

Mr. Blanford joined the Geological Survey in 1855; but left it in 1861, and became Professor at the Presidency College. Six years later, he was appointed Meteorological Reporter to the Government of Bengal; and in 1875 became Meteorological Reporter to the Government of India. Mr. Blanford was Secretary to the Society from 1864 to 1868, and has long been a most valuable member. He contributed in 1871 a Note on the error of the Calcutta Standard Barometer compared with those of Kew and Greenwich. In 1875, he read a paper in which he showed the variation of the sun's heat to be so considerable as to have an appreciable effect on all terrestrial phenomena, and recommended direct actinometric observations as the only means of ascertaining the variation in the absolute quantity of heat. The *Journal* for 1876 contains his observations on "The irregularities of atmospheric pressure in the Indian monsoon region," besides a paper on "Comparisons of dewpoint temperature," and another on the "Physical explanation of the inequality of the two semidiurnal oscillations of barometric pressure." In the first of these papers it is shown, that amid all the changes to which atmospheric pressure is subject, certain peculiar features tend to perpetuate themselves, though they never become permanent; and that these peculiarities in the distribution of barometric pressure exercise an important influence on the rainfall, by affecting the course and velocity of the winds which bring the rain. The second paper brings together the results of a number of experiments made in various parts of India with the object of comparing the observed hygrometric state of the atmosphere ascertained by Regnault's Hygrometer, with that computed with the help of the dry and wet-bulb thermometers. In the last-named article, Mr. Blanford attributes a great part of the diurnal irregularity of the barometric tides to the transfer of air from land to sea and *vice versâ*, and to a similar transfer which may be proved to take place between the plains and the mountains. In 1877, the Society received two contributions from Mr. Blanford, one "On the Variation of the Barometric Tides in connection with diurnal land and sea breezes," and the other "A Catalogue of the recorded Cyclones in the Bay of Bengal up to the end of 1876;" and the following year, a paper was read by him on the "Diurnal Variations of the Rainfall frequency at Calcutta." In January 1880, Mr. Blanford showed that the excessive pressure of 1876—78 was the maximum phase of a cyclical variation in India and the Malay region, but in Northern Asia it was quite anomalous, and most probably so in Australia. In April 1881, he discussed the circumstances chiefly determining those marked variations of temperature which characterize the corresponding seasons of different years in India, and the variations in the density of the lower and higher strata of the atmosphere, as shown by a comparison of the barometric pressure at hill-stations with the pressure on the plains. The last of his long and valuable series of contributions appeared in the last volume of the *Journal*, in which he gave some further results of his sun thermometric investigations with reference to atmospheric absorption and the supposed variation of the solar heat.

§ 4.—*Tidal Observations.*

J. Kyd. 1829.

The earliest Register of Tidal Observations extant in this country is that of the day and night tides in the Hugli at Kidderpúr from 1805 to 1828, by James Kyd, the founder and the then proprietor of the Kidderpúr Dockyard. The observations were published in the first part of the eighteenth volume of the *Researches*.

The heights of the tides are exhibited in maps showing the state of the river throughout the year. In 1833, a table (the earliest of the kind in Western India), showing the rise of spring tides in Bombay Harbour during night and day, was communicated by Benjamin Noton. In the same year Dr. Whewell's "Suggestions to persons who have opportunities to make or collect observations of the tides" appeared in the *Journal;* and the observations which were received in conformity with these suggestions were published in the

J. T. Walker and J. Waterhouse. 1878.

Journal between 1837 and 1850. About the year 1865 or 1866, the late Dr. Oldham, Superintendent of the Geological Survey of India, drew the attention of the Government of India to certain questions which had been raised regarding secular changes in the relative level of the land and sea, which are believed to be going on in various parts of the Bombay Presidency and more particularly at the head of the Gulf which separates the Province of Cutch from Kattiwar, and he recommended that accurate tidal and levelling observations should be made in that part of the country and repeated at intervals of time sufficiently great to allow the secular changes to reach an appreciable magnitude, and so settle the question. The Government of India sanctioned the proposal, and after some delay operations were commenced in 1872 by Captain A. W. Baird, under the direction of Lieut.-General J. T. Walker, Superintendent of the Great Trigonometrical Survey. An interesting account of the early operations during the years 1873 to 1875 was compiled by Major (then Captain) J. Waterhouse and communicated by General Walker in 1878. Tidal observations are now taken regularly at several stations round the coasts of the Indian Ocean and Bay of Bengal.

§ 5.—*Law of Storms.*

H. Piddington. 1839—1851.

The indefatigable Piddington, who was Foreign Secretary to the Agricultural Society of India, Sub-Secretary to the Asiatic Society, Curator of our Museum of Economic Geology, President of the Marine Court of Enquiry, and Coroner of Calcutta, presented the Society with a series of twenty-three Memoirs accompanied by Charts on the Law of Storms, the first of which appeared in the eighth volume of the *Journal.* His experience had been most varied. "He was one of the few who escaped from the massacre of Amboyna. . . . . . . In the early days of his residence in India he was engaged in the culture of coffee and indigo, and the manufacture of sugar, and during that period he contributed various notices on agricultural subjects to the *Transactions* of the Agricultural and Horticultural Society." Piddington was once in the merchant navy; and the subject of storms was to him connected with many associations of his early life, "and more especially," says he in the opening paragraph of his first memoir, "with one instance in which to the veering of a hurricane alone I owed my safety from shipwreck, after cutting away the mainmast of a vessel which I commanded." He continued giving accounts of all important cyclones that occurred in the East from 1839 to 1851. This required a vast amount of patience and industry, and no small ability and judgment in the arrangement of the materials.

§ 6.—*Electrical Researches.*

W. B. O'Shaughnessy. 1840—42.

Sir W. O'Shaughnessy,* Professor of Chemistry at the Medical College, and for some time Joint Secretary to the Society, contributed

* Sir W. O'Shaughnessy was the first Director of Telegraphs in India. He was Secretary of the Society in 1838-39, and again from 1846 to 1850.

various papers, among which were several on electrical subjects, the most notable among these being entitled "Memoranda relative to Experiments on the communication of Telegraph Signals by induced electricity."

L. Schwendler. 1871—81.

To the late Mr. Schwendler, who was for many years a most active member, the Society owes a number of valuable papers. A votary of science in the true sense of the expression, he took a prominent part in the scientific movements of the day, and will be long remembered as one of the founders of the Zoological Gardens—an institution which promises to be a centre of zoological study in India. The first paper he read was on a practical method for detecting bad insulators on Telegraph lines, published in the *Proceedings* for March, 1871. He found that a great many lines in India contained electrically defective insulators; some to such an extent as to lower the insulation to a degree which is fatal to the direct and regular working of long lines. Mr. Schwendler exhibited an apparatus for testing the resistance of insulators, and explained in detail the advantages of his method. In February 1874, he communicated an article "On the Theory of Duplex Telegraphy." Considering the line as a variable conductor only, but not acting perceptibly as a Leyden Jar, Mr. Schwendler found that, by using the Bridge Method, the branches of the bridge, with the exception of the one which lies opposite to the line, should be made each equal to half the measured conductor resistance of the line; while the branch opposite to the line should be equal to the sixth part of this resistance. Further, that this branch, the smallest of all, should be invariably used for readjusting balance when disturbed. In June 1874, he read a paper on Earth-currents, in which he pointed out that though the two phenomena, 'earth-magnetism' and 'earth-currents,' were undoubtedly connected with each other, it was by no means established as yet that they were cause and effect, or parallel effect of one and the same general, but entirely unknown, cause. Mr. Schwendler proposed to the Council of the Society to urge on Government the introduction of a system of observation of earth-currents; the Council took up the proposal most warmly, and appointed him, along with Colonel Hyde, who was then President of the Society, and Mr. R. S. Brough, to work out a practical system.

In 1876, General Strachey had recommended to the Secretary of State for India that a trial of illuminating Indian railway stations by the electric light should be made. In February 1877, Mr. Schwendler, as Superintendent Electrician of Government Telegraphs in India, was requested to institute detailed inquiries, which led him to propose that it would be advisable to make some more experiments before a practical trial at Indian railway stations should be attempted. The Directors of the East Indian Railway agreed to this, and sanctioned the necessary outlay. The experiments, which were made at the India Office Stores, occupied Mr. Schwendler till November, 1878. The results of these experiments he laid before the Society in March 1879, and they are printed in the *Proceedings* for that month. Next month he read a paper on a "New Standard of Light," which consists of an U-piece of pure sheet platinum cut accurately to fixed dimensions. When a sufficiently strong electric current is made to pass through the platinum, it becomes white-hot and emits a brilliant light. The author showed experimentally how the intensity of this light could be varied,—*i. e.*, the magnitude of the standard altered,—by varying the currents, and also that when the current was kept constant, the light was rigorously constant also. In November, he communicated a paper, in which he described a method of using an insignificant fraction of the main current, produced by a dynamo-electric machine, for Telegraph purposes. The method in question is simple and ingenious. A strong current is produced through a comparatively small resistance by a dynamo-electric machine, which is an arrangement for converting mechanical power direct into magnetism and electricity, according to the laws of Faraday's Magneto-induction. This strong main current, while available for any kind of useful work, can, without perceptible loss, supply the very weak current required for signalling. Mr. Schwendler made a number of experiments to test the practicability of his new method of supplying signalling currents, and the results of these experiments he communicated to the Society in November, 1880.

R. S. Brough. 1877.

Mr. Brough, who has been mentioned above in connection with the "Earth-currents" Committee, published several interesting papers in the *Proceedings*.

§ 7.—*Photography, Process of Coining, &c.*

J. Waterhouse. 1874—.

Major Waterhouse* of the Survey of India, who has for many years been a most zealous member of the Society, was appointed Superintendent of the Photographic Branch of the Surveyor-General's Office in 1866. He was associated with Colonel Tennant in observing the transit of Venus in 1874, and took above a hundred photographs of the solar disc while the planet was on it, besides five showing the egress of the planet from the sun. He contributed a paper containing the results of the photographic operations in connection with the observations of the transit of Venus at Rúrki, 9th December, 1874, printed

* Major Waterhouse was General Secretary of the Society from 1872 to 1879.

in the forty-fourth volume of the *Journal.* In 1878, Major (then Captain) Waterhouse read a paper on the "Application of Photography to the reproduction of maps, plans, &c., to the photo-mechanical and other processes." It opens with an introduction, in which the history of the rise and progress of the system of reproducing maps and plans by photography is briefly sketched. The article contains a review of the various photographic processes employed for the reproduction of maps under the heads of Printing on Sensitive Papers, Photo-zincography, Photo-collotype, Woodbury-type, Photo-engraving, Photo-typography, and miscellaneous processes. In 1875, he exhibited some photographs of the extreme red end of the spectrum taken on stained dry collodion plates. The only previously known photographs of this end of the spectrum were taken by Dr. H. W. Draper. In the following year he drew the attention of the Society to the action of the then newly discovered dye called 'eosin' in extending the photographic action of the solar spectrum on sensitive dry collodion plates, a discovery which has since been turned to practical account by various French photographers in photographing paintings and other coloured objects.

J. F. Tennant. 1871—.

In the *Proceedings* for 1871, Col. (now Major-General) Tennant, Master of the Mint, one of our oldest and most valuable contributors, published a memorandum on the total eclipse of December 11th-12th, 1871, in which he briefly drew attention to the principal phenomena it was proposed to observe; and in the following year he exhibited some enlarged copies of the photographs of the corona on that occasion at Dodabetta in the Neilgherry Hills. General Tennant communicated the results of his experiments made on coining silver into rupees in April, 1879. The paper contains an account of some experiments made by the author to ascertain the cause and extent of the apparent refining that takes place when an alligation containing fine silver and copper is melted, and of the further changes in the alloy during the processes of coining. In the following year, Colonel Tennant described a method, by which a portion of the weights of an English bullion set were compared and their values found in terms of a Standard Ounce, known in terms of the English Standard Pound. Colonel Tennant gave full details showing how the comparison and valuation can be systematically carried out in some cases, and how an exceptional case can be dealt with. Tables are given in an Appendix for reducing the results of weighings in air to what they would have been in a vacuum, and for determining specific gravities. The author also compares the advantages of several systems of weights, and discusses the best value of a standard weight, and describes the results he has arrived at, and by which he has been guided, in making a set of standard Tolah weights for the Mint.

§ 8.—*Mathematical Sciences of the Hindus.*

The Mathematical Sciences had been cultivated by the Hindus from very remote times. But the history of the progress and civilization of that nation closes with the end of the twelfth century. Every work that has the stamp of originality had been written before the close of that century. Bháskarácharya, the last of the noble band of mathematicians which it is the glory of this country to have produced, completed his great work on Algebra, Arithmetic, and Mensuration about A.D. 1150. Since then, the degenerated Hindus, who, for want of better occupation, employed, or rather wasted, their time in inventing an infinity of absurd, frivolous stories about gods and goddesses, demigods and *avatárs*, forgot the principles of their sciences, which were thus reduced to mere arts practised by ignorant astrologers and needy physicians to earn a living. To rescue those sciences from oblivion was one of the noble objects which the Asiatic Society set itself from its very foundation to accomplish. The task was by no means an easy one. Though ample stipends were offered by Sir W. Jones to any Hindu astronomer who could name in Sanscrit all the constellations which he would point out, and to any Hindu physician who could bring him all the plants mentioned in Sanscrit books, he was assured by the Bráhmans whom he had commissioned to search for such instructors, that no *Pandit* in Bengal even pretended to possess the knowledge which he required!

A set of Hindu Astronomical Tables had been taken to Europe from Siam as early as 1687 by a Frenchman named LaLoubère. They passed from hand to hand as a sort of scientific curiosity, until they were explained by Cassini, one of the most eminent astronomers of his age. Two more sets of tables were sent from Southern India by the Jesuit Missionaries about the middle of the last century. The best known and most important set, however, was one from Travalúr on the Coromandel Coast, which was taken to Europe by M. Le Gentil, who visited India for the purpose of observing the transit of Venus in 1769. He communicated an account of these tables and of the astronomy of the Hindus to the French Academy in 1773. The subject was then most zealously taken up by M. Bailly, one of the most distinguished mathematicians of his day, the contemporary of Laplace, Lagrange, and D'Alembert. He published his "History of Astronomy from its origin to the establishment of the Alexandrian Schools" in 1775, in which he stoutly maintained the antiquity and excellence of the Hindu Astronomy. His great work, however, was his "History of Indian Astronomy," in which his views are more clearly expounded, and the subject treated more fully and in greater detail. That work appeared in 1787, a year before the publication of the first number of the *Asiatic Researches*.

S. Davis and Sir W. Jones.

The second volume of the *Researches* contains a paper by Mr. Samuel Davis, of Bhágalpur, on the "Astronomical Computations of the Hindus," and another by Sir William Jones "On the Antiquity of the Hindu Zodiac." Mr. Davis had procured a copy of the *Súryasiddhánta*, one of the most ancient of Indian astronomical works, and translated portions of it bearing upon the prediction of eclipses and other phenomena. Sir William Jones undertook in his paper to prove that the Indian Zodiac was not borrowed mediately or directly from the Greeks; and that since the solar division of it in India is the same in substance as that used in Greece, both the Greeks and Hindus received it from an older nation, who first gave names to the luminaries of heaven.

R. Burrow.

Reuben Burrow, whose mathematical work has been noticed at the commencement of this chapter, was the first to attempt a translation of the Indian works on Algebra and Arithmetic. There is a very interesting article by him entitled "A Proof that the Hindus had the Binomial Theorem," in which he adduces evidence to show that the Hindus had a differential method similar to Newton's. The earliest notices of Indian Algebra and Arithmetic which reached Europe were from Burrow. He made a good collection of mathematical manuscripts, which he bequeathed to his friend, Mr. Dalby, of the Royal Military College, who communicated them to those interested in the subject in 1800.

In the second volume of the *Researches* is published an advertisement calling upon the learned Societies of Europe to transmit to the Secretary to the Asiatic Society "A Collection of short and precise queries on every branch of Asiatic History, Natural and Civil, on the Philosophy, Mathematics, Antiquities, and Polite Literature of Asia, and on eastern Arts, both liberal and mechanic; since it is hoped that accurate answers may in due time be procured to any questions that can be proposed on those subjects, which must in all events be curious and interesting, and may prove in the highest degree beneficial to mankind."

J. Playfair, 1795.

This advertisement led Professor Playfair, of Edinburgh, to submit a few questions and remarks relating to the Astronomy of the Hindus, in 1792. Two years previously he had read a paper before the Royal Society of Edinburgh, in which he declared himself a convert to M. Bailly's views with regard to the antiquity of the Hindu Astronomy. Notwithstanding the "most profound respect" he had for the "learning and abilities of the author of the *Astronomie Indienne*," he "entered on the study of that work, not without a portion of scepticism, which whatever is new and extraordinary in science ought to excite, and set about verifying the calculations and examining the reasoning in it with the most scrupulous attention. The result was an entire conviction of the accuracy of the one and of the solidity of the other." In concluding his queries (published in the fourth volume of the *Researches*), Professor Playfair declares himself so deeply interested in the subject of Indian Astronomy, that he "would not lose even the feeblest ray of a light which, without the exertions of the Asiatic Society, must perish for ever."

J. Bentley. 1797—1805.

In 1797, Mr. J. Bentley, one of the best mathematicians of the time in India, contributed some remarks "On the principal æras and dates of the ancient Hindus." In a subsequent paper "On the antiquity of the *Súryasiddhánta*," published in the sixth volume of the *Researches*, he made instructive observations on the principles of the Hindu Astronomy and on the manner in which their cycles were formed, and exhibited useful formulæ showing their application in discovering the actual position of the heavenly bodies. He, however, dissented from Bailly and Playfair, and threw doubts on the antiquity of Indian Astronomy. This led to a severe critique in the *Edinburgh Review;* and Bentley replied in the pages of the *Asiatic Researches* (Vol. VIII).

H. T. Colebrooke. 1807—1816.

Henry T. Colebrooke, perhaps the most cautious and erudite orientalist that England has produced, who combined in himself the double qualifications of a sound mathematician and a thorough oriental scholar, and who for some time occupied the presidential chair of this Society, now entered the field with a paper on the "Indian and Arabian divisions of the Zodiac," in which he maintains that the Arabs had adopted, though with slight variations, a division of the zodiac familiar to the Hindus. In the twelfth volume of the *Researches* appeared his Treatise "On the Notion of the Hindu Astronomers concerning the precession of the equinoxes and motions of the planets." These articles by Colebrooke are, according to Principal Mill, "the best correction to the extravagant notions of Indian antiquity, which the preceding speculations of Bailly and others had deduced from imperfect notices of the Hindu observations, and also to the crude and fanciful speculations with which Mr. Bentley had unhappily adulterated some valuable and interesting calculations."

To the general degeneracy of the Hindus since the thirteenth century there have been a few exceptions. Foremost among these stands the name of the Astronomer Jai Sing, Rájá of Dhundar, who flourished about the beginning of the eighteenth century.* He was chosen by Mahammad Shah, Emperor of Hindustan, to construct a new set of Astronomical Tables, which were completed in 1728. Finding that brass instruments which were in use in his time did not come up to his ideas of accuracy, "because of the smallness of their size, the want of division into minutes, the shaking and wearing of their axes, the displacement of the centres of the circles, and the shifting of the planes of the instruments, he concluded that the reason why the determinations of the ancients, such as Hipparchus and Ptolemy, proved inaccurate must have been of this kind; he therefore constructed in Dar-ul-khelafet, Shah Jehanabad [Delhi]," instruments of his own invention, "of stone and lime, of perfect stability, with attention to the rules of geometry, and adjustment to the meridian and to the latitude of the place, and with care in the measuring and fixing of them; so that the inaccuracies from the shaking of the circles, and the wearing of their axes, and displacement of their centres, and the inequality of the minutes might be corrected." In order to test the accuracy of the observations made at Delhi, Jai Sing constructed similar instruments at Jaipúr, Mathurá, Benáras, and Ujain. Dr. W. Hunter, the author of several valuable papers on astronomical subjects in the earlier volumes of the Society's *Transactions*, gave in the fifth volume a detailed account of the Delhi Observatory, and some account of the tables of Jai Sing.

W. Hunter. 1895—97.

---

* He was the founder of Jaipúr, the only Indian city which is built on a regular plan with streets bisecting at right angles.

CHAPTER II.

GEOLOGY.*

[§ 1. Preliminary. § 2. Strategraphical Geology: (*a*) Southern India — Voysey — Benza — Malcolmson — Newbold. (*b*) Northern India — Voysey — Franklin — Coulthard—Hardie — Everest — Finnis — Spilsbury — Adam — Sherwill — Homfray — Oldham — Haughton — Hislop — Blanford — Godwin-Austen. (*c*) The Himalayas — Herbert — Falconer — Everest — Hutton — Hay — Medlicott — Godwin-Austen — Verchère. (*d*) The Salt Range — Fleming — Theobald. (*e*) Burma, the Islands in the Bay of Bengal, &c. — Low — Blanford — Ball. § 3. Dynamical Geology (*a*) Volcanoes and Earthquakes — Colebrooke — Halstead — Baird Smith — Asam Government. (*b*) Glacial Action — Hodgson — Batten and Manson — Weller — Madden — Strachey — Godwin-Austen — Blanford — Campbell — Medlicott. (*c*) River-Action — Everest — Piddington.]

§ 1.—*Preliminary.*

It was in 1790, six years after the foundation of the Asiatic Society, that Werner propounded, to his pupils at Freiburg, his doctrine of 'Formations.' In the same year, William Smith, an English surveyor, published a "Tabular View of the British Strata," in which he proposed a classification of the secondary formations in the West of England, each marked by its peculiar organic remains. A most animated controversy was then being carried on in Europe between the followers of Werner (Neptunists) and those of Hutton (Vulcanists). "The two parties," in the words of Sir C. Lyell, "had been less occupied in searching for truth than for such arguments as might strengthen their own cause or serve to annoy their antagonists." And it

---

* See Indices, pp. xxvi—xlii, and lxxxviii—xci.

was not until 1807, seventeen years after the publication of Smith's "Tabular View," that the good work of which it laid the foundation could be said to have fairly commenced. In that year, the Geological Society was founded in London by a new school of Geologists, who adopted the words of Lord Bacon in inviting "those to join them as the true sons of science who have a desire and a determination, not so much to adhere to things already discovered and to use them, as to push forward to further discoveries, and to conquer nature, *not by disputing an adversary*, but by labor, and who, finally, do not indulge in beautiful and probable speculation, but endeavour to attain certainty in their knowledge."

In the following year (1808), a Committee of the Asiatic Society was formed "to propose such plans, and carry on such correspondence as might seem best suited to promote the knowledge of Natural History, Philosophy, Medicine, improvements of the Arts and Sciences, and whatever is comprehended in the general term Physics." The Committee does not appear to have prospered, and ceased to meet after some time. It was revived on the 2nd of January, 1828, under the auspices of Sir Edward Ryan and Mr. James Calder, and set itself to work most energetically. It met once a fortnight; and hardly a year had elapsed before materials were ready to fill 266 pages of a quarto volume, and furnish twenty maps, plates, and charts. These formed the first part of the eighteenth volume of the *Researches*, published in 1829. Though the subjects to which the attention of the Physical Committee was to be principally directed are stated to be the Zoology, Meteorology, Mineralogy and Geology of Hindustan, it was the two last named subjects which received most attention. Of the sixteen articles contained in the publication just mentioned, no less than twelve are on geological subjects.

§ 2.—*Strategraphical Geology.*

(*a*) *Southern India.*

H. W. Voysey. 1820—1823.*

Dr. Voysey was the father of Indian Geology. In 1818, he was attached as Surgeon and Geologist to the Surveying Party of Colonel Lambton. It reflects no little credit on the Honorable East India Company that they were only a few years behind the most enlightened Governments of Europe in undertaking the measurement of an arc and starting a geological survey.

Colonel Lambton and Dr. Voysey were both very talented men. It is a remarkable coincidence, that not only did these pioneers of Indian Science work together, each in his own department, with unsurpassed energy and ability, but that they died in the same year, under strangely similar circumstances, both performing their onerous duties almost literally to the last moments of their lives.†

Voysey's first contribution was on the "Diamond Mines of Southern India." Though published in the fifteenth volume of the *Researches*, dated 1825, it was probably written about 1820. This paper contains, besides an account of the mode of occurrence of the diamond, a geological sketch of the Nalla Mala Mountains, situated between Kambham in the Cadapa district and Amrábád, a town in the province of Háidarábád, north of the Krishná. It has been asserted that he belonged to the Wernerian school. But he does not appear from his writings to have belonged to either school. With

* See note above, p. 2.

† The last words of the last journal kept by Dr. Voysey, and published in the thirteenth volume of the Society's *Journal* are "Rocks of Coliapal. The same—micaschist with quartz veins. One specimen of quartz reminded me of axinite." After writing this he caught a fever, and was found dead in his *palki* on its arrival at Howrah.

regard to the geological structure of the Nalla Mala Mountains, he says : "It is difficult to understand, and it cannot be easily explained by either the Huttonian or Wernerian theories." Owing to the predominance of clay slate, he applied the name of "Clay Slate Formation" to the rocks of which the mountains are composed. He gives an account of the mining operations as carried on in his time, and remarks upon the poverty of the miners who were all *Dhers* or outcasts.

After Dr. Voysey's death in 1823, his numerous manuscripts came into the possession of the Asiatic Society, and were placed in the hands of some of the members of the Physical Committee, in order to be digested for publication, which was delayed, however, owing to an unseemly opposition from a professional artist, who appears to have given Dr. Voysey a few hints in sketching. "Dr. Voysey's valuable collection," wrote this artist, "his writings, and my drawings have been seized upon by some calling themselves the Asiatic Society ; they are about to publish a selection from his writings without consulting his friends, or making them any compensation." The Asiatic Society succeeded in getting over this difficulty; and Dr. Voysey's Reports on the Geology of Háidarábád, written between 1819 and 1820, were given to the world in 1833, ten years after his death.

P. M. Benza. 1835.

Dr. P. M. Benza, Surgeon to the Governor of Madras, contributed a paper on the Geology of the Nílgiris, which may be considered as the southern termination of the Western Gháts, here terminating in almost vertical precipices, and which rise abruptly from the table-land of Maisúr in stupendous cliffs. He considers the granitoid rocks, which form the highest hills of the group, as intrusive, and notices the basaltic dykes. The article, however, is mainly mineralogical, describing specially the different varieties of iron ore in the locality. Accompanying the paper is a note on some specimens from the Northern Circars, which Dr. Benza had sent to the Museum of the Asiatic Society. Amongst these was the highly fossiliferous Intertrappean Limestone (with oysters and other shells) of Rájámahendrí, now so well known.*

T. G. Malcolmson. 1833–36.

Dr. Malcolmson, also of the Madras Medical Service, who was one of the earliest and ablest contributors on the Geology of India, and especially on that most interesting formation, the Deccan Trap, discovered, about 1832, fossiliferous Intertrappean Limestone in the Nirmal Hills, north of the Godávari, an account of which he furnished in a letter to the Society.† He notices the remarkable alteration of the limestone by the bursting through it of basaltic dykes. But the most remarkable part of the letter is his account of the Lonar Lake, which he had examined some years previously. He describes it as a "vast crater nearly 500 feet deep, and four or five miles round on the upper margin;" the water, "green and bitter, supersaturated with alkaline carbonate, and containing *silex* in solution, as well as some iron." Dr. Malcolmson had, in May 1833, forwarded to the Society's Museum a selection of geological specimens collected in May, 1833, between Háidarábád and Nágpur. In 1836, he furnished some notes‡ on these, in which he treats of the Geology of the metamorphic country between Háidarábád and the

---

* This is the first notice of the limestone in question; that published in the *Madras Journal of Literature and Science* appeared two years later, in 1837.

† *Journal*, Vol. III (1834), p. 302.

‡ These notes were reprinted in *Madras Journal of Literature and Science*, Vol. IV (1836).

Nirmal Hills, of the Sichel Hills (Nirmal Range), and of the basaltic tract between Edelábád and Nágpur.*

J. T. Newbold. 1836—47.

But the ablest Geologist of his day in India was unquestionably Captain Newbold† of the Madras Native Infantry, who was subsequently appointed Assistant Resident at Karnúl. His first contribution was in 1836, when he presented to the notice of the Society specimens of a calcaro-silicious scoria, forming a small hill about eleven miles west of Ballári. But it was in 1842, in the tenth volume of the *Journal*, that he began that admirable series of papers on the Geology of Southern India, the conclusions established in which have, in the main, been but little altered by the far more detailed and systematic examinations of the officers of the Geological Survey of India. In his two articles on the Geology of the country between Ballári and Bijápur, he refers to the granitoid hills in the Raíchur Doáb, known as the Berar Hills, and notes the remains of an iron-smelting industry crushed by Mahomedan oppression. He observed the chloritic band to the north-west of Tarugiri, as well as the clay-iron beds near Kamdigal. An admirable sketch of the Geology of the ancient Mahomedan city of Bijápur and its vicinity is given. His third paper contains some pregnant remarks on the origin and age of *kankar*, and on the supposed decrease of the temperature of India. In his paper on the Geology of the country between Masulipatam and Goa, Captain Newbold presented the results of his study of the *Regur* (or black cotton soil) and the Laterite—

* Dr. Malcolmson subsequently communicated an elaborate Memoir on the "Deccan Trap" formation to the Geological Society of London. He became Secretary to the Bombay Branch of the Royal Asiatic Society, and died at Dhulia, while engaged in geological pursuits, in February, 1844.

† Captain Newbold joined the army in 1827. He was an accomplished oriental scholar. He died in 1850.

both problems of considerable interest in Indian Geology. He was the first to detect the occurrence of manganese veins in the latter. Brongniart, on the authority of M. de Luc, had spread the idea in Europe, that the rounded blocks of granite around, and in the vicinity of, Háidarábád (Deccan) were truly erratic boulders. Captain Newbold, however, after a long and careful survey, the results of which were communicated to the Society in 1845, came to the conclusion that the blocks in question are *in situ* (since they invariably rest upon, or near, a granite of the same petrological character) and that they owe their globular and rounded form to concentric exfoliation. He did observe certain marks and furrows, but these could not be referred to glacier-action; and he found nothing which could not be explained by the action of existing subaerial agencies. In his Geological Notes on the South Mahratta country, he dwells on the Geology of the Sítádinga Hills, the plain of Bagulcata, the country between Kaladgi and the Falls of Gokak, and the tract between these Falls and Belgaum along the western slope of the Gháts. He then gives the geographical position and extent of the various rocks of the South Mahratta country, the extent of the Limestone and Sandstone rocks, the distribution of the Laterite, Kankar, Regur, &c., and winds up his valuable discourse with a classification of the rocks of the South Mahratta country as follows :—

Regur Old kankar Laterite Laterite sandstone Overlying trap	1st Group [Tertiary].
Basaltic greenstone Granite Sandstone	2nd Group [Devonian or Carboniferous ?]

Basaltic greenstone Granite Hypogene schist	3rd Group [Silurian or Cambrian ?]

The *Journals* for 1845 and the two succeeding years contain a number of other important geological contributions from the pen of Newbold. Of these some are mainly Mineralogical, and contain most accurate accounts of the gold tracts and of the mines of various other minerals in Southern India. "It may be said with truth," says Mr. King,* of Captain Newbold's researches, "that each paper is about the most clear and careful description of whatever it was intended to illustrate that has been given by any of the explorers of Southern India; whatever errors he has fallen into are almost all due to his not having been able to make a thorough investigation of the rocks ...... In fact, it may almost be affirmed of Captain Newbold, that the only work incorrectly done, or not done at all, was such as could alone be accurately determined and settled by the continuous and systematic working of men trained to such investigations. He examined the rocks quite as closely for organic remains as we have done, and with equal non-success, lingering only over some peculiar minute spherical and oval bodies in an oolitoid silicious rock, and coming to the same doubtful conclusions, as we have been compelled to do, regarding their organic or inorganic structure."†

(*b*) *Northern India.*

W. Voysey. 1821.

The fifteenth volume of the *Researches* contains a paper by Dr. Voysey on the Building Stones of Ágrá, in which the sandstone, of which

* Memoirs, Geological Survey of India, Vol. VIII, pt. i. p. 9.

† The other contributors on the Geology of Southern India were Drs. H. Walker and A. Christie (1841), and Messrs. Schlagintweit (1855-56).

that city is built, is referred by him to the Old Red Sandstone formation. He regarded it as highly probable that the sandstone forms part of the great Sandstone Formation of India, the north-eastern boundary of which is formed by Fatepur-Sikri, Kalinjar, Machkund, Dholpur, Gwalior, Chunár, and Rotasgar—a most happy conjecture, the correctness of which has since been well established by the officers of the Geological Survey.

In the eighteenth volume of the Society's *Transactions*,* which, as observed before, is chiefly devoted to Geology, appear several long and elaborate Memoirs on the Geology of Central India.

J. Franklin. 1829.

Captain James Franklin explored a large portion of Central India, and described the great Sandstone Formation, now known as the Vindhyan, identified by him (though wrongly) with the New Red Sandstone of England. He also notices the great Trap Formation, which covers such an extensive area in the Deccan and on the Málwa plateau, and forms one of the most striking features in the Geology of India. This formation, as represented in the district of Ságar, is dealt with in detail by Captain Coulthard, who describes its general appearance, petrology, &c.

C. Coulthard. 1829.

* It opens with some "General Observations on the Geology of India" by James Calder, Vice-President of the Physical Committee. He pays a fitting tribute to the memory of Voysey. "In the field of Geology," says he, "some steady progress has been made, which the superintending care of the lamented Voysey promised to ripen into a rich harvest; fatally, however, for science, this ardent philosophic enquirer was a martyr in the cause to which he was devoted." [Mr. Calder's paper gives a succinct review of the information then available about the Geology of India and Ceylon. The distribution of that strange formation, the Laterite, is carefully noted, as well as the coalfield occupying both sides of the River Damuda.]

Mr. J. Hardie, of the Bengal Medical Service, also read a paper on the Geology of Central India, which was published in the second part of the eighteenth volume of the *Researches.* He classifies the rocks described by him under the heads of (1) Granite; (2) Gneiss; (3) Quartz rocks; (4) Micaceous Schist; (5) Chlorite Schist; (6) Talcose Schist, &c. The paper is chiefly mineralogical. Mr. Hardie also contributed some geological remarks which he made in a march from Barodá to Udayapur.

J. Hardie. 1829.

The Rev. R. Everest, whose observations on the quantity of earthy matter brought down by the Ganges we shall have occasion to notice later on, and whose physical researches have been reviewed in the preceding chapter, described the Sandstone and Trap Formations west of Mirzápur between Ságar and the Jamuná.

R. Everest. 1833.

Lieutenant Finnis brought before the Society, in 1829, a very fair Geological description of the country between Nágpur and Hoshangábád, which was published in the third volume of the *Journal.* In it he divides the country into four parts according to the lithology of the rocks met with. He was followed by Dr. Spilsbury,* of the Bengal Medical Service, who (1833) discovered important Mam-

J. Finnis. 1834.

G. Spilsbury. 1833—40.

* The following is an extract from a Resolution passed at a meeting of the Council (see *Journal,* Vol. XXIV, 1855, p. 171):—" Dr. Spilsbury's merits were not merely those of a collector of fossils; in most cases he accurately defined and identified his specimens; and it was probably the want of necessary means of reference and comparison in a remote locality, and the innate modesty of his character that prevented Dr. Spilsbury from giving to the world a full and complete account of his researches in a connected form. Dr. Spilsbury's contributions have further been marked by as great liberality as zeal in behalf of the

malian remains in the Narmadá Valley. He contributed two Geological papers, one in 1834, and the other a few years later. In the former, the Valley of the Narmadá, from Tendukheri to the table-land of Pánchmárí, is described; while the latter gives the results of Dr. Spilsbury's observations on the country between Brimhan Ghát to Amarkantak, the holy source of the Narmadá. Dr. J. Adam, also of the Bengal Medical Service, wrote on the Geology of the country previously traversed by Captain Franklin. The formations occurring there are classified by him into Granite, Trap, Sandstone, and Gravel; in the last of which the diamond-mines are stated to be situated.

J. Adam. 1842.

Captain W. S. Sherwill, of the Revenue Survey, contributed important geological articles on the districts of Sháhábád and Behár, and gave, in the twentieth volume of the *Journal*, a highly interesting sketch of the Rájmáhál Hills, containing valuable geological information. He was the first to examine the structure of these hills; and the conclusions arrived at by him were so sound, that they have been but little shaken by the subsequent detailed examination of the ground by the officers of the Geological Survey of India. The true position of the Sandstones as regards the Volcanic Rocks was pointed out by him. He also discovered the coal of the Chuparbhita Pass, and described the known seams with accuracy.

W. S. Sherwill. 1845—51.

Society. The Council consider that they have served alike to enrich the Society's Museum and to advance the progress of science. On these grounds, they are of opinion that Dr. Spilsbury is entitled to a public recognition of his services; and the Council propose that a subscription be entered upon among the members and the friends of science for a portrait of Spilsbury to be hung up in the Society's rooms."

Mr. J. Homfray's* description of the Dámudá Valley is the first published account of the Ránigan field. It is accompanied by a map, in which the boundaries are laid down with tolerable accuracy. Mr. Homfray shows the absurdity of the view which then prevailed as to the former connection of the Dámudá and Sylhet coal areas.

J. Homfray. 1842.

Dr. Oldham, who was five times elected President of the Society, and whose bust graces their Meeting Hall, was a most active and zealous member of the Society. He had, as Director of the Geological Survey of Ireland, established a wide reputation in Europe before his arrival in India in 1851. He created the present Geological Survey of India. During the working season of 1852-53, he examined the Rájmahál Hills, and the results of his observations were communicated to the Society by the Government of Bengal. He came to the important conclusion, that the entire group of the coal-producing rocks of Bengal Proper (including the Dámudá, Ajaya, Rámgar, and Karharbári Coalfields) are quite distinct from the true coal measures of England, and belong to the same great geological era as the Oolites of Europe,—an opinion which, afterwards, as we shall presently see, he found reason to change. At the May meeting of the Society in 1856, Dr. Oldham gave a résumé of the valuable researches of his talented and energetic colleagues in Central India. He proposed the name of 'Vindhyan' for the great Sandstone Formation of Northern and Central India, which had been referred by Voysey, and subsequently by Sherwill and others,

T. Oldham. 1854—76.

---

* Mr. Homfray was manager of Messrs. Jessop and Co.'s Colliery at Náráyanpuri. In 1837 he was deputed by the Coal Committee to report on the coalfields of Palamow.

to the Old Red Sandstone;* by Franklin, to the New Red Sandstone; and by Dr. Carter, of Bombay, to the Jurassic Epoch, along with the coal-bearing strata of Bengal. He pointed out that, owing to the absence of organic remains, the Vindhyan could not be safely correlated to any of the great European formations, but that they might be Cambrian. Reposing unconformably upon the Vindhyan was a vast thickness of sandstones and shales with numerous plant fossils, which enabled Dr. Oldham to establish their identity with the coal groups of Bardwán, of Házáribág, and of Catak, which had previously been shown to be of Jurassic age. Resting unconformably upon these, there was found another series of very thick, often ferruginous sandstones, forming the Pánchmárí scarp, for which he proposed the name of *Mahádevas*. With regard to the Intertrappean beds, facts had been adduced by the Survey to show that their hardening was due to the subsequent overflow of igneous matter, and not to intrusive sheets of basalt, as advocated by some. He concluded his brief but pregnant remarks with a classification of the Rock Groups, which has since been but little altered. In May 1861, on the occasion of laying before the Society a collection of rocks and fossils from the vicinity of Sydney, presented by Sir William Denison, Dr. Oldham made some interesting remarks on the age of the Indian coal-bearing strata, which had been regarded by Hislop, Carter, and a number of other Geologists, as *all* referable to the Jurassic or Oolitic beds, without admitting of any separation into distinct groups or systems. He contended against this erroneous view, and brought forward the important results of the valuable researches of Mr. W. T. Blanford. Dr. Oldham

* See *ante*, p. 34.

held out a prospect, that future investigations would establish an accurate parallelism between the rocks of India and those of Australia, portions of which were, even then, known to be synchronous ; and "that, while in all probability it would be found that, starting from the common datum line of the coal-bearing rocks in either land, the sequence upwards would be established from Indian researches in this country, apparently supplying links wanting in Australia ; on the other hand, we should be enabled to supplement the evidence of the succession downwards (which is deficient in India), by a reference to Australian Groups." No marine deposits in this country, of the same age as the 'Wollonggong' Sandstones of Australia, had as yet been discovered, but he found nothing in the plant remains of the Talchir beds which would "militate against their being of the same general age."

R. H. Keatinge and T. Oldham. 1858.

Previous to 1857, rocks of the Cretaceous Epoch were known to occur in India only between Trichinopoly and Pondichery. Dr. Carter, in his "Geology of India," had ingeniously suggested, that the beautiful limestone, well known as the "coralline limestone," used at the now ruined city of Mándu, formerly the capital of Malwa, was derived from near Bág, though he had wrongly assigned it to the Oolitic age. Dr. Oldham, during his tour in the Narmadá Valley in 1856, meeting Captain (now Colonel) Keatinge, Political Agent at Mandlesar, then the capital of British Nimar and a military cantonment, strongly urged him to visit the locality. In 1856-57, Colonel Keatinge collected a large number of fossils, which established the Cretaceous age of the coralline limestone beyond question. These were sent to the Museum of the Geological Survey, along with some notes, which were communicated to the Society by Dr. Oldham.

I. C. Haughton. 1854.

Colonel Haughton submitted his geological investigations in Singbhúm and the adjacent country in 1854. He was the first to detect the existence of two subdivisions of the Metamorphics, which he describes as (i) Gneiss passing in some places into Granite, and (ii) Schists, Slates, &c.

S. Hislop. 1855.

The Rev. S. Hislop,* the well-known Missionary of Nágpur, contributed a short but well-digested paper on the age of the coal measures of Bengal and Central India, which he referred to the Oolite of Europe.

W. T. Blanford. 1860.

Mr. Blanford, who joined the Geological Survey in October, 1855, and has lately retired after a distinguished service of twenty-seven years, was President of the Society in 1878 and 1879, and is now an Honorary Member.† He was engaged in the survey of the Rániganj coalfield from 1858 to 1860, the results of which he laid before the Society. He arrived at the following classification in descending order correlative of the Rániganj beds :—

	Ranigunj.		Rajmahal.	Orisa.	Narmadá Valley.	Nágpur.
1.		......	......	Mahadevas.	Mahadevas, Lametas.	Mahadevas.
2.		......	Rajmahals.	......	......	......
3.	Panchet	Upper	Conglomerates.	......	Upper Damudas of Jabalpur.	Mangli Shales.
		Lower	......			
4.	Damuda	Raniganj Series	......	......	......	Damudas.
		Ironstones	......	......	......	
		L. Damudas.	L. Damudas.	L. Damudas.	L. Damudas.	......
5.	Talchirs	Talchirs.	......	Talchirs.	Talchirs.	

* He arrived at Nágpur early in 1845. He was accidentally drowned in crossing a river.

† The Wollaston gold medal, one of the earliest recipients of which was the distinguished Falconer, has this year been awarded to Mr. Blanford by the Geological Society of London.

Colonel Godwin-Austen, late of the Topographical Survey, the well-known naturalist, described the geology and physical features of the Khási and Jaintiá Hills. The oldest rocks, the Metamorphic, were found by him overlaid by sandstones with seams of valuable coal, which had previously been referred to the Cretaceous period by Oldham. These sandstones are followed by Nummulitic limestones, succeeded at places by highly fossiliferous rocks of still younger age, the equivalents probably of the Siváliks. The Lakadong Nummulitic coal is specially noted.

H. Godwin-Austen. 1869—.

(c) *The Himálayas.*

Captain Herbert was among the foremost pioneers of Indian Geology. "As a man of great talent and of sound and extensive scientific culture, he may stand with Captain Newbold, who did so much for the Geology of Southern India . . . The Mineralogical Survey of the Himálayan districts was one of the earliest attempts at a geological map of a considerable area made officially in India. The work was entrusted to Captain Herbert by the Marquis of Hastings. . . . . Captain Herbert* does not assume any pretensions to authority. He tells us very plainly that he made up his Geology for the occasion, but it is plain, too, from his observations and reflections, that he thoroughly mastered his authors. His suggestions in correction of current views are often very judicious, and display a truly scientific turn of mind. . . . He divides all the rocks of the mountains into two great 'primary formations'—one for the Gneiss occupying the central region, and one for the Micace-

J. D. Herbert. 1815—1830.

* Captain Herbert's Report was published in the eleventh volume of the *Journal.*

ous, Chloritic, Hornblendic, and Argillaceous Schists, to which also he joins the limestones. He makes a third zone of the narrow strip of secondary rocks, mostly, if not entirely, the Newer Red, or Saliferous Sandstone."*

H. Falconer. 1831.

Dr. Falconer† commenced his geological explorations among the Sivâlik Hills in 1831, a year after his arrival in India. Cautley and Herbert had found lignite in the sandstones which compose them. Captain Herbert, in his paper on the "Occurrence of Coal in the Indo-Gangetic Mountains," published in the sixteenth volume of the *Researches*, considered these sandstones as forming part of an extensive secondary formation. It was in 1831 that Falconer inferred the Tertiary age of the Sivâlik formation, and placed it on the horizon of the *Molasse* of Switzerland. Three years later, Dr. Falconer contributed to the third volume of the *Journal* a brief account‡ of the geology and physical features of the Range, accompanied by a rough section exhibiting its relation to the Himâlayas.

R. Everest. 1833—1835.

Dr. Gerard, whose geographical contributions will be noticed later on, was the first discoverer of fossil shells in the Spiti Valley. The Rev. R. Everest contributed a memorandum on them in 1833; and two years later brought before the Society some observations which he had made on a journey from Masuri to Gangautri. He mentions the following formations in ascending order :—

(1) Granite ; (2) Gneiss and Mica Slate ; (3) Talcose

---

* Mr. H. B. Medlicott "On the Geology of the Himâlayan Districts," in the "N. W. P. Gazetteer," pp. 112-113.

† For Falconer's Palæontological Researches, see *infra*, Chap. III, p. 58.

‡ The article is on the aptitude of the Himâlayan Range for the culture of the tea plant, and will be found in the "Index," under Section VII.

Gneiss and Talc-Slate; (4) Clay Slate; (5) Masuri Limestone; and (6) Quartz Rock.

T. Hutton. 1839—1841.

Towards the close of 1837, Lieutenant Hutton proposed to the Society to undertake with their patronage and assistance an expedition into the Spiti Valley in order to follow up the discoveries of Dr. Gerard by a geological examination of the country. The Society warmly approved of the idea, and sanctioned substantial pecuniary assistance. A long and interesting account of his trip by Lieutenant Hutton was the result.

W. C. Hay. 1850.

Lieutenant Hutton was followed by Captain Hay, whose Report on the Spiti Valley contains some note-worthy geological observations, though they are vitiated, like those of Hutton, by ill-founded theories and hasty generalisations.

H. B. Medlicott. 1861.

Mr. H. B. Medlicott, Superintendent of the Geological Survey, and twice President of the Society, has long been a most active and earnest member. Formerly of the Geological Survey of Great Britain, he joined the Geological Survey of India in March, 1854. In 1857, he began his examination of the Himálayas, and, in March, 1861, communicated to the Society an abstract of some of the principal results of that highly important survey, which was concluded in the following year (1862).

Captain R. Strachey, in his account to the Geological Society in 1851, had left the massive sandstone at the base of the mountains where Herbert had placed it in the Saliferous period of the secondary era. Major Vicary's discovery of nummulitic fossils at Subathu had been announced in 1854. Falconer and Cautley had also paid almost exclusive attention to fossils, so much so that their description left it to be inferred that the fossiliferous beds of Náhan overlay those of the outer hills. Mr. Medlicott reduced all this confusion to a more intelligible strategraphical order. He showed that the so-called saliferous sandstone of Kumáun corresponds at least in part to the Náhan sandstone, and that there is a great physical break between this latter and the newer Siválik rocks of the outer hills, and also between it and the older Tertiary rocks of Upper Sirmur (Vicary's Nummulitics).

Godwin-Austen. 1865.

Colonel Godwin-Austen, having heard of a field of coal near Santrabári, Bhután Duárs, went to the spot. The geological results of the trip are contained in a paper published in the *Journal* for 1865. He found some lignite in sandstones overlaid unconformably by horizontally bedded conglomerates, but no coal. Two years later, he read a paper on the geological features of the country near the foot of the hills in the Western Bhután Duárs, in which he announced the discovery in the bed of the Diama River, a short distance west of Buxá, of the fossil molar of an elephant probably washed out of the conglomerates just mentioned. He expressed his opinion that "the elevatory force that has raised the Tertiary sandstones into the position they are found in along the whole base of the Himálayas, often to a height of nearly 3,000 feet above the sea, has here been extended in a less degree, and that they are to be sought for yet below the upper conglomerates, more or less deeply seated, at a short distance from the base of the hills."

In 1875, Colonel Godwin-Austen contributed a paper on the Geology of the Daflá Hills, in which he brought to notice certain beds on the Dikrang River, considered by him to be the representative of the Dámudá Series. Some recent river-terraces are described, as well as the alluvium of the Bisnáth plain.

Dr. A. M. Verchère, of the Bengal Medical Service, contributed a voluminous paper on the Geology of Káshmir, the Western Himálaya, and the Afghan Mountains. Previous to the Carboniferous, and probably during the Silurian Epoch, there existed, according to Dr. Verchère, in the centre of Asia (which was then probably a sea uniting the Arctic to the Indian Ocean), linear volcanoes, arranged in a direction parallel to the present general direction of the Himálaya, *i. e.*, N.W. and S.E. Other linear volcanoes were directed from the N.E. to the S.W., where the Afghan Mountains now stand. Dr. Verchère traces the geological history of the area described by him through the Mesozoic and Tertiary Epochs to prehistoric times. The fossils collected by him were examined by M. E. de Verneuil, the distinguished Palæontologist, who contributed a note on them.

A. M. Verchère. 1866-67.

(*d*) *The Salt Range.*

Sir Alexander Burnes, in his paper on the Salt Mines of the Punjab, had given a few geological details ; as had also Dr. Jameson, who was for some time Curator of the Society, in his report on the Indus Inundation, published in the twelfth volume of the *Journal*. Some mineralogical information is also contained in the itinerary papers by Agha Abbas of Shiráz, and Munshi Mohan Lál, both of whom explored under the patronage of Major Leech. But the geology of the Salt Range was first properly and systematically studied by Dr. A. Fleming, of the Bengal Medical Service. In his first Memoir he describes the height and course of the Salt Range ; the red sandstone conglomerate last seen on the Indus below Kálibág and supposed (though wrongly) to underlie the saliferous marl with gypsum and rocksalt ; the variegated sand-

A. Fleming. 1848—53.

stones which come above the marl, superposed by fossiliferous calcareous strata. Above these last named beds he noticed a yellow marl followed by bituminous shales including seams of coal. The highest strata noted by him were those of a compact, fine-grained fossiliferous limestone with flints, described by him as Nummulitic. He gives mineralogical details about Gold, Coal, Iron-ore, Petroleum, Sulphur, Lead-ore, and Salt. In an Appendix, the alum manufacture of Kálibág is described in detail. Dr. Fleming's second contribution consisted of the diary kept by him of his trip to Pind Dádan Khan and the Salt Range, which was communicated by Sir H. M. Elliot, Secretary to the Government of India. In 1851, Dr. Fleming was placed in charge of the Geological Survey of the Salt Range, and had Mr. W. Purdon, an able engineer, and Mr. W. Theobald, late of the Geological Survey of India, as his assistants. His long and elaborate report published in the twenty-second volume of the *Journal* is almost exhaustive. The map which accompanies it, the first of the Salt Range executed from a regular survey, was prepared by the able assistants just mentioned. The Memoir opens with a description of the general physical features of the Salt Range. It then goes on to describe the various formations in the following strategraphical order :—

Devonian ...	*a.*	Red Marl, with Gypsum and Rocksalt.
	b.	Lower Red Sandstone and Grits.
	c.	Micaceous Sandstone and Shales.
	d.	Variegated Sandstones, Grits, &c.
Carboniferous ...	*a.*	Lower Limestone, Calcareous Sandstone, and Shales.
	b.	Grey Sandstone and Shales.
	c.	Upper Limestone (sometimes Magnesian).
Oolitic ...	*a.*	Quartzose Sandstones, Grits, and Shales.
	b.	Cherty Limestones, with Shales.
	c.	Belemnite Sandstone and Shales.

Eocene	...	Calcareous Sandstone, Nummulitic Limestone, Marls and Alum Shales, with Lignite.
Miocene (?)	...	Sandstones, Argillaceous Grits, Conglomerates, &c.
Recent	...	Alluvium.

W. Theobald. 1854.

Mr. Theobald, late Deputy Superintendent of the Geological Survey of India, began his career as assistant to Dr. M'Clelland in 1848, and retired from the service last year. He explored the Salt Range along with Dr. Fleming; and brought together his observations before the Society in 1854. The Physiography of the Range is minutely described, and the strategraphical geology of the area is treated of in the following order :—

Formations.	*Thickness in feet.*
1. Red Marl and Gypsum, with Rocksalt	1,500
2. Dark Red Sandstone	700
3. Dark Arenaceous Shales	250
4. Cupriferous Purple Shales, &c.	400
5. Sandstone, with Conglomerate Bands	700
6. Productus Limestone	1,100
7. Spotted Shales and Sandstones	600
8. Carbonaceous Shales, &c.	80
9. Nummulitic Limestone	1,100
10. Nummulitic Limestone, Conglomerate, Ossiferous Sands, &c.	10,000

(e) *Burma, Malay Peninsula, and the Islands in the Bay of Bengal.*

J. Low. 1829.

Captain J. Low, of the Madras Army, contributed "Some Observations on the Geological Appearances and General Feature of portions of the Malayan Peninsula, &c.," in which the geology of Perak, Penang, Tenasserim, Tavoy and Martaban is described.

Mr. Blanford, in 1862, gave an account of the extinct

W. T. Blanford. 1862.

volcano of Puppadoung in Upper Burma, in which he clearly established the fact of an active volcano having existed in Pegu during the deposition of beds of comparatively recent geological date.

Professor Ball, late of the Geological Survey of India,

V. Ball. 1870.

who has been one of the most industrious members of the Society, and who acted as treasurer in 1881, has made numerous contributions to Natural History, among which are those on the Geology of the Nicobar Islands and of the vicinity of Port Blair. Dr. Hochstetter had, in the "Records of the Geological Survey of India," given an account of the Nicobars; and Mr. Ball's observations were chiefly confirmatory of those held by that distinguished geologist. The rocks which, in the Nicobars, determine the character of the soil were pointed out by Mr. Ball to be :—

1. Coral rocks.
2. Magnesian Claystone, with Conglomerates.
3. Gabbro and Serpentine rocks.

In his second paper Mr. Ball describes the geological features of Ross Island, the southern coast-line of Port Blair, Mount Harriet, Viper Island, islands north-east of Port Blair, and of Narkandam Island. The article concludes with an enumeration of the useful products contained in the rocks of the Andamans — Coal, Serpentine, Iron, &c.

§ 3.—*Dynamical Geology.*

(*a*) *Volcanoes and Earthquakes.*

The earliest geological contribution to the Society's *Trans-*

R. H. Colebrooke. 1795.

actions is a note on "Barren Island and its Volcano by Lieut. R. H. Colebrooke," published in the fourth volume of the *Researches.* On the 12th of May, 1787, on a voyage to Pulo Penang, he saw a column of smoke ascend from the summit of Barren Island. By the help of his glasses he perceived the smoke to arise from a hill nearly in its centre, around which appeared an extensive valley. He quotes Captain Blair's description of an eruption which he had witnessed on the 24th of March, *i.e.*, about two months previously. It runs thus :—" The volcano was in a violent state of eruption, bursting out immense volumes of smoke, and frequently showers of red hot stones. Some were of a size to weigh 3 or 4 tons, and had been thrown some 100 yards past the foot of the cone. There were two or three eruptions while we were close to it. . . . . The base of the cone is the lowest part of the island, and very little higher than the level of the sea."

Colonel Colebrooke concludes his note with some speculations, which, considering the time they were written (about 1790), are very interesting. Europe, as we saw before, was then being agitated by the disputes between the rival factions of the Neptunists and the Vulcanists. Colonel Colebrooke, like most other Indian Geologists, probably had no previous geological training, and certainly did not belong to either of these parties. " From the very singular and uncommon appearance of this island," he remarks, " it might be conjectured, that it has been thrown up entirely from the sea by the action of subterranean fire. Perhaps, but a few centuries ago, it had not reared itself above the waves ; but might have been gradually emerging from the bottom of the ocean, long before it became visible, till at length it reached the surface. . . . The cone or volcano would rapidly increase in bulk, from the continual discharge of lava and combustible matter. . . . . If this conjecture should gain credit, we may suppose not only many islands, but a great portion of the habitable globe, to have been thrown up by volcanoes, which are now mostly extinguished. . . . . A ground-plan of Barren Island would so exactly resemble some of the lunar spots as seen through a good telescope when their shadows are strong, that I cannot help thinking there are also many more volcanoes in the moon than have yet been discovered by a celebrated modern astronomer." A sketch of the volcano accompanies the paper.

E. P. Halstead. 1841.

Edward Halstead, Commander of Her Majesty's Sloop "Childers," contributed an elaborate report on Cheduba, in which a chapter is devoted to Geology. He mentions the fact of an elevation of the island having taken place within the memory of man, and of the extension of the elevatory movement over all the shoals and islands from the Terribles, off the north end of Ramri, to Foul Island. The movement in question has been about thirteen feet at the Terribles, twenty-two feet on various parts of the north-western reef of Cheduba, sixteen feet at the north point of the island, thirteen feet at the centre of the island on the west coast, twelve feet at the southern end, and from twelve to nine feet in the islands south of Cheduba as far as Foul Island. Commander Halstead met with a man, aged 106 years, who gave him an account of the elevation of Cheduba, accompanied by an earthquake, which had occurred when he was 15 years, *i.e.*, about 1751. "The earthquake was very violent, the sea washed to and fro several times with great fury, and then retired from the grounds, leaving an immense quantity of fish; the feasting on which is a favourite story throughout the island; no lives were lost, no rents in the earth occurred, nor fire from the volcanoes of the island." These, known as "mud volcanoes," were all visited. The larger volcanoes when in eruption, which is stated to take place during the rains, are described as occasionally ejecting fluid mud, mixed with angular fragments of stone (to some of which small portions of copper ore are found attached) torn from the strata, through which the vent is forced.

R. Baird Smith. 1843—45.

Colonel Baird Smith, of the Bengal Engineers, was the first to record and analyze the phenomena of Indian earthquakes. The first part of his long and admirable Memoir is a register of Indian earthquakes for 1842. An historical summary of known shocks from 1803, with remarks on the general distribution of subterranean disturbing forces throughout India and its frontier countries, is given in the second part. Colonel Baird Smith then proceeds to give an analysis of the Indian earthquakes, and concludes with remarks on the points to be observed during earthquake shocks, and on the means of making the requisite observations. In 1845, he furnished a record of Indian and Asiatic earthquakes for 1843.

S. Hannay and Assam Government. 1839—43 & 1874—80.

The earthquakes in Assam for 1839—43 were recorded by Captain Hannay, who was one of our most zealous contributors; and those from 1874 to 1880 by the Assam Government. Scattered through the pages of the Society's *Journal* are registers of various earthquakes in other parts of India.

(*b*) *Glacial Action.*

I. A. Hodgson. 1822.

Captain Hodgson, in his account of a visit to the source of the Ganges in 1817, published in the fourteenth volume of the *Researches*, describes the Ganges as issuing from under "a very low arch at the foot of the grand snow-bed," about a mile and-a-half in width, with small hollows, and "the snow stuck full of rubbish and rocks imbedded in it." These *débris* are described as being supported in the snow, sinking as it sinks.

J. H. Batten and Manson. 1842.

Mr. J. H. Batten, who was for some time resident in Kumáun, and was long one of our most zealous members, edited in the eleventh volume of the *Journal* Captain Manson's Diary of a trip to Milum and the Anta Dhura Pass. Captain Manson noticed at the source of the Gori River, about a mile north-west from Milum, "a mass of dark-coloured ice," covered with rock-fragments forming a succession of low hills. The bases of the hills on either sides are described as a succession of landslips; but from their distance, Captain Manson could not believe it possible, "that the *débris* in the centre of the snow-bed valley can have fallen there from the side hills. Lieutenant Weller, Executive Engineer in Kumáun, also visited this glacier on a visit to the Bulaba and Anta Dhura Passes.

J. A. Weller. 1843.

E. Madden and R. Strachey. 1847.

Captain E. Madden, of the Bengal Artillery, made an excursion to the Pinder (or Pindir) glacier in September, 1846, and contributed his observations in the form of a diary to the sixteenth volume of the *Journal*. But it was Lieutenant R. Strachey who first systematically studied the Himálaya glaciers. In May, 1847, he paid a visit to the Pindir and Kuphine glaciers, both in the Kumáun Himálaya; and an interesting paper was the result, in which he came to the conclusion, that "in the Himálaya, as in the Alps, almost every valley that descends from the ranges covered with perpetual snow has at its head a true glacier."

Lieutenant R. Strachey again visited the Pindir glacier in May, 1848, chiefly with a view to the accurate measurement of its motion; and the result of his operations was published in the seventeenth volume of the *Journal.* The mean motion of the ice in 24 hours is thus given in inches :—

		On the lateral moraines.		On the middle of the glacier.
Lower part of the glacier	...	4·8	...	9·4.
Upper part of the glacier	...	5·3	...	10·0.

H. Godwin-Austen. 1868—75.

Colonel Godwin-Austen, in an article on the "Pangong Lake District of Ládak," pointed out numerous instances of evident ice-action in the Káshmir territory. He detected traces of a glacial period, even as low as the valley of the Jhelum at Baramúla. "When the glaciers extended down to 5,000 feet," he remarks, "what must have been the appearance of the Upper Shayok, Indus, and Chang Chungmo, where 12,000 to 13,000 feet is the lowest level of the country. Contemplation of such a scene in the mind's eye renders the formation of lakes and the accumulations of detrital matter a natural sequence very easy to imagine."

In August, 1875, he read a paper, in which he showed that on so low a latitude as 25° 30′ N., glaciers of considerable dimensions must have once filled the valleys of the Burail Range, the main ridge of the Nágá Hills. He observed moraines at a height of 9,890 feet above the level of the sea, and met with huge transported blocks of sandstone, one of which measured 4,320 cubic feet, as low as 4,800 feet.

W. T. Blanford. 1871.

Mr. Blanford, in his account of a visit to the eastern and northern frontiers of Independent Sikkim,* described traces of former glaciers

---

* See Geographical Index, p. lxxviii.

which he had observed in the Upper Tístá Valley at between 5,000 and 6,000 feet, and especially noticed the great moraines of the Láchung and Láchen Valleys described by Dr. Hooker in his "Himalayan Journal."

J. F. Campbell. 1877.

Mr. Campbell, author of "Frost and Fire," while travelling in India, contributed some remarks on Himálayan glaciation. Between the Ganges and the Ravi, which included the Masuri Hills and the country to the north-west of Simla, he could find no evidence of glacial action, no "perched block," "hogbacked ridge,' or rounded valley. He failed to detect even in the coarsest conglomerate any trace of an erratic boulderbed or anything approaching to a moraine. The great blocks so abundant in the Kángrá Valley, which had been first brought to the notice of geologists by Mr. H. B. Medlicott, were attributed by him to river deposits.

H. B. Medlicott. 1877.

The only direct evidence of presumed glaciation that came within the range of Mr. Campbell's immediate observations, were the great blocks of gneiss along the base of the Dhuládhár in the Kángrá Valley within an elevation of 3,000 feet, which Mr. Medlicott had described in 1864 as probably due to glacial action. While pointing out that Mr. Campbell had overlooked the principal point upon which that opinion had been based, Mr. Medlicott indicated possible by-gone conditions in the Kángrá Valley, whereby the position of the great boulders might be due to ordinary diluvial action as suggested by Mr. Campbell, but at the same time Mr. Medlicott insisted that the conditions aforesaid were presumably connected with a great former extension of glacial action in the Himálaya, probably contemporaneous with the Glacial Period.

(c) *River Action.*

The Rev. R. Everest instituted, in 1831,a series of experiments to ascertain the quantity of earthy matter brought down by the Ganges at Gházipur, the results of which laid before the Society in June, 1832, were :—

R. Everest. 1832.

Season.	*Average breadth in feet.*	*Velocity in feet per hour.*	*Cubic feet discharged per second.*
Rains (4 months) ...	2,080	23,800	494,208
Winter (5 months) ...	1,780	7,435	71,200
Hot weather (3 months) ...	1,730	7,445	36,330

The average quantity of solid matter suspended in the water during the 122 days of the rains was found to be $\frac{1}{428}$th part of solid matter by weight; taking the specific gravity of the water at one-half that of the dried mud; the solid matter discharged amounted to 577 cubic feet per second, giving a total of 6,082,041,600 cubic feet for the discharge in the 122 days of the rains.

Mr. Piddington,* Curator of the Society's Museum of Economic Geology, gave, in 1854, a tabular statement of the quantity of silt held in suspension by the water of the Hugli at Calcutta for each month of the year 1842. Two years later, he contributed a far more elaborate series of measurements. Tabular statements are given of the amount of silt held in suspension at the surface as well as at a mean depth of about three fathoms, by the waters of the Hugli at Calcutta, and at the mouth of the Hugli below Saugor. Observations on the width, mean depth, sectional area, mean velocity per second, and discharge

H. Piddington. 1854—56.

---

* *Vide ante*, p. 15.

per second, of the river, by Lieutenant-Colonel Goodwyn, Bengal Engineers, at Calcutta, and by Mr. A. Bedford at Mayápur, thirteen miles below Calcutta, and at the Jagaháli Semaphore below Diamond Point, are also tabulated.*

---

* It was originally intended to have a section on Mineralogical papers and notices, as historically they are highly important. But being mostly mere chemical analyses, their review would have required an amount of time and space, which, even if I had it at my command I would consider unnecessary, as they have been distinguished in the accompanying Geological Indices , so that the reader may pick them out and ascertain their nature with but little trouble.

CHAPTER III.

ZOOLOGY.*

[§ 1. Introductory. I. Vertebrata. § 2. Mammals, Birds, Reptiles, and Amphibia — Hodgson —Falconer — Cautley — Baker — Durand — Blyth —Tickell — Blanford — Theobald — Godwin-Austen — Stoliczka — Anderson — Lydekker. § 3. Fishes — M'Clelland — Blyth — Cantor — Day. II. Invertebrata — Benson and Hunter — Theobald — H. F. and W. T. Blanford — Godwin-Austen — G. & H. Nevill— Stoliczka — Wood-Mason — Marshall — Nicéville.]

§ 1.—*Introductory.*

SIR W. JONES was averse to zoological study. "Could the figure, instincts, and qualities," says he in one of his anniversary discourses,† "be ascertained either on the plan of Buffon, or on that of Linnæus without giving pain to the object of our examination, few studies would afford us more solid instruction, or more exquisite delight; but I never could learn by what right, nor conceive with what feeling, a naturalist can occasion the misery of an innocent bird, and leave its young, perhaps, to perish in a cold nest, because it has gay plumage, and has never been delineated, or deprive even a butterfly of its natural enjoyment, because it has the misfortune to be rare or beautiful." These are noble and humane sentiments. So feelingly and eloquently declared and by a man of Sir William Jones's position and influence, they no doubt tended seriously to discourage zoological research. As a consequence, we had none worth the name until the year 1828.

* See Indices, pp. xliii and xcii—xciv.

† Tenth Anniversary Discourse, *Asiatic Researches*, Vol. IV.

I.—Vertebrata.

§ 2.—*Mammals, Birds, and Reptiles.*

In that year the systematic study of the Vertebrata of India was commenced by Mr. Bryan Houghton Hodgson, for many years Resident at the Court of Nepal, and perhaps the oldest Member of the Society now living. His contributions on the Bird and Mammalian Fauna of Nípál, Sikim, and Tibet, published in the *Researches* and the *Journal*, amount to no less than ninety. They are all characterized by "deep research and great acumen, and are very full in details of structure."

B. H. Hodgson. 1829—48.

At the June meeting of the Society in 1831, Mr. Secretary Prinsep read the following letter from Dr. H. Falconer, dated from Sáhá-ranpur :—

Hugh Falconer. 1831—59.

"Sir,—In No. 3 of the *Journal of the Asiatic Society* [Vol. I, p. 97], Mr. Royle has announced the discovery by me of the fossil bones in the range of hills which skirts the valley of Dehra on the southwest. I regret that Mr. Royle did not confine himself to a simple announcement of the fact, without giving an extract from the letter in which it is mentioned. The communication was made immediately after I had met with the fossils, and was an unguarded expression to an intimate friend of what I imagined them to be, and not an opinion intended for a public journal in the *ipsissima verba* of the letter. Beyond, therefore, the fact of fossil bones occurring in these hills, I do not wish to stand responsible for any opinion regarding their specific determination in the present imperfect state of the inquiry. As yet they have been found in a small quantity only, and consist of a few fragmented portions of bones. The lignite occurs in great abundance. The "fragments of the shells" (not the 'skull' as stated in the *Journal*) of tortoises resemble those found by Mr. Crawfurd and Dr. Wallich on the banks of the Iráwadi, and others contained in the Museum of the Asiatic Society. The "fragment of a bivalve shell" is very imperfect, and therefore very questionable.

"I conceive it necessary to state that Lieut. Cautley, Superintendent of the Doab Canal, is the original discoverer of fossils in these hills. The most perfect portion I have yet seen of these fossil bones has been in his possession several years, without, however, his being aware of its nature."

This is the earliest published communication from the pen of Dr. Falconer, and the first on those grand discoveries which have immortalized his name, and added so much to the fame of the Asiatic Society. Brief as the communication is, and though it was written at the early age of twenty-two, it shows admirably that caution and that spirit of scientific research which characterize the subsequent writings of that truly great man. He was cautious almost to a fault, and never committed himself to an opinion until he felt quite sure about it. "And thus," remarks his biographer, "as too often happens under such circumstances, he constantly deferred publishing his views, and others reaped the credit of observations originally made by him." Superficial people, who measure the energy of a man by the amount of his published writings without regard to their quality, have brought the charge of idleness against Falconer. He was certainly not a voluminous writer, but whatever he wrote are models of what scientific papers should be.

Dr. Falconer arrived in Calcutta as an Assistant Surgeon in the East India Company's service, in September, 1830. He at once undertook an examination of the fossil bones from Ava in the collection of our Society, and communicated a short paper on them, which was published in the third volume of "Gleanings in Science." While at Mírat, to which station he was ordered early in 1831, he made the acquaintance of Dr. Royle, then Superintendent of the Botanical Garden at Sáháranpur. The acquaintance developed into friendship; and on the retirement of Dr. Royle in 1832, Falconer succeeded him in charge of the garden. He was then only twenty-three.

Proby T. Cautley, W. Baker, H. Durand.

At that time three eminent Engineers, whose names stand foremost in the early history of Indian Irrigation, Sir (then Captain) Proby Cautley, Sir (then Lieutenant) William Baker, and Sir (then Lieutenant) Henry Durand, were engaged on the Jumna Canals, the heads of which are close to Sáháranpur. A friendship sprang up between Falconer and Cautley, and their names are henceforth linked together in connection with the Sivâlik Fauna, as are those of Baker and Durand.

On the 16th of November, 1834, Lieutenant Baker sent to the Secretary of the Asiatic Society a sketch of a fossil elephant's tooth, which had been presented to him by the Rájá of Náhan. Having heard of the tooth, Falconer made inquiry, and had a fragment of a similar tooth presented to him also. He says, in a letter to the Secretary dated Masuri, 3rd January, 1835:—

"I got a hint where they [the teeth] came from, and on going to the spot, I reaped a splendid harvest. Conceive only my good fortune; within six hours, I got upwards of 300 specimens of fossil bones. This was on November 20th, a couple of days after Lieutenants Baker and Durand had got their first specimens through their native collectors."

The nineteenth volume of the *Researches* contains Memoirs by Falconer and Cautley on the *Sivatherium Giganteum*, the *Felis Cristata*, and the *Ursus Sivalensis*, and on fossil species of the camel and the hippopotamus. In the same volume is published also a paper on "The Hippopotamus and other Fossil Genera of the Sub-Himálayas in the Dádupur Collection," by Lieutenant Durand.

The discoveries near the valley of Markunda were enthusiastically followed up by similar ones in other parts of the Sub-Himálayan Range; and the fourth, fifth, and sixth volumes of the *Journal* are rich in contributions on the remarkable fauna thus brought to light by Messrs. Falconer, Cautley, Baker, and Durand. Unequalled for richness and extent in any other region then known, the fossils created no little sensation throughout the scientific world. The Wollaston Medal in duplicate was awarded in 1837 to Dr. Falconer and Captain Cautley by the Geological Society; and the learned Societies of Europe and America hastened to mark their appreciation by the bestowal of appropriate honours. Sir Charles Lyell announced the award of the Geological Society in terms which must have been no mean incentive to young Falconer—for he was at the time under thirty. "When," remarked Sir Charles, "Captain Cautley and Dr. Falconer first discovered these remarkable remains, their curiosity was awakened, and they felt convinced of their great scientific value; but they were not versed in fossil osteology, and being stationed on the remote confines of our Indian possessions, they were far distant from any living authorities or books on comparative anatomy to which they could refer. The manner in which they overcame these disadvantages, and the enthusiasm with which they continued for years to prosecute their researches, when thus isolated from the scientific world, are truly admirable."

From 1843 to 1847, Dr. Falconer was in England, engaged in the determination and illustration of the Sivâlik fossils in the British Museum and the East India House.

In February, 1848, he returned to India as Superintendent of the Calcutta Botanic Garden. For some years after his arrival, he was mainly occupied with botanical pursuits. The Society, however, largely availed itself of his presence at Calcutta, and the result was "a Descriptive Catalogue of the Fossil Remains of Vertebrata from the Siválik Hills, the Narmadá, Perim Island, &c., in the Museum of the Asiatic Society of Bengal." There was no man better qualified for the task than Dr. Falconer. He was well acquainted with the ordinary characters and appearance of the Siválik fossils, and was familiar with those of Perim Island, having examined and, in part, described a large collection presented by Captain Fulljames to the Geological Society of London. He knew the Ava collections made by Crawfurd in 1826 well, having carefully gone over the whole series in the Geological Society's Museum in London before he left for India, and was conversant with the characters of the Narmadá specimens through the collections taken to England by Mr. Charles Fraser. The catalogue was finished in 1855, and published in 1859. Six years later, Falconer breathed his last. A committee, including the Presidents of the Royal, Linnean, Geological, Geographical, and Ethnological Societies, was formed to raise a 'Falconer Memorial' fund; and a marble bust by Timothy Butler was placed in the rooms of the Royal Society. By a separate subscription raised here, another marble bust has been placed to the right of the main entrance to our meeting hall—a fitting tribute to the memory of a man who has done so much to raise the reputation of this noble institution.

E. Blyth. 1841—63.

While Falconer was so busy, exhibiting the connexion between the extinct species of the Siválik formation and their living representatives, these latter were being studied with unsurpassed assiduity and earnestness by another eminent zoologist. Even before his departure for India to be Curator of the Society's Natural History Museum, Mr. Blyth had made his mark in England as an ardent student of zoology. On his arrival here, he set himself to the performance of his duties with characteristic zeal and devotion, which were more than once acknowledged by the Society; but it was his devotion to the cause of science that mainly supported him in his twenty-two years' hard work in a tropical climate and at an inadequate remuneration. His work was the work of love; and it is such work alone that keeps one up—as it certainly did keep up Blyth—in the midst of struggles and difficulties.

As Curator, Blyth was required to furnish monthly reports. Besides these, each of which occupies from fifteen to twenty pages, his contributions to the *Journal*, mostly on Reptiles, Birds, and Mammals, amount to no less than forty. His Catalogue of Birds in the Asiatic Society's Collection was published in 1849, and that of Mammalia in 1863. The last sheets of the latter work were seen through the press by his friend, Jerdon. Twenty-one years of incessant work —and not a little of it was pure drudgery—had seriously affected Blyth's health; and in the summer of 1862, it broke down so completely that he was compelled to retire and proceed to England. During the last three years of his life there, he was engaged in the preparation of a catalogue of the Mammals and Birds of Burma at the request of Sir A. Phayre. He did not live to publish it; and it was printed by the Asiatic Society as an extra number in 1875, two years after his death, with a biographical notice by Mr. Grote and a portrait of the author.

Darwin frequently quoted Blyth as an "excellent authority;" and Gould refers to him as "one of the first zoologists of his time." Blyth was certainly the founder in this country of a school of what may be called field-zoologists. The active correspondence he kept on with the sportsmen-naturalists—most of the zoologists in India are such—in various parts of the country, and his elaborate notices of the presentations which were made by them to the Society, not to speak of his numerous Memoirs, "contributed an impetus to the study of natural history that has done more to its extension in India than all the previous publications."

Since the time of Blyth, the scientific contributions received by the Society have been mainly zoological. Foremost among his successors stand the names of Jerdon, Blanford, Theobald, Tickell, Godwin-Austen, Dobson, Brooks, and Tytler, whose contributions enrich the pages of the *Journal* for the last twenty years.

S. R. Tickell. 1838-65.

Colonel S. R. Tickell was one of the pioneers of Indian Ornithology. As early as 1833, he presented the Society with a list of Birds collected by him in the jungles of Barábhum and Dholbhum. His contributions on Birds, Reptiles, &c., extend down to 1865.

W. T. Blanford. 1868—.

Mr. W. T. Blanford* has long been a most active contributor. Wherever he has been — and his duties have carried him to various parts not only of Asia, but also of Africa—he has most zealously collected the Mollusca, Reptiles, Birds, and Mammals of the locality, and described them for the Society. His numerous papers on these branches of Zoology are characterized by that ability, judgment, and thoroughness which mark his equally, or perhaps still more, numerous geological researches.

W. Theobald. 1866—.

Mr. Theobald† will be long remembered for his valuable contributions to the Herpetology and Malacology of India and Burma. The

---

* See above, Chapter II, p. 40. † *Ibid*, p. 47.

latter will be noticed later on; with regard to the former his most important works are his Catalogues of the Reptiles. The first of these is his "Catalogue of Reptiles in the Museum of the Asiatic Society of Bengal," which was published as an extra number to the *Journal*, Part II for 1868.

H. Godwin-Austen. 1869—78.

Colonel Godwin-Austen, whose geological work was reviewed in the last Chapter, described and catalogued the Birds collected by him in various parts of Assam for the Society in a number of highly valuable papers.

G. E. Dobson. 1871—75.

Dr. G. E. Dobson, of the Netley Hospital, author of the "Monograph of the Asiatic Chiroptera," communicated a number of articles on the *Chiroptera* in the Society's *Journal* for 1871. He is one of the highest authorities on that order of the Mammalia; and his descriptions are thorough and accurate.

F. Stoliczka. 1869—74.

That accomplished naturalist, the late lamented Stoliczka, who held the Natural History Secretaryship for over five years, contributed several important papers which comprise nearly all the classes of the Vertebrata, and several of the Invertebrata, which latter will be noticed in the next section.

T. Anderson. 1871—.

The mantle of Blyth fell on Dr. J. Anderson,* the present accomplished Superintendent of the India Museum. In 1871, he contributed a paper on "Reptilian Accessions to the Indian Museum from 1865 to 1870, with a description of some new species." The *Journal* for 1877 contains his descriptions of some new and little-known Asiatic shrews in the collections of the Indian Museum; and that for the following year a monograph on the Indian species of the *Erinaceus*.

* Dr. Anderson was Natural History Secretary of the Society from 1865 to 1867.

The pages of the *Proceedings* also contain descriptions by Dr. Anderson of various new or little-known Vertebrate forms.

R. Lydekker. 1877—.

To Mr. R. Lydekker, late of the Geological Survey of India, an accomplished Comparative Anatomist, who acted for some time as Natural History Secretary, the Society is indebted for a number of contributions, among which is his "History of the Fossil Vertebrata of India."

§ 3.—*Fishes.*

J. M'Clelland, T. Cantor, E. Blyth, and F. Day.

Dr. M'Clelland's Monograph of the Indian *Cyprindiæ*, published in the second part of the nineteenth volume of the *Researches*, laid the foundation of the study of the Fishes of India. The next important contributor on the subject was Dr. Cantor, of the Bengal Medical Service, whose "Catalogue of Malayan Fishes" was published in the *Journal* for 1850. Mr. E. Blyth was the author of several interesting papers on the Fishes of India, Pegu, Port Blair, &c., printed in the *Journal* for 1858, 1859, and 1860. The last and best known writer is Dr. F. Day, the author of two handsomely illustrated volumes on the "Fishes of India." His articles were communicated between 1870 and 1872. Of these the longest and most important is his Monograph of the *Cyprinidæ* printed in six parts in the *Journal* for 1871 and 1872.

II.—INVERTEBRATA.

H. Benson and T. Hunter. 1830—55.

Mr. W. H. Benson and Lieutenant T. Hunter were the earliest contributors on the Land and Freshwater-Shells of India. Their numerous papers are scattered through the pages of the "Gleanings in Science" and the *Journal* of the Society for a quarter of a century, from 1830 to 1855.

W. Theobald. 1857—.

In 1857-58, Mr. Theobald commenced a highly important series of papers on the Land and Freshwater-Shells of Burma and India, which were continued with but little intermission down to 1881.

W. T. Blanford and H. F. Blanford. 1860—.

In 1860, Mr. W. T. Blanford, in conjunction with his brother, Mr. H. F. Blanford, contributed the first of a series of Malacological contributions. The second of the series appeared under their joint authorship in the following year; and henceforth the articles were continued by Mr. W. T. Blanford till 1880, when the twelfth and last of the series appeared. Besides the Mollusca contained in these papers, Mr. Blanford has described many more from India, Burma, and Ceylon.

H. Godwin-Austen. 1868—.

Colonel Godwin-Austen has presented the Society with a series of valuable descriptions of the Shells collected by him in Assam.

G. and H. Nevill. 1870—.

All these writers confined their attention to Land and Freshwater Mollusca, which they had mostly collected themselves on survey expeditions. To Messrs. H. and G. Nevill, especially to the latter, we are indebted for accurate descriptions of a number of marine and estuarine Mollusca.

F. Stoliczka. 1869—74.

The distinguished writers, whose work we have just noticed, wrote mainly upon Mollusca and almost exclusively upon the *shells* or their solid parts. It was in 1869 that Ferdinand Stoliczka first commenced in this country the systematic study of the Anatomy, Physiology, and Morphology of the *animal*, not only of Mollusca, but of other Invertebrata. He was a zoologist of the new school—a laboratory-zoologist. Even before he joined the Geological Survey of India in 1862, he had established a reputation as naturalist and geologist in connection with the Imperial Geological Survey of Austria. As Palæontologist to the Indian Survey, his work on the Cretaceous Fauna of Southern India testifies at once his great ability and untiring industry. Besides enriching the pages of our *Journal* with his researches, always thorough and profound, he did our Society most useful service as Natural History Secretary. The Natural Science part of the *Journal* for 1869 contains three papers by Stoliczka; one on the "Anatomy of *Sagartia Schilleriana* and *Membranipora Bengalensis;*" the second on "*Onchidium;* and the third on "Indian *Arachnoidea.*" In all these papers special attention is paid to the soft parts of the animals, to the anatomical and morphological details. In all his subsequent communications, the same feature is characteristically prominent. In 1874, Dr. Stoliczka accompanied the mission of Sir Douglas Forsyth to Káshgár, and died on the 9th of June—a martyr in the cause of science.

J. Wood-Mason. 1871—.

To Mr. Wood-Mason, of the Indian Museum, our late Natural History Secretary,* we are indebted for numerous memoirs. He has paid special attention to the *Arthropoda*, and to the *Crustacea* and *Insecta* among them. His first article, entitled "Contributions to Indian Carcinology," was communicated in 1871, two years after his arrival in India.

G. F. L. Marshall and L. de Nicéville.

During the last four years we have been presented with a series of valuable contributions from Major Marshall and Mr. de Nicéville on Butterflies.†

* Mr. Wood-Mason was Natural History Secretary from 1874 to 1877, and again from 1880 to 1882.

† Some explanation is perhaps due to our Zoological Contributors for the apparently meagre notice taken of their numerous and valuable papers. A bare enumeration of them was considered unnecessary, as that is already done in the appended Indices. To give any further information about their contents than what can be gathered from their titles, long lists of orders, genera, and species would have had to be inserted, which, even if we could make room for them, would, unless accompanied by the diagnostic characters of the species, be, it was thought, of questionable utility in a review of this nature.

CHAPTER IV.

BOTANY.*

[§ 1. Indian Flora—Sir W. Jones—Roxburgh—Wallich—Griffiths—Hooker—Thomson—Anderson—Edgeworth. § 2. Burmese Flora—Kurz. § 3. Palæo-Botany—Feistmantel.]

§ 1.—*Indian Flora.*

Sir W. Jones. 1788—1794.

IN the Anniversary Discourse to which allusion was made in the opening lines of the last Chapter, the President-Founder of the Society calls Botany "the loveliest and most copious division in the Science of Nature." He began his study of Botany under the confinement of a severe and lingering illness. The last paper he read at this Society was a description of select Indian plants, with their Sanscrit and vulgar names. As long ago as 1676, Henry Van Rheede, the Dutch Governor of Malabar, had made a large collection of Indian plants through the agency of a Brahman. These were sent to Cochin, where they were figured and described in Latin. The work, which was published at Amsterdam in twelve folio volumes with seven hundred and ninety-four plates, between 1686 and 1703, appears to have stimulated our worthy President. "When we complain," says he, "and myself as much as any, that we have no leisure in India for literary and philosophical pursuits, we should consider that Van Rheede was a

* See Indices, pp. lxviii and xcv.

nobleman at the head of an Indian Government, in his time very considerable, and that he fully discharged all the duties of his important station, while he found leisure to compile those twelve large volumes, which Linnæus himself pronounces *accurate.*"

Sir William Jones describes the plants under their Sanscrit names, and gives the vulgar and Latin names as synonyms, and he was fully persuaded that Linnæus himself would have adopted the same plan had he known the learned and ancient languages of this country.

The foundation of the Botanic Gardens at Calcutta in 1786, and those at Sáháranpur in 1823, and the munificent patronage which was early accorded to Botany by the Court of Directors of the East India Company, removed that science from the special care and attention of the Society; and when the Physical Committee was formed (or rather revived) in 1828, Botany was excluded from the objects of their research. The explanation of this exclusion is contained in the following passage from the introductory paper of Mr. J. Calder, published in the first part of the eighteenth volume of the *Researches:*—

"In the colonial possessions of other nations, the whole field of nature has been explored and described by scientific and enlightened travellers: whilst in India it has been almost entirely neglected with one splendid exception, in which the munificent patronage of the East India Company has enabled a distinguished member of our Society to make magnificent discoveries in the Vegetable Kingdom. May we not hope that the same patronage may be extended to other departments of Physical Science, and that as Indian Botany has found its Linnæus, we may yet see the treasures of the Animal and Mineral Kingdoms unfolded to us by a Humboldt and a Cuvier."

William Roxburgh was this "Indian Linnæus." He first reduced the plants of the East to the form of a flora, and was appointed Superintendent of the Calcutta Botanic Gardens in 1793, which office he continued to fill until 1814, when he went home and died at Edinburgh in April, 1815. He was a most active member of the Society, and was for many years a member of the Committee of Papers. His contributions to the Society, though few, were most valuable, especially his descriptions of the Indian *Cannaceæ.*

W. Roxburgh. 1793–1814.

Dr. N. Wallich, a Dane, who came to India as Surgeon of the Danish settlement of Serámpur, was taken prisoner when that place was captured by the English. His reputation as a botanist, however, induced the Government not only to liberate him, but place him in charge of the Botanic Gardens in 1815. In 1820, appeared in the thirteenth volume of the *Researches* his descriptions of rare Indian plants, which were afterwards developed into his grand work, The "Plantæ Asiaticæ Rariores," in three folio volumes with three-hundred coloured plates, published by the East India Company in 1832.

N. Wallich. 1815–1833.

William Griffiths, one of the most distinguished botanists of the age, arrived at Calcutta as Assistant Surgeon in 1835. That very year he presented the Society with descriptions of several interesting plants, published in the nineteenth volume of the *Researches*, and was at once appointed to accompany Dr. Wallich to Assam. He explored the country between Sadiyá and Ává, making magnificent collections of plants and animals; and contributed several important botanical papers on the flora of that country to the sixth and seventh volumes of the *Journal.* He

W. Griffiths. 1835–38.

traversed the Bhután country as Surgeon to Pemberton's Embassy, and subsequently joined the army of the Indus in a scientific capacity. He went to Malacca at the end of 1847, and there died early next year.*

J. D. Hooker. 1848—49.

Dr. J. D. Hooker, Honorary Member of the Society, while on his memorable visit to this country, contributed two papers, one entitled "Observations made when following the Grand Trunk Road across the hills of Upper Bengal, Paresnáth, &c., in the Sôn Valley, and on the Kymore Branch of the Vindhyan hills;" and the other, "Notes chiefly Botanical, made during an excursion from Darjeeling to Tonglo, a lofty mountain on the confines of Sikkim and Nepal."

T. Thomson. 1856.

Dr. T. Thomson, who, in conjunction with Dr. Hooker, began the "Flora Indica," contributed in 1856 "Notes on the Herbarium of the Calcutta Botanic Garden," of which he was the Superintendent, with special reference to the completion of that grand work, which, however, was never completed, owing to the refusal of the Court of Directors to give any assistance.

---

* The following letter of condolence was addressed to Mrs. Griffiths:—

MADAM,—I am directed by the Asiatic Society of Bengal to express its deep and heartfelt condolence with you for the irreparable loss which you have sustained.

The Asiatic Society had not been inattentive to the great scientific ability, untiring zeal, and thorough disinterestedness of the late Doctor Griffiths; and it looked forward to the day when, had it been so permitted, he might have been associated, and that in a position worthy of him, to the labours of its members; in aid of which he had already contributed so valuably and ably.

This hope no longer exists, but the Asiatic Society have deemed it right to express how deeply it mourns, in common with the scientific public of India and Europe, the loss of one from whose labours so much had already resulted and much more was hoped for.

MUSEUM, *The 7th Nov.*, 1845.

(Sd.) H. TORRENS,
Vice-President and Secy., Asiatic Society of Bengal.

To Dr. T. Anderson, who succeeded Dr. Thomson at the Calcutta Gardens, we are indebted for two valuable articles, *viz.*, "Notes on the Flora of Lucknow, with Catalogues of the cultivated and indigenous Plants;" and "The Flora of Behar and the mountain Paresnath, with a list of the species collected by Messrs. Hooker, Edgeworth, Thomson, and Anderson." Mr. M. P. Edgeworth, who was an active contributor for ten years, from 1842 to 1852, did much for the promotion of Botanical Science in India.

T. Anderson. 1859-63.

M. P. Edgeworth. 1842-52.

§ 2.—*Burmese Flora.*

Sulpiz Kurz came to Calcutta as Curator of the Herbarium of the Botanical Gardens early in 1864. He became a member of our Society in 1869, and in 1872 began in the forty-first volume of the *Journal* that series of highly valuable papers on the Burmese Flora, the last of which appeared in 1877, a few months before his death. These researches formed the most important work of his life, which "has placed the name of Kurz in the first rank of Indian Botanists."

S. Kurz. 1872—77.

§ 3.—*Palæo-Botany.*

The fossil floras of India were first systematically investigated by Dr. O. Feistmantel, the accomplished Palæontologist to the Geological Survey of India. In 1876, he presented us descriptions of a number of plants from the Dámudá series, the richest and most important of the Gondwáná system.

O. Feistmantel. 1876.

A few years later Dr. Feistmantel contributed an able résumé of his valuable work in connection with the Flora and Fauna of the whole of the Gondwáná system. The fossils, the great majority of which are plants, are enumerated in biological order, with their range in space and time.

CHAPTER V.

GEOGRAPHY.*

[§ 1. The Himálayas — R. H. Colebrooke — Webb — Raper — Moorcroft — Gerard — H. T. Colebrooke — Herbert — Csoma de Körös — Baron Hugel — Cunningham — H. Strachey — R. Strachey — Campbell — Hodgson — Montgomerie — P. S. Sherwill — J. L. Sherwill — W. T. Blanford — Nain Sing. § 2. Assam and the North-Eastern Frontier — Wilson — Hannay — Grange — Bigge — Yule — Peal. § 3. Burma, the Islands in the Bay of Bengal, China, &c. — Hannay — Richardson — McLeod — Des Granges — Foley — Tickell — Williams — Louis — Newbold — Colebrooke — Fontana — Barbe. § 4. Southern India — Stirling — Kittoe. § 5. Western India and the North-Western Frontier — E. De la Hoste — Postans — Leech — Falconer — Montgomerie — Obbard — Pratt — W. T. Blanford — Fenwick. § 6. Afghanistan and Central Asia — Burnes — Wathen — Vigne — E. Conolly — A. Conolly — Gardiner and Edgeworth — Raverty — Waterhouse.]

§ 1.—*The Himálayas.*

ONE of the most interesting geographical problems at the commencement of the present century was the position of the source of the Ganges. All that was known of the Upper Himálayas and Tibet at the time was derived from Chinese authorities through Jesuit missionaries. As early as the beginning of the eighteeth century, a map of Tibet had been constructed by persons in the retinue of a Chinese Ambassador to that country, and was given to Father Regis, one of the missionaries at Pekin. He pointed out its defects; and the Chinese Emperor, resolved to have one more accurate, deputed two Lamas to Tibet, who had studied arithmetic and geometry in a Chinese college, with instructions to prepare a map of the country from Siuing

* See Index, pp. lxxi.

to Lhásá, and thence to the sources of the Ganges. The map which they executed was placed for examination in the hands of the Jesuit missionaries in 1717; and, based chiefly on it, the latter prepared a map of Tibet, which is published in Du Halde's description of China.

Anquetil du Perron, who showed good grounds to reject the authority of the Lamas for the sources of the Ganges, published in 1784 the result of the geographical researches of Father Tieffenthaller, a Jesuit missionary in India. But though Tieffenthaller delineated the course of the Sarayu from the lake of Mánassarovara to the plains, and that of the Ganges to Gangautri, his conclusions were not based upon personal observations; and the question of the source of one of the largest rivers in the world still lay involved in considerable doubt and uncertainty. An actual survey of the Ganges above Haridwar, where it enters British territory, to the farthest accessible point, was necessary, and the man who now guided the operations of the Geographical Departments at Calcutta took up the idea most warmly.

R. H. Colebrooke. 1803—1810.

Colonel R. H. Coolebrooke, whose astronomical and geological observations we have noticed already, became Surveyor-General in 1803. He had in 1795 contributed to the *Researches* papers on the Andaman Islands and the islands of Nancowry and Comarty; and in 1801, one on the course of the Ganges through Bengal. In 1808, he obtained the sanction of the Government for an expedition to the source of the Ganges. But while making preparations for his journey, he was seized with a fatal illness; and the execution of the enterprise devolved upon his assistant, Lieutenant Webb, who was accompanied by

Lieutenant Webb and Captain Raper. 1810.

Captain Raper and Captain Hearsay. The journal of Captain Raper and a summary of the results of the survey by Lieutenant Webb are published in the eleventh volume of the *Researches*, prefaced by an historical introduction from the pen of H. T. Colebrooke, the orientalist, a kinsman of the Surveyor-General. This enterprise was followed up with indefatigable perseverance by Moorcroft, who, accompanied by Hearsay, visited in 1812 the western shores of the celebrated lake Mánassarovara in which the Ganges was long supposed to take its rise. The country had never before been explored by any European ; and Moorcroft's "Journey to Mánassarovara, in Undes," published in the twelfth volume of the Society's *Transactions*, first supplied accurate information regarding it. He established the fact that the lake does not give origin either to the Ganges or any of the other rivers reputed to flow from it.

W. Moorcroft. 1812.

Dr. Gerard followed Moorcroft, and ascended the Spiti Valley. He crossed various ridges at elevations between 15,000 and 16,000 feet, and found the snowy zone to be of great breadth, and, instead of being a single line of peaks, to present consecutive ranges. His geographical and ethnological observations on the Spiti Valley are recorded in a paper published in the second part of the eighteenth volume of the *Researches.*

J. G. Gerard. 1833.

The great height of the Himálayas had long been suspected, but upon insufficient evidence. In 1816, H. T. Colebrooke brought together all the observations that had been made on the subject up to that date in a paper "On the Height of the Himálaya Mountains," which set all doubts at rest.

H. T. Colebrooke. 1816.

At the conclusion of the Nepál war, Captain Hodgson and Lieutenant Herbert were appointed by Lord Hastings to survey the Himá-

J. D. Herbert. 1815—20.

layas between the Satlaj and the Ganges; and Captain Webb to continue the survey through Kumáun. Some of the results of these important operations were given to the world through the Asiatic Society. In 1819, Captain Herbert penetrated as far as Shipki in Chinese Tartary, and presented an interesting account of his journey, which was printed in the fifteenth volume of the *Researches*. Herbert was the first geographer who attempted a detailed and systematic account of the physical geography of the Himálayan region and the country beyond; about the latter, however, his information was most imperfect. Humboldt had not yet undertaken his Asiatic Expedition; and his "Fragmens Asiatiques" and "Asie Centrale" appeared long after the conclusion of Herbert's geographical studies. He was struck by a large central space in the map of Asia, which is strongly marked by the circumstances of being but little intersected by rivers, while numerous streams flow from it on every side, and unite to form some of the largest rivers of the world; and inasmuch as the source of every river must be higher than any other part of its course, he inferred, that the zone in which these rivers originate is higher than the plain through which they flow to seek the ocean. But he clearly saw at the same time, that the line of water-parting is by no means synonymous with the line of greatest elevation. "It may be," says he, "that the central tract is not of such great elevation as has too hastily been presumed."

Herbert's observations on the physical geography of the Himálayas were published by the Society in 1842, nearly ten years after his death, under the title of a "Report of the Mineralogical Survey of the Himálaya Mountains." In this admirable Memoir, Herbert speculates "upon the relation between the height of the sources of rivers and the length of their courses, and gives a most interesting account of the Duns, the parallel chain of the Siváliks, the forest belt at their bases, and the Terai region beyond."

The first volume of the *Journal* has a short but excellent geographical notice of Tibet from the pen of that distinguished Hungarian traveller and scholar, M. Alex. Csoma de Körös. It treats of the different provinces of Tibet, its lakes, glaciers, mines, medicinal waters, &c.

Alex. Csoma de Körös. 1832.

Baron Hugel explored Káshmir in 1835, shortly after Jacquemont, and placed the main results of his researches before the Society in a short paper published in the fifth volume of the *Journal.*

Baron Hugel. 1836.

General A. Cunningham, the illustrious Archæologist, who was elected an Honorary Member of the Society in 1868, has enriched the pages of the *Journal* with several valuable contributions on Himálayan geography. In August and September, 1846, he penetrated to the Chu Mureri Lake in Ládák, passing through Kulu and Lahul. An account of the trip in the form of a diary appeared in the *Journal* for 1848.

A. Cunningham. 1846.

While Cunningham was exploring Ládák, Lieutenant H. Strachey was engaged in a most arduous enterprise—a trip to Rakas Tal and Mánassarovara, and the valley of Pruang in Nári-Hundes; a detailed narrative of it was given to the public in the second part of the seventeenth volume of the *Journal.*

H. Strachey. 1846—48.

On the data furnished by Webb, Gerard, Herbert, and Moorcroft in the papers alluded to above, Von Humboldt arrived at the conclusion, that the limit of perpetual snow on the southern declivity

R. Strachey. 1849.

of the Himálayan chain is 13,000 feet above the sea-level; while his investigations on the northern declivity, on the peaks which rise above the plateau of Tartary, led him to fix their limit at 16,600 feet,—the difference being attributed by him to the result "conjointly of the radiation of heat from the neighbouring elevated plains, the serenity of the sky, and the infrequent formation of snow in very cold and very dry air." In April, 1849, Lieutenant R. Strachey submitted some valuable remarks on the Snow-line in the Himálayas between the north-western portion of Nepál and the Satlaj, which were published in the *Journal* for that month. He showed that the southern edge of the belt of perpetual snow in this portion of the Himálayas is at an elevation of 15,000 feet, while on the northern edge it rises to 18,500 feet; and that on the mountains to the north of the Satlaj exceeds that limit by 500 feet or more. "The greater elevation which the snow-line attains on the northern edge of the belt of perpetual snow is," he concludes, "a phenomenon not confined to the Tibetan declivity alone, but extending far into the interior of the chain; and it appears to be chiefly caused by the quantity of snow that falls in the northern portion of the mountains being much less than that which falls further to the south, along the line where the peaks covered with perpetual snow first rise above the less elevated ranges of the Himálayas."

A. Campbell and B. H. Hodgson. 1848-52.

Dr. Campbell, who was at first attached to the Residency at Kátmandu, and subsequently posted to Dárjiling as Superintendent, was the author of many important papers on Himálayan geography. He had long wished to visit Sikkim, but in vain. In September, 1848, he obtained the authority of Lord Dalhousie to procure the permission of the Sikkim Raja for Dr. Hooker to travel in his territory ; and addressed the Raja in suitable terms. But under various pretexts, the chief of which was the dreaded wrath of the Sikkim deities if their sacred land were visited by an European, the permission was refused. The whole of Sikkim was declared to be thus sacred, and Kanchanjingá, the special object of Dr. Hooker's journey, the most sacred of all. Dr. Campbell tried hard, but to no purpose. Resolved to see the Raja himself, he made a trip to Sikkim, a highly interesting narrative of which is published in the eighteenth volume of the *Journal.* The map accompanying contained a good deal of the geography of Sikkim previously unknown. He made another journey about the end of 1849, in company with Dr. Hooker, to the frontiers of Tibet, the details of which were laid before the Society and published in 1852. A map of Sikkim and Eastern Nepál, executed by Dr. Hooker, showing his routes, accompanies the paper.

Mr. Hodgson contributed several geographical papers, the most noteworthy of which is one on the physical geography of the Himálayas, which appears in the nineteenth volume of the *Journal.*

T. G. Montgomerie. 1857.

Perhaps the most important of the topographical surveys executed in Sir Andrew Waugh's time was that of Káshmir, in which some of the most eminent members of the Survey of India, such as Basevi, Montgomerie, Godwin-Austen, and Brownlow, were engaged and distinguished themselves. The explorations which were under the immediate charge of Captain Montgomerie were fruitful of the most important results. In 1857, he announced to the members of the Society the great height of the Nanga Parbat, which

H. E. Thuillier. 1859—. he estimated at 26,629 feet.* In 1859, Colonel (now General Sir H. E.) Thuillier,† one of our oldest living members, who, though not contributing much to the *Journal*, always had the interests of the Society at heart, and afforded us material assistance in reproducing and printing maps, communicated the results of the measurement of another stupendous peak by the same Surveyor, which is second only to Mount Everest, its height being 28,278 feet. A brief report of the work of the field season of 1860 was submitted by Captain Montgomerie. The triangulation of the Káshmir series had made good progress up the Indus; and among the more noticeable achievements were the fixing of the position of Leh, the capital of Ládák and of several points in China.

In 1852, Captain W. S. Sherwill, of the Revenue Survey, W. S. Sherwill. 1853. made a tour to the Sikkim Himálayas in order to ascertain the geological formation of Kanchanjingá and of the perpetually snow-J. L. Sherwill. 1861. covered peaks in its vicinity; and in 1861, Major J. L. Sherwill, also of the Revenue Survey, undertook a trip, in company with Dr. B. Simpson and Captain E. Macpherson, to explore the glaciers of the Kanchanjingá group of the Sikkim Himálayas. Since the time of Drs. Hooker and Campbell, very few Europeans had penetrated far into Sikkim; and the accounts of these two journeys, published in our *Journal*, were the only ones extant in 1871, when Mr. W. T. Blanford, of the W. T. Blanford. 1871. Geological Survey, and Captain Elwes made a trip into the interior of that country with a view especially to explore its fauna.

* Hitherto it had been put down as only 19,000 feet above the sea.

† Sir H. E. Thuillier was President of the Society in 1863.

Nain Sing.

The jealousy with which the Trans-Himálayan regions are guarded, prevent their proper exploration by Europeans; and Major Montgomerie originated a plan of employing Indians for the purpose while he was engaged in the survey of Káshmir and Ládák. Of those that have been thus employed the most distinguished by far was the Pandit Nain Sing, who, in 1877, was awarded one of the Royal Gold Medals by the Council of the Geographical Society of London. He was distinguished in the Survey Reports as the Chief Pandit or Pandit (A). A narrative report of the very useful work done by him and his colleagues was presented to the Society by Major Montgomerie in 1870.

§ 2.—*Assam and the North-Eastern Frontier.*

War and conquest have done more than any other cause to extend geographical knowledge and widen the area of scientific observation, however much they might be deplored on other grounds. It was the Maisur war which, as we saw, led to the first steps towards a systematic geographical survey of India. The Nepál war afforded another occasion for important discoveries. The breaking out of the war with Burma first furnished accurate information with regard to Assam and the Eastern Frontier. In October, 1824, several of the officers employed in Revenue Surveys were placed under Major Schalch during the war, in order that, accompanying the several divisions of the army and receiving his instructions, they might avail themselves of the opportunities so suddenly and unexpectedly opened of pushing investigations beyond those barriers which the jealousy of neighbouring nations had hitherto opposed to the British.

R. Wilcox. 1825—28.

Lieutenant R. Wilcox was appointed to act as Captain Bedford's assistant; and Assam was the province allotted to them. Captain Bedford was instructed to pay special attention to the Brahmaputra. "He was to endeavour to unravel the mystery in which was enveloped each notice or tradition respecting its fountain-head by proceeding up its streams as far as the influence of the neighbouring force, or the safeguard of a detached escort, might permit." Lieutenant Wilcox was engaged in his exploration for four years from 1825 to 1828. In one journey he passed beyond the frontier up the Brahmaputra Valley; and in another succeeded in reaching the Iráwadi. Captain Bedford went up the rivers Dihong and Dibong. The results of these surveys were placed before the Society in a Memoir by Wilcox, accompanied by a map published in 1832. To this day that Memoir is the chief authority on the country of which it treats; and the information conveyed by it has not been much added to by later explorers.

S. C. Hannay.
1838.

Captain S. C. Hannay and Lieutenant E. R. Grange were the authors of several articles on Assamese geography. The latter undertook an expedition into the Nágá Hills in 1840, an account of

E. R. Grange.
1839-40.

H. Bigge.
1841.

which was communicated to the Society by the Government of India, as was the despatch sent the year after by Lieutenant H. Bigge, on the same country, to Captain Jenkins, Agent to the Governor General, North-Eastern Frontier.

H. Yule.
1844—61.

In 1844, Colonel Yule contributed some valuable notices on the Khási Hills; and some sixteen years later he ably edited an important Memorandum on the country between Tibet, Yunan, and Burma, by the Very Rev. Thomène D'Mazure, Vicar-Apostolic

S. E. Peal.
1879.

of Tibet. From Mr. S. E. Peal, one of our zealous contributors, we have lately had several important papers on the North-Eastern Frontier.

§ 3.—*Burma, the Islands in the Bay of Bengal, China, &c.*

The exertions of Bedford, Wilcox, Neufville, and Burlton brought an enormous accession to geographical and ethnological knowledge. The journeys of Wilcox and Burlton had proved the absence of communication between the Iráwadi and the great Tsánpo of Tibet; but they were unable to extend their observations further east, and the greater portion of the valley of the Iráwadi still remained a *terra incognita*, owing to the jealous vigilance of the Burmese officials. The course of the lower portion of the Iráwadi had been delineated by Lieutenant Wood, who accompanied Captain Symes on his embassy to the court of Ava; and the topographical features of the surrounding country had at the same time been represented by Buchanan Hamilton.

S. Hannay and R. B. Pemberton. 1835—37.

But as regards the upper Iráwadi Valley, there was still a vast gap; and the expedition of Captain S. Hannay to the south-east frontier of Assam from the capital of Burma about the end of 1835 was the first important contribution towards a knowledge of that region. The scientific results of the expedition were embodied in a paper by Captain R. Boileau Pemberton and printed in the Society's *Journal* for 1837. Between 1830 and 1837, Dr. Richardson and Captain McLeod made several journeys from Moulmein to Ava and the Chinese frontier, the accounts of which appeared in the second, fifth, and sixth volumes of the *Journal;* the eighth and ninth contain Dr. Richardson's Journal of a Mission to the Court of Siam.

D. Richardson and McLeod. 1830—40.

Otto des Granges. 1848.

In 1848, Baron Otto des Granges contributed a paper, in which he showed the great commercial and political importance of the Burmese town of Bhámo, and the practicability of a direct trade overland between Calcutta and China. Accounts of different parts of Burma and the adjoining country by Lieutenant W. Foley, Major Tickell, Dr. C. Williams, and others are scattered through the pages of the *Journal.*

W. Foley. 1835-36.
S. R. Tickell. 1841—59.
C. Williams. 1864.

The Right Rev. Jean Louis, Bishop of Isauropolis, Vicar-Apostolic of Cochin China, and Honorary Member of the Society, contributed two articles on the geography of Cochin China. In these he cleared up several points in which previous writers had contradicted each other: — so much so, that Malte-Brun, the great geographer, declared that the knowledge of the country had become more obscure, the more it had been handled by successive writers.

Jean Louis. 1837-38.

Captain Newbold, the eminent geologist, was the author of a series of papers on Perák and various other states in the Malay Peninsula.

T. J. Newbold. 1834—36.

The islands in the Bay of Bengal have been described by Colonel R. H. Colebrooke, Nicolo Fontana, Foley, Williams, Dr. Adam, and Rev. P. Barbe.

R. H. Colebrooke. 1790.
N. Fontana. 1792.
P. Barbe. 1846.

§ 4.—*Southern India.*

The first part of Stirling's well-known Memoirs on Orissa, published in the thirteenth volume of the *Researches*, treats of its boundaries, ancient and modern; soil, productions, rivers, towns, commerce, population, &c. Captain M. Kittoe, a most energetic member of the Society, and one of Prinsep's indefatigable colleagues, was, in 1838, deputed by the Coal and Mineral Committee to explore the supposed coalfields of Orissa, which had been

A. Stirling. 1825.
M. Kittoe. 1838-39.

reported by him in the previous year. He started on his journey with a determination to make the most of his time, and of the small grant made for the purpose, in antiquarian and other researches beyond the mere exploration of coal-fields. The *Journals* for the following years witness the manner in which he acted up to this laudable resolution. Of his numerous papers several treat of the geography of the country travelled through, especially of Orissa.

§ 5.—*Western India, and the North-Western Frontier.*

One of the earliest contributions on the geography of this part of India was from Captain De la Hoste, who reported on the country between Karáchi, Táttá, and Schwan. The next important paper is one by Lieutenant J. Postans on Upper Sind and the eastern portion of Cutchee, which is accompanied by a map of the route from Sakkar to Dádar and Kahan in the Marri country, and a description of the various routes in Sind compiled from the Bombay official documents and communicated by the Government of India.

E. P. De la Hoste. 1840.

J. Postans. 1843.

To Major Leech, Political Agent at Candahar, we are indebted for various contributions on Afghanistan, Beluchistan, and the North-Western Frontier of India. Besides exploring himself, he employed native agents as explorers, and translated and put their itineraries into shape for our *Journal.*

R. Leech. 1844–45.

Dr. H. Falconer wrote a letter to the Secretary of the Society on the Cataclysm of the Indus of 1841, and "suggested, as an explanation, a temporary obstruction of the river with snow or ice above Iskardoh. This he supposed had dammed up the water and caused the river to be so low, that at Attock, in place of being, as usually, many fathoms, it was fordable.

H. Falconer. 1841.

All at once the obstacle had given way, and a mighty flood coming down had swept everything before it."

The great flood of the Indus in August, 1858, brought together a number of observers at Attock. Captain Montgomerie, Mr. Obbard, and Archdeacon Pratt contributed memoranda on it.

T. G. Montgomerie, J. Obbard, and J. H. Pratt. 1860.

Mr. Blanford has contributed a thoughtful paper on the physical geography of the Great Indian Desert, in which he comes to the conclusions, that, in very recent geographical times, the Ran of Kach was part of an inlet of the sea, which certainly extended for a considerable distance up the eastern edge of the area now occupied by the Indus alluvium, and perhaps occupied the whole alluvial area of the Indus Valley; that the central portion of the desert about Jaysalmir and Bálmir was not covered by the sea, but formed either an island or a promontory, and that the sand of the desert is mainly derived from the old seacoast, and its transport into the interior of the country is due to the south-west wind.

W. T. Blanford. 1876.

The navigation of the Narmadá was for many years an important geographical problem; and several enterprising officers undertook expeditions for its solution. The most difficult part of the passage, that between Chikaldá and Broach, was attempted by Captain Fenwick in 1849, who had in the previous year shown the river to be navigable without very serious difficulty from the Falls of Dhári to the Hiranphal.

Capt. Fenwick. 1849.

§ 6.—*Afghanisthan and Central Asia.*

In 1832, Lieutenant (afterwards Sir A.) Burnes, accompanied by Dr. Gerard, set out on his memorable journey to Bokhara. Their

A. Burnes. 1832-33.

letters giving accounts of their trip appeared in the pages of the *Journal;* and Burnes wrote a glowing description of the city of Bokhara, its people, and its sights..

In 1834, W. H. Wathen, Persian Secretary to the Bombay Government, contributed a Memoir on the Usbek State of Khokand (ancient Ferghánâ); and three years later G. J. Vigne gave an account of the valley of Ghazuri and Cabul.

W. A. Wathen. 1834.

G. J. Vigne. 1837.

Captain E. Conolly contributed in 1840 a sketch of the physical geography of Seisthan, in which he describes the physical features of the country, and remarks upon its flora, fauna, soil, climate, &c. In the following year the journal kept by him while travelling in Seisthan was published. His brother, Captain A. Conolly, who was despatched on a mission to Khorassan, wrote an able Memoir on the country, which was communicated to the Society by the Political Secretariat.

E. Conolly. 1840-41.

A. Conolly. 1841.

Mr. Gardiner was for many years a traveller in Central Asia. The journals kept by him were lent to Sir A. Burnes in Cabul, and were partly destroyed during the Cabul disasters. Such portions as were recovered were edited by Mr. M. P. Edgeworth, a most energetic member of the Society. They contain, amongst other valuable matter, notes on the sources of the Oxus.

Mr. Gardiner and M. P. Edgeworth. 1853.

Major Raverty has furnished the *Journal* with many excellent papers on the geography of Afghanisthan and Central Asia. The volume for 1857 contains three papers by him—one on the mountainous district forming the western boundary of the Lower Deráját; another on Kokan, Káshgár, Yárkand,

H. G. Raverty. 1857—62.

and other countries in Central Asia; and the third on Káfiristhan. A few years later he contributed an account of the Upper and Lower Seewát and the Kohisthan, to the source of the Seewát river.

J. T. Walker and J. Waterhouse, 1879.

The last Afghan War of 1879 added considerably to our knowledge of the geography of Afghanisthan. The officers of the Surveyor-General's and Quartermaster-General's Departments, aided by the Political and Military authorities, zealously carried on the survey operations, an account of which, compiled from their letters and diaries, was prepared by Major Waterhouse, and communicated by General Walker, who has for upwards of twenty years been a most active member of the Society, and materially assisted it in various ways.

CHAPTER VI.

ETHNOLOGY.*

[§ 1. Preliminary. § 2. Tribes of Mongolian or doubtfully Mongolian Affinities—Eliot—C. Reynolds—Rawlins—McRae—Walters—Yule—Wilcox—Rowlatt—Dalton—Hodgson—A. Campbell—O'Donel—H. Reynolds—Mason. § 3. Kolarians—Tickell—Sherwill—Samuells—Dalton—G. Campbell. § 4. Dravidians—Shaw—Dalton—G. Campbell.]

§ 1.—*Preliminary.*

INDIA is unquestionably one of the best and most attractive fields for ethnological study. Races and tribes of radically different origin, in various stages of savagery and civilization, and with languages as remote from each other as Hebrew is from English, occupy that vast and extensively varied country. Broadly speaking, they are divisible into two distinctly defined groups—the Aryan and the non-Aryan. More than four thousand years have elapsed since a colony of the former from the Highlands of Central Asia settled on the banks of the Indus and its tributaries. But the settlement of the Aryans would appear to have been preceded by several waves of immigration. The Dravidians, comprising the Gonds, Khonds, Tudás, Oráons, Málers, and the tribes of Southern India, speaking the Curg, Tulu, Canarese, Telugu, Támil, and Malayalan dialects, were probably the earliest race that entered India from the North-West; and they probably found the country

* See Index, pp. lxxix—lxxxii and xcvi. Ethnological studies from the side of philology are, I need hardly remark, beyond the scope of this Part of the "Review." The present chapter is to be taken as supplemental to the Philology Part.

already occupied by the aborigines of the Kolarian group—the Kols, Santáls, Hos, &c.—whom they possibly drove into the unhealthy jungle-clad hills, where they live, like numberless other tribes of India, as so many fossils of the Pre-historic period. Besides the Dravidians and the Kolarians, there is a heterogeneous mass of other non-Aryan tribes inhabiting the Himálayas, the elevated hilly tracts of Assam and the North-Eastern Frontier, whose affinities have not yet been satisfactorily ascertained, but who would appear to approximate to the Mongolian type, and have been denominated the "Indo-Chinese."

§ 2.—*Mongolian or doubtfully Mongolian Tribes.*

Mr. John Eliot was the first European to travel amongst the *Gáros.* He was deputed in 1788 to investigate the duties collected on the Gáro Hills, and to secure the good-will of the people who had hitherto known no intercourse with Europeans. The Government had seen that, by good treatment and kindness, the hill tribes could in a large measure be rendered at least peaceable and inoffensive, if not serviceable ; and Mr. Eliot was given some scarlet cloth to be distributed amongst the people. His intercourse with the Gáros was of a most open nature ; and in the third volume of the *Researches* he furnishes a lucid description of their appearance, mode of living, nuptial and funeral ceremonies, &c. The next important account of the people is by Captain C. S. Reynolds, Principal Assistant to the Commissioner of Assam.

J. Eliot. 1792.

C. S. Reynolds. 1849.

The earliest notice of the *Kukis* is one in Persian by Mr. John Rawlins in the second volume of the *Researches*, translated by Sir W. Jones. It treats briefly of the manners, religion, and laws

J. Rawlins. 1790.

of the people. The next account, contributed by Dr. J. McRae of Chittagong, is much fuller. The information embodied in it was obtained from a native of Ránganiá, who had long resided among the Kukis as their captive. They are all described as hunters and warriors, divided into a number of distinct tribes, totally independent of each other, but all admitting more or less the authority of three different Rájás. The great similarity of the *Mag* and *Kuki* languages, many words being common to both, is pointed out; and the character, food, funeral ceremonies, religious belief, &c., of the people described.

J. McRae. 1801.

It was in 1826 that the attempt to open direct communication between Assam and Silhet brought the officers of the British Government into contact with the *Khásiás.* They were first properly brought to the notice of the civilized world in a paper by Mr. H. Walters, published in the seventeenth volume of the *Researches.* He describes them as a stout, athletic race, fairer than the inhabitants of the plains, devoted to chewing *pán*, and fond of spirituous drink. He notices those singular stone monuments (*cromlechs*) formed of large stone slabs, supported by upright stones set on end, which form such a characteristic feature in the Khási hills, specially about Nanklo, and saw the urns with the ashes which had been deposited in them after cremation. Colonel Yule visited the Khási hills about 1844, and contributed a Memoir on the country and its people, whose physiognomy, food, arts, laws, festivals, amusements, government, religious belief, astrological notions and local traditions are described in detail. He also notices the *cromlechs* which he saw in great profusion.

H. Walters. 1832.

H. Yule. 1844.

Wilcox's admirable Memoir on Assam contains numerous notices of the tribes he met with,
R. Wilcox. 1832. such as the *Khámtis*, the *Abors*, the *Mishmis*, &c. The last-mentioned tribe, who inhabit the mountainous country on the extreme north-eastern frontier of Assam, is noticed at length by Lieute-
E. A. Rowlatt. 1845. nant (afterwards Colonel) Rowlatt, who penetrated to the Du and up that river, in a northerly direction, to the village of Tuppang, in a letter to Major F. Jenkins, then Governor-General's Agent, N.-E. Frontier, communicated to the Society by the Government of India.

The custom, religion, language, &c., of the *Abors* and *Miris* were admirably treated by Colonel
J. G. E. Dalton. 1845. Dalton in a communication which was published in the fourteenth volume of the *Journal.*

Mr. Hodgson, the well-known naturalist and orientalist, contributed a number of ethnological articles, in which the languages of the *Singphos*, *Mithan Nágás*, *Tablung Nágás*, *Khari Nágás*, *Angami Nágás*,
B. H. Hodgson. 1828—56. and various other aboriginal tribes are elaborately compared. From the Himálayan region, to which his personal observations were specially directed, to the island of Ceylon, and from the extreme eastern frontier of Assam to the westernmost limit of India, the aborigines were studied by him with that ability and devotion which characterized him in all his pursuits. His ethnological researches, which extend over a quarter of a century, and amount to twenty-one articles, began with the people of Nepál and its vicinity, but gradually included the aborigines of the north-eastern frontier, of the Nilgiris, of Central India, &c. In 1849, he gave an intensely interesting account of the *Kácháris* (or Bodo) and *Dhimals*, who mainly occupy the malarious forest belt extending from 25°

to 27° North Lat., and from 88° to 93½° East Long.,* the Dhimals being restricted to the most westerly part of this region—the sál forest lying between the Konki and the Dhorlá.†

A. Campbell. 1840—42.

Dr. Campbell, Superintendent of Dárjiling, who was one of our most energetic contributors, furnished accounts of the *Lepchás* of Sikkim, and of the *Limbus* and other hill tribes.

J. H. O'Donel and H. J. Reynolds. 1863.

Mr. O'Donel, Revenue Surveyor of Arácán, and the Hon. H. J. Reynolds, our present President, contributed a few notes on Some Tribes of the Eastern Frontier, *viz.*, the *Khumis*, the *Kús*, the *Khyens*, and the *Tipperahs* (or Kukís). The last-mentioned people are described by Mr. Reynolds as distinct from the Kukís of Chittagong. The majority resemble the Khásiás, having strongly marked Mongolian features. Mr. Reynolds was "struck with the fair complexions of many of them, scarcely darker than a swarthy European."

F. Mason. 1866—68.

The Rev. Dr. Mason has minutely described the *Kárens*, who are scattered over Burma and Siam through nine degrees of latitude and eight degrees of longitude. Though small in stature, they are well proportioned, with complexion similar to that of the Chinese, and the hair straight, coarse, and usually very black. The head is pyramidal ; the breadth of the face across the cheek bones wider than across the temple ; and the nose is much depressed. The face is lozenge-shaped, and the type of the countenance, Mongolian.

---

* The meridional limits, according to Colonel Dalton, might be put much further apart.—" Ethnology of Bengal," p. 84.

† The *Kooch*, who are also noticed in the paper in question, apparently as related to the Bodos and Dhimals, are believed by Dalton to be a branch of the Bhuiyá family, whom he classes with the Dravidian.

§ 3.—*The Kolarians.*

Colonel (then Lieutenant) Tickell, whose contributions to Indian ornithology will be noticed hereafter, wrote an entertaining paper on the *Hodesun* or *Hos*, also known as *Larka Kols*, who inhabit the country to the south-east of Chotá Nágpur Proper, called Kolehan, between 22° and 23° North Lat. and 86°53′ and 85°2′ East Long. It is accompanied by a vocabulary of the Ho language. In the course of his annual tour through the Kolehan District in 1842, Lieutenant Tickell discovered a people calling themselves "*Bend-kars*,"* and occupying a small range of hills, an extremely wild country to the north of Keonjhar, and he contributed a short note on their appearance, language, &c.

S. R. Tickell. 1840–42.

The next important contribution on the Kolarian group of the non-Aryans was from the pen of Colonel Sherwill, Revenue Surveyor. He was the first to explore the hilly country extending from Sikrigallí on the Ganges, in 26°10′ North Lat. and 87°50′ East Long., to the boundary of the district of Bírbhum, a distance of seventy miles, and known as the Rájmáhál hills. It is inhabited by two perfectly distinct races, the hillmen or *Málers* and their kindred, who are Dravidians and will be noticed in the next section, and the lowlanders or *Santháls*,† who are confined to the valleys. Colonel Sherwill's now almost classical paper contains accurate and interesting accounts of both these peoples, especially of the latter. The Santhál is described as a

W. S. Sherwill. 1851.

* Since ascertained to be "a somewhat isolated fragment of the Savaras," the "Suari" of Pliny, and the "Sabaræ" of Ptolemy.

† The Santháls inhabit the districts of Bhágalpur, the Santhál Parganás, Bírbhum, Báncurá, Házáribág, Mánbhum, Mednipur, Singhbum, Mayurbhanj, and Bálásur.

short, well-made, and active man, quiet, inoffensive, and cheerful; with the thick lips, high cheekbones, and spread nose of the Bhils and Kols; beardless or nearly so; intelligent, obliging, and timid. "The Santhál is an industrious cultivator of the soil, and as he is unfettered with caste, he enjoys existence in a far greater degree than does his neighbour, the priest-ridden and caste-crushed Hindu."

H. Piddington. 1855.

Mr. Piddington contributed a memorandum to the twenty-fourth volume of the *Journal* on two individuals of an unknown forest race, supposed to occupy the jungles south of Pálámáo.

E. A. Samuells. 1858.

Mr. Samuells of the Bengal Civil Service, Superintendent of the Tributary Máháls of Catak, considered them as probably *Patuás* or *Juángás*, who are found in the states of Dhekenal and Keonjhar, and who were noticed by him in a paper accompanied by interesting sketches. They are described as diminutive, and seemingly weak, with broad face, flat nose, and wide nostrils. The sole garment of the women consists of two large bunches of leaves, hence the name of the tribe, Patuá, or "leaf-bearing."*

E. T. Dalton. 1865-66.

Colonel Dalton, late Commissioner of Chotá Nágpur, who had long been engaged in ethnological researches in Assam and Chotá Nágpur, gave an account of a tour in Bonai, Gangpur, Udayapur, and Sirgujá, in which he described the *Korwas* found in Jushpur, as well as in the wildest parts of Sirgujá, and the mountainous country intervening between this last-named place and Pálámáo, and akin to the Santháls, the Bhumij, and the Mundás of Chotá Nágpur; the *Birbors*

* "The Juángs," observes Colonel Dalton, "are in habits and customs the most primitive people I met with or read of."—Ethnology of Bengal, p. 153.

(literally foresters), a nomadic tribe of limited numerical strength; the *Kaurs*, scattered through the jungles of Chattisgar, Udayapur, Sirgujá, &c., and claiming descent from the Kurus of Kuru Pándava fame, but characterized by Colonel Dalton as one of the ugliest races he had ever met with—dark, coarse-featured, wide-mouthed, broad-nosed, and thick-lipped ; the *Bogthás* of Sirgujá; and also several tribes with Dravidian affinities to be noticed in the next section.

In 1866, Colonel Dalton communicated an excellent account of the non-Aryan population of Chotá Nágpur, the so-called 'Kols.' In addition to the Kolarian tribes mentioned above, he noticed the *Kharriás*, closely allied to the Juángs, and most abundant on the banks of the southern Koel river, the source of the Bráhmani, into which they throw the ashes of their dead, and which they venerate, much as the Santhâls do the Dámúdar ; the *Patuás* or *Juángs* first noticed by Samuells; the *Bhumij*, a ramification of the Mundás, whose home is in Dhalbhum (or Ghassilla), but who form the majority of the population in all the estates of the Mánbhum district to the south of the Kassae river, and are also found in Keonjhar and Mohurbhanj; and the *Mundás*, most nearly related to the Hos or Larkakols of Kolehan. These latter are described as "the nucleus of the Moondah nation, the most compact, the purest, most powerful, and most interesting division of the whole race, and in appearance decidedly the best looking. In their erect carriage and fine manly bearing the Hos look like a people that have maintained and are proud of their independence. . . . . . The inhabitants of the imperfectly reclaimed hill forests are more savage-looking, but they seldom deteriorate to the almost simian physiognomy that the Oráons are found with under similar circumstances."

At a meeting of the Natural History Committee, held on the 11th of February, 1862, Mr. A. Grote, then President of the Society, made a proposal for bringing together collections of crania illustrative of the various peoples inhabiting India and the adjacent countries; and a circular letter was issued soliciting the co-operation of members and others towards this object.* Some skulls were sent by Colonel Dalton, Colonel Tytler, and others in response to this call. But the number was small, and leisured men competent to work them out were wanting. In December, 1865,† Dr. J. Fayrer submitted to the Society a proposal for a grand Ethnological Exhibition in Calcutta, which would afford the anthropologist an opportunity for the systematic study of the various races of the Old World. The idea was cordially approved of by the Society, and a Committee, consisting of Dr. Fayrer, Mr. A. Grote, Dr. D. B. Smith, Mr. W. L. Heeley, Dr. J. Anderson, and Dr. S. B. Partridge, was appointed to carry it out. But there were difficulties in the way; the plan was found impracticable and was ultimately abandoned. In the meantime, however, the Government of India had, at the request of the Council of the Society, called on the local authorities to furnish reports on the tribes found within their respective jurisdictions. Colonel Dalton, who had utilized the splendid opportunities afforded to him of making ethnological investigations in various parts of Assam and Chotá Nágpur, was selected to edit the reports. But the material contained in these was found to be very insufficient, and Colonel Dalton proposed "to draw up an account of the tribes in Bengal from all available sources of information." The proposal was warmly received by the Society, and the Council gave

---

* *Proceedings*, 1865, p. 158.

† *Proceedings*, 1866, p. 82.

Colonel Dalton all the assistance in their power. The result was the publication in 1872 of a handsomely illustrated quarto volume—"The Ethnology of Bengal."

G. Campbell. 1866.

When the Government of India, at the suggestion of our Society, consented to call upon its officers in all parts of India to submit lists of the races and tribes found in the various districts, Sir George (then Mr. Justice) Campbell, with a view to assist the collation of such data, drew up a capital general account of the Ethnology of India. He had made careful notes during his visits to the Panjáb frontier, to the Bombay Presidency, and to the Maisur country, and had taken a most prominent part in the anthropological discussions at the Society. His inquiries were directed to the peculiarities in physical appearance, language, religion, laws, manners, and mental characteristics presented by the various peoples of India. These are classed by him as—1. Aborigines. 2. Modern Indians. 3. Borderers. Under the first head, Sir George Campbell described the Southern or Dravidian tribes, the Northern or Kolarian tribes, the tribes of Western India, the tribes under the Himálayas, and the *Bhuiyás* of the Bengal Borders. The second division includes the *Bráhmans*, the *Játs*, the *Rájputs*, the *Kurmis*, some Punjab tribes, the Mahomedan settlers, pastoral tribes (*Gujars*, *Ahirs*, &c.), the *Mális* and others, the *Kshatriyas*, the *Beniás* and other trading tribes, the *Káyasthas* and other writer tribes, the artisans, and the inferior helot classes, and some tribes of the South. The third class comprises the *Tirmen* or Islanders, the *Mophlás*, the tribes of the Bombay coasts, the *Sindhis*, the *Beluchis*, the *Páthàns* or Afgháns, the aboriginal Arians of the Caucasus, the mixed tribes of the Thibetan frontier, and the tribes of the Eastern frontier.

§ 3.—*The Dravidians.*

The *Málers* or *Páháris* (hillmen) of the Rájmáhál hills were first noticed by Lieutenant T. Shaw, whose account, though written nearly ninety years ago, is still the only authority on that interesting tribe, the northernmost known fragment of the great Dravidian race.

T. Shaw. 1795.

In his account of a tour in Bonai, Gangpur, Udayapur, and Sirgujá, Colonel Dalton noticed the *Bhuiyás*,* an interesting and widely-spread tribe, being found in Bhágalpur, Bihár, Dinájpur, &c.; the Jushpur *Oráons*, extremely ugly, "with foreheads 'villainous low,' flat noses, and projecting maxillaries," approaching "the negro in physiognomy much closer than do their brethren in Chotá Nágpur;" and the *Gaurs*, completely hinduized in Sirgujá and Udayapur, but considered by Colonel Dalton as affined to the *Gonds*. The Oráons were treated of more at length in Colonel Dalton's paper on the 'Kols' of Chotá Nágpur.

E. T. Dalton. 1865-66.

Sir George Campbell, in his excellent handbook on the Ethnology of India, describes various Dravidian tribes.

G. Campbell. 1866.

---

* The *Bhuiyas* form an important constituent of the population of Singbhum. Their ethnological relations have not yet been satisfactorily settled. They are affiliated to the Dravidians by Colonel Dalton.

CHAPTER VII.

CHEMISTRY.*

[§ 1. Preliminary. § 2. Calcutta Water-supply, &c. — Waldie — Pedler.]

§ 1.—*Preliminary.*

THERE are important branches of Geology and Biology, which are best and most profitably studied in the field; and Geography is pre-eminently a subject for out-door work. In a country, parts of which are even now but little explored, anyone with a little general culture and some amount of observational power can, with a few simple, inexpensive, and easily portable appliances, make material additions to our knowledge of these subjects; and not a few of the contributions we have reviewed hitherto, important as they are, are of this preliminary nature. It is far otherwise with Chemistry. That is a subject which can be prosecuted only in the laboratory. In India, until recently, there have been but few laboratories worth the name, and we have had but few competent men with leisure to devote to lengthened chemical research. Under these circumstances, our Chapter of Chemistry at the Asiatic Society is near being as brief as the proverbial Chapter on Snakes in Ireland.

§ 2.—*Calcutta Water-supply, &c.*

D. Waldie. 1866—.

Mr. Waldie, one of our oldest and most zealous members, made between 1866 and 1867 an extensive series of observations on the

* See Index, p. lxxxiii.

water of the Hugli at Calcutta, the results of which, communicated to the Society, went to show that the water of that river was the purest that could be obtained—a conclusion that was at first controverted, but the correctness of which has since been confirmed. In 1873, Mr. Waldie contributed a paper "On the Muddy-water of the Hugli during the rainy season, with reference to its purification and to the Calcutta Water-supply," in which the causes of the difficulties attending filtration were examined and explained.*

A. Pedler. 1878.

Mr. Pedler, Professor of Chemistry at the Presidency College, Calcutta, has been a most active member.† In 1876, he contributed a note on the use of the Radiometer as a Photometer, published in the *Proceedings* for that year. Mr. Crookes, the well-known Physicist, had, in a paper which appeared in the Quarterly Journal of Science for July 1875, come to the conclusion that the radiometer is a perfect photometer. Mr. Pedler instituted a series of experiments to test the validity of this conclusion, with the result that he could not speak with great confidence of the radiometer as a photometer. In 1880, he read a paper on the Water-supplies of Calcutta. The first part of it is devoted to the consideration of the quantity and quality of the old supply which existed before the introduction of the present hydrant water. As for the quantity, Mr. Pedler's researches led him to conclude that, at the time when Calcutta depended for its water-supply on its tanks and wells, the inhabitants must have used the same water over and over again,

* Mr. Waldie contributed to the *Journal* for 1869 the results of his Analysis of the Khetri Meteorite. The paper will be found in the Geology Section of the 'Index.'

† Mr. Pedler was General Secretary for 1880-81.

though of course without knowing it. The state of affairs as to quality was even worse. Of the two hundred samples of Calcutta tank and well waters examined, Mr. Pedler found 44 per cent. were true sewages, 22 per cent. diluted sewages, 20 per cent. contaminated with considerable quantities of sewage, 9 per cent. "dirty waters," and about 4 per cent. only moderately safe waters. The second part of the paper dealt with the present water-supply of Calcutta, which consists of the Hugli water pumped from the river at Paltá, where it is collected in settling tanks, and after subsidence filtered through sand and supplied to Calcutta. The analysis of the hydrant water led to the result, that the Calcutta water falls just outside the class of waters of "great organic purity," but that it is high in the class of waters of "fair organic purity." In the third division of his long and interesting paper, Mr. Pedler considers the extension of the present water-supply. It is shown by the analytical results, that water collected from within three or four miles of Calcutta would be decidedly impure, and a strong opinion is expressed that the water for the extension of the supply should be collected at Paltá as has been hitherto done.

CHAPTER VIII.

THE MUSEUM.

THE Asiatic Society of Bengal is one of the oldest Scientific Institutions in the world, and is, certainly, the oldest in this country. For nearly three-quarters of a century, its publications were the principal vehicle of information on many subjects of interest and importance in India. But for it, many valuable researches would never have been undertaken, many important papers would never have seen the light. From the days of Colonel Colebrooke and William Lambton, to very recent times, the pages of its *Transactions* were the only source available to the public for authentic information on all interesting operations of the Topographical and Trigonometrical Surveys, and without the channel of publicity afforded by the Society, the results of the important surveys of Lambton, Webb, Hodgson, Herbert, Wilcox, and others would have lain buried among musty piles of official records: some, no doubt, consigned to oblivion, and some, more fortunate, to be rescued moth-eaten and perhaps almost illegible and unrestorable, years after their usefulness or interest had been partly or entirely lost. The early publication which the Society's *Transactions* secured to the observations of cultured travllers like Moorcroft, Gerard, and Hodgson, in remote parts of India and the adjacent countries, stimulated and helped other explorers; and it is thus that a considerable portion of our accessions to geographical and ethnological knowledge has been effected. The grand series of the Mammalian Fauna of the Sub-Himálayas, the Narbadá Valley, and Perim Island owe their collection and elucidation, in no small degree, to the warm encouragement and cordial assistance of the Asiatic Society. Falconer, Cautley, Colvin, Baker, Durand, and Spilsbury were all among the Society's most ardent and energetic contributors. "As I am neither a geologist, nor have the leisure to make myself one," wrote Colvin, "I have obviously no motive for collecting a cabinet myself; I propose, therefore, excavating and collecting for the Museum of the Asiatic Society."* Previous to the commencement of the publications of the Geological Survey of India, the Society's *Transactions* were the principal channel for communications on Indian geology. The Society has been ever forward in the promotion of any scientific movements that have been set on foot in this country. It was under its superintendence that the boring operations in Calcutta, which revealed the geological structure of Lower Bengal, were conducted; and it was with its help or instrumentality that the investigations of Franklin, Hutton, Csoma de Körös, and of a host of other explorers were carried on.

But one of the most conspicuous and permanent monuments of the Society's work is unquestionably its Museum, which was taken over by the Government some years ago, and which is now located in one of the grandest edifices in the best situation in this city. As early as the 29th of September, 1796, the Society announced their intention of establishing a Museum, and invited donations.† But it was not until the beginning of 1814 that any steps were taken to carry

---

* *Journal*, Vol. IV, p. 56.

† Asiatic Researches, Vol. VI, pp. 591, 593.

out that intention. Contributions of animals, plants, minerals, &c., were solicited; and arrangements were made for their reception. By the year 1835, the collections had grown to such dimensions that the services of a paid curator were found necessary; and in May, Dr. J. T. Pearson, of the Bengal Medical Service, was appointed at a salary of Rs. 200 a month. The appointment was renewed in 1836. But in May, 1837, the condition of the Society's finances compelled it to solicit Government aid for the support of the Museum; and the following resolution was passed :—

"That—viewing the maintenance of the Museum as a national object, and calculated to be of immense importance to science if placed upon a footing of efficiency, with a professional Naturalist at the head, directing researches and systematizing informations obtained from various sources, both public and private, in all the branches of Physical Science, but more particularly in regard to the Natural History of British India and Asia at large—it is incumbent on the Society to make a full and urgent representation to Government on the subject, and to solicit such support as is accorded in most other countries to similar institutions of national and scientific utility."

An application was forwarded to the Court of Directors in accordance with this resolution. It was refused ; but on further representation to the Governor-General, a monthly grant to the Museum was authorized, and sanctioned by the Court of Directors in a Despatch dated the 18th September, 1839.

The Society was thus placed in a position to engage the services of a highly competent curator, Edward Blyth, whose work we have noticed in the Chapter on Zoology. His services to the Museum were invaluable, and the following resolution in recognition of his efforts was unanimously passed by the Society in November, 1864 :—

"On the eve of transferring the Zoological collections of the Society to Government, to form the nucleus of an Imperial Museum of Natural History, the Society wishes to record its sense of the important services rendered by its late curator, Mr. Blyth, in the formation of the collections. In the period of twenty-two years during which Mr. Blyth was curator of the Society's Museum, he has formed a large and valuable series of specimens richly illustrative of the Ornithology of India and the Burmese Peninsula, and has added largely to the Mammalian and other Vertebrate collections of the Museum; while, by his numerous descriptive papers and catalogues of the Museum specimens, he has made the materials thus amassed by him subservient to Zoological Science at large, and especially valuable to those engaged in the study of the Vertebrate Fauna of India and its adjoining countries."*

In the meantime the Society had become the custodian of an important series of Geological and Palæontological collections which had been yearly growing in richness; but before the year 1839, these latter appear to have suffered much from neglect, and were in almost chaotic confusion. In that year, at the December meeting, the then 'Committee of Papers' submitted a Report on the Museum, in which it is stated, "that the first object of the Society in remodelling its Museum should be to form a grand collection of minerals and fossils, illustrative of the Geology, Geography, and Palæontology of our British Indian possessions. A few of the existing minerals and some superb fossils in our Museum are

* *Journal*, Vol. XXXIII, p. 582. For an account of the transfer of the Society's Collections to Government, see *Calcutta Review*, Vol. XLIII (1866), p. 427.

available for this object, but it is clearly within the scope of the Society's influence to procure, within a few months, collections of specimens from every part of India, and in such numbers as would find the Curator in ample employment."*

In 1840, the Geological and Palæontological collections were separated from the rest under the appellation of the Museum of Economic Geology, which began to thrive under the care of Mr. Piddington, who then officiated as Curator. On Mr. Blyth taking charge of the Curator's office early in September, 1841, Mr. H. Torrens, Secretary of the Society, wrote asking him to take special care of the new Museum. In his reply dated the 22nd September, 1841, Mr. Blyth said :

" . . . . I think I may crave some indulgence on the part of the Society, if I do not, at the very first, prove alike proficient in every one of these several departments, confidently appealing to the experience of any practical naturalist for an acknowledgment of the reasonableness of the plea which I have here ventured to offer.

"It is in the Mineralogical Department, unfortunately, that I am at present less qualified by previous study to devote my immediate and first labours advantageously for the Society."

In 1842, the Society succeeded in securing a separate Government grant for the Museum of Economic Geology, to which Mr. Piddington was appointed curator. The Museum grew under the custody of the Society until 1856, when the Government portion of the collection was trans-

---

* *Journal*, Vol. VIII (1839), p. 1061. The Report is signed by Sir Edward Ryan, President of the Society; Mr. H. T. Prinsep, Vice-President; Messrs. W. P. Grant, H. Torrens, J. C. C. Sutherland, W. B. O'Shaughnessy, David Hare, Col. D. McLeod, Dr. D. Stewart, Sir H. W. Seton, Major W. H. Forbes, and Dr. N. Wallich.

ferred to the newly-established Museum in connection with the Geological Survey of India. The Society's own collections of Geology and Mineralogy were also asked for, but were refused. A careful inquiry into the condition of the Museum, its growing importance, and the poor accommodation available in their building had impressed the Society with the necessity for the institution of a grand public Museum in Calcutta, to which the whole of the Society's collection might be transferred under certain restrictions, as any partial transfer would probably have been detrimental to the accomplishment of this noble object. Negotiations were opened by the Council of the Society with the Government on the subject, which terminated in the establishment of the present Indian Museum, the Society offering to make over its collections on the condition that a suitable building should be erected and that the collections should be placed under the management of a body of Trustees, which conditions were carried out and legally instituted by Act XVII of 1866.

CLASSIFIED INDEX

TO THE

SCIENTIFIC PAPERS

IN THE SOCIETY'S PUBLICATIONS

FROM 1788 TO 1882.

I.

MATHEMATICAL AND PHYSICAL SCIENCE.

[*N. B.*—Articles marked with * are partly antiquarian.]

As. Res. Vol.	
I. (1788.)	Astronomical observations in Fort William, and between Madras and Calcutta. T. D. Pearse, Col. 57
	Friction in Mechanics. R. Burrow 171
	A method of calculating the moon's parallax in latitude and longitude. R. Burrow 320
	Remarks on the artificial horizons. R. Burrow 327
	Demonstration of a theorem concerning the intersection of curves. R. Burrow.. 330
	Meteorological Journal from 1st March, 1785, to 28th February, 1786. Col. Pearse.............................. 442
	Correction of the Lunar method of finding the longitude. R. Burrow 433
II. (1790.)	*Astronomical computations of the Hindus. S. Davis. 225
	*Antiquity of the Hindu Zodiac. Sir W. Jones 289
	Meteorological Journal 1784-85. H. Trail 419
	Observations of some of the eclipses of Jupiter's Satellites. R. Burrow 483
	A proof that the Hindus had the Binomial Theorem R. Burrow 487

As. Res.	
Vol. III. (1792.)	*Demonstration of one of the Hindu rules of Arithmetic. R. Burrow .... 145 *On the Musical modes of the Hindus. By Sir W. Jones .... 55 Method of reducing practical tables. R. Burrow ...... 141 The Lunar year of the Hindus. Sir W. Jones 257
IV. (1795.)	Astronomical observations in upper Hindusthan. W. Hunter........ 14 A treatise on Barometers. F. Balfour........ 195 *Questions and remarks on the Astronomy of the Hindus. John Playfair, A. M., Professor of Mathematics at Edinburgh .... 159 Astronomical observations made on a Voyage to the Andaman and Nicobar Islands. R. H. Colebrooke........ 317 Astronomical observations made on a Survey through the Carnatic and Mysore, R. H. Colebrooke .... 321 Latitudes and longitudes of some principle places of India determined from astronomical observations. R. Burrow .... 325 Astronomical observations. W. Hunter 359
V. (1797.)	*Account of the Hindustanee Horometry. J. Gilchrist 81 On Indian weights and measures. H. T. Colbrooke .. 91 *Some account of the Astronomical labours of Jaya Singha, Raja of Ambhere. W. Hunter .... 177 *Chronology of the Hindus (Hindu Astronomy). Capt. F. Wilford .... 241 *Remarks on the principal æras and dates of the Ancient Hindus. J. Bentley .... 315 Astronomical observations made in the upper provinces of Hindusthan. W. Hunter........ 413
VI. (1799.)	Observations on the theory of walls. W. Lambton .. 93 Maximum of Mechanic powers and the effects of Machines when in motion. Lieut. W. Lambton........ 137 *The antiquity of the Súrya Siddhánta. J. Bentley... 537
VII. (1801.)	An account of a Method for extending a Geographical Survey across the Peninsula. Brigade Major Lambton .... 312 Demonstration of the 12th Axiom of the first Book of Euclid. Rev. Paul Lim. 449

As. Res.	
Vol. VIII. (1805.)	Observations respecting the remarkable effects of Sol-Lunar influence on the fevers of India, with the scheme of an Astronomical Ephemeris for the purposes of Medicine and Meteorology. F. Balfour .... 1 An account of the Measurement of an arc on the meridian on the Coast of Coromandel, and the length of a degree deduced therefrom in the latitude 12° 32′. W. Lambton 137 *On the Hindu systems of Astronomy, and their connection with history in ancient and modern times. J. Bentley 193
IX. (1807.)	An account of experiments made in the Mysore country, in the year 1804, to investigate the effects of terrestrial refraction. Lieutenant Warren .... 1 Description of a very sensitive Hygrometer. Lieut. Kater .... 24 *On the Indian and Arabian divisions of the Zodiac. H. T. Colebrooke .... 323 Description of an improved Hygrometer. Lieut. T. Kater .... 394 On the grámas or musical scales of the Hindus. J. D. Paterson 445
X. (1808.)	An account of Trigonometrical operations in crossing the peninsula of India and connecting Fort St. George with Mangalore. Captain William Lambton. Communicated by the Honorable William Petrie, Governor of Fort St. George .... 290 An account of Astronomical observations taken at the Honorable Company's observatory near Fort St. George in the East Indies, in the years 1806 and 1807. To which are added some remarks on the declination of certain Stars and of the Sun when near the Zenith of that place. Capt. John Warren of H. M. 33rd Regiment of Foot 513
XI. (1810.)	An account of experiments made at the observatory near Fort St. George, for determining the length of the simple pendulum beating seconds of time at that place. Capt. J. Warren 293

As. Res.	
Vol. XII. (1816.)	An account of the measurement of an Arc on the Meridian, comprehended between the latitudes 8° 9′ 33″ 39‴ and 10° 59′ 48″ 93‴ north being a Continuation of the grand Meridional Arc commenced in 1804 and extending to 14° 6′ 19″ north. Lieut.-Colonel William Lambton, His Majesty's 33rd Regiment of Foot 1
	On the early history of Algebra. Edward Strachey. 158
	An account of observations taken at the observatory near Fort St. George, in the East Indies, for determining the obliquities of the Ecliptic in the months of December 1809, June and December 1810. Capt. John Warren His Majesty's 33rd Regiment of Foot 192
	*On the notions of the Hindu Astronomers, concerning the precession of the Equinoxes and motions of the Planets. H. T. Colebrooke. 209
	On the heights of the Himalaya Mountains. H. T. Colebrooke 251
	An account of the measurement of an Arc on the Meridian extending from latitude 10° 59′ 49″ to 15° 6′ 0″ 65‴ north. William Lambton...................... 286
XIII. (1820.)	An account of the measurement of an Arc on the Meridian, extending from latitude 15° 6′ 2″ to latitude 18°, 3′, 45″ being a further continuation of the former Arc, commencing latitude 8°, 9′, 38″. Lieutenant-Colonel W. Lambton 1
	On the Binomial Theorem; as known to the Arabians. J. Tytler. Communicated by R. Tytler, M. D. 456
XIV. (1822.)	Latitudes of places in Hindustan and the northern mountains; with observations of Longitude in the mountains, according to Immersions and Emersions of Jupiter's Satellites. Capt. J. A. Hodgson 153
	An account of Trigonometrical and Astronomical operations for determining the heights and positions of the principal peaks of the Himalaya Mountains. Captain J. A. Hodgson and Lieut. J. D. Herbert.......... 187
	On an Indian method of constructing Arches. Captain Makintosh 476
XV. (1825.)	Observations on the climate of Subathu and Kotgarh. Lieut. P. Gerard, Beng. Nat. Inf.................. 469

As. Res.	
XV. (1825.)	Extracts from the Proceedings of the Benares Corresponding Society—Latitude of the Hindu observatory at Benares. W. Cracroft and J. Prinsep .... i Table of Multipliers for ascertaining the Deviation of a Transit Instrument from the Meridian. William Cracroft .... vi Meteorological Journal. J. Prinsep.............. vii Description of a Pluviometer and an Evaporometer constructed at Benares. James Prinsep .... xiii Abstracted results of marine observations. G. A. Prinsep xv
XVI. (1828.)	On a new method of determining the longitude, from the observed interval between the Transit of the Moon's enlightened limb, and that of the Sun, or of one or more Stars. Captain P. W. Grant.................. 235
XVII. (1832.)	An Essay on the Extraction of the roots of integers, as practised by the Arabs. John Tytler 51
XVIII. pt. 1. (1829.)	Tables exhibiting a daily register of the tides in the river Hoogly, at Calcutta, from 1805 to 1828, with observations on the results thus obtained. James Kyd.... 259
pt 2. (1833.)	Observations on the inclination and declination of the magnetic needle. Lieut.-Colonel J. A. Hodgson and Monsieur de Blossville, communicated by Captain J. D. Herbert.................................... 1 On the Formulae for calculating Azimuth in Trigonometrical operations. Captain G. Everest .... 93 On the compensation measuring apparatus of the great Trigonometrical Survey of India. Captain Everest 189 Experiments on the Strength and Elasticity of Indian woods. Captain H. C. Baker 215
Journal Vol. I. (1832.)	Summary of Meteorological observations made at the Surveyor General's Office in Calcutta during the years 1829-30-31 23

Journal.	
Vol. I. (1832.)	On the temperature and saltness of the river Hugli, from Calcutta to the Sea. G. A. Prinsep 104
	Abstract of Meteorological tables, kept at Bancura. J. MacRitchie for 1830 and 1831 154
	Some observations on the quantity of Earthy matter brought down by the Ganges river. Rev. R. Everest 238
	Meteorological Averages at Canton and Macao 303
	Observations of the Transit of Mercury. James Prinsep, Sec. 408
	Description of an Instrument for Trisecting Angles. Lieut. T. S. Burt, Engineers 499
	Some additional observations on the quantity of Earthy matter brought down by the Ganges, its depth and velocity, made during the rainy season of 1832, at Ghazipur. Rev. R. Everest 549
	Meteorological registers for March, May, June, July, August, September, ... 168, 216, 264, 326, 374 and 430
II. (183	Trisection of an Angle. Lieut. Nasmyth Morrieson .. 71
	An Experimental inquiry into the means employed by the natives of Bengal for Making ice. T. A. Wise, M. D. 80
	Abstracts of observations of the Temperature, Pressure and Hygrometrical state of the air at Nasirabad. Major T. Oliver 128
	Catalogue of the most remarkable Celestial objects visible in the Horizon of Calcutta, arranged in order of Right Ascension 252
	Description of a Compensation Barometer and observations on wet Barometers. J. Prinsep 258
	Meteorological table kept at Bancura, for the year 1832. John MacRitchie 383
	Note on the extraordinary fall of the Barometer during the gale of the 21st May last. James Prinsep, Sec..... 427
	Culminating Stars observed with the Moon at Nasirabad. Lieut.-Col. Thomas Oliver 432
	An inquiry into the laws governing the two great powers, attraction and repulsion, as operating on the Aggregation and Combination of Atoms. By Julius Jeffreys, Bengal Medical Service 441, 506

Journal.	
Vol. II. (1833.)	Determination of the Constant of Expansion of the standard 10 feet iron-bar of the great Trigonometrical Survey of India, and Expansions of gold, silver and copper by the same Apparatus. James Prinsep 130
	Table of ascertaining the heights of mountains from the boiling point of water. James Prinsep, Sec. 194
	On the climate of Nagpur. W. Geddes, Surgeon, Mad. Eur. Reg.................................... 239
	Table shewing the rise of spring tides in Bombay Harbour during night and day for the year 1832, communicated by Ben Noton 247
	Description of a Sun Dial in the Court of the Moti Masjid, in the fort of Agra. Capt. J. T. Boileau, Engineers 251
	Defence of Lt. Burt's Trisection instrument 485
	Additional note on the climate of Nágpur. J. Prinsep, Sec. As. Soc. 542
	Abstract of a Meteorological Journal kept at Kotgarh (Lat. 31° 11′ 45″ N. Long. 77° 27′ 49″ E.) Subathu, and the intermediate places in the Himalaya Mountains for 1819—20. Capt. E. Smith, Bengal Engineers 622
	Meteorological register at Barelly in 1831. H. S. Boulderson 641
	Meteorological tables, January to November, 656, 104, 160, 216, 272, 328, 384, 440, 496, 570, 608
III. (1834.)	Register of the weather at Futtehgar, (Lat. 27° 21′ Long. 79° 30′ E.) from April 1832, to October 1833. M. P. Edgeworth, C. S. 46
	Abstract of a Meteorological register kept at Mozaffarpur, in Tirhut (Lat. 26° 7′ 29″ N. Long. 85° 24′, 80″ F.) T. Dashwood, C. S............................... 79
	A Catalogue of Stars to be observed with the moon, in March and April, with the view of determining the difference of Longitude of the places whereat they may be observed. John Curnin, F. R. A. S. 94
	Climate of Seringapatam. Latitude 12° 45° N. Long. 76° 51′ E. 138
	Catalogue of Stars to be observed with the moon in May, 1834.. 139
	Meteorological register for 1833 kept at Bancura. J. MacRitchie 190

Journal.	
Vol. III. (1834.)	Experiments on the preservation of sheet iron from rust in India. James Prinsep 191
	Latitude of the Church Bungalow at Nasirabad, by altitudes (170) of Polaris out of the Meridian, observed with a Troughton's 18-inch Altitude and Azimuth circle. Col. Thos Oliver 243
	On Catadioptric Microscopes. J. W. Laidlay........ 288
	Observations of the Moon and Moon-culminating Stars at Seharanpur, Nasirabad and Dholeswar with the Longitudes deduced 297
	On the influence of the moon on Atmospherical Phenomena. Rev. R Everest, M. G. S., M. A. S.,.......... 345, 631
	On the Measurement of the Ilahy Guz of the Emperor Akbar. W. Cracroft 360
	Table of the Times of high water at the principal places between Calcutta and Point Palmiras. P. G. Sinclair 403
	Note on the Brown liquid, contained in the cylinders, from Manikulya. Jas. Prinsep 567
	Meteorological registers, January to December, .. 56, 104, 152, 208, 256, 312, 368, 424, 480, 544, 600, 656
	Abstract of a Meteorological Register kept at "Caineville," Masuri. S. M. Boulderson 230
	Comparison of the Heights of the Barometer, with the distance of the Moon from the Celestial Equator. Rev. R. Everest 252
	Collimation Error of Astronomical Instruments. J. G. Taylor, H. C. Astronomer, Madras 258
	Results of the observations made on the Tides at Madras, from the 31st May, to the 10th October, 1821, by means of a Tide-gauge fixed near the north-east angle of the Fort 325
	Register of the Thermometer at Ambala, for 1834. M. P. Edgeworth, C. S. 405
	Horary, Meteorological observations made at Calcutta on the 21st—22nd September. James Prinsep, Secretary 574
	Application of iron Rods, proposed to compensate for the strain occasioned by the tension of the strings upon Piano Fortes, thereby to prevent warping, and to render them more durable and better adapted to keep longer in tune. Col. D. Presgrave 634

Journal.	
Vol. IV. (1835.)	Extracts from a Meteorolgical Journal, kept at Kandy, Ceylon. Captain Ord, R. E. 709
	Abstract of Meteorological observations at Nasirabad. Lieut.-Col. Thomas Oliver 48
	Longitude of Nasirabad by lunar transits and by observations of Moon Culminating Stars. Lieut.-Col. Thomas Oviler 52
	Roof of the new iron foundery at Kasipur near Calcutta 111
	On the amount of rain-fall at Calcutta, as affected by the Declination of the Moon. Rev. R. Everest...... 207
	Rules for Calculating the lengths of the Drop-bars of suspension Bridges, the length and deflection of the chain rise of the roadway. Capt. J. Thomson 222
	Table shewing the weight or pressure which a cylindrical wrought-iron bolt will sustain when supported at the ends and bonded in the middle of its length. Capt. J. Thomson 225
	A table of the Scantlings of Beams of Teak or Saul Wood, to sustain a Terrace roof not exceeding seven inches in thickness; the deflection not to exceed one-fortieth of an inch for each foot of length. Capt. J. Thomson .. 227
	On the temperature of deep wells to the west of the Jamna. Rev. R. Everest 229
	Range of the Barometer and Thermometer, at Port Louis, Mauritius, in 1828. L. Geoffroy................ 715
	Meteorological Registers for Jan. to Dec..... 64, 120, 184, 240, 296, 360, 476, 412, 532, 588, 652, 716
V. (1836.)	Horary Observations of the Barometer, Thermometer and Wet-bulb Thermometer, made at Calcutta on the 21st and 22nd of December, 1835 and on the 21st and 22nd March, 1836. H. Barrow 51
	On the method employed to remove the Vaulted Roof of St. Peter's Church in Fort William, illustrated by a Section 208
	Note on the occasional existence of fresh-water on the surface of the Ocean. C. Brownlow 239
	On the Revolution of the Seasons. Rev. R. Everest 281
	Meteorological Register kept at Bangalore. Dr. J. Mouat 296

Journal.	
Vol. V. (1836.)	Meteorological observations taken every hour at Bangalore in the Hospital of H. M. 13th Dragoons from 6 A. M. of the 21st to 6 P. M. of the 22nd March, 1836, in conformity with Sir J. Herschel's instructions. Dr. J. Mouat 293
	Horary observations taken at Dadupur, in conformity with Sir John Herschel's circular by Col. Colvin, Lieut. Baker, Lieut. Druand, Engineers 299
	Experimental Researches on the Depressions of the Wet-bulb Hygrometer. James Prinsep, Sec. 396, 828
	Note on the Nautical Instruments of the Arabs. J. Prinsep.......... 784
	A comparative view of the daily range of the Barometer in different parts of India. J. Prinsep, Sec. 816
	Meteorological Registers for April, May, September, and December 256, 320, 600, 836
VI. (1837.)	Meteorological Register 160
	On the Revolution of the Seasons, Rev. R. Everest.... 303
	Observations of the Magnetic dip and intensity at Madras. T. G. Taylor, H. C. Astronomer 374
	Barometrical elevations taken on a journey from Katmandu to Gosainsthan, a place of pilgrimage in the mountains of Nipal. Chhedi lohar, a smith in the employ of Captain Robinson 696
	Meteorological Registers kept in Darjiling from April to August, 1837. Dr. H. Chapman 700, 888
	Abstract of Meteorological Register kept at Kathmandu for July and August, 1837. A. Campbell, Nipal Residency 889
	Notes on the Musical, Agricultural and other instruments of the Nipalese. A. Campbell, M. D.......... 953
VII. (1838.)	Abstract of a Meteorological Register kept at the Kathmandu Residency for September, 1837. A. Campbell, Nepal Residency 83
	Meteorological Register kept at Darjiling, for September to November, 1837 84
	On a remarkable heat observed in masses of brine kept for some time in large reservoirs. G. A. Prinsep 207

Journal.	
Vol. VII. (1838.)	On the Reg-Ruwan or moving sand, a singualar phenomenon of sound near Cabul with a sketch. Capt. Alex. Burnes .... 324 Account of the Hurricane or Whirlwind of the 8th April, 1838. J. Floyd (communicated by J. H. Patton, Magistrate of the 24-Pergunas) .... 422 On the spontaneous heating of brine. G. A. Prinsep 1014 Meteorological Registers for January, February, and August to December. 92, 172, 750, 838, 918, 990, 1064
VIII. (1839.)	Remarks upon the Rain and Drought of the last eight seasons in India. Rev. Everest, Landour .... 313 On the use of Wells, &c., in Foundations, as practised by the natives of the Northern Doab. Captain Cautley, Superintendent of the Doab Canal........ 341 Researches on the Gale and Hurricane in the Bay of Bengal on the 3rd, 4th, and 5th of June, 1839; being a First memoir on the Law of Storms in India. Henry Piddington .... 559, 631 Memoranda relative to the experiments on the communication of Telegraph signals by an induced Electricity. W. B. O'Shaughnessy, M. D., Professor of Chemistry, Medical College, Calcutta, and Officiating Joint Secretary to the Asiatic Society, Bengal .... 714 On an Aerolite presented to the Society .... 822 Description of an Astronomical Instrument presented by Raja Ram Sing of Khota to the Government of India. J. J. Middleton, of the Hindu College, Calcutta.... 831 Memorandum on the explosion of gunpowder under water by the Galvanic battery; with a notice of the successful destruction of the "Equitable," at Fultah Reach. W. B. O'Shaughnessy. .... 851 Meteorological Registers for January, February, and July to November 76, 158, 621, 692, 777, 867, 971
IX. (1840.) Pt. I.	Memorandum on the differences of the Meridian of the Observatory at Madras and the Flagstaff of Fort William and of the Cantonment of Futtehgar in the Doab. Col. J. A. Hodgson, late Surveyor General of India 75 A Second Memoir with reference to the Theory of the Law of Storms in India being researches relating to the Storms

Journal.	
Vol. IX. (1840.) Pt. I.	of the 19th to the 21st Sept. at the head of the Bay of Bengal; to the great Hurricane at Coringa on the 16th Nov. 1836; and to another off the island of Preparis on the 22nd Nov. Henry Piddington 107, 397
	Meteorological Tables 95, 217
Pt. II.	Report on a line of Levels taken by order of the Right Honorable the Governor-General, between the Jumna and Sutlej rivers. Lieut. W. E. Baker, Supt. of Canals W. of Jumna 688
	A Third memoir with reference to the theory of the Law of Storms in India; being researches relating to the Hurricane in the Bay of Bengal and at Cuttack, from 27th April to 1st May, 1840. H. Piddington 1009
	The Galvanic Battery in its various practical applications as an igniting Agent. Lieut. R. Baird Smith, Bengal Engineers 1149
X (1841.)	On Lightning Conductors to Powder Magazines. W. B. O'Shaughnessy. 6
	Succinct review of the observations of the tides in the Indian Archipelago, made during the year 1839 by order of His Excellency the Governor-General of his Netherlandish Majesty's possessions, 20th October 1838 302
	A Fourth memoir on the Law of Storms in India being remarks and documents relative to the loss of the ship Golconda, in the Tyfoons of 22nd to 24th Sept. 1840, in the China Sea. Henry Piddington 895
	Remarks on the Construction of Newman's improved Portable Barometer, and on the mode of renewing the Guage when lost. Capt. J. T. Boileau 957
XI. (1842.)	A Fifth memoir on the Law of Storms in India, being researches about the Madras Storms of May 16th, 1841, and an account of a whirlwind experienced by the French ship "Paquebat des Mers du sud" off the Cape. Henry Piddington 6
	On equations of condition for a quadrilateral common or re-entrant. Capt. R. Shortrede 28
	On improvement in Irrigation. Lieut. A. Murray McGregor................................ 39

Journal.	
Vol. XI. (1842.)	Compendious Logarithmic tables. Capt. Shortrede...... 40
	Tables of Barometrical and Thermometrical observations, made in Affghanistan, Upper Sind and Kutch Gundava, during the years 1839-40. Dr. Griffith............ 49
	Register of the rise and fall of the tide at Prince of Wales' island and Singapore, October 1840............. 149
	Notes regarding the Meteorology and climate of the Cape of Good Hope. Robert Trotter.................... 211
	On the theory of Angular Geometry. S. G. Tollemache Heatly 230
	Remarks on the Essay "on the theory of angular geometry." Captain Shortrede 240
	Notes on the recent earthquakes on the North-Western Frontier. Lieut R. Baird Smith 242
	Register of the rise and fall of the tide at Prince of Wales' Island and Singapore 263, 359
	Report upon the Construction of Philosophical instruments in India. Capt. J. Campbell.................. 293
	A Sixth Memoir on the Law of Storms in India, being Storms in the China seas from 1780 to 1841. Henry Piddington.. 605
	Comparison of the Areas of Plane and Spherical Triangles. Capt. Shortrede 779
	A note on Capt. Shortrede's remarks in page 240 of this volume 782
	A Seventh Memoir on the Law of Storms in India, being the Calcutta hurricane of 3rd and 4th June, 1842. Henry Piddington 971
XII. (1843.)	A perpetual Moon table. Capt. R. Shortrede 103
	On the treatment of Geometry as a branch of Analysis. S. G. Tollemache Heatly......................... 110
	Barometrical observations taken to ascertain the Altitude of the station of Purulia, Ramghur district. Capt. Hannyngton 226
	A Companion to the Moon table. Capt. R. Shortrede 231
	Remarks on some of the disturbing causes in Barometric observations. Capt. R. Shortrede 293
	On Barometric heights. Capt. R. Shortrede 298
	Memoir on the application of Asphaltic Mastic to Flooring, roofing, and Hydraulic Works in India. Capt. Goodwyn, Engineers 534

Journal.	
Vol. XII. (1843.)	A general statement of the weather at Kotgarh and Subathu, for 1819-20-21. Capt. Patrick Gerard 749
	Meteorological register kept at Kathmandu. Capt. G. H. Robinson 768
	A Ninth Memoir on the Law of Storms in India; being the Puri and Cuttak storms of 2nd, and the Gya and Patna storms of the 5th and 6th October, 1842. Henry Piddington 771
	A note on the winds, as influencing the Tracks sailed by Bermuda Vissels; and on the advantage which may be derived from sailing on curved Courses, when meeting with revolving winds. Lieut.-Col. Reid, Governor of Bermuda 1104
XIII. (1844.)	Tenth Memoir on the Law of Storms in India, being the Madras and Masulipatam storm of 21st to 23rd May, 1843. Henry Piddington 69
	Tables for determining the Elastic Force of Aqueous Vapour in the Atmosphere and the temperature of the dead-point by observations of a dry and wet bulb Thermometer; computed agreeably to Dr. Apjohn's Hygrometric formula, under the direction of Capt. J. T. Boileau. 135
	On the Specific Gravity of sea water. J. Middleton, 766
XIV. (1845.)	Mr. Ivory's tables of mean Astronomical refractions, revised and augmented. Major J. T. Boileau, ... 1
	A Eleventh Memoir on the the Law of Storms in India; being the storms in the Bay of Bengal and Southern Indian Ocean, from 26th November to 2nd December 1843. Henry Piddington. 10
	Observations on the rate of Evaporation in the open sea; with a description of an instrument used for indicating its amount. T. W. Laidlay 213
	A Twelfth Memoir on the Law of Storms in India, being the Storms of the Bay of Bengal, 9th to 14th November, 1844. Henry Piddington 357
	A Thirteenth Memoir on the Law of Storms in the Indian and China Seas being the Charles Heddle's Hurricane

Journal.	
Vol. XIV. (1845.)	in the Southern Indian Ocean, 22nd to 27th February, 1845. Henry Piddington........................ 703 A Fourteenth Memoir on the Law of Stoms in India; being the Bay of Bengal, Ceylon, Malabar Coast, and Arabian Sea Storms of 29th November to 5th December, 1845. Henry Piddington 878
XVI. (1847.)	Easiest method of taking and preparing drawings for Lithograph. Capt. M. Kittoe. .... 368 Refinage, on a large scale, by means of Nitre, of brittle or understandard silver, for Coinage purposes, and a ready mode of approximate assaying of silver. W. B. O'Shaughnessy, ... 557 Chart of the Bay of Bengal, note to accompany, with the average courses of its Hurricanes from 1800 A D. to 1846. H. Piddington........................ 847 Meteorological registers from July to November...... 850, 1002, 1094, 1182, 1278
XVII. (1848.)	A notice of a remarkable Hot wind in the Zillah of Purneah. H. Piddington........................ 144 On the fall of rain at Patna. C. E. Ravenshaw, ... 150 Temperature of the hot springs at Pir Mangal or Manga 230 Daily rate of Evaporation in Calcutta .... 236 A tabular view of the fall of rain, and of other Meteorological Phenomena in Calcutta from 1829 to 1847. Capt. H. E. L. Thuillier .... 349 Method of determining the neutral point of Barometers. Capt. J. C. Hannyngton .... 533 Fifteenth and Sixteenth Memoirs on the Law of Storms. H. Piddington .... 27, 517 Meteorological registers from July to December 1848.... 125, 239, 353, 475, 591 Resultant System for the construction of Iron Tension bridges. Major H. Goodwyn.............. 412
XVIII. (1849.)	Note on Iron Tension bridges. Rev. J. Pratt........ 249 A Seventeenth Memoir on the Law of Storms in India. H. Piddington 252

Journal.	
Vol. XVIII. (1849.)	Deviation of the Compass near Saugor in Bundelkund, a notice of a remarkable local phenomenon H. Piddington........ .... 410 Meteorological registers from January to June, 1849; 88*a*; 182*a*; 286*a*; 418*a*; 552*a*; 647*a*;.................. Embankments of rivers; and the nature of over-flowing rivers in Diluvial Plains. Capt. J. D. Cunningham.. 697 Influence of forests on climate. W. H. Parish ...... 791 An Eighteenth Memoir on the Law of Storms in India being the Cyclone of the 12th to 14th October 1848, in the Bay of Bengal. H. Piddington .... 826, 869 Meteorological registers for July, to September .. 759, 866, 987
XIX. (1850.)	Memorandum on the Storms experienced in Tartary, with suggestions relative to them. H. Piddington .... 242 A Nineteenth memoir on the Law of Storms in the Indian and China Seas. H. Piddington .... 349 Dust Storms of India. P. Baddeley .... 390 Tables for determining heights by the Barometer. Captain Hannyngton .... 394 Encrustation of Steam Boilers and pipes in India. Dr. G. Buist .... 419 Answers to Mr. Piddington's queries about Winds, Storms, &c., in Tibet. Dr. A. Campbell .... 457 Meteorological registers from January, to December of 1850 ...89, 189, 169, 349, 429, 499, 573, 575 577, 579, 581, 583
XX. (1851.)	A Twentieth memoir on the Law of Storms, in the Indian and China Seas, being the April Cyclone of the Bay of Bengal, 23rd to 28th April, 1850. H. Piddington .... 13, 195 Chronometers, on the rates of, as influenced by the local attraction of ships and by Terrestrial Magnetism. H. Piddington. .... 61 Aneroid and Marine Barometers and Sympiesometers in Cyclones. H. Piddington...................... 219 Influence of the Moon on the weather. J. Middleton 275 On the adaptation of the Aneroid for the purposes of Surveying in India. G. Buist 320

Journal.	
Vol. XX. (1851.)	Meteorological registers from January to December of 1851 112, 217, 289, 369, 449, 451, 454, 535, 622, 627, 633
	Monthly means of maximum and minimum pressures for 1841 to 1849, taken from the Meteorological register kept at the Surveyor General's Office, Calcutta 528
XXI. (1852.)	An Apparatus for distilling off the Mercury from an Amalgam of gold and silver. Henry Piddington........ 403
	Daily register of temperature during a part of 1850, at Mirut in the Upper Doab. C. Gubbins 563
	Dust Whirlwinds and Cyclones. P. F. H. Baddeley 140, 264, 333
	On Filtering waters of tanks in large quantities for the use of towns. H. Piddington 473
	Influence of the Moon on the weather. J. W. Beale.. 501
	Twenty-first Memoir on the Law of Storms in the Indian and China Seas. Henry Piddington 283
	Meteorology of Rampur Bauleah for the year 1851. J. R. Bedford 593
	Meteorological registers kept at the Surveyor General's Office, from January to December, 1852...103, 193, 280, 363, 443, 557, 558, 560, 562, 643, 645, 647.
	Meteorological observations kept at the Rangoon field hospital. Dr. J. Fayrer 520, 622
	Abstracts of Registers of temperature and fall of rain kept by Medical Officers in different parts of India. Dr. Lamb 383
XXII. (1853.)	Barometric waves in a Cyclone, Geometrical measurement of the distance from crest to crest of. Henry Piddington, President Marine Court 7
	Meteorological registers kept at the Surveyor General's Office, Calcutta, for Nov. and Dec. 1852 117
	Meteorological register kept at the Office of the Secretary to Government, N. W. P., from August to December, 1852, and Jan. to Oct., 1853. ....217, 327, 424, 707
	Meteorological observations, abstract of the results of the hourly, taken at the Surveyor General's Office, Calcutta 508, 599
	Meteorological registers kept at the field hospital, Rangoon, for October to April...........113, 317, 421, 502, 596

3

Journal.	
Vol. XXII. (1853.)	A Twenty-second Memoir on the Storms of the Indian and China Seas, Cyclones and Tornadoes of the Bay of Bengal, from 1848 to 1852. H. Piddington... 1
XXIII. (1854.)	Notes upon some Atmospherical Phenomena observed at Darjiling in the Himalaya Mountains during the summer of 1852. Capt. W. S. Sherwill .... 49 Report of the dust whirlwinds of the Punjab. Dr. A. Gardon .... 365 A Twenty-third Memoir on the law of Storms in the Indian and China Seas, being the Peninsular and Oriental Steam Navigation Company's Ship *Precursor's* Cyclone of October, 1854. H. Piddington 505
XXIV. (1855.)	On a simple method of manipulation in the Calotype process J. J. Gray .... 287 A Twenty-fourth Memoir on the law of Storms, being the Calcutta and Sunderban Cyclone of 14th and 15th May, 1852. H. Piddington 397
XXV. (1856.)	Report upon the progress of the Magnetic Survey, and the researches connected with it in Sikkim, the Kasia hills and Asam, April to December, 1855. Adolphe and Robert Schlagintweit........ .... 1 Report upon the progress of the Magnetic Survey of India and of the researches connected with it in the Himalaya Mountains, from April to October, 1855. A. and R. Schlagintweit .... 105 Report on the progress of the Magnetic Survey from January to May, 1856. Hermann Schlagintweit 554
XXVI. (1857.)	Mean temperature and fall of rain at Darjiling, 1848 to 1855 J. R. Withecombe .... 63 Reports on the Progress of the Magnetic Survey and of the researches connected with it; from November, 1855, to April, 1856. A. and R. Schlagintweit .... 54, 97 Report on the proceedings of the officers engaged in the Magnetic Survey of India 208

Journal.	
Vol. XXVII. (1858.)	Discussion of some Meteorological observations made at Parasnath hill. Dr. G. Von Leibig 1
	*Bháskara's knowledge of the Differential Calculus. Bapu Deva Shastri, Professor of Mathematics, Sanskrit College, Benares 213
	On Hypsometrical measurements by means of the Barometer and the boiling point Thermometer. James Burgess 337
	A register of the temperature of the Surface of the Ocean from the Hooghly to the Thames. A. Campbell .. 170
	Account of a Cyclone in the Andaman sea, on the 9th and 10th April, 1858. Dr. G. Von Leibig 323
	Twenty-fifth Memoir on the Law of Storms in India, being the Honorable Company's Steamer Pluto's Cyclone in the Gulf of Martaban, 23rd and 24th April, 1854. Henry Piddington 177
	The great Indian Arc of Meridian and the Figure of Earth. The Venerable Archdeacon Pratt 20
XXVIII. (1859)	Reply to Mr. Pratt's letter to the Asiatic Journal on the Indian Arc of Meridian. Capt. J. F. Tennant, B. E., G. T. Survey of India.. 17
	Second letter on the Indian Arc. J. H. Pratt 22
	On the influence of Mountain-attraction on the determination of the relative heights of Mount Everest near Darjiling, and the lofty peak, lately discovered near Kashmir. J. H. Pratt 150
XXIX. (1860.)	Memorandum on the great flood of the river Indus which reached Attock on the 10th August 1858. Capt. T. G. Montgomerie 128
XXX. (1861.)	On the translation of waves of water with relation to the great flood of the Indus in 1858. J. Obbard......... 266
	On the Physical difference between a rush of water like a torrent down a channel and the transmission of a wave down a river, with reference to the inundation of the Indus, as observed in Attok, in August, 1858. J. H. Pratt 274

Journal.	
Vol. XXX. (1861.)	Notes on the rainfall in the basin of the river Mahanady and the floods consequent thereupon. Capt. J. C. Harris, 216 The great Comet of 1861. Rev. Dr. W. S. Mackay .. 279 Discovery of the new planet, *Asia.* N. R. Pogson.... 291
XXXI. (1862.)	*On Colebrooke's determination of the date of the *Vedas.* Ven'ble Archdeacon J. H. Pratt 49
XXXII. (1863.)	Progress of the Trigonometrical Survey, being extracts from a report from Major J. T. Walker .... 111 Abstracts of the results of the hourly Meteorological observations taken at the Surveyor General's Office, Calcutta, for July to December, 1862, and January to July, 1863 .... i, xxv, xlix, lxxii
XXXIII. (1864.)	Extract from report of the operations of the great Trigonometrical Survey of India during the year 1862-63. Major J. T. Walker .... 381 Abstract of the results of the hourly Meteorological observations taken at the Surveyor General's Office, Calcutta, for April to June, 1864 .... xxv Abstract of the Meteorological observations taken at Gangaroowa, near Kandy, Ceylon, September 1863 to February, 1864 .... xvii, lxi Note on the hailstorm of Thursday the 24th March. Henry F. Blanford...... .... 530 Abstract of the results of the hourly Meteorological observations taken at the Surveyor General's Office, Calcutta for July to December, 1864 xlix
XXXIV. (1865.)	On the degree of uncertainty which local attraction, if not allowed for, occasions in the map of a country, &c.; and speculations on the constitution of the Earth's crust. Archdeacon Pratt .... 34 On the Pendulum operations about to be undertaken by the Great Trig. Survey of India. J. P. Basevi, R. E., Trig. Survey .... 251 Meteorological observations at the Surveyor General's Office, i, ix, xxv, xxxiii

Journal.	Meteorological observation taken at Gangaroowa, near Kandy xvii
Vol. XXXIV. (1865.)	
XXXV. Pt. II. (1866.)	Observations on the Astronomical points determined by the brothers Schlagintweit in Central Asia. Capt. Golubief .... 46 Comparative Hypsometrical and physical tableau of High Asia, the Andes, and the Alps. Robert Schlagintweit, Professor at Giessen .... 51 Meteorogical Observations at the Surveyor General's Office, lvii Ditto ditto taken at Gangaroowa, near Kandy, Ceylon, in May, 1864 lxii
XXXVI. Pt. II. (1867.)	Meteorological observations at the Surveyor General's Office . xvii, xxxiii, xli
XXXVII. Pt. II. (1868.)	Diagram of monthly mean curves of Barometer and Thermometer, and of rainfall, Calcutta, 1856-65. Col. T. E. Gastrell .... 77 The adjustment of the Hindu Calendar. P. Ch. Ghose 181 Meteorological observations at the Surveyor General's Office lxv
XXXVIII. Pt. II. (1869.)	Meteorological observations at the Surveyor General's, September 1861 to October 1869 .... i, lxix
XXXIX. Pt. II. 1870.	Meteorological observations at the Surveyor General's Office . i, lxxxiii
XL. Pt. II. (1871.)	Meteorological observations at the Surveyor General's Office lxxiv Note on the error of the Calcutta Standard Barometer compared with those of Kew and Greenwich. H. F. Blanford .... 446 On the discharge of long Overland Telegraph Lines. H. Schwendler .... 78 On a quantitative method of testing a "Telegraph earth." W. E. Ayrton 177

Journal.	
Vol. XLII. Pt. II. (1873.)	On differential Galvanometers. L. Schwendler 144
XLIII. Pt. II. (1874.)	On the General Theory of Duplex Telegraphy. L. Schwendler Part I .... 1 Part II 218
XLIV. (1875.)	On some recent evidence of the Variation of the Sun's heat. H. F. Blanford .... 21 On the general theory of Duplex Telegraphy, Part III. L. Schwendler .... 47 Photography in connection with the observations of the Transit of Venus at Rurki, 9th December 1874. J. Waterhouse 64
XLV. Pt. II. (1876.)	On certain protracted irregularities of Atmospheric Pressure in the Indian Monsoon region, and their relations to variations of the local Rainfall. H. F. Blanford...... 27 An account of experiments made in 1875 and 1876 in various parts of India for the purpose of comparing the observed temperature of the Dew point with that computed from the Psychrometer by different methods of reduction. H. F. Blanford .... 53 On the Physical explanation of the Inequality of the two Semidiurnal oscillations of Barometic Pressure. H. F. Blanford .... 319 On the General Theory of Duplex Telegraphy. L. Schwendler 1
XLVI. Part II. (1877.)	Note on the variation of the Barometric Tides in connection with diurnal land and sea-breezes. H. F. Blanford ... 45 Catalogue of the recorded cyclones in the Bay of Bengal up to the end of 1876. H. F. Blanford .... 328 Memorandum on the diurnal variation of atmospheric pressure at the Sandheads. C. Harding 339
XLVII. Pt. II. (1878)	On the proper relative sectional area for Copper and Lightning Rods. R. S. Brough .... 191 Great snowfall in Kashmir. R. Lydekker 177

Journal.	
Vol. XLVII. Pt II. (1878.)	An account of the Tidal observations in the Gulf of Cutch conducted by the Trigonometrical Survey. J. Waterhouse .... 26 The application of Photography to the reduction of Maps and Plans by Photo-Mechanical and other processes. J. Waterhouse 53
XLVIII. (1879.)	On the diurnal variation of rainfall frequency in Calcutta. H. F. Blanford .... 41 On the operations for obtaining the discharges of the large rivers in Assam during 1877-78. H. J. Harman ...... 4 On a new standard of Light. L. Schwendler .... 83 On some experiments made at H. M.'s Mint in Calcutta on coining silver into rupees. J. F. Tennant 56
XLIX. Pt. II. (1880.)	On a simple method of using an Insignificant fraction of the main current produced by a Dynamo-Electric Machine for Telegraph purposes. Louis Schwendler .... 1 Account of the verification of some Standard Weights, with considerations on Standard weights in general. J. F. Tennant .... 41 On the high Atmospheric pressure of 1876-78 in Asia and Australia in relation to the Sun Spot Cycle. H. F. Blanford. .... 70 On some experiments instituted to supply all the lines terminating at the Calcutta Telegraph office with current tapped from the main current produced by a Dynamo-electric machine. Louis Schwendler 167
L. Pt. II. (1881.)	On the relations of Cloud and Rainfall to Temperature in India, and on the opposite variations of Density in the higher and lower Atmospheric strata. H. F. Blanford 69
LI. Pt. II. (1882.)	Some further results of Sun-thermometer observations with reference to atmospheric absorption and the supposed variation of the Solar heat. H. F. Blanford........ 72
Proceedings (1865.)	On whirlwind at Pandua. Chunder Shekhur Chatterjee 124

Proceedings	
	Recorded solar eclipses. Major Ellis 172
(1867.)	
(1868.)	On discrepancies in the observations of the Cyclone of 1867........ 66
	On an instrument used by native Captains for determining their latitude. T. Oldham 201
	On the Eclipse. T. Oldham........218, 228
	Notes on the eclipse. Major F. Tennant 127
	Results deducible from the Eclipse. Major F. Tennant 273
(1870.)	On North-Westers. H. F. Blanford 95
	On the Assay of Silver. Dr. H. E. Busteed 276
(1871.)	On Inertia and Time. W. E. Ayrton 160
	On a new Galvanometer. W. E. Ayrton........ 217
	On the total Eclipse of December 11th. J. F. Tennant 128
(1872.)	On Syphon Recorder. W. E. Ayrton 51
	New joint detector. L. Schwendler 92
	On Whirlwind at Satkhira. W. G. Willson 96
	Meteorological observations at the Surveyor General's i
(1874.)	On the correction of Copper-plates by Electrodeposition. J. Waterhouse........ 1
	Meteorological observations at the Surveyor General's i
(1875.)	On specimens of telegraph cable penetrated by grass. L. Schwendler 158
	Meteorological observations at the Surveyor General's i
(1876.)	On the influence of Eosin on the Photographic action of the solar spectrum upon the Bromide and Bromoiodide of silver. Capt. J. Waterhouse 12
	Meteorological observations at the Surveyor General's i

Proceedings	
(1877.)	A theoretical deduction of the best resistance of a Telegraph receiving instrument. R. S. Brough 184
	Note on Professor Graham Bell's Telephone. R. S. Brough 252
	On a case of lightning; with an Evolution of the Potential and quantity of the discharge in absolute measure. R. S. Brough 56
	On the diameter of the wire employed in winding an electro-magnent to produce the Maximum Magnetic effect. R. S. Brough 134
1878.	Autographic records of Nor'-Westers. H. F. Blanford 103
	On Meteorological Charts. H. F. Blanford 104
	On tidal observations. Col. J. T. Walker 106
	Solar Photographs. Capt. J. Waterhouse 119
	Peculiarities in hailstones at Khulná. H. G. Rainey 125
1879.	Photograph of the solar disc. J. Waterhouse........ 140
1880.	Balfour Stewart's Actinometer. H. F. Blanford ... 51, 52
	Drawings of hailstones. Col. H. H. Godwin-Austen... 103
	Crook's Electrical Radiometers. Rev. E. Lafont 91
1881.	Van Rysselberghe Meteorograph. H. F. Blanford...... 65
1882.	Spirit-levelling operations in connection with the tidal observations of the Indian Survey. J. T. Walker... 78

II.

GEOLOGY.*

(*N. B.*—Mineralogical contributions are distinguished by [M.])

As. Res. Vol. I. 1788.	[M.]	Gold of Limong. Macdonald 336
V. 1795.		Barren island and its Volcano. Lieut. R. H. Colebrooke 397
		Geology of Perwattam. C. Mackenzie 303
VI. 1799.	[M.]	Petroleum wells in Burma. Capt. H. Cox 127
XI. 1810.		An account of the Petrifactions near the Village of Truvikera in the Carnatic. Capt. J. Warren 1
XII. 1816.		Boring made near the river Hooghly, in the vicinity of Calcutta, from May to July 1814, in search of a Spring of pure water. Sir Edward Hyde East 542
XIV 1820.	[M.]	Analysis of the Snake-stone. J. Davy............... 317
XV. 1825.		On the Diamond Mines of Southern India. H. W. Voysey 120
		On the building Stones and Mosaic of Akberabad or Agra. H. Voysey 429
XVI. 1828.	[M.]	On the *Zehr Mohereh* or snake-stone. Capt. J. D. Herbert 382
	[M.]	Notice of the occurrence of Coal and Lignite in the Himalaya. Lieut. P. T. Cautley 387
	[M.]	Note on the occurrence of Coal, within the Indo-Gangetic Tract of Mountains. Capt. J. D. Herbert 397

* Some Geographical papers not included in this section contain information on Geological subjects. Palæontological papers are to be looked for under Zoology and Botany.

As. Res. Vol. XVIII. Pt. I. 1829.

General observations on the Geology of India. James Calder 1

On the Geology of a portion of Bundelkhand, Boghelkhand and the districts of Sagor and Jabalpur. Capt. James Franklin 23

The Trap Formation of the Ságar District and of those districts westward of it, as far as Bhopalpur, on the banks of the river Newas, in Omatwara. Capt. S. Coulthard 47

Geology of the country, on the route from Baroda to Udayapur viâ Birpur and Salembher. James Hardie 82

Diamond mines of Panna in Bundelkhand. Capt. James Franklin 100

Geological and Mineralogical Structure of the hills of Sitábaldi, Nágpur, and its immediate vicinity. H. W. Voysey 123

Geological and general features of portions of the Malayan Peninsula, and of the countries lying between it and 18° North latitude. Capt. James Low.................. 128

Description of the North-West Coal district, stretching along the river Dámudá, from the neighbourhood of Jeria or Jeriagerh, to below Sanampur, in the Purgunnah of Sheargarh, forming a line of about sixty-five miles. Mr. Jones of Calcutta 163

[M.] Iron Ore from Burdwan. H. Piddington 171

[M.] An account of some Minerals collected at Nagpur and its vicinity with remarks on the Geology &c. of that part of the country. Capt. F. Jenkins 195

[M.] Notice of the occurrence of Gypsum in the Indo-Gangetic tract of mountains. Capt. J. D. Herbert 216

[M.] Mineral productions of that part of the Himalaya mountains, lying between the Satlej and the Káli. Capt. J. D. Herbert 227

Pt. II. 1833.

Sketch of the Geology of Central India, exclusive of Malwa. James Hardie 27

Geology of the Peninsula. Lieut. S. C. Macpherson... 115

Short Sketch of the Geology of Pulo Pinang and the neighbouring islands. T. Ward 149

Spiti valley and circumjacent country within the Himalaya. Surgeon J. G. Gerard 238

As. Res. Pt. II. 1833.

[M.] Note on the discovery of Platina in Ava. James Prinsep 279

Journal Vol. I. 1832.

[M.] Examination of Minerals from Ava. J. Prinsep, Sec. ... 14
Earthquake at Lahore, 25th Jan. 1832 34
[M.] Salt mines of the Panjab. Lieut. A. Burnes 145
[M.] Mode of extracting the gold dust from the sand of the Ningthie river.................................. 148
[M.] Smelting of Iron in the Kasia hills 150
[M.] Chinese Vermilion 151
Geological Sketch of Masuri and Landour in the Himalaya. F. H. Fisher, ... 183
[M.] Gypsum of the Himalaya. Capt. P. T. Cautley 289
[M.] Litharge of Ava 305
[M.] Oriental accounts of the precious Minerals 353
[M.] Remarks on a late paper in the Asiatic Journal on the Gypsum of the Himalaya. Rev. R. Everest 450
Some observations on the quantity of earthy matter brought down by the Ganges. Rev. R. Everest 238, 549

II. 1833.

[M.] Discovery of the Silhet Coal Mines 47
[M.] Short description of the Mines of Precious Stone in the district of Kyakpyau in the Kingdom of Ava 75
Geology of Hyderabad. H. W. Voysey........... 298, 392
[M.] Native Sulphate of Alumina from the Alumious Rocks of Nipal. J. Stevenson. 321
[M.] Native Sulphate of Iron from the Hills of Behar and used by native Dyers of Patna. J. Stevenson 321
[M.] Description of the salt works at Panchpadder, Mewar. Lieut. A. Burnes 365
Report of the Committee appointed on the 27th March, 1833, to consider the expediency of recommending to the Government the continuance of the Boring experiment 369
Some Geological remarks made in the country between Mirzapur and Ságar, and from Ságar northwards to the Jumna. Rev R. Everest 475
[M.] Alum or Salajit of Nipal. A. Campbell, ... 482

Journal Vol. II. 1833.

[M.] A visit to the Gold Mine at Batting Moring, and summit of Mount Ophir or Gunong Ledang, in the Malay peninsula. Lieut. J. T. Newbold 497

An Earthquake at Kathmandu. A. Campbell ... 564, 636

[M.] Note on the Coal discovered at Khyuk Phyu, in the Arracan district 595

Notes on the specimens of the Kankar Formation, and on fossil Bones collected on the Jamna. Capt. E. Smith, 622

III. 1834.

Climate of the fossil Elephant. Rev. R. Everest 18

Chirra Punji and a detail of some of the favourable circumstances which render it an advantageous site for the erection of an Iron and Steel manufactory. Lieut.-Col. T. C. Watson 25

Tufa formation in Persia 54

Geology of the country between Hoshungábád on the Narbada and Nágpur, by the direction of Baitul. Lieut. John Finnis 71

Explanation of the sketch giving a Geological Section of the strata from Nimach to Merta published in the Asiatic Researches, Vol XVIII. James Hardie........ 238

Notes relative to the collection of some Geological Specimens, in the Kasia Hills between Asam and Nanklow. W. Cracoft, ... 293

Note on the Temperature of wells at Náhan 366

Geological Section across the Valley of the Narbada, from Tendukheri to Bittoul. J. G. Spilshury, ... 388

[M.] Observation on the Golden ore, found in the Eastern Provinces of Mysore in 1802. Lieut. John Warren.... 463

[M.] Nepalese method of refining Gold. Dr. A. Campbell... 622

Notice of some fossil impressions occurring in the Transition Limestone of Kumaon. Dr. J. McClelland ....

Temperature of Wells 655

IV. 1835.

Jumma Alluvium. Edmund Dean 261

[M.] Gold-washing of the Gumti river. Lieut. Cautley...... 279

Geological sketch of the Nil-giris. Dr. P. N. Benza, 413

Mr. Stevenson on the Pea Stalactite of Tibet 520

[M.] On the composition of the Rángun Petroleum with remarks on the composition of Petroleum and Naphtha in general. William Gregory, ... 527

Volume		Title	Page
Journal Vol. IV. 1835.	[M.]	Minerals of the Trappean rocks of Bombay	530
	[M.]	Notice of two beds of Coal discovered. Captain J. R. Ouseley,	648
		Geological observations made in a journey from Masuri to Gangautri. Rev. R. Everest	690
	[M.]	Copper Ore from Nellore. James Prinsep	574
	[M.]	Mineral Exudation from Ghazni. H. Piddington	696
	[M.]	Coal beds in Asam. Captain T. Jenkins	704
V. 1836.		Notes explanatory of a Collection of Geological Specimens from the country between Hyderabad and Nágpur. J. G. Malcolmson,	96
		Notice of a visit to the Valley of Cashmir in 1836. Baron Hugel	184
		Notes on the Geology of the country in the Neighbourhood of Maulmyeng (Moulmein). Capt. W. Foley	269
		Volcanic Scoria in the Southern Peninsula. Lieut. J. T. Newbold	670
		Geological notes on the Northern Conkan and a small portion of Guzerat and Kattywar. Charles Lush	761
VI. 1837.		Memorandum of the progress of sinking a well in the bund of Chandpur, near the foot of the hills. William Dawe	52
		Hot Spring of Lohand Khad. Capt. C. M. Wade	153
		Report of the progress of the Boring Experiment in Fort William. Major T. M. Taylor. With notes, by J. Prinsep	234
	[M.]	Catalogue of Geological Specimens from Kumaon presented to the Asiatic Society. Dr. McClelland	653
		Strata passed through in a Boring at Gogah, Gujerat. Lieut. George Fulljames	786
VII. 1838.		On the difference of level in Indian Coalfields, and the causes to which this may be ascribed. J. McClelland	65
		Section of a Hill in Catak supposed to be likely to contain Coal. M. Kittoe	152
	[M.]	Table of Indian Coal analyzed at the Calcutta Assay Office, including those published in the "Gleanings in Science," September 1831, arranged according to localities, extracted from the Report of the Coal Committee	191

Journal Vol. VII. 1838.

[M.] Native account of Washing for Gold in Asam. Muneeram. 621

[M.] Further information on the same, extracted from Capt. Hannay's communication to Capt. Jenkins, Agent to the Governor-General in Assam 625

[M.] Coal discovered in Tenasserim Provinces. Dr. Helfer . 701

[M.] Report on ten specimens of Coal from Capt. Burnes ... 848

Supposed Coal Field at Bidjeygurh (Vijayagar). George Osborne 839

[M.] Copper mines of Kumaon. Capt. Drummond 934

VIII. 1839.

[M.] Report upon the Coal beds of Asam. The Coal and Iron Committee 948

[M.] Coal and Iron Mines of Talchir. M. Kittoe 137

[M.] Papers relative to the New Coal Field of Tenasserim.. 385

[M.] Report by Lieut. John Glasfurd, on the progress made up to the 1st May 1839, in opening the experimental Copper mine in Kumaon 471

Mr. Middleton on the Meteors of August 10th, 1839... 495

[M.] Note by Messrs. Jessop & Co. of Calcutta, on the smelting of Iron Ore of the district of Burdwan 683

Note on the river Gumti, with a section of its bed. V. Trigear 712

Trip through Kunawur, Hungruq and Spiti undertaken in the year 1838, under the patronage of the Asiatic Society of Bengal. Lieut. Thomas Hutton 901

Geology etc. of the country extending between Bhar and Simla 1037

[M.] Note on the process of washing for the Gold dust and Diamonds at Heera Khoond. J. R. Ouseley 1057

IX. Pt. I. 1840.

[M.] Memoranda respecting the existence of Copper in the territory of Luz, near Bela. Capt. De la Hoste 30

[M.] Note on discoveries of gems from Kandahar. Lieut. Conolly 97, 100

[M.] Report of the Coal Committee 198

Note on the Map attached to the report of the Coal Committee. Capt. Macleod, ... 582

Boring operations in Fort William, from their commencement in December 1835, to their close in April, 1836. Col. D. McLeod 677

Physical Geography of Seistan. Cap. Conolly 710

Journal Vol. X. 1841.

[M.] Mines and Mineral resources of Northern Afghanistan. Capt. Drummond 74

Valley of the Spiti and the route from Kotgar. Capt. Hutton 198

[M.] Memoir on the Coal found at Kotah, with a note on the Anthracite of Dumtimnapilly, (H. H. the Nizam's dominious). W. Walker 341

[M.] Discovery of Coal in a new site. W. Dunbar. 300

Geology of Hunumkunda (Nizam's Territory) &c.—A. W. Walker 471, 725

[M.] Tin of the Province of Mergui. Capt. G. B. Tremenheere 845

[M.] Manganese of Do. Do. ... 852

Observations of Meteors, on the night between the 12th and 13th Nov. 1841, made at the Magnetic Observatory at Simla. Captain J. T. Boileau 964

[M.] On Porcelain Clay found at Mangalore. A. T. Christie, 967

XI. 1842.

Additions to Capt. G. B. Tremenheere's report on the Tin of Mergui, communicated to the Asiatic Society, through the Secretariat of the General Department...... 24, 289

[M.] Extract from a letter to Government on the above from Dr. McClelland, Secretary to the Coal Committee 25

Notes on the recent Earthquakes on the North-Western Frontier. Lieut. R. Baird Smith 242

[M.] On a cylinder and certain gems collected in the neighbourhood of Herat. Major Pottinger 316

Geology of Bundlecund and Jubbulpur. Dr. J. Adam 393

Report of the Mineralogical Survey of the Himalaya Mountains lying between the rivers Sutlej and Kali. Illustrated by a Geological Map. Capt. J. D. Herbert,... i

Coal field of the Dámuda Valley and the adjacent countries of Birbhum and Purulia. J. Homfray... 728

[M.] Contributions towards a history of the development of the Mineral resources of India. S. G. Tollemache Heatly 811

[M.] Second report on the Tin of Mergui. Capt. G. B. Tremenheere 839

[M.] Notes on the Iron of the Kasia hills. Lieut. Yule, ... 853

Notes, principally Geological, on the Tract between Bellary and Bijapore. Capt. Newbold,.. 929, 941

Journal.	
Vol. XI. 1842.	Meteors observed at Allahabad on the 10th of August, 1842 Capt. Shortrede, ... 959
	On Specimens offered to the Asiatic Society of Bengal. Capt. Newbold ... 1131
XII. 1843.	First report by Dr. Jameson of his deputation by Government to examine the effects of the great inundation of the Indus ... 183
	Brigadier Twemlow on Artificial Fuel (received from the Agricultural Society) ... 228
	Account of a luminous Meteor seen at Charka, lat. 24° 06′ long. 81° 02′ on the morning of the 11th April, 1842. Capt. Shortrede ... 235
[M.]	Analysis of Iron ores from Tavoy and Mergui, and of Limestone from Mergui. Dr. A. Ure, London ... 236
	Memoir on Indian Earthquakes. Pts. I and II. Lieut. R. Baird Smith ... 258, 1029
[M.]	Report on the Government experimental workings of the Copper Mines of Pokri in Ghurwal, with notices of other Copper Mines. G. S. Lushington ... 453, 769
	Report of visit to the Pakchan river, and of some Tin localities in the southern portion of the Tenasserim Provinces. Capt. G. B. Tremenheere, ... 523
[M.]	Contributions towards a History of the development of the Mineral resources of India. S. G. Tollemache Heatly 542
	As-Soyuti's work on Earthquakes, called, *Kashf-as-salsalah' au wasf Az-Zal-Zalab*, translated from the Arabic. A. Sprenger ... 741
[M.]	Native Copper found in Round Island Cheduba group, south-east of Ramri, forwarded to the Society by Capt. Campbell. S. Mornay ... 904
	Memoranda of Earthquakes and other remarkable occurrences in Upper Assam from January, 1839, to Sept., 1843. Capt. Hannay ... 907
XIII. 1844.	Geological Map of Capt. Herbert's Himalaya Survey .. 171
	Note on a recent fossiliferous fresh-water deposit in Southern India, with a few remarks on the origin and age of Kunkur. Capt. Newbold ... 313

Journal.	
Vol. XIII. 1844.	Red sandstone from the junction of the Diamond limestone and Sandstone at Narnur, Karnul. Osseous Deposit in the caves of Billa Surgans. Capt. Newbold, H. Piddington 336
	Geological remarks during a march from Benares (old road) *viâ* Hazaribag, Bankura, and Burdwan, to Barakpur. Dr. J. Row 862
	An account of a remarkable Aerolite, which fell at the village of Manicgaon, near Eidulabad, in Khandeish. Capt. James Abbott, and H. Piddington 880
	Memoir on Indian Earthquakes. Pt. III. Lieut. R. Baird Smith 964
	Notes, chiefly geological, across the Peninsula from Masulipatam to Goa, comprising remarks on the origin of the Regur and Laterite, and the occurrence of Manganese veins in the latter. Capt. Newbold 984
XIV. 1845.	On the Alpine Glacier, Iceberg, Diluvial and Wave translation theories; with reference to the deposits of Southern India, its furrowed and striated rock basins. Capt. Newbold 217
	Notes on the South Mahratta country. Falls of Gokanth—Classification of rocks. Capt. Newbold 268
	Report, from Capt. G. B. Tremenheere, with information concerning the price of Tin Ore of Mergui 329
	Notes across the Peninsula of Southern India, from Kistapatam, on the Western Coast, comprising a visit to the falls of Gairsuppa. Capt. Newbold 398
	On Kunker formations. Capt. J. Abbott 442
[M.]	Notes on the Pokri and Dhanpur Copper Mines, Gharwal. Siegmund Reckendorf 471
	Note on a curious sandstone formation at Sasseram, Zillah Shahabad. Lieut. W. S. Sherwill 495
	Madras to Goa by the Baulpilly Pass and ruins of Bijayanagar, Capt. Newbold 497
	Asiatic Earthquakes in 1843. R. Baird Smith 604
	Mangalore to Madras. Capt. Newbold 641
[M.]	On the Iron Ores of Birbhum 754
	Agate splinters found in the clay stratum bordering the river Narbada. Capt. J. Abbott 756

Journal			Page
Vol XIV. 1845.		Notes, chiefly geological, across South India from Pondicherry, to Beypoor, through the great gap of Palghautcherry. Capt. Newbold	759
	[M.]	On the Asam Petroleum beds. Capt. P. S. Hannay	817
		Remarks upon the occurrence of granite in the bed of Narbada. Capt. J. Abbott	821
XV. 1846.		Notes, on the Coast of Coromandel, from Pennour to Pondicherry. Capt. Newbold	204
		Geological features of Zillah Behar. W. S. Sherwill	55
	[M.]	From Kumpta on the western Coast (S. India), by the Devamunni and Nundibaunama Passes, easterly to Cumbum, and thence southerly to Chittur; comprising a Notice of the Diamond and Lead excavations of Buswapur. Capt. Newbold	380
		From Seringapatam, by the Hegulla Pass, to Cannanore. Capt. Newbold	315
		Western Coast of South India. Capt. Newbold	224
XVI. 1847.	[M.]	Account of the process employed for obtaining Gold from the sand of the river Beas; with a short account of the Gold mines of Siberia. Capt. J. Abbott	226
	[M.]	Coal, a new kind of, from Aracan. H. Piddington	371
		Singapore, including Notices of Sumatra and the Malay peninsula. J. R. Logan	519 667
		Zillah Shahabad or Arrah. Lieut. W. R. Sherwill	279
	[M.]	Tremenheerite, a new carbonaceous Mineral. H. Piddington	369
		Notes, chiefly geological, from Gooty to Hydrabad, South India, comprising a brief notice of the old Diamond Pits at Dhone. Capt. Newbold	477
		Notes of an Excursion to the Pindri glacier, in September, 1846. Capt. Ed. Madden,	226 596
	[M.]	Notice on the Ferruginous Spherules imbedded in sandstone from Lullutpore, Bundlecund. H. Piddington	711
		A description of the glaciers of the Pindur and Thuphinu rivers, Kumaon Himalaya. Lieut. R. Strachey	794
XVII. 1848.	[M.]	Extract from a Memoir of some of the natural productions of the Angami hills and other parts of Upper Asam. J. W. Masters	57

Journal Vol. XVII. 1848. Pt. I.	[M.]	The ball Coal of the Burdwan Mines. Henry Piddington 59
		Correspondence regarding the Coal beds in the Namsang Naga hills; Communicated by Capt. T. E. Rogers... 89
	[M.]	Diamond in the possession of the Nizam. H. Piddington 151
	[M.]	A few observations on the probable results of a Scientific research after Metalliferous deposits in the Sub-Himalayan range around Darjiling. R. H. Irvine, ... 137
Pt. II.		Note on the motion of the glacier of the Pindur in Kumaon. Lieut. R. Strachey 203
	[M.]	Report on the Salt Range and on its Coal and other Minerals. Dr. Andrew Fleming 500
	[M.]	Meteoric iron from the Kharakpur hills. H. Piddington 538
		Notes on the eastern desert of Egypt, from Gebel Sprit by the ancient Porphyry quarries of Gebel Dukhan, near to Gebel Gir. Hekekyan Bey 584
XVIII. 1849.	[M.]	Capt. Sherwill's supplementry note On Meteoric Iron. H. Piddington 171
		Earthquakes in Assam 172, 173, 174
	[M.]	Ball Coal of the Burdwan Mines. H. Piddington...... 412
		Pind Dádud Khan and the Salt Range. A. Fleming... 661
		Note on the limits of perpetual Snow. Capt. J. D. Cunningham 694
		On the Physical Geography of the Himalayas. B. H. Hodgson 761
		Remarks on the Snow line in the Himalaya. Capt. Thomas Hutton.. 954
XIX. 1850.	[M.]	Ball Coal of the Burdwan Mines. H. Piddington...... 57
	[M.]	On Calderite, an undescribed Silicio-iron-and-manganese Rock. H. Piddington 145
		On the general Vibration, or Descent and Upheaval which seems, at a recent geological period, to have occurred all over the Northern Hemisphere. George Buist 302
	[M.]	Haughtonite. H. Piddington 452
	[M.]	Note on specimen of Iron from the Dhunakar hills, Birbhum. H. Torrens 77

Journal Vol. XIX. 1850.		Note on the formations and Lead mines of Kohel et Terafeh. Hekeykian Bey........................ 217
	[M.]	An orange yellow earth from Sikkim. H. Piddington 143
		Note on Patna Boulders. Capt. E. L. Ommaney 136
		Extracts from Voysey's private journal,...........190, 269
		Wadi Araba, Note on the strata cut through in exacavating for coal in. Hekeykian Bey.......................... 139
	[M.]	Note on the Zinc Mines of Jawar. Capt. J. C. Brooke 212
XX 1851.	[M.]	Copper Ores of the Deogur Mines. H. Piddington ... 1
	[M.]	On a series of Calderite rocks. H. Piddington... 207
		Floods in India, for 1849. Dr. G. Buist.............. 186
	[M.]	Behar Mica Mines. Capt. W. S. Sherwill 295
	[M.]	Shalka Meteorite. H. Piddington 299
		Rájmahal Hills. W. S. Sherwill 544
XXI. 1852.	[M.]	On the Argentiferous Ores of Deoghur................ 74
	[M.]	Table of Analysis of Indian Coals. H. Piddington ... 270
XXII. 1853.		Laterite, Rangun. Capt. C. B. Young 196
		The Salt Range. A. Fleming 229, 333, 444
		Note on the discharge of water by the Irawady. J. McClelland, ... 480
		Memorandum on the prospect of remuneration in working the Iron Mines of the Ranigunj District by Major W. E. Baker, with a report on the same subject by T. Oldham 484
	[M.]	Note on the Gold fields of upper Asam. Maj. Hannay... 511
XXIII. 1854.	[M.]	Notes on the Iron ore of Korana in the Jetch Dooab of the Punjab. Dr. A. Fleming 92
		Memorandum on the Geological structure and Mineral resources of the Singbhum Division of the South-West Frontier Agency. Capt. J. C. Haughton 103
	[M.]	On the Nepaulite, a new Mineral from the neighbourhood of Kathmandu. H. Piddington 170
		Rájmahal Hills. T. Oldham.......................... 263

Journal Vol.	
XXIII. 1854. [M.]	Examination and analysis of Dr. Campbell's Specimens of Copper Ores obtained in the neighbourhood of Darjiling. H. Piddington 477
[M.]	Coal from Darjiling and from Ava. H. Piddington 381, 714
	Notes on the geology of the Punjab Salt range. W. Theobald 651
XXIV. 1855.	On the age of coal strata in Western Bengal and Central India. Rev. S. Hislop 347
[M.]	Report on the Kulu iron Mines, and on a portion of the Manikurn Valley. M. Marcadien........ 191
[M.]	Memorandum on the Kunkürs of Burdwan, as a flux for smelting iron ores. H. Piddington 212
[M.]	Report on two specimens of Cuttak Coal, from the Talchir mine, forwarded by E. A. Samuells. H. Piddington 240
[M.]	Examination and analysis of a Coal from Cherrapunji. H. Piddington 283
[M.]	Observations on the Graphite or Plumbago of Kumaon and of Travancore. Dr. Royle 203
XXV. 1856.	Notes on the iron ore statistics and Econimic Geology of Upper Assam. Lieut.-Col. S. F. Hannay 330
XXVI. 1857.	Report on the progress of the Magnetic Survey and of the researches connected with it; from November, 1855 to April 1856. Adolphe and Robert Schlagintweit 97, 208
XXVIII. 1859.	Geological specimens from the Persian Gulf, collected by Lieut. E. G. Constable. H. Carter 41
XXIX. 1860.	On the rocks of the Damuda group and their associates in Eastern and Central India as illustrated by the re-examination of the Ranigunj field. W. T. Blanford 352
	Specimens from the Persian Gulf, &c. collected by Capt. E. G. Constable. H. G. Carter 359

Journal.	
Vol. XXIX. 1860.	Memorandum on the Irawadi River, with a monthly register of its rise and fall from 1856 to 1858, and a measurement of its minimum discharge. Lieut.-Col. A. Cunningham 175
	Notes upon some remarkable waterspouts seen in Bengal between the years 1852 and 1860. Maj. W. S. Sherwill 366
XXX. 1861.	Report on the Shalka, Futtehpore, Pegu, Assam and Segowlie Meteorites sent from the Asiatic Society of Bengal, to the Imperial Museum of Vienna. Dr. W. Haidinger 129
	Notes on the rainfall in the Basin of the river Mahanady, and the floods consequent thereupon. Capt. J. C. Harris 216
	On the Sub-Himalayan rocks between the Ganges and the Jumna. H. B. Medlicott, ... 22
XXXI. 1862.	Account of a visit to Puppa-doung, an extinct Volcano in upper Burma. W. T. Blanford 215
XXXII. 1863.	Account of a visit to the hot springs of Pai, Tavoy district. Captain J. H. Stevenson, ... 383
XXXIII. 1864.	Enumeration of the hot springs of India and high Asia. Robert De Schlagintweit 49
	Note on a tank Section at Sealdah, Calcutta. H. F. Blanford, ... 154
	Observations on the geological features &c. of the country in the neighbourhood of Bunnoo and the Sanitorium of Shaikh Boodun. C. P. Castello 378
[M.]	The Mines of Khetri in Rajpootana. Col. J. C. Brooke.. 519
XXXIV. Pt. II. 1865.	Notes to accompany a geological map and section of the Lowaghur or Sheenghur range in the district of Bunnoo, Punjab; with analysis of the lignites. Albert M. Verchére 42

Journal.	
Vol. XXXIV. Pt. II. 1865.	Note relating to Sivalik Fauna. H. B. Medlicott ..... 63 Notes on the sandstone formation, &c., near Buxa Fort, Bhutan Duars. Capt. H. H. Godwin-Austen, ... 106
XXXV. Pt. II. 1866.	Catalogue of meteoric stones and meteoric irons in the Museum of the Asiatic Society of Bengal, collected up to January, 1866. Dr. F. Stoliczka and H. F. Blanford 43 Kashmir, the Western Himalaya and the Afghan Mts. Albert M. Verchére, with a note on the fossils by M. Edouard Verneuil, Pts. I, II 89, 159
XXXVI. Pt. II.	Do. Do. Pts. III, IV, V 9, 83, 201
XXXVII. Pt. II. 1868.	Pangong Lake District of Ládak. H. H. Godwin-Austen 84 Geological structure of the country near foot of hills in the Western Bhutan Duars. H. H. Godwin-Austen 117
XXXVIII. 1869. [M.]	Geology of the Khasi hills. H. H. Godwin-Austen ... 1 Do. of the Jaintia hills. Do. ... 151 Analysis of Khetri Meteorite. D. Waldie 252
XXXIX. Pt. II.	Nancowry Harbour, Nicobar Island. V. Ball ...... 25 Port Blair, Andaman Island. V. Ball 231
XLIII. Pt. II.	Record of the Khairpur Meteorite of 23rd Sept., 1873. H. B. Medlicott 33
XLIV. Pt. II.	Dafla Hills, Asam. H. H. Godwin-Austen .... 35 The evidence of past glacial action in the Naga Hills, Asam. H. H. Godwin-Austin 209
XLV. Pt. II. 1876.	The Physical Geography of the great Indian desert with special reference to the former existence of the sea in the Indus Valley; and on the origin and mode of formation of the Sand-hills. W. T. Blanford 86

Journal.	
Vol. XLVI. Pt. II. 1877.	On Himalayan glaciation. J. F. Campbell .... 1 Note on Mr. J. F. Campbell's remarks on Himalayan glaciation. H. B. Medlicott .... 11 Record of Earthquakes in Asam during 1874-75-76. R. H. Keatinge 294
XLVII. Pt. II. 1878.	Physiographical notes, &c., on Tanjore. R. B. Branfill 179 Earthquake in the Punjab of March 2nd, 1878. A. B. Wynne... 187 Earthquakes in Asam in 1872. R. H. Keatinge 2
XLVIII. Pt. II. 1879.	The country between Kala Abdullah Khan in the Khojak Pass and Lugari Barkhan. R. C. Temple 103
L. 1881. [M.]	Identification of certain Diamond mines in India with a note on the history of the Koh-i-nur. V. Ball ... 31, 219 Record of Earthquakes in Assam during 1879 and 1880. 61
Proceedings 1865.	On Gopalpur Aerolite. Gaurdas Bysak 94
1867.	On the Kuyahinya Meteorite. Dr. Duke .... 21 On November Meteors. W. Masters 17, 20
1868.	On Meteorites. T. Oldham .... 203, 208 The action of the Ganges. W. Oldham........ 225, 229
1869. [M.]	On the ancient copper mines of Singhbhum. V. Ball 170 Meteorite at Jullunder in April, A. D. 1621 according to the *Iqbalnamah-i-Jahangiri*. H. Blochmann ...... 167 Notes on the Cachar Earthquake. Capt. Godwin-Austen 91 Account of a Meteor in Cooch Behar, April 30th, 1869. Col. Haughton.............................. 169 On the Jullunder Meteorite. Dr. T. Oldham........... 168 On the Cachar Earthquake. Dr. T. Oldham 115

Proceedings 1870.	[M.]	On the fall of an Aerolite. Col. G. H. Saxton 64
		On a New Mineral from Burma. D. Waldie 279
1873.		On stone implements from the Narbada Valley. H. B. Medlicott.................................... 138
1875.		Damuda rocks in Asam; H. B. Medlicott 139
1876.		An Ancient Kitchen-midden at Chandwar. V. Ball ... 120
		Meteorites from Raipur. H. B. Medlicott...... 115, 221
1878.		On the Geology of Sind. T. W. Blanford 3
1879.		Geological specimens collected by Lieut. R. C. Temple. H. B. Medlicott 176
1880.		On some geological specimens from Afghanistan. H. B. Medlicott 3
	[M.]	Rock salt from Afghanistan. H. B. Medlicott 123
1881.		On the so-called Kharakpur Meteorite. V. Ball 140

N. B.—For Geological notices published in the Proceedings before 1865, *vide infra.*

III.

ZOOLOGY.

1.—VERTEBRATA.

[*N. B.*—P = Pisces. R = Amphibia and Reptilia. F R = Fossil *Reptilia*. A = Aves. M = Mammalia. F M = Fossil Mammalia. G = General or mixed. F G = Fossil general or mixed.]

As. Rs.			
Vol. I. 1788.	[M]	Pangolin of Behar. M. Leslie	376
II. 1790.		Dissection of the Pangolin. L. A. Buist	353
IV. 1795.	[A]	Dhanesa or Indian *Buceros*. Lieut. C. White	119
	[M]	*Loris* or slow-paced *Lemur*. Sir W. Jones	135
VI. 1799.	[R]	Poison of the Serpents. W. Baog	103
VII. 1801.	[M]	A new species of Delphinus. Dr. Roxburgh	170
VIII. 1805.	[M]	Ox, named Gayal. H. T. Colebrooke	487
XIII. 1820.	[R]	Venomous Sea-snakes, on the coast of Madras. Dr. Mackenzie	329
	[M]	Tapir found in the Peninsula of Malacca. Maj. Farquhar. Communicated by the Honorable A. Seton	417
XIV. 1822.	[M]	On the *Sorex Glis*. Messrs. Diard and Duvaucel	44
XV.	[M]	On the black deer of Bengal. Mons. A. Duvaucel	157
	[M]	Some account of an orang-outang of Sumatra presented to the Asiatic Society by Capt. Cornfoot. Clark Abel	489
XVIII. 1829.	[A]	On a new species of *Buceros*. B. H. Hodgson	178

Volume	Class	Title and author	Page
As. Res. Pt. II. 1833.	[A]	*Aquila circautus* and *A. dicrurus.* B. H. Hodgson ...	13
	. [A]	On the Migration of the *Natatores* and *Grallatores*, as observed at Khathmandu. B. H. Hodgson	122
	[M]	The wild Goat, and the wild Sheep of Nepal. Hodgson	129
	[M]	On the Katwa Deer of Nepal. B. H. Hodgson	139
	[A]	*Buceros Homrai* of the Himalaya. B. H. Hodgson ...	169
	[M]	The wild Dog of the Himalaya. B. H. Hodgson......	221
XIX. Pt. I. 1836.	[F M]	*Sivatherium gigantium*, a new fossil Ruminant genus from the Valley of the Markanda. Hugh Falconer and Capt. P. T. Cautley	1
	[F R]	Crocodile of the Sivalik hills. Capt. P. T. Cautley	25
	[F R]	The Gharial of the Sivalik hills. Capt. P. T. Cautley	32
	[F M]	Sivalik Hippopotamus. H. Falconer, and Capt. Cautley	39
	[F M]	Hippopotamus &c. in the Dadupur collection. Lieut. H. M. Durand	54
	[M]	A new genus of the Carnivora. B. H. Hodgson.......	60
	[M]	Note of the *Eurinorynchus griseus.* J. T. Pearson ...	69
	[M]	Three new species of Paradoxurus. Hodgson	72
	[R]	An undescribed Hooded serpent. Dr. Th. Cantor	87
	[F M]	Sivalik Camel. Falconer, and Cautley	115
	[F M]	*Felis cristata* and *Ursus Sivalensis.* Falconer and Cautley	135
	[R]	Ornithology of Nepal. B. H. Hodgson	143
Pt. II.	[P]	Indian *Cyprinidæ.* J. M. Clelland	
Journal. Vol. I. 1832.	[M]	*Antilope Hodgsonii.* B. H. Hodgson......................	59
	[M]	The Jarai. B. H. Hodgson	66
	[M]	Catalogue of Mammalia (Dekhan). W. H. Sykes ...	161
	[A]	Catalogue of Indian Birds. W. H. Sykes	261
	[M]	On the Mammalia of Nepal. B. H. Hodgson........	335
II. 1833.	[G]	Catalogue of the Mammalia and Birds belonging to the Museum of the Asiatic Society. Dr. W. Warlow ...	96
	[G]	On progressive development in the cold-blooded Vertebrata. D. W. Nash	465
	[A]	Birds of Borabhum and Dholbhum. Tickell	569
	[F M]	Fossil bones near Jabalpur. J. Prinsep	583

Journal II. 1833.

[G] Report on a collection of Natural History. The Curator of the Museum, Asiatic Society.................. 588

III. 1834.

[M] Note on the Chiru Antilope. B. H. Hodgson 138

[F M] Note on the fossil bones of the Narbada Valley discovered by Dr. G. G. Spilsbury, near Narsingpur. J. Prinsep 396

[A] Catalogue of Birds of the Raptorial and Insessorial Orders observed in the Dukhun. Lieut.-Col. W. H. Sykes .. 418

[A] Bearded Vulture of the Himalaya. Lieut. Hutton.... 522

[A] Catalogue of Birds of the Insessorial Order in the Dukhun Colonel Sykes 536

[A] Catalogue of the Rasorial, Grallatorial, and Natatorial Orders, Dukhun. W. H. Sykes 597, 639

[F M] Fossil Elephant's Tooth from Somrotee, near Nahun. Lieut. W. E. Baker 638

IV. 1835.

[P] The (so-called) mountain Trout of Kumaon. Dr. J. M'Clelland 39

[R] On a new species of Snake discovered in the Doab 217

[M] Fœtus of the *Squalus maximus*. Dr. J. T. Pearson ... 324

[A] Bearded Vulture of the Himalayas. B H. Hodgson ... 454

[A] Red-billed Erolia. B. H. Hodgson 458, 701

[M] Thar and Gharal antelopes. B. H. Hodgson 487

[M] On the wild Goat and wild Sheep of Himalaya with remarks on the genera, Capra and Ovis. B. H. Hodgson 490, 710

[F M] Fossil bones of the Jumna river. Dean and Prinsep 495, 500

[F M] Fossil Elk of the Himalaya. Lieut. W. E. Baker 506

[F G] Sub-Himalayan Dádupur collection. Lieut. W. E. Baker 565

[M] A new species of Cervus. B. H. Hodgson 649

[F M] Camel of the Sub-Himalayas. Lieut. W. E. Baker ... 694

[M] *Vespertilionidae* of Nipal. B. H. Hodgson 699

[M] Description of a little Musteline animal, denominated Kathiah Nyul. B. H. Hodgson 702

[F G] Sivalik collection. Capt. P. T. Cautley and H. Falconer 706

Journal. Vol. V. 1836.

[F M] *Sivatherium Giganteum.* Falconer and Cautley 38
[A] A new species of Columba. B. H. Hodgson 122
[F G] Catalogue of a second collection of fossil bones presented to the Asiatic Society's Museum. Col. Colvin 179
[A] Some new species of *Falconidae.* B. H. Hodgson 231
[G] Some new animals, enumerated in the catalogue of Nepalese Mammals. B. H. Hodgson 231
[M] Note on the *Cervus Duvauceli* 240
[F M] Recent Discovery of fossil bones in Perim Island, by Baron Hugel and Mr. Geo. Fulljames 288
[F G] Sub-Himalayan Dádupur collection. Baker and Durand 291, 486, 661, 739
[F M] Teeth of the Sivalik Mastodon. Cautley 294
[M] *Canis Vulpes montana*, or Hill Fox. J. T. Pearson ... 313
[A] Two new Merceline birds. B. H. Hodgson 358
[A] On a new genus of the Meropidæ. B. H. Hodgson ... 360
[A] On a new Piscatory genus. B. H. Hodgson 362
[F M] Carnivora from the Sub-Himalayas. Lieuts. Baker and Druand 579
[M] Postscript to the account of Ursitaxus, printed in the 19th Vol. of *Researches*, Asiatic Society. B. H. Hodgson 671
[F M] Mastodons of the Siváliks. P. T. Cautley 768
[A] Ornithology of Nepal. B. H. Hodgson 770

VI. 1837.

[A] On three new long-legged Thrushes. B. H. Hodgson... 107
[A] Three new species of Woodpecker. B. H. Hodgson ... 104
[A] A new Incessorial bird. B H. Hodgson 110
[F M] Sivâlik Quadrumana. Falconer. Cautley 354
[A] On some new genera of Raptores with remarks on the old genera. B. H. Hodgson 361
[F M] Fossils in the Narbada Valley. Dr. G. G. Spilsbury ... 487
[A] New species of Indian Snipes. B. H. Hodgson 489
[R] On the *Python Tigris.* Lieut. T. Hutton 528
[F R] A gigantic Batrachian. Dr. T. Cantor 538
[M] On a new genus of the Plantigrada. B. H. Hodgson 560
Testudo Geometrica. Lieut T. Hutton 689
[M] On the Bibos. B. H. Hodgson 745
[A] Nest of the Bengal Vulture with observations on the power of scent ascribed to the vulture tribe. Lieut. Hutton 112
[M] Notes on a Musk deer. A. Campbell,........................ 118
[F M] Additional fragments of the Sivatherium... 152

Volume		Entry	Page
Journal Vol. VI. 1837.	[M]	Specimen *Bos Gaurus.* Dr. George Evans	223
	[M]	On the Gaur and Gayal. J. T. Pearson	225
	[A]	On a new genus of the *Sylviadæ* with description of three new species. B. H. Hodgson	230
	[F G]	Bones from the Sivâlik Range east of Hardwar. Falconer	233
VII. 1838.	[A]	Himalayan Vulture Eagle. Lieut. T. Hutton	20
	[F M]	A Sivâlik Ruminant allied to *Giraffidæ.* Capt. Cautley	658
	[M]	A species of *Arctonix* from Aracan. Dr. G. Evans,	732
	[A]	A new Pheasant from Tibet. B. H. Hodgson	863
	[P]	Six new *Cyprinidæ*, with an outline of a new classification of the family. J. McClelland	941
	[M]	On the genus *Hexaprotodon.* J. McClelland	1038
VIII. 1839.	[A]	Distribution of European Birds. W. Jameson	21
	[A]	New genus of the Fissirostal Tribe. B. H. Hodgson	37
	[M]	Three new species of Musk. B. H. Hodgson	202
	[M]	Four new species of Otter. B. H. Hodgson	319
	[A]	On the Geographic Distribution of *Vulturidæ*, *Falconidæ* and *Strigidæ.* W. Jameson	321
	[M]	Dissection of the *Arctonix Collaris.* G. Evans	408
	[P]	The ground fish of Bhootan. J. T. Pearson	551
	[F G]	Various Fossil Sites on the Nerbudda	950
IX. Pt. I. 1840.	[M]	Wild Sheep of the Hindu Kush. Capt. Hay	440
	[G]	Catalogue of the Museum of the Asiatic Society. Pearson	514
		On *Bos Gaurus.* Dr. Spilsbury	551
	[F M]	*Camelidæ* of the Sivâliks. Capt. Cautley	620
Pt. II.	[M]	Common Hare of the Gangetic Provinces and of the Sub-Himalaya; with a notice of a Himalayan species. B. H. Hodgson	1183
	[M]	Three new species of Monkey; with remarks on the genera, *Semnopithecus and Macacus.* Hodgson	1211
X. 1841.	[M]	Two wild species of Sheep inhabiting the Himalayan region, with remarks on the craniological character of Ovis and its allies. Hodgson	230
	[F M]	Discoveries in the Narbadá valley. Spilsbury	626

Journal	Class	Entry
Journal Vol. X. 1841.	[G]	Birds and Mammals in the Society's Museum.... 628, 660
	[M]	The species of true stag. E. Blyth 736
	[M]	*Cervus elaphus* (?) Marmots, &c. Hodgson 721, 777, 795
	[M]	*Lagomys Nepalensis.* B. H. Hodgson.............. 854
	[A]	*Conostoma Æmodius Glancopinæ.* B. H. Hodgson ... 856
	[M]	The Species of wild Sheep. E. Blyth.............. 858
	[M]	Catalogue of Nepal Mammals. Hodgson 907
	[M]	Three species of Taphozous. E. Blyth 971
XI. 1842.	[A]	Indian and Malayan birds, with descriptions of some new species. E. Blyth 160
	[M]	Predatory and sanguinivorous habits of Magaderma, with remarks on the blood-sucking propensities of other *Vespertilionidae.* E. Blyth......................... 255
	[M]	Mammals of Tibet. B. H. Hodgson 275
	[M]	A Monograph of the species of Lynx. E. Blyth 740
	[M]	*Taphozous longimanus* (Hardwicke) E. Blyth 784
	[A]	Malayan species of *Cuculidæ.* E. Blyth 897, 1095
XII. 1843.	[A]	A new genus of *Falconidæ.* Hodgson 127
	[A]	Indian and Malayan Species of *Cuculidæ.* E. Blyth ... 240
	[A]	Catalogue of Nepalese birds, presented to the Asiatic Society, named and classified by the Donor, Mr. Hodgson 301, 447
	[M]	Two Marmots, and a *Rhinolophus.* Hodgson........... 409
	[F M]	Antelope in the Dadupur Museum. Capt. Baker 769
	[M]	On a Tiger killed near Darjiling. Lieut. Tickel...... 814
	[M]	*Cervus dimorphe.* Hodgson 897
XIII. 1844.	[M]	Two new flying Squirrels. B. H. Hodgson, ... 67
	[M]	Descriptions of many new species. E. Blyth 463
	[F G]	Osseous Breccia and deposit in the caves of Billa soargum, Lat. 15° 25′ Long. 78° 15′ Southern India. Capt. New bold 610
	[F M]	Notes on Narbada fossils. Dr. G. G. Spilsbury 765
	[M]	The osteology of the Elephant. 915
	[A]	"On the Leiotrichane birds of the Sub-Himalayas." B. H. Hodgson, with some additions and annotations and a synopsis of the Indian Pari, and of the Indian Tringillidæ. E. Blyth 93

Journ.		
Vol. XIV.	[A]	Various new or little known birds. Blyth 173, 546
	[M]	Caprologus, a new genus of Leporine Mammalia. Blyth 247
	[M]	Zoology of Candahar, and the neighbouring district. Capt. Hutton, with note by Ed. Blyth 340
	[A]	Drafts for a *Fauna Indica*, comprising the animals of the Himalaya mountains, those of the Valley of the Indus, of the provinces of Asam, Sylhet, Tipperah, Arracan, and of Ceylon. Ed. Blyth 845
XV.	[G]	Notes on the fauna of the Nicobar islands. E. Blyth... 367
	[M]	Malayan Fauna. Theodore Cantor 71, 241
	[A]	Various new birds. E. Blyth....................1, 280
	[M]	A new Tibetan antelope. B. H. Hodgson 334
	[M]	Rough Notes on Zoology of Candahar and the Neighbouring districts. Capt. Hutton ; with notes by Blyth 135
XVI.	[M]	On a new form of *Suidæ*. Hodgson 423, 593
	[M]	On the Hispid Hare of the saul forest. B. H. Hodgson 572
	[A]	New or little known birds. Blyth 117, 428
	[M]	*Ovis Ammonoides* of Hodgson. T. Hutton 568
	[M]	The species of wild Sheep. E. Byth.............. 350
	[M]	On the Charj or *Otis bengalensis*. B. H. Hodgson...... 883
	[M]	On a new species of Porcupine. B. H. Hodgson 771
	[M]	On a new species of *Plecotus*. B. H. Hodgson 894
	[A]	Candahar Fauna. Capt. Thomas Hutton 775
	[R]	Malayan Fauna. T. Cantor 607, 897, 102
	[A]	*Magaderma schistacea*. B. H. Hodgson 889
	[M]	Tibetan Badger, *Taxidia Cucurus*. Hodgson......... 763
	[M]	On the tame Sheep and Goats of the Sub-Himalayas and of Tibet. B. H. Hodgson 1003
	[M]	Various Genera of Ruminants. B. H. Hodgson 685
XVII. Pt I.	[A]	Oology of India :—A description of the Eggs, also Nests, of several birds of the Plains of India. Capt. S. R. Tickell 297
XVII.	[M]	Ailurus, Porcula, and Stylocerus. Hodgson 475
Pt. II.	[A]	The Nidification of Indian Birds. Hutton 3, 681

Journ. Vol.		
[M]	The Sciuri from Ceylon and Tenasserim. E. Blyth ...	600
[M]	The Polecat of Tibet. B. H. Hodgson	446
XVIII. [A]	A supplemental note to the Catalogue of Birds in the Asiatic Society's Museum. E. Blyth	800
[P]	Catalogue of Malayan fishes. Dr. T. Cantor	983
XIX. [M]	Description of a new Species of Mole. E. Blyth......	212
[A]	Ornithology of India. E. Blyth	229, 319, 501
[M]	On the shou or Tibetan stag. B. H. Hodgson ...	466, 518
[M]	*Budorcas taxicolor.* B. H. Hodgson	65
[A]	Variation of nearly affined species or races of birds, chiefly of India. E. Blyth	229
XX. [G]	Report on the Mammalia, and more remarkable species of Birds inhabiting Ceylon. E. Blyth........................	153
[G]	Notice of a collection of Mammalia, Birds, and Reptiles from Cherra Punji. E. Blyth	517
[M]	*Cervus affinis.* B. H. Hodgson	388
XXII. [M]	Remarks on Orangutan. E. Blyth	369
[R]	Catalogue of Indian Reptiles. T. C. Jerdon	462, 522
[R]	Various reptiles, new or little known. Blyth...........	639
XXIII. [A]	A Monograph of the Indian species of Phylloscopus and its immediate Affines. E. Blyth	479
[R]	Various reptiles, new or little known. Blyth	287
[A]	Nidification of birds of the Salt range &c. Theobald...	591
XXIV. [M]	A Memoir on the Indian species of Shrews. E. Blyth	24
[G]	Zoological collection from the Somáli country. Blyth	291
[M]	The different species of Orangutan. Blyth	518
[A]	Catalogue of Nepalese Birds. B. H. Hodgson	572
[A]	On Indian Oology. W. Theobald	520
[A]	A new species of Hornbill. Capt. Tickell	285
XXV. [A]	On a new Bird from Tibet. B. H. Hodgson	165

Journ. Vol.		
XXVI.	[A]	A new Indian Pigeon, akin to the 'Stock-Dove' of Europe; with notices of other *Columbinæ*. Blyth 217
	[M]	On a new Lagomys, and a new Mustela. Hodgson ... 207
XXVII.	[M]	A new species of Mole, *Talpa Macrura*. B. H. Hodgson 176
XXVIII.	[M]	The different animals known as wild Asses. Blyth...... 229
	[M]	On the great Rorqual of the Indian Ocean. E. Blyth 481
XXIX.	[M]	Note on the races of Rein Deer. E. Blyth............... 376
	[G]	On the flat-horned Taurine Cattle of S. E. Asia, with a note on the races of Rein Deer, and a note on domestic animals in general. E. Blyth 282
	[P]	Fishes from the Sitang river, and its tributary streams, Tenasserim Provinces. Blyth 138
	[P]	The cartilaginous fishes of lower Bengal. E. Blyth ... 35
	[M]	Memorandum on Mr. Blyth's paper on the animals known as wild Asses. Major R. Strachey 136
	[A]	Ornithology of Amoy. Robert Swinhoe 240
XXXI.	[M]	The living Asiatic species of Rhinoceros. Blyth 151
	[M]	Wild Asses and alleged wild Horses. Blyth 363
	[R]	A little described species of Turtle. Tickell 367
	[M]	A Memoir on the Rats and Mice of India. E. Blyth... 327
	[M]	Description of a new species of Paradoxurus from the Andaman islands. Lieut.-Col. R. C. Tytler 188
	[M]	Gibbon of Tenasserim. S. R. Tickell 196
XXXIII.	[A]	Notes on the *Didunculus strigirostris* of the Navigator islands, Sir W. Denison 313
	[R]	Observations on a few species of Geckos alive in the possession of the Author. Lieut.-Col. R. C. Tytler 535
XXXIV. Pt. II.	[A]	Description of a supposed new genus of the *Gadidae*, Arakan. Lieut.-Col. S. R. Tickell 32
	[M]	Note on *Lagomys Curzoniæ*. F. Stoliczka 108

Journal.	
Vol. XXXVI. Pt. II.	Contributions towards a history of *Panolia Eldi*. R. C. Beavan 175
XXXVII. Pt. II. [A]	Ornithology of the Sutlej Valley. F. Stoliczka 1
[A]	Birds of the Goona district. G. King 208
[R]	Catalogue of Reptiles in the Museum of the As. Soc. of Bengal. W. Theobald .... Extra number
[A]	Ornithological notes chiefly on some birds of Central, Western, and Southern India. W. T. Blanford ... 164
[R]	Descriptions of two new species belonging to the genera *Varanus* (*Psammosaurus*) and *Feranioides*, respectively. H. C. L. Carlleyle 192
XXXIX. Pt. II. [P]	On the genus *Hara*. F. Day 37
[R]	Indian and Malayan *Amphibia* and Reptilia. F. Stoliczka 134, 157
[A]	Observations regarding some species of Birds noticed by W. T. Blanford in his "Ornithological notes." A. O. Hume 113
[A]	Birds obtained in the north Cachar Hill range. H. H. Godwin-Austen 264
[A]	Contributions to Malayan Ornithology. F. Stoliczka . 279
[A]	Birds from Port Blair. V. Ball 240
XL. [R] Pt. II.	Accessions to the Indian Museum from 1865 to 1870 with a description of some new species. T. Anderson 12
[A]	On Mc. Master's list of Nagpore Birds. W. T. Blanford 216
[A]	List of Birds collected or observed in the Wardha valley and its vicinity near Chanda. W. T. Blanford 268
[G]	Zoology of the Alpine and Subalpine regions on the Eastern and Northern frontiers of Independent Sikkim, part I. W. T. Blanford........................... 367
[P]	Monograph of the Indian *Cyprinidæ*. F. Day, Pts. I, II, III 95, 277, 337
[M]	A new species of *Vespertilio*. G. E. Dobson 186
[M]	New species of *Cheiroptera*. G. E. Dobson 260, 455
[A]	Notes on Birds observed in the neighbourhood of Nagpore and Kámpti, Chikaldá and Ákola. A. C. McMaster 207
[R]	Indian and Burmese *Ophidians*. F. Stoliczka 217

Journ. Vol.			Page
	[A]	Notes on Birds collected in the Andaman islands by G. E. Dobson. V. Ball	273
XL.	[A]	Notes on a Sikkim collection. W. T. Blanford	152
Pt. II.	[A]	Notes on the Ornithology of Kashmir. W. E. Brooks	73
	[A]	Two undescribed Kashmir Birds. W. E. Brooks	327
	[P]	Monograph on Indian *Cyprinidæ*. F. Day	1, 171, 318
	[P]	Dr. Stoliczka's Kachh collection. F. Day	258
	[M]	Osteology of *Triænops Persicum*. G. E. Dobson	369
	[M]	Osteology of some new species of Bats. G. E. Dobson	334
	[M]	New species of *Rhinolophine* Bats. G. E. Dobson	336
	[A]	Birds, Kásiá Hills. Godwin-Austen	142
XLI.	[R]	New or little known Indian Lizards. F. Stoliczka	86, 77
Pt. II.	[G]	Mammals and Birds inhabiting Kachh. F. Stoliczka	21
XLII.	[R]	On the genus *Gymnops* (*Lacertidæ*). W. T. Blanford	144
Pt. II.	[A]	On an undescribed *Lophopdianus*. W. E. Brooks	57
	[A]	*Aquila bifasciata* and *A. orientalis*. W. E. Brooks	145
	[A]	On the *Certhiinæ* of India. W. E. Brooks	255
	[M]	*Pteropidæ* of India and its islands. Dobson	195
	[M]	A new *Vespertilio* from N. W. Himalaya. Dobson	205
	[R]	Malayan Amphibia and Reptilia. F. Stoliczka	111
	[R]	Andamanese and Nicobarese reptiles. Stoliczka	162
XLIII.	[A]	Ornithological notes and corrections. W. E. Brooks	239
Pt. II.	[P]	Remarks on some Indian Fishes. F. Day	31
	[M]	Asiatic species of *Molossi*. G. E. Dobson	142
	[M]	List of *Chiroptera* inhabiting the Khasi hills with description of a new species. G. E. Dobson	234
	[M]	Description of new species of *Chiroptera* from India and Yunan. G. E. Dobson	237
	[A]	Birds principally from the Naga Hills and Manipur. H. H. Godwin-Austen	151
	[A]	Occurrence of supraorbital chain of bones in the *Arboricolæ* (Wood Partridges). J. Wood-Mason	254
XLIV. Pt. II.	[M]	On the Scientific evidence of the Sind "Ibex," the Markhor, and the Indian Antelope. W. T. Blanford	12

Journ. Vol.			
XLIV. Pt. II.	[M]	List of Mammalia collected by the late Dr. Stoliczka, when attached to the embassy under Sir. D. Forsyth in Kashmir, Ládak, Eastern Turkestan, and Wakhán, with description of new species. W. T. Blanford	105
	[M]	On the species of Marmot inhabiting the Himalaya, Tibet, and the adjoining Regions. W. T. Blanford	114
	[R]	List of *Reptilia* and *Amphibia* collected by the late Dr. Stoliczka in Kashmir, Ládak, &c. W. T. Blanford...	191
	[R]	*Elachistodon Westermanni* &c. W. T. Blanford......	207
	[M]	Note on a large hare inhabiting high elevations in Western Tibet. W. T. Blanford	214
	[M]	Note on the occurrence of a partially ossified Nasal Septum in *Rhinocerus Sondaicus*. O. L. Fraser	10
	[G]	Catalogue of the Mammals and Birds of Burma. E. Blyth (Extra Number)	
XLV. Pt. II.	[R]	On some Lizards from Sind with descriptions of some new species. W. T. Blanford	18
	[M]	Deseription of *Felis Shawiana*. W. T. Blanford	49
	[M]	*Golunda Ellioti* from Sind. W. T. Blanford	165
	[A]	List of the Birds from Dafla Hills, Asam, and from Darrang Terai. H. H. Godwin-Austen	64
	[A]	Birds from the hill ranges on the N. E. Frontier of India. H. H. Godwin-Austen	191
XLVI. Pt. II.	[M]	Description of some new and little known Asiatic Shrews in the Indian Museum. J. Anderson	261
	[M]	Weasel from Yarkand. W. T. Blanford	259
	[M]	On the Metád Rat (*Golunda Meltada*, Gray) with a note on *Golunda Ellioti*. W. T. Blanford	288
	[M]	Notes on two species of Asiatic Bears, and on an apparently undescribed Fox from Beluchistán. W. T. Blanford	315
	[M]	On an apparently New Hare, and some other Mammals from Gilgit. W. T. Blanford......................	323
	[M]	Notes on a collection of *Chiroptera* from India and Burma, with descriptions of new species. G. E. Dobson	310
	[A]	Three new species from Saddya. Godwin-Austen....	41
	[M]	Sheep from the Central Hill of Kelat. A. O. Hume...	327
	[M]	Notes on the Mammalian Fauna of the Wardwan and Upper Chenab Valley. R. Lydekker	283

Journ. Vol.		Page
[M]	Indian species of *Erinaceus*. J. Anderson	193
XLVII. Pt. II. [M]	On *Arvicola indica*, Gray, and its relations to *Nesokia*, with a description of the species of *Nesokia*. J. Anderson	214
[A]	*Ruticella schisticeps*, Hodgs. W. T. Blanford	1
[R]	On some *Reptilia* from the Himalayas and Burma. W. T. Blanford	125
[M]	On some Mammals from Tenasserim. W. T. Blanford	150
[M]	*Erinaceus niger* from Muscat. T. W. Blanford	212
[A]	Birds from the hill ranges of the North-East Frontier of India. H. H. Godwin Austen	12
[M]	Aberrant dentition of *Felis Tigris*. R. Lydekker	4
XLVIII. Pt. II. [R]	Notes on a collection of Reptiles and Frogs from the neighbourhood of Ellore and Dumagudem. W. T. Blanford	110
[R]	Notes on a collection of Reptiles made by Major O. B. St. John at Ajmere. W. T. Blanford	119
[R]	Notes on Reptilia. W. T. Blanford	127
[M]	Mammalia from Gilgit. W. T. Blanford	95
XLIX. [M]	Occurrence of the Musk-Deer in Tibet. R. Lydekker	4
Pt. II. [M]	Note on some Ladák Mammals. R. Lydekker	6
[G]	History of Fossil Vertebrata of India. R. Lydekker	8
[M]	On the Blue Sheep of Tibet. R. Lydekker	131
[M]	Dentition of Rhinoceros. R. Lydekker	135
[A]	*Trochalopterum* from Travancore. W. T. Blanford	142
[M]	*Arvicola* from the Panjab Himalayas. W. T. Blanford	244
L. [M] Pt. II.	On the Voles (*Arvicolæ*) of the Himalayas, Tibet and Afghanistan. W. T. Blanford	88
[M]	On *Myospalax fuscicapillus*, Blyth. W. T. Blanford	118
[G]	A sketch of the history of the fossils of the Gondwana System. O Feistmantel	168
[R]	An apparently undescribed *Varanus* from Tenasserim, and other *Reptilia* and *Amphibia*. W. T. Blanford	239
[G]	A numerical estimate of the species of Animals, chiefly land and fresh water, hitherto recorded from British India and its dependencies. W. T. Blanford	263

Journ. Vol. LI. Pt. II.	[M]	On an abnormality in the horns of the Hog-deer, *Axis porcinus*, with an amplification of the theory of the evolution of antlers in Ruminants. J. Cockburn	45
	[R]	On the habits of a little known Lizard, *Brachysaura ornata.* J. Cockburn	50
Proc. 1865.	[M]	On supposed new species of rats. R. C. Tytler	76
1866.	[M]	On *Nesokia Indica.* W. Theobald	239
	[A]	On *Vultur monachus.* R. C. Tytler	74
1868.	[M]	Remarks on elephants. V. Ball	129
	[M]	On the Lion of Abu. Dr. G. King	178, 198
	[G]	On rare Malayan animals. A. C. Maingay	127, 177, 194
1870.	[A]	New species of Birds. T. C. Jerdon	59
1871.	[R]	On a new *Scincus.* J. Anderson	115
	[R]	On a new *Mabonia*, and on two genera of *Eurylepis* and *Plocederma.* J. Anderson	180
	[R]	Notes on *Hemidactylus Marmoratus* and *Ablabes Humberti.* W. T. Blanford	173
	[A]	On new *Abrornis.* E. Brooks	248
	[A]	On a new Flamingo. E. Brooks	284
	[M]	On a new *Kerivoula.* G. E. Dobson	77
	[M]	On Malayan Bats. G. E. Dobson	105
	[M]	On Persian Bats. G. E. Dobson	133
1872.	[A]	On a new Indian *Sylvia.* W. E. Brooks	66
	[A]	On the imperial Eagles of India. W. E. Brooks	37, 64
	[A]	On a new *Reguloides.* W. E. Brooks	148
	[A]	On a new *Phyllopneuste.* W. E. Brooks	4
	[A]	On the Swans of India. W. E. Brooks	4, 63
	[M]	On *Taphozous.* G. E. Dobson	151
1873.	[A]	Notes on Eagles. W. E. Brooks	173
	[R]	On a double-headed snake. G. E. Dobson	23

Proc.			
1873.	[M]	On the genera *Murina* and *Harpyiocephalus* of Gray G. E. Dobson	107
	[R]	On Type specimens of *Batrachia*. W. Theobald	110
1874.	[M]	On occurrence of *Tupaia Ellioti*, Waterhouse, in the Satpura Hills	95
	[A]	Ornithological Notes and Corrections. W. E. Brooks	229
	[A]	Birds, new species of. A. O. Hume..................	106
	[G]	Note on two undescribed species of Goat, and a new Dove. A. O. Hume...	240
	[R]	On Indian and Burmese *Trionyx*. W. Theobald ...	59, 75
1875.	[A]	On an apparently unnamed species of *Phœnicopterus*. W. E. Brooks..	17, 48
	[M]	*Ailurus fulgens*. L. Schwendler	93
	[M]	A four-horned Sheep, from Sind. L. Schwendler	186
	[M]	On photographs of *Rhinoceros Sondaicus* and *R. Indicus*. J. Wood-Mason	230
	[R]	On the young of certain species of *Trionyx* and on the colours of extinct animals. J. Wood-Mason	179
1876.	[M]	*Pelomys Watsoni*, a from Sind. W. T. Blanford	181
	[M]	Remarks on the habits of wild Pigs. W. T. Blanford	92
	[F M]	Jaw of *Tetraconodon magnum*. R. Lydekker	172
1877.	[M]	A Bamboo-rat. J. Anderson..............................	148
	[M]	Notes on certain Mammals occurring in the Basin of the Mahánadí. V. Ball	168
	[M]	Notes on some recent researches on the origin of the domestic Dog. W. T. Blanford	114
1878.	[F M]	On the palate of the anthropoid Ape from the Siváliks. R. Lydekker	191
	[M]	On the absence of a horn in the female of the Sundarban Rhinoceros. H J. Rainey	139
1879.	[M]	On the Mamb, or Beluchistan Bear. W. T. Blanford	4
	[M]	*Ovis Pali*. J. Wood-Mason..............................	280

Proc. [M]	Zoological Notes. L. Schwendler 55
1880. [M]	Rat from the Safed Koh Ranges. J. Wood-Mason ... 173
1881. [M]	On the occurrence of the Lion in Palamow. V. Ball 3
1882. [M]	On polydactylism in a Horse. J. Cockburn 115
[G]	Habits and instincts of some animals. J. Cockburn ... 106

N. B.—For notices of the Vertebrata published in the "Proceedings" before 1865, see below.

2.—INVERTEBRATA.

[N. B.—C = Cœlenterata. A = Arthropoda. M = Mollusca. F M = Fossil Mollusca.]

As. Res. Vol. XIV. [C]	Description of a Zoophyte commonly found about the Coasts of Singapore island. T. Hardwicke 180
XVIII. Pt. I. [F M]	On the Petrified shells found in the Gawilgar range of hills, in April 1823. H. W. Voysey 187
Pt. II. 1833. [F M]	Memorandum on the fossil shells discovered in the Himalayan mountains. Rev. R. Everest 107
Journ. [M] Vol. I.	Account of a new genus of Land snails, allied to the genus *Cyclostoma*. W. H. Benson 11
1832. [M]	On the habits of the *Paludinæ*. T. Hunter 411
II. [M]	Note on the *Spiraculum*. J. T. Pearson............ 590
1833. [M]	Shells from Ságar. H. H. Spry 639
III. [M] 1834.	On the land and fresh water Shells of India. T. Hutton 81, 520

Journ. [M] Vol. IV.	Account of *Oxygyrus*, a new genus of Pelagian Shells with a note on some other Pelagian shells. W. H. Benson 173
[M]	Characters of three new species of Indian fresh-water Bivalves. Isaac Lea; with notes by W. H. Benson 450
[M]	Dr. M'Clelland on the fossil shells of Chirrapunji 520
[M]	Character of the genus *Cuvieria*. W. Benson 698
V. [M]	Terrestrial and Fluviatile *Testacea*, chiefly from the North-East Frontier of Bengal. W. H. Benson 350, 741
[M]	*Nematura*, a new genus of Mollusca. W. H. Benson .., 781
[M]	Note on the genus *Ptercyclos* (Benson) and *Spiraculun* (Pearson). Dr. William Bland.................. 783
VI. [M]	On *Balantium*, a genus of *Pteropodous Mollusca*, with the characters of a new species inhabiting the Southern Indian Ocean. W. H. Benson 150
[M]	On *Oxygyrus* and *Bellerophon*. W. H. Benson....... 316
VI. [M]	On the land and fresh water shells of the western Himalaya. T. Hutton and W. H. Benson 211
[M]	Note on the affinities of *Galathea* of Lamarck. W. H. Benson 420
[A]	Note on the New Zealand Caterpillar. G. Evans .. 187
VIII. [F M]	On fifteen varieties of fossil shells found in the Saugor and Narbadá territories. George G. Spilsbury 108
IX. [F M]	Fossil shells discovered by Captain Hay, in the neighbourhood of Rájgar, Afghanistan 1126
XII. [A]	On Genus *Paussus*. W. J. E. Boyes 421
XVI. [M]	On *Teredo Navalis*, T. Cantor 487

Journal.	
Vol. XVII. [A]	The land shells of the Tenasserim provinces. Rev. F. Mason .... 62 *Coleoptera* of Hongkong. Capt. Champion 572
XVIII. [M]	Notices of some land and fresh water shells occurring in Afghanistan. Capt. T. Hutton..................... 649
XIX. [A]	Note on the bird-devouring habits of a species of Spider. Captain Sherwill 474
XXIV. [M]	On the Chusun Shells, collected by Dr. T. Cantor. W. H. Benson 119
XXV. [A]	New Ceylon *Coleoptera*. John Neitner......... 381, 523
XXVI. [M]	Notes on the distributions of some of the land and fresh-water shells of India, Part I. W. Theobald........ 245
XXVII. [M]	Notes on the distribution of some of the land and fresh-water shells of India, Part II. W. Theobald...... 313
XXVIII. [M]	New Burmese and Indian *Helicidæ* with remarks on some previously described species. W. Theobald 305
XXIX. [M]	Contributions to Indian Malacology, No. I. W. T. and H. F. Blanford 117
XXX. [M]	Contributions to Indian Malacology, No. II. H. F. and W. T. Blanford 347
XXXI. [M]	Contributions to Indian Malacology, No. III. Descriptions of new operculated land-shells from Pegu. W. T. Blanford 135

Journ.	
Vol. [F M] XXXII. 1863.	On Dr. Gerard's collection of fossils from the Spiti Valley, in the Asiatic Society's Museum. H. F. Blanford 124
[M]	Contributions to Indian Malacology, No. IV. Descriptions of new land shells from Ava, and other parts of Burma. William T. Blanford 319
[M]	Notes on the distribution of Indian terrestrial *Gasteropoda* considered with reference to its bearing on the origin of species. W. Theobold 354
[F M] XXXIII.	Note on the fossils in the Society's Collection reputed to be from Spiti. T. Oldham 232
1864. [M]	Notes on the variation of some Indian and Burmese *Helicidæ* with an attempt at their re-arrangement, together with descriptions of New Burmese *Gasteropoda.* W. Theobald 238
XXXIV. Pt. II. [M] 1865.	Observations on certain strictures by W. T. Blanford on W. Theobald's paper on the distribution of Indian *Gasteropoda* in J. A. S. W. Theobald 60
[M]	Contributions to Indian Malacology, No. V. Descriptions of new land shells from Arakan, Pegu, and Ava; with a note on the distribution of described species. W. T. Blanford 66
[M]	Notes on a collection of land and fresh-water shells from the Shan States collected by F. Fedden, 1864-65. W. Theobald 273
XXXV. Pt. II. [M] 1866.	Contributions to Indian Malacology, No. VI. Descriptions of new land shells from the Nilgiri and Anamullay hills, and other places in the Peninsula of India. W. T. Blanford 31
[M]	Contributions of Indian Malacology, No. VII. List of species of *Unio* and *Anodonta* described as occurring in India, Ceylon, and Burma. W. T. Blanford 134
XXXVI. Pt. II. [M] 1867.	Contributions to Indian Malacology, No. VIII. List of Estuary shells collected in the delta of the Irawady in Pegu with descriptions of the new species. W. T. Blanford 51
	On the intimate structure of muscular fibre. M. D. Macnamara 71

Journ. [M]	Contributions to Indian Malacology, No. IX. Descriptions of New *Diplomatinæ* from Darjiling and the Kasia hills. W. T. Blanford 77
Vol. XXXVII. Pt. II. [M]	Figures of the species of *Diplomatinæ* (Benson) inhabiting the Himalayas, Kasia hills, &c. Godwin-Austen 83
[C & M] XXXVIII. Pt. II.	Anatomy of *Sagartia Schilleriana* and *Membranipora Bengalensis*, a new Coral and a Bryazoon living at Port Canning. F. Stoliczka 28
[M]	On some new Marine *Gasteropoda* from the Southern Provinces of Ceylon. G. & H. Nevill 65, 157
[M]	Contributions to Indian Malacology, No. X. W. T. Blanford 112
[M]	The Malacology of Lower Bengal—on *Onchidium*. F. Stoliczka 86
[A]	Indian *Arachnoidea*. Dr. Stoliczka................. 201
[M]	New species of *Diplomatinæ* from the Kasia hills. Col. H. Godwin-Austen 1
XXXIX [M] Pt. II.	Contributions to Indian Malacology, No. XI. W. T. Blanford 9
1870. [M]	On the Land Shells of Bourbon. G. Nevill 403
[M]	New species of Land Shells from the Shan States of Pegu. W. Theobald........................... 395
XL. [M] Pt. II.	Species of *Camptoceras* and other land Shells. H. Blanford 39
1871. [M]	The *Alycæinæ* of the Kasia hills. Godwin-Austen ... 87
[A]	Mollusca from the Eastern regions. G. & H. Nevill.. 1
[M]	Notes on Terrestrial Mollusca from the neighbourhood of Moulmein. F. Stoliczka 143, 217
[A]	Contributions to Indian Carcinology. J. Wood-Mason 189, 201, 449
XLI. [M] Pt. II. 1872.	Account of a visit to the Eastern and North-Eastern Forntiers of Independent Sikkim, &c., Part II. W. T. Blanford 30
[M]	Monograph of Himalayan, Asamese, Burmese, and Cingalese, *Clausiliæ*. W. T. Blanford 199

Journ. [M]	
	Postscript to above. F. Stoliczka 207
Vol.	Land Shells of Penang Island, Part I, *Cyclostomaceæ*. F. Stoliczka 261
XLI. [M] Pt. II. 1872.	Burmese and Arakanese Land Shells. Theobald and Stoliczka 329
XLII. [M] Pt. II. 1873.	On the Landshells of Penang Islands with descriptions of the Animals and Anatomical notes; Part II, (*Helicidæ*.) F. Stoliczka 11
[A]	Indian species of *Thelyphonus*. F. Stoliczka........ 126
[A]	Contributions towards a Monograph of the Indian *Passallidæ* F. Stoliczka 149
[A]	Two new species of Indian Landshells. Stoliczka 169
[M]	Two new species of *Unionidæ*. W. Theobald........ 207
[A]	On *Nephropsis Stewarti*. J. Wood-Mason.......... 39
[A]	New or little known species of *Phasmidæ*, Part I, genus *Bacillus*. J. Wood-Mason 45
[A]	On *Rhopalorhynchus Kröyeri*, a new genus and species of *Pycnogonidæ*. J. Wood-Mason 171
[A]	On a new genus and species of Land Crabs from the Nicobar Islands. J. Wood-Mason 258
XLIII. Pt. II. [M] 1874.	Description of nine species of *Alycæinæ* from Asam and the Naga hills. H. H. Godwin-Austen 145
[M]	Descriptions of New Marine Mollusca from the Indian Ocean. G. & H. Nevill 21
XLIV. [M] Pt. II.	*Cœlostele*, (Benson) and *Francesia* (Paladilhe), and some species of Land shells from Aden. W. T. Blanford 41
[M]	*Helix* and *Glessula* from the Khasi hills and Manipur. H. H. Godwin-Austen 1
	Zonitidæ, from the N. E. frontier of Bengal. H. H. Godwin-Austen 4
[M]	Descriptions of some operculated Land shells from the Naga Hills and Asam. H. H. Godwin-Austen 7
[M]	Marine Mollusca from the Indian Ocean. G. and H. Nevill 83

Journ.		
Vol. XLV. Pt. II.	[M]	On new or little known species of *Phasmidæ*. J. Wood-Mason 215
	[M]	On the *Cyclostomaceæ* and *Helicidæ* of the Dafla Hills, Asam. H. H. Godwin-Austen............... 171, 311
	[M]	New Land and Fresh water Shells from India and Burma. W. Theobald 183
	[A]	A new species of *Phasmidæ*. J. Wood-Mason 47
	[A]	A new species of *Cetoniidæ*. J. Wood-Mason 52
	[A]	A new species of *Blattidæ*. J. Wood-Mason 189
XLVI. Pt. II.	[M]	Description of *Spiraculum Mastersi*. W. T. Blanford 313
	[M]	Mollusca brought by Dr. J. Anderson from Yunan and Upper Burma, with descriptions of new species. G. Nevill... 14
	[A]	Notes on *Phasmidæ*. J. Wood-Mason 342
XLVII Pt. II.	[A]	Preliminary Diagnoses of new Coleopterous Insects belonging to the families *Dytiscidæ*, *Staphylinidæ*, and *Scarabæidæ*. D Sharp 169
	[M]	Notes on the Land and Freshwater Shells of Kashmir, more particularly of the Jhilum Valley below Srinagar and the hills north of Jamu. W. Theobald 141
	[A]	On some *Hymenoptera*. J. Wood-Mason 167
	[A]	A New Lepidopterous insect. J. Wood-Mason 175
	[A]	A new Homopterous insect. J. Wood-Mason 194
XLVIII Pt. II.	[C]	Hydroid Zoophytes from the Indian Coasts and Seas. J. Armstrong, ... 98
	[A]	*Hemiptera* from U. Tenasserim. W. L. Distant, ... 37
	[M.]	On new species of the genus *Plectopylis* of the family *Helicidæ*. H. H. Godwin-Austen, ... 1
	[A]	Preliminary notice of a new genus of *Phasmidæ* from Madagascar with brief descriptions of its two species. J. Wood-Mason, ... 117
XLIX. Pt. II.	[A]	The species of *Chæradodis*, a genus of *Mantodea* common to India and Tropical America. J. Wood-Mason, 82
	[A]	A new species of Diurnal *Lepidoptera* belonging to the genus *Hebomoia*. J. Wood-Mason 134

Journ. Vol.			
XLIX. Pt. II.	[A]	On a new species of *Papilio* from South India, with remarks on the species allied thereto. J. Wood-Mason, ...	144
	[A]	The Female of *Hebomoia Rœpstorffii*. J. Wood-Mason	150
	[M]	Notes on, and drawings of, the Animals of various Indian land Mollusca (*Pulmonifera*). H. H. Godwin-Austen	151
	[M]	New species of Brackish-water mollusks. G. Nevill...	159
	[A]	On the *Lepidopterous* genus *Æmona*, with description of a new species. J. Wood-Mason	175
	[A]	A new *Papilio* from the Andamans. J. Wood-Mason	178
	[M]	Contributions to Indian Malacology, No XII. Descriptions of new Land and Freshwater shells from Southern and Western India, Burma, the Andaman islands. W. T. Blanford	181
	[A]	Some new species of Rhopalocerous *Lepidoptera* from the Indian region. Capt. G. F. L. Marshall and L. de-Nicéville	245
	[A]	List of Diurnal *Lepidoptera* from Port Blair, with descriptions of some new or little known species, and of a new species of *Hestia* from Burma. J. Wood-Mason and L. de Nicéville.............	223
	[A]	Description of *Parantirrhœa Marshalli*, the type of a new genus and species of Rhopalocerous *Lepidoptera* from South India. J. Wood-Mason	248
L. Pt. II.	[M]	*Mollusca* of the Indo-Malayan Fauna. G. Nevill....	125
	[M]	A new species of *Rostellaria* from the Bay of Bengal. G. Nevill	262
	[A]	A list of Butterflies taken in Sikkim in October 1880 with notes on habits. L. de Nicéville	49
	[M]	List of Mollusca from the hills between Mari and Tandiani. W. Theobald	44
	[A]	On some Lepidopterous insects belonging to the Rhopalocerous genera *Euripus* and *Penthema* from India and Burma. J. Wood-Mason	85
	[G]	A sketch of the history of the fossils of the Gondwana System. O. Feistmantel............................ ..	168
	[A]	Description of a new species of the Lepidopterous genus *Euripus* from N. E. India. J. Wood-Mason	272
	[A]	List of Diurnal *Lepidoptera* inhabiting the Nicobar Islands. J. Wood-Mason and L. de Nicéville	224
	[A]	Second list of Rhopalocerous *Lepidoptera* from Port Blair. J. Wood-Mason and L. de Nicéville	243

Journ. Vol. LI. Pt. II.	[A]	Second list of butterflies taken in Sikkim in October 1882. L. de Nicéville	54
	[M]	Notes on and drawings of the animals of various Indian *Pulmonifera*. H. H. Godwin-Austen	68
	[M]	On a Collection of Japanese *Clausiliæ* made by Brigade Surgeon R. Hungerford. O. F. Möllendorf	1
	[M]	*Clausilia Nevilliana* (Nicobars). O. F. Möllendorf	11
	[M]	New Asiatic *Clausiliæ*. O. F. Möllendorf	12
	[A]	Some new or rare species of Rhopalocerous *Lepidoptera* from the Indian region. G. F. L. Marshall	37
	[A]	A new species of *Hipparchia* from the N. W Himalayas. G. F. L. Marshall	67
	[A]	On new and little known *Mantodea*. J. Wood-Mason	21
	[A]	Second list of Diurnal *Lepidoptera* inhabiting the Nicobar islands. J. Wood-Mason and L. de Nicéville	14
Proc. 1865.	[M]	On land Mollusca of Burma. W. T. Blanford	72
1866.	[A]	On fire-flies. F. Fedden	19
1868.	[G]	On rare Malayan animals. A. E. Maingay	127, 177, 194
	[M]	On *Nanina pollux* and *Helix propinqua*. A. E. Maingay	263
1871.	[M]	On the Anatomy of *Cremnoconchus*. F. Stoliczka	108
1872.	[A]	On *Nephropsis stewarti*. J. Wood-Mason	151
1873.	[A]	Australian *Phasmidæ*. J. Wood-Mason	150
	[A]	On *Carcinus mænas*. J. Wood-Mason	172
1874.	[A]	On a secondary sexual character in *Squilla raphidea*. J. Wood-Mason	2
	[A]	Drawings of blind Crustaceans. J. Wood-Mason	180
	[A]	On *Trictenotoma childrenii*. J. Wood-Mason	181

Proc.			
	[A]	A spider of the genus *Mygale.* Wood-Mason....	197
1875.	[A]	Three new species of *Paratelphusa.* J. Wood-Mason...	230
	[A]	On a specimen of *Astacus modestus.* J. Wood-Mason	231
	[A]	New Stomapod Crustaceans. J. Wood-Mason........	231
1876.	[A]	A new species of *Astacoides*, with remarks on the Systematic position of the New Zealand *Astacidae.* J. Wood-Mason	4
	[A]	Species of *Iapyx*, *Scolopendrella*, &c. J. Wood-Mason	174
	[A]	Femoral Brushes of *Mantidae.* J. Wood-Mason ..	123, 176
1877.	[A]	Note on the floral simulation of *Gongylus gongylodes*, Linn, J. Anderson	193
1880.	[A]	Butterflies from the Andamans, Masuri and Sibságar. J. Wood-Mason	102, 123
1882.	[A]	On the Anatomy of the Scorpion Spiders (*Thelyphonus*) Part I. The scent-glands. J. Wood-Mason	59
	[M]	On the structure of the "foot" in certain Terrestrial *Gasteropoda.* J. Wood-Mason	60

N. B.—For notices of the Invertebrata published in the 'Proceedings' previous to 1865, see below.

IV.

BOTANY.

Papers on the Burmese Flora are marked [B].

As. Res.		
Vol. I.	Mahwa Tree. Lieut. C. Hamilton	306
II. 1790.	A treatise on the plants of India. Sir W. Jones	345
	Spikenard of the Ancients. Sir W. Jones	405
III. 1792.	A description of the Plant *Butea*. W. Roxburgh	469
IV. 1795.	Plant *Morinda* and its uses. W. Hunter	35
	Select Indian plants with their Sanscrit and Vernacular names. Sir W. Jones	229
	Selected Indian plants. Sir W. Jones............. ...	257
	Jonesia Asoka. W. Roxburgh	356, 405
	Botanical observations on the Spikenard, *Valeriana Jatamanse* of the ancients. W. Roxburgh	
V. [B]	Description of a Tree, called by the Burmas, Launzan. F. Buchanan	123
[B]	*Urceola elastica*, or Caout-chouc Vine of Sumatra and Pulo-Penang. W. Roxburgh........................	167
VI. 1799.	Plants collected between Hardwar and Srinagar. T. Hardwicke	348
	A Botanical and Economical account of *Bassia Butyracea* or East India butter tree. W. Roxburgh	477
IX. 1807.	On *Olibanum* or Frankincense with desciption of *Boswellia serrata*, Roxb. H. T. Colebrooke	377
X. 1808.	The Plant, which furnishes the medicine called *Columb* or *Columba Root*. Dr. A. Berry	385
XI. 1810.	A Catalogue of Indian Medicinal Plants and Drugs, with their names in Hindustáni and Sanscrit. John Fleming ...	153
	Descriptions of several of the Monandrous Plants of India, belonging to the natural order called *Scitamineæ* by Linnæus, *Cannæ* by Jussiu, and *Drimyrhizæ* by Ventenant. W. Roxburgh, ...	318
XII. 1816.	On the *Dryobalanops Camphora* of Sumatra. H. T. Colebrooke	
	Two new species of *Sarcolobus*, and some other Indian Plants. N. Wallich	
XIII. 1820.	Some rare Indian Plants. N. Wallich..............	369
	New *Camellia*, Nepal. N. Wallich	428

As. Res.	
XIX. Pt. I.	Two genera of the Family of *Hamamelideæ*, two species of *Podostemon*, and one of *Kaulfussia*. William Griffith 94
Journ. I.	Botanic Garden at Saharanpur. J. H. Royle 41
II. 1833.	List of Indian woods collected by N. Wallich 167
	Note on the fossil Palms lately discovered on the Table-land of Saugor in Central India. H. H. Spry 639
V. 1836.	Some grasses, from the Jheels of the District of Sylhet. William Griffith 570
	Development of Pollen. William Griffith 732
	Remarks on a Collection of Plants made at Sadya, upper Asam, from April to September, 1836. W. Griffith 806
VII. 1838.	The Caoutchouc Tree of Assam. William Griffith 132
	Botanico-Agricultural account of the protected Sikh States. M. P. Edgeworth, ... 151
VIII. [B]	Burmese and Manipur Varnish Tree. N. Wallich...... 70
	Note on the Scapes of *Xanthorhæa* and Fossil Stems of *Lepidodendra*. Lieut. N. Vicary 685
X. 1841.	On Lichens in the Himalayas. Henry Cope 828
	A connected view of the species of Lichens, with the Botanical relationship existing between them and the Indian productions. Henry Cope 888
XI. 1842.	Botanico-Agricultural account of the protected Sikh States, M. P. Edgeworth 26
	Observations on the genus *Spathium*. M. P. Edgeworth 145
XIII. 1844.	Flora of the Naga Hills. J. W. Masters 707
XVI. 1847.	Herborisation at Aden. M. P. Edgeworth 1211
Pt. II.	The Liquidamber tree, Tenasserim. Rev. F. Mason ... 532
XVII. [B] Pt. I.	Observations made when following the Grand Trunk road across the hills of upper Bengal, Parasnath, &c. Dr. J. D. Hooker 355
XVIII. [B]	The Pine tree, Tenasserim. Rev. F. Mason 73
	Notes, chiefly Botanical, made during an excursion from Darjiling to Tonglo, a lofty mountain on the Confines of Sikkim and Nepal. J. D. Hooker 419
XXI. 1852.	Catalogue of Plants found in the Banda district 1847-49. M. P. Edgeworth 151, 240, 563
XXV. 1856.	Notes on the Herbarium of the Calcutta Botanic garden, with especial reference to the completion of the *Flora Indica*. Thomas Thomson 405
XXVIII.	Notes on the Flora of Lucknow with Catalogues of the cultivated and indigenous plants. T. Anderson 89

Journ. [B]		
XXVIII.	Notes during a tour from Moulmein to the three Pagodas, and in Shan States. Rev. C. Parish	457
XXXII. 1863.	On the flora of Behar and the mountain Parasnath, with a list of the species collected by Messrs. Hooker, Edgeworth, Thomson and Anderson. Thomas Anderson	189
	Flora of the Peshawur Valley. J. L. Stewart.......	219
XXXIII.	Vegetation of the Jhelum (Punjab). J. E. Aitchison	290
XXXIV. Pt. II.	Remarks on the vegetation of the islands in the Indus river. J. E. T. Aitchison	53
XXXVI. Pt. II.	On the Reproductive functional relations of several species and varieties of *Verbasca*. J. Scott	143
	Pandanophyllum and allied genera. S. Kurz	70
	Notes on the Flora of Manbhum. V. Ball	112
XXXIX. Pt. II.	New or imperfectly known Indian plants. S. Kurz ...	61
	Gentiana Jæschkei re-established as a new genus of *Gentianaceæ*. S. Kurz..	229
XL.	New or imperfectly known Indian plants. S. Kurz	45
Pt. II. [B]	*Algæ* collected by Mr. S. Kurz in Burma and adjacent islands. G. von Martens	461
XLI. [B] Pt. II.	New Burmese plants. Pt. I, S. Kurz	29
XLII. Pt. II	Do. Do. Pts. II and III	59, 227
XLIII. [B] Pt. II.	Contributions towards a knowledge of the Burmese Flora. S. Kurz	39
	Descriptions of a few Indian plants. S. Kurz	181
[B]	Enumeration of Burmese Palms S. Kurz	191
XLIV. [B]	Burmese Flora. S. Kurz	128
Pt. II.	Notes on a few new Oaks from India. S. Kurz.........	196
	Description of a new species of *Tupistra*. S. Kurz ...	198
	Descriptions of new Indian Plants. S. Kurz...........	199
XLV.	Vegetation of the Nicobar Islands. S. Kurz	105
Pt. II. [B]	Burmese Flora. S. Kurz	204
	Fossil Flora in India. O. Feistmantel	329
XLVI. [B]	Burmese Flora. S. Kurz	49
L. Pt. II	Fossils of the Gondwana System. O. Feistmantel......	168
Proc. 1866.	On *Eurya chinensis*. Dr. T. Anderson	109
	On Comestible jungle fruits. V. Ball	237
1882.	On torsion in the awns of Spear Grass. J. Cockburn...	49

V.

GEOGRAPHY.

[*N. B.*—[A] = Afghanisthan and Central Asia. [B] = Burma, the Islands in the Bay of Bengal, &c. [H] = Himalayan Geography. [N I] = Northern India. [C I] = Central India. [E I] = Eastern India. [W I] = Western India. [S I] = Southern India.]

As. Res.			
Vol. I.	[H]	Account of a journey to Tibet. S. Turner	206
II.	[H]	Account of Nepal. Father Guiseppe	307
	[B]	A short description of Carnicobar. G. Hamilton	337
III.	[B]	On the Nicobars. Nicolas Fontana	149
IV.	[B]	Nancowry and Comarty. Lieut. R. H. Colebrooke	129
	[B]	Andaman islands. R. H Colebrooke	385
VI.	[C I]	Narrative of a journey form Agra to Ougein. W. Hunter	7
VII.	[N I]	On the Course of the Ganges through Bengal. Major R. H. Colebrooke	1
	[C I]	Narrative of a Route from Chunár to Yertnagoodum, (Ellore). Capt. J. T. Blunt	57
	[S I]	An account of a method for extending a Geographical Survey across the Peninsula of India. W. Lambton	312
XI.	[H]	On the sources of the Ganges. H. T. Colebrooke	429
	[H]	Narrative of a survey for the purpose of discovering the sources of the Ganges. Capt. F. V. Raper	446
XII.	[H]	Height of the Himalayas. H T. Colebrooke	251
	[H]	A journey to lake Manasarovara in Undes. W. Moorcroft. With introductory note by H. T. Colebrooke	375
XIII.	[H]	An account of a Journey to the Sources of the Jumna and Bhagirathi rivers. J. B. Fraser	171
	[H]	Memoir relative to a survey in Kumaon. Capt. W. S. Webb	293
XIV.	[H]	The principal peaks of the Himalayass. Capt. J. A. Hodgson and Lieut. J. D. Herbert	187
XV.	[H]	On Bhutan. Kishen Kant Bose	128
	[S I]	Orissa Proper or Cuttack. A. Stirling	163
	[H]	Tour made to lay down the course and levels of the river Sutlej or Satudrá, performed in 1819. Capt. J. D. Herbert	339
XVI.	[E I]	Geography of Asam. Capt. John Bryan Neufville	331

As. Rs. [E I] XVII.	Memoir of a Survey of Assam and the Neighbouring countries, executed in 1825-6-7-8. Lieut. R. Wilcox ... 314
[E I]	Journey across the Pandua Hills. H. Walters 499
[H]	Route from Cathmadu to Tazedo on the Chinese Frontier. B. H. Hodgson 513
XVIII. [H] Pt. II.	Observations on the Spiti Valley and circumjacent country within the Himalaya. J. G. Gerard 238
Journ. [H]	Geographical notice of Tibet. Csoma de Körös....... 121
I. [B] 1832.	Account of the Barren islands in the Bay of Bengal drawn up by the late Dr. J. Adam 128
[A]	A sketch of the route and progress of Lieut. A. Burnes and Dr. Gerard. By a recent Traveller 139
II. [A] 1833.	The route of Lieut. A. Burnes, and Dr. Gerard, from Peshawar to Bokhara, and Bokhara to Meshed......... 1, 143
[B]	Ava to Kendat. D. Richardson 59
[A]	Description of Bokhara. Lieut. A. Burnes.............. 224
III. [C I] 1834.	Some remarks upon the country to the South-West of Hoshungabad and Káliabheet hills. R. H. Miles 61
[E I]	Journal kept by Capt. F. T. Grant, during a tour of Inspection on the Manipur Frontier along the course of the Ningthi river, &c. 124
[A]	Dera Ghazi Khan, through the Veziri country to Kabul. Dr. Honigberger 175
[A]	Note of a pilgrimage undertaken by an Usbek and his two sons from Khokend or Kokan, in Tartary, &c., to Mecca. W. H. Wathen 379
	Georgia, Persia, and Mesopotamia. R. Mignan....... 576
[B]	Naning, in the Malayan Peninsula. Lieut. J. T. Newbold 601
IV. 1835.	Georgia, Persia and Mesopotamia. Capt. Mignan 271, 332
[A]	Memoir on Khokend. W. H. Wathen...................... 369
[B]	Island of Rambree. Lieut. Wm. Foley........20, 82, 199
[E I]	An excursion to the Tea Hills which produce Ankoy Tea. G. J. Gordon 95
	Report on the island of Socotra. Lieut. J. R. Wellsted 138
	Voyage from England to Calcutta in 1831. Lieut. T. Hutton 167
[B]	Naning in the Malay Peninsula. J. T. Newbold...... 297
	Heavando Pholo, the Northern Atoll of the Maldive islands. Lieut. T. Powell 319
	Notes of a tour through Palestine...................... 438

Journ. Vol.		Subject	Page
IV. 1835.	[B]	Sungi Ujong one of the States in the interior of Malacca. Ensign T. J. Newbold	537
	[B]	Journal of an attempted ascent of the river Min, to visit the Tea plantations of Tumkin Provinces of China. G. J. Gordon	553
		Territory and Government of Iskardoh. Capt. C. M. Wade	589
		Georgia, Persia, and Mesopotamia. Capt. R. Mignan	602
V.	[B]	Rambowe in Malacca. T. J. Newbold	61
1836.	[B]	Johole and its former dependencies of Jompole Gominchi. T. Newbold	257
	[B]	The neighbourhood Moulmein. Capt. W. Foley	257
	[W I]	Peshawar and the country comprised between the Indus and the Hydespes. M. A. Court	468
	[B]	Perak, Sincenanti, and other States in the Malaya Peninsula. Lieut. T. J. Newbold	505, 561
	[B]	Petty States lying north of Tenasserim drawn up from the Journals and reports of D. Richardson	601, 688
	[W I]	A brief account of Masud, known by the name Farid Shakarganj or Shakarbar. Munshi Mohun Lal	635
VI. 1837.	[E I]	Journal of a route travelled by Capt. S. F. Hannay, from Ava to the Hukong valley on the South-East Frontier of Assam. Capt. R. Boileau Pemberton	245
	[E I]	Mishmee hills, Assam. W. Griffith,	325
	[B]	Cochin China. Rev. Jean Louis	737
	[H]	Valley of Kashmir, Ghazni and Kabul. G. J. Vigne	766
	[B]	Expedition to Kiang Hung on the Chinese Frontier. Lieut. T. E. MacLeod	989
	[B]	Expedition from Moulmein to Ava through the Karen country. D. Richardson	105
VII.	[W I]	Kala Bagh on the Indus. Mohun Lal	25
1838.	[S I]	Journal of a tour in Orissa. Lieut. Markham Kittoe	1060
	[H]	Note of a visit to the Niti Pass. J. H. Batten	310
	[B]	Geography of Cochin China. Rev. Jean Louis	317
	[A]	The plain of Koh-i-Daman, and the country from the Indus to Kabul. P. B. Lord,	521
	[E I]	Account of the country occupied by the Bor Senaputtee. S. C. Hannay	671
	[B]	A portion of Mergui. Capt. R. Lloyd	1027
VIII. 1839.	[W I]	Account of a journey to Beylah, and Memoir on the Province of Lus. Lieut. Carloss	184

Journ.		
Vol. VIII.	[H]	Journal of the Mission, which visited Bhootan in 1837-38 under Capt. R. Boileau Pemberton. W. Griffith 208, 251
1839.	[S I]	Account of a journey from Calcutta *viâ* Cuttack and Puri to Sambalpur, thence to Midnapur through the Forest of Orissa. Lieut. M. Kittoe 367, 474, 671
	[E I]	Narrative of an Expedition into the Naga territory. E. R. Grange 445
	[H]	Journal of a trip through Kunawur, Hungrung and Spiti. Lieut. T. Hutton 901
	[B]	Report on Tenasserim. John William Helfer 973
IX.	[B]	Journal of a Mission from the Supreme Government to the
1840.		Court of Siam. Dr. Richardson 1016
	[B]	Mission to the Court of Siam. Dr. Richardson 1, 219
	[W I]	Some account of a journey from Kurrachee to Hinglaj, in the Lus territory. Capt. Hart 134
	[H]	Journal of a trip through Kunawur, Hungrung and Spiti. Lieut. T. Hutton.......................... 489, 555
	[A]	Physical Geography of Seisthan. Capt. E. Conolly .. 710
	[C I]	Notes of a march from Brimham Ghat on the Narbada to Amarkantak, the source of that river. G. Spilsbury 889
	[W I]	Report on the country between Karáchi, Tatta and Schwan, Sind. Capt. E. P. De la Hoste 907
	[E I]	Extracts from the journal of an expendition into the Naga hills on the Assam Frontier. Lieut. Grange 947
X.	[H]	Abstract journal of the routes of Lieuts. A. Broome and A.
1841.		Cunningham to the sources of the Punjab rivers... 1, 105
	[A]	Extracts from demi-official reports, by Capt. Arthur Conolly, on a Mission into Kharássan 116
	[E I]	Despatch from Lieut. H. Bigge, Assist. Agent detached to the Naga hills to Capt. Jenkins, ... 129
	[B]	Province of Arracan. Henry Harper Spry 138
	[A]	The country of the Toorkoman tribes. Capt. Edward Stirling 290
	[A]	Journal kept in Seistan. Capt. E. Conolly 319
	[B]	Report on Cheduba. Edward P. Halsted............ 349
	[W I]	The recent Cataclysm of the Indus. Falconer 615
XI.	[A]	Valley of Jellalabad. Lieut. MacGregor............ 117
1842.	[B]	The isle of St. Martin's. C. B. Greenlaw 309
	[H]	Narrative of a Journey from Subathu to Shipke, in Chinese Tartary in 1818. Lieut. A. Gerard 363
	[B]	Pakung Yeh in Ava to Aeng in Arracan. Lieut. Trant 1136

Journ. [H] Vol. XI.	Capt. Manson's journal of a visit to the Melum and the Oonta Dhura Pass in Juwahir. J. H. Batten 1157
XII. [W I] 1843.	Report on Upper Sind and the Eastern portion of Cutchee. Lieut. J. Postans 23
[W I]	Various routes in Sind, from official documents from Bombay, of March 1840 44
[W I]	Road from Sind, and from Subzul to Shikarpur. Mr. Nock 59
[H]	Journal of Lieut. J. A. Weller on a trip to the Bulcha and Oonta Dhoora Passes. J. H. Batten, ... 78
[B]	Report of a visit to the Pakchan river, and of some Tin localities in the Southern portion of the Tenasserim provinces. Capt. G. B. Tremenheere, ... 523
[W I]	Journal of a tour through parts of the Panjab and Affghanistan, in the year 1837. Agha Abbas of Shiraz, arranged and translated. Major R. Leech 564
XIII. [A]	A description of Seisthan. Lieut. R. Leech, ... 115
1844. [A]	Routes from Candahar to Herat, ... 121
[H]	Notes on Moorcroft's travels in Ladak, and Gerard's account of Kunáwar, including a general description of the latter district. Lieut. J. D. Cunningham.............. 172, 223
[A]	Herat to Simla, *viá* Cándáhár, Cábul and the Punjab. Major Tod 339
[W I]	Route from Derá Gházi Khan to Cándáhár. Maj. R. Leech 527
[E I]	Notes on the Kasia hills and people. Lieut. H. Yule ... 612
[A]	Notes taken on a tour through parts of Beluchisthán, in 1838 and 1839. Hajee Abdul Mubee. Arranged and translated by Major Robert Leech 667, 786
[H]	Journal of Captain Herbert's tour from Almora through parts of Kumaon and British Gurhwal. J. H. Batten ... 734
[E I]	Journey into the Naga hills. Wood................ 771
[W I]	Itinerary from Yezd to Herat 827
[W I]	A geographical Notice of the Valley of Jellalabad. Capt. G. H. MacGregor 867
XIV. [E I] 1845.	The neighbourhood of the Soobanshiri river, Assam. Lieut. E. T. Dalton 250
[C I]	The course of the Narbadá. Lieut-Col. Ouseley 354
[E I]	The Mishmee hills to the north-east of Sudyah. Lieut. E. A. Rowlatt.. 477
[W I]	Account of parts of the Cabul and Peshawar territories, and of Sama, Sudaom, Bunher, Swat, Dur and Bajour, visited by Mulla Ahem-Ulla. Major R. Leech 660

Journal.		
[W I]	Account of the Panjkora Valley and of lower and upper Kashkar, by Raja Khan of Cabool. Translated by Major Leech	812
Vol. XIV.		
XV. [B]	Notice of the Nicobar islands. Rev. J. Barbe	344
XVII. [H] 1848.	Phari in Thibet to Lassa, with appended routes from Darjeeling to Phari. A. Campbell	257
Pt. I. [B]	The practicability of a direct trade overland between Calcutta and China. Baron Otto des Granges	132
Pt. II. [H]	Narrative of a journey to Cho Lagan, (Rakastal), Cho Mapan (Manasarovar) and the Valley of Pruang in Guari, Hundes, in September and October 1846. Lieut. H. Strachey	98, 127, 327
[C I]	Dhari falls to the Hiruphal. Capt. Fenwick	210
[H]	The British Himalayan frontier in Kumaon and Gurhwal. Lieut. H. Strachey	532
[H]	The seven Co'sis of Nepal. B. H. Hodgson	646
[H]	Routes from Darjiling to Thibet. A. Campbell	488
[H]	Route from Katmandu to Darjiling. B. H. Hodgson	634
XVIII. [H]	Snow line in the Himalaya. Lieut. R. Strachey	287
1849. [H]	Kohistan of the Jullunder. Lieut. W. H. Parish	360
[H]	Darjiling to Tongló, a lofty mountain on the confines of Sikim and Nepal. J. D. Hooker	419
[H]	Journal of a trip to Sikim. Dr. A. Campbell	482
[W I]	Narbadá from Chikulda to Broach. Capt. Fenwick	461
[A]	Western Afghanistan. Major W. Anderson	553
[H]	The Turan and outer mountains of Kumaon. Major E. Madden	603
[W I]	Pind Dadud Khan and the Salt Range. A. Fleming	661
[H]	Physical Geography of the Himalayas. B. H. Hodgson	761
XIX. [W I]	The district of Jhilum. L. Bowing	43
[H]	Notice of a trip to the Niti Pass. Lieut. R. Strachey	79
XX. [N I]	The Rajmahal hills. Capt. W. S. Sherwill	544
1851 [W I]	Report on the Turan Mall hill. Capt. Thurburn	502
XXI. [H]	Sikim to the Frontier of Thibet. Dr. A. Campbell	407, 477
[N I]	Kurrukpore hills. Capt. S. R. Sherwill	195
XXII. [A] 1853.	Ibu Huakul's account of Khorasan. Major W. Anderson	152
[A]	Notes on the sources of the Amoo or Oxus, extracted from the journal of Mr. Gardiner. M. P. Edgeworth	431
[H]	Central Asia, Abstract of a journal kept by Mr. Gardiner, with introduction. M. P. Edgeworth	283

Journ. [E I]	
Vol. XXII.	Account of a visit to Juglu and Sisi rivers in Upper Assam. Capt. E. T. Dalton 511
1853. [H]	Sikim Himalaya. W. S. Sherwill.............. 540, 611
XXIII	
[W I]	Notes on the Topography of Murree. Dr. A. Gordon 461
XXV [H] 1856.	Nepalese Embassies to Pekin, with remarks on Tibet. B. H. Hodgson 473
XXVI [A] 1857.	District forming the Western boundary of the lower Derajat. Lieut. H. Raverty 177
[A]	Notes on Kokan, Kashgar, Yarkand, and other places in Central Asia. H. Raverty........................ 257
[H]	Memorandum on the Nanga Parbat, and other snowy mountains of the Himalayan range adjacent to Kashmir. Lieut. T. G. Montgomerie 266
XXVIII [A]	Notes on Kafiristan. Capt. H. G. Raverty 317
1859. [B]	Amherst, Tenasserim. Major S. R. Tickell............ 421
XXIX [B]	Barren island. G. Von. Liebig.......................... 1
1860. [H]	Memorandum on the survey of Kashmir in progress under Capt. T. G. Montgomerie. Major H. L. Thuillier ... 20
XXX [H] 1861.	Memorandum on the progress of the Kashmir series of the great trigonometrical survey of India. T. G. Montgomerie 99
[B]	Notes on the river Yangtse-Kiang from Hankow to Pingshan. Lieut.-Col. H. A. Sarel 222
[H & E I]	Memorandum on the countries between Thibet, Yunan and Burmah. The very Rev. Thomine de Mazure; with notes and a comment by Lieut.-Col. Yule 367
XXXI [A] 1862.	The upper and lower Suwat and the Kohistan to the source of the Suwat river. H. G. Raverty 227
[B]	Report on a route from the mouth of the Pakchan to Kran and thence across the isthmus of Kran to the gulf of Siam 347
[H]	Trip to the Kanchunjingah group in the Sikkim Himalaya. Major J. L. Sherwill 457
[H]	Simla to the Spiti Valley and Chomoriri (Tshomoriri) lake W. Theobald 480
XXXIII	
1864. [C I]	On the dependency of Bustar. Capt. C. Glasfurd, ... 44
[B]	Trip to Bhamo. Dr. C. Williams.......................... 189
XXXIV	
Pt. II. [C I] 1865.	Tributary Mahals, under the Commissioner of Chota Nagpore, Bonai, Gangpore, Odeypoore, and Sirgooja. Lieut. Col. T. Dalton 1

Journ. [A] Vol. XXXIV Pt. II. [B] 1865.	Notes on Central Asia. M. Semenof. Communicated by Lieut. Col. J. T. Walker ... 113
	Notes of a trip up the Salween. Rev. C. Parish 135
XXXV [A] Pt. II.	Russian Geographical operations in Central Asia. (Communicated by Lieut. Col. F. T. Walker) ... 77
XXXVII. Pt. II. [H]	Lake districts of Ladakh. H. Godwin-Austen 84
XXXIX. Pt. II. [H]	Trans-Himalaya explorations. Major T. G. Montgomerie 47
XL, Pt. II. [H]	Independent Sikkim. W. T. Blanford ... 367
XLVIII. 1879. [E I]	The route over Patkai *viâ* Nongyang. S. E. Peal 69
[A]	Survey operations in Afghanisthan in connection with the Campaign of 1878-79. J. Waterhouse ... 146
[E I]	Report on a Visit to the Nongyang Lake, on the Burmese Frontier. S. E. Peal ... 1
Proc. [A] 1866.	Physical Geography of High Asia. R. Schlagintweit... 21
1878. [A]	Trans-Frontier Explorations. Col. Walker 107

VI.

ETHNOLOGY.

[*N. B.*—Notices of the Kolarian tribes are distinguished by [K]]

As. Res.		
Vol. II.	The Arabs. Sir W. Jones	1
1790.	The Tartars. Sir W. Jones	19
	The Persians. Sir W. Jones	43
	The Kukis of Tripura. J. Rawlins	187
	The Chinese. Sir W. Jones	365
III. 1792.	Borderers, mountaineers and islanders of Asia. Sir W. Jones	1
	On the Garos. J. Eliot	17
IV. [K]	Inhabitants of the hills near Rajmahal. T. Shaw	45
VI. 1799.	The inhabitants of the Paggyar Nassau islands lying off Sumatra. J. Crisp	77
VII. 1801.	The Kukis. John MacRae	183
	Bazeegurs (denominated *Nats*). D. Richardson	457
XII. 1816.	On the Malaya Nation. T. Raffles	102
XVI. 1828	On the population of Assam. J. B. Neufville	331
	Notice of the Khyen Tribe inhabiting the Yunan mountains, between Ava and Aracan. T. A. Trant	261
XVII.	Memoir of Asam [Khamtis &c.] R. Wilcox	314
1829.	Journey across the Pandua Hills near Silhet [Kásiás &c.] H. Walters	499
Journal.	The Military Tribes of Nipal. B. H. Hodgson	217
Vol. II.	The Játs of Bharatpur. G. T. Lushington	273
III. 1834.	The Siah Posh tribe or reputed descendants of the Macedonians. Mohan Lal	76
	Aborigines of Nepal Proper. B. H. Hodgson	215
IV. 1835.	The inhabitants of Ramri. Foley	20, 82, 199
	The tribes of the Piney Hills, Madura. Ward	66
V. 1836.	Mountain Tribes on the N. E. Frontier. McCosh	193
VII. 1838.	On the Siah Posh Kaffirs. Capt. Alex. Burnes	325
	The Moa-Morah sect. Capt. S. C. Hannay	671
VIII. 1839.	The Nagas. B. Otto de Grange	445
	The inhabitants of Tenasserim. J. W. Helfer	973
IX.	The Lepchas of Sikkim. A. Campbell	379
1840.	The Limbus and other hill tribes. A. Campbell	595
[K]	The Hodesum. Lieut. S. R. Tickell	694, 783, 1063

Journal.	
Vol. IX.	The Eusofzye tribes of Afghanistan. E. Conolly 924
	On the Nagas. Otto de Grange 947
1840.	The Kujjukzyes (Upper Sind). Capt. N. Hart........ 1214
X. [K]	On the Hodesun. S. R. Tickell.............................. 30
1841.	On the Nagas. H. Bigge 129
	Note on the Brahoons. Capt. Hart.................... 136
	The Toorkoman Tribes. E. Stirling.................. 290
XI. 1842.	Certain hill tribes in Sikkim. A. Campbell............... 4
[K]	Notes on the Bendkar, a people of Keonjhar (Savaras). Lieut. S. R. Tickell 205
XIII. 1844.	On the Migratory tribes in Central India. E. Balfour 1
	The Mijjer Theya Somalees. Lieut. C. J. Cruttenden 319
	On the Kasias. Lieut. H. Yule 612
XIV. 1845.	The early Ghiljai and the Hazaras. R. Leech...... 306, 333
	The hill tribes, district of Chittagong. Rev. M. Barbe 380
	The Miris and Abors (Asam). Lieut. E. Dalton 426
	On the Mishmis. E. A. Rowlatt 477
	The Esafzai Affghans. Khásh Ali 736
XVI. 1847.	Aborigines of the Sub-Himalayas. Hodgson........... 1235
XVII. 1848.	*Addenda et Corrigenda* to the above. B. H. Hodgson 73
	The Aborigines of Central India. B. H. Hodgson..... 550
	Tibetan Type of Mankind. B. H. Hodgson 222
XVIII.	Dushani and Chianni Garos. C. S. Campbell 45
1849.	Aborigines of Southern India. B. H. Hodgson 350
	Aborigines of Nor.-Eastern India. B. H. Hodgson .. 451
	Note on Indian Ethnology. B. H. Hodgson 238
	Aborigines of the Eastern frontier. B. H. Hodgson ... 967
	The Kooch, Bodo, and Dhimal tribes. B. H. Hodgson 702
XIX. 1850.	Aborigines of the N.-E. frontier and of the South. B. H. Hodgson 309, 461
XX. 1851.	On the Dophlas. W. Robinson 126
[K]	Inhabitants of the Rajmahal hills. Col. W. Sherwill . 544
XXI. 1852	The Henma or Shendoos, (N. Aracan). S. R. Tickell 207
	Two heads found in the Punjab. W. Jackson 511
XXII. 1853.	Caucasian and Mongolian Affinities. B. H. Hodgson 26
	Indo-Chinese Borderers. B. H. Hodgson 1
XXIII.	Origin of the Afghans. Lieut. H. G. Raverty 550
XXIV.	Indian Veddas, south of Palamow. H. Piddington... 207
XXV. 1856.	Aborigines of the Nilgiris. B. H. Hodgson 31, 498
[K]	Puttooas or Juangas, Catak. E. A. Samuells............ 295
XXVI. 1857.	Hill tribes of the Western boundary of the lower Derajat. H. G. Raverty 177

Journal. Vol.		
XXXII. 1863.	People of the Shan States. R. H. Schomburgk	387
	The tribes of the Eastern frontier. J. H. O'Donel, and H. J. Reynolds	400, 404, 407
XXXIII.	Memoranda relative to three Andamanese. Colonel S. R. Tickell	162
[K]	The Tributary Mahals. Lieut. Col. T. Dalton	1
XXXIV. Pt. II. 1865.	The Boksas of the Bijnour district. Dr. J. L. Stewart	147
	The Karens. Rev. F. Mason, D. D.	173, 195
XXXV. Pt. II. 1866.	Physical character of the Karens. F. Mason	1
	The Ethnology of India. Justice Campbell. Extra Number	1
[K]	The "Kols" of Chota Nágpur. Lieut. Col. E. T. Dalton Extra Number	153
XXXVII. Pt. II. 1868.	Northern Frontier of Assam. Hessellmeyer	192
	Dwellings, works of art &c., of the Karens. F. Mason	125
	The Tribes of Bhutiana and Harniana. W. A. Minas	171
XLVIII. 1879.	Notes on some implements from the Khasi Hills and the Banda and Vellore districts. J. Cockburn	133
Proc. 1865.	Stone implements. V. Ball	127
	Stone implements. W. Theobald	126
1866.	Ethnology of Mergui. W. Abbey	243
	The worked agates of stone-age. W. T. Blanford	230
	Ethnology of Travancore and Cochin. E. M. Ross	242
1867.	Ethnology of India. J. B. Davis	121
	Aboriginal tribes of India. E. Schlagintweit	127
1868.	Stone implements. V. Ball	177
	Celts. H. F. Blanford	59
1869.	On the Minas, Central India. Lieut.-Col. Showers	238
	Stone implements from Burma. W. Theobald	181
1870.	On the Andamanese. F. Day, and V. Ball	53, 177
	On Asam Celts. V. Ball	268
1871.	On Chipped implements. W. T. Blanford	179
1872.	Celts in Western Yunán. Dr. Anderson	47
1873.	Stone implements from the Narbadá Valley. H. B. Medlicott	138
1874.	Identification of Aboriginal tribes noticed in the "Ethnology of Bengal. Col. E. T. Dalton	7
1875.	The Khyeng of the Sandowy district Arakan. G. E. Fryer	96
	The cranial characteristics of Mongoloid tribes of N. E. Frontier. J. Wood-Mason	97

Proc. 1875.	Stone implements from Kharakpur. V. Ball 103
	On some stone implements of the Burmese type found in Dalbhum and Singhbum (Chutia-Nagpur). V. Ball 118
	Specimens of flint-cores and flakes from Sakhar and Rohri, on the Indus, Sind. W. T. Blanford 134
	Stone implements found in the river Mun. Lockwood 102
1876.	On stone implements from Burma. Sir A. Phayre ... 95
1878.	Stone implements from Pares-Nath. V. Ball 125
1881.	The Nicobarese. Dr. A. F. Roepstorff 104

VII.

CHEMISTRY.*

As. Res.	
Vol. XV.	Analysis of a Mineral water. James Prinsep........... xiv
XVIII. Pt. I.	The Fertilising principles of the inundations of the Hugli. H. Piddington.. 224
Journal. Vol. II. 1833.	A method of preparing Strychnia. J. T. Pearson...... 42
	Analysis of the Ashes of four Indian Plants. J. Stevenson 322
	Chemical Analysis. James Prinsep 427
III. 1834.	Efflorescence of Sulphate of Soda, as found native in the Soil of Tirhut and Sarum, Behar. J. Stephenson ... 188
IV. 1835.	Chemical Analysis. James Prinsep 509
V. 1836.	Soil suitable for Cotton, Tobacco, Sugar and the Tea plant. H. Piddington.. 314
	Soil and Salt from the Sumbhur lake salt works. J. Stephenson 792
VIII. 1839.	Arsenical Poisons etc. W. B. O'Shaughnessy 147
X. 1841.	Soda Soils of the Barramahol. Capt. Campbell......... 159
	Reports on the Soils brought from Cheduba by H. M. S. Childers. H. Piddington 436, 447
	Puckwah and *Phul Khari.* H. Piddington....... 939
XII. 1843.	Experiments relating to the effects of Sea-water on iron. W. B. O'Shaughnessy 1066
XVI. 1847.	Atmospheric dust from Shanghai. H. Piddington ... 193
XXIII. 1854.	Quantity of silt held in suspension by the waters of the Hooghly at Calcutta in each month of the year. H. Piddington 283
XXV. 1856.	Quantity of Silt held in suspension by the Hooghly etc. H. Piddington.. 151
	Bengal Mineral Waters. H. Piddington..................... 190
XXXV. Pt. II.	Calcutta Water Supply, Pt. I. D. Waldie 203
XXXVI. Pt. II.	Calcutta Water Supply, Pts. II and III. D. Waldie 1, 115
XLII. Pt. II.	Muddy water of the Hugli and the Calcutta Water Supply. D. Waldie 210
XLIX. Pt. II.	On the Past and Present water supplies of Calcutta. Alexander Pedler 85
Proc. 1865.	On Peat. Tween 86
1866.	Burmese Paraffine. D. Waldie.............................. 72
1876.	Radiometer as a photometer. A. Pedler................. 187

* Analyses of Minerals will be found among the Geological articles distinguished by [M].

VIII.

ECONOMIC SCIENCE AND STATISTICS.*

As. Res.		
Vol. I.	Method of distilling at Ramgur.	309
1788.	Process of making Atar. Col. Polier	332
III. 1790.	On the Manufacture of Indigo. Lieut.-Col. C. Martin	475
IV. 1795.	Natural Productions of Sumatra. J. Macdonald	19
V. 1797.	The Elastic Gum Vine of Prince of Wales' Island. J. Howison	157
IX. 1807.	Pepper (Prince of Wales' island). W. Hunter	383
XII. 1816.	Population of Burdwan. W. B. Bayley	547
XVI. 1828	Sketch of Kumaon. G. W. Traill	137
	Statistical Sketch of Arakan. C. Paton	353
XVII. 1832.	Bhutia Mahals of Kamaon. G. W. Traill	1
	Census of population of Benares. J. Prinsep	470
	Census of the city Dacca. H. Walters	535
XX. 1836.	Mortality in British India. H. B. Henderson	190
Journal.	Nepalese method of making paper. B. H. Hodgson	8
Vol. I.	Population of Allahabad	34
1832.	The Lacquered ware of Ava. H. Burney	169
	Native manufacture of Steel in India. Dr. Voysey	245
	Estimate of the risk of life to Civil Servants of the Bengal Prisidency. H. T. Prinsep	277
	Timber trade in Cachar	305
	Articles of *Materia Medica*, obtained in the Bazars of India. J. F. Royle	458
II. 1833.	Manufacture of Saltpetre in Tirhut. J. Stevenson	23
	Native manufacture of Turpentine	248
	Area of the Kingdoms and Principalities of India	488
	Population of the city and district of Murshidabad, taken in 1829	567
	Nipal paper stuff. G. Swinton	93
III. 1834.	Manufacture of common Salt. J. Stephenson	36
	The aptitude of the Himalayan range for the culture of the tea plant. H. Falconer	178
	Population of the city and district of Allahabad	244
	Abstract statement of 412 villages in district Bareilly. H. S. Boulderson	475

* Meteorological Statistics have been included in section I, and Statistics of Earthquakes in section II.

Journal. Vol.	
III. 1834.	Price of grain at Aligar from the year 1804 to 1832. E. Stirling 620
IV. 1835.	The Nepalese Spirit Still. A. Campbell 282
	Analysis of raw silk. J. W. Laidlay 710
V. 1836	The preparation of Opium for China. D. Butler 165
	Returns (agricultural, &c.) of Mathura District, made up to 1st October, 1835. R. Wroughton 216
	Cotton Spinning, Weaving, Printing, Dyeing in Nepal. A. Campbell 219
	The Satin embroidered Scarfs of the Tibetan Priests. T. H. A. Llyod 383
VI. 1837.	The Silkworms and Silks of Assam. Thomas Hugon 21
	The indigenous Silkworms of India. T. W. Helfer ... 38
	The risk of life to Civil Servants of the Bengal Presidency. H. T. Prinsep 341
	Silk cloth dyed from the leaves of Teak. B. Burt...... 242
VII. 1838.	Botanico-Agricultural account of the protected Sikh States. M. P. Edgeworth 751
	Table of Mortality for ages from birth to twenty years, framed from the Registers of the Lower Orphan School, Calcutta. H. T. Prinsep 818
	Population and Mortality in Calcutta 888
	Weights, &c., of Cabul and Bokhara. Furdoonjee 892
VIII. 1839.	Isinglass in *Polynemus sele*, Buch. J. McClelland .. 203
	The cultivation of Roses, and the Manufacture of Rosewater and *Attar* at Ghazipur 411
	The Native mode of preparing the perfumed oils of Jasmine and Bela. Dr. Jackson 496
	The Manufacture of Tea, and the extent and produce of the Tea Plantations in Asam. C. A. Bruce 497
	The habits of the Coel, and the discovery of Isinglass. Major Davidson 684
	Table of Mortality among Hindu Females. Dr. Kean 704
	The Indian hemp. W. B. O'Shaughnessy 732, 838
	Soil produce, &c., of Afghanistan and the neighbouring countries. Lieut. Irwin 745, 779, 1005
	The duration of diseases in 13,019 fatal cases in Hindus. Extraordinary mortality among lying-in Women. Dr. D. Stewart 816
IX. 1840.	The soil, produce, &c. of Afghanistan and the neighbouring countries. Lieut. Irwin 33, 189

Journal.	
	Wool and Woollen manufactures of Khorásán. Capt. Hutton........ 327
Vol. IX.	Silk trade between Shikárpur and Khorásán, and Indigo in Sind. J. Postans 843
X. 1841.	Trade between Shikarpur and Candahar. J. Postans... 12
	N. W. Frontier trade with Afghanistan 251
	Productions and manufactures in the District of Hunumkunda, Nizam's Territory. A. M. Walker 386
	Manufactures of Rori in Khyrpur. G. Westmacott 393, 479
	Memorandum on Nurma Cotton. H. Piddington 713
	Memorandum on some Articles of Trade sent by Lieut. Postans from Khorásán. H. Piddington 718
	The Nurma Cotton of Bundelcund. J. G. Bruce 822
XI. 1842.	The protected Sikh States. M. P. Edgeworth 26
	Report upon the improvement of the Silk manufactured in Mysore and the Salem districts. J. Campbell 218
	On the *Nurma* cotton in Guzerat. A. Burn 29
	Nurma cotton of Gwalior. Dr. Irvine........ 311
	Building materials of Catak. Lieut. Rigby........ 839
	Manufacture of natural steel in S. India. Capt. Campbell 895
	The *Nurma* or Chanderi cotton. J. Abbott 1188
XII. 1843.	Comparative tables of the law of mortality, the expectation of life, and the values of Annuities in India and England. J. C. Hannyngton 1057
XIII. 1844.	The agriculture of Shoa. Capt. Graham 253
XVI 1847.	Explosive cotton. W. B. O'Shaughnessy 177
XVIII. 1849.	Recorded revenues of states beyond the Sutlej, about 1750 to 1800. W. Anderson 822
XIX. 1850.	Statistics of Bándá. M. P. Edgeworth 89
	Tables of Mortality according to the experience of the Bengal Civil Service, with the values of Annuities, &c. J. C. Hannyngton 250
XXI. 1852.	On Hircine, a new Resin. H. Piddington 76
XXII. 1853.	On Hircine a new Resin. H. Piddington 279
	Income, Expenditure and Food in Bengal. J. R. Bedford 387
XXVIII. 1859.	Account of Mahoba, district Humeerpur, Bundelcund. J. H. Freeling........ 369
XXXIII. 1864.	British trade with China *viâ* Burma. C. Williams ... 407
	Mode of keeping Salt water fish alive for a considerable time. R. C. Tytler 534

Journal.	
Vol. XXXVI. Pt. II. 1867.	Jungle products used as articles of food by the Inhabitants of the districts of Máubhum and Hazaribag. V. Ball 73
XXXVII. Pt. II. 1868.	Additions to the knowledge of silk. Capt. T. Mitchell 169
XXXIX. Pt. II. 1870.	Statistical data of Asiatic Russia. R. Mitchell 41
XLVIII. 1879	Ravages of Rats and Mice in the Dakhin, 1878-79. S. B. Fairbank 143
Proc. 1869	The Famine Food of Marwar. G. King 116
1881.	The nature and use of fire sticks. V. Ball 72

INDEX OF NOTICES PUBLISHED IN THE PROCEEDINGS (1832-64).

I

GEOLOGY.

N. B.—Mineralogical notices are distinguished by [M].

Vol. of Journal (Proceedings).

Vol.		Notice	Page
I		Elephant Hill, Queddah coast. Dr. Ward	157
„		Boring in Fort William. Dr. Strong	473
II		Sandstone of Sikrigali, with vegetable impressions of ferns, &c. Dr. Langstaff	45
„	[M.]	Wood-oil from the Tenasserim provinces. G. Swinton	93
„		Voysey's geological specimens. Dr. Malcolmson	94
„	[M.]	Copper ore from Nellore. Mr. Kerr	*ib.*
„		Specimens of the coprolite. Dr Wallich	151
„		Borings in Fort William. Major Benson	153
„	[M.]	Minerals from Manipur, Kachar, and Assam. Pemberton	205
„	[M.]	Peshawar Coal. Lieut. Burnes	267
„	[M.]	Coal in the Arracan district. W. Foley	368
„	[M.]	Hoshungabad Coal. Capt. J. R. Ouseley	647
„		Fossil bones, Kankar, and rocks. Lieut. T. S. Burt	648
„	[M.]	Coal from the sandowy district. H. Walters	263
„	[M.]	Himalayan coal and gold. E. J. Ravenshaw	264
III	[M]	Coal near Bhullea, 14 miles south of Házáribág. J. Wilkinson	142
„	[M]	Lead, copper, antimony, iron and arsenic from Ava. Burney	194
„		Geological specimens from S. India. Lieut. Braddock	*ib.*
„	[M.]	Limestone in Asam. Capt. F. Jenkins,	303
„		An aerolite at Hissar. R. Everest	413
IV	[M.]	Minerals from the neighbourhood of Kábul. Syed Keramat Ali	517

Vol.		Title	Page
VI		Elastic sandstone. Dr. H. Falconer	240
,,	[M]	A new site of coal in Upper Assam. Lieut. H. Bigge	243
,,	[M]	Coal beds in the Ungool and Hindon, near the Kursua and Baitarani rivers. Lieut. Kittoe	320
,,		Boring operations at Fort William. D. M. M'Cleod	498
VII	[M]	New sites of coal in Assam. Dr. McClelland	169
,,	[M]	Coal from the neighbourhood of Házáribág. Dr. A. Drummond	170
,,	[M]	Coal from a new site near the Damuda. Lieut. J. Hannyngton	285
,,	[M]	Coal and iron of Assam. Captain Hannay	368
VIII	[M]	Coal near Jabalpur. G. G. Spilsbury	530
IX		Society's Museum of Economic Geology. H. Piddington,	1148
XI		The Earthquake, 11th November, 1842. H. T. Prinsep	1201
XII		Eruption at Khyuk Phyu. Howe 255, 336,	622
,,	[M]	Newly discovered sulphur bed, at Kurachee	833
,,	[M]	Copper mine in Round Island. D. Williams	915
,,		Earthquakes in Asam. Capt. Hannay	919
,,		Volcanic island off Cheduba	1014
,,		Geology of the Cheduba group. Captain Russell	1114
XIII	[M]	Iron ores of Hirápur (Bundelkhund). J. N. Oldfield	vii
,,	[M]	Lignite of Beypoor, near Calicut. Captain Newbold	xxxiv
,,		Volcanic eruption in False Island. T. R. Davidson	xxxv
,,		Geological specimens from Western India	xxxvi
,,		Specimens of rocks and soils, Lower Assam. J. N. Martin	l
,,	[M]	Sitajeet of Behar. Lieut. Sherwill	lxxxiii
XIV		Volcano of Killauea. J. H. Low	xxii
,,		Hot Springs of Chittagong. R. Price	xxiii
,,		Eruption of a submarine volcano seen from Khyouk Pheyoo. D. Williams	xxv
,,	[M]	Graphite from Trevandrum. Major-General Cullen	lxiv
XV	[M]	Ore of Cerium from Southern India. H. Piddington	lxii
,,	[M]	Lead and Antimony from Hisato, Chota-Nagpore. H. Piddington	lxiv
,,		Volcanic eruption at Kyouk Phyoo. Major Williams	xcii
XVI		Earthquake or eruption near Mandla. D. Briggs	380
,,		Volcanic island off the coast of Coromandel, from the Annual Register, Vol. 1st, 1758	499

XVI Fossil bones in the "secondary formation" of the Himalayas. Capt. Vicary 1266

XVII [M] Coal from Jaipur, Assam. Major Hannay 167

„ [M] Ball coal from the Sitárámpur colliery. J. Homfray 703

XIX [M] Coal from Laboan. Wallage 156

„ [M] Silver ores of Deoghur. H. Piddington 565

XX [M] The coal and Pyrites from near Afzulpoor on the Adji Nullah, 16 miles north of the Ranigunge collieries. W. S. Sherwill and H. Piddington ... 365

„ [M] Coal from Gomeah, near Házáribág. Capt. Haughton 439

XXI [M] Graphite from Kurseong. Captain Sherwill 538

XXII [M] Iron ore, Hill of Karona, 10 miles from Lahore. Major Baker 207

„ Fossiliferous limestone from Girbee in the Straits of Malacca. Dr. Cantor 311

„ [M] Sulphuret of copper, Barragunda copper mine. H. Piddington 312

„ [M] Jet coal from the Chawa Nuddee, a tributary of the Tistá. H. Piddington 313

XXIII [M] Copper mines of Dholbhum. Mr. Ricketts 396

„ Minerals and fossils form about two miles north of Rajahmundry near the Village Káteru. Walter Eliott 399

„ Peats of Bengal. H. Piddington 400

„ Sub-Himalayan range, south of Darjiling, the Khasia hills and the Rajmahal hills. T. Oldham 616

XXIV [M] Iron ore from the Gangpur Raja's territory. Capt. Saxton 185

„ [M] Coal fields of Talchir on the Brahminee river. E. A. Samuells 248

„ [M] Gold dust and gold sands, Midnapore. W. D. Short 250

„ [M] Copper ore of Darjeeling. Dr. Campbell 251

„ Burdwan Paving stone. Taylor 704

„ [M] Coal from Thayet Myo, Pegu. Capt. Niblett and H. Piddington, ... 709

XXV Meteorite from Sugauli, near Bettia. Dr. McDonell 170

„ Hot Springs in the village of Kujoorah, nine miles from Jessore. Dr. Watson 224

„ Water-fall in the Bonai province of the south-west Frontier Agency. Capt. G. H. Saxton 230

XXV	Geology of Central India. T. Oldham	249
„	[M] Alum stone from the Sung-Yang hills bordering on Foh Kien. Dr. McGowan	366
XXVI	Meteoric stones near the village of Parnáli, Manduhasoli. H. S. Taylor	287
XXVII	Cretaceous rocks of India. T. Oldham and Capt. Keating	112
„	An Earthquake, Cuttack. G. H. Saxton	366
XXVIII	Meteorites in the Society's collections	259
„	Central India. J. G. Medlicott	303
„	Curia Muria, southern shore of Arabia. Dr. Buist	507
XXIX	Wazeeree country. T. Oldham and J. L. Stewart ...	314
„	Aerolite at Dhurmsálá. H. Cope	410
XXI	Earthquake at Ballygunge and Krishnanagor. Lieut. Col. H. Bruce and Mr. Masters	161
„	The Indian Coal-bearing strata. T. Oldham	177
„	Meteorite at Peprossu and Bullooach, Sarun district. T. F. Peppé	396
XXXI	Zanskar and other glaciers. Captain Montgomorie	209

II.

ZOOLOGY.

1.—VERTEBRATA.

I	*Felis* of the Midnapur jungles. Dr. J Pearson	75
II	Fossil bone from Jabalpur. Benson	151
"	Bone from a Cave in the neighbourhood of Hyderabad. Dr. Malcolmson	204
"	A fragment of a large fossil bone from Jabalpur. Dr. Spilsbury	263
III	Fossil bones from Zenang-goung and the neighbouring hills in Ava. Major Burney	365
IV	Sivalik Fossils,..............................	57
"	Fossils in the Sewalik range. F. Cautley, ...	585
"	Mammalia and birds. Dr. McCosh, ...	587
V	Fossil bones from the Cape of Good hope. J. Trotter	518
VI	Indian sucking fish. W. Ewin	321
VII	Two small fish from a hot spring at Puri. Dr. McClelland	465
X	List of mammalia and birds contained in the Museum of the East India Company	38
"	Reports for September to November, 1841. E. Blyth 836, 917,	936
XI	Reports from Jan. to June, 1842. E. Blyth 95, 129, 444,	585
"	Report for July, 1842, with appendices on the Asiatic Drongos and Quails. E. Blyth	788
"	Report for August, 1842 (mainly *Reptilia*). E. Blyth,	865
"	Reports for September to November, 1842. E. Blyth, 880, 969,	1202
XII	Report for February, 1843 (revision of reports, with observations on Asiatic *Simiadæ*). E. Blyth	166
"	Report for November, 1843 with comments on collections from Darjeeling. E. Blyth	925
XIII	Report for May, 1844 (the Mynahs &c.) E. Blyth	361
XV	Report for November, 1845, ...	xcix
XVI	Reports for February to May, 1847. Blyth 209, 385, 502,	603
"	Report for June, 1847 (*Quadrumana* in the Society's Collection.) E. Blyth, ...	725
,	Report for July, 1847 (*Sciuridæ* in the Society's collection). E. Blyth	863

XVI	Report for August, 1847 (the Hornbill group). E. Blyth	992
"	Report for December, 1847 (Pangolins). E. Blyth..	1271
XVII	Reports for Jan. to June, 1848. E. Blyth.. 82, 247,	559
XVIII	Report for January, 1849. E. Blyth	80
XIX	Reports for June to Octobor, 1850. E. Blyth 426, 490, 497,	561
"	Hippopotamus from Narsingpur. Dr. Spilsbury ..	489
XX	Reports for January to August, 1851. E. Blyth 108, 213,	443
XXI	Reports for April and May, 1852. E. Blyth .. 341,	433
XXII	Reports for May, to October. E. Blyth .. 408, 580,	589
XXIII	Report for February, 1853 (with note on Orangutans). E. Blyth	210
"	Report for October, 1854 (with note on the series of Indian and Tibetan foxes in the Society's Museum). E. Blyth	729
XXIV	Reports for February and March, 1855. E. Blyth 178,	187
"	Report for April, 1855 (Rüppell's contributions from Abyssinia and Tickell's and Frith's discoveries of Adjutant's nests). E. Blyth	252
"	Report for May, 1855. E. Blyth, ...	359
"	Report for July, 1855 (with note on the smaller squirrels in the Society's collection). E. Blyth ..	469
"	Report for October, 1855 (Theobald's contributions of reptiles and other specimens from the Tenasserim Provinces). E. Blyth	711
"	*Colossochelys Atlas.* Falconer and Cautley	173
XXV	Report for August, 1856 (the two supposed wild types of the Domestic cats of India). E. Blyth	439
"	Fossils from Kohat. From Lieut. Trotter and Lieut. Garnett	359
"	Fossils from the nummulitic rocks of Sind. H. F. Blanford, ...	581
XXVI	Reports for May to October, 1857. E. Blyth 238, 284,	314
"	Report for December, 1857 (with note on the species of *Palæornis*). E. Blyth	81
XXVII	Report for May, 1858 (describes Dr. Liebig's contributions from the Andaman islands, and fishes obtained in the neighbourhood of Calcutta). E. Blyth....	267
XXVIII	Reports from February to May, 1859 (Andaman collections, and the series of flying squirrels). E. Blyth	271

XXVIII	Report for September, 1859 (Tickell's contributions from Tenasserim). E. Blyth	411
XXIX	Report for March, 1860 (Swinhoe's contributions from Amoy and Formosa; Cape specimens from Layard; collections from the Andamans). E. Blyth	87
”	Reports for April and May, 1860. E. Blyth	447
”	Report June, 1860 (collections from China, the Philippine islands, and Cape of Good Hope). E. Blyth	490
”	Dr. Bronn's work on the laws of development of organised beings. H. F. Blanford	428
XXX	Report for July, 1861 (Stag and Staghorns). E. Blyth	185
XXXI	Report for February, 1861 (collections from British Burma, and a note on the ascertained species of *Sciuridæ* in that province). E. Blyth	331
XXXII	Report for February, 1861, continued, (collections from Burma and Port Blair). E. Blyth	451
XXXIII	Report for December, 1863 (Comments on Milne-Edward's Monograph of the *Chevrotains*. E. Blyth).	48
”	A fossil Amphibian from the Pachmari hills. Mr. Blanford, ...	336

2.—INVERTEBRATA.

I	Land and fresh water shells of the Doab, and of the Gangetic provinces. Benson	75
II	Fossil shells of the Himalayas. Captain P. Gerard,	151
”	Fossil shells from Jabalpur. Dr. Spilsbury	205
”	Fossil shells discovered by Dr. H. H. Spry	549
III	Fossil shells in Hyderabad. Dr. Malcolmson	302
VI	Fossil Conchology of the Chari range in Cutch. Captain A. Burnes	159
XIV	Fossil shells and Zoophytes of Roree, Tatta and Kurachee. T. C. Blagrave, ...	liii
XV	Shells from Danish and Swedish localities. T. Cantor	xii
XXV	Fossils from the Nummulitic rocks of Sind. H. F. Blanford	581
XXIX	Dr. Bronn's work on the laws of development of organised beings. H. F. Blanford	428
XXXIII	Himalayan fossils in the Oxford Museum. Prof. J. Phillips	577

III.

BOTANY.

XXIV Fossils from the Rev. S. Hislop and the Rev. R. Hunter 364
„ Impressions of ferns From Rajmahal. J. Pontet .. 365

IV.

ETHNOLOGY.

XXXI	Celts found in Bundlekund and chert implements from the Andamans. W. Theobald	323
XXXII	Flint implements from the Andamans. Col. J C. Haughton	306
XXXIII	Stone implements near Madras discovered by Messrs. King and Foote	67

ERRATA AND ADDENDA.

p. ii. As. Res. VII. For "Lim." read "Limrick."
„ xxii. line 1 (from top) p. 144 refers to Vol. XLI of the "Journal."
„ „ Against Vol. XLII insert "On Differential Galvanometers. L. Schwendler .... 1."
„ xxiv. In the "Proceedings" for 1871, insert "A new Photo-Callographic printing process. J. Waterhouse, 239."
„ xli. Vol. XLVII. For "Earthquakes, &c. in 1872" read "Earthquakes, &c., in 1877."
„ xliii. For "F R = Fossil *Reptilia*" read "F R = Fossil Reptilia."
„ xlviii. line 5 (from top) for "Glancopinæ" read "Glaucopinæ."
„ „ line 1 (from bottom) for "93" read "933."
„ xlix. line 2 (from top) for "Caprologus" read "Capro-lagus."
„ li. Vol. XXXI. Draw a line after "A little described species of Turtle, &c."; insert Vol. XXXII against "A memoir on the rats, &c," and draw a line after it; and omit the line after "Gibbon of Tenasserim, &c.
„ „ Vol. XXXIII. For "Notes on the *Didunculus*, &c. ...... 313" read "Notes on the *Didunculus*, &c. ...... 373."
„ lxii. line 7 (from top) for "Bryazoon" read "Bryozoon."
„ lxiv. line 1 (from top) for [M], read [A].

PROCEEDINGS

OF THE

SPECIAL CENTENARY MEETING

OF THE

ASIATIC SOCIETY OF BENGAL.

A Special Meeting to celebrate the Hundredth Anniversary of the First Meeting of the Asiatic Society of Bengal was held in the Society's Rooms, on Tuesday, the 15th January, 1884, at 7-30 P.M.

The Hon'ble H. J. Reynolds, B.A., C.S., President, in the Chair.

The following six gentlemen, duly proposed by the Council at the last Ordinary Meeting of the Society, were unanimously elected Special Centenary Honorary Members :—

1. James Prescot Joule, LL.D., F.R.S., discoverer of the laws of the evolution of heat, of the induction of magnetism by electric currents, of the mechanical equivalent of heat, and the originator of the kinetic theory of gases ; presented by the Royal Society in 1850 with its medal, and in 1870 with the Copley medal, for his experimental researches on the dynamical theory of heat.

2. Dr. Ernst Haeckel, Professor in the University of Jena, for his morphological and embryological discoveries, and his many valuable papers on the Medusæ and other forms of sea and fresh-water animals.

3. Charles Meldrum, M.A., F.R.S., F.R.A.S., Port Louis, Mauritius, on account of his valuable researches into the meteorology of the Indian Ocean.

4. A. H. Sayce, Deputy Professor of Comparative Philology in the University of Oxford, on account of his distinguished services to Comparative Philology generally, and especially to the knowledge of the Assyrian, Accadian, and Hittite languages.

5. E. Senart, Member of the Institute of France, on account of his distinguished services to Páli Scholarship, especially in the decipherment of the ancient inscriptions of Asoka, and in editing Páli and Gáthá texts.

6. Monier Williams, Boden Professor of Sanskrit in the University of Oxford and founder of the Indian Institute in the same University, on account of his distinguished services to the interests, literary and social, of India, and his valuable grammatical and lexicographic contributions to Sanskrit Philology.

The Review of the Society's History and Researches during the century of its existence, drawn up by the Secretaries and Dr. Rájendralála Mitra, was laid upon the table. A vote of thanks to the Compilers of the Review was unanimously passed.*

The following addresses from learned Societies, congratulating the Society on the celebration of its Centenary, were read :—

C F

I.

Royal Prussian Academy of Sciences.

An die Asiatische Gesellschaft von Bengalen zum XV. Januar MDCCCLXXXIV.

Berlin, *6th December*, 1883.

Geehrte Herren!

Am 15ten Januar 1784 gegründet, feiert Ihre Gesellschaft im Beginn des nächsten Jahres ihr 100jähriges Bestehen.

Als die älteste aller zur Zeit vorhandenen morgenländischen Gesellschaften, steht sie an der Spitze jener glorreichen Entwickelung der orientalischen Studien, welche wir der Kenntniss des Sanskrit verdanken.

Wenn die europäische Gesittung unter dem Schutze der britischen Herrschaft im Laufe dieses Jahrhunderts reichen Segen über Indien gebracht hat, so hat in umgekehrter Richtung während dieses Zeitraumes auch Indien seinerseits durch seine Sprache und Literatur tiefeingreifende Wirkungen auf Europa ausgeübt. Es möchte wenige Gebiete der historischen und der sprachlichen Wissenschaft geben, welche von dem Einfluss der Sanskritstudien gänzlich unberührt geblieben wären. Das Sanskrit hat uns eine indogermanische Urzeit erschlossen, — eine vergleichende Sprachwissenschaft erstehen lassen, — hat das alte Persien uns aufgethan,

---

* See Proceedings for February.

und die geistigen Denkmäler Zarathustra's sowohl wie die steinernen der Achaemeniden eröffnet, — hat endlich von da aus dann weiter auch die alten Culturländer, Babylon und Assyrien, aus dem Todesschlaf ihrer Keilschriften wiedererweckt und zum Reden gebracht.

Von diesen in ihrer Bedeutung annoch unabsehbaren Folgen der Erschliessung des Sanskrit konnten allerdings die Männer, welche als die Pioniere dieser Studien dastehen, konnten Ihre Jones, Wilkins, Colebrooke, Wilson nur erst einen Theil bereits ahnen. Ihr Streben war Indien speciell zugewendet. Aber ihre Arbeiten haben dennoch weithin befruchtend und schöpferisch gewirkt.

Eine grosse Vergangenheit liegt hinter Ihnen. — Dass aber auch Sie, Ihrer Väter werth, die Erforschung Indiens, seiner Sprache und Literatur, als ein kostbares Erbe betrachten, das Sie immer aufs Neue zu "erwerben" suchen, "um es würdig zu besitzen," dafür legt, neben Ihrem auch den Naturwissenschaften reiche Ausbeute bietenden Journal, die Bibliotheca Indica ein vollgültiges Zeugniss ab, jene grossartige Text-Publication, welche, seit nunmehr 35 Jahren unter Ihrer Aegide erscheinend, die wichtigsten literarischen Erzeugnisse des indischen Geistes der Wissenschaft allgemein zugänglich zu machen bestimmt ist.

Die Königlich Preussische Akademie der Wissenschaften hat in Wilhelm von Humboldt und in Franz Bopp zwei Männer zu ihren Mitgliedern gezählt, welche die hohe Bedeutung des Sanskrit in ihrem vollen Werthe erkannten und auch bei uns zu allgemeiner Anerkennung zu bringen nach Kräften bemüht waren. Bopp besonders kann, wie er als der Begründer der vergleichenden Sprachforschung dasteht, so auch geradezu als der Vater der Sanskritstudien in Deutschland betrachtet werden, die seitdem daselbst eine feste Stätte gefunden haben.

Im Hinblick auf diese ihre beiden hervorragenden Mitglieder erkennt es daher die Königliche Akademie als eine besondere Ehrenpflicht, Ihnen geehrte Herren, zu dem bevorstehenden Ehrentage Ihrer Gesellschaft den Tribut dankbarer Anerkennung und Huldigung darzubringen. Möge der Geist, in dem sie begründet wurde, auch in dem neuen Saeculum in ihr fortdauernd in voller Wirksamkeit bleiben!

Die Königlich Preussische Akademie der Wissenschaften.

(Sd.)	E. Curtius.	(Sd.)	Websky.
„	E. du Bois-Reymond.	„	Zeller.
„	Th. Mommsen.	„	Wattenbach.
„	A. Auwers.	„	Landolt.
„	Diels.	„	Eichler.

(Sd.)	Schrader.	(Sd.)	v. Helmholtz.
„	Weber.	„	Siemens.
„	F. Kirchhoff.	„	Tobler.
„	Ewald.	„	A. Kirchhoff.
„	Schwendener.	„	Rud. Virchow.
„	Beyrich.	„	Lepsius.
„	A. W. Hofmann.	„	Kiepert.
„	Roth.	„	G. Waitz.
„	Kronecker.	„	Sybel.
„	Herm. Munk.	„	Dillmann.
„	Tringsheim.		

II.

From the German Oriental Society, Halle.

Der Asiatischen Gesellschaft von Bengalen, welche während der hundert Jahre ihres Bestehens die ihr von ihrem grossen Begründer Sir William Jones gestellte Aufgabe, die Geschichte, die Künste und Wissenschaften, und die Literatur Asiens zu erforschen, glänzend erfüllt und dadurch den Dank aller orientalischen Philologen sich verdient hat, der ältesten Asiatischen Gesellschaft widmet die aufrichtigsten Glückwünsche zu ihrem Jubiläum am XV. Januar MDCCCLXXXIV die Deutsche Morgenländische Gesellschaft.

Der geschäftsführende Vorstand:

(Sd.)	Dr. Chr. Bartholomae.	(Sd.)	Dr Julius Wellhausen.
„	Dr. Ludolf Krehl in Leipzig.	„	Dr. Ernst Windisch in Leipzig.
			Halle A. S.

III.

Royal Asiatic Society,

22, Albemarle Street, London, W.,

December 20, 1883.

Sir,

The Council of the Royal Asiatic Society having heard that their Parent Society, the Asiatic Society of Bengal, are about to celebrate, on the 15th January, 1884, the Centenary of their Foundation, desire to offer to the Council and Members of the Society their heartiest congratulations on this auspicious occasion.

I have the honour to be,

Sir,

Yours very faithfully,

(Signed) H. B. E. Frere, *President, R. A. S.*
W. S. W. Vaux, *Secretary, R. A. S.*

To the Secretary of the Bengal Asiatic Society.

IV.

Royal Institute for the Philology, Geography,
and Ethnology of Netherlands India.

The Hague (Holland),
18*th December*, 1883.

Gentlemen,

On the 15th of January, 1884, the Asiatic Society of Bengal will have to commemorate a glorious past. The century so splendidly inaugurated by the researches of Sir William Jones and Henry Thomas Colebrooke, and so remarkable by the discoveries and labours of John Prinsep, Horace Hayman Wilson, Brian Haughton Hodgson and so many other illustrious names, has been fruitful in results more striking and marvellous than the fairy tales of the East. By steadily promoting and encouraging scientific research in every direction, your Society has earned the thanks of scholars in general, and especially of those who have devoted themselves to Oriental studies.

As representatives of a Society which for many years has stood in friendly relations with yours, we beg to offer our sincere congratulations for the memorable day of 15th January. We rejoice at the flourishing condition and unabated vigour of the centenarian, and we hope that the future may be as bright and glorious as the past.

(Signed) H. Kern,
President of the Royal Institute for the Philology, Geography, and Ethnology of Netherlands India.
P. C. L. Wijnmalen,
Secretary.

V.*

DIRECTION DES KÖNIGL. ZOOLOGISCHEN UND DES ANTHROPOLOGISCH-ETHNOGRAPHISCHEN MUSEUMS ZU DRESDEN.

The 20th December, 1883.

To

THE ASIATIC SOCIETY OF BENGAL,

CALCUTTA.

The Society's Centenary induces me to give expression to the most cordial and sincere wishes from the part of the Royal Museum of Dresden and to the hope that the Society may flourish in all future as hitherto, and may increase in influence and importance to science.

The Director of the Royal Zoological, Anthropological and Ethnographical Museum,

(Signed) A. B. MEYER, M. D.

The occasion was further celebrated by a dinner immediately after the meeting, at which the following were present:—

GUESTS.

H. E. the Marquess of Ripon, K.G., P.C., G.M.S.I., G.M.I.E, Viceroy and Governor-General of India.

H. W. Primrose, Esq., Private Secretary to H. E. the Viceroy.

Capt. E. H. Clough-Taylor, Aide-de-Camp to H. E. the Viceroy.

His Grace Archbishop Goethals.

The Hon'ble Lieut.-General T. F. Wilson, C.B., C.I.E.

The Hon'ble Sir Steuart Bayley, K.C.S.I., C.I.E.

The Hon'ble C. P. Ilbert, C.I.E.

The Hon'ble W. W. Hunter, LL.D., C.I.E.

Prof. Monier Williams, C.I.E., D.C.L.

MEMBERS.

The Hon'ble H. J. Reynolds, B.A., C.S., *President, in the Chair.*

The Hon'ble J. Gibbs, C.S.I., C.I.E., F.R.G.S., M.R.A.S., *Vice-President.* H. B. Medlicott, Esq., M.A., F.R.S., F.G.S., Dr. D. Waldie, F.C.S., J. Westland, Esq., C.S., Nawab Abdul Latif Khan Bahadur, C.I.E., Major J. Waterhouse,

---

* This address was received subsequently to the meeting, and was read at the Ordinary Monthly Meeting of the Society in February.

B.S.C., Alex. Pedler, Esq., F.C.S., A. W. Croft, Esq., M.A., *Members of Council.* Dr. A. F. R. Hoernle, *Philological Secretary.* L. de Nicéville, Esq., *Offg. Natural History Secretary.* F. W. Peterson, Esq., F.C.S., *Honorary Treasurer.* Dr. H. W. M'Cann, *General Secretary.* Sayyid Amir Ali, M.A., Barrister-at-Law; Dr. J. Anderson, F.R.S., F.L.S.; E. F. T. Atkinson, Esq., B.A., C.S.; Nawab Sayyid Ashgar Ali Diler Jang, Khan Bahadur, C.S.I.; Dr. R. A. Barker; Rev. K. M. Bannerjee, LL.D.; Dr. A. Barclay; R. R. Bayne, Esq., M.R.I.B.A.; the Hon'ble H. Beverley, M.A., C.S.; J. F. Browne, Esq., C.S., M.R.A.S.; Surgeon-Major H. Cayley; Dr. Aghorenath Chatterjee; J. Cockburn, Esq.; J. C. Douglas, Esq.; J. Eliot, Esq., M.A.; F. Fedden, Esq.; Prince Mahomed Firukh Shah; Monmohun Ghose, Esq.; Raja Satyananda Ghoshal; G. A. Grierson, Esq., B.A., C.S.; Beharilal Gupta, Esq., C.S.; J. Hart, Esq.; Surgeon-Major C. J. J. Jackson; Moulvie Kabiruddin Ahmed, Khan Bahadur; P. Kennedy, Esq., M.A.; Dr. G. King, F.L.S.; Rev. Father Lafont, C.I.E.; Major-General G. B. Mainwaring, S.C.; Babu Jadulal Mullick; the Hon'ble A. B. Miller; J. R. Napier, Esq.; A. M. Nash, Esq, M.A.; J. C. Parker, Esq.; T. F. Peppé, Esq.; Col. W. F. Prideaux, B.S.C.; Babu Bipin Chunder Rai, B.L.; Dr. W. Schlich; Dr. Mohendralal Sirkar; Lieut.-Col. Sir O. B. St. John, R.E., C.S.I.; J. Schaumburg, Esq.; Lieut.-Col. A. C. Toker, B.S.C.; R. Turnbull, Esq.; Prince Jahan Qadr Muhammad Wahid Ali Bahadur; Dr. G. Watt; W. T. Webb, Esq., M.A.

After dinner, the following toasts were proposed and speeches delivered:—

The PRESIDENT said:—The first toast on our list, as the first in our hearts, is one which needs no words of recommendation from me. Wherever her subjects, whether English or native, are gathered together, the health of the Queen-Empress is received with an acclamation in which we combine the tribute due to every excellence which can adorn womanhood, with the homage which we gladly pay to the virtues of the Sovereign. But it seems to me that the occasion on which we are assembled to-night is one to which this toast is specially appropriate. The founder of our Society declared that its enquiries should extend, within the limits of Asia, to whatever is performed by man, or produced by nature. Nothing within those limits is more wonderful or stupendous than the mighty Empire which has been built up by the succession of statesmen and warriors whom England has sent forth to establish in India the blessing of peace, the supremacy of law, and the development of material wealth. The pole-star of that Empire is the gracious Lady whom we trust Providence may long preserve to rule over us, and whose name we welcome with no mere conventional loyalty of the lips, but with the devotion of our hearts and the service of our lives. The toast I give you is the health of the Queen-Empress.

The President then proposed the next toast as follows:—Gentlemen, the next toast I have to propose is the health of Her Majesty's representative in this land, the Viceroy and Governor-General. In the name of the Society, I beg to thank His Excellency for honouring our Centenary celebration with his presence to-night. The Asiatic Society has owed much to the encouragement and fostering care of the rulers of India. Though we are proud to claim Sir William Jones as our founder, it would ill-become us to forget that his efforts for the establishment of our Society were supported, and eventually rendered successful, by the assistance which he received from the first Governor-General of India. Since the days of Warren Hastings, successive Governors-General have extended to the Society the same favour as he showed to it. Some of them, among whom I may name Sir John Shore and the Marquis of Hastings, have filled the presidential chair, and all of them have accepted the office of patron of the Society. This patronage of the Society by the head of the Governm-nt has been, I believe, creditable and beneficial to both the parties concerned in it; and in our present Patron we are glad to welcome a nobleman who has not only won distinction as a statesman and a ruler, but who is honourably known by the interest he has taken in education, both in England and in this country.

His Excellency the Viceroy said:—Mr. President and Gentlemen, I thank you sincerely for the toast which you have just drunk. I thank you, Mr. President, for the terms in which you have proposed, and you, gentlemen, for the reception which you have accorded to it. I can assure you that it is a great pleasure to me to be present here this evening, and thus to mark the strong interest which I feel in the prosperity of this Society. The occasion which has brought us together to-night is one which must command the sympathy of all who care for Oriental literature and learning; for we are assembled here to-day to celebrate the Centenary of a Society which has for its special object the promotion of the study of Asiatic languages, literature, history, and science. England may be called the home of societies. They spring up there of every kind and for every conceivable purpose. Some of them are extremely ephemeral, and are born to-day to die to-morrow, and but few of them can count a hundred years of life. The fact, therefore, that the Asiatic Society of Bengal has now completed a full hundred years of existence is a proof of the importance of the objects for which it has been established, and of the earnestness and zeal with which its members have laboured to promote those ends. It seems to me that Englishmen may well be proud when they recollect that this Society was first established in the year 1784, and when they call to mind how soon it was after the real commencement of our political rule in this country that we began to take a deep interest in the language, literature, and history of India. Within less than thirty years of the battle of Plassey, Englishmen were found looking forward with most prophetic eyes to the future which lay before them, and they set themselves to work to master the hidden treasures of Eastern learning, and thus to lay a solid foundation for our power in an intelligent knowledge of the people of the country, with whom, in so marvellous a manner, they had just been brought into close and intimate relations. To me, as a public man, it is peculiarly interesting to see that the founders and the first members of this Society—most of them administrators, or Judges, or men with official duties,—approached the problem of Government from one of its most important sides, and sought to obtain a real and substantial comprehension of the feelings and genius of the people among whom their lot was to be cast. It is true that this was not their only object. It may not even have been consciously a foremost object with them at all, but it was embodied in their undertaking; and by its promotion they conferred great benefits upon this country. From that time, up to the present hour, this Society has steadily pursued its work; by its library and museum, by the publication of original papers and of many most valuable works in Sanskrit, Arabic, Persian, and other languages, and by providing a centre of intercourse for Oriental scholars and of information for Oriental students, it has laboured to promote the end which its founders had in view. Time will not permit to detain you by entering upon any biographical sketches of the many eminent men who have been connected with this institution, or I might recall to you the lives and the services to literature and science, both in England and in India, of Sir William Jones, of Sir John Shore, of Colebrooke, of Wilkins, of H. H. Wilson, of James Prinsep and of the other remarkable men who have adorned the Asiatic Society of Bengal,—men who were all distinguished in their respective ways, zealous members of this Society, of varied learning and constant study, and who won for themselves the admiration not only of their own countrymen, but of learned men in all parts of the world. Guided by these men, and by such as these, this Society has maintained its position down to the present time, and even now, in these days, with that widened attention to

Eastern learning which has of late been given to it by learned men of all countries, this Society has received no check, and continues to preserve the respect of all who are acquainted with its labours. And now, gentlemen, I am about, I fear, to commit what may be considered an unpardonable sin in an after-dinner speaker, but I trust to you to forgive me if I yield to the strong temptation which prompts me to read to you an extract from the words of one whose memory must be foremost in our recollections to-night. There is no name that could come before us on this occasion with the same force of reality as that of Sir William Jones. I was much struck last year in reading the interesting lectures of Professor Max Müller, which were published under the title of "India and what she has to teach us," by an account which I found there, given by Sir William Jones himself, of the feelings with which he first landed in this country. I will read you the words, because they are far more eloquent and heart-stirring than any that I could myself command, and because it is well that we should to-night have brought before us the actual thoughts of him whose memory we are met to honour, for, though we are primarily assembled here to celebrate the Centenary of the Society which he has founded, we are here also to mark our veneration of his character and our gratitude for his services. This is what he said of himself when he approached the shores of India when he first came out to this country:—" When I was at sea last August" (that is in August 1783) "on my voyage to this country (India), which I had long and ardently desired to visit, I found one evening, on inspecting the observations of the day, that *India* lay before us, *Persia* on our left, whilst a breeze from *Arabia* blew nearly on our stern. A situation so pleasing in itself, and to me so new, could not fail to awaken a train of reflections in a mind which had early been accustomed to contemplate with delight the eventful histories and agreeable fictions of this Eastern World. It gave me inexpressible pleasure to find myself in the midst of so noble an amphitheatre, almost encircled by the vast regions of Asia, which has ever been esteemed the nurse of sciences, the inventress of delightful and useful arts, the scene of glorious actions, fertile in the productions of human genius, and infinitely diversified in the forms of religion and government, in the laws, manners, customs, and languages, as well as in the features and complexions of men. I could not help remarking how important and extensive a field was yet unexplored, and how many solid advantages unimproved." It seems to me, gentlemen, that in these glowing words we have the germ of this Society; for within a few months after they had sprung up in the mind of your distinguished founder, they found their natural realization in the establishment of this institution. During the whole time which has since elapsed, the Asiatic Society of Bengal has pursued its way instinct with the same feelings, and bent upon the same aims as those which rose up before Sir William Jones as he approached the shores of India. It is in the earnest hope that, for long years yet to come, it will continue to labour earnestly and successfully for these most valuable ends, that I now ask you to join with me in drinking to its prosperity, and I couple with the toast the name of one so well qualified by his high character and varied attainments to fill the honourable office of President, as my friend Mr. Reynolds.

The PRESIDENT replied as follows:—In rising to respond, on behalf of the Asiatic Society of Bengal, to the toast which your Lordship has so kindly proposed, I cannot but feel that the duty imposed on me by the office I hold would have been more worthily discharged by a President better qualified than myself to represent a Society which was founded for the advancement of a learning to which I can lay no claim, and for the prosecution of researches to which I am unable to contribute. The fitting mouthpiece of the Asiatic Society, on an occasion like the present, would have been a Colebrooke, a Wilson, or a Prinsep. When I look round this room, and see the effigies, in marble or on canvas, of the distinguished men who have preceded me in the occupation of this presidential chair, my feelings are something like those which the poet ascribes to the Greek minstrel, when he lamented the decay of his country, and complained that the national lyre, so long divine, had degenerated into unworthy hands. My only apology must be that, in accepting the post with which the Society thought fit to honour me, I was showing, in the only way possible to me, my loyalty to the Society's cause, and my desire to promote what it considered to be its interest. "They also serve who only stand and wait." I would ask those who hear me to-night to forget, if they can, the humble individual who addresses them, and to turn their thoughts to the illustrious Society on behalf of which I speak.

The Asiatic Society of Bengal enters to-night upon the second century of its career, its inaugural meeting having been held on the 15th January, 1784. It was founded in the last year of the rule of Warren Hastings, a time which historians are pleased to describe as a period of comparative tranquillity. The tranquillity may have been comparative, but it was assuredly neither positive nor superlative. In the south we were at war, or had very lately been at war, with Tippoo: in Benares, Cheyt Singh had just before been deposed: in the west, the Mahratta power was growing into a formidable rival. The rejection of

Fox's India Bill, only a few weeks previously, had hurled the Coalition Ministry from power. It was then that thirty gentlemen, conspicuous among whom were Sir William Jones, Mr. Justice Hyde, Sir John Shore, John Harington, Sir G. Barlow, Sir Robert Chambers, Jonathan Duncan, and Sir Charles Wilkins, formed themselves into a Society for the purpose of enquiring into the civil and natural history, the antiquities, arts, sciences, and literature of Asia. They obtained the patronage of the Government, and Warren Hastings was invited to become their President. He declined the honour in favour of Sir William Jones, who filled the chair for ten years till his death in 1794. Then were laid the foundations of that magnificent series of essays and dissertations which are the true glory of our Society, and which, embodied first in the twenty volumes of the Asiatic Researches, and afterwards in the Society's Journal, have thrown a flood of light on the literature, antiquities, and natural history of the East. The torch of knowledge was handed on from one distinguished Orientalist to another. *Uno avulso non deficit alter Aureus.* After Sir William Jones came Colebrooke, Carey, Harington, Horace Hayman Wilson, Bryan Hodgson, James and Henry Prinsep, Henry Torrens, and many others whom time would fail me to enumerate—a galaxy of illustrious names, whose labours more than realized the highest expectations which the founder of the Society had formed. The dignitaries of the English Church showed their sympathy with an institution which is identified with the great continent from which all the religions of the world have sprung. I believe all the Bishops of Calcutta have been members of the Society : Bishop Middleton was our Vice-President in 1816, Reginald Heber in 1824, Daniel Wilson in 1850. The military profession has given us many of our most distinguished members, such as Francis Wilford, Sir Proby Cautley, and Sir Henry Durand ; while to the profession of the law we owe our very existence. The service to which I have the honour to belong has taken its full share in the labours and the triumphs of the Society.

It is worthy of notice that, for many years after the establishment of the Society, no natives were enrolled in its ranks. This was assuredly from no narrow or exclusive spirit on the part of its Founder. I find among the rules laid down by Sir William Jones one which declares that "no qualification shall be necessary for membership beyond a love of knowledge and zeal for the promotion of it." But, from whatever cause it may have happened, no natives seem to have joined the Society for nearly fifty years after its foundation. It is said that some natives were proposed for election in 1818, but the list of 1832 is the earliest in which

I have observed the entry of natives, and in that list I find the honoured name of Dwarka Nath Tagore. It is probably something more than a coincidence, that, in the year in which native members first joined the Asiatic Society, the patron of the Society was Lord William Bentinck.

Into the history of the Society, during the hundred years of its existence, I need not here enter in detail. A Centenary Review has been drawn up for this occasion by some of the Society's officers, and the first part of that Review, for which we are indebted to the careful research and practised pen of Dr. Rájendralála Mitra, gives an excellent summary of the labours, the vicissitudes, and the progress of the Society. We have passed through some periods of trouble and difficulty. On one occasion our whole collection of coins was stolen, and we have twice been sufferers by the failure of our bankers. But, on the whole, the record of the century is a record of development and success. The house in which we are assembled to-night was built for us in 1808; the Museum was formed in 1814. Some of the finest manuscripts in our library were once the property of Tippoo Sultan, and were received in 1808 from the Seringapatam Prize Committee: others were made over to the Society on the abolition of the old College of Fort William. Among the claims which the Society has on the gratitude of the public, may be mentioned its supervision of the publication of the series of Oriental works issued under the title of the Bibliotheca Indica; its labours for the conservation of Sanskrit manuscripts; and last, but assuredly not least, the fact that it was largely due to the Society's exertions that the Government consented to establish the Indian Museum, to which the Society's collections in the departments of archæology, natural history, and geology were removed a few years ago.

The Society has now lived and laboured for a hundred years, and I have sometimes heard it said that if it has not left its first love, it has in some measure ceased to do its first works. I have known critics point to the illustrious names which adorned its earlier annals, and ask where their successors are to be found at the present day. If there is any ground for this complaint—and when I look at the learning and genius displayed in the volumes of the Asiatic Researches, I am sometimes tempted to doubt whether these critics have not reason on their side—I believe the causes are not very far to seek. It must be remembered in the first place that, when our Society was founded, the treasures of Indian literature and science were almost unknown to European students. The early members of the Asiatic Society were sustained and stimulated by the excitement of discovery, and by the interest which attaches to the exploration of new and untrodden fields of knowledge. In the second place, the pressure of business, both official and mercantile, is far heavier now than it was then. When Horace Hayman Wilson was leaving India, just half a century ago, the Society presented him with a valedictory address, in his reply to which he said that his labours on behalf of the Society had made many hours of leisure in this country glide happily away. The gliding away, whether happily or otherwise, of many hours of leisure, is a sensation to which we in these days are entire strangers, and if Wilson had left India in 1883 instead of in 1833, he would hardly have found time to elaborate the learned contributions with which he enriched the records of the Society. But another reason remains, which is, perhaps, the strongest of all. In the early part of this century, the author of a paper on any Oriental subject generally gave his thoughts to the world through the medium of the Asiatic Society of Bengal. The Society was not only the recognized channel of such communications, but hardly any other channel existed. At present there are numerous societies, numerous magazines and periodicals, through which an audience can be addressed on Oriental questions. If the stream of knowledge may seem to be less deep, it is only because it is more widely diffused; if the treasure appears to be less splendid and massive, it is because it is distributed among a larger number. We take a pardonable pride in the recollection that our Society is the parent institution, from which other Asiatic Societies, both in India and elsewhere, have sprung. The Royal Asiatic Society of London came into existence in 1823, and its first Director was that very Henry Colebrooke who had been President of our Society for nine years, from 1806 to 1815. The Bombay Society was established in 1827, that of Ceylon in 1845. The effect of our Society's labours has been felt far beyond the limits of the British Empire and of the English tongue. We were the pioneers in that field of research in which the scholars of France and Germany have since won such splendid triumphs; and across the Atlantic the stimulus of our investigations has quickened into sympathetic activity the intelligence and industry of the Oriental Societies of the United States.

If, therefore, there were any grounds for saying that the Asiatic Society of the present day is less useful and less energetic than of yore, these considerations would, I think, be sufficient to account for the change. But I am not willing to admit that such an imputation is in any way deserved. On this point I might refer to the addresses which we have received, on the occasion of this Centenary celebration, from the Asiatic

Societies of London, the Hague, Berlin, and Halle. The wording of these addresses will show that, in the opinion of those institutions, the Bengal Society has not ceased to maintain the reputation it formerly enjoyed. It would be presumptuous in me to attempt to balance claims which I can so imperfectly appreciate, and it would not be altogether seemly that I should speak of the merits and achievements of living members of the Society. But those whom I address will know to whom I refer when I say that our present roll of members includes the names of men whose researches in literature, in archæology, in natural history, and in physical science, will bear comparison with those of the giants of a former day. When the next anniversary of this kind comes round, and the Society completes its second century, there are members of the Society now living to whom the men of that age will refer with something of the veneration with which we now pronounce the names of Henry Colebrooke and Horace Hayman Wilson.

I will not venture to look forward to a still more distant future. I will not presume to say that when that artistic personage, the New Zealand traveller, after completing his sketch of the ruins of St. Paul's, takes his ticket, by balloon or submarine railway, for India, he will find the Asiatic Society of Bengal still flourishing in undiminished vigour and activity. But I believe that the Society has still before it a long career of usefulness, and that, even if it could be extinguished to-morrow, it would leave behind it much which the world would not willingly let die. It would leave behind it something more precious than its collection of coins and manuscripts, or even than the records in which its history is enshrined. It would leave an example and a remembrance of patient research and self-denying labour, undertaken not from any motive of greed or any desire of glory, but with the single aim of advancing the interests of science, and extending the boundaries of human knowledge. And now, before I sit down, I will ask all present to join me in a toast which ought not to be omitted on such an occasion as this. I give you "The Honoured Memory of our Founder, Sir William Jones."

The Hon'ble Mr. Gibbs proposed the last toast as follows:—Mr. President, Your Excellency, and Gentlemen,—The next toast has been entrusted to my charge. It is one which it is always a pleasure to the hosts to propose and the company to honour, being that of "Our Guests." In the Society which celebrates its hundredth birthday this evening, it has been the practice hitherto to treat its guests with "the feast of reason and the flow of soul," but for its indulging in the more substantial feast of this evening, though we have necessarily no precedent, we feel we need none, as the exceptional circumstances of the occasion justify an exceptional entertainment.

When the Society, therefore, determined that its members should meet and celebrate this auspicious event in the truly English manner we have done, it could not forget that a Society which was formed to enquire, among other subjects, into the literature of Asia, and which by its publications has enabled the Oriental scholars of Europe to acquire the knowledge which was buried in many valuable MSS., was bound to remember the admonitions to be found therein as regards guests and their duty to them. In the well-known Sanscrit law-book, the *Vishnu Smriti,* it is thus laid down.—Before such a learned assembly as the present, it might be expected that I should give the extract in the original, but, being under the immediate eye of my excellent friend and former preceptor in Sanscrit, I prefer to follow the example lately set by a high official at Oxford and, " to prevent mistakes," give it in English.—

" By honouring guests a householder obtains the highest reward. Let him assiduously honour guests who arrive in the evening. Let him not suffer guests to stay at his house unfed."

With this appeal to our duty sweetened by the promise of reward, we invited our guests, and we trust the concluding portion of the programme has been carried out to their satisfaction. Among those who have honoured us with their presence this evening, we have representatives of the clerical, military, civil, legal, literary, and educational professions. In the Archbishop of Western Bengal we have a distinguished representative of a religious society, which has laid the people of this city, as well as that of Bombay and other towns, under a deep debt of gratitude for the excellent educational institutions it has established; whose schools and colleges are patterns to all others both in management and results. In my honourable colleague, General Wilson, the army is well represented by one who, having filled with credit the most important offices of his rank, is now the adviser of His Excellency in Council in all matters relating to that army the welfare of which he has warmly at heart. The Civil Service is ably represented by my honourable colleague, Sir Steuart Bayley, whose large administrative experience, added to his intimate knowledge of Bengal, its tenures and its people, make him a most valuable adviser. My learned friend and honourable colleague, Mr. Ilbert, by his highly distinguished academical career, and his great knowledge of the science and practice of law, fitly represents the legal profession; while literature has the good fortune to find itself represented by Dr. Hunter, whose facile pen has done so much to remove the ignorance which prevailed at home with regard to India, its races, and its creeds. There is yet one more of our guests whose name I have been asked to couple more particularly with this toast—Professor Monier Williams—the Boden Professor of Sanscrit, a gentleman well known as an able Oriental scholar, and kindly remembered as one of our professors by those who, like myself, were students at the old East Indian College at Haileybury.

This Society has done honour to itself this evening by electing him one of the Centenary Honorary Members, a special rank we have introduced to mark this day's auspicious event; but I venture to think that, however widely he may be remembered for his learning, he will, as far as India is concerned, be remembered by its people with respect and gratitude, as the Founder and Director of the Indian Institute which he has established at Oxford for the reception of native youths, wherein they may reside free from the temptations of a large city like London, and acquire, under due academical discipline, the benefits of an English University education. With these observations, Mr. President, Your Excellency, and Gentlemen, I call upon you to drink the health of Our Guests, coupling with it the name of Professor Monier Williams.

Professor Monier Williams said:—I feel a great difficulty in replying to this toast, in the capacity of a guest, because I am profoundly conscious that there are other more worthy representatives of the visitors here to-night; but if you will allow me to thank you in the capacity of a debtor, then no person can possibly be more indebted to this Society than I am. The rôle I have played in the free republic of Oriental letters has—to speak honestly—been a humble one, notwithstanding the kind expressions of my old friend, the Hon'ble Mr. Gibbs, and notwithstanding the great distinction you have this evening conferred upon me by electing me an Honorary Member of your Society. The student of Sanscrit—when I began its study—had to traverse, so to speak, a difficult country abounding in steep mountains, deep ravines, and dense jungles. All I can claim to have done is to have formed one of a band of Oriental Macadams. I have done something towards smoothing the road and facilitating the progress of plodding students who might otherwise have turned back in despair. It is in my performance of this task that you have made me your insolvent debtor. And I am not the only person who is glad of an opportunity, such as this Centenary celebration affords, of acknowledging his obligations to you. At the recent Oriental Congress held at Leyden, a strong opinion was expressed by Dr. Weber and others, that Oriental scholars generally should unite in a common effort to commemorate the Centenary of your

Society by an international tribute of honour. I wish, indeed, that some representative of every branch of Eastern lore, from every University in Europe, were present here to-night, so that no time might be lost in taking action in this matter. Speaking as Boden Professor of Sanscrit at Oxford, and as a student of Sanscrit for more than forty years, I fearlessly maintain that no Society has done so much for Sanscrit literature during that period as the Asiatic Society of Bengal.

In the Vaisvadeva ceremony performed every day by orthodox Hindus there is a prayer 'may I live for a hundred years!' This seems to indicate that a hundred years is the natural term of life in India, but I am glad to see that your Society, though commencing its second century of existence, shows as yet no signs of decrepitude. On the contrary, its vitality appears to be more vigorous than ever.

Bear with me for a few minutes while I refer to the labours of four of your most illustrious members—Sir William Jones, your founder, Sir Charles Wilkins, Henry Thomas Colebrooke, and Horace Hayman Wilson. In my address at the Berlin Congress of Orientalists, three years ago, I ventured to remind German scholars of their obligation to these four great men. I said—"Permit me, as an Englishman, to speak with pride of those great pioneers of Sanscrit learning, Sir William Jones, Wilkins, Colebrooke, and Wilson. These are the men, without whose labours you German scholars would never have advanced with such rapid strides on the path of Sanscrit learning." I need scarcely add that this remark was received with applause by all present. Bear with me yet a little while longer, whilst I trouble you with a few of my personal reminiscences in connection with these four great men. Veteran as I am, I am not quite old enough to have had any personal dealings with your founder, Sir William Jones; but it may not be known to all here that he has two monuments at Oxford, one in the ante-chapel of University College, and the other at St. Mary's University Church. Your founder and I were therefore related as sa-tírthyáh, and my Oriental ambition was early stimulated by reading his epitaph, feebly expressed though it was, on my way in and out of chapel. If Sir William Jones had done nothing else but translate the laws of Manu and invent a system of transliteration which forms the basis of that now adopted by all scholars, including my friend Dr. Hunter himself, he would have immortalised his name; but he was what in Sanscrit we call náná-sástra-visáradah; and it may truly be said of him that *nihil tetigit quod non ornavit.* And now a word on Sir Charles Wilkins. I confess my early recollections of him were not quite so pleasant. He was the Socrates of Sanscrit grammar, who brought down that god-given grammar from the clouds to dwell among plain Englishmen. In my early days his grammar was the only one procurable. It cost three guineas, and like the work of all pioneers, was very roughly done and swarmed with mistakes. To him also belongs the honour of having written a Sanscrit inscription on the gold medal awarded to all who were highly distinguished in Sanscrit at Haileybury, which few could translate—and to this day I am not quite certain how it ought to be translated. It ran thus:—Átma-buddhi-prasáda-jam yat sukham tat sáttvikam; "the happiness resulting from the cultivation" (such, at least, I suppose, is the meaning) "of one's own intellect is the only true happiness." Of the great Colebrooke, I will only say that, in common with other scholars, I constantly do pújá to him as to an incarnation of the spirit of accuracy. He is the only English grammarian worthy of a niche in the same temple with the great Indian grammarian Pánini, and the only English scholar to whom Patanjali's description of Pánini—Pramánabhútácárya—is justly applicable. Truly, India is a land of contradictions and inconsistencies. It has produced an immense series of accurate grammarians and accurate writers, and has fostered the mathematical precision of a Colebrooke, yet I feel sure that if Mr. Matthew Arnold were to take a walk through the Calcutta Exhibition, he would blame Indians for their inaccuracies, as much as he blamed Englishmen the other day for their want of lucidity. Here is an amusing specimen of one of the notices in the Exhibition.—"The refreshment-rooms for Mahamedians is on the East-West Corner." Other inaccuracies have a vein of satire; for instance, an image of *Bali*, the demon king of the infernal regions, is labelled by the native artist "King of the Netherlands." All honour, then, to such apostles of accuracy as Pánini, Kátyáyana, Patanjali, Colebrooke, in this land of inaccuracies. And now, what shall I say of my illustrious predecessor in the Boden chair, Horace Hayman Wilson? To him I owe most of all. I remember as a youngster, soon after I received my appointment in the Indian Civil Service, I was made to go and call on him, and that my first exclamation on leaving his presence was—"What a dry old stick!" But I soon found out that beneath that dry exterior a warmer and truer heart never throbbed, and that the stick possessed an intellect as pointed as the Kusa-grass (Kuságra-buddhi) and full of the fire of genius like the Vedic *Arani*. His death was to me like the death of a father; and I have ever since been an ardent worshipper of his memory and a humble follower in his footsteps. Before I sit down, allow me to claim for the Oxford Indian Institute—now in its infancy—some kinship with your great and ancient

Society. The first object of that Institute will, of course, be the teaching of young men; but I feel sure that when some of you eminent scholars—members of this ancient Society—visit it, as I hope you will one day do, you will be conscious of a thrill of sympathy on reading the inscription carved over its portal—Ísánakampayá nityam árya-vidyá mahíyatám Aryávartángla-bhúmyos ca mitho maitrí vivardhatám. By the favour of God, may the learning and literature of India be ever held in honour, and may the mutual friendship of India and England constantly increase.